CW01372577

Matthew Boulton's Naval Medals

Featuring the Otaheite / Resolution & Adventure,
St Eustatia, Lord Howe's Glorious First of June,
Davison's Nile, King Ferdinand IV's,
Earl St Vincent's and Boulton's Trafalgar medals.

Matthew Boulton holding a medal and with a view of the Soho works in the distance.
Portrait painted by Charles Frederick von Breda, 1792.
Photo © Birmingham Museums Trust

Matthew Boulton's Naval Medals

Featuring the Otaheite / Resolution & Adventure,
St Eustatia, Lord Howe's Glorious First of June,
Davison's Nile, King Ferdinand IV's,
Earl St Vincent's and Boulton's Trafalgar medals.

Sim Comfort

Sim Comfort Associates
2017

Published by

Sim Comfort Associates
127 Arthur Road
Wimbledon Park
London, SW19 7DR

Tel: 44 (0) 208 944 8747
Website: www.simcomfort.co.uk
Email: sim@simcomfort.co.uk

First Edition

ISBN 978-0-905887-11-1

The contents of this work are copyright to the image holders and to the author with all rights reserved. Please contact the image holder or publisher if you wish to reproduce any image or section of text.

Production Credits

Book Design and Origination:	Sim Comfort
Paper:	Munken Arctic Matt White 90 gsm Munkendal, Sweden
Printing:	Optichrome Limited Woking, Surrey
Binding:	Skyline Bookbinders, Dorking, Surrey

Certificate

To: Graham Hunt

The publisher certifies
that this is copy number

25

of a limited edition
of 500 copies.

Sim Comfort
Sim Comfort Associates

To

Nicola Campbell

and

Gillian Hughes

Acknowledgements.

This work is the result of a long quest where many people have helped me on the way. Amongst them are John Adams, Phillip Attwood, Michael Broadbent, Laurence Brown, Nimrod Dix, Christopher Dixon, Ray Eddy, Christopher Eimer, Mark Grimwade, Thomas A. Hardy, John Hayward, Peter Hore, Graham Hunt, Nigel Israel, Brian Lavery, Skyler Liechty, Randy Mafit, Charles Miller, Timothy Millet, Michael Naxton, Anthony Payne, Richard Price, Tim Slessor, Glenn Stein, Barbara Tomlinson, Peter Warwick, Sir John Wheeler and Sam Willis.

Nicola Campbell is a good friend who has provided inspiration and has kept pushing me to keep digging until the truth behind a medal and its design are finally revealed.

The information pertaining to the men whose medals are discussed really is the work carried out by Gillian Hughes at the National Archives, Kew. Gillian has been researching these men for me for thirty years or more and I'm very grateful to her and her great skill in learning their stories.

Daniel Fearon has been my medal collecting confidante for many years. Wonderful medals Daniel has found for me and I'm very grateful for his advice and friendship over the years.

David Vice of Format Coins in Birmingham has been my sheet anchor and has often kept me on course as to understanding both Matthew Boulton and his work carried out at the Soho Mint.

Martyn Downer with his work *Nelson Purse* has provided the most complete biography of Alexander Davison and has been a regular help with my research.

Peter Clayton as a numismatist, naval historian and Egyptologist is the perfect man to apply his red biro to this offering and he has and it is better for it!

Jonathan Betts at the National Maritime Museum unlocked the information surrounding the metallic composition of the Boulton Trafalgar medals.

James Hammond was a pioneer in recording named Davison Nile and Boulton Trafalgar medals and the two of us have spent some lovely times together comparing lists of named medals.

Virginia Medlen, an extraordinary American lady now sadly deceased, who would on her many trips to London visit the National Archives and ultimately create a complete muster list for all of the officers and men on board Nelson's ships at the Battle of the Nile. She was also an early collector of named Davison Nile and Boulton Trafalgar medals.

Pam and Derek Ayshford created the digital *Ashford Complete Trafalgar Roll* which has proved invaluable in cross checking named Boulton Trafalgar medals.

My sister Marcy Berry keeps my American identity in shape with our daily chats about tennis and what is going on in Greeley, Colorado and elsewhere in the States.

xii

Contents

Acknowledgements	xi
Background and References	xiv - xvi

Part One - The seven Boulton naval medals

Matthew Boulton and the Soho Mint	2 - 9
The Otaheite or Resolution and Adventure Medal and Captain Cook	10 - 47
The St Eustatia Medal and Admiral Lord Rodney	48 - 53
The Glorious First of June Medal and Admiral Lord Howe	54 - 61
The Davison Nile Medal and Admiral Lord Nelson	62 - 70
The gilding of Davison Nile medals on board ship	71 - 72
Supplying the glazed cases for 48 mm Boulton medals	73
Engraving Nile and Trafalgar medals	74 - 75
Creating the die	76 - 77
A Friend in Need is a Friend Indeed, by Martyn Downer	78 - 97
Captain Ralph Willett Miller's account of the Battle of the Nile	98 - 108
Dominique Vivant Denon's account of the Battle of the Nile	108 - 116
King Ferdinand IV Medal and Nelson's support for the King	117 - 121
Earl St Vincent's Medal of Approbation	122 - 129
Matthew Boulton's Trafalgar medal	130 - 145
Boulton's Trafalgar Medal by David Vice	133 - 141
Boulton Trafalgar medal metal analysis	144 - 145
The Forger's Detective	146 - 149

Part Two – The Catalogue of named and provenanced medals 150 - 387

Earl St Vincent medals	152 - 161
Davison Nile medals	162 - 319
Boulton Trafalgar medals	320 - 387

Image Credits	388
Index	389 - 405

BRITISH NAVAL MEDALS:

COMMEMORATIVE MEDALS,
NAVAL REWARDS, WAR MEDALS,
NAVAL TOKENS, PORTRAIT MEDALLIONS,
LIFE-SAVING MEDALS,
ENGRAVED PIECES, &c., &c.

BY

ADMIRAL
THE MARQUESS OF MILFORD HAVEN
(PRINCE LOUIS OF BATTENBERG UNTIL 1917)
P.C., G.C.B., LL.D., &c.

FELLOW OF THE ROYAL NUMISMATIC SOCIETY
HONORARY MEMBER OF THE BRITISH NUMISMATIC SOCIETY
MEMBRE D'HONNEUR DE LA SOCIÉTÉ FRANÇAISE DE NUMISMATIQUE
MEMBRE D'HONNEUR DE LA SOCIÉTÉ ROYALE DE NUMISMATIQUE DE BELGIQUE
HONORARY MEMBER OF THE AMERICAN NUMISMATIC SOCIETY
HONORARY MEMBER OF THE NEW YORK NUMISMATIC CLUB

[Foreign Naval Medals are dealt with in two similar Volumes]

LONDON
JOHN MURRAY, ALBEMARLE STREET, W.1
MCMXIX

Background and References

Picture it, an American coin collector who married an English girl and the two of them have just returned to London in February 1968. Fortunately Mary was able to get her old job back at Banker's Trust in Grosvenor Square. I had the presence of mind to sell my American coins in St Louis before we left, and to use that money to buy British coins which were dirt cheap in Missouri. So, while looking for a proper job as a salesman, I was a street coin dealer, i.e. dress in a suit, pin plastic envelopes which contained coins on the inside of the jacket, stuff my pockets with more coins and catch the District Line into town. There was a large coin shop at Trafalgar Square which was rarely open but had a big display window showing coins, so I would stand outside that shop window and when several people were looking at the coins in the window, I'd say, 'What a pity the shop is closed, but if you'd like to buy some coins, I have stock!' And then I'd open my jacket so they could see what coins I had. And it worked!

I do remember one occasion when I sold a number of coins to a Sergeant in the Guards. We had to return to his post where he kept his money. He'd just paid me when outside somebody called, 'Officer on Parade!', and my customer quickly opened a cupboard door and pushed me in! There was then a conversation between the Sergeant and the Officer who then left, cupboard door was opened and I left, not too sure what had happened, but I had the money and I was on my way to Spink's in St James to look at naval medals. Those days in the late '60s and during the '70s were a collector's dream. At Spink's, you were let behind the counter and placed in front of a very tall and wide mahogany medal cabinet. I'd have a chair and just sit and go through the cabinet drawer by drawer and rarely left without finding some new treasure.

My interest in naval history was well in place prior to returning to London and as I began to get to know the several coin dealers in the West End, I found these wonderful naval medals struck by Boulton and Hancock which celebrated the British naval victories of the French wars 1793-1815. And they were cheap, £3 or £5 would buy a very nice medal. I would use spare profits from coin sales to buy naval medals and coin collecting gave way almost entirely to medal collecting. I continued to have a weak spot for early American Large Cents mainly due to my training via *Penny Whimsy* by Sheldon, Pascal & Breen.

I do like a good sea story and although a coin dated 1805 certainly puts you in touch with the year of Trafalgar, it can't compare with a named Boulton Trafalgar medal that brings you on board a man's ship at Trafalgar and what he went through during the battle.

In leaning about naval medals, I have relied greatly on the people who have preceded me. The Marquess of Milford Haven (Prince Louis of Battenberg) and his monumental *British Naval Medals* which is the first complete survey taken of the subject, and invaluable from the date it was published by John Murray in 1919. In 1980 Seaby published Laurence Brown's *British Historical Medals 1760-1960*, which provided information on the full British series from the reign of King George III to modern times and includes the naval medals of the French Wars and has been of great use.

Prior to Milford Haven, one had to rely upon *Historical Record of Medals* by George Tancred, published by Spink in 1891 which is valuable for a number if interesting anecdotal items; and *Medals and Decorations of the British Army and Navy* by J. H. Mayo, published by Archibald Constable & Co. in 1897 which contains much of the early information regarding Mr Boulton's naval medals.

H. W. Dickinson's *Matthew Boulton* published by Babcock and Wilcox Ltd. at the University Press Cambridge, 1936, provides an excellent biography of Matthew Boulton. *The Numismatic Chronicle* for 1970 contains an extensive article by J. G. Pollard: *Matthew Boulton and Conrad Heinrich Küchler*, which produces a complete survey of all the medals created by this partnership and has a great deal of background information regarding the designs for each medal.

We then have the four articles written by James Hammond. Two were published by *Coin and Medal News*: *Mr Davison's Medal* in January 1987 and *Mr Boulton's Trafalgar Medal* in September 1988 in which James produces the first survey of known named examples for each of the two medals; and two articles published by *The Military Chest*, which are *The Minotaur at Aboukir Bay* in January 1986, and *An Introduction to Medal Research* in February 1988.

Without question, the most important article written about the Boulton Trafalgar Medal is the piece done by David Vice for *Medal News* in May of 1997 entitled *Boulton's Trafalgar Medal*. For that reason the whole of his article is reprinted in this volume.

Then we come to *Matthew Boulton's Otaheite Medal* written by Arthur Westwood and published by the Birmingham Assay Office in 1926 which includes the correspondence between Boulton and Banks held in Birmingham. Another very important work is *The Resolution and Adventure Medal* by L. Richard Smith, published by the Wedgwood Press, Sydney in 1984. Mr Smith was able to draw upon correspondence from Boulton to Banks held in the Mitchell Library, which hadn't been seen by English authors. I incorporate the key documents from both works in this volume.

More recent publications are the scholarly work by Richard Doty, *The Soho Mint and the Industrialization of Money*, published by Spink in 1998 which provides both a fine biography of Boulton but also how his skill as an engineer and flair as a salesman changed the world of coinage and medals. The two works by Thomas A. Hardy, *Remember Nelson* and *Trafalgar 200*, provide the most complete catalogue of all the medals that relate to Nelson and are published by The Nelson Society. For the bicentennial of the death of Boulton in 2009, Birmingham City Council and the Birmingham Museum and Art Gallery staged a conference with the main publication being a fine booklet by Nicholas Goodison entitled, *Matthew Boulton's Trafalgar Medal*, which has proved a valuable source. Lastly is the magnificent *British Commemorative Medals and their values* by Christopher Eimer, published Spink in 2010 which is extremely useful as a survey for the medals from Elizabeth I to modern times, all accompanied with the finest of photowork.

So there is a fair amount of reference material available to the collector, however when it comes to understanding the learning curve that Matthew Boulton went through as a medallist, which resulted in some of the finest naval medals ever created, and relating the medals to the historic naval battles or events the medal represents, there are things to learn and discoveries to be made, which is what this book is about. I hope you enjoy the voyage.

Sim Comfort
14 February 2017
Wimbledon Park

Part One

The seven Boulton naval medals

At Covent Garden Theatre, shortly after the news of Lord Nelson's death had arrived, the following interesting incident occurred:-

'In the pit, at an early part of the evening, a sailor, apparently about thirty years of age, and of a very healthy appearance, with the blunt and honest manner of a real tar, bawled loudly for those aloft (meaning the galleries) 'to Stow their Jabber' (or cease their noise), increasing thereby the confusion which prevailed. Jack, at length, raising himself on one of the seats, exclaimed – 'Messmates aloft - three hearty cheers for Nelson and the Nile!' Jack was obeyed, nor were the shouts confined to the galleries only.

'Jack, from the attention paid to him, was now inclined to indulge himself further, and producing a medal, to which he had fastened a black riband, he gave the audience to understand that 'it was a Medal which had been struck to commemorate the Battle of the Nile, and which as the brave Nelson was no more, and it bore his head, he offered it to their notice (pointing to the black riband) in mourning!' - Much applause followed, and the medal in mourning was waved conspicuously by the sailor many times during the remainder of the night.' (Ref: *Naval Chronicle*, vol. 15, pp. 18-20.)

And by coincidence, also from volume 15, page 18 of the *Naval Chronicle* (which is for January to June, 1806) is the following note:

'Boulton's Trafalgar Medal

'Mr Boulton, the scientific and venerable proprietor of Soho, whose public exertions have so uniformly been distinguished by a patriotism the best directed, has solicited the permission of Government, that he might be allowed to strike a Medal, at his own expense, in commemoration of the brilliant victory off Cape Trafalgar, and to present one to every seaman who served that day on board the British Fleet. The permission was immediately granted, with the warmest approbation of so laudable a design. In a short time the Medals will be sent down to the several ports, to be distributed among the valorous tars by His Majesty's Commissioners, thus enabling the heroic defenders of their country to carry to their wives, and sweethearts, the most honourable testimony.

That their own true Sailor he was one!'

It was in 1970 and John Hayward was still trading from the Piccadilly Arcade, when I stopped by and asked if he had anything interesting relating to Nelson. A minute later, there was before me a bronze-gilt Davison Nile. The piece had been mounted in a bronze-gilt glazed case with a watch style suspension and loop. All this was in a fitted green leather case and all original. Under the glass in the reverse field one could read '*George Thompson, HMS Defence, 1798*'. The medal is listed as DN 19 in the following Catalogue. With this purchase began the long road that was the start for me in collecting named Davison's Nile, Boulton's Trafalgar and Earl St Vincent's Medal of Approbation. However, we have to go back and take a look at how all this came about. Who made these wonderful medals, who received them, who designed them, who paid for them, how were they distributed, what are they like and so many more questions?

Matthew Boulton was an ingenious as Lord Nelson was brave. And curiously enough, he was as well (if not better), connected in certain Royal, Government and Naval circles. Matthew Boulton was at the time of his first medal, an aware and enterprising engineer who felt very strongly that function and design were of equal importance. Through his emphasis on design, he made a name for himself in the highest circles of both industry and authority. His correspondents (and customers) included Benjamin Franklin, Sir Joseph Banks, Josiah Wedgwood, James Watt, James Boswell, James Adam, Alexander Davison (prize agent to Lord Nelson), Earl St Vincent, Lady Hamilton and many more luminaries of an age filled with light. It is during the great period of exploration through the efforts of Captain Cook and of war through the likes of Earl St Vincent and Lord Nelson, that we see a close parallel between the rise of Matthew Boulton's industrial and medallic contribution and the general success of Britain at Sea. This book is produced to bring all of the detail together for the first time. Hopefully we will get to know the men involved, the events and the processes which produced such wonderful reminders of the great age of Exploration and War under Sail.

Matthew Boulton was born in Birmingham on September 3rd, 1728. In later life, he was particularly pleased with his birth year, as the number equalled the number of cubic inches found in a cubic foot. His father was also a Matthew, and spelled his surname as either Bolton or Boulton.

Birmingham of the early 18th century was a place of great industry. The main reasons for this being are its location near supplies of iron and coal, with ample water power for driving lathes and hammers. The elder Matthew owned a small works which specialised in the manufacture of 'Toys'. These were not the things children played with (although they may well have done!), but was a generic term meaning all things small and made of metal, i.e. small boxes, pin ornaments, snuffers, tweezers, ear scoops, buttons, fasteners, and buckles. It is this last item in which the elder Boulton specialised. Buckles for shoes and stockings were all the rage in Britain, the Continent and the American colonies.

The younger Matthew appears to have had a normal schooling and joined his father in the business at the age of 14. Upon reaching his majority, his father made him a partner and generally left the running of the total enterprise to his enthusiastic and energetic son. In 1756, at the age of 28, Matthew took Mary Robinson as his wife. A most fortunate match. Mary brought with her nearly £14,000 in capital as she was the joint heir (with her sister Anne) to her father's estate. Tragedy struck after just a few years when she died sometime around 1759-1760. A fragment in Boulton's hand tells of his state of mind, 'Upon seeing the corps of my dear wife Mary many excellent Qualitys of Hers arose to my mind which I could not then forbear acknowledging extempory with my pen & depositing it in her Coffin.' (Ref: Dickenson's *Matthew Boulton*, p. 30.)

As a double blow, Matthew's father also died about this time. And with these events, Boulton was now the sole proprietor of his father's works and had available his deceased wife's estates to expand the business.

Staying with domestic history, we next note that Boulton had in or about 1767, married his deceased wife's sister Anne, whom he called Nancy, and in so doing had secured the remaining half of his wife's family estate. That the match was one of love, there is no doubt, but one cannot help seeing the financial wherewithal coming to be which was to act as the capital base for his various and successful enterprises. A widower, marrying his sister-in-law in the middle of the 18th century was definitely considered an immoral thing to do. To counter this, Boulton bought 180 copies of *Fry on Marriage* in which the argument that to marry ones wife's sister is 'fit and convenient being opposed neither to law nor morals.'

Undoubtedly, Boulton placed a copy in the pocket of any and all who felt a bit squeamish about this less than orthodox pursuit of marital bliss. Further it is noted that the book retailed for 2s. each. Matthew paid a total of £9 (or 180s.) for all 180 copies, thus gaining a 50% discount. A solid mark of his business approach to all matters of the heart! (Ref: Ibid. p. 34.)

There is a wonderful added reference toward this marriage, when a friend, Richard Lowell Edgeworth, was in the process of deciding to marry his deceased wife's sister, and wrote to Boulton for advice. The response still exits: 'The only advice I can give you upon the subject of your letter is to read a small book upon Marriages between near kindred by Fry. When you have taken your resolution I advise you to say nothing of your intentions but go quickly and snugly to Scotland or some obscure corner of London, suppose Wapping, and there take Lodgings to make yourself a parishioner. When the month is expired and the Law fulfilled, Live and be happy. The propriety of such a marriage is too obvious to men who think for themselves to need my comments....I recommend Silence, Secrecy & Scotland.' (Ref: Ibid. pp. 35-36.)

Boulton's marriage was a success bearing two children, Anne and Matthew Robinson. Unfortunately, his beloved Nancy lived only until 1783. Matthew Robinson would succeed his father, who passed away in 1809, and continued the business until his death in 1842, although with much less flair and care for design than shown by his father.

So, back to business. Why Birmingham? Noted above is that the geographical location was important. There was something else of equal importance, i.e. that Birmingham was not an incorporated city. As such, had no ruling body of Guilds which produced restrictive practices in order to protect their own interests. Birmingham was the Tiger within the Lion's realm. With no restrictions as to who produced what, the city grew very rapidly as a safe haven for the industrially bright. Between the period 1617 to 1853, Birmingham stood supreme over all other British cities in putting forward patents. Her closest rival was Manchester, with Birmingham producing something around three times as many patents. It is this loose approach to enterprise which allowed Matthew Boulton to excel in the initial area of Toy Manufacture which brought him into contact with Wedgwood. Boulton produced very fine cut steel frames for many of Wedgwood's ceramic miniatures, then onto silver plate and silver objects. The perfection of a method of producing Ormolu (gold flake mixed with mercury and then annealed to bronze, brass or steel) which was a closely guarded French craft, the secrets of which Boulton mastered. He produced dazzling results in Ormolu as furniture embellishments, the gilding of medallions and the adornment of sword blades. His association with James Watt and their efforts in harnessing steam power became one of the main contributions toward the start of the Industrial Revolution. Lastly his involvement in coinage, both in the traditional manner and then later with the introduction of revolutionary steam presses which completely changed the standard of world coinage. With such a vast range of activity and manufacture, Birmingham was the only place in the world where such a maestro as Matthew Boulton could thrive.

Another measure of the man is found in a rather testy reply toward the end of his life to Philip Thickness, who had referred to Boulton as Tradesman of Birmingham and queried why with his wealth secure at an early age, he hadn't taken up the pursuits of a Gentleman! 'Early in life Fortune gave me the option of assuming the character of an idle man commonly called a Gent., but I rather chose to be of the class which Le Baron Montesque describes as the constant contributors to the purse of the commonwealth rather than of another class which he says are always taking out of it without contributing anything towards it.' (Ref: Ibid. pp. 36-37.)

Birmingham did have one drawback though. It was known as a producer of cheap goods that worked, but may not be of the highest quality and certainly did not make a contribution in terms of design. This is where Matthew Boulton made a very conscious decision by endeavouring wherever possible to seek out the very best artisans in England and elsewhere, and involving their design into his wares. To this end, Boulton established in 1761 his, soon to be world famous, works at Soho, Birmingham. He also in 1762 took a partner, John Fothergill. The general relationship was that Boulton would run the business and manage the British market, while Fothergill concentrated on securing business on the Continent. Further, it is noted that in addition to securing outlets for the products of Soho, Fothergill was to visit the great collections in Rome and elsewhere and bring back accurate drawings of classical design, the keel upon which Georgian Design sailed.

The following description of the Soho works is taken from the holograph Memorandum written by James Watt and dated Glasgow, September 17th, 1809: 'Memorandum concerning Mr Boulton, commencing with my first acquaintance with him. I was introduced at Soho by Dr Small in 1767 but Mr Boulton was then absent; Mr Fothergill his partner & Dr Small showed me the works. The goods then manufactured there were steel-gilt & fancy buttons, steel watch chains & sword hilts, plated wares, ornamental works in Ormoulu. Tortoise shell snuff boxes, Bath metal buttons inlaid with steel & various other articles, which I have now forgot. A mill with a water wheel was employed in Laminating metal for the buttons, plated goods &c and to turn Laps for grinding & polishing steel work & I was informed that Mr Boulton was the first inventor of the inlaid buttons, & the first who had applied a mill to turn the Laps. Mr B at that (time) also carried on a very considerable trade in the manufacture of buckle chapes, in the making of which he had made several very ingenious improvements. Besides the Laps in the mill, I saw an ingenious lap turned by a hand wheel for cutting and polishing the steel studs for ornamenting buttons, chains, sword hilts &c, and a shaking box put in motion by the mill for scouring button blanks & other small pieces of metal which was also a thought of Mr B – there was also a steel house for converting iron into steel, which was frequently employed to convert the cuttings & scraps of the chapes & other small iron wares into steel which was afterwards melted & made into cast steel for various uses.' (Ref: Ibid. Appendix I.)

In order to fully capitalise upon this combining of art and artifice, Boulton wanted to be in the position of both manufacturer and retailer. To this end, and to avoid the extreme cost of a London store, he found that Mr Christie and Ansell's sale rooms in Pall Mall were well suited as an outlet for his goods. Audacious to say the least, Boulton felt his new wares were of such interest that they could be auctioned successfully. Indeed they were and with success he certainly never imagined. A close supporter of his sales was King George III, who with his Queen were busy outfitting Buckingham Palace (as well as refurbishing apartments at Windsor Castle), with Mr Boulton's wares. Boulton wrote to his dear Nancy in 1770, 'The King hath bought a pair of cassolets, a Titus, a Venus clock and some other things and enquired this morning how yesterday's sale went. I shall see him again I believe. I was with them, the Queen and all her children, between two and three hours....Never was man so complimented as I have been; but I find that compliments don't make fat nor fill the pocket. The Queen showed me her last child which is a beauty but none of 'em are equal to the General of Soho or the Fair Maid of the Mill. God bless them both and kiss them for me.' The General and the Fair Maid were the pet names for their two children, Matthew Robinson and Anne. (Ref: Ibid. pp. 56-57.)

Matthew Boulton had an inquiring mind which was extended by his association with the Lunar Society of Birmingham, so named because its members met once a month when the moon was full. Within this circle of scientific men, Boulton met Dr William Small who introduced him to Benjamin Franklin in 1765.

Steam engines where of interest to members of the Society even before James Watt became a member. Josiah Wedgwood was also a member and with his experiments in the properties of different clays and Boulton's interest in metallurgy, one can see how the scientific endeavours of the Society led to practical ends and greatly assisted both Wedgwood and Boulton and others in becoming leaders in their respective businesses.

As a note, Boulton was well respected in the wider circle of science and he was elected a Fellow of the Royal Society in 1785 and a member of the Society of Civil Engineers in 1792. The true combining of science with industry.

Steam power, however, changed everything for Matthew Boulton. When he became acquainted with James Watt and fully appreciated the potential of his invention, Boulton wanted it and got it, but in the best way possible with Boulton and Watt forming a partnership in 1775 that worked very well for the rest of their lives. One would be mistaken if it was felt that Boulton's side of the business was sales and Watt's was invention, because Boulton's mind was constantly employed at improving his products and with the steam engine, he made a number of innovations. However, one would consider Boulton as the master for manufacturer and sales as well as looking for new ways to get the best from the steam engine, which in the end was the cornerstone for the Industrial Revolution in Britain.

Again, like Wedgwood, Boulton believed in a vertical structure to his business wherein everything associated with his manufacturer was combined at one site, which was Soho outside Birmingham, a model facility complete with housing for his workforce.

We then see the most remarkable coming together of various skills and circumstances which are all centred upon Matthew Boulton and had the most dramatic effect upon the minting of coinage and medals.

The most important use of the steam engine for Boulton and Watt was to pump water from tin and copper mines in Cornwall. If the mine could be freed of water, more ore was mined and the steam engine was the tool for achieving this. Over time, Boulton gained a financial interest in some copper mines and began to build stocks of copper and tin from his mining customers. One imagines that money may have been tight for the miners, so what better way to pay Boulton than to give him smelted copper and tin. At the same time, Boulton realised that by incorporating steam power into minting, he could very accurately regulate the pressure of the press which would result in a perfect coin with each strike. This had never been achieved before and resulted in a new business which would become world famous for Boulton.

The first Soho mint was established in 1788 / 1789. As Richard Doty notes, '[Boulton] was totally unprepared to coin at the beginning of 1788; had he then received orders [from the Royal Mint] to do so, he would have been exposed to official and popular ridicule. Matthew Boulton had no idea what he was doing in January 1788 and would only learn his chosen craft the hard way, through time, until he would finally be ready to back his claims with solid evidence.'

I don't entirely agree with Dr Doty's assessment of Soho at that time. Boulton's driving ambition as an industrialist was that through invention and steam power, he would be able to reduce the cost of production and increase the quality of his products. He and his workforce were striking coins and learning new skills as they incorporated new techniques and machinery, particularly where steam power was involved. Certainly, Boulton and his team hadn't achieved all the core skills by 1788, but they were well on their way.

The brilliant Swiss die maker and coiner, Jean-Pierre Droz (1746-1823), became the central figure who would turn any lack of skill at Soho into a centre of excellence, or at least that was hoped by Boulton. The relationship between Boulton and Droz was stormy to say the least, but Boulton felt he needed the skills that Droz brought to the business and in July 1790, work between the two men began in earnest. However it is felt that in the end, Boulton and his team of craftsmen taught themselves through trial and error more than Droz contributed.

Tenacity, ambition and hard work are the essential ingredients to success and Matthew Boulton had all of these characteristics. As Richard Doty notes, 'Serious work on the mint machinery began in the autumn of 1788. The number of presses to be powered by the overhead wheel now rose from six to eight, and drawings were commissioned and parts devised for connecting the [steam powered] driving wheel to the individual presses.'

We then have a document by Boulton dated September, 1789 and quoted by Q. David Bowers in, *The History of United States Coinage as illustrated by the Garrett Collection*. Here Boulton enthused about the current capability of his steam powered coining press. This looks like a document sent to Philadelphia in the hope of the Americans buying Boulton's new technology:

'It will coin much faster, with greater ease, with fewer persons, for less expense, and produce more beautiful pieces than any other machinery ever used for coining.

'The quantity of power or force requisite for each blow is exactly regulated and ascertained and is always uniformly the same, for the same pieces, thereby the dies are better preserved.

'One of my coining machines will work much faster by the attendance of one boy than others can do by any number of men.

'Can stop these machines at an instant by the power of a child and the same child can as instantaneously set them to work again.

'Can increase or diminish the force of the blow at pleasure, in any proportion.

'Can lay the pieces or blanks upon the die quite true and without care or practice and as fast as wanted.

'Can work day and night without fatigue by two sets of boys.

'The machine keeps an account of the number of pieces struck which cannot be altered from the truth by any of the persons employed.

'The apparatus strikes an inscription upon the edge with the same blow that it strikes the two faces.

'It strikes the ground of the pieces brighter than any other coining press can do.

'It strikes the pieces perfectly round, all of good diameter, and exactly concentric with the edge, which cannot be done by any other machinery now in use.'

In 1791, Boulton gained a large contract for supplying copper coinage for the East India Company in Bombay and was busy minting tokens for merchants up and down the land. The use of tokens was popular due to the scarcity of regal copper coinage.

The Americans had also courted Droz because the new Philadelphia Mint was being formed at this time. Although Boulton wished to establish a mint in the United States, this wasn't to be, however Soho did supply finished planchetts to the Americans until the commencement of the War of 1812 when trade ceased with America.

The American's first penny, the Chain Cent, was struck in 1793 from dies by Henry Voigt. A highly interesting coin which with its die breaks etc., shows just how much the Americans had to learn. By contrast, in the same year, Droz and Boulton struck the really superb Bermuda penny, which has to be one of the finest colonial coins ever issued.

But Droz wasn't to stay in Soho. It was with the Flemish medallist, Conrad Heinrich Küchler (1740?-1810) arriving in Soho in 1793, that Boulton found the artistic partner which between them would create wonderful medals and coins that changed everything in terms of minting in England. A total of 33 medals were produced by Boulton and Küchler with the first recording the execution of King Louis XVI of France in 1793. It was with Küchler as die maker that in 1797 came the first contract for the supply of regal copper coinage in England with the introduction of the Cartwheel twopence and penny.

Of all the enterprises that Matthew Boulton was involved in, it was the Mint and the striking of coins and medals that he liked best. The enterprise would expand further with Boulton supplying to a number of countries complete working mints and the men to set them up and teach the customer how to get the best from them.

We will see that the Otaheite medal, struck by Boulton in 1772, demonstrated just how eager Boulton was to be a medallist and how very unprepared he was for the task. By the time of the arrival of Küchler in 1793, the Soho mint had matured. Boulton and his team had gained much experience plus the added skills provided by Droz helped them move forward. With the production of the first Küchler naval medal, Earl Howe's First of June 1794 medal, we see one of the finest English naval medals produced to that date. This success was then followed with the Davison Nile, Ferdinand VII, Earl St Vincent and lastly the Boulton Trafalgar medal. With Boulton dying in 1809 and Küchler in 1810, the standard set by these two men for English naval medals came to an end, but their memorial is found in their medals. Possibly, not until the fine polar medals for the Royal Geographical Society by Bayes and Bowcher, have the Boulton and Küchler medals been equaled.

The last word is given to Richard Doty who wrote, 'Matthew Boulton's career affords a splendid illustration of how one activity might lead to another in the career of an eighteenth-century man of business. Thus, while it would surely be an oversimplification to say that his connection with James Watt and the improved steam engine led him to an interest in Cornish copper mining, and that in turn to a [financial] interest in Cornish copper mining companies, and that, in turn to an interest in a market for their wares, and the copper coinage, one could nonetheless make an argument for each and every link in the chain. In the case of copper coinage, Matthew Boulton was a reformer, and in the application of steam to the coining process, he was a visionary; but he was also a businessman, and the remembrance of earlier journeys helped determine his arrival at this particular destination.'

The American Chain Cent struck in Philidelphia in 1793. This is the first Federal coinage of the United States. The Bermuda Penny with dies by Droz and struck by Matthew Boulton at Soho in 1793, a coin stuck for distribution within the Island of Bermuda in the Caribbean. Chain Cent images courtesy of Stack's Bowers Galleries. Bermuda Penny images from the Sim Comfort Collection.

The Otaheite or Resolution and Adventure Medal

The early 1770s takes us to Matthew Boulton's first naval medal, which is also his first medallic effort.

1) The Otaheite Medal or the *Resolution* and *Adventure* Medal, 1772. (MH 373 / BHM 165 / Eimer 744)

Description:

Obverse: Laureate head of George III facing right. GEORGE . III . KING . OF . GR . BRITAIN . FRANCE . AND . IRELAND ETC (on the shoulder of the King) B : F (Boulton : Fothergill)

Reverse: Two ship rigged sloops (barks) viewed from astern. RESOLUTION   ADVENTURE. In exergue: SAILED . FROM . ENGLAND / MARCH MDCCLXXII.

Diameter: Type I 42 mm, Type II 44 mm.

Type I: Platina / Brass: 2,000 made to Admiralty order and a few copper examples. A copper-gilt suspension was originally fitted to the Type I examples, but is rarely found today. As a note, platina is a brass alloy based on copper and zinc, but as platina is the term used by Boulton, I'll use it here instead of brass. It is only the Type I medals that sailed with Captain Cook for distribution amongst newly discovered peoples.

Rarity: Type I: Copper RR £4,500, Copper-gilt RR £4,500, Platina N £4,500.

Type I copper example sold by Glendining's on 18 November 1987, lot 19. Very possibly the finest example known with its original loop suspension. Image courtesy of Glendining's.

Type II silver example, purchased from Spink in the 1980s. Sim Comfort Collection.

Type II: Gold: Two made to Joseph Banks' order with one known in the British Museum, ex King George III. Silver: 142 made to Joseph Banks' order. Copper: Quantity unknown, but very small, probably less than a dozen. It is possible that Boulton struck some silver and copper examples for his own use as presents or to sell.

Rarity: Type II: Gold RRRR £NA, Silver R £5,000, Copper RR £3,500.

Varieties:

Type I: This is the original reverse die which has a die crack running through the left part of the exergue, affecting the words SAILED and MARCH. Further, the anchor on the starboard bow of the left-hand ship is hanging down into the water which looks a little unusual as she is in full sail! This reverse is coupled with an obverse which has a die flaw which is about 10 mm long and is located near the letter K in the obverse field. There is also a small elongated flaw / lump, horizontally situated on the upper middle of the King's neck. Also the words KING and ETC. (as well as all the rest of the legend in the obverse die) are well and clearly struck. The orientation of the obverse and reverse dies is usually off centre by about 10 degrees, i.e. both the obverse and reverse dies are upright, but the top point for each is roughly 10 degrees off centre from the other. I say usually, as the platina example in the British Museum and the copper in Sim Comfort Collection (SCC), have a 180 degrees difference in orientation between the obverse and reverse, i.e., top of obverse to bottom of reverse. It is only this Type I die set which is found with either the top rim pierced (centred on either the portrait of the King or the *Resolution* and *Adventure*) to receive a screw to which is attached a bronze-gilt loop suspension, or the complete suspension and screw are fitted in place. Lastly, the rim of the Type I examples is slightly convex, i.e., there is some curvature out from the edges. This die combination constitutes the original striking in late February or early March, 1772 with delivery to and / or agreement to pay by the Admiralty in April, 1772. Type I is only known in platina and copper. The full diameter is 42 mm. The internal edge diameter for both obverse and reverse dies is 40 mm.

Type II: The Second Reverse die which has no die breaks in the exergue, but does have a small die crack between the letters E and N in ADVENTURE and the ship on the left- hand side now has its starboard bow anchor firmly stowed horizontal to the ship's side. The obverse die is as before, but with a possible variation. The gold and silver examples in the British Museum (gold being ex the Royal Collection and acquired by the British Museum in 1825, and silver being ex Sarah Sophia Banks, Joseph Banks' sister) are as near to what today would be called proof examples with frosted devices within both the obverse and reverse images. The silver example in SCC and others noted are less well struck, but definitely of the same dies. The result of this proof striking is that the die flaws under the letter K and upon the King's neck are well defined as well as the die crack between the letters E and N on the reverse. Also, the obverse die of the British Museum examples, has the word KING less strong than found in the Type I striking, and the word ETC. is now weak. In the SCC example (the weaker and perhaps regular striking) the words KING and ETC. are both quite weak and the die flaws found under the letter K and on the King's neck for the obverse and between the letters E and N on the reverse are just a shadow of their former selves. There may have been a polishing of the obverse die used in the SCC example in order to reduce the effect of the flaws. This, coupled with (the presumed) less pressure being applied when striking in order to preserve a deteriorating set of dies, may well account for this lack of sharpness in the obverse legend

For the Type II examples, none have been met with which have the loop suspension affixed, nor do they have the tell-tale hole in the rim where the suspension screw would have been set. Further, the orientation of all examples is with the obverse and reverse dies sharing the same top point. Lastly, the rim of the Type II examples has a definite outward bulge, and what looks like hand filing and polishing of the rim. There is a curious minute step from the rim to the top edge of the obverse plane. This is not repeated on the reverse and looks to be caused by the reverse die being 1mm larger in diameter than the obverse die. The rim features and lack of suspension are applicable to all Type II examples. Type II is only found in gold, silver and copper with no platina examples encountered. They were probably struck in late March, 1772 and (for the gold and silver) delivered and invoiced to Mr Joseph Banks in April, 1772. There is the possibility that Type II examples were struck after this date (particularly the copper and perhaps some silver medals) as Matthew Boulton supplied / sold some examples to interested parties. The full diameter is 44 mm with the internal edge diameters being 41 mm for the obverse and 42 mm for the reverse dies.

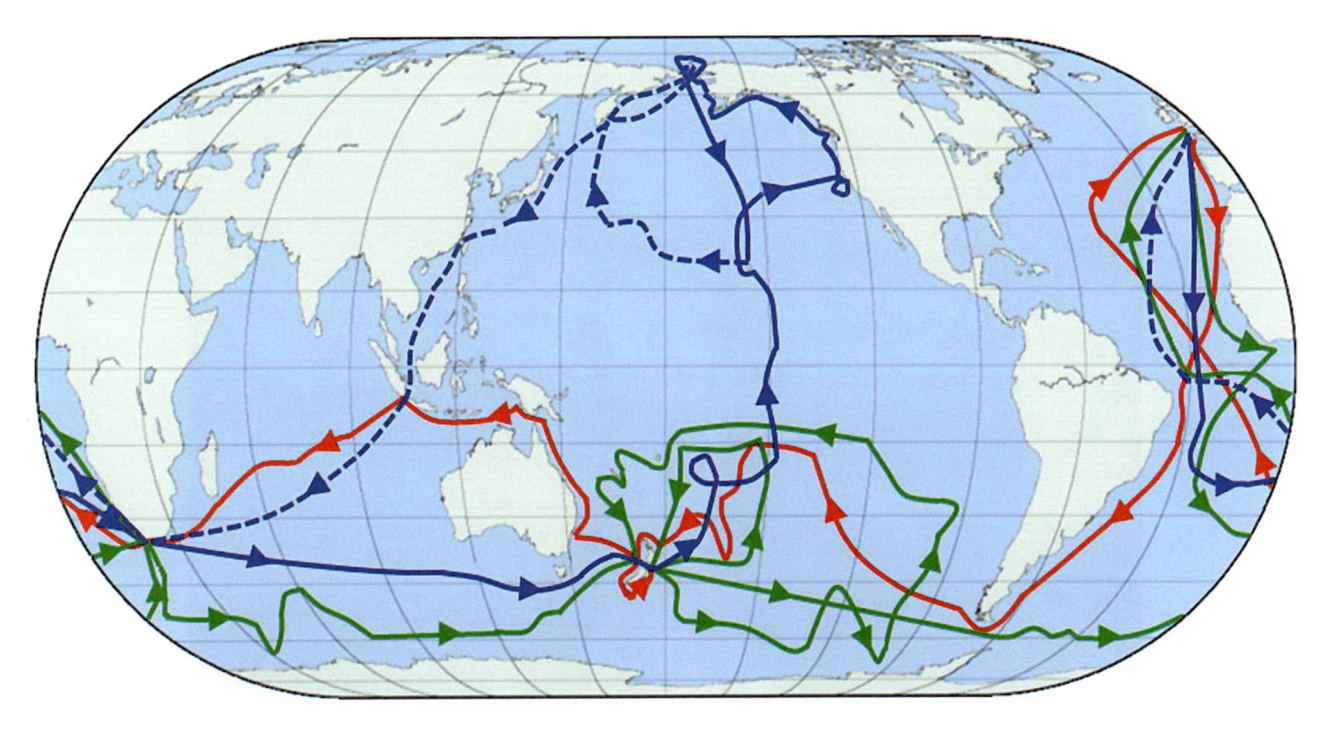

The routes of Captain James Cook's voyages. The first voyage is shown in red, second voyage in green, and third voyage in blue. The route of Cook's crew following his death is shown as a dashed blue line. Image courtesy of Wikipedia.

Background to Cook's voyages and the Otaheite Medal

Otaheite: 'There is no general agreement that Tahiti is the most beautiful island in the Pacific; but it is generally agreed that it is a beautiful island, and to its first discoverers it seemed paradisal. Coming to it after so many atolls, lagoons encircled by a broken rim of sand and coral, isle-studded, they saw a great volcanic upthrust high in the sea, rising from mere hilly slopes to five thousand, six thousand, seven thousand feet, forested and green till the final peaks; a land also of deep valleys and quick rivers. Almost round, the slashed mountainous mass runs a narrow band of level fertile ground, widest at the north-west end, in places failing altogether, so that the steep hillside falls straight to the rocks of the sea. The name the island was known by to its inhabitants was learnt soon enough - Otaheite, O Tahiti, 'It is Tahiti!' (Beaglehole, *Life of Captain Cook*, pp. 172 and 174.)

Having shown where our Otaheite Medal was going, we now have to look back a few years before that event and understand what was behind these great voyages of discovery.

At the time we are writing about there were several pressing issues for both the Admiralty and the scientific community represented by the Royal Society: How to determine Longitude?; What is the distance from the Earth to the Sun?; How large is the Universe?; Where is the great Southern Continent and what is its extent?; Can Britain control the key gates into the Pacific (via Cape Horn and the rumoured North-West Passage)?; and perhaps lastly, how can Britain in the Pacific Ocean out manoeuvre her rivals of France, Spain, and Holland and consolidate her position of Mistress of the Seas? All major issues which we will see both science and government co-operate to resolve.

Portrait of Captain Cook painted by John Webber who accompanined Cook on his third voyage on board the *Resolution*. Image courtesy of the Wellington Museum, Wellington, New Zealand.

To determine the distance from the Earth to the Sun, and from this gain the first true perspective as to the extent of the Universe, was the trigger which brought the Royal Society and the Admiralty into co-operation. One way to achieve the measurement is to measure the distance between Venus and the Earth. This can be done during a total eclipse of Venus and the Sun. A rare occasion which occurred in 1761, but the data gained was faulty. The next opportunity would be on 3 June 1769. Following this date, the event wouldn't occur again until 1874. The method employed was to measure the time Venus took to completely cross the face of the Sun (The Transit of Venus), and then incorporating the surveyor's technique of parallax to equate the time and angle to achieve the distance. The measurement would be made by many people in a number of countries, a truly global effort. As a note, the reason why a measurement of the distance between the Earth and the Sun was not possible using parallax is because the distance is so great that on Earth, the base line measurement is so minute, that it was deemed not measurable. Therefore, use parallax to gain the distance to Venus, whose proximity allowed a measurable base line, and then consider the relationship between Venus, the Earth and the Sun in order to gain the distance to the Sun.

Britain's global power was just taking shape. Following the defeat of the French at Quiberon Bay and Quebec in 1759, and the conclusion of the French and Indian War (Seven Years War), the British were now master of the Atlantic and all of North America. Spain still ruled South and Central America. India was coming under the influence of Britain. The Dutch and the French were established in the East Indies on the doorstep of the Pacific. There was no doubt that the Pacific Ocean was to be the settling ground for future mastery of the seas. Even more enticing was a total continent yet to be discovered, yet to be explored, colonised and used as yet another significant addition to Britain's might at sea. Everyone knew there had to be a continent in the Southern Pacific. A countering mass of land had to balance the mass of Europe and Africa in a Pacific Ocean which to date was mainly devoid of land. Sightings of Australia's north western coast had already been made by the Dutch which they named New Holland. The whole issue of finding Terra Australis Incognita had become very important to Britain and the race was on.

To determine Longitude, a robust and accurate time piece was needed. As you will see, even in the most skilled hands, the taking of Lunar sightings and figuring the longitude could produce a result that may be off target. For the navigator, this result could produce anything from not arriving to actual shipwreck. Longitude was such a pressing issue for the Admiralty that as far back as 1714, the Lords of the Admiralty had offered a prize of £20,000 (probably £2,000,000 in today's money), to anyone who could sail for six weeks and at the end of this period produce a longitudinal reading which was accurate to within thirty nautical miles or half a degree of Longitude. Thirty miles may seem a vast margin of error today, but in 1714 it would demonstrate an enormous improvement and at least put the mariner in a position to refine his position through other means. Mr John Harrison, watchmaker, in 1764 won the prize with his 'Time Machine', and from this began the development of the world's first chronometers. With an accurate timepiece, the determination of Longitude was no longer a problem. In order to calculate Longitude, one records the local time for sunrise or moonrise or the rise of Venus or Mars at any given location on the Earth. If you know the precise time for the event at Greenwich (Greenwich Mean Time), then for every hour's difference between the time at the spot where your are taking the reading and GMT, every hour difference equals 15 degrees of Longitude.

The technology, the event, and the need were all coming together. The Royal Society of London was the prime mover on the scientific front. The Admiralty was aware of the opportunity and proposed a programme of voyages of discovery which would answer the questions regarding Longitude, the

Southern Continent, and the northern and southern gates to the Pacific Ocean. The only modern equivalent to this task was putting a man on the moon, and certainly the results of the following voyages had more effect upon us earth bound creatures!

In all, there were six official voyages of discovery into the Pacific Ocean carried out by the Royal Navy during the 1760's and 1770's. The first two voyages used the *Dolphin*, a frigate of 6th rate which, especially for her voyages of discovery, had her bottom coppered, the first instance in the Royal Navy. For the voyages of Cook, and Bligh something altogether different was used. Tough coasting vessels as opposed to the streamlined naval frigates of the day. The new emphasis was on strength and shallow draft as opposed to speed. The men were as tough as the ships. Men like Cook, Bligh, Riou, Vancouver and many others. However, there was another man who was involved with each of the four latter voyages. He sailed on Cook's first, nearly did so on the second and helped promote the remaining two. He was Sir Joseph Banks, the commissioner of the Otaheite Medal. In order to put the voyages into perspective, this narrative will take each in turn:

   * Captain John Bryon in the frigate *Dolphin* carried out a circumnavigation of the globe during the years 1764 to 1766. This voyage is unique in that Captain Byron appears to have discovered nothing. The *DNB* reflects, 'it appears he had not the nose for such work!'

   * Captain Samuel Wallis, again in *Dolphin*, had much better luck. During his voyage of 1766 to 1768 he secured a base near Cape Horn (the Falkland Islands) and then he explored west into the Pacific in search of the Southern Continent. Although Wallis did not achieve his objective (mainly through extreme hardship in rounding The Horn), one critical discovery was made. Otaheite. Upon Wallis' return, the Royal Society immediately recognised the importance of this discovery as being in the most preferred area for observing the Transit of Venus in all of the Pacific. Further, Wallis did sight the North Cape of New Zealand which was an important influence on the orders given to Captain Cook.

   * Captain James Cook's first voyage was aboard His Majesty's Bark *Endeavour* (a converted Whitby collier of 369 tons) took place during the years 1768 to 1771. The major mission was to observe the 'Transit of Venus' at Otaheite and to search for, and chart, the Southern Continent, and record any other useful discoveries along the way. The ship's compliment consisted of Lieutenant James Cook as Captain, and Lieutenant John Gore, an American who had been Master's Mate to both Captain John Byron in the *Dolphin* and more recently, Captain Wallis, also in the *Dolphin*. Certainly, Gore was the most knowledgeable South Sea traveller amongst the officers. Also present were Lieutenant Zachary Hicks and Midshipman Charles Clerke, a farmer's son from Essex who had a knack for being at the right place at the right time. He was in the mizzen-top of the *Bellona* when the mast was shot away in a celebrated action with the *Courageux* in 1761. He managed to swim to the surface and crawled half drowned into the chains. He too had been aboard the *Dolphin* with Byron, but was in the West Indies during Wallis' voyage. He was to thrive under Cook's command, and command the *Discovery* during the fatal Third Cook Voyage. Following Gore from the *Dolphin*, came Master Robert Molyneux, and Master Mates Richard Pickersgill and Francis Wilkinson. The Surgeon was William Brougham Monkhouse and as Surgeon's Mate, William Perry. Young gentlemen (1st class volunteers) were Isaac Manley aged 12, who later became an Admiral and the last survivor (died in 1837) of the *Endeavour* voyage, Jonathan Monkhouse (the Surgeon's brother), and Isaac Smith (Mrs Cook's cousin aged 16). An amusing note relates to the appointment of the ship's cook. As was normal, this post was reserved for a man who had suffered the loss of a limb and therefore was not a

full fighting man-of-war's man, but suitable as a cook. When Cook observed what the Admiralty had sent him as a 'lame infirm man and unable to do his duty', the Admiralty immediately obliged by appointing John Thompson who was only missing his right hand! Captain Cook again complained, which this time the Admiralty ignored. John Thompson managed well during the voyage. The total compliment was now 85 souls including a dozen Marines.

Lastly, we add the scientific contribution. Mr Joseph Banks, Naturalist, who was very well connected within English society. Here, I want to give you a wonderful assessment of Banks, given by J. C. Beaglehole in his *The Life of Captain Cook*. 'It now became fortunate that he [Captain Cook] had Banks with him: the young man, with plenty of time at his disposal while Solander worked on plants and fishes, revealed a universal interest and the happiest gift for getting on with people, whether men or women; and his susceptibility to the latter–who can forget 'the very pretty girl with a fire in her eyes'? ~ was welcomed and echoed by them. As a coadjutor, as a junior manager, he was invaluable; as an observer he was excellent; he was excited but not often thoughtless~ he could, even, be more cautious than Cook; he was sympathetic, amused, accurate. It is obvious that his journal and Cook's lay open before each other; obvious that he was baffled by some things as much as Cook was. It is obvious that neither was sentimental enough at that time to nourish the thought of Noble Savages.' In short, it is the enthusiasm of Joseph Banks which seems to drive the voyages of Captains Cook and Bligh. Although not a naval man, and still only 25 years old when *Endeavour* set sail, he managed over the years to be the bridge between interested parties including the Admiralty, the Royal Society, Cook, Bligh and Matthew Boulton. 'Happiest gift of getting on with people!'

As a note, the reference to 'the very pretty girl with a fire in her eyes' comes from *The Endeavour Journal of Joseph Banks* (edited by J. C. Beaglehole) and tells of the first meeting with the Royal Family of Otaheite, wherein: 'After this ceremony was over we walked freely about several large houses attended by the ladies who shewd us all kind of civilities our situation could admit of, but as there were no places of retirement, the houses being entirely without walls, we had not an opportunity of putting their politness to every test that maybe some of us would not have faild to have done had circumstances been more favourable; indeed we had no reason to doubt any part of their politness, as by their frequently pointing to the matts on the ground and sometimes by force seating themselves and us upon them they plainly shewd that they were much less jealous of observation than we were.

'Our Chief's own wife (ugly enough in concience) did me the honour with very little invitation to squat down on the mats close by me: no sooner had she done so than I espied among the common croud a very pretty girl with a fire in her eyes that I had not before seen in the countrey. Unconscious of the dignity of my companion I beckond to the other who after some intreatys came and sat on the other side of me: I was then desirous of getting rid of my former companion so I ceas'd to attend to her and loaded my pretty girl with beads and every present I could think pleasing to her: the other shewd much disgust but did not quit her place and continued to supply me with fish and cocoa nut milk. How this would have ended is hard to say, it was interupted by an accident which gave us an opportunity of seeing much of the peoples manners.' And so the scene closes with the discovery that Dr Solander and another gentleman had just had their pockets picked, this followed the admonishment of the crowd by Mr Banks with his gun, which then sent the girl with fire in her eyes running for cover.

On a further note, Banks in his capacity within the Royal Society actually had put forward the great hydrographer Alexander Dalrymple to head the expedition as opposed to Captain Cook. This recommendation ran foul of the Admiralty's insistence that Royal Navy ships must be commanded by a Royal Naval officer and as Cook had fully demonstrated his skill as a hydrographer and chart maker in the St Lawrence Seaway, during Wolf's Quebec campaign, Cook was the best choice of all. Interesting to note that in 1795, Dalrymple was appointed by the Admiralty as chief hydrographer and established the Admiralty Chart office. Dalrymple gained permission to recruit engravers so that the creation of the copper plates for printing charts would remain under his watchful eye. Later in 1800, Dalrymple ordered from Matthew Boulton a 'rolling-press', which was used to take refined copper bars and turn them into copper plates. For Boulton the process was necessary to create the plates from which coin planchettes would be cut out, for Dalrymple, he would now have the complete production of copper printing plates in house and under his control.

Next we meet the Swedish Dr Daniel Carl Solander, who was a pupil of the great Linnaeus. Dr Solander was a professional botanist associated with both the British Museum and Royal Society. We have an episode prior to the voyage which links Dr Solander with Matthew Boulton, but in a most curious way. There was great commercial rivalry between Britain and Sweden at this time, particularly in the area of industrial process. Under an Act of Parliament dating back to the reign of George I, there was a fine of £100 or three months in prison for those who tried to entice British artisans to migrate to Sweden and in so doing reveal secrets of industry. A correspondence exists in the Public Record Office (quoted by Dickenson in his *Matthew Boulton*) from Mr L. Stanhope (secretary to the Earl of Halifax, then Secretary of State) and Dr John Roebuck. In the letter dated 3 July 1765, Stanhope writes:

'About a year ago you applied to the Earl of Halifax to stop some artificers who were going to Sweden to establish a manufactory of Iron and Steel in that country, which his Lordship effectually did for that time but his Lordship has lately received advices that such a project is now on foot again and that one Dr Solander who is thoroughly acquainted with the affair is employed to negociate the business and there are reasons to believe he has been at Birmingham with proposals to one Boulton who the Sweeds are very desirous to engage to leave this country and settle amongst them.'

Mr Stanhope then asks Roebuck to act practically as a spy: 'It would be particularly usefull to his Lordship to know if Dr Solander has been at Birmingham or Boulton in London, or absent for any time within a few months past.'

In reply, James Farquaharson, clerk to Roebuck, who was away in Scotland on an extended trip, replied on 6 July, 1765:

'I have made all the secret inquiry I can to learn if Dr Solander hath been in Birmingham this year but I dont find that he has been.....but I find about 2 years agoe he recommended 2 or 3 Swdish Gentn from London to come to the Manufactures of this place. Mr Boulton is a man of very considerable property in & about Birmingham & I think very unlikely to attempt going to Sweden. I am very well acquainted with him & within this 4 years he has laid out above £4,000 in building Shops, Mils & Utensils for manufacturing of buttons & steel toys....etc.'

This is followed by another letter from Farquaharson on 19 Sept. 1765:

'I can now inform you for certain that Mr Boulton has no intention of going to Sweden, tho' he has very advantageous offers made to him. On the contrary he would spare no expense to detect any scheme of that nature which he considers so prejudicial to his country. Mr Boulton has lately rec'd a letter from Doctor Solander wherein he says that he had wrote to him 4 times & that he imagines they have miscarried for want of a proper direction. The Doctor presses Mr Boulton for an interview, but he declines either writing to him or to meet him but he intends to send you copy or the original letter from Dr Solander.' (Ref: Dickinson *Matthew Boulton*, pp. 48-50.)

Dr Solander is clearly busier than just considering the flora and fauna of these fair Isles!

As astronomer for the voyage, Mr Charles Green, who had served as Bliss' assistant at The Royal Observatory at Greenwich and had made in 1763 the voyage to Barbados with Maskelyne (Astronomer Royal and Head of the Board of Longitude), to test the accuracy of Mr Harrison's 'Time Machine'. Further, in Mr Banks' retinue were two artists (Sydney Parkinson and Alexander Buchan, the latter unfortunately died of an epileptic fit shortly after arriving at Otaheite), one secretary, four servants and two dogs.

Lastly we have an unnamed goat who had sailed with Wallis on the *Dolphin* and whose consistent production of milk was such, that with great recommendation, Captain Cook signed her on.

His Majesty's Barque *Endeavour* set sail from Plymouth on 25 August 1769. As first proof of Cook's good luck and precise navigation, it was a near perfect voyage into the Pacific. Only four deaths as compared with the near ruin of all previous crews brave enough to risk Cape Horn. This, as with so many things which relate to Cook, is down to his attention to detail and planning. The bringing of sauerkraut as an anti- scorbutic is one, and its use gives us a chance to hear from Captain Cook how his men were brought to like it:

'The Sour Krout the Men at first would not eate untill I put in practice a Method I never once knew to fail with seamen, and this was to have some of it dress'd every Day for the Cabbin Table, and permitted all the Officers without exception to make use of it and left it to the option of the Men either to take as much as they pleased or none atall; but this practice was not continued above a week before I found it necessary to put every one on board to an Allowance, for such are the Tempers and dispossions of Seamen in general that whatever you give them out of Common way, altho it be ever so much for their good yet it will not go down with them and you will hear nothing but murmurings gainest the man that first invented it; but the Moment they see their Superiors set a Value upon it, it becomes the finest stuff in the World and the inventer a damn'd honest fellow.' (Ref: Beaglehole *Life of Captain James Cook*, pp. 170-171.)

Further, Cook's changing the routine on board ship to three watches (instead of the normal two), where practical to work the ship, his stowing the cannon below in readiness for The Horn, and perhaps most importantly of all, his general rule that while strict discipline was necessary, the way to achieve it was not through the lash. While men on board *Endeavour* did not escape flogging for very severe infractions of the Standing Orders, it was indeed a rare occurrence. As Beaglehole comments that Cook clearly considered 'the sailor's mind rather than his back as the effective area of persuasion.' It is interesting to think that this was in fact Captain Cook's first long voyage as Captain, and his first time South of the Line. He made his land fall as expected and *Endeavour* dropped anchor in Matavai Bay, Otaheite on 13 April 1769, in plenty of time to make all of the preparations for the important observation of the Transit of Venus.

A portrait of 19 year old Poedua by John Webber, painted during Cook's third voyage, circa 1777. She lived on Raiatea, (Ulietea), one of the Society Islands neighbouring Tahiti. She wears a white drape of tapa cloth beneath her bare breasts and long black hair cascades over her shoulders. Jasmine blossom is positioned in her hair at her ears. Her right arm falls by her side and she holds a 'fly whisk' in her right hand, a mark of chiefly rank. Her arms and hands are covered with small tattoos.

BHC 2957 © National Maritime Museum, Greenwich, London.

With this arrival (or to be more accurate with Wallis's arrival on 18 June 1767), 'he came to an island such as dreams and enchantments are made of' and as such we have an encounter which was to become the stepping stone for the future exploration of the Universe and the Pacific Ocean, and, perhaps, a more subtle exploration within the longings of all men for all time.'

There followed the successful recording of the Transit at Otaheite. Tupaia (a Priest of Otaheite), and a small boy, Taiata, as his servant were taken on board to help with the further charting of the Society Islands. It is during the charting of the remaining islands that an interesting event occurred. Upon reaching the island of Huahine, about 100 miles distant from Otaheite, on 16 July, Cook and Tupaia and others were met on shore by Chief Ori, father of Poedua, who John Webber would paint on a later voyage in 1777. Upon exchanging names, Captain Cook and Chief Ori struck up an immediate friendship. Prior to Cook departing on the 19th, and as a token of regard, Cook presented Ori with 'a few medals as testimony of his discovery, but, more particularly, a small pewter plate inscribed with the words *His Britannick Maj. Ship Endeavour, Lieut. Cook Commander 16th July 1769. Huaheine.* The Chief promised never to part with it, and he did not.' (Ref: Ibid. pp. 193.) What were the medals given? I'm afraid we will never know. They may have been examples of a coronation medal of George III, or something else with his portrait. In the Banks' Journal is a footnote by Beaglehole, the items are described as 'medals or counters' which makes me think of the brass counters which are effectively guinea counters used in games and made to look like guineas with a portrait of the King on the obverse. This is a likely possibility as there would surely be the necessity for games on board *Endeavour*, particularly amongst Banks and his suite. If they had been coins, I think that they would have been described as such. Either way, this presentation to Chief Ori leaves no doubt that the presentation of a specifically struck medal for such occasions would be a boon to the discovery business! This must have left a lasting impression on Mr Banks as he was to make sure that on the second voyage, Captain Cook would not go without a purpose made medal with a fine portrait of the King as well as a representation of the ships taking part in the quest.

Progress was then made to New Zealand, where for the first time, the total extent of the coasts of both North and South Islands were charted. On 31 January, 1770 upon an island (Motuara) within the Cook Strait between North and South Island, Cook had erected a wooden post with 'ENDEAVOUR 31 Jan. 1770' carved on it. To an old man who is viewing these activities, Cook presents several 'silver threepenny pieces and spike (ship's) nails stamped with the (Admiralty) broad arrow', which were things Cook viewed as likely to be preserved. This was all in aid of encouraging the people not to pull the marker down and to care for it over time. Here a coin is specifically referred to. (Ref: Ibid. pp. 214.)

With the completion of the circumnavigation of both the North and South Islands, Cook produced the first chart delineating them. But the fixing of the Longitude for New Zealand was still by the Lunar method without the aid of an accurate chronometer. Even though John Harrison had solved the problem with his 'Time Machine', the clock was deemed far too delicate for regular use at sea. It wasn't until the second voyage that Cook was outfitted with chronometers robust enough to perform for years on end. Captain Cook was to find on his return to New Zealand, his original charts made during the *Endeavour* voyage had placed the islands between 30 and 40 minutes East of the actual Longitude, an error of about half a degree or 30 nautical miles.

Then Australia, the Southern Continent was at last sighted by Lieutenant Hicks at the main masthead on 19 April 1770. The survey of the eastern coast commenced from just north of Tasmania

Tahiti Revisited A View taken in the bay of Oaite Peha [Vaitepiha] Otaheite by William Hodges who was with Cook during the *Resolution* and *Adventure*, voyage of 1772-75.
BHC 2396© National Maritime Museum, Greenwich, London.

(Point Hicks) and did not end until York Cape in the Torres Straits. On 28 April, a fair bay was found, and Cook's wife's young cousin, Isaac Smith became the first Englishman to set foot in Botany Bay and all of Australia. Meetings with the local inhabitants did not prove fruitful. First, the language was not Polynesian based, so Tupaia was not able to converse as he had been in New Zealand. Secondly, the people didn't want to talk! Beads are offered, but all ignored. There is no mention of medals, counters or coins being exchanged. As a note, some of the natives used as adornment a slender four inch long piece of bone which was pierced through the bridge of the nose. Amongst the sailors, this was called a spirit-sail yard! Cook then set sail again and headed North / North West, but he didn't appreciate that as he moved north, he sailed deeper into a funnel which is formed by the Great Barrier Reef to the east and the shore to his west. Finally, on a hair raising day (Sunday, 10 June 1770), *Endeavour* struck the reef at high tide. It wasn't until the morning of the 13th that she managed to break free following the heaving overboard of her guns and all non essential material, and then on the 16th she sailed into what came to be known as Endeavour Bay. Repairs continued until the 4th of August, when the progress north recommenced. *Endeavour* finally (after many more near misses with the reef and shoal water) reached the Torres Strait, and with passage through, Cook was at last able to prove that Australia and New Guinea were separate bodies of land and that the Southern Continent was well and truly discovered.

Arriving at Batavia Road on 10 October (where Cook learned it was 11 October) effectively brought to an end the discovery part of the voyage. There followed a terrible period where malaria attacked the ship's company as all waited for the refit of *Endeavour* to be completed. Monkhouse, the Surgeon, both Taiata and Tupaia, Green's servant John Reynolds, and a number of seamen all died at Batavia. At last, on 26 December 1770, the restored *Endeavour* set sail, but the sickly state of the crew took its toll with Sporing, Green, the astronomer and the artist Sydney Parkinson along with a few others all perishing shortly after. These were followed by Midshipman Jonathan Monkhouse and a number of petty officers and men. On 15 April, Robert Molyneaux, the Master died. It wasn't until 25 May when the sharp-eyed Lieutenant Zachary Hicks died, that the dying finally stopped. In all malaria took nearly a third of the crew. At last home to England. Dover was sighted on 12 July 1771 and The Charmed Goat survived the trip!

Upon arrival, Mr Banks and Dr Solander ascended to the limelight and became the heroes of the age. As Beaglehole sums up: 'they had touched a near forty undiscovered islands, they had brought back over a thousand different species of plants unknown to Europe before....and although Banks did not bring back a lion or a tiger or a Tupaia; he was [now] a lion himself, and the nobility called at his house.' And such was the mania for information about the new discoveries. (Ref: Ibid. p. 273.)

As for Captain Cook, he was presented to the King by the new First Lord of the Admiralty, John Montagu, 4th Earl of Sandwich. The King expressly wanted to meet Captain Cook and have him describe his new discoveries. During Cook's presentation, the King found the moment to reward him with his new commission as Commander, Royal Navy. One can imagine the restrained enthusiasm of Cook as he described the adventures and achievements of the voyage. Never had a voyage taken so long, nor had the results been so complete. No longer would a 'glimpse' of unknown lands add to the Chart. As Nelson was to change the standard of success for a fighting command, so had Cook forever changed the standard for those in search of the unknown.

We are now in the late summer of 1771. The question for Captain Cook was, would the Admiralty support another voyage of discovery? His answer came on 25 September, when the Admiralty instructed the Navy Board to purchase two more Whitby coasters. From this point on, Cook became a busy man, selecting two ships for the purpose, testing new devices for purifying water, making beer, new types of pre-cooked food, a myriad of items which Commerce, Science, The Admiralty and sometimes even Cook himself, wanted to try out on the next voyage. He also allotted time to spend with his family, who with the loss of two children through illness, had suffered perhaps more than he while he was gone to Otaheite. Mr Banks was also busy (after all, this was to be His voyage!). Recruiting the artist Zoffany, securing two horn players, bringing Parliament to grant £4,000 for payment to Dr Lind, the physician to join the team. On and on it went. And there was the contact between Mr Banks and Mr Boulton of Soho to see about the manufacture of a medal which would be taken on the next voyage and distributed amongst the newly discovered peoples.

By early February, 1772, things were moving very fast. *Resolution* and *Adventure* were in the Thames being made ready for the voyage. Captain Cook made the formal address to Earl Sandwich as to his plan for the next voyage which was to go as far south as possible in search of the land of Antarctica. When it was deemed no longer possible to continue south or land had been reached, then to proceed east and either follow the coast of the new land or hopefully find it. If all fails and no new land is discovered, then proceed north in the longitude of New Zealand. The unknown land at the bottom of the World will be found! All was accepted by Earl Sandwich and all looked favourable for a Spring start. During this time, Cook had become increasingly aware that Mr Banks was making preparations in terms of added personnel and accommodation aboard the ships, which frankly could not be met. Things came to a head when Banks rejected the *Resolution* as she was, and required an additional deck to be built upon her in order to accommodate all 17 people in his party, and to give them ample living and work space. Cook (appreciating the politics?) allowed the changes to be made. On 2 May, Mr Banks entertained the French Ambassador and a number of other notables to a pre-departure party aboard *Resolution*, during which Banks probably distributed examples of the new Otaheite Medal. On 10 May, *Resolution* headed for the Downs. At the Nore, on 14 May, the Pilot gave up! She was too top heavy and couldn't carry a stitch of sail. Lieutenant Clerke told Mr Banks, 'By God I'll go to Sea in a Grog Tub, if desir'd, or in the *Resolution* as soon as you please; but must say, I think her by far the most unsafe Ship I ever saw or heard of.' And so it was that Mr Banks, and the Admiralty parted company and *Resolution* returned to dock where she was altered to her original lines. (Ref: Ibid. p. 294.)

Mr Banks and Dr Solander then changed tack and decided to explore Iceland, which they did for a month that summer. The medal discussed below probably was planned to be used on that voyage, but the medal was never struck or delivered.

Sir Joseph Banks painted by Josuha Reynonds, 1772.
Image © National Portrait Gallery, London.

Images courtesy of Heritage Auctions and Skyler Liechty

While all of this was in play, in Birmingham, Matthew Boulton was trying to produce his first medal. It is generally accepted that the design and die cutting came from John Westwood Sr. (1744-1792), who was an engraver and medallist in Birmingham. The attribution to Westwood is based on a unique cliché in the Skyler Liechty collection of the Type I medal with the obverse signed in place of the letters B:F, with the name 'Westwood' in full on the truncation of the King's neck. The portrait of King George III looks to be largely based on the obverse portrait used by Thomas Pingo in his recently published (1768) Royal Academy Prize Medal. There is also a note from Boulton's partner, John Fothergill to Boulton and dated 27 June 1772, in which he says: 'I am favor'd wth. yours of 24 Inst & another today. The dyes for the medals of Mr Banks and Dr Solander will be finish'd this day fortnight by Westwood [John senior] at 12 Guineas so that we shall have 9 days to finish the order wch. Moore [the Soho foreman] says shall be executed in L (ead?)'. This note is dated several months too late to relate to the now completed Otaheite Medal and probably has to do with an entirely new commission, never completed, which celebrates Banks and Solander as explorers in Iceland. It does, however, show that Boulton and Fothergill did use Westwood to cut dies for them.

What equipment would Matthew Boulton have used to produce the Otaheite Medal? Boulton had built his manufacture based on water power. Although he was in discussion with James Watt about exploiting his steam engine as early as 1767 and 1768, it appears that they didn't reach a business arrangement until 1774 when Watt moved to Birmingham to work with Boulton. From the previously quoted description of the Soho works by James Watt, we know that water power was available and that Matthew Boulton was using it to make buttons. The manufacture of a metal button (which is like a small medal) and to strike medals themselves is not a very great step. The obverse and reverse dies are produced, sheets of metal are produced and planchets or round blanks are punched or cut from the metal sheet. The images are struck on one or both sides of the button planchet by either a drop hammer or a Swing (or Fly) press. For a drop hammer, a simple arrangement is used wherein there is a substantial working station which has a fixed place for seating the planchet or blank on top of the reverse die, which for a button may be blank. Above this point is a hammer head which has the obverse die affixed to it. The hammer is raised within guides by either muscle or water power, and then at its peak is released to effect the blow or striking upon the seated planchet, which is now impressed both sides and ready for finishing.

If a Swing or Fly press was used, the process is the same except that the obverse die is secured to a rod which is brought down by swinging two perpendicular bars (with each swing bar being manned) which activates a descending screw, which in turn creates the downward thrust which sends the obverse die into contact with the planchet. The strike from above creates the obverse impression and the continued push creates the reverse impression on the other side of the planchet.

To create a better impression, more than one strike or blow is made with either a drop hammer or Fly press.

Lastly, what sort of collar was used? By a collar we mean a sort of a hollow circular die which forms the edge of the medal as the rim of the medal is pushed outward upon the strike being made. I don't think that the Otaheite Medal had a collar used in its production. Again from Watt's observations, Boulton hand finished buttons with water powered grinders and polishers. There is also a tell tale curiosity about Type II medals, i.e. the obverse die appears to be about 1mm less in diameter than the reverse die. Imagine a paddy of dough. If it is sitting on a flat surface and you push something circular into it, there is a raising up of a rim around the impression. An uncollared medal planchet will behave the same way. My view is that after striking each medal, Boulton had its rim lightly machined or hand filed to create a rounded even rim. Particularly on the Type II not 'proof-like' silver medals, one can see these light file / machining lines.

We have an revealing notation from Boulton's Pocket Book of 1772:

'Silver Banks Medals took 5 blows each. He [the pressman] could stamp 4 Gro. [gross, i.e. 12 x 12 = 144] per day, but if a Boy could lay 'em in [the planchets onto the die] he could stamp 10 Gro or 12 [gross] once over [one strike each]. Our big hammer is 7 Score.' [7 x 20 = 140 lbs.]

There then follows a calculation, which I include, if only to show how Boulton's business mind is working:

'3s. each \ 144 \ 432s. = £21.12s viz. £20 per Gross' [keep in mind 20 shillings to a Pound].

Note: Here Boulton is taking the unit sale (or is it cost?) price of 3 shilling each and finding out what to sell a gross or 144 units for. His math is a little out as 432 shillings equals £21. 6 shillings, but he is working fast and rounds it all down to £20 per 144 units.

'144 x 50 = 7,200 plus 3,600 equals 10,800 or 10,000 or 75 Gross equals £1,500.' [i.e. total sale price for 75 Gross].

'Say 10 per Minute equals 600 per Hour or 6,000 per day, or say 10,000 in 2 days. 5000 devided by 144 equals [say] 35 Gross per day.' (Ref: Westwood, *Matthew Boulton's Otaheite Medal*, p. 4.)

Several things may be deduced from the above. First, only one man was operating the press. The drop hammer required only one operator, while the Swing Press required two. Secondly, the Silver Medal required five blows (even sounds like a drop hammer compared with the more delicate Swing Press). Boulton then speculates what the effect of using the Big Hammer of 140 pounds will have on the rate of production. My interpretation is that some lesser hammer was used which required five blows, but if the Big Hammer was used, Boulton thinks it might produce a medal with only one blow. This equation may not work in that one has to keep in mind the ability of the planchet to receive one very big blow compared with several medium blows. Worst case, the planchet and the dies will all split asunder!

Lastly, I think that what we are looking at here is not so much a critique regarding the production of Otaheite Medals, but the early notes by Boulton which assess the potential revenue in this type of new manufacture. To expand, he is looking at £1,500 per 75 Gross. He thinks he can produce this over two days. His next item would be that if he could find people who could stand a press 10 hours a day and produce every day of the year, he would have produced £136,875 worth of goods, which in 1772 was indescribable wealth! Mr Boulton was starting to see what coinage and medallic manufacture could mean.

However, it certainly isn't plain sailing as Boulton writes to Dr Solander on 10 March 1772:

'I here send you Such part of a Letter (I some time ago wrote to a certain Southern Voyager, i.e. Banks) as relates to the Distinguishing of Minerals. I cannot but consider it as somewhat presuming in myself to write to a Gentn. so much more learned in every branch of natural knowledge but such presumption is more excusable than not fullfilling my promise. I was very unfortunate in ye Cracking of one of the Medal Dyes, but hope nevertheless that they will Ansr. all the purposes intended. [and then referring to glass beads and ear drops ordered by Banks], The Bead I was forced to Manufacture myself there being no such thing made in Birmingham. I have also got the Ear drop done which appear'd to me in so rough a Style that I have ventured to put you to the expence of grinding one half of 'em which suppose will make 'em more profitable to you. They with every thing else shall be at Mr Banks on Saturday evening next per Coach. May the God of all things preserve your Body that I may once more have the happiness of Saluting you, farewell, remember me who am &c.'

As Boulton wrote this, he was not expecting to see either Banks or Solander for several years. You will note that the date on the Otaheite Medal is March 1772. All should have been finished with the medals struck (Type I only with the cracked reverse die) and on board ship. Not to be! (Ref: Ibid. p. 6.)

In the Mitchell Library, Sydney, there are letters from Boulton & Fothergill to Banks in the file labelled *Volunteers, Instructions, Provisions for 2nd Voyage* pp 291-300, which are quoted here. With this letter from Matthew Boulton to Mr Banks dated Soho, 11 March 1772, Boulton reveals just how depressed he is with his efforts:

'Dear Sir,

'So stupid are all our Birmingham glass pinchers that I could scarcely get anyone to undertake ye making of ye drops, beads &c: but at length prevail'd upon one to promise them, who, when ye day ariv'd for ye delivery, informed me that he could not make them. I then set one of our own workmen to Soho about them & I believe he will compleat them by Tuesday eveng so that you will receive them on Thursday pr coach & at the same time you shall receive all the Medals. I durst not strike any Silver ones as the dye for ye reverse provd unsound & cracked in a very ugly manner the very first blow. As I am this evening sending several Boxes pr Coach to Lord Kerry in Portman Square I have inclosed 2 Doz of medals that you may see their faults they are seald up & I beg you send some body on Wednesday morng for them. If time wd have permitted I would have sunk a new reverse dye but I durst not attempt it. The loop [suspension] being forgot until ye dyes were hardened we were obliged to be at an extroadinary expence in putting a pendant to each medal wch we shall not charge to you.'

Letter from Matthew Boulton to Mr Banks dated Soho, 16 March 1772:

'Dear Sir,

'I am fac'd with yours of ye 14th int by which I perceive you want 12 more Silver Medals, ie in all 12 medals (plus) 20 (total) 32, also 2 Gold ones. Now you must know that a flaw in a Medal dye like a hole in ones Stocking increases in a greater ratio than ye squares if ye uses or wear of it, so that ye dye for ye reverse is now so bad that I cannot think of disgracing the Cabinet of the King or your Friends with impropious of so tatterd a dye. I have therefore come to a resolution this afternoon (wch I wish I had done a week ago) to have a new reverse dye gravd & that I hope to get done so that the 2 Gold & ye 32 Silver ones shall be deliverd to your order in London on Tuesday evening the 24th int. Although it will be attended with some little expence yet it shall not be such a one as to give you any reason to complain. I know you dont mind four or 5 guineas or thereabouts. It is probabl but you may sail before the 24th but if you should you may leave your orders respecting the distribution of them. I have venturd to make some wrist rings & some cheap braseletts, of a kind that we once had orders before for East India wch hope will suit your purposes haveing made them on purpose. We have now sent by this & last nights coach all the remains of your orders except ye Medals & some of ye long Ear drops wch wth the Invoyce of ye whole shall be sent tomorrow ex (post?) haste & believe me to be with exteem Your much obliged humle serv. Matthw. Boulton'

If you have any occassion to write to me again do intimate when you think you shall leave London as I think there is some chance of my seeing you again.

Letter Invoice from Boulton & Fothergill to Jos. Banks, dated Birmingham, 18th March 1772:

'Inclos'd We take the freedom of handing you Invoice of all the Goods already forwarded from hence viz:

Sundries		the 5th Marchin three Casks	p. Waggon		Nett £48/17/-
Medals	14th	do in one do	p.	do	Nett £50/1/6
Sundries		do in a box p. Machine		do	Nett £15/11/-
do	17th	do do	do	do	Nett £12/4/-

         In the Whole   £126/13/6

'which We doubt not will be found right, and to satisfaction. You have inclos'd a Certificate to receive a drawback of £1/7/2 upon our Agent Mr William Matthews / at No. 14 Cannon Street in London / hath already deliver'd the nails to your order & furnish'd you with Invoice thereof. You can also adjust every thing respecting these goods with said Mr William Matthews, as He is properly authoriz'd to transact Business on our behalf with the same power that We could do if personaly present.

'The Silver &c Medals are not yet ready owing to the accident that befel the Reverse Side of the Die, but We presume our Mr Boulton hath wrote you the needfull relative thereto.

'P.S. Our Servant who is to Sink the Reverse, or the Ship Side of the Medal die, hath not been able to Work since we recd. your order for the Silver Medals But we are Hopes He will be able to do a little Tomorrow, and defend not a moment of time shall be lost to complete the execution.'

During this time between the 18th and 25th of March, Westwood was able to cut a new reverse die and production of the gold and silver medals has commenced.

We next have a letter from Boulton & Fothergill to Jos: Banks Esq., New Burlington Street, London, dated 25 March 1772:

'Above you have Invoice of the Gold & Silver Medals which we forwarded in a Box directed for you pr to Night fly [flying Waggon] amounting to £43/16/0 for which your account stands debited. We have been obliged to make Use of fine Gold for fear of the Medals being too hard for the dyes, and as the shortness of the time wou'd not admit of our getting proper Shagreen Cases made for them, we leave it to you to buy such Cases as you will think most suitable to the purpose. The Earings we have not been able to get dõne having been disappointed in the Opinion we had of the Workman we intrusted with the making of them, who at first did not succeed in his Attempts, but however got to day 2 pair of them done, which we send you along with the Medals (Otahite), altho there is no time left to send you any More of them. By the several Experiments we have made respecting the Beads we are now able to make 'em as good as they can be wish'd for, but for want of time we cannot send you more of 'em. We wish you sincerely a happy and successfull Voyage and are with perfect Esteem.

'At last we cannot send you the silver Medals to Night for the above being wrote we perceive that we cannot get 'em done; how ever we send the 2 Gold ones to our Agent, Mr Wm. Matthews, No. 14 Cannon Street, with strict Orders to deliver them to you imediately on reciption and shall forward you the Silver Ones by to Morrow.' (Ref: Westwood, *Matthew Boulton's Otaheite Medal*, p. 7.)

And again on 29 March: 'We are extremely glad to observe by your kind favour to 25 inst, that your departure is delay'd for a fortnight longer as it affords us the satisfaction to know that we have sent you the Gold and Silver Medalls yet in time and struck out of the new dye, and as said delay gives us time to execute some green Glass Ear-drops we hope to send you some of 'em, so as to arrive in London by Wednesday or Friday night. Our Mr Boulton who intends to be soon in London hopes to have the pleasure of seeing you yet before you leave the Island.' (Ref: Ibid. p. 7.)

Further we have: Boulton & Fothergill (written by Fothergill) to M. Boulton Esqr (in London) and dated between 4 and 7 April, 1772:

'The 100 Silver Medals for Mr Banks being done, I shall forward them along with 12 pair of Green Glass Ear drops (which is all Thacker has made of them 'till now) by tomorrow morning's Coach, but as I am rather doubtfull or not the Charge I have made for the fashion &c. &c. will be agreeable to you, I shan't advise Mr Banks thereof but leave it to you to settle the fashion as you think most proper, mean while I have debited him as follows in our Books:-

'100 Silver Medals wt 145 Ounces @ 5/9 each   £41 / 13 / 9
        fashion & waste in Silver &c.   15 /   /
        12 pair Ear drops @ 1/6 each   /18 /
                Box   / 6

                                                       £57 / 12 / 3

'It is very possible that as I do not know how to apreciate properly the fashion I may have charged it too high, but it will be an easy matter to alter it afterwards agreeable to your direction. All the Ear drops Thacker will get done shall be sent to Mr Banks in the Course of this Week. I have charged the Ear drops 1/6 p pair - for Bently says they cost 1/- p pair.' (Ref: Ibid. pp 7-8)

We then have a detailed list from the Admiralty Secretary to Captain Cook, dated 11 April:

'It being judged necessary that the several things mentioned in the enclosed Account, should be provided & sent on board the *Resolution* & *Adventure* in the proportions therein Mentioned, in order to be exchanged for Refreshments with the Natives of such New discovered or unfrequented Countries as they may touch at, or to be distributed to them in presents towards obtaining their friendship, & winning them over to our Interest, And their Lordships having directed Mr Boulton of Birmingham to pack up in proper Cases, & send to the Storekeeper at Deptford to be put on board said Sloops the Several Articles Mark'd B in the said Account,....etc.' (Ref: Beaglehole, *The Journals of Captain Cook*, vol. II, pp 923-924.)

For the items marked B, we have quite an impressive selection. Adzes 20, Axes 340, Broad Axes 40, Hatchets 500, Spike Nails 800 Lbs, Nails 40 pence and upwards 800 Lbs., Chizzles 40, Saws 20, Coopers Augers 80, Tweezors 10 dozen, and lastly Hammers 40. No doubt this was also in aid of keeping the natives and the men from using actual parts of the ships to 'seal the pact of friendship!'

On 16 April, there is a note from the Admiralty to the Navy Board: 'Messrs Boulton and Fothergill of Birmingham to be paid £80 / 14 / 3 for articles provided for *Resolution* and *Adventure* [this would probably refer to the goods noted in the 11 April note to Captain Cook] and further £50 for making a die and striking off 2,000 medals to be distributed to natives of such new discovered countries as the sloops may touch at.' (Ref: Ibid: p. 925.)

So, with this note, we know that the 2,000 medals have either been shipped or have arrived in London at a price to the Admiralty of £50, hence the authority being given to pay Boulton and Fothergill. We also know that the dies for the (still unknown medal) made by Westwood cost 12 guineas (£12 / 12 / 0) and considering one of the dies had to be recut, (say) £18 to round up for the total cost of the dies, which leaves £32 to produce and deliver the medals. In the pound (at that time) there were 240 pence. £32 equals 7,680 pence.

We are familiar with the Penny and Cartwheel Twopence minted by Boulton in 1797. The Otaheite Medal has more metal than the Penny, but if Platina, would probably cost about the same to produce. Therefore, the relationship is 2,000 units of equivalent value of one pence each, versus 7,680 pence in revenue. Plus suspension for another 2,000 units, total 4,000 units. Not bad!

And then on 19 April 1772 from Boulton & Fothergill to William Matthews (their agent in Cannon Street, London): 'You'll find herewith a parcel for Mr Banks containing the 6 Silver Medals, shall send the metal ones soon after you please to acquaint Mr Boulton that Banks is charg'd for them as follows, but wrote to (viz)

6 Silver Medals wt. 8 oz 13 dwt. @ 5/9 each	£2 / 9 / 9
fashion waste in Silver &c.	/ 12 / 3
	£3 / 2 /

We should also be glad to know what alteration Mr Boulton has made in Bank's Account that we may pass it accordingly.' (Ref: Westwood, *Matthew Boulton's Otaheite Medal*, p. 9.)

From The Mitchell Library is the key document, a statement from Boulton & Fothergill to Mr Banks dated 20 April 1772, wherein the total supply is stated:

March	5th To a Cask of Edged Tools & Two casks of Glass	£48/17/-
	14th To 2000 platina medals and the cask	50/1/6
	ditto To sundry glass and other Toys	15/11/-
	17th ditto ditto ditto	12/4/-
	26th To 2 Gold and 36 Silver Medals	43/16/-
	30th To 18 Casks of Nails	12/11/-
April	4th To 100 Silver Medals and 12 pair Ear Drops	57/12/3
	9th To 23 pair Green Glass Ear Drops	1/14/6
	11th To sundry Glass and other Toys	2/8/8
	13th ditto ditto ditto	-/10/6
		£245/6/5
	20th To 6 Silver Medals	3/2/0
		£248/8/5

Now with Mr Banks definitely not making the voyage, a letter from Boulton & Fothergill to William Matthews dated 6 June 1772: 'Mr Boulton desires you'll return the medals you have if you have not opportunities to dispose of 'em, for if you have not we have many of 'em here.' (Ref: Westwood, *Matthew Boulton's Otaheite Medal*, p. 9.)

Lastly for John Fothergill in Soho to Matthew Boulton in London, dated 27 January 1773: 'I will send you some Bankes Medals by next Coach.' (Ref: Ibid. p. 9.)

One doesn't know whether these medals were charged to Banks and perhaps not collected by him, or are these medals that Boulton struck to his own account for sale to interested collectors? Probably the latter.

With the above, we can draw some conclusions:

* We have the invoice dated 16 March from Boulton & Fothergill to Mr Banks which includes one Cask of Medals shipped on 14 March via Waggon. The cost was £50/1/6. We don't know how big the cask was, but if 2,000 medals are involved, something like a cask would be used to ship them.

* We have the Admiralty order to the Navy Board dated 16 April wherein £50 is allowed for 'making a die and striking 2,000 medals.' This is the proof that the Admiralty accepted the transfer of the order from Banks for the 2,000 medals that went on the Voyage.

* We also know that from the Boulton to Banks letter dated 16 March that the silver and gold have not been struck due to the reverse die breaking.

* The letter dated 25 March from Boulton & Fothergill to Jos. Banks confirms that the two Gold Medals were now struck, and apparently some silver and that the total bill is £43/16/0. The gold and silver Medals were struck with the new die for the reverse. Situation is still a bit confused, but with the letter of 29 March, the gold and silver are on their way.

* From the Statement of Account dated 20 April, it is now clear that Banks had ordered medals struck from the new reverse die as 2 x gold and 142 x silver medals. Whether Boulton struck more medals to his own account is not known, but one has to think very likely particularly as the Type II medals in copper don't appear in the accounts to Banks.

From the above, the conclusions we can draw are that 2,000 Type I medals were struck for a price of about £50 and paid for by the Admiralty for use on the second Cook voyage. We will have to look at the physical evidence to see exactly which medals these were, but for now it certainly looks to be platina, with some copper examples included. The two gold and 142 silver medals for Banks to be given to his friends were struck for a total cost of £104/10/3 with some ear drops included.

Review of some known medals and comments:

Images © The Trustees of the British Museum, London.

OM 1) The Gold Medal in the British Museum came from the collection of King George III. The example is absolutely stunning (and heavy as Boulton noted he had to use 'fine Gold for fear of the Medals being too hard for the dyes.' The dies used are Type II, with a glorious strike which has produced frosted images for both the obverse and reverse. The strength of the striking has accentuated the die breaks in the obverse field under the letter K in KING and the elongated lump on the upper middle of the King's neck. Also, there is a less strong impression of the word KING as in the obverse striking found in Type I examples. Further, the word ETC. is now in real trouble, with the E and T coming up particularly weak. The rest of the obverse legend is relatively strong. For the reverse die, the die crack between the letters E and N in Adventure is just starting. The rim has a distinct convex curve and a minute step from the rim to the obverse edge, plus the rim has been dressed in a high polish. The diameter is 44 mm. There is no suspension, nor is there a tell-tale hole where the suspension may have been fitted. The orientation is perfect with both the obverse and reverse dies sharing the same top point. A truly impressive piece!

OM 2) This Silver Medal in the British Museum is from the collection of Sarah Sophia Banks (sister of Joseph Banks, and an indefatigable collector of coins and medals). In later years, Matthew Boulton presented her with an example of every coin and medal he struck. An interesting note from Sir Joseph Banks to Boulton in December, 1791 reads: 'As you allow me to write to you when I want anything, I take the liberty to acquaint you, first, that my sister is a great pusher, she has seen your 5 sous piece and has not got one of them. If you fear a lady's resentment or wish to court her favour, I would advise you to furnish her with one as speedily as convenient, and if you add to it any other new tokens it may be well, as the sight of them will certainly work favourably in her eyes.' To this Boulton replied: 'Please to present my most respectful compliments to Miss Banks with assurances that I remember the promise I made and that my religion will not suffer me to break my promises and particularly when made to a Lady. I hope to have the honour of contributing to Miss Banks' Collection of Coins in the course of a Month, but the principal pieces are not yet out of the Mint.' (Ref: Westwood, *Matthew Boulton's Otaheite Medal*, p. 5.) Again, a proof-like very strong striking of the Type II set of dies. You can almost see that immediately following the striking of the gold, the silver medals were struck. In Miss Banks' silver example, the new die crack found

Images © The Trustees of the British Museum, London.

in the reverse die of the gold between the letters E and N in ADVENTURE suddenly increases and wields up a significant lump of metal at the left foot of the letter N. Everything else is exactly as the gold, same orientation, same 'dressed and polished' convex rim, same 44 mm diameter and no suspension nor drill hole in the rim. Again, a magnificent piece! For another example, reference the medal illustrated as BHM 165. In past discussions with Laurence Brown, we couldn't be sure which metal it was made of, but with its proof-like qualities and the state of the die flaw in the reverse die between the letters E and N, it looks the same state as the Sarah Banks silver example and is probably another silver.

OM3) The silver medal in SCC is from the Type II set of dies, but with a much less crisp obverse

legend with the words KING and ETC, bordering on the faint. I'm speculating that this was caused by a polishing of the dies and working with a much reduced force in striking in order to preserve the dies from further damage. The flaw in the obverse field under the letter K is just barely noticeable, as is the elongated lump in the upper middle of the King's neck. The die flaw on the reverse die between the letters E and N in ADVENTURE is there, but not very menacing, i.e. it is now just a line between the letters, whereas in the Miss Banks example, there is a significant lump of metal at the left foot of the letter N. The devices are not frosted, but still very attractive. The orientation is perfect with the obverse and reverse dies sharing a common top point. The rim again is convex and there is no doubt that it has been machined and polished, although not to the degree of the Miss Banks Silver. The diameter is again 44 mm. There is no suspension affixed, nor is there any trace of a suspension having ever been fixed to the rim. For two more examples of the 'not proof-like' Type II versions, reference Spink Australia sale of 16 and 17 March 1988, Lot 986. and Christie's sale of 8 December 1987, Lot 305.

Copper examples are found struck with both the Type I and Type II sets of dies. Examples in copper may be in a class of their own, in that they are scarcer than the silver and usually found in excellent condition wherein the platina examples are frequently well worn. Of the Type I Copper pieces, it appears that the die break is always in its earliest stages, therefore my thinking is that in copper, these pieces are probably trial pieces.

OM 4) For this Type I Copper medal see Glendining's sale of 18 November, 1987, lot 19 for one of the finest known example in existence. This piece has its original suspension and it is oriented to the reverse die, but with the top point being off centre by about 10 degrees. Of particular interest is the state of the reverse die flaw in the exergue, which is at an early stage, i.e., a very thin line crack

which comes up from the bottom edge below the letter H and then catches the foot of letter C going off to the left where it crosses the letter R and finally stops at the foot of the letter L. There is also a small lump of metal, which may have started life as part of the design, located under the stern of the left hand ship (*Resolution*) and is placed on the bar which forms the upper extent of the exergue. In 1987, this medal made £3,300 and was again sold in the Bowers & Marena auction of the Lucien La Riviere collection on 17 March 2001 as lot 2133. At that time the price was £5,980 which to me was still cheap considering the extreme rarity of the piece.

Although this medal is a very early strike, it has none of the characteristics of the 'proof- like' frosted images and near mirror fields of the Gold and Silver Type II examples in the British Museum. The rim (working from the Glendining's photograph) appears to be slightly convex and the example has a 42 mm diameter.

OM 5) The SCC Copper Type I example was purchased from Baldwin's in 1995. The die break is in its early stages. The medal has lost its suspension and is only very good to fine condition, i.e. it is very evenly worn as if it has been a pocket piece for many years, perhaps kept by somebody with a dry pocket to keep it in, could have been a crew member who made the trip. The really surprising thing about this example is the orientation. It has shifted to 180 degrees and so far is the only copper Type I recorded as such. The suspension hole is placed for displaying the obverse.

For Copper Type II examples, the assumption is that they are as the Type II Silver (but not proof-like) issue, which looks correct from viewing the photographic and catalogue detail of three examples to have been auctioned. Ref: Spink Australia of 16 and 17 March 1988, Lot 987 where there is no notation of the piercing of the edge for suspension. This example looks to me to be right at the end of the production of the Otaheite Medal, as the obverse legend is now suffering very greatly with KIN in the word KING being barely discernible, as well at ET in ETC. being extremely weak. On the reverse die, there is now a quite noticeable die break between E and N in ADVENTURE which runs from the outer edge, down between the letters and stops with a considerable lump of metal at the left foot of the letter N. The diameter is 44 mm. This piece is ex George Mackaness Collection, and is discussed in his *The Art of Book Collecting in Australia*, Sydney, 1956, ref: pp. 10-12. Mr Mackaness (who also wrote the definitive biography of William Bligh), tells us of an urgent message from a friend in Newcastle, NSW: 'You had better come up here on Saturday because one of the pilots (Captain Anderson) has some rare Cook material that he wants to sell.' He then recounts that Captain Anderson's father and grandfather had both been Master Mariners at Grimsby in Yorkshire (which is not far from Cook's home in Whitby), and that his grandfather had collected the material in England and this included the above Otaheite Medal. The author then recounts a hurried deal with an eye on the clock so that he doesn't miss his train home, and the general excitement of at last finding one of these wonderful pieces.

Another Type II Copper was sold at Sotheby's sale of 30 Sept. 1988, lot 692, where the previous lot (691) is a platina example lacking its suspension and noted as such in the catalogue; while this copper example in lot 692 has no mention of lacking suspension, therefore one thinks there is no rim hole which would be present if there had been a suspension fitted. The photographs of the piece and the above example match very closely with the noticeable lump of metal at the left foot of the letter N in ADVENTURE on the reverse die. The die break is very similar to the Miss Banks' silver example, but then the obverse legends are much less well defined. The diameter is 44 mm.

At Woolley & Wallis, 21 January 2015, lot 821, a Copper Type II in near EF condition made £4,200 hammer, around £5,000 all in. Not bad for a very rare medal.

OM 6) A holed Platina specimen in SCC. To my knowledge platina examples are found only with the Type I set of dies and are always pierced for suspension. Ref: Glendining's sale of 18 Nov. 1987, Lot 20, which is the Sim Comfort Collection example. The hole for the suspension (the original screw is still embedded in the rim) orientates to the obverse portrait of King George III with both the obverse and reverse sharing the top, but with the 10 degree shift. The rim itself is as the Type I Copper, i.e., it is slightly convex, and is machine finished, but not polished. The rim is not as convex as the rim found in the Type II Gold and Silver (and assumed Copper) that I have inspected. The diameter is 42 mm. The dies conform

completely to the Type I statement, while the reverse die flaw in the exergue has taken on rather dramatic proportions. As in the Type I Copper it commences its journey at the edge below the letter H (in MARCH) moves north-west, connects with the foot of C and then kind of explodes into a massive lump of metal which almost entirely overlays the letters A and R, then continues north-west and terminates in the foot of L in SAILED. But there is more! Like a San Andrea's fault, under the surface of the medal one can see a bulge which is parallel to the above line. This bulge starts in the letter I and goes north-west and then erupts into what is now a large mass of metal on the exergue top border line under the stern of *Adventure*. As it looks to be part of the sea, many may mistake it as a monster from the deep!

The piece itself is an evenly worn VF with another special feature. A large and neat round hole centred above the King's head (which makes it off centre for the two ships on the reverse). How awful! Well not exactly, for this is a very special hole. First, this hole allows us to be quite definite about the medal being made of platina and not copper or bronze-gilt. You can look inside the hole and between the encrusted elements you are in a tiny mine of Pinchbeck Gold / Brass. It glimmers and shimmers just like the real thing! It doesn't take too long to ask, 'Where did the hole come from?' Indeed, where did it come from? I don't know, but you can be pretty sure that Matthew Boulton didn't put it there. And as the platina pieces are the pieces that made the trip with Cook, someone on board Cook's ships could have put it there, or SOMEONE who it was given too! We'll never know, but my money is on 'the very pretty girl with a fire in her eyes.'

On a more serious note, a visit to the Museum of Mankind in London gave me the answer I was looking for. Throughout Polynesia, drilling holes by the use of a spindle top type device was used with great effect. The drill point could be of the hardest material available, i.e. flint, shark's tooth, coral, or small mineral alloys created by volcanic action. The results are dramatic, particularly in South Island, New Zealand where the extremely hard nephrite or 'Green Stone' is worked and drilled with perfectly round holes, just like the one in this Platina Type I Otaheite Medal. And as yet another aspect of something as trite as a carefully drilled hole in this platina medal, it may well represent a very early instance for the culture who fashioned it; an early instance of manufacture in metal as there was no metal common to Otaheite or Polynesia prior to the arrival Captain Cook with his ship's nails and Otaheite Medals.

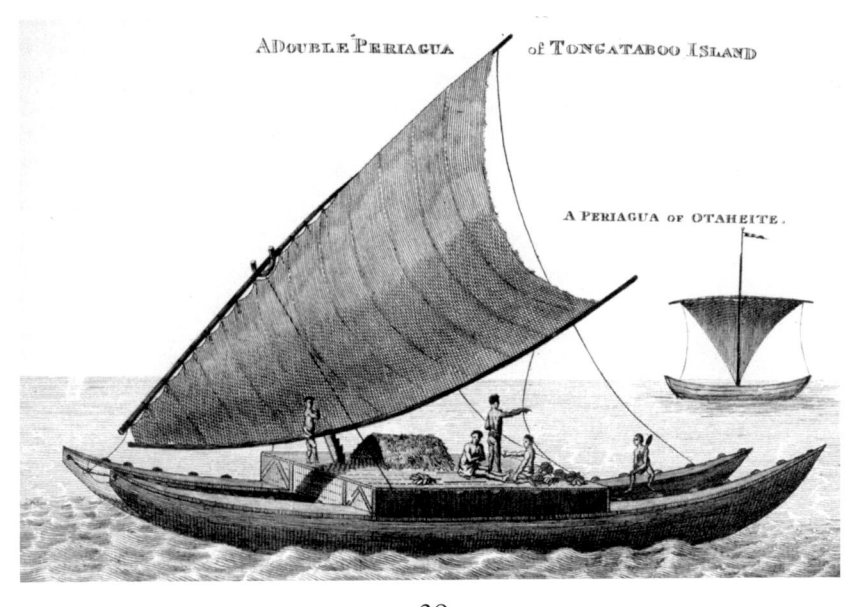

OM 7) This Type I Platina medal is another example from SCC which is lacking its suspension but bears the suspension hole which is situated to display the two ships with the obverse and reverse sharing a common top point, but 10 degrees out. There are references to medals which are copper-gilt and this could be one of them, although if the gilding was done at Soho, the surface wouldn't have deteriorated in this fashion. This medal does have one strange feature though and that is almost the total loss of the letters AND in ENGLAND in the reverse exergue. I think this has been caused by the letters AND being clogged and therefore not struck up.

Again the suspension orientation would have been to the obverse portrait of King George III (you can see a bulge in the reverse die behind the letter A which gives proof of this), and in fact is like another pea from the same pod as the OM 6. The die crack in the reverse die exergue is just as dramatic, and under a strong glass looks to be at very nearly the same state of progression. The diameter is 42 mm.

OM 8) Another Type I Platina specimen from SCC which is very similar to OM 6, but without the hole. There is a lot of copper colour, but the medal I'm pretty sure is platina. The suspension is centred on the obverse and with the obverse and reverse sharing the same top point but being 10 degrees out. The diameter is 42 mm.

Next we have the Type I Platina example in the British Museum which is also ex Miss Banks. The dies conform completely with the Type I with the reverse die crack at the earliest stage. It commences at the edge and moves north-west to the foot of C in MARCH. It then moves left to, and through, the letter R where it stops at the upper left of R. But the orientation of the obverse and reverse dies is at 180 degrees, i.e. the top of each die is at the other end of the medal. The piece was mounted with suspension, but the loop has broken off leaving the screw still imbedded in the rim. Although the piece is EF, it unfortunately has suffered an attack of some form of oxidation which has left it with a very unpleasant surface and not suitable for photography.

Last, we have probably the best preserved platina example which was auctioned by Spink Australia on 16 and 17 March, 1988, lot 985. Like the British Museum example, it has the same 180 degrees orientation, and best of all, its original suspension is still in place with the suspension oriented to the reverse view of the ships, but upside down! The piece is graded EF and looks it. What is also interesting is that the reverse die crack most closely resembles that of the Miss Banks' example and is at an earlier stage than the copper with original suspension auctioned by Glendining's (lot 19) in November, 1987, i.e. the die crack is in its very early stages and is not the mature die crack detailed in the other platina pieces. This medal made £3,260.

As a comment, we have seen one copper and two platina examples with orientation at 180 degrees. All three examples have the reverse die break at early stages. We then have the have two platina examples with orientation of the dies both being up, but 10 degrees off centre and both with a very extensive die flaw in the reverse exergue. Looks like a fairly safe conclusion that the three 180 degree orientation pieces are very early specimens which caused Boulton to rethink the orientation (keeping in mind that the suspension had an effect on the medal as either obverse or reverse could be displayed when the medal was worn), because on one side the King's head is correctly displayed facing up, while when turned over the two ships are upside down. Better to have them both right side up. Even better to have them right side up and sharing the same top point. Boulton had learned many lessons by the time Type II was produced!

Discussion:

The Otaheite Medal is in a class all by itself. I believe it to be the only medal in the British series which is expressly made and sanctioned by the Crown to be given to such new peoples as are found on a voyage of discovery. In a way, it is like an Indian Peace Medal, but then it isn't, because the recipients of the Peace Medals where known and recognised and the occasion was invariably concluding a Treaty of Peace. The use of the Otaheite Medal was an offering of introduction upon which it was hoped friendship would follow. There is perhaps a more subtle purpose. To let those future travellers know that the representatives of King George have been here and that these lands are deemed his. All in support of Britannia Rules the Waves!

How do the two types of medals fit into the chronology of the correspondence and events? First let us recount what happened. It is clear that Boulton's skill of medal making was in its infancy, just as it is clear that his manufacturer of 'Green glass ear drops' was something he hadn't contemplated. As a businessman, his cause was to gain the order and serve his customer. But there is something else. Perhaps this relates to the vision of doing something very important, i.e. being a participant in a History making Enterprise. This is something which we will see again in connection with Matthew Boulton. It wasn't just business, it was much more important than that. All of this is seen with each of his naval medals, and culminates in the Boulton Trafalgar Medal which had no business basis at all, a pure gesture of recognition by himself personally to those who made History.

So we have Boulton with this very important commission. The first medals are struck, and the reverse die breaks. Somewhere along the line, someone notes that the *Resolution* shouldn't be shown in full sail with her anchor down. A double disaster! Mr Banks is in high tension because it is now March and the expedition should set sail very soon and the medals aren't ready. Well, at least the platina pieces are ready and already stowed in the hull of *Resolution*. Boulton's very weak note to Solander on 10 March reveals his dismay: 'I was very unfortunate in ye cracking of one of the Medal Dyes, but hope nevertheless that they will Ansr. all the purposes intended.' And it looks like he got away with it for the 2,000 platina pieces were supplied to the Admiralty. But what of the silver pieces for distribution to the friends and admirers of Mr Banks? It was not acceptable to serve up a broken piece with this joke of a ship sailing as fast as she could with her anchor down! And Banks wouldn't be put off. And then the note of 25 March to Banks which states: 'we have sent you the Gold and Silver Medalls........struck out of the new dye.' But then they don't seem to show up! 100 Silver Medals were then sent between 4 and 7 April. A further six medals on 19 April, and then the much later note on 27 June by Westwood to Boulton stating that 'the dyes for the medals of Mr Banks and Dr Solander' will be finished in mid July, which probably relates to their Icelandic trip. By the time this letter was written, Mr Banks and Dr Solander are no longer a part of the voyage, and *Resolution* and *Adventure* have already sailed.

And finally the cryptic note to Boulton's London agent Matthews dated 6 June: 'return the medals you have if you have not opportunities to dispose of 'em, for if you have not we have many of 'em here.' Does this reference medals Boulton struck to his own account for sale to collectors or are these silver medals rejected by Banks, i.e. return them as Boulton wants to melt them down and at least get the silver value back? I don't think this was the case because Banks ordered a further six medals on 20 April, which indicates that he had given all of his silver medals to friends by that date and that these medals were part of Boulton's inventory.

The difficult note is the one of 27 June in which Westwood reports that he has completed new dies for the 'medals of Mr Banks and Dr Solander.' There is another piece of evidence though. Matthew Boulton didn't produce a new medal (or coin) until some years following the Otaheite Medal, with the only exception being the ill fated Regimental Medal for the 37th Foot which was struck in 1774. Again massive die breaks greatly blemish the piece. (Ref: Balmer, *Regimental and Volunteer Medals*, Vol. I, pp. 152-153.) It may well be that the note of 27 June relates to a new medal which would depict Banks and Solander. Indeed in Sweden in 1783 (BHM 252), a Solander medal was struck. If one considered that the 27 June letter relates to a different medal than the Otaheite Medal and probably to mark the expedition to Iceland that Banks and Solander made together, and that the new Otaheite reverse die was in place late March, then Types I and II make sense.

The platina pieces were produced with the Type I dies and delivered to Captain Cook on board

Resolution by 16 April. The copper medals are usually in much better condition that the platina, and the few really wonderful copper pieces with their original suspension do look like they went straight from Boulton or Banks into collector's cabinets. Beaglehole is specific as to the brass / platina medals being the Admiralty supply. But then Banks rejects the gold and silver specimens and the Panic is on. Finally in April, the silver medals for Banks are delivered to him. These are Type II, 'struck out of the new dye.' It's even singular, i.e. only one 'new dye'. Examples were struck in the 'proof-like' state, and then a more regular less well struck supply is made. The 27 January 1773 note from Fothergill to Boulton in London, 'I will send you some Banks Medals by next Coach' most likely relates to some surplus of the Type II, which would include both copper and silver. The suspension is ignored as a requirement as the pieces are for collectors and with suspension, they wouldn't fit so well in a cabinet drawer. These last medals really do look like production to Boulton's own account for sale to collectors.

And now the big conundrum! The Copper and Platina Type I have a slightly convex rim which is machine finished and measures 42 mm in diameter. Further, the inside edge diameter for both the obverse and reverse dies is 40 mm. The Copper, Silver and Gold Type II have the bulging convex machine finished and polished rim and measure 44 mm in diameter. The inside edge measurements are 41 mm for the obverse and 42 mm for the reverse. This accounts for the minute, i.e. .5 mm step in the rim just as it joins with the reverse plain which is only seen on the Type II examples. Type I has suspension and Type II doesn't. What does it all mean? A clue may be found in examining Westwood's *Jubilee in honour of William Shakespeare* medal (BMH 136) which was produced in 1768. The rim is very slightly convex and machine finished. If you compare the rims of medals by Pingo and Kirk of the same period, the rims are typically collar formed and never machine finished. The Otaheite Medal appears to have been struck without a collar. For the Type I medal, the result is a slightly convex rim, but the Type II with the reverse die being larger than the obverse die, has resulted in a much more convex rim which required special finishing because of the difference in diameter of the two dies.

It has been suggested that the Type I medal was made by somebody other than the maker of the Type II medal. Westwood was in Birmingham and was already involved as a die maker and medallist. Westwood prepared the dies for the Otaheite Medal. It is also interesting to note that Boulton's Pocket Book calculation (unfortunately there is no date to the entry other than it being a book for 1772), references the production of silver medals only. If one were to discuss output into the 75 gross level, the production of 2,000 platina examples would have been more appropriate as the discussion example. But no mention of platina production, only silver. I think it is tempting to consider that the difference in rim between the Type I and II is significant enough to conclude that perhaps Westwood produced both the dies and the 2,000 Platina examples. However, the difference in the rims is undoubtedly caused by the reverse die being larger in diameter than the obverse die. As Boulton wrote, 'I was very unfortunate in ye cracking of one of the Medal Dyes', there is a clear call from a wounded man who wants to produce a fine medal, but just hasn't the skill to do so. I really think that Boulton struck all of the Otaheite medals.

What we are seeing is the struggle between business risk and the realities of production. What today is called, 'The Learning Curve'. I can imagine Boulton's thinking as he deals with each of the problems. He starts with a Type I set of dies which creates a significant reverse crack with their first use. There is also confusion as to how the dies should be oriented (common top point or 180 degrees opposite), and the decision of a common top point that is still 10 degrees off centre. Someone notices that the design in the

Type I reverse die needs to be altered as well (anchor stowed!). OK, understand all of the problems now. Order a new die, letters to the customer, push the finished 2,000 platina examples for acceptance by the Admiralty which will go to people who have never seen a medal before and they might think the die crack is part of the process! We are all set. Type II is produced with a new reverse die. Anchor is where it ought to be. No significant die breaks. Orientation is now perfect with a common top point for obverse and reverse. This is real progress. What do you mean, the new reverse die is 1 mm greater in diameter than the obverse die! I Don't Believe It! And we are supposed to have a gold medal to be given to the King by Friday!

This is where I think we all can feel what Matthew Boulton was going through. Personally, I am looking more toward this scenario that describes what actually happened simply because I don't see in the record of medal manufacturer anything that is so obviously struggling as the Otaheite Medal. However, Boulton ends up with a fine Type II medal by hand finishing the rim and gaining the resulting compliments from those fortunate in receiving an example. Today, the medal is just exquisite!

As a further note, my preference as to the meaning of B : F is now firmly placed as Boulton : Fothergill. My reasoning is that most of the correspondence to Banks is presented in the official Boulton & Fothergill style which is understandable as this was the company Banks was doing business with. Further, Boulton & Fothergill was a relatively new partnership, and in such cases partners are usually very sensitive to ensuring that the corporate image is established, i.e. one is restrained in just putting forward yourself, you want to share. If B : F stood for Boulton Fecit, this would have been a terrible slight against Fothergill, and Matthew Boulton was too canny for that! When Boulton regains control of the Soho works in 1782, upon the death of John Fothergill, he then trades as Matthew Boulton for all manufacture, with the exception of manufacture and supply of steam engines which is through the partnership of Boulton & Watt. For later pieces (mainly Küchler designs), the only signature is usually that of Küchler though several forms, the most frequently met with being 'C.H.K.' In 1798, for the Davison Nile Medal, Boulton does sign it with 'M.B.SOHO'.

Captain Cook's second and third voyages.

Time to get underway and follow Captain Cook to see what he did with his 2,000 Otaheite Medals.

For Cook's second voyage (1772 to 1775), he had as ships, *Resolution* (462 tons) and *Adventure* (340 tons). The ship's compliment was 112 for *Resolution* which included, Captain James Cook, 1st Lieutenant Robert Palliser Cooper, 2nd Lieutenant Charles Clerke and as 3rd Lieutenant Richard Pickersgill. Joseph Gilbert was the Sailing Master and for Midshipmen, John Elliott, Isaac George Manley, William Harvey and Isaac Smith. Also as Midshipmen, Henry Roberts, James Burney (whose younger sister was Fanny), Charles Loggie, James Maxwell and the young 15 years old George Vancouver. As an AB was Alexander Hood (1758 - 1798), who was the son of Samuel Hood, purser RN, and first cousin to both Lord Hood and Lord Bridport. Alexander was but 14 when he joined *Resolution*, is perhaps better known as Captain of the *Mars*, when he was killed during the desperate fight with the French *Hercule* in April, 1798. The surgeon was James Patten, and his two mates were William Anderson and Benjamin Drawwater. In addition was William Hodges, artist, who brought to life so much that was seen and visited. And lastly, the father and son team of John Reinhold Forster and young George Forster, these two now took over the duties of Mr Banks and Dr Solander as naturalists.

Adventure had 81 officers and men with Captain Tobias Furneaux and as 1st Lieutenant Joseph Shanks (who was to die early at the Cape. 'Smitten by gout', 2nd Lieutenant Arthur Kemp, and with the death of Shanks, James Burney was moved from *Resolution* to *Adventure* to serve as 2nd Lieutenant under Kemp, who was promoted to 1st Lieutenant. Peter Fannin was Master.

Captain Cook was to seek out the continent at the bottom of the Earth. To sail south to Cape Town and make final preparations. From there, to sail due south as far as you can go, and then east staying in the high latitudes, until in the longitude of New Zealand, when Cook would head north again. During this voyage will take place the first full sea trial for several new chronometers selected by Mr Maskelyne, a duplicate of Mr Harrison's 'Time Machine' made by Kendall and three chronometers by Arnold. The real test of reliable time machines versus Lunar Observations in order to secure reliable Longitudinal readings was on! In addition, Mr William Wales (who following the voyage was to teach at the Mathematical School at Christ's Hospital, and to have as pupils the likes of Lamb, Coleridge and Leigh Hunt), and Mr William Bayly along with two portable observatories, were to accompany the expedition to both facilitate the testing of the chronometers and to make astronomical observations.

With a final meeting at Plymouth with Sandwich and Palliser (Comptroller of the Navy and key to all supplies Cook required), both ships set sail on 13 July 1772. The passage to Cape Town was uneventful. From there, they sailed due south. On 17 January 1773, the two ships crossed the Antarctic Circle, the first time this feat had been achieved. Still not finding land and the clear strain of learning to live with mountainous bergs of ice as sailing companions; Cook notes: 'great as these dangers are, they are curious and romantick Views many of these Islands exhibit and which are greatly heightened by the foaming and dashing of the waves against them and into several holes and caverns which are formed in most of them, in short the whole exhibits a View which can only be discribed by the pencil of an able painter and at once fills the mind with admiration and horror, the first is occasioned by the beautifullniss of the Picture and the latter by the danger attending it, for was a ship to fall aboard one of these large pieces of ice she would be dashed to pieces in a moment.' (*Life of Captain Cook*, p. 321.) On 8 February, the two ships parted company in fog. On 17 March, Cook finally made the decision to head north again as he reckoned that Tasmania should be there. On 25 March, Dusky Bay in South Island, New Zealand was sighted and at Anchor Island, a rest break was taken.

From the Captain's log: Monday, 29th March, 1773: 'After the rain was over one small double Canoe in which were Eight of the natives appeared again and came within musquet shott of the Ship where they (were) looking at us for about half an hour or more and then retired, all the signs of friendship we could make notwithstanding. After dinner I took two Boats and went in search of them in the Cove where they were first seen, accompaned by several of the officers and gentlemen, we found the Canoe hauled upon the Shore, near two small mean hutts where there were several fire places, some fishing netts, a few fish lying on the beach and some in the Canoe; we however saw no people, they probably had retired into the Woods. After a short stay and leaving in the Canoe some medals, Looking glasses, Beads &c. I embarked..... '

Thus we have the first mention of the Otaheite Medal in the Captain's log. The story goes on though. Three days later, the Otaheite Medals and other presents are still undisturbed in the canoe. On 6 April, on his way back from an exploring expedition, Cook met an elderly man and two younger women by chance. George Forster takes up the story: 'He [Captain Cook] went to the head of the boat, called to the man in a friendly way, and threw him his own and some other handkerciefs, which he would not pick up. The captain then taking some sheets of white paper in his hand, landed on the rock unarmed, and held the paper out to the native. The man now trembled very visibly, and having exhibited strong marks of fear in this countenance took the paper: upon which Captain Cook coming up to him, took hold of his hand, and embraced him, touching the man's nose with his own, which is their mode of salutation.' Beaglehole then notes that half an hour later which was spent in 'chitchat' uncomprehended on either side, the younger of the two women being most voluble, which occasion'd one of the Seamen to say, 'that women did not want tongue in no part of the World!' (Ref: Beaglehole, *The Journals of Captain James Cook*, Vol. II, pp. 112-113.)

But this dark and rainy place wasn't what his men needed after spending three months searching the Antarctic seas, so on 29 April, *Resolution* set sail and headed north. On 18 May, as they entered Cook's Strait, canon fire was noted from *Adventure*, who was waiting as planned in Ship's Cove. But the New Zealand winter is now fast approaching, and dreaded scurvy is beginning to tell on the ship's company, so on 7 June sail was set for Otaheite, which was sighted on Sunday, 15 August, 1773.

There followed cruising amongst the Society Islands, returning to New Zealand and further attempts to find the land mass of the Antarctic Continent, but to no avail. Cook returned to England on 30 July 1775 having been away for just over three years during which he lost only four men, which was a remarkable achievement.

L. Richard Smith published in Sydney in 1985 his limited edition monograph *The Resolution and Adventure Medal*, and it is here that much of the Boulton and Banks correspondence held by the Mitchell Library was first published. As part of his research, Mr Smith collated all of the incidences noted by Cook and others on the voyage where Otaheite medals were distributed. He notes, 'It is also worth noting that the medals were always given as gifts, and never used for trade or barter..' Smith records medals as having been distributed in Tasmania, New Zealand, Tahiti and other Society Islands, Tonga, Easter Island, Cook Islands, Fijan Islands, New Hebrides, New Caldonia and Tierra del Fuego.

Richard Smith was a great collector of Cook related medals. The Noble, Australia sale of 22-24 November 2005 saw his collection of *Resolution and Adventure* medals auctioned. Included were 3 x Silver Type II, a Platina Type I with original suspension still in place, another Platina Type I with part of the suspension in place, but with the orientation being 180 degrees and two other Platina Type I medals. There was also a Copper uniface obverse struck medal and an Iron uniface casting of the obverse medal. All the medals made very good money with a silver EF making £9,300 and a good VF medal making just under £6,000. The platina with full suspension made £6,700 and without suspension £3,400.

Upon the return to England in July 1774, there were medals still remaining which were taken on the next trip (*Resolution* and *Discovery*) in July 1776. On 18 January 1778, Captain Cook sighted the island of Kauai, in the Hawaiian Islands which he named the Sandwich Islands after Lord Sandwich, first lord of the Admiralty and sponsor of the voyage. During this trip, medals were distributed in the Hawaiian Islands and along the Canadian coast at Nootka Sound.

In Australia, the Aborigines largely ignored such gifts as they only carried that which was needed for survival. The people of Polynesia accepted and treasured the medals which continue to be discovered amongst the islands.

The Fatal third Cook voyage (1776 to 1780) comprised his old ship *Resolution* with the little *Discovery* (229 tons) as her tender. Amongst the officers where such men as (aboard *Discovery*) Commander Charles Clerke, Lieutenants James Burney and John Rickman. Thomas Edgar was Master, and as Midshipmen were George Vancouver and 'the gallant good Riou', who died on board *Amazon* at Copenhagen, 1801. On board *Resolution*, Cook had Lieutenants John Gore, James King and John Williamson (who captained the *Agincourt* at Camperdown, 1797, and was cashiered for cowardice following the action). The Master was William Bligh, who turned near ruin in the Fourth voyage into personal triumph, and who later Commanded the *Director* at Camperdown and the *Glatton* at Copenhagen in 1801. John Webber was the artist.

The mission was to again gain more detail of the newly discovered Australia and New Zealand, to return to the ever inviting Otaheite, visit Hawaii and then undertake the search for the North West Passage from the Pacific Ocean. In Hawaii on 14 February, 1779 Captain Cook was murdered by the natives he so much wanted to reach out to. On 22 August, 1779, on the far northern Russian coast, Captain Clerke died. The command of the two ships fell to Lieutenant Gore of the *Resolution* and Lieutenant King of the *Discovery* with Mr Bligh managing most of the navigation for the rest of the voyage.

The last voyage was the creation of Sir Joseph Banks, who became president of The Royal Society in 1778 and Knighted in 1781. Working closely with Evan Nepean, Under-Secretary of State at The Home Office, a plan was developed to transplant breadfruit from Otaheite to the West Indies in order to provide a cheap staple diet for the many slaves there. Lieutenant Bligh was Banks' personal recommendation for the voyage, and *Bounty* was the ship. *Bounty* left Spithead, 27 November 1787, and she never returned. Her timbers were found in 1957 deep beside Pitcairn Island where Mr Christian sailed her with some of the Mutineers. On 28 April 1789, having just departed that scented isle Otaheite, Mr Christian (Mate and acting Lieutenant), and a party of the crew, seized Captain Bligh and all who would follow the captain and cast them away in the whale boat. The remaining Mutineers were deposited at Otaheite while Bligh and his twenty-two stalwarts, made the epic 2,000 mile sail in the open whale boat to Timor, finally reaching England on 17 March, 1790.

The romance associated with the *Mutiny of the Bounty* has caught the imagination of the general public via books and movies which all tell the story of tropical islands with beautiful beaches, palm trees and beautiful women and men who wished to escape forever to this island paradise. Don't we all!

The Death of Captain Cook. Courtesy of the Wellington Museum, Wellington, New Zealand.

Painted by Hugh Barron. Engraved by V. Green, Mezzotinto Engraver to his Majesty & the Elector Palatine.

Sir George Brydges Rodney, Bar.
ADMIRAL of the WHITE,
and Rear Admiral of Great Britain.

Publish'd June 1st 1780, by V. Green, No. 29 Newman Street, Oxford Street.

The Saint Eustatia Medal

As a commercial venture, Boulton struck this medal and considering its rarity one imagines that the venture wasn't that successful. Having said that, the problems encountered with the Otaheite medal have been overcome, and the examples appear to be free of die faults.

2) The Saint Eustatia Medal. (MH 382 / BHM 230)

Description:

Obverse: Uniformed bust of Admiral Rodney with cocked hat, facing right. G. B. RODNEY

Reverse: THE HERO / WHO HAVING / SPENT HIS YOUTH / IN THE SERVICES OF / HIS COUNTRY, / IS AMPLY REPAID / BY THE CAPTURE / OF ST EUSTATIA / FEBY 3D 1781

Diameter: 34 mm.

Metals used: Silver RRR £500; Copper RR £350; Tin RR £250.

MH 382, BHM 230, MEC 1445 © National Maritime Museum, Greenwich, London.

In the northern Leeward Islands of the West Indies near Saint Kitts and Nevis, is Saint Eustatius or Sint Eustatius as it is named in Dutch today. In Rodney's time, the name was Saint Eustatia. Although not large, Saint Eustatia does have with Oranje Bay, a deep anchorage which became the central trading port for the Dutch West Indies Company. From 1756, Saint Eustatia became duty free which made the transportation of everything, particularly arms and ammunition during the American Revolutionary War, critical to the supply of the American military. So successful was Saint Eustatia in trade, that the island became known as the Golden Rock.

It came to be that on 16 November, 1776, the American brig *Andrew Doria*, Captain Isaiah Robinson, arrived off Fort Oranje and fired a 13-gun salute to the governor. This was returned with the required 11-gun salute from the fort and thus was the first diplomatic recognition of the new founded United States of America.

Edmund Burke had said of Saint Eustatias in 1781, 'It had no produce, no fortifications for its defence, nor martial spirit nor military regulations ... Its utility was its defence. The universality of its use, the neutrality of its nature was its security and its safeguard. Its proprietors had, in the spirit of commerce, made it an emporium for all the world ... Its wealth was prodigious, arising from its industry and the nature of its commerce.'

Lord Stormont declared in the House of Commons that 'if Saint Eustatias had sunk into the sea three years before, the United Kingdom would already have dealt with General Washington.'

Nearly half of all American Revolutionary military supplies were obtained through Saint Eustatia. Nearly all American communications to Europe first passed through the island. As a result of the ongoing trade between Holland and the rebellious Americans, Great Britain declared war on Holland on 20 December 1780. Rodney was ordered to the West Indies to destroy the weapons depot and communications centre that the island had become.

Admiral Rodney appeared in Oranje Bay on 3 February 1781 with his fleet of 15 ships of the line and numerous smaller craft and 3,000 troops. Rodney's fleet had over 1,000 cannon compared with the Dutch defences of a dozen cannon and sixty men. Rodney offered Govenor De Graaff the opportunity to surrender, which the governor accepted, after firing two cannon as a demonstration of resistance.

With the surrender of the island, came the surrender of the 130 merchantmen then riding in Oranje Bay. The treasure captured by Rodney was estimated to be in excess of £3,000,000, probably the most valuable capture made during the 18th century.

The island passed to the control of the French later in 1781 and returned to the Dutch in 1784, but the status as a trading centre was never regained.

Rodney was later criticised for staying too long at Saint Estatias and not seeking out Count de Grasse's fleet, which had taken station off Chesapeake Bay and cut off supplies to General Cornwallis. Rodney did dispatch part of his fleet under Admiral Graves, but too late to assist Cornwallis. Count de Grasse sparred with the British on 5 September 1781 which resulted in stalemate, however because de Grasse maintained control of Chesapeake Bay, it proved a strategic disaster for the British as Cornwallis, due to lack of supply, was forced to surrender to General George Washington and his French allies.

1780 proved to be a golden year for Admiral Rodney. With the advent of the American Revolutionary War, Spain felt it was a good time to reclaim Gibraltar which had been lost to the British in 1704. Early in January 1780, Rodney was dispatched with a convoy to relieve the Spanish blockade of Gibraltar and deliver essential supplies to the garrison. As he headed down the coast of Portugal, he encountered and captured a Spanish supply convoy on 8 January. Rodney added the ships that contained supplies useful to Gibraltar to his own convoy, and sent the rest of the captured ships back to Portsmouth.

Then on 16 January, Rodney's fleet of eighteen ships of the line met the Spanish fleet of only nine ships under the command of Admiral Lángara off Cape Saint Vincent, Lángara realising the great risk he had against Rodney's superior numbers tried to get south and into Cadiz. Rodney's ships were faster and managed to block the way and as the sun set, the two fleets commenced battle which continued into the night and became known as the famous Moonlight Battle. Rodney took fours ships of the line and destroyed two in a resounding victory. He then pushed south, broke the Spanish blockage at Gibraltar and provided the supplies so desperately needed. He then sailed to Minorca to resupply that station and then headed for the West Indies.

In 1780 as news reached England about each succeeding success of Admiral Rodney, made him an instant hero. The accompaning mezzotint portrait of Rodney on board his flagship during the Moonlight Battle by Valentine Green appears to be the basis for the obverse of a number of Rodney medals, including the Saint Eustatia medal.

Rodney's fame was further established with his resounding defeat of Count de Grasse's fleet during the four day Battle of the Saints where four French ships of the line were captured and one destroyed. Count de Grasse's flagship was amongst the captured ships. Thus Admiral Sir George Rodney became Britain's most famous admiral until the rise of Nelson, and this celebration was recorded in the many medals that proclaim his victories.

From David Vice of Format Coins in Birmingham, who has for many years studied the Boulton archive held in the Birmingham Museum, we have: 'Boulton & Fothergill definitely struck a piece commemorating the capture of St. Eustatius, seemingly in silver, copper, gilt and tin. The silver piece contained silver of an intrinsic value of 4/6d [approximately the value of a Spanish 8 Real]. All these factors seem to suggest that BHM 230 is the likely medal. B&F sold the medals through the Birmingham and London toyshops on a sale or return [to B&F] basis. In addition, Mathew Boulton's son asked for three copies of the medal and one of these in silver may have passed through the family to be sold amongst the coins and medals formerly belonging to M. P. W. Boulton [which were] sold at Sotheby's in April 1912.' Ref: Letter from John Hodges at Soho to Matthew Boulton in London dated 9 April 1781, Boulton Archive: MS 3782/12/63.

It appears that Boulton continued to use the drop hammer that was used to strike the Otaheite medal for the Saint Eustatias medal. Although the partnership between Boulton and James Watt commenced in 1775, the Soho Mint wasn't established until 1788/1789. As Boulton produced the Otaheite medal within his then current workshops, it is most probable that he struck the Rodney medal in the same way, with the drop hammer. Lessons, however, have been learned, the copper uniface trial strike of the reverse of BHM 230 clearly demonstrates a very even and strong strike with all of the legend in high relief. One can also see with BHM 230, that one finds none of the problems with die breaks, obverse and reverse not sharing the exact same top point and both dies being the same diameter, all of these issues are now resolved and the medal looks about as perfect as one would hope.

Uniface copper trial piece for the St Eustatius Medal. Sim Comfort Collection

But is this the only Rodney Saint Eustatius medal that Boulton produced?

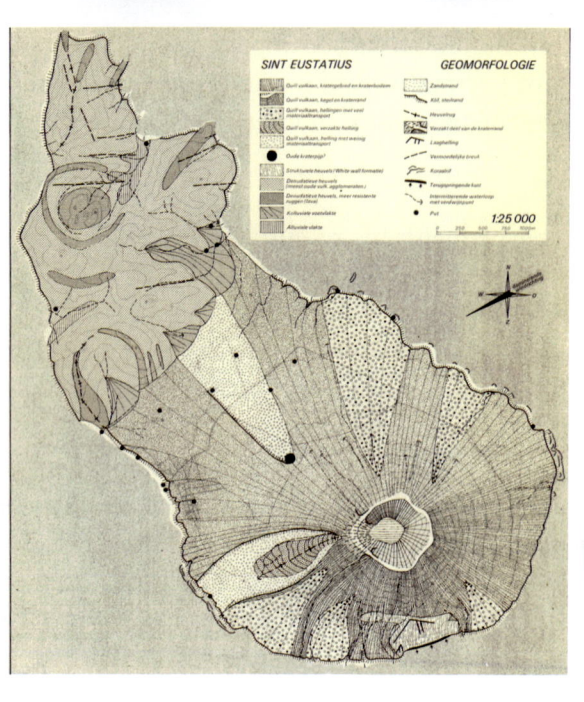

Upper left: AE, BMH 229 / MH 381,
Upper right WM, BMH 230 / MH 382,
Middle left WM, BHM 231 / MH 383,
Lower left AE, BHM 232 / MH 384 (courtesy the Adams Collection),
Bottom left AE gilt, BHM 233 / MH 326,
Middle right is a WM Mule with obverse of BHM 243 / MH 390 and reverse of BHM 231/ MH 383. Sim Comfort Collection

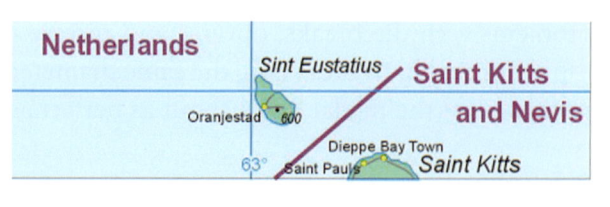

Let's take a look at the other medals that celebrate the same event and may have been struck by Boulton and try decide if BHM 230 is his only Rodney medal or are there others.

BHM 229 / MH 381, BHM 230 / MH 382, BHM 231 / MH 383, BHM 232 / MH 384, BHM 233 / MH 326

All of these pieces share pretty much the same obverse design, so is there something that would differentiate one from the other? Compare the lettering in RODNEY with 229 and 231 and you will find that they are the same. Look at the distance between the O and D and again at the distance between E and Y. Also the closeness of RODNEY to the rim, it is much closer in 229 and 231 than in 230. One will also see differences in the uniform coat and the tie for Rodney's hair and well as his hat.

So BHM 229 and 231 are struck by someone else.

When we look at BHM 232, we see a slightly different portrait of Rodney and the change in the legend from G. B. to ADM for Admiral, so this is by someone else. The production of the medal isn't to the same quality as the other three Rodney medals.

Looking at the text used for the reverse of 229, 231 and 232, they all echo 'Punish the Dutch' where with 230 the message is simply an applaud to the great achievement of Rodney with his capture of Saint Eustatia. To me, I can't see Boulton being part of the populist angst. His circle of friends and customers reached the very highest levels of society and most particularly with his production of the Otaheite medal, he aligned himself with those on a higher plain than the hack medallists of his day. Boulton wouldn't want to 'Punish the Dutch', he would prefer to do business with them!

From *Matthew Boulton, Industry's great innovator*, by Tann & Burton we have an account of Boulton taking a trip to Holland in 1779 by a fast packet from Harwich to Rotterdam:

'I soon went to my hammock to prevent sickness but about Midnight the Wind blew hard & I became sick. The Vessell roll'd from one Side to ye other. The Capt. & all hands were upon deck all night managing ye Sails as Violent Squalls often returned. Mr. & Mrs. Cummins were very sick & puked although they declar'd they had crossed the Atlantick 4 times & had been accustomed to ye sea 19 years without ever being sick before...'

Boulton was greatly taken with Holland - 'prudence, industry, decency & seriousness are characteristics of the Dutch' and he particularly noticed how clean everything was, even the barges on the canals. But he was not in Europe for sightseeing. He made his usual calls on likely aristocratic customers.'

Lastly, 233 has a changed obverse while the reverse depicts two ships in action with one on fire. This didn't happen at the capture of Saint Eustatia, but did happen in the next year during Rodney's victory over De Grasse at the battle of the Saints when the French ship of the line *César* caught fire and finally blew up when the fire reached her magazine.

So, it really looks like BHM 230 / MH 382 is the Matthew Boulton Rodney Saint Eustatia medal.

54

The Glorious First of June Medal

Again this medal was a commercial venture. Although the result is very fine and rates this as one of the finest of the British naval medals, Boulton could have made it even better by having more accurate information regarding the uniform of Earl Howe and the fight between the *Brunswick* and *Vengeur du Peuple*, although one can understand the need for a really dramatic view of this important action.

3) The Glorious First of June Medal. (MH 417 / BHM 383 / Eimer 854)

Description:

Obverse: Uniformed bust of Earl Howe right, hair long tied with ribbon. RIC . COMES HOWE THALAS-SIARCHA BRITAN (Richard, Earl Howe, British Admiral), Below bust: PATRIAE DECVS ET TVTAMEN (The country's glory and defiance). Under the right shoulder: C.H.K.

Reverse: A view of the battle between Captain John Harvey's 74-gun ship *Brunswick* and *Vengeur du Peuple* (People's Avenger) of 74 guns, which later sank. NON SORTE SED VIRTUTE. (Not by luck but by valour). In exergue: GALLOR . CLASSIS PROFLIG. / DIE 1 JUNI . / MDCCXCIV. (French fleet routed on the 1st June 1794). Along the top right hand side of the exergue: C. H. KUCHLER . F .

Diameter: 48 mm. by C. H. Küchler. The medal is found with both thick and thin planchettes being used, about half a millimetre difference between the two.

Metals used: Silver RR £900; Copper CC £370; Copper-gilt RR £750; Tin RR £250.

There is in the British Museum a trial piece in tin, ex the collection of George III, with a spelling error THESSALLIARCHA and a different arrangement of the obverse text. It appears that another example of the medal was sent to Joseph Banks to be given to his sister Sarah Sophia. Boulton notes in his cover letter that the die for this medal has been destroyed.

With the arrival of Conrad Küchler in Birmingham in 1793, British historic medals entered a phase marked by very fine designs and equally fine production. At last Matthew Boulton had the elements together in terms of minting technology, artistic excellence and a collaboration which was even tempered and produced outstanding results.

For Earl Howe's medal, which celebrated his victory over the French fleet of Admiral Villaret de Joyeuse over a three day period which culminated on the Glorious First of June, 1794, Boulton relied on Küchler to establish the design of the medal which was then approved by Boulton, but always with consensus between the two men being the way they worked together.

We have from J. G. Pollard's article in *The Numismatic Chronicle* of 1970, which provides a full discussion for all the medals created by Boulton and Küchler, a letter from Boulton to Küchler, who appears to have been in London at the time, dated 29 October 1794:

'I approve of doing a medal of Lord Howe, provided it can be done expeditiously & a good portrait of him – perhaps you can find one at Mr Bacon's or perhaps Mr Bacon can inform you where you can see a Bust or picture of him. I like your design of Lord Howe's ship sinking a French ship, but I think there should appear at some distance a fleet of ships something like the sketch marked B enclosed. I have likewise sent you a medal with a ship upon it for you to take any [details?] from you please. I am told some person in London has advertised to receive subscriptions for a medal that is engraving of Lord Howe but perhaps if you are expeditious you may come first to market & I will advertise yours before it is finished...

'I think you should distinguish the 3 coloured Flag in the French ship & suppose you may see one of their flags at St Paul's.

'When a man of war fires a Broadside I presume the recoil of the guns turns the ship on one side at least it will not be so perpendicular as you have drawn it.'

We have a lot of information from this letter. It is clear that Küchler is putting forward the ideas for new medals and that Boulton is deciding if the subject warrants a speculative venture or not. It is also clear that the design of the medal is coming from Küchler and that Boulton is providing critique. I think this is also echoed in the bold signing of the medal in the reverse exergue: C. H. KUCHLER . F . We can also see Boulton's eye at work for the business end, let's move fast and be the first to market with the medal.

I haven't found the portrait of Lord Howe that the obverse is based on, perhaps the likeness was taken from a bust, but it is a very good portrait of the Admiral. The uniform is a bit whimsical, but it serves well. For the reverse battle scene, we have something that is very dramatic indeed. One would really like to know what medal Boulton sent to Küchler. The design echoes the great Dutch medals of the 17th century.

In Milford Haven, Brown and Pollard, the reverse is described as showing: 'A quarter view of Howe's flag ship, the *Queen Charlotte*, sinking a French ship.' What is really curious about the reverse is that it actually doesn't depict Howe's flagship the *Queen Charlotte*, which was a 100-gun three-decker, but Captain John Harvey's 74-gun two-decker *Brunswick* as she grappled with the French 74-gun *Vengeur du Peuple* (the People's Avenger). The scene has condensed the time between the fight and the ultimate sinking of *Vengeur*, but that's understandable considering how long it took for *Vengeur* to finally sink. It also adds drama to one of the greatest big ship fights of all time. The most sensational act of heroism from the 1st of June was Harvey's fight with *Vengeur*, and it is this that Küchler has so well captured in his design for Lord Howe's medal. I have to think something was lost in communication between Boulton and Küchler as it appears that Boulton expected Howe's flagship *Queen Charlotte* to be portrayed, but Küchler went for the most dramatic event during the battle and depicted the *Brunswick* and *Vengeur* in mortal combat instead.

There is another medal which comes to mind and that is the fabulous John Paul Jones Comitia Americana medal by Dupré, commissioned by Thomas Jefferson and struck at the Paris Mint in late 1789 and early 1790, which was the time when Boulton was in discussion with Droz. The depiction of the fight between the *Serapis* and the *Bonhomme Richard* is possibly the greatest view of a single ship action ever conceived for a medal. Küchler's work with the battle scene for the 1st of June medal certainly places it as the best depiction of single ships in action for the British series of naval medals. Was he influenced by Dupré's work, we don't know, but could well have been? The following example is from the Sim Comfort Collection.

Tensions between England and France became very strained with the onset of the French Revolution in 1789. With the execution of King Louis XVI on 23 January, 1793, war was inevitable between England and France and on the 1st of February war was declared. Europe was now in turmoil and would remain so during the next twenty-odd years, with the ever present threat of invasion by the French something the Admiralty had to protect against.

The encounter between Rear-Admiral Villaret-Joyeuse and Admiral Lord Richard Howe, known as 'Black Dick' to his sailors, would be the first and the greatest encounter at sea between the French and the British during the French Revolutionary Wars. The object Villaret-Joyeuse had was to effectively see into port a large convoy of desperately needed grain arriving from Virginia. Howe would like to intercept that convoy as well; however both admirals knew that if they met, National Honour was really the issue at stake.

The two fleets manoeuvred for advantage and brushed each other during the days of 28 and 29 May. The next two days were foggy and the fleets didn't make contact, however on the 1st of June 1794 they did meet about 400 miles west of Ushant. Admiral Howe held the weather gage, which meant the French fleet was down wind to his fleet which allowed Howe to time the attack and choose how he wished his fleet of 25 ships of the line to engage the French fleet of 26 ships of the line.

In past wars, two major fleets such as this would conduct a sort of parade, where the opposing ships would pass one another line ahead and cannonade as the line advanced. The problem with this tactic was that usually nothing was achieved in terms of clear victory and Lord Howe knew he had to demonstrate Britain's command of the sea.

His tactic was to bring his long line of ships abreast of the French line, and then on his command for each of the British ships to turn into the French line and by doing so cannonade the vulnerable bows and sterns of the French ships as each British ship passed through the line, and then for each British ship to engage closely a French ship.

Although, the tactic did work to some degree, not all of the captains under Howe's command obeyed his order to cut the French line. Some of his captains appeared to be less than eager to commit their ship to action at all. However there were enough who understood exactly what Howe wanted and fought all during the day like tigers with the result that seven French ships of the line were captured and many of those that escaped back to Brest, were so damaged that they weren't seen at sea again for some time.

However, the American convoy did reach France and in so doing, the French were able to claim a victorious action despite their losses in ships and men.

The high point of the battle was reached with the fight between the *Brunswick* and *Vengeur du Peuple*. The *Brunswick* was trying to obey Howe's order to break the French line, but was having difficulty in doing so. The story is best told by Sam Willis in his *The Glorious First of June*:

'*Brunswick* had enjoyed the 'honour' of covering the *Queen Charlotte* from much of the fire of the French centre and rear as she had approached. Now, already damaged, her captain John Harvey searched desperately for a gap through which to lead his ship. Harvey thought he saw a sufficient gap between *Le Patriote* and *Le Vengeur* but the captain of the *Vengeur*, spotting Harvey's intention, trimmed his sails to catch more wind and instantly increased his speed to close the gap. The *Brunswick*, therefore, did not break clean through the French line but crashed with such force into the side of the *Vengeur* that both ships became locked together as the three starboard anchors of the *Brunswick* caught the larboard fore-channels and the fore-shrouds of the *Vengeur*. Mr Stewart, the *Brunswick*'s Master, then asked Captain Harvey if he should cut the ship clear, and Harvey replied, 'No; we have got her, and we will keep her', British sailors kept his word and later in the action carefully shot any Frenchman trying to cut the ships apart. At the start of the battle, however, the sailors of the *Vengeur* where not prepared to accept this violent imposition and her men fought with sustained ferocity. Eventually the momentum of the British attack seems to have turned both ships, and together they sailed off to leeward, directly downwind, leaving the rest of the battle behind. This battle within a battle was caught in one of the Age of Sail's most evocative images by Pocock, who was watching the battle from the decks of the *Pegasus*.

'We have a good record of the fight..., one of them written by a woman named Mary Anne Talbot who was serving aboard *[Brunswick]* in disguise as John Taylor. Mary was stationed at the second gun on the vulnerable quarter deck, responsible for handing fresh cartridges to the men. It was not long before she, ..was injured by a piece of grapeshot that took her in the ankle. She wrote: 'I attempted to rise three times, but without effect, and in the last effort part of the bone projected through the skin in such a manner as wholly to prevent my standing.' She was then shot by a musket ball straight through her thigh and taken down to the surgeon...She survived the battle but the lead pellet remained in her ankle for the rest of her life.

'At the start of the action, the *Brunswick* was crushed so close to the *Vengeur* that the British gunners were unable to open the nine sternmost gunports on the starboard-side lower deck. Desperate to start the fight they fired their cannon anyway, blowing off their own gunport lids.

'Captain Harvey was then wounded three times. First a piece of langridge took off three fingers from his right hand, a wound he kept hidden from his officers, before a large splinter, breaking clear of the ship's hull, struck him on the right arm. Moments later he was struck on the head and forced to go below for medical attention.

'Harvey was just one of the *Brunswick's* casualty list, the longest in the British fleet with forty dead and 113 wounded. ...At one stage the *Brunswick* was on fire in four different places, and the *Vengeur* alight twice. When the ships finally pulled apart, the *Vengeur* tearing the *Brunswick's* anchors from her bows, the *Brunswick* was so shattered that [she] was left to the mercy of the sea.'

With the two ships now apart, the *Vengeur* began to settle as water rushed through her torn gunports and hull, finally sinking by the stern. It was reported that 356 of her ship's company were either dead or wounded. Captain John Harvey succumbed to his wounds and died ashore at Portsmouth on 30 June. He is remembered by a memorial in Westminster Abbey.

Pictured are copper and copper-gilt medals. In this collection is a well worn and holed for suspension copper medal which was probably purchased by a man who fought at the 1st of June. No doubt Boulton looked at the sailors who took part in the action as potential customers.

The copper example is in its steel shells, which Boulton medals are regularly found with. This author feels fairly confident that the use of shells to protect the medal is a Boulton innovation. It would be easy for him to produce the shells as it is just another stamping process that his works at Soho were well equipped to carry out. A full discussion of the shells will be found in the Trafalgar medal section.

So, it is with the Lord Howe First of June medal that we begin the series of five Boulton and Küchler naval medals that remain unsurpassed in quality of design and production. Having said that, this appears to be the last speculative naval medal by Boulton and Küchler as the Davison Nile, Ferdinand VII and Earl St Vincent medals were each a commission, while the Boulton Trafalgar wasn't a commercial medal, but a simple gift from Matthew Boulton to the men before the mast who fought with Nelson on that fateful day off Cape Trafalgar in 1805.

Aquatint by Nicolas Pocock showing the *Brunswick* in the centre with the *Vengeur* to the right and *L'Achille* to the left. There is a swell running which has caused *Vengeur* to tilt to the left.

Aquatint by Nicolas Pocock depicting the sinking of the *Vengeur* and the damage caused to the *Brunswick* during the action.

Rear-Admiral Horatio Nelson painted by Lemuel Francis Abbott in late 1797, when Nelson had returned to England to recuperate from the loss of his arm. He is wearing the Star and Ribbon of the Bath and the Naval Gold Medal for Cape St Vincent.   Image © The National Portrait Gallery, London

The Davison Nile Medal

Alexander Davison was Rear-Admiral Nelson's prize agent for the Battle of the Nile, 1 August 1798. So successful was Nelson in destroying Napoleon's invasion fleet at Aboukir Bay that Davison took it upon himself to commission a medal to be distributed amongst Nelson's officers and men who took part in the action. The level of care given to this medal by many of the recipient sailors shows just how much the gift was appreciated.

4) The Davison Nile Medal (MH 482 / BHM 447 / Eimer 890 / Hardy 5)

Description:

Obverse: The allegorical figure Hope standing on a rocky shore holding in her right hand an olive spray and supporting with her left hand an oval shield with a bust of Lord Nelson. EUROPE'S HOPE AND BRITAIN'S GLORY. Above: REAR-ADMIRAL LORD NELSON OF THE NILE. Signed on the rock: C. H. K.

Reverse: A view of the British fleet going into action against the French. Above: ALMIGHTY GOD HAS BLESSED HIS MAJESTY'S ARMS. In exergue: VICTORY OF THE NILE / AUGUST. 1. 1798. Along the top border of the exergue: M. B. SOHO   C. H. KÜCHLER. FEC.

Edge: Incuse legend: FROM ALEXR DAVISON, ESQR ST . JAMES'S SQUARE = A TRIBUTE OF REGARD.

Diameter: 48 mm. by C. H. Küchler.

Metals used: Gold RRR £20,000+, Silver RR £1,500; Copper C £450; Copper-gilt R £600. Named or provenanced medals will fetch a very considerable premium.

Original Soho gilding, Colonel William Stewart's medal.

From David Vice we have this regarding the 48 mm diameter of the medal, and most of the subsequent commemorative medals produced by Boulton and Küchler: 'With regard to Boulton's 48 mm medals, I think that Boulton was the originator of this size. Küchler initially worked for Boulton whilst based in London and Boulton simply sent along blank dies to be filled in with a mutually agreed subject. Having once established a size of 48 mm, Boulton tried his best to keep it. I suppose he could keep the same cutting out tools and collars. The initial request for Davison's medal was based on a smaller flan, but Boulton managed to convince him that a larger flan would be more normal and appropriate for such a design.'

Having also discussed the 48 mm size with the horologist Richard Price to see if this was a normal size for a Georgian pocket watch, he assured me that it wasn't and that the 48 mm cases which one finds with Davison Nile and Boulton Trafalgar medals would have been expressly made just for medals of that size.

From Pollard, *The Numismatic Chronicle* of 1970, one finds the correspondence regarding the design and striking of the Davison Nile medal. Suffice it to say that Davison supplied the original design for the medal, drawn by himself, and that Boulton wasn't satisfied with the drawings and had the marine artist Robert Cleveley commissioned to work up a design based on the Davison drawings.

Again, we can see Boulton drawing upon his friends and associates to bring the best skills and information toward the creation of something. Boulton suggested that Mr Joseph Banks should be consulted as Robert's brother John Cleveley had sailed with Banks and Solander on their Icelandic expedition of 1772 as draughtsman. Boulton described Robert as: 'a friend of Nelson, lieutenant R.N. and a correct ship painter.'

Following this description of the Davison Nile medal is an essay written by Martyn Downer which describes the very close relationship between Davison and Nelson and provides some compelling insights regarding the design of the medal and its possible relationship to Masonic design and icons.

For the portrait of Nelson, Boulton turned to Josiah Wedgwood who had commissioned John de Vaere to sculpt a profile of Nelson which was used in a Wedgwood jasper ware plaque. De Vaere (1755-1830) was born in France and settled in England sometime prior to 1786 and travelled to Rome in the following year where his talents were recognised by the Pope. He later became the assistant to the English neo-classical sculptor John Flaxman. Upon his return to England in 1790, he worked for Wedgwood and produced naval portraits in profile of Admiral Lord Howe, Admiral Adam Duncan, Earl St Vincent and Lord Nelson along with other designs for Wedgwood.

The battle of the Nile occurred in Aboukir Bay on 1 August 1798. It was the culmination of a long and frustrating search by Nelson for Napoleon's Egyptian invasion fleet. When Nelson, just as the sun was setting, found the French fleet at anchor, he immediately attacked and effectively destroyed Napoleon's fleet during a hard fought action through the night. I would recommend *Nelson and the Nile* by Brian Lavery as the most complete account of the battle. In my catalogue section where the individual Davison Nile medals are described, the actions of each ship in Nelson's fleet are given, so I will leave the discussion of the battle for you to explore in the catalogue.

From Martyn Downer's *Nelson's Purse*, we find the most complete statement as to the numbers of each type of medal made: 'In the end Boulton struck 7,216 medals, not including 100 struck in error. This was more than enough for all the survivors. Küchler's dies were given to Davison and destroyed. Boulton's bill, which took another two years to arrive showed 25 gold medals [in red morocco cases] at just under £11 each, 154 silver medals at 11s 6d each, 506 in copper-gilt at 4s each and 6,531 in bronzed copper at 2s 6d each. The total came to a little over £1,200, far less than the £2,000 generally quoted by historians. After Davison complained about the lateness of the bill and reminded Boulton that he had once airily promised to make the medals at cost, the amount was reduced by a further £100. Boulton had met his match.'

The order from Davison to Boulton included 25 gold medals in red morocco cases which would go to the fourteen captains of ships of the line plus Nelson, but not including Hardy as the *Mutine* was just a brig and not a ship of the line engaged in the battle. The remaining ten gold medals were for Davison to distribute as he wished. The silver medals went to lieutenants, masters and marine officers of the fourteen ships of the line. The copper-gilt medals went to the afterguard and petty officers, which included chaplains, school teachers, master's mates, boatswains, gunners and all manner of petty officers. Lastly bronze medals were distributed amongst the men and marines before the mast. Nelson retained a quantity of these medals for his own personal distribution during the rest of his life. See DN33 for details regarding the copper gilt medal given by Nelson to Colonel William Stewart who was on board the *Elephant* with Nelson at the Battle of Copenhagen, 2 April 1801.

At Christie's on 19 October 2005 was auctioned possibly the most interesting gold Davison Nile medal which came from the descendant family of Captain Thomas Hardy, who was captain of *Victory* at Trafalgar and captain of the *Mutine* brig at the Nile. As noted, Hardy didn't receive the Naval Small Gold medal from the King or the Davison Nile in gold, but when the shipment of gold Davison Niles reached Nelson at Palermo in August 1799, Nelson visited Hardy and gave him the gold medal that was intended for himself and after having done that and realised that he did want a gold example wrote to Davison on 24 August: 'Poor dear Miller is dead: so will be your Nelson, but I trust till death that your friend longs to wear your [gold medal] present; therefore I have kept Millers's, and hope you will send another to his family.' Hardy's medal, after a long fight in auction, finally made £65,000 hammer and with the premium, cost the new owner something over £80,000. See DN28 in the Catalogue for more about this medal. Nelson also gave a gold medal to Sir William Hamilton in recognition of his support for Nelson's fleet after the battle.

Although the Davison Nile medal has always been described as an unofficial private medal, it did receive the support of Henry Dundas, the Secretary of War and certainly the Admiralty. Its place in history is also well established as being the first instance of a medal being expressly struck for a British battle and all of the victorious combatants receiving the medal. Matthew Boulton would repeat the gesture with his presentation of his Trafalgar medal to all of the men before the mast in Nelson's fleet. That medal also received Government and Admiralty sanctions. It wasn't until Waterloo in 1815 when the Crown and Government had a medal issued to all of those who took part in a battle.

As a further note, you will see two medals in the Catalogue which have engraved both the male recipient's name and a woman's name. Andrew Nicol was a landsman on board the *Goliath* and his sea wife was Mary Williams. William Flinn was a private Marine on board the *Alexander* and his sea wife was Ann Crumwich. I use the term sea wife because I can't think of any other reason for a man to have a woman's name engraved with his on a Davison Nile medal. These men shared their medal with women who were at the battle with them. We know women were on board the ships, this was common knowledge at the time as demonstrated by the painting by Thomas Stothard showing a gun crew in action and a woman dragging away a wounded man. You will learn more from the detail provided with these two medals in the Catalogue records: DN04 and DN30. (Painting is SCC)

We now turn our attention to the most vexing issue regarding this wonderful medal and that is the reverse design. *The Attack at Sunset* oil painting by Robert Dodd was published as an aquatint by Dodd in February 1799 and became an instant success. Dodd captured the drama of the moment when Nelson decided not to wait for the morning. His willingness to risk a night action just underlined his aggressiveness.

Davison and Boulton were still in correspondence regarding the number of medals to be struck in May 1799 which makes me think that the medal was being struck about that time. Deliveries to Nelson ships occurred in August 1799.

We then consider a couple of things. Ralph Miller's chart of the attack upon the French fleet shows Nelson ships coming from the north-east on a south westerly bearing. The French fleet was roughly oriented in an east-west line in Aboukir Bay with the old fort towards the head of the French line in the west.

Dodd and Pocock both decided to paint the view of the British attacking into the sunset, but Davison and Cleveley depict the British having arrived at the western head of the French fleet and turning east as the ships decided to sail either between the anchored enemy and the shore or to pass on the open seaward side of the French fleet.

Robert Dodd's *Attack at Sunset* and a section of Captain Miller's chart of the attack

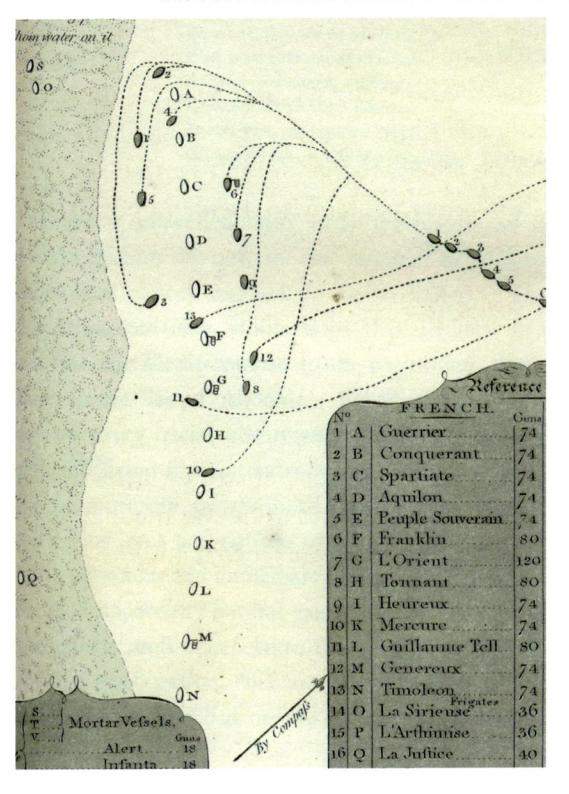

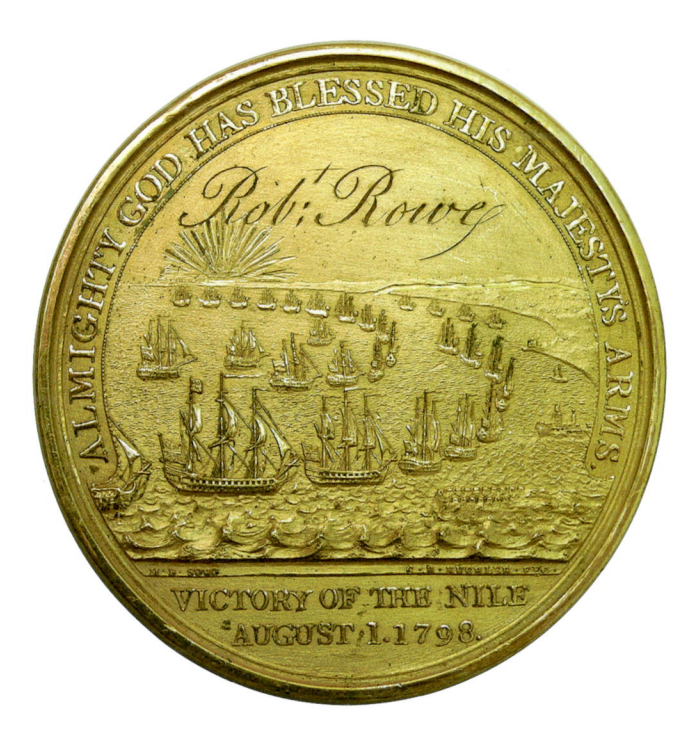

Therefore the perspective depicted by Cleveley has the British headed east with the shore to the right and a battery of the old castle in the right foreground. The sun is behind the point Cleveley chose as his viewpoint which is confirmed by the print of Cleveley's drawing published in *The Anti Jacobin Review and Magazine* in March 1799 and held in the National Maritime Museum. There is no sunset in Cleveley's drawing for the scene of the attack. It's interesting that Cleveley did make a mistake by having too many British ships pass between the enemy fleet and the shore. The Laurie and Whittle broadsheet of the battle plan was published on 28 October 1798, so there was ample information available for Cleveley to depict the correct number of inshore ships. (PU 4121 © NMM, Greenwich)

Who decided to add the sunset? In the essay by Martyn Downer, Martyn thinks that this was Davison who desired a Masonic reference to a raising sun as an echo of Hope and Peace. Although there was a fair amount of correspondence between Boulton and Davison regarding the medal, there isn't any discussion about including a sunset, and as the published finished Cleveley drawing, which has no sunset, was made available by Davison, I don't think the decision came from him. That just leaves Boulton and Küchler with the decision.

The one thing we can be sure of is that the alteration to the design to include a sunset was very easily achieved. Just take a graver and cut a dozen or so radiant lines into the horizon. We have seen Boulton out of his depth when it came to sea scenes, the anchor down on *Resolution* in the Otaheite medal, the *Brunswick* instead of the *Queen Charlotte* in the First of June medal and now a sunset that shouldn't be there on the Davison Nile. I guess in the end, it should have been both Boulton and Küchler who decided upon it, but the next paragraph may have the answer.

The next Boulton – Küchler medal celebrates the return to Naples of King Ferdinand IV on board one of his own frigates. Although the medal shows a 74 gun ship entering the Bay of Naples from the south on 10 July 1799, it wasn't Nelson's *Foudroyant* as she was already there and at anchor, although the King transferred the next day to the *Foudroyant*, along with his staff. Küchler has depicted *Foudroyant* as the ship entering the Bay and included a sun rising in the east. This again is curious because the original artwork for the medal didn't include a sunrise. It appears that Kuchler has made use of artist's license and as he was the man with the graver, my opinion is that he simply decided to add the sunrise to the Ferdinand medal and the sunset to the Davison Nile medal because they filled in a vacant space and looked good.

How was the medal viewed by the men who received them? Very well indeed is the answer. In the catalogue section are 34 named or provenanced Davison Nile medals which include at least one medal for each of Nelson's line of battle ships. With regard to the sunset, it appears that only the men on board *Bellerophon* considered it a mistake and on the four medals from that ship, the sunset has been removed from three of them. Everybody else just accepted it as part of the design and if the detail of the medal was to be heightened by a jeweller chasing the design, the sunset is given due attention with the rays normally chased.

What becomes fairly obvious is that both on board ships and on shore, both the men and jewellers were set to work personalizing the medals by engraving the recipient's names and ships onto them. For very fine work, the medal was fitted in a glazed case with a loop for suspension, so the medal could be worn and preserved. Both the Davison Nile and Boulton Trafalgar medals are 48 mm in diameter and both include examples which are found in a glazed case which suits that size perfectly. Many of the cases look to be the same and have a Birmingham look about them, so one wonders if an enterprising jeweller at (say) Gibraltar, where many of the Nile ships went to be refitted, had a supply of cases shipped to him. This would not have been that difficult as communication between Gibraltar and English ports was a regular occurrence. Or, perhaps, Boulton had some cases sent along with the medals. We just don't know, but the cases were certainly available either in the Mediterranean or back home in Portsmouth or other English ports.

There is a discrepancy amongst the gilt medals. As noted above these medals were intended only for petty officers and staff members of the afterguard. One can easily distinguish a Boulton gilt medal as its gilding is so very rich and distinctive. What has happened, I'm pretty sure, is that men before the mast received their copper-bronzed medals, but saw petty officers with their gilt medals and simply decided that they would like a gilt medal as well. It was easy to take your medal to a jeweller and ask for it to be named and gilt and cased. However, many of these medals are clearly not engraved by a jeweller, but are engraved by men on board ship. This is proved by examining medals from both the *Minotaur* and the *Bellerophon* where one finds a distinctive graver's hand at work that is not found on any other ship and certainly isn't the hand of a jeweller. Following this article is a short essay that describes how Boulton gilt his medals and also discusses how the process may have been carried out on board ship.

One can't understate this medal in terms of its importance to the men who received them. They were one of Nelson's 'Band of Brothers' and had just taken part in the most audacious and successful and hard fought fleet action of the Georgian era to that date. They had just beaten Napoleon, the first time he had been stopped as he conquered country after country. They had saved India! The consequences of this victory were even to be felt in North America as this defeat became one of the reasons for Napoleon selling the Louisiana Territory. He realized that at sea he was at risk and only via the sea could he reap the rewards of that vast land. His defeat at the Nile would forever stay in his mind.

Nelson was to use the medal as a token of regard to be presented to men he respected. There are a couple of instances of this to be found in the Catalogue, DN 33 and 34. One may also remember that the effigy of Nelson in Westminster Abbey is adorned with a Davison Nile medal being hung by a blue ribbon around his neck. I also think of the shipboard dinner scene in *Master and Commander* where Captain Jack Aubrey sits at the head of the dinner table wearing his glazed and cased Davison Nile medal. With great drama one of the dinner guests asks if he had met Nelson, and Aubrey replies, 'Yes I have and it was at a dinner just like this one.' Then he was asked, 'Did he speak to you?' 'Why yes he did.' 'And what did he say?' 'Well he said, pass the salt please!' Laughter all round followed. Such was the mystic that surrounded Nelson after the Nile that such a story would have been told time and time again and everybody loved the teller of the story because they all loved Nelson.

I can remember visiting Nimrod Dix in the 1991 and that Nimrod had the medals of Captain Thomas Foley, who as captain of the *Goliath* led the British ships inshore which set the stage for the destruction of Napoleon's fleet at the Nile. As I recall, there were the Naval Small Gold medals for both St Vincent and the Nile and a gold Davison Nile medal. The price was £35,000 and I didn't buy them and have regretted that decision ever since! Glendining's auctioned them for £40,700 hammer on 20 June 1991.

I shouldn't complain though. One of the reasons I've preferred collecting named Davison Nile, Earl St Vincent and Boulton Trafalgar medals is that the men who received them typically did important things on board ship. The Naval General Service medal wasn't authorised until 1848 and the recipient had to still be alive in order to receive the medal. Captain Foley of the *Goliath* died in 1833, so there was no NGS amongst his medals. This also meant that the recipients were often boys or very young midshipmen and not officers or petty officers or senior gunners, etc. The other issue is that the NGS has been faked by taking common named Syria clasp medals and swapping clasps for, say, the Nile as surplus clasps were, and still are, available within the war medal trade.

Deciding to collect medals which are engraved with the men's name and his ship is also something that should be approached with caution. Over time, I think I have developed an eye for what is contemporary engraving and what is modern. But be assured that Davison Nile medals will be engraved today by the unscrupulous who are only out for a fast profit. Unfortunately, after this book has been published and more examples of contemporary engraving are made available to the fraudster, well, one must be careful in making the decision to buy a medal. Having said that, the price of a named Davison Nile that is correct will still be a lot less than an NGS with a Nile clasp and the man who received the Davison Nile will probably be more interesting than the NGS recipient, so it is worth your while learning about what is genuine and what isn't.

Perhaps, the last comment comes from an inventory which appears to have been made by Captain Hardy and included the effects from Nelson's cabin in the *Victory* and sent to Lady Hamilton on 8 December 1805. Some of Mr Davison's medals were included in the list of Nelson's possessions. Nelson really liked this medal and kept a supply with him to the end of his life.

Gilding of Davison Nile Medals on board ship

Boulton charged Davison 2 shillings for each bronzed Davison Nile medal. Gilt medals cost 3/6.

The method used by Boulton was to first stamp out the circular planchets from sheet copper. The blank planchets would then be gilt using the mercury based fire gilding technique. Next, the planchets would be struck to form the finished medal. The tell-tale signs of Boulton / Soho original gilt medals are that the gold colour is more yellow than red and that the devices of the medals are often frosted.

On board ship and amongst the jewellers of the seaports, mercury fire gilding would be the norm and certainly could be carried out on board ship. With over 500 officers and men on board a 74 gun ship, and that the men before the mast came from all walks of life, the skill for engraving and gilding would be found amongst them, as is evidenced by the shipboard engraved and gilt medals found.

As the level of heat required to effect the gilding is not that great, the process could take place at either the ship's galley stove or the Armourer's portable forge which would be set up near the foremast hatchway when the ship was at anchor in calm waters. The process could be carried out by any number of jewellers in Mediterranean ports, however one does think that as the sailors were typically not allowed off their ships and as it appears that skills on board ship could carry out both the engraving and gilding of the copper bronzed Davison Nile medals, that the whole of the process was carried out on board ship. The same process could be used with silver as the additive, instead of gold, to create a silvering of a tin Boulton Trafalgar medal.

Mercury gilding:

- Reduce gold to a fine dust, i.e. file down a gold guinea and then reduce it further by use of a mortar and pestle. One can also add either copper or silver to increase the amount of gold amalgam, but this would decrease the carat content, i.e. more copper would produce a red gilt, silver, a pale gilt while 24 carat would be a fine yellow gilt.

- Heat the gold (or mixture of gold, copper, silver amalgam), until it is mildly hot and turns to a liquid and then throw it into previously heated mercury until the mixture begins to vaporise, or as Matthew Boulton called it, 'to smoak', i.e. smoke. If you continue to heat the mercury too much, then it will all evaporate, so keeping the heat low is important. The ratio of metal to mercury is usually one part metal to six to eight parts mercury.

- Stir the mixture with an iron rod. The gold will disappear and a mercury solution created. When cold, squeeze the solution though a chamois to get rid of the excess mercury. What is left inside the chamois is a paste that should have the consistency of butter.

- The surface of the medal to be gilt should be cleaned with nitric acid and then dipped in quicksilver water, a solution of mercury nitrate which acts as a key for the gilding paste.

- Thinly paint / spread the paste over the surface and edges of the medal.

- Gently heat the coated medal just sufficiently to vaporise the remaining mercury. Too much heat will make the gold amalgam pool and / or run off.

- Treat the surfaces of the medal with gilding wax, essentially beeswax mixed with a number of ingredients which will heighten the colour of the gilding. The medal is again exposed to gentle heat to drive off the wax.

- What is left is a gilt medal. One would gently burnish the finished metal with a chamois or soft cloth.

As a note, mercury would be available on board a man-of-war because mercury was needed by the Surgeon to cure the venereals; also used in the ship's barometer and added to paint as an anti-fouling agent. Mercury would be available from most chemists and jewellers who could supply ships via the many small trading boats used in port.

From Matthew Boulton's notebook held at the Birmingham Library, we have his recipe 'to have gilding of the finest Colour'. Firstly he takes great pains to ensure that the Mercury is pure. His notes escape the full deciphering by this author however it is a process which involves dissolving and then filtering the mercury which when pure is retained in an iron retort.

For the preparation of the gold, it appears that firstly the ground gold dust is dissolved in Aqua Regia [three parts hydrochloric acid and one part nitric acid], and then left to stand for 12 or 24 hours to settle. Green Vitriol / Ferrous Sulphate is then added to precipitate the gold out of the gold chloride solution. The excess liquid is then siphoned off leaving a gold powder which should be washed, but not let to dry.

At this point, the gold and mercury should be combined in an iron pot with a lid and heated until the mercury begins to smoke / vaporise. The contents should then be poured into a cool vessel and strained through a chamois. The remaining paste is applied to the copper metal planchets and gently heated which further vaporises the mercury, thus leaving the finished gilt copper planchet.

Boulton states that the fire should be entirely free of smoke which would contaminate the gilding. A charcoal fire is best. Keep in mind that mecury is highly poisonous, so protective gloves and glasses should be worn.

Lastly, it is thought that the cheap 48 mm glazed cases that the Davison Nile, and later the Boulton Trafalgar medals, are often housed in were made in Birmingham and that a supply of them was shipped with the Davison Nile medals to the Mediterranean in the spring of 1799, or that an enterprising merchant at Gibraltar ordered a supply. The issuance of the Davison Nile medal was the first time that a medal was struck for distribution amongst an entire fleet and with the quantity of medals being around 7,000, it would appear obvious to create a mass produced glazed case that would protect the medal and provide a suspension for wearing the medal. Because petty officers received the gilt Nile medal, the seaman and marines who received the bronze medals appear to have decided to enhance their medals with gilding and engraving, which is how you often find them today.

This article has been written with the assistance of Mark Grimwade of The Goldsmiths' Company, London.

Discussion with the well known horologist Richard Price about watch cases

SC: Was 48 mm a standard watch size for the period 1798-1805?

RP: Certainly not, they would have been larger by up to 50%.

SC: Would a watch be 3 mm thick?

RP: Certainly not, they would be 10 mm thick at a minimum.

SC: Would a watch be in a copper gilt case?

RP:: Certainly not, they would be in gold and possibly silver, but never copper gilt.

SC: Would a watch case have a glazed front and back?

RP: Certainly not, the outer case would be solid metal both sides with the front lid being spring loaded etc. It would take about ten craftsmen to make a watch case during that period.

And I think we know the answer to would a watch case have a loop for suspending the watch from a ribbon? Certainly not!

Conclusion: Thanks to Richard and I hope he doesn't mind this somewhat whimsical reportage. What we see are purpose made glazed cases for just the Davison Nile and Boulton Trafalgar medals and possibly other 48 mm Boulton medals. They are very cheap gilt copper cases that were almost certainly made in Birmingham. They may have been contracted by Boulton or by an enterprising Birmingham maker for supply to ports in Britain and the Mediterranean. From the ports, bum boats would be able to take them to men on board ships and sell them along with all of the other wares the bum boatmen supplied.

Medals engraved by men on board Nelson's ships

The first book I wrote was entitled *Forget Me Not* and was a study of naval and maritime engraved coins and plate. From the 138 engraved examples illustrated and discussed in this book there is ample proof of the engraving skill of 18th century shipboard seamen who where also engravers. Part of the reason for this is that the 'graver' or tool used for engraving is a simple four sided steel awl which would have had common usage on board ship. All that was needed was for the tip of the awl to be sharpened to the point which best suited the engraver and he was ready to practice his art. The engraved coins of this period, which were often booty captured from enemy ships, really are the harbingers to the great age of scrimshaw which one would see in the 1830s and beyond with the growth of the whaling industry. However, it is in the 18th century that the sailor's skill reached heights rarely achieved in the 19th.

When this you see, Remember Me is an oft found message on a sailor engraved coin. The theme of separation is the most prominent. Jack Tar is going away and surely he will return, but then maybe he won't. The engraved coin served as the seal to his promise to return.

There once was a topman named Jack
Whose hair tail went all down his back
He loved a true lass
Who lacked any cash
And pined at the thought of his sailing

So, Jack scribed an old William shilling
With his ship, heart, arrow and dove
He holed it for wearing and she was quite willing
So at her bosom, always rested her love
(SC 12/95)

With the gift from Alexander Davison of a medal for all those officers, men and boys, seamen and marines who fought with Nelson at the Nile was created an opportunity for shipboard engravers to personalize their medals by inscribing their name and sometimes the name of their ship as well. Although medals were also engraved by jewellers, one can see medals to men on board the *Minotaur* and *Bellerophon* which were engraved by a unique hand that was on board each of those two ships and is discussed in the Catalogue.

The Boulton Trafalgar medal doesn't appear to have had the same attention paid to it by men on board ship, more jeweller engraved pieces are found. There are the interesting examples of BT 21 and BT 32 where the Plymouth jeweller has confused the men and ships the two medals belonged to, which proved a challenging puzzle to resolve.

Perhaps the most satisfying discovery from the engraved Davison and Boulton medals is the inclusion of sea wives' names with those of the men who fought with them at the Nile and Trafalgar. Women were there and on these medals, as with the engraved coins, they are remembered.

The montage of engraved coins is created from pieces in the Sim Comfort Collection.

DEFIANCE 74
COURAGEUX
The NAMURE
FEBY
Cleopatra
William & Mary
LEVIATHAN ENGAGEING THE LE AMERICA
STOCKER
1781
FORMIDABLE
THIS YOU SEE REMEMBER ME
Jno Walsh
ELISABETH
HANAH
GORGON
VILLE DE PARIS
1790
The Gift is small but Love is all

Creating the die

This article is based on conversations with Malcolm Appleby, who has worked in die cutting in association with the Royal Mint, Philip Attwood of the British Museum and British Art Medal Society, Christopher Eimer, author of *British Commemorative Medals and their values*, Daniel Fearon, who has dealt with and catalogued historic medals for many years and David Vice of Format Coins, who has studied Matthew Boulton and the operations of the Soho Mint for many years.

The object of the die cutter is to transfer the agreed design for a medal from the drawing to a reverse mirror image cut incuse into a steel die. There isn't anything published which details the steps in achieving this end and that is because the die cutter / engraver isn't limited to just one process. The men, particularly in the late 18th century, had many skills and were regularly experimenting on new techniques to achieve the desired result. In addition to this, the management of the metal, typically steel, from soft to tempered hardness for striking was a skill in its own right, and particularly with Matthew Boulton's works at Soho, the backroom team that supported both the die maker and those carrying out the striking of medals and coins were very skilled in creating just the right finished steel dies.

- The simplest process is to engrave the artwork incuse and in reverse / mirror image onto a soft steel die which would then be hardened and become the die for striking a medal. To transfer the image of the original artwork to a reverse image on the die, I understand that such was the skill of die cutters of that time, they could do this by eye alone, however one could also make a tracing of the original artwork on a material that would allow the transfer of the design in reverse onto the face of an uncut soft steel die and then cut the die following that pattern, which would then be hardened for use.

- The problem with using the single die is that if it breaks, then one is left with only that die to strike further medals. This appears to have been what happened with the Otaheite Medal, when despite a severe break in the reverse die, Boulton continued to use it for the striking of the 2,000 platina medals ordered.

- To protect against this happening, one could produce a master die as above. From this hardened steel master, it could be struck into a hot soft steel hobb (also called a hob and hub), which would now be in relief and be the same image as the artwork. This steel hobb would then be hardened and from it could be made several identical inverse incuse dies for use in striking medals and for backup dies.

- For more complex designs, more than one process may be used. Take for example an obverse image which includes a profile portrait which is then surrounded by a legend in letters. The first step would be to sculpt the portrait in soft steel in relief called a matrix, so that the sculpted portrait and the artwork display the same image. This soft steel matrix would then be hardened. It would then be struck with a soft steel die which would have the image as an incuse inverse / mirror image. While still working in soft steel, the die cutter could then use letter punches to create an incuse / reverse legend to surround the portrait. This soft steel die would then be hardened and the fields polished to provide a mirror surface to the fields. It would act as the master die which would then be struck in hot soft steel to create a hobb in relief and be the same as the artwork. This hobb would then be hardened and struck again and again with soft steel dies which would then be hardened. These would contain incuse and reverse / mirror images, which would be used after hardening to strike the actual medals and act as backup dies.

- There is an article in *The Numismatic Chronicle* for 1971 by J. G. Pollard where he describes Matthew Boulton's disappointment with Droz in 'discovering a more efficient means than the conventional use of hand-cut puncheons and a multiplying press for the duplication of dies.' Never satisfied, Boulton continued writing to Foucault in Paris and was introduced in 1790 to Jean Baptiste Dupeyrat (1759-1834), who had invented a lathe for creating steel dies. In the end, Boulton did secure the lathe which was able to create from a steel bas-relief matrix, the finished master die. The additional innovation was that the lathe could work from a model that was larger in size than the finished medal would be. All of this was couched in great secrecy by Boulton who had built a special room with limited access to preserve his technological advantage.

Although we don't know exactly how Küchler created his dies, it is probable that he sculpted his total image in bas-relief in soft steel as the matrix. This soft steel matrix would then be hardened and from it via the Dupeyrat lathe, the finished master die would be cut incuse and as a reverse / mirror image. After polishing the fields, this master would be struck with a hot soft steel hobb to create a relief image die which would be the same as the bas-relief original design. This hobb after hardening, would be struck again and again with soft steel dies which would create the image incuse and in reverse. When hardened these dies would be used for striking medals and backup.

However, mixed process may still be at work here. One can think of the Lord Howe, First of June medal with a spelling mistake in the obverse legend. Boulton was able to react to this fault immediately which may mean that the portrait of Howe was copied by the Dupeyrat lathe and then the legends were punched into the fields and so on. With a master portrait, changing the legend would take very little time along with making new working dies. Or it is possible that Küchler sculpted the design images and legends and that the Dupeyrat lathe created the finished master die. Either way, the Küchler medals are just stunning.

A trick in PhotoShop allows us to view the incuse reverse image of the Davison Nile reverse die and then the finished struck medal.

Alexander Davison by Lemuel Abbott, image courtesy of the Martyn Downer Collection.

A Friend in need is a friend indeed
by Martyn Downer

'A friend in need is a friend indeed': writing to his agent Alexander Davison in February 1803, Nelson described these words 'an old adage, but not the less true'.[1] Davison and his family were marooned in lodgings at Calais, a tour of France during the Peace of Amiens truncated by the sudden illness of one of their children. Yet even in extremes Davison did not neglect the material needs of his 'dear friend' who was seeking funds to improve Merton Place the house the admiral shared in Surrey with his mistress, Emma Hamilton. 'Command the purse of your ever unalterably affectionate friend' Davison had written without hesitation and with no certainty of being repaid.[2] Although Nelson only needed a few thousand pounds - small beer to a man like Davison who estimated his fortune at £300,000[3] - his agent's casual offer of financial assistance was material proof of the deep well of affection that existed between the two men in the last years of the admiral's life.

They had met in Quebec twenty years before, during the American War of Independence. Nelson, then captain of *Albemarle*, was on North Atlantic convoy duty while Davison was running a successful business in the town supplying goods to the British troops arriving in Canada to fight the war as well as to the loyalist émigrés refugees who were pouring across the border from the colonies. Through his carefully nurtured contacts within government, Davison had also secured the lucrative agency to supply presents to the Native American tribes whose allegiance to the crown - so critical to the success of the Canadian fur and fish trades - was being severely tested by the blandishments of the American rebels. The idea of using sweeteners to secure loyalty was a lesson Davison learnt early in his career.

At first glance it might appear that the young officer and the merchant had little in common. Nelson, who was twenty-four, had already spent half his life at sea while Davison, the elder of the two men by eight years, had been immersed in trade since his youth. The nature of international trade in the eighteenth century, however, - which rested so heavily on the sea - caused their worlds to be in constant contact, even before the exigencies of war made Davison rely on the Royal Navy for the safe transport of his goods across the Atlantic. This mutuality was reinforced by the similar backgrounds, social position and outlooks of the young men attracted to both sea and City, similarities which were typified by Davison and Nelson. Each, for instance, had passed their childhoods in remote rural areas close to the sea – Nelson in Norfolk, Davison in Northumberland. Nelson's connections with the navy are well recorded yet Davison, too, was in close proximity to several naval families from a young age. His elder sister Katy married captain, later admiral, Roddam Home[4] and at least two of his contemporaries and near neighbours in Northumberland: Cuthbert Collingwood and John Orde, rose to prominence alongside Nelson in the Navy.

As sons, respectively, of a clergyman and a farmer, Nelson and Davison were products of the 'middle gentry', that mildly impoverished yet ambitious and upwardly mobile breed which was spreading rapidly across the country. In many material respects the interior life of the Davisons' stone farmhouse in the Cheviot Hills would have closely resembled that of the Nelsons' parsonage in Burnham Thorpe.

Beyond the physical landscape that cast the young men was empathy in their upbringing, for each was the fourth son to his parents and as such was denied the attention afforded to their elder brothers. For example, neither of them received the benefits of an extended education nor was there enough money to buy either of them a commission in the army or an apprenticeship with one of the large, 'moneyed' firms in the City of London such as the East India Company. Growing up at opposite ends of the country, both boys must have realised that to a great degree they would have to make their own way in the world. Nelson chose the sea; Davison chose trade.

There were, however, two striking differences in the backdrop to the boys' emotional lives. Perhaps the most significant was the early loss of Nelson's mother when he was just nine years old. By contrast, from surviving family correspondence it is clear that Davison enjoyed a warm and supportive rapport with his mother until her death in his early middle age. Subsequently Nelson's relationships with women were often awkward, even destructive. 'I know your determination about women' Davison warily told his friend in 1801 whereas he himself was at ease in female company enjoying a long and happy marriage to Harriett Gosling whilst forging an affectionate friendship with Nelson's wife Fanny.[5] Another notable distinction between the boys was their religious upbringing. Nelson grew up under the watchful eye of his father Edmund, the local parson and a stern advocate of religious orthodoxy. Yet although the Davisons were baptised, married and buried in their local Anglican church, their faith was informed by the prevailing dissenting beliefs of many of their neighbours in the borders. It is known, for example, that they patronised the Presbyterian chapel in Morpeth. Religious non-conformity gave Davison an independence of thought denied to Nelson whose strict spiritual upbringing often left him struggling painfully at moments of personal crisis.

Despite the limitations of their backgrounds, the ambitions of both boys stretched far beyond the bleak view from a draughty Norfolk rectory or an isolated north Northumbrian farmhouse. But desire alone was not enough to succeed. To reach their goals – distinction, respectively, in business and in the navy – Davison and Nelson needed to develop a network of well placed social and professional patrons. For aristocratic endorsement the Nelsons looked to the Walpoles at Houghton Hall, with whom they could claim a distant kinship, while in Northumberland the Davisons fostered a relationship with the powerful Percy family at Alnwick Castle. Meanwhile within their chosen careers Nelson could rely on the support of his uncle Maurice Suckling while Davison's early life in the City of London prospered under the careful supervision of the eminent trans-Atlantic fur trader Robert Hunter.

Nelson and Davison viewed their patrons as 'friends' but not in the modern sense of mutually supportive friends chosen voluntarily. Davison later described Hugh Percy, the second duke of Northumberland, as his "best" friend, but the duke would never have returned the compliment.[6] The professional lives of the patron and patronised might overlap but their social spheres rarely did. Indeed, despite eventually achieving prominence in their respective fields, both Davison and Nelson were humiliated when they tried to meet their socially superior patrons on an equal footing. Hubris allied with the jealousy of his business rivals would lead Davison to Newgate prison, while Nelson was snubbed at court following the disclosure of his affair with Emma Hamilton.

For social relationships based on disinterested sentiment outside their families, Nelson and Davison looked within their own circles for like-minded acquaintances of similar status. Those circles touched when HMS *Albemarle* moored in the Saint Lawrence River off Quebec in September 1782. It is not known for certain where Davison and Nelson were first introduced, perhaps at the chateau of the governor or in one of the coffee houses or taverns in the lower town. With Quebec overflowing with troops and refugees it seems likely that Davison offered to put up the young officer at his house on St Peter Street. The only other option for Nelson was to remain in the cramped conditions in his ship.

During Nelson's short stay in the town he forged a friendship with Davison based not simply on their similar backgrounds but on their broad emotional and intellectual affinity. Nor was it the first occasion on which the thrusting young naval officer had befriended a like-minded merchant. Until his death Nelson would remain in friendly contact with Hercules Ross, another agent of provisions of Northern British descent who he had met in Jamaica in the late 1770's.[7] The personal characteristics Nelson recognised in Davison included a rigorous independence of spirit verging on arrogance; nonconformity in the face of authority and a propensity to impulsiveness which was typified by events involving both men on 14 and 15 October 1782.

Early on the morning of 14th October, just hours after *Albemarle* unmoored to move downriver to rendezvous with a convoy of troop transports bound for New York, Nelson unexpectedly returned ashore determined to precipitously propose marriage to Mary Simpson, a local beauty he had met in the town during his stay. Fortunately for his career, Nelson was intercepted on the quay by Davison who was able to dissuade his new young friend from taking such a calamitous step. The incident left such an impression on Davison - who had suffered youthful rejection by a sweetheart himself - that he specifically recalled it after Nelson's death. And although Nelson never mentioned it himself, the memory of Davison's timely intervention in such a sensitive matter may have informed his later decision to employ his friend in the unpleasant business of separating from his wife Fanny.

Within twenty-four hours, Davison himself was embroiled in a potentially far more serious affair. As *Albemarle* sailed downriver, Davison fought a duel on the Heights of Abraham, outside the town gates, the result of a hot-headed clash with a business rival. No harm was done to either man, yet the incident leaves the impression of a man sensitive to criticism, and one not afraid to act to protect his reputation.

Beyond the record of a brief meeting in London the following year, there is no record of any further contact between Nelson and Davison until May 1797. Yet they must have occasionally written to each other in the interim, for that month their surviving correspondence bursts precipitously into life with a letter from Nelson addressed to 'My dear friend'[8] – terms he generally reserved for his closest male acquaintances, men like Cuthbert Collingwood and William Locker. This intimacy; the nature of the letter's businesslike content and the subsequent exhortation of Sir Nicholas Harris Nicolas, the Victorian editor of Nelson's letters, for Davison's son to 'let me have the letters before 1798'[9] suggests that some early material has been lost. Perhaps it was not until Nelson's eye-catching exploits at the battle of St Vincent in February 1797 that Davison thought it worth preserving his friend's letters. (Nelson's habit of burning many of his incoming letters probably accounted for Davison's.)

Even so there is scant evidence that the friendship formed in Canada was well maintained before 1797. For instance, Davison's congratulations to Nelson for the daring part he played in the battle of St Vincent, were forwarded to the Mediterranean by Nelson's elder brother Maurice, a clerk at the Navy Office with whom Davison was familiar through his constant business dealings with the Navy Board. In fact Davison's friendship with Maurice can be seen as bridging the lost years of his relationship with Nelson. For a time the two men even worked alongside each other. In 1793, following his appointment as commissary-general to Lord Moira's expeditionary army, Davison invited Maurice to be his assistant. Maurice, who had chafed at the lowliness of his position in the Navy Office, leapt at the chance to double his wages (the commissariat paid him £1 5s a day.) He was also undoubtedly flattered by the patronage of his younger brother's influential Canadian friend. After joining Davison at commissariat headquarters on the Isle of Wight,

Maurice commented proudly to his wife that: 'I live with Mr D but not lodge, if I may be allowed to judge his friendship increases.'[10] Indeed the friendship between Maurice and Davison grew to become one of genuine affection; greater perhaps in sentimental terms than Davison's relationship with Maurice's illustrious, but generally absent, brother. 'I have lost my Bosom and sincere friend!'[11] Davison cried, following Maurice's early death in April 1801. Terms that can be compared to his regret, after Trafalgar, at the death of 'my late valuable friend Nelson'.[12]

Although sceptical of the wisdom of abandoning the Navy Office for the commissariat Nelson, like the rest of his family, was grateful to Davison for helping his hapless brother. When the commissariat was wound up in 1796 and Maurice safely restored to his former position at Somerset House; Nelson thanked Davison for the 'kind method you have taken for effectually serving my dear brother'.[13]

And nor, it seems, was the help Davison extended towards Nelson's family limited to Maurice. As early as 1791 Davison - whose contacts with the government were well known - had been approached by Nelson's brother-in-law George Matcham for help in securing land in the newly settled colony of New South Wales. Presumably the introduction was made either through Maurice or Nelson himself (who was living in Norfolk at the time) for Matcham, a successful businessman himself, was clearly acting on a known family interest. So even if direct contact with Nelson himself was limited before 1797, Davison was already widely recognised by Nelson's extended family as a source of valuable patronage. Fanny Nelson later praised his 'very disinterested friendship to all the family'.[14] The debt of gratitude that Nelson felt towards Davison undoubtedly informed his otherwise surprising decision to award his friend the prize agency for the battle of the Nile in August 1798. Nevertheless (and even though he had more reason than most to thank Davison for his help in the past) the appointment shocked Maurice who felt that his kinship to the Victor of the Nile should have secured him a role that was seen as a valuable perk by his colleagues at the Navy Office. 'I am free to confess to you' Maurice wrote to his brother:

'that I feel myself not a little hurt at my not having been named with Mr D as one of the agents to your squadron. It might have put something in my pocket, at least it would have stopped people's mouths who repeatedly say there must have been some misunderstanding between me and you...I have no doubt you have sufficient reason and content myself in present degrading situation, degrading I call it because I cannot reach the top of my profession.'[15]

There were other, more personal reasons, why Nelson risked incurring the wrath of his brother in making the appointment. Not only was he sensitive to charges of nepotism - an accusation that could harm his growing reputation - but he was also alert to the shift in official attitude towards Navy Office employees moonlighting as prize agents. Yet there was one further compelling reason why Nelson chose Davison for this prestigious and lucrative job, the roots to which can be traced to their meeting in Quebec fifteen years earlier. This was a reason, moreover, which had remained hidden to biographers of Nelson until the recent discovery of Davison's collection of papers and artefacts. Its emergence confirms the importance of looking beyond the documentary record to reveal the entirety of a person's life.

Among Davison's treasures was a pair of wine coolers commissioned by him from the Derby porcelain factory following the battle of the Nile. (The Derby showroom in London was next door to Davison's army clothing factory in Covent Garden.) The prominent use of Nelson's coat of arms on the coolers, however, which had been newly-augmented by a baron's coronet and the Sultan of Turkey's chelengk, make it unfeasible that anyone else except for the admiral himself could have displayed the coolers without causing offence. In all probability the coolers were a gift from Davison to Nelson by way of thanks for his appointment as prize agent. On 21 February 1799 – while Nelson still lingered in the Mediterranean after the battle – Fanny Nelson thanked Davison: 'for some of the most beautiful china I have ever seen'.[16] Unfortunately Fanny does not describe the exact nature of her gift beyond describing 'the devices' decorating it as 'elegant'. In the letter Fanny also reveals how, after she received Davison's lavish present, she passed a happy day with her father-in-law Edmund Nelson: 'in admiring them and disposing of them in various parts of the room' – terms which accord with an attempt to find the best position to display the coolers. And she cheerfully complained that Davison's generosity had un-intended consequences for 'one expense brings on others for I shall exert my judgement in forming a plan for something quite out of the ordinary for them to stand on'. For Davison, however, who had long experience of the terms under which gifts were given and received, Fanny's most satisfying comment came towards the end of her letter. 'Your china has been shown and name told' she wrote, 'so that the Bath talkers will soon be undeceived'.[17] If, as seems likely, the Derby wine coolers were the 'beautiful china' which Fanny received on her husband's behalf in February 1799, they were probably returned to Davison after Trafalgar as Emma Hamilton began haphazardly selling the contents of Merton Place in her struggle to keep her creditors at bay.

Lot 19, Pair of Darby wine coolers made £80,000 hammer. Images courtesy Sotheby's.

And yet the full significance of Davison's gift is only revealed by examining the complicated iconography decorating the tableau on the reverse of the coolers. These were painted with images symbolic of Nelson's victory off the coast of Egypt, such as a flag draped cannon, a pyramid, palm trees and a sphinx. Yet on close inspection several discrepancies become apparent in the iconography, notably the prominent display of a Roman Corinthian column at the heart of the ostensibly Egyptian landscape. The key to this mystery is, however, literally staring the viewer in the face. Alongside the Corinthian column is a mason wearing an apron.

Their shared interest in freemasonry did not forge the friendship between Nelson and Davison but it did invisibly bind them together. It may also account for the otherwise often enigmatic character of a relationship that survived the acrimonious break-up of Nelson's marriage in 1801 and Davison's imprisonment for electoral corruption in 1804. Nelson's contact with masonic culture also informed the loyalty he felt towards other male friends and colleagues in his circle regardless of their often-manifold faults. By comparison this hidden sense of duty was often lacking in his uneasy dealings with women, who were excluded from freemasonry, most notoriously in his treatment of his wife Fanny. By contrast Emma Hamilton may have had at least some knowledge of freemasonry from her marriage to the antiquarian Sir William Hamilton. Emma had accompanied her husband and Nelson on a tour of the famous masonic gardens at Wörlitzpark during their journey through Germany on the way back to England from Naples in 1800. A few months later all three passed Christmas as guests of the exotic aesthete and prominent freemason William Beckford. Intriguingly in one of the letters he wrote to Emma during Nelson's lifetime, Davison even overtly referred to the 'All Ruling Power', indicating that he knew she would recognise this masonic allusion to God. [18]

There are no surviving records of Nelson's formal membership of a masonic lodge beyond his acceptance - in 1801 - of the regalia for the so-called Ancient Gregorians in Norwich, one of the many fashionable pseudo-masonic friendly societies that were springing up around the country at the time. Davison was initiated as a master mason - the third and highest degree of freemasonry – during a ceremony in Quebec on 22 October 1785. His attainment of this degree indicates that he had been a freemason for some years and almost certainly before Nelson's arrival in the town in 1782. Davison's membership of Merchant Lodge No.1 in Quebec was not surprising, for freemasonry was the principal social and intellectual activity among the small British merchant community in the province, as it was in other British colonies. By participating in it Davison would have enjoyed the mutual support and encouragement of his peers.

In typical fashion the first lodges had arrived in Canada embedded in the regiments that secured the country after the conquest in 1759. Freemasonry - with its emphasis on equality and fraternity – not only offered the officers a forum for philosophical debate free from the handicaps of status but gave them an opportunity to wine and dine in congenial company thus contributing to esprit de corps. Freemasonry struggled, however, to take hold in the less familial atmosphere of the navy compared to the tight knit culture of the army. Its rituals may also have been hampered by space restrictions on board a warship. [19] Indeed compared to the dozens - even hundreds - of lodges recognised in the army, only three ships in the Royal Navy were granted warrants to hold freemason meetings by the Grand Lodge in London: *Vanguard*, *Prince* and *Canceaux*.[20] Nelson, of course, became very familiar with *Vanguard* during the Nile campaign[21] while, by coincidence, *Canceaux* was moored in the River St Lawrence when he arrived at Quebec in September 1782. [See DN 10 which is a medal that belonged to a Marine on board *Vanguard*, who was a mason as indicated by the masonic device engraved on his medal.]

In Quebec Nelson would have recognised the colonial masonic milieu that he had experienced earlier in his career in the West Indies. Indeed on at least two occasions he had lodged in Jamaica at the house of Admiral Sir Peter Parker, the provincial Grand Master of the freemasons in the West Indies who later became his mentor. By the time of Nelson's state funeral at St Paul's Cathedral twenty-five years later - where he controversially led the official mourning in place of the First Lord, Earl St Vincent - the ageing Parker had risen to become the Deputy Grand Master of the freemasons in England, a position second only in executive importance within the masonic hierarchy to the acting Grand Master, and another conspicuous guest at the ceremony, the earl of Moira. (In the Cathedral Moira stood alongside the Grand Master, the Prince of Wales, who was prevented by protocol from leading the official mourning himself.)

Moira, subsequently the Marquis of Hastings, played a major role in Davison's life and a greatly underestimated one in Nelson's. At Davison's trial for fraud in 1809, Moira claimed that they had met on the outbreak of war in 1793 when Davison had been recommended to him as the commissary-general for the army he was preparing to take over the channel to invade France. Davison's name may have been proposed by the duke of Northumberland who had fought alongside Moira in the American War, and who shared the earl's aristocratic, Whiggish outlook. When Moira became embroiled in a plot to oust the Prime Minister William Pitt from office in 1797, he instinctively turned to the duke for help, using Davison as a secret go-between, a role Davison would reprise for Nelson and Emma. In a similar manner, Moira used Davison's influence with Nelson to harness the Victor of the Nile's political appeal. In 1802 Davison told Nelson that Moira was on the verge of being appointed to Henry Addington's new cabinet. Persuaded by the hope that Moira's influence might secure a longed-for government pension for Emma Hamilton, Nelson gave the earl his proxy in the House of Lords believing him 'a distinguished officer, an enlightened statesman and a man of too much honour to abuse so sacred a trust'. [22] Nelson's disappointment was profound, therefore, when not only was Moira not invited to join the cabinet but he began to wield his vote against his interest. On his last leave in England in September 1805 Nelson felt compelled to ask the earl for the return of his proxy, an embarrassing and unpleasant task which he bitterly resented having to do, believing it was Davison's responsibility, but his agent was out of town.

Nelson saw his lavish Derby wine coolers for the first time on his return to England in November 1800. An educated eye would have recognised the obvious Egyptian motifs: obelisks, pyramids and palm trees as well as the conventional symbols for a naval victory: a flag draped gun, trident and anchor. An initiated observer, however, could decipher the hidden masonic code, for each of the images was loaded with rich allegorical meaning. The most striking of these was the Roman Corinthian column which a freemason would recognise as emblematic of strength and wisdom. The column stood alongside an obelisk, another striking masonic image. In due course both would become physical realities. For, with its empty pedestal, the column on the coolers eerily foreshadowed the vast stone monument erected in Trafalgar Square forty years after Trafalgar, whereas Davison himself raised an obelisk in Nelson's memory on his estate in Northumberland.

The coolers offer vivid proof of Davison's guiding philosophy and of his enthusiasm for the voguish masonic conviction that freemasonry could be traced to the ancient world of the Egyptians. Yet the physical manifestation of this previously hidden aspect to Davison's friendship with Nelson did not end there. In November 1798 Davison embarked on an ambitious, and expensive, scheme to give a medal to every man who fought the battle of the Nile - all 6,000 of them. Davison's grand project - which eventually cost him £1,200 - was authorised by his political friend the Secretary for War Henry Dundas. Dundas insisted that the medal should not glorify Nelson, rather that it should celebrate the victory as a stepping stone to peace. However, as a prominent freemason himself, the minister turned a blind eye to the encoding of the Nile medal with masonic symbols. In accordance with the government's instructions Davison – who painstakingly designed the medal himself – placed a figure of Hope on the obverse of his medal, to represent the official desire for peace. In contrast the image of Nelson was relegated to a small shield, in blatant contravention of the precedent set by earlier medals for naval victories – such as Earl Howe's victory on the Glorious First of June – when a bust of the commander-in-chief was given prominence. The figure of Hope served a dual function. Alongside her traditional representation as a source of comfort was her providential role as one of the three principal theological virtues of freemasonry (the others being Faith and Charity). To emphasis this point still further, in his design Davison depicted Hope with her right breast bared, in imitation of the masonic initiation ritual. He also insisted that the anchor supporting the figure of Hope – her traditional and, in the context of a naval victory, highly appropriate emblem – should appear exactly as he had sketched it, intending that its partially obscured stock should appear like a coffin, another discrete masonic reference. Matthew Boulton, the famous steam engineer and industrialist who was entrusted with the manufacture of the medal, was unimpressed by the use of so much symbolism believing it to be confusing and in very bad taste. Boulton's objections were ignored and it is only by understanding the deliberate ambiguities within Davison's Nile medal that a solution can be found to its most abiding mystery.

This is the appearance of the sun on the reverse of the medal which depicted the scene within Aboukir Bay shortly before the battle commenced. As the action took place at night, the orientation of the Egyptian coastline on the medal suggests that the sun is setting in the east. This impossibility had always been assumed to be the unintended error of Matthew Boulton's master die-cutter, a German émigré called Conrad Küchler. Yet from the extensive - almost obsessive - correspondence between Davison, Boulton and Henry Dundas' office in Downing Street over the manufacture of the Nile medal, it seems inconceivable that such an obvious mistake would have been tolerated. Indeed in the final design of the medal – which Davison arranged to be published in the *Anti-Jacobin Review and Magazine* – the sky above the bay was left entirely blank. Why then was the sun added to the design, apparently at the last moment?

The answer to this riddle is found in other masonic jewels of the period notably those of the Ancient Gregorians, the obscure pseudo-masonic friendly society which later counted Nelson among its members. In these jewels a rising sun often appears as symbolic of the influence of the masonic 'All ruling Power'. The use of the sun to represent Divine Providence is analogous within masonic iconography to the more familiar 'Eye of Providence'. The 'Eye of Providence' is seen in 'The Thanksgiving Medal', another medal struck after the battle to celebrate the victory. 'The Thanksgiving Medal' was available to the public in a variety of metals from a leading jeweller in the Strand and it seems impossible that Davison was not aware of it. Placing 'The Thanksgiving Medal' with its pyramid, palm tree, and masonic bi-morph figure, alongside Davison's Nile medal and the Derby wine coolers it is impossible to ignore the extraordinary amalgamation of masonic influences. It seems that Davison was not alone in expropriating Nelson's victory as a triumph of masonic virtues over the threat of tyranny.

There was also a political dimension to Davison's very public act of generosity. Prevented by their constitution from publicly defending themselves, the freemasons, led by Lord Moira, had recently embarked on a discreet campaign to secure exemption from emergency legislation which, although designed to outlaw the secret meetings of Jacobins and Irish revolutionaries, would have severally restricted their own activities. Within this highly charged political context, Davison's medal can be seen as a mute demonstration of masonic loyalty to crown and country. Accordingly, in addition to the medals struck for the men who fought the battle, Davison ordered a further quantity for his own, carefully targeted, distribution. Two of the first medals were sent to Earl St Vincent and Admiral Sir Peter Parker, neither of whom had been at the battle, while Davison presented one to the King in person, reporting happily to Nelson that they were received 'most graciously and with much joy and pleasure'. [23] St Vincent subsequently returned the favour presenting Davison with one of the gold medals he commissioned from Boulton after he struck his flag for the final time in 1800. Like Nelson, no record survives of St Vincent's membership of the freemasons yet his medal is elegant proof that he, too, was steeped in the masonic culture which informed the very highest levels of the government and military. The medal depicts a marine and a naval officer making a masonic handshake against the backdrop, following the recent union with Ireland, of the newly instituted Union Jack. Above them is the motto 'Loyal and True' - sentiments which resonated through the military and political elite.

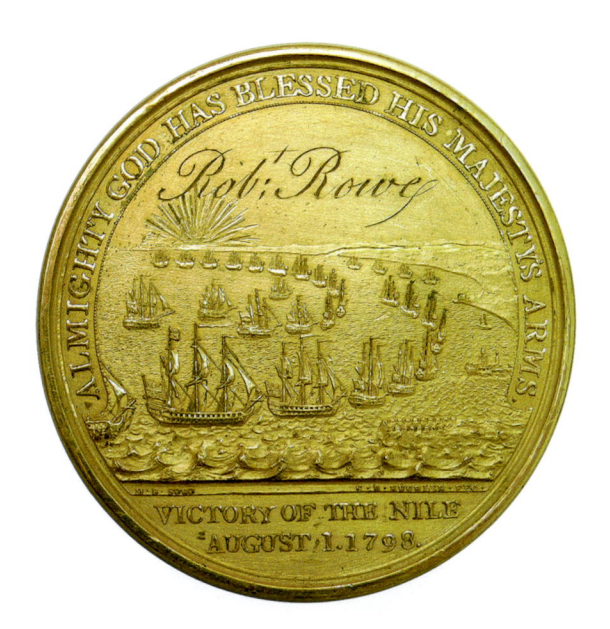

3 medals Sim Comfort Collection. Lot 8, Nelson's Davison Nile made £26,290. Image courtesy Sotheby's.

The government took the opportunity of Davison's largesse for some strategic gift giving of its own. Lord Grenville, the foreign secretary, asked Davison to send medals to the emperors of Russia and Germany, the sultan of Turkey and the king of Naples. Davison happily obliged, waving aside offers of payment satisfied as he was with the political capital he was reaping. Nelson – who understood the currency of gift giving - doled out Nile medals liberally until his death. His own medal, which he wore on a ribbon around his neck, was returned to Davison after the battle of Trafalgar. [24]

8 obverse   8 reverse

8 ALEXANDER DAVISON'S MEDAL FOR THE BATTLE OF THE NILE, 1798, IN GOLD

The material expression of the friends' interest in the culture of fraternity was matched by the language they employed, famously in Nelson's description of his Nile captains as his "band of brothers". This striking term is taken, of course, from the king's speech in *Henry V* yet it seems the idea of employing it in the aftermath of the battle was given to Nelson by his wife. In a letter to her husband written in March 1797, Fanny Nelson

89

casually mentions Lady Spencer, the wife of the First Lord, speaking "of the admirals and captains as a chosen band, they all can do the same great actions." [25] "The band of brothers" was certainly a propitious term in the context of the fraternalism of the freemasons and by expropriating it (then modifying it to the "brethren of the Nile"), Nelson defined the intellectual environment in which the battle was fought.

So compelling was the prevailing instinct to ritualise fraternal bonds forged in war that barely twenty four hours after the battle the "band of brothers" instituted the elite "Egyptian Club". With its rules and designated meeting place (though it never seems to have only met once), the Egyptian Club mimicked the freemasons and other friendly societies with which the captains were familiar. Back in London, Davison was given the task of organising a deluxe gold and bejewelled presentation sword with its hilt designed as a crocodile for the members of the club to present to Nelson. Replica swords were made for the captains and an elite group of invited members, including the prince of Wales. Davison himself owned at least two Egyptian Club crocodile swords. One was bequeathed by his son, Sir William Davison, to the Royal Naval Hospital at Greenwich in 1873 while another was found among his collection of artefacts.

Lot 13 Egyptian Club Sword made £240,000. Image courtesy Sotheby's

The Nile medal and the Derby wine coolers indicate the high importance that the friends placed in gift giving. Yet Nelson faced a dilemma. With only limited resources, what could he give a man who quite literally had everything? The answer is found in the will he made out shortly before joining HMS *Victory* in May 1803. In the will, he bequeathed to Davison "my Turkish Gun, Scimitar and Canteen." [26] Although of uncertain provenance - Davison subsequently claimed they had been presented to Nelson after the battle of the Nile by the Sultan of Turkey - these three items of otherwise modest value were carefully selected by Nelson as emblematic trophies of war. As such they held a resonance for Davison far beyond anything Nelson could have purchased and were of inestimable value to him. At the earliest opportunity after receiving his bequest in 1806, Davison was painted by Arthur William Devis – the artist who had just completed his famous work "The Death of Nelson" - ostentatiously carrying Nelson's "scimitar" (in reality, a captured French cavalry sabre.) At a stroke the painting identified Davison to posterity as an intimate of the nation's hero. The sabre was included in Sir William Davison's bequest to the Royal Naval Hospital although in the event only its gilt scabbard was received with the sabre believed lost until it resurfaced among Davison's lost treasures. [27]

Lot 84 French Officer's sword made £336,650. Image courtesy Sotheby's.

Nelson relics © National Maritime Museum, Greenwich, London. Lot 67 Diamond brooch made £140,000.

Alongside his bequest to Davison, Nelson gave another indication in his will of the significance he attached to those objects he felt were invested with emotional significance. This was his mention of a diamond star which he left to Emma Hamilton "as a token if my friendship and regard". Nelson had previously described the star - which was incontrovertibly a gift from the Sultan of Turkey - in a letter to Emma as a "memento of friendship, affection, and esteem" [28] presumably because it had witnessed the onset of their affair. After Nelson's death, Emma asked Davison to take the diamond star to John Salter, her jeweller on the Strand, "as he is to do something to it". [29] Thereafter the star disappears, to be replaced in Emma's collection by a "brilliant anchor"; probably the same jewel - decorated with Nelson's initials – which was found two hundred years later with Davison's descendants and which was the key to the discovery of his lost treasures. As with the Derby wine coolers, Emma presumably sold the diamond anchor to Davison as her fortunes dramatically declined after Nelson's death.

91

Davison's role in altering the diamond star is one practical demonstration of his integration into Nelson's closest inner circle, placing him at the heart of a dense web of relationships. Following his appointment as Nelson's prize agent in 1798, Davison used his experience in business to quickly extend his interests until they encompassed virtually the entire management of Nelson's civilian life including the admiral's legal and financial affairs, his domestic household, his tax returns, even the management of his post. When called upon, Davison was also expected to lend his friend money without charging interest something which he happily, and frequently, did - although the scale of his debt came to trouble Nelson. This mixing of private and professional duties between friends was characteristic of a period where there were few other outside resources to rely on. In this way Davison's mansion in St James's Square became the hub of Nelson's world, a place to which all those in the admiral's inner circle looked for advice, or influence; and none more so than Nelson's wife Fanny.

Davison's papers reveal that during her husband's long absence in the Mediterranean after the battle of the Nile – as his affair with Emma Hamilton gathered momentum – Fanny was effectively adopted by the Davison family. Her letters mention shared suppers, walks, evenings of whist and her warm affection for Davison's children and for his young wife Harriett. In June 1799 Fanny stood as a sponsor to the Davisons' sixth child, Alexander Horatio Nelson Davison, though she excused herself from the baby's christening pleading the lack of a suitable gown.

It was against this intimate background that Davison received Nelson's deplorable instruction in April 1801 to "signify to Lady N. that I expect, and for which I have made such a very liberal allowance to her, to be left to myself". [30] Davison dutifully replied that "I shall implicitly obey and execute your wishes at the proper time...I will break the subject in the most delicate manner I possibly can and in a way to give least offence to Lady N". [31] And yet, handicapped by his close friendship Davison did nothing. Indeed to the contrary, despite all he knew, he continued to give Fanny hope that rapprochement with her husband was still possible. Davison may even have believed this himself, anticipating that widespread social and professional opprobrium at Nelson's behaviour, combined with the admiral's jealous regard for his own reputation, would crush the affair. Also found among Davison's papers was a revealing letter from Captain Edward Parker, one of Nelson's young protégés, written in August 1801. In his letter Parker referred to Emma Hamilton as a "B[itch]" who would "play the deuce with him [Nelson]" .[32] That Parker felt able to describe Emma in such withering terms to Nelson's closest male friend indicates not only that he believed he had a sympathetic ear, but that he was expressing a widely-held sentiment.

So Davison did nothing, his duty to Nelson outweighed by compassion for Fanny. In this perilous state he received a startling letter from Fanny which reveals her as every bit as passionate as her glamorous rival. "You or no one can tell my feelings" she wrote:

"I love him I would do anything in the world to convince him of my affection – I was truly sensible of My good fortune in having such a husband – surely I have angered him – it was done unconsciously and without the least intention - I can truly say, my wish, my desire was to please him – and if he will have the goodness to send for me – I will make it my study to obey him in every wish or desire of his – and with cheerfulness – I still hope – He is affectionate and possesses the best of hearts – He will not make me miserable – I hope I have not deserved so severe a punishment from him."[33]

Davison took a month to reply. "I have long wished to write to you" he began, his words betraying his obvious discomfort:

"Which nothing but the want of something to say to you prevented. I have nothing to relate in particular, yet it is with unspeakable pleasure I can assure you, that Lord Nelson is in better health that I had ever reason to expect...I hardly need to repeat how happy I should have been to have seen him with you, the happiest. His heart is so pure and so extremely good that I flatter myself he never can be divested from his affection. I have the same opinion I ever had of his sincere regard for you. I have no right to doubt it. "[34]

Davison's letter is further evidence of an emerging consensus that Nelson had been led astray by his mistress. Fanny described her husband as "deluded"[35] while the Reverend Edmund Nelson lamented that his son "is gone a little out of the straight road – He will see his error – and be as good as ever".[36] This attitude brought with it some comfort, and a little hope, but made the inevitable denouement still more devastating. This arrived in December 1801 when Fanny sent a letter to her husband under cover to Davison's house in St James's Square, the one place where she believed her husband might read it away from the gaze of Emma Hamilton. "My dear husband" she wrote:

"The silence you have imposed is more than my affections will allow me...Do, my dear husband, let us live together. I can never be happy till such an event takes place. I assure you again I have but one wish in the world, to please you. Let everything be buried in oblivion, it will pass away like a dream. I can now only entreat you to believe I am most sincerely and affectionately your wife, Frances H. Nelson [37]

Davison was now forced to choose between his friends. His decision was inevitable, given the value to him of his role in Nelson's life and the strength of the hidden loyalties that existed between them. But it was none the less painful. The same evening Fanny received her letter back. On the address leaf was written – like a short stab to her heart: "Opened by mistake by Lord Nelson, but not read. A. Davison".[38]

Davison's loyalty to his friend, which he pursued at great personal cost (the thoughts of Harriet Davison on her husband's role in the separation of the Nelsons may be imagined), was not entirely reciprocated. From Nelson's surviving correspondence to Emma Hamilton it seems that in the last months of his life the admiral was cooling in his regard for his old friend, a situation exacerbated by his anger and embarrassment at the abuse of his proxy vote by Davison's patron Lord Moira. The news in 1804 that Davison had been imprisoned in the King's Bench for electoral corruption was greeted with a distinct smug satisfaction. "I am quite hurt about his getting into such a scrape" Nelson commented, "he always told me: "Oh! I know my ground – leave me alone – I cannot be deceived". It often turns out that these very clever men are oftener deceived than other people". [39]

Emma, who had clashed with Davison over the cost of her improvements to Merton Place, undoubtedly stirred things up. Matters deteriorated to such an extent that in one of the last letters Nelson wrote to Emma, he confided that: "I don't think Davison a good hand to keep such a secret as you told him. I fear I cannot even write him a line." [40] The nature of the "secret" which Emma divulged to Davison is not known. Perhaps she revealed to him the true parentage of her four year old "ward" Horatia. Nelson was also eager to escape from Davison's financial grasp, confiding to Emma in May 1805 that: " I know I am most deeply in debt to Davison, and I want his account that I may close it, for it must not run on in the way it has, but I cannot get it, nor do I know how I stand with their banking house, I get no account." [41]

Yet despite his inner thoughts, the last letter Nelson wrote to his friend, from *Victory* on 13 October 1805 owed no sign of any lessening of affection. In the letter – which Davison carefully preserved – Nelson expressed his hope that "some happy day I hope to get at their fleet and nothing shall be wanting on my part to give a good account of them." [42]

Davison stayed loyal beyond Nelson's death. He erected an obelisk on his estate dedicated to their "Private Friendship" and, to his credit, did his best to support Emma Hamilton as she struggled with her rising debts. Learning that Davison had raised a consortium of investors to bale her out of her debts, Emma wrote that: "to my last breathe I shall feel a glory in having had Alexander Davison as my friend; as did Nelson, to his death, die loving & respecting you more than he did any man living. Relations not excepted."[43] In the event, Davison's unhappy fate was scarcely less humiliating than Emma's. In 1809 he was found guilty of defrauding the public purse in his capacity as a government contractor and was again sent to prison, this time for two years. On his release Davison embarked on an ill advised and costly attempt to clear his name. Although eventually vindicated, his campaign, combined with the failure of his bank, cost him much of his vast fortune. In 1817 his mansion in St James's Square was sold and the contents auctioned in a spectacular fourteen day sale. Alongside his magnificent collection of works of art and paintings were numerous souvenirs of his relationship with Nelson although Davison preserved those of particular sentiment, including the diamond anchor, Nelson's Nile medal, the Derby wine coolers and the bloodstained purse which his friend had carried to his death at Trafalgar.

Lot 972 on the last day of the auction was a copy of Jeremy Taylor's *Doctor Dubitantium or The Rule of Conscience*. Taylor, an influential seventeenth century theologian, believed that a good friend should be "wise and virtuous, rich and at hand, close and merciful, free of his money and tenacious of a secret, open and ingenuous, true and honest" for "a fool cannot be relied upon for counsel; nor a vicious person for the advantages of virtue, nor a begger for relief, nor a stranger for conduct, nor a tattler to keep a secret, nor a pitiless person trusted with any complaint, nor a covetous person with my child's fortune…nor a suspicious person with a private design".[44] In subsequent biographies of Nelson and even - as a contemporary caricature reveals - during his lifetime, Davison has been vilified for exploiting his friendship with the hero. Yet it seems that he largely fulfilled Taylor's dictum and that, on balance, it was Davison who was ill-advised in his choice of friend.

Portrait of Nelson by George Perfect Harding after Devis, circa 1840.
Cast of Tassie intaglio after Filippo Rega of Emma Hamilton circa 1800. Sim Comfort Collection.

Footnotes

1. Nelson to Davison, 8 February 1803, H.N. Nicolas, *The Dispatches and Letters of Vice-Admiral Lord Viscount Nelson* (1846), V, p. 42
2. Davison to Nelson 3 February 1803, T. J. Pettigrew *Memoirs of the Life of Vice-Admiral Lord Viscount Nelson, K.B.* (1849), II, p.282.
3. In "State of my affairs according to my books to the 31st December 1803", Davison estimated his net personal worth at £307,940. (Private collection)
4. Davison introduced his nephew William Home, then serving in *Blanche*, to Nelson during a visit to Yarmouth in February 1801 shortly before the fleet sailed on the Baltic campaign.
5. Quoted by Nelson in a letter to Emma Lady Hamilton 7 March 1801 Pettigrew,
6. Davison to his son William Davison, 8 December 1810, (Private collection.)
7. Davison and Ross must have known each other, if only by repute. In a letter dated 11 June 1801 Nelson asked Davison for assistance in matter involving Ross' nephew. Nicolas, IV, p. 408.
8. Nelson to Davison 27 May 1797, Nicolas, VII, p.cxxxviii.
9. Sir Nicholas Harris Nicolas to Percy Davison, 17 December 1844, BL EG MSS 2241
10. Maurice Nelson to Sukey Ford, 27 March 1794. NMM HAM/81
11. Davison to Nelson, 24 April 1801, NMM CRK/3
12. Davison to Admiral Cuthbert Collingwood NMM DAV/52 fo.44
13. Nelson to Davison, 27 May 1797, Nicolas, VII, p.cxxxviii
14. Frances Nelson to Davison, 3 May 1801, NMM DAV/2/43
15. Maurice Nelson to Nelson, 25 November 1798, BL ADD MSS 34988
16. Frances Nelson to Alexander Davison 21 February 1799 NMM DAV/2 fo.6
17. ibid
18. Davison to Emma Hamilton, undated probably November 1804. in A. Morrison, *The Hamilton and Nelson Papers* (1893), II, p.247.
19. J. Harland-Jacobs, "The Essential Link" : *Freemasonry and British Imperialism, 1751-1918*, unpublished D Phil dissertation (2000) p.46n
20. F. Smyth, "The Master-Mason-at-Arms: *A short study of Freemasonry in the Armed Forces*" in Ars Coronatorum 104 (1991)
21. In *Horatio Lord Nelson Was he a Freemason* (1998) John Webb points out that during Nelson's tenure the Great Cabin of Vanguard was carpeted by a piece of sailcloth marked out in black and white squares as if for a masonic ritual. Webb states that this checkerboard sailcloth was subsequently transferred to *Victory*.
22. Nelson to William Haslewood, quoted in T.Pocock *Horatio Nelson* (1987) p.310
23. Davison to Nelson, 6 April 1799, BL ADD 34910
24. In 1866 the medal was recorded in a family inventory by Davison's son, Sir William Davison, as "the gold nile medal worn by the immortal Nelson when he fell 21st October 1805 at Trafalgar". It was Lot 8 in *The Alexander Davison Collection*, Sotheby's London, 21 October 2002 selling for £26,290.
25. Frances Nelson to Nelson, 11 March 1797, in G.P.B.Naish Nelson's letters to his wife and other documents 1785-1831 (1958) p.350
26. The will is printed in full in Nicolas VII, pp. ccxxi-ccxl.
27. The sabre was Lot 84 in *The Alexander Davison Collection*, Sotheby's London, 21 October 2002, selling for £336,650
28. Nelson to Emma Hamilton, undated but probably February 1801, Pettigrew, I, p.428.

29. Emma Hamilton to Davison 7 June 1806, NMM LBK/7
30. Nelson to Davison, 23 April 1801, Nicolas, VII, p.ccix
31. Davison to Nelson, 4 May 1801, in Lot 70 *The Alexander Davison Collection*, Sotheby's London, 21 October 2002.
32. Edward Parker to Davison, 9 August 1801, in Lot 53 *The Alexander Davison Collection*, Sotheby's London, 21 October 2002
33. Frances Nelson to Davison 26 June 1801 NMM DAV/2 fo. 50
34. Davison to Frances Nelson 12 July 1801, Naish, p.588.
35. Frances Nelson to Davison 15 March 1801 NMM DAV/2 fo. 32
36. Quoted in Frances Nelson to Davison 27 July 1801 NMM DAV/2 fo. 51
37. Frances Nelson to Nelson, 18 December 1801, Naish, p.596
38. Ibid
39. Nelson to Emma Hamilton, 22 May 1804, Pettigrew, II, p.392.
40. Morrison
41. Nelson to Emma Hamilton 13 May 1805, Pettigrew, II, p474
42. Nelson to Davison, 13 October 1805, *The Alexander Davison Collection*, Sotheby's London, 21 October 2002, Lot 76.
43. Emma Hamilton to Davison, 21 December 1808, NMM MSS 9640
44. *A Discourse of the Nature, Offices and Measure of Friendship* Jeremy Taylor (London 1671) p27-28

Service dish part of the Baltic service used at Paradise Merton. Sim Comfort Collection.

PLAN of the BATTLE of the NILE on the 1st of AUGT. 1798,
by the late R.W. Miller, Esqr. Captain of H.M.S. Theseus.

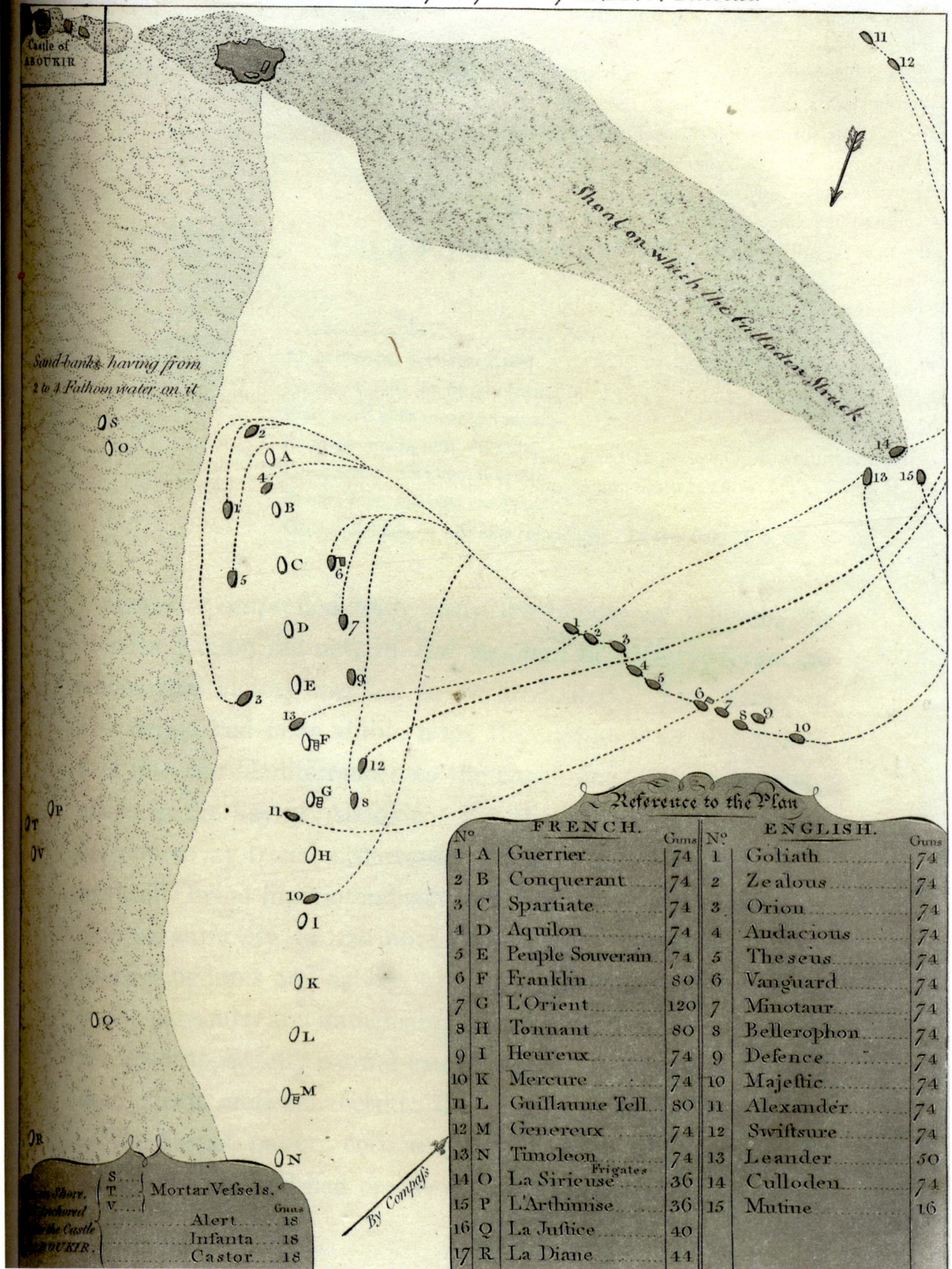

Reference to the Plan

No		FRENCH	Guns	No	ENGLISH	Guns
1	A	Guerrier	74	1	Goliath	74
2	B	Conquerant	74	2	Zealous	74
3	C	Spartiate	74	3	Orion	74
4	D	Aquilon	74	4	Audacious	74
5	E	Peuple Souverain	74	5	Theseus	74
6	F	Franklin	80	6	Vanguard	74
7	G	L'Orient	120	7	Minotaur	74
8	H	Tonnant	80	8	Bellerophon	74
9	I	Heureux	74	9	Defence	74
10	K	Mercure	74	10	Majestic	74
11	L	Guillaume Tell	80	11	Alexander	74
12	M	Genereux	74	12	Swiftsure	74
13	N	Timoleon	74	13	Leander	50
14	O	La Sirieuse	36	14	Culloden	74
15	P	L'Arthimise (Frigates)	36	15	Mutine	16
16	Q	La Justice	40			
17	R	La Diane	44			

Mortar Vessels.

	Guns
Alert	18
Infanta	18
Castor	18

98

Captain Ralph Willett Miller's
Account of the Battle of the Nile, 1 August 1798

In 1899 and 1900, The Navy Records Society of London published *The Logs of the Great Sea Fights (1794 – 1805)*, edited by Rear-Admiral T. Sturges Jackson. If there were two volumes that would provide essential information for naval historians during the decades that followed, these two volumes certainly achieved that.

One of the important contributions is the publication of Captain Ralph Miller's account of the battle of the Nile. Miller captained HMS *Theseus* and his account, which was sent to his wife on 19 October 1798 when his ship was being repaired at Gibraltar, is clearly based on his own recollections, but also contains information that he gained from his fellow captains. Today, his account still stands as the best contemporary description of the battle and for that reason it is here published in its entirety.

[After Napoleon and his fleet left Toulon on 19 May 1798, there began a long frustrating search by Nelson to discover where the enemy fleet was bound, which was only resolved on 28 July.]

'On the 28th of July, being off the Gulf of Coron in the Morea [southern most peninsula of mainland Greece], the *Culloden* stood into it and learnt from the Turkish Governor that the enemy were at Alexandria and brought out with her a French brig loaded with wine. Soon after she joined the Admiral [Nelson], he bore up for Alexandria with the signal flying, that he had intelligence of the enemy, and, constantly keeping the worst sailing ship under all sail, he arrived off that port the 1st of August, at noon, and seeing nothing of the French there, stood alongshore to the eastward, when, about three-quarters past 2, the *Zealous* made the signal for 16 sail of the line at anchor, and soon after we discovered them from this ship [HMS *Theseus*].

'Here let me pause till I can make you perfectly understand the state of the fleet at that moment. We had a fine breeze of the north wind, smooth water, and fair weather, the body [of the British squadron], extending about three miles easterly and westerly without being in any order of sailing, and going about five miles an hour under topsails, generally. The *Culloden* under all sail about seven miles astern, with the wine brig in tow (an article of which the fleet was running short), the *Alexander* and *Swiftsure* being far ahead on the look out, and, chasing when we were steering. SE by E, were thrown considerably to leeward by our change of course after making Alexandria; and at the time of the enemy being discovered. I should think were full nine miles to the southward of us. The *Zealous* and *Goliath* were the most advanced ships next to the Admiral [in the *Vanguard*], and a posse of us near him; the *Majestic* and *Leander*, I believe, the sternmost, exclusive of the *Culloden*; the general signal of recall having been made about 2 o'clock, the *Swiftsure* and *Alexander* standing towards us with all sail on a wind, and the *Mutine* within hail of the Admiral.

'The *Zealous*, after previous signals, announced to the Admiral, at three-quarters past 2, that 16 sail of the line were at an anchor E b S, and in a few minutes after, we all discovered them. At 3, the Admiral made the signal to prepare for battle – at half-past 3, for the *Culloden* to quit her prize. At 25 minutes past 4, to prepare for battle with the sheet cable out of the stern port, and springs on the bower-anchor, &c, &c. – at 54 minutes past 4, that it was the Admiral's intention to attack the van and centre of the enemy. At 40 minutes past 5, to form the line of battle as most convenient ahead and astern of the Admiral; and immediately after, for the leading ship to steer one point more to starboard.

'The *Goliath* was leading, the *Zealous* next, then the *Vanguard*; the *Theseus* followed close to her stern, having the *Bellerophon* close on the weather quarter, and *Minotaur* equally so on the lee quarter: I do not recollect the order of the other ships.

'We wore gradually round, preserving our order till we brought the wind on the starboard beam, when the Admiral hove to, to speak the *Mutine* [Captain Hardy], about three miles from the enemy, who were making signals and heaving on their springs. I took this opportunity to pass the Admiral to leeward and endeavour to obtain the honour of leading the fleet into battle, as the *Culloden*, the only ship ahead of us in the regular line, was still considerably distant; but Captain Berry hailed as we passed, and gave me the Admiral's order to become his second ahead, in consequence of which I hove to close ahead of him, and the *Orion* and *Audacious* passed us. We had before got springs on both our bower-anchors, the stream cable passed out of the stern port, and bent to its anchor; and were now doing the same by the sheet, being in all other respects in the most perfect order for battle.

'The enemy had 13 large ships anchored in close order of battle, in the form of a bow, with the convex part to us, *l'Orient*, of 120 guns, making the centre of it, the string of the bow being NW & SE, and four frigates a little within them, with a gun and mortar battery on a small island about three-quarters of a mile from their van ship, and three mortar boats placed near the frigates.

'In about five minutes after bringing to, the Admiral made the signal to make sail again, the leading ship first, when the *Goliath*, in a very gallant and masterly manner, led along the enemy's line, gradually closing with their van, which, as well as the battery on the island, opened its fire. At 40 minutes past 6, the Admiral made the signal to engage the enemy close, the *Goliath* passing round and raking the enemy's van ship (the *Guerrier*), brought up with her stern anchor inside of and abreast their second ship (the *Conquerant*). *Zealous* following likewise raked the *Guerrier*, brought down her fore mast, and came to with her stern anchor on her inner bow. The *Orion*, from her previous situation, described a little wider circle, passed the off side of the *Zealous*, and made a wide sweep in order to come to with one of her bowers; in doing which she completely knocked up the *Serieuse* frigate, which lay in her way, having made such a wreck of her, that on her driving, presently after, on a shoal, all her masts fell, and she filled with water.

'I think the *Orion* must have touched the ground from the time between her passing the *Zealous* and her coming to nearly abreast the inner side of the fifth ship (the *Peuple Souverain*); for, through she passed the *Zealous* before us, we had completely brought up abreast the inner beam of the *Spartiate*, the third ship, and had been in action with her four or five minutes before the *Orion* came to. In running along the enemy's line in the wake of the *Zealous* and *Goliath*, I observed their shot sweep just over us, and knowing well that at such a moment Frenchmen would not have the coolness enough to change their elevation, I closed them suddenly, and running under the arch of their shot, reserved my fire, every gun being loaded with two and some with three round shot, until I had the *Guerrier's* masts in a line, and her jib-boom about six feet clear of our rigging; we then opened with such effect, that a second breath could not be drawn before her main and mizzen mast were also gone. This was precisely at sunset or 44 minutes past 6; then passing between her and the *Zealous*, and as close as possible round the off side of the *Goliath*, we anchored exactly in a line with her, and as I have before said, abreast the *Spartiate*; the *Audacious* having passed between the *Guerrier* and the *Conquerant*, came to with her bower close upon the inner bow of the latter. We had not been many minutes in action with the *Spartiate* when we observed one of our ships (and soon after knew her to be the *Vanguard*) placed herself so directly opposite to us on the outside of her, that I desisted firing on her, that I might not do mischief to our friends, and directed every gun before the main mast on the *Aquilon*, and all abaft it on the *Conquerant*, and giving up my proper bird to the Admiral; the *Minotaur* following the Admiral, placed herself on the outer side of the fourth ship (*Aquilon*), and the *Defence* on the fifth, or *Peuple Souverain*.

Attack at Sunset by Robert Dodd. Note that Nelson is flying his Rear-Admiral's blue flag at the mizzen of *Vanguard*. The red pennant and blue and red flag are signalling Number 5, however Dodd has misunderstood the colour of the flag which should be yellow and blue and not red and blue. Number 5 commands 'To Engage the Enemy' and in the signal book is the further instruction, 'If [the flag is] alone, then a red pennant will be shown over the flag', which is just what Dodd has painted. Sim Comfort Collection.

'The *Bellerophon*, I believe, dropped her stern anchor well on the outer bow of *l'Orient* (seventh ship), but it not bringing her up, she became singly opposed to the fire of that enormous ship before her own broadside completely bore, and then sustained the greater part of her loss; she then either drifted or sailed along the French line, and came to anchor about six miles eastward of us, where we discovered her next morning (without a mast standing), with her ensign on the stump of the main mast. Captain Darby was wounded at the beginning, and poor Daniel, 1st lieutenant, as well as the 2nd and 4th, killed.

'As well as I can learn, the *Majestic*, whether owing to the thickness of the smoke at the shutting in of the evening, or that her stern cable did not bring her up in time, ran her jib-boom into the main rigging of *l'Heureux*, ninth ship, and remained a long time in that unfortunate position suffering greatly; poor Westcott was almost the first that fell, being killed by a musket-ball in the neck. She got disentangled, and brought her broadside to bear on the starboard bow of the *Mercure*, the tenth ship, on whom she took a severe revenge; having laid that bow almost open, she also had only a fore mast standing at daylight.

'My noble and glorious neighbour, on the 14th February, the gallant Captain Troubridge, of the *Culloden*, had the misfortune to strike and stick fast, spite of all his efforts, on a shoal, but little out of gunshot of the battle, to his inconceivable mortification, though individually it could not have happened better than to him, or publicly worse, as no naval character for indefatigable zeal, courage, and ability stands higher than his, or is built on a broader basis; while, on the other hand, it was to us the loss of force of a ship that is without a superior. I think it very likely she saved the three following ships from the same mischance.

'My worthy friends Hallowell and Ball got among us a few minutes after 8 o'clock, the *Swiftsure* coming to, with her stern anchor upon the outer quarter of the *Franklin* (the sixth ship), and bow of *l'Orient*. When the five headmost ships of the enemy were completely subdued, which might have been 9 or half-past, the *Leander* came to with her stern-anchor upon the inner bow of the *Franklin*, having thus late by proffering assistance to the *Culloden*.

'Having now brought all our ships into battle, which you are to suppose raging in all magnificent, awful, and horrific grandeur, I'll proceed to relate the general events of it as I saw them. The *Guerrier* and *Conquerant* made very inefficient resistance, the latter being soon stripped of her main and mizen masts, they continued for a considerable time to fire, every now and then, a gun or two, and about 8 o'clock, I think, were totally silent.

BATTLE of the NILE, Augt 1st 1798.

'The *Spartiate* resisted much longer, and with serious effect, as the *Vanguard's* killed and wounded announces, who received her principal fire; her larboard guns were fired upon us in the beginning with great quickness, but after the Admiral anchored on his starboard side, it was slow and irregular, and before or about 9 o'clock she was silenced, and had also lost her main and mizen masts; the *Aquilon* was silenced a little earlier, with the loss of all of her masts, having the whole fire of the *Minotaur* on her starboard side, and, for some time, near half ours on her larboard bow.

'*La Peuple Souverain* was, about the same time, entirely dismasted and silenced, and drifting between the *Franklin* and *Orion*, when the *Leander* came into the battle, and took her place immediately on the *Franklin's* larboard bow, the *Swiftsure* having been long on her starboard quarter, and *Defence*, after *le Peuple Souverain* drifted away, firing upon her starboard bow; while she was thus situated, scarcely returning any fire, *l'Orient* caught fire on the poop, when the heavy cannonade from all the *Alexander's* and part of the *Swiftsure's* guns became so furious, that she was soon in a blaze, displaying a most grand and awful spectacle, such as formerly would have drawn tears down the victor's cheeks, but now pity was stifled as it rose by the remembrance of the numerous and horrid atrocities their unprincipled and blood-thirsty nation had and were committing; and when she blew up, about 11 o'clock, though I endeavoured to stop the momentary cheer of the ship's company, my heart scarce felt a single pang for their fate. Indeed, all its anxiety was in a moment called forth to a degree of terror for her, at seeing the *Alexander* on fire in several places; and a boat that was taking in a hawser, in order to warp the *Orion* further from *l'Orient*, I filled with fire-buckets, and sent instantly to her, and was putting the engine in another just returned from sounding, when I had the unspeakable happiness of seeing her get before the wind, and extinguish the flames.

'There was now no firing, except towards the French rear, and that quite a broken, disconnected one. Just after *l'Orient* blew up, I discovered by the moonlight a dismasted frigate on our inner beam, and sent Lieutenant Brodie to take possession of her if, on hailing, she surrendered, and, if not, to burn false fires, that we might compel her to it; the first took place, and he sent me the captain and three officers of the *Serieuse* frigate, which, having been severely handled by the *Orion*, had got aground, and filled with water in trying to escape, and all her masts gone; her crew, except thirty, had abandoned her.

'I, at this time, also perceived a group of the enemy's ships about a mile and a half within us, which must have moved there after the attack, and sent one of the mates to sound between us and them (the master being employed sounding within us, and examining the state of the *Serieuse*); and being, as well as the officers and people, greatly fatigued, I was happy to snatch half an hour's sleep, from which, in a little time I was roused by Captain Hood of the *Zealous*, who came to propose that our ships and the *Goliath* should go down to the group of ships; when, finding that my boat was sounding between us and them, it was agreed to wait the report of the officer on that service; meanwhile we prepared for it, and were lifting our bower-anchor, when an officer from the *Swiftsure* came to say, the Admiral wished us all to go to the assistance of the *Alexander* and *Majestic*, then exchanging an irregular fire with the enemy's rear; and while we were lifting our stern anchor for that purpose, a lieutenant of the *Alexander* came from the Admiral to us, and any other ships that could renew the action, to desire us to go down to these ships, and slip our cable if necessary.

'All firing had now ceased about ten minutes, I therefore hove up the stern anchor, and ran down under staysails, till I passed the *Majestic*, when we dropped our sheet-anchor, and, having run out a cable, let go our bower, so as to present our broadside to the enemy in a line with the *Alexander*, and leave a clear opening for the *Majestic* (who appeared to have suffered much) to fire through. We were not at first holding;

but happily the enemy made no use of the opportunity, though three of their broadsides bore on our bow from the different distances of about 2 ½ to 5 cables; besides these, which were two 80 and two 74's and one of which appeared not to have suffered anything, there were two 74's on our starboard quarter that did not appear to have been at all in action, about half gun shot from us; a 36-gun frigate, about the same distance, whose broadside bore immediately on our stern, and two others of 40 guns, at the longest range of shot, being the group I have before mentioned.

'Finding myself thus situated, a principal object to all the French ships, and the sole one to the group, I was resolved to remain quiet as long as they, and the *Alexander* and *Majestic*, chose to be so, to give time to the *Goliath*, *Zealous*, and *Leander* to join us, neither of which were yet moving; and I sent an officer to tell Hood I waited for them. My people were also so extremely jaded, that as soon as they had hove our sheet-anchor up they dropped under the capstan-bars, and were asleep in a moment in every sort of posture, having been then working at their fullest exertion, or fighting, for near twelve hours, without being able to benefit by the respite that occurred, because, while *l'Orient* was on fire, I had the ship completely sluiced as one of our precautionary measures against fire or combustibles falling on board us, when she blew up.

'It was some time before daylight that we reached our new position; observing the *Guillaume Tell* moving, and having the *Genereux* and her exactly in one, as she passed under our stern, I could no longer wait, particularly as none of the other English ships were yet in motion, but precisely at sunrise, opened my fire on these two ships, as the *Alexander* and *Majestic* did immediately after; this was directly returned, principally by the *Guillaume Tell* and *Tonnant*. After a little time, perceiving they all increased their distance, we veered to two cables on each anchor, and soon after the *Leander* came down, and having anchored without the *Alexander*, commenced a very distant fire.

'These four ships, having at length by imperceptible degrees got almost to the utmost range of shot, we turned our whole fire upon the two line-of-battle ships that were on our quarter, and whom we had now long known to be on shore; the *Majestic* and *Alexander* firing a few shot over us at them, as the *Leander* may perhaps have done. In a short time we compelled *l'Heureux* 74, to strike her colours, and I sent Lieutenant Brodie to take possession of her, and from her to hail the other ship to strike immediately, or she would else soon be involved in so much smoke and fire, that we, not being able to see her colours come down might, unintentionally, destroy all on board her.

'Just as the boat got there, the *Goliath*, anchored on our outer quarter and began to fire, but desisted on my hailing her; and, presently after, *Mercure*, of 74 guns, hauled her colours down; also as *l'Artemise*, 36, after firing her guns shotted, had done just before. I sent Lieutenant Hawkins to take possession of *Mercure*, and Lieutenant Hoste of *Artemise*; the former, on a lieutenant of the *Alexander* afterwards coming, delivered her into his charge, and returned on board; and when the latter got within about a cable's length of the *Artemise*, perceiving she was set on fire by a train, and that her people had abandoned her on the opposite side, he also returned on board; after burning about half an hour, she blew up. This dishonourable action was not out of character for a modern Frenchman; the devil is beyond blackening.

'We were now thus situated in the *Theseus*; our mizen mast so badly wounded that it could bear no sail; our fore and main yards, so badly wounded that I almost expected them to come down about our ears, without sail; the fore topmast and bow-sprit wounded; the fore and main sails cut to pieces, and most of the other sails much torn; nine of our main and several fore and mizen shrouds, and much of our other standing and running rigging shot away; eight guns disabled, either from the deck being ploughed up under themselves, or carriages struck by shot, or the axle-tree breaking from the heat of the fire; and four of them lower deckers.

'In men we were fortunate beyond anything I ever saw or heard of; for though near 80 large shot struck the hull, and some of them through both sides, we had only 6 men killed and 31 wounded: Providence, in its goodness, seemed willing to make up to us for our heavy loss at Santa Cruz. Hawkins and myself were the only officers from whom blood was drawn, and that in a very trifling way.

'The enemy were anchored again at the long range of shot, and many large boats from the shore were passing to and fro among them; and the *Justice* frigate was playing about under sail, and at length stood out of the bay, as if to make her escape. The *Zealous*, after being some time under way without the fleet, was, at this time standing down towards us, but stood out again as the Admiral made her signal to chase the frigate, who stood back into the bay, the *Zealous* remaining outside.

'Hearing it was the enemy's intention to take their men out of their line of battle ships and set them on fire (for, from what information we had, we supposed them on shore, being ourselves in 4 ½ fathoms), I caused a cool and steady fire to be opened on them from our lower deckers only, all of which being admirably pointed by Lieutenant England, who commanded that deck, they soon drove the boats entirely away from all their ships, and doubtless hulled them frequently, particularly the *Timoleon*. The boats having abandoned them, the *Guillaume Tell*, the *Genereux*, the *Timoleon*, and the *Justice* and *Diane* frigates, got under way, and stood out of the bay in line of battle; the *Timoleon*, being under our fire all the time, cast in shore, and, after appearing to make another attempt to wear, stood directly for the shore, and, as she struck, her fore mast went over the bows; the *Tonnant* being dismasted, remained where she was.

'The Admiral made the *Zealous's*, *Goliath's*, *Audacious's*, and *Leander's* signals to chase the others; the *Zealous* very gallantly pushed at them alone, and exchanged broadsides as she passed close on the different tacks; but they had so much the start of the other ships, and now of the *Zealous*, who had suffered much in her rigging, and knowing also they were remarkably fast sailors, the Admiral made the general signal of recall, and these four ships were soon out of sight.

'The ships under way being readier, having suffered less damage in the action, been not half the time engaged, or done half as much as ourselves, I gave up all further thoughts of the *Tonnant*, except sending a boat to see if she had surrendered, which, being menaced by her guns, returned. In the evening I went on board the Admiral, who I before knew was wounded. I found him in his cot, weak but in good spirits, and, as I believe every captain did, received his warmest thanks, which I could return from my heart, for the promptness and gallantry of the attack. I found him naturally anxious to secure the *Tonnant* and *Timeleon* and that the *Leander* was ordered to go down for that purpose in the morning; I told him if there was any difficulty I would also go down in the morning, notwithstanding the state of the ship. Seeing the *Leander* get under way we hove up to our best bower; sent our prisoners and their baggage, which lumbered our guns, on board the *Goliath*, and got a slip buoy on the end of the sheet cable. The *Swiftsure's* boat returning from having been with a flag of truce to summons the *Tonnant*, informed us the answer of the captain was, that he had 1,600 men on board and unless the Admiral would give him a ship to convey them to Toulon, he would fight to the last man – a true French gasconaded; we immediately slipped the sheet cable, and hoisted our topsails, and seeing the Admiral make the *Leander's* signal to engage the enemy, which must have been the moment of his receiving this French reply, we hove up our best bower and ran down directly for the *Tonnant* with the master sounding in a boat ahead; as we cast so as to open the view of our broadside to her, she hoisted true colours; when we got within a cable and half of her, having only 25 ½ feet water, we let go our anchor, veered to within half a cable of her and hauled upon our spring, which was parted. It was now, however, of no consequences, as just after we came to, she allowed the *Leander's* boat to come on board, and was soon after under English colours; the *Leander* had brought to about two or three cables without us while we were going down. The *Timoleon* being abandoned by her crew, was set on fire with her colours flying, and soon blew up.

'There being no longer an enemy to contend with, we beat the retreat and solemnly returned thanks to Almighty God through whose mercy we had been instrumental in obtaining so great and glorious a victory to his Majesty's arms, and I believe from the body of men more fervent gratitude never mingled in prayer. I had desired the chaplain to introduce a prayer for the slain, which was attended to with a degree of feeling that could not but delight every good heart. Previous in the public service I had returned my own thanks to the officers and ship's company for their gallantry and good conduct; and observing to them, that our business was not finished till the prizes were fit for sea, exhorted them to obtain by their work as much credit as by their courage. Captain Oldfield of marines, having very handsomely volunteered going into any of the prizes, I sent him with his whole party on board the *Tonnant*, and Lieutenant England, to take charge of her without one seaman, and gave him orders to secure the magazines, store-rooms &c, immediately, and having examined below to see every person and every light from them, and to have sentinels to prevent anyone going on any pretence below the lower deck, and to render it unnecessary I would send provisions and water daily from the *Theseus*; I was thus cautious from knowing some of the other ships had been on fire since their capture.

'I now felt the benefit of the pains I had taken to get carvel-built boats, and more capacious than the regular allowed ones, and of having had them out of the way of shot during the action. Of those in, two were destroyed and the launch shot through; I turned all the carpenters to patch her up for present use, merely while the people were dining, and then turned heartily to work, and having made one strong cable fast to the *Tonnant*, and desired sentinels to be placed on it on board her, we warped the *Theseus* about a mile and three quarters till we got hold of the end of the sheet cable we had slipped and put it on board the *Tonnant* to secure her; this, from the freshness of the northerly wind and the swell, was not accomplished till the evening of the 6th; meanwhile England was getting as much of the *Tonnant's* wreck cleared away by the French carpenters as he could, and we repairing our own damages with ours.

'Before daylight on the 7th I sent the first lieutenant, the master, and all our best petty officers, the boatswain, carpenter, and all his crew, two complete watches, and all the seamen of the *Theseus* with everything necessary to erect shears and clear away wreck, both fore and main masts having fallen within board.

'I had enjoyed the pleasure of finding the Admiral much better on the 6th, and he had given into my care the fitting of the *Tonnant* and told me I should not in the least be interfered with, and he hoped I should see her all the way to England; that after so many services to the public I owed it to myself to pursue my own happiness. Though I had thought this before, I was pleased to find a man of his activity think so likewise, and am infinitely obliged to him for his consideration in putting me unasked in the fair way to return to my long wished for home – but let me keep down the thousand emotions that rise in my soul till this narrative is finished, in which I am the more particular for the twofold purpose, it will give you the more information and be a more satisfactory account to B——, and it will remain in your hands as a record for me hereafter of the battle, the share the *Theseus* had in it, and the mode of conduct I found beneficial.

'As most of the ships were able to commence their equipment and that of the prizes under their charge on the 2nd, which I could not do till the 7th, I feared we should retard the sailing of the first batch to which we were fixed, and I determined it should be as short a period as possible. To encourage and enable all my people to do much work in little time, I ventured to make very day a meat day, and to give them an additional half allowance of wine. I sent her as many spars as we had unwounded, one spare topsail, and topgallant sails to be coursers and topsails for her, and had every man that could use a sail-needle at work to alter some of her own sails, and some we got from the *Serieuse* to make up a set for her; and with the few men remaining in this ship we got up and sent to her two French bower-anchors, and one smaller one, with two cables and four or five hawsers; and also a bower-anchor we have since given to the *Peuple Souverain*, and by that labour which no other ship did, and which could not be at all expected from us especially, we added a £1,000 value at least to the prizes.

'By these means, seconded by the indefatigable exertions of the officers and men in both ships, I was enabled to say to the Admiral we were both ready to sail as early as he pleased on the 10th, and I had the pleasure to find *Tonnant* the first prize ready – we, however, continued to have the same party on board daily till the noon of the 13th, by which we made her the more complete, and were enabled to set her new rigging up five times before she sailed. In the afternoon of that day I sent Lieutenant Hawkins, first lieutenant, Brodie, the second, master, a lieutenant and 12 marines, and petty officers and seamen, making up together 133 souls. On the following morning of the 14th, the following ships sailed under the command of Sir James Saumarez to receive Lord St Vincent's orders off Cadiz: - *Orion, Bellerophon, Defence, Minotaur, Audacious, Theseus, Majestic*; with the following prizes in charge, *Peuple Souverain, Franklin, Aquillon, Conquerant, Tonnant* and *Spartiate*. The three prizes we left there were burnt by the Admiral's orders, The *Guerrier* being so much cut up in the action, the *Mercure* and *Heureux* from what they suffered in the action and getting on shore, being found so much damaged that they could not be repaired without detaining the squadron in Aboukir Bay longer than was consistent with the necessities of his Majesty's service; most of their stores &c, were previously taken out.

'I have omitted to say the *Franklin* did not submit till after *l'Orient* had been some time on fire. I do not vouch for what I have said of the *Bellerophon* and *Majestic*, as among several disagreeing, I have been unable to collect what I could say is certainly exact history; but speaking generally, there appears to be a glorious emulation among all, to do service to their King and country and honour to themselves. On more particular inquiries respecting the *Majestic* and *Bellerophon*, it appears to me that the *Majestic*, as I have mentioned before, did not bring up on letting go her anchor till she got her bowsprit foul of the bowsprit of *l'Heureux*, in which position she lay one hour, able to make use of but a few guns; and the *Tonnant* firing into her quarter with her stern chase in addition to such guns as *l'Heureux* could bring to bear; on getting disentangled, she lay athwart the *Mercure's* bow, raked her with great effect. On *l'Orient* taking fire the *Tonnant, Heureux* and *Mercure* cut their cables, the former dropped a little way past the *Guillaume Tell* and anchored again, the other two, each with a staysail or two set, ran aground.

'The *Timoleon, Guillaume Tell* and *Genereux* veered I fancy to two cables, by which several means, and *l'Orient* blowing up, a vacancy of about a mile was left in the French line. The *Bellerophon* remained alongside *l'Orient* till near 8 o'clock, when Captain Darby who had been severely wounded in the head came on deck again, and seeing *l'Orient* on fire between decks, ordered the cable to be cut and drifted away as before described, without main or mizen mast, and his fore mast fell soon after this fire was extinguished on board *l'Orient*.

'There cannot be much error in time for these reasons – a prisoner now on board this ship who was a lieutenant of the *Tonnant*, and speaks very good English, describes an English ship dismasted by *l'Orient* and the *Tonnant*, and that after she cut her cable and dropped away from *l'Orient*, two other ships came, one on her bow and one under her stern; these ships were the *Alexander* and *Swiftsure*, who came in about 8 o'clock.

'Oct 17. We are now in sight of Gibraltar with all our prizes; we stopped at Augusta in Sicily 6 days, to get water, fresh beef, and vegetables.'

NB: Unfortunately, Captain Miller never made it back to England. *Theseus* was directed in February, 1799 to join Sir Sidney Smith in the Eastern Mediterranean and took part in the defence of Acre. Sadly, Captain Miller died on board his ship on 14 May due to an accidental explosion of shells on her poop deck. See DN 07 for further details.

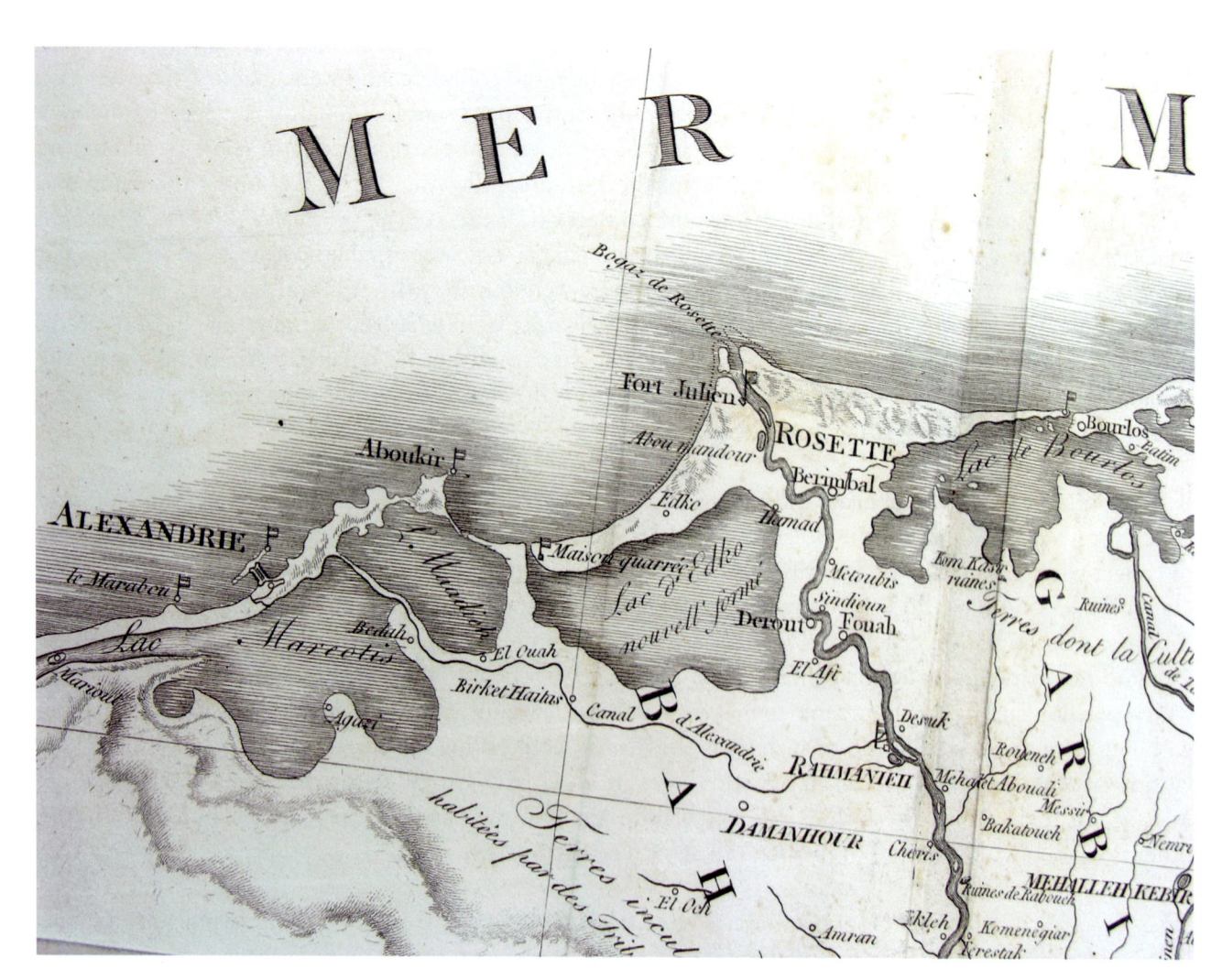

Chart of Alexandria and Aboukir made for Napoleon's Armée d'Orient from Vivant Denon's *Travels of Lower and Upper Egypt during the Campaigns of General Bonaparte* published in Paris in 1802 and London in 1804.

M. Denon, dans le Désert de la Haute-Égypte se préparant à dessiner les Ruines d'Hiéraconpolis.

Denon at Aboukir

Dominique Vivant Denon (1747 – 1825), was born in Burgundy as minor nobility. His given surname was de Non, but this was altered to Denon following the French Revolution. A man of many talents which included the speaking of several languages, being fluent in both Italian and English, a man of letters having briefly studied law and then changed his efforts to pursue literature and the arts. He had written a successful comedy for the Parisian stage, was an antiquarian with a keen interest in archaeology and a man of art whose pencil was very precise in depicting both portraits and ancient monuments. He was a formidable conversationalist and also a man most popular with ladies which is well accounted for by his erotic novella, *No Tomorrow*, which was originally published in 1777 and is still in print.

He had served as Chevalier de Non in the diplomatic corps for both Louis XV and XVI. Having previously served in St Petersburg, Stockholm and Geneva, he then gained a posting to Naples. He arrived in 1779 as secretary to the then ambassador and upon the ambassador's return to France, became chargé d'affaires to the court of Ferdinand IV where he remained until 1786. Also in Naples and serving the court of Ferdinand, was Sir William Hamilton who shared many of the same interests as Vivant de Non, but during this period Britain and France had been brought to war due to the American Revolution and one wonders if archaeology and collecting antiquities surmounted national agendas and if de Non and Hamilton became fast friends. It is known that Sir William, with his new bride Emma Hart / Lady Hamilton, while on honeymoon in 1791 and in Geneva spent some time with Vivant Denon who sketched Lady Hamilton. He had also sketched her famous attitudes and this may well have occurred while he was still in Naples as he knew her as Emma Hart.

With the terror of the French Revolution, de Non came under the scrutiny of the Committee of Safety as being bourgeois, which he certainly was, however his friend the artist J-L David spoke on his behalf describing him as a skilled engraver of plates and with the change of his name to Denon he escaped the guillotine while he worked for David as a designer of costumes for revolutionary pageants, which he also turned into engraved printer's plates.

He had come under the notice of Napoleon and with the outfitting of the Egyptian expedition in 1798, gained a post amongst the artists and scientists that accompanied Napoleon's army in Egypt. Although over fifty years old and suffering many hardships as well as taking part in a number of battles, Denon was simply unstoppable in his search for the interesting in this neglected land and became the first Egyptologist thanks to his very skilled observations and accurate drawings of ancient temples and the hieroglyphs that adorned them. His efforts resulted in the publication in 1802 of a two volume work entitled *Voyage dans la basse et la haute Egypte*, which quickly gained popularity and was published in English with a fine folio of plates in 1804. Denon was a major influence in creating the Egyptian Revival in decorative arts. In the same year, he was appointed Director-General of Museums and Director of the new Museum Napoleon in Paris which he actively worked toward filling with the finest art available from Napoleon's conquered lands, particularly Italy, with a great many of these pieces now residing in the Louvre.

Intérieur du Temple d'Apollinopolis à Edfou.

Temple d'Apollinopolis magna à Edfou.

Napoleon also made Denon the Director of the Mint, which he presided over from 1804 until 1815. During this period, many medals were struck which celebrated Napoleon's victories with the medals being signed by the engraver and Denon Director. Most of the designs for these medals were created by Denon with the engraver completing the finished medallic design. In 1804 Napoleon had embarked on his plan to invade England by assembling his army and 2,000 barges at Boulogne which was recognised by two medals under Denon's direction. A third medal was designed and trials struck, which was to be minted in London following the successful invasion. Only a lead trial piece survives, now located in the British Museum collection. However, Edward Thomason (1769-1849) in about 1820 created a fantasy medal based on the reverse of the original with an altered legend that reads 'Frappe a Londres' instead of 'Frappee a Londres en 1804'. Thomason had been an apprentice at Boulton's Soho works and established his own manufacturer in Birmingham in the early 1790s and a mint in 1807. Napoleon's invasion plans were thwarted by Admiral Calder who in 1805 prevented the combined Spanish and French squadrons from entering the Channel. Any future plans of invasion died with the destruction of the combined fleets at Trafalgar by Lord Nelson.

Upper left medal celebrates Napoleon awarding the Légion d'honneur to his men and the assembledge of barges to invade England. The lower medal anticipates a successful invasion while the medal above (an electrotype of the unique example in the BM), was to have been struck in London following the invasion. Sim Comfort Collection.

What most interests us here about Denon is that he was an eyewitness to the Battle of the Nile. He landed with the French Army of Egypt at Alexandria on 2 July 1798, endured the long march to Cairo and took part in the Battle of the Pyramids on 21 July. Following that victory over the Mamelukes, Denon returned to Rosetta and was there on the 1st of August. In his journal, he notes that immediately following the landing of troops on the Egyptian shore:

'Bonaparte, perceiving the advantages of this position, was desirous to secure it by bringing the fleet within the harbour of Alexandria. He offered two thousand sequins to anyone who should discover the means. The captains of some merchantmen, it was said, had discovered a passage into the old harbour; but the evil destiny of France persuaded the admiral to moor his fleet in Aboukir; and dissipate in one day the advantages of a long course of success.

'In the afternoon [1 August 1798], chance brought us to Abu-Mandur, a convent of which I have spoken about seven leagues [twenty miles] from the anchored French fleet and which terminates an agreeable walk from Rosetta on the banks of the river. On coming to the tower which commands the monastery, we saw twenty sail of ship arrive, range in line of battle, and attack in a moment. It was five o'clock when we heard the first shot, and the smoke soon obstructed our view of the two fleets. At night we could distinguish better, but could give no account of what was passing. The danger which we ran of being taken even by the smallest troop of Bedouins could not withdraw our attention from a scene of such awful importance. The dreadful firing which we heard left us no doubt but that the combat was sustained with equal obstinacy on both sides. On our return to Rosetta [that evening], we ascended to the roofs of the houses, and beheld about ten o'clock a blaze which denoted a great fire. In a few minutes we heard a dreadful explosion, which was followed by a profound silence. We had seen a firing from the left to the right upon the object which was inflamed, and were thus induced to believe that it was one of the ships of the enemy which we had destroyed. The succeeding silence we thought occasioned by the retreat of the English, who might continue the contest or desist as they chose, since they possessed the full space of the sea. At eleven o'clock a slack fire recommenced, and the combat began anew at midnight, and lasted till two in the morning.

'At daylight I went to the advanced posts, and ten minutes after, the engagement was renewed. At nine o'clock another ship blew up: at ten, four ships, the only ones which seemed not disabled, and which we recognised to be French, spread their sails and left the field of battle, of which, as they were neither attacked nor pursued, we thought them in possession. Such was the vain hope arising from the enthusiasm of the moment.

'From the tower of Abu-Mandur I counted twenty-five ships, half of which were only wrecks, and the rest unable to assist them. This uncertainty lasted for three days. With my glass in my hand, I took to drawing of this scene, in order to know if the next day would produce any change. In this illusion we rejected all rational evidence; but the bar being broken, and the communication with Alexandria intercepted, we learned that our situation was changed, and that, divided from our country, we were become the inhabitants of a remote colony, condemned to subsist as we could till the time of peace. We were now apprised that the English fleet had doubled our line, which did not lie sufficiently close to the land to be defended by the batteries; and that the enemy, forming a double line, had attacked our ships one after another, a manoeuvre which prevented more than half from acting, and compelled them to be spectators of the ruin of their companions. We learned likewise that it was the *Orient* who blew up at ten o'clock and the *Hercule* in the morning; and that the commanders of the *Guillaume Tell* and *Genereux*, and of the frigates *La Diane* and *La Justice*, seeing the rest of the ships in the enemy's power, had seized the moment of lassitude on the part of the English to escape.

'We learned lastly, that the first of August had broken the unity of our forces, and diminished our glory; that the destruction of our fleet had restored to the enemy the empire of the Mediterranean, an empire torn from them by the valour of our armies, and which had now fallen from our hands with the loss of our ships.'

We then have the melancholy scene of Denon visiting Aboukir Bay some days following the battle when he had joined a caravan for protection and had headed west from Rosetta:

'At midnight we reached the sea, and the rising moon displayed a new scene. The shore for the space of four leagues [twelve miles] was covered with the wrecks of our ships sustained at the battle of Aboukir. The Arabs, in order to procure a few nails or a few iron hoops, were burning the masts, gun carriages, and boats, along the beach, which had cost us so much in building, and the ruins of which were valuable in a country so destitute as this.

'The robbers fled at our approach, leaving only the carcases of the wretched victims, drifted on the sands, and half covered by them, but exhibiting even in this state a sublime and terrific spectacle. The sight of these objects filled me with a melancholy; I endeavoured to avoid them; but all that I saw arrested my attention, and made different impressions upon my mind. A few months ago, and they were all young, and in health, full of courage and hope. By a noble effort they had torn themselves from the arms of their mothers, sisters, wives, and tender infants. All these to whom they were dear, thought I, are now offering up prayers for their welfare and return, in the confidence and certainty of their success. Greedy to hear the news of their

Vue du Port-neuf d'Alexandrie.

Vue du grand Pharillon.

triumphs, they are preparing feasts, and counting the moments of their absence, - whilst the objects of their love lie on a distant shore, burnt up by a burning sand; their heads already bleached. Whose mangled trunk is that? Is it thine, intrepid Thevenard? Impatient to suffer the amputation of thy fractured limbs, thou didst covet no other honour but to die on thy post!

'Thy ardour would not submit to a slow operation: thou had no hope of life; but thou might have given a useful order, and was fearful that death might prevent it. Another spectre succeeds; his arm raised above his head, which is buried in sand. Killed in battle, - remorse seems to have survived thy noble end. ....Farewell! A tomb will not enclose thy ashes, but the tears of a hero that regrets thee are a monument which will ever recall thy memory to the sons of France. ....He still looks towards the English fleet, and like Bayard, scorned to die but with his face turned to the enemy: his hand is stretched out towards a corpse decaying, and almost gone. I can distinguish the neck and the arms. It is you young hero, noble Casabianca! Death, death alone, could unite thee to thy father, whom thou preferred to life. Sensible and respectable young man, thy youth held out a promise of glory, but filial piety was best content with death: receive our tears, the reward of thy virtues.

'I arrived at the suburb of Aboukir, which resembles the city, from which it is distant about a hundred and fifty paces. Both together consist of forty or fifty houses in ruins, dividing the peninsula into two parts, at the extremity of which the fortress stands. This fortress looks well at a distance; but the bastions would tumble upon a third discharge of the guns upon the rampart, which are in ruins. One of the guns is brass, fifteen feet long, and able to carry a fifty-pound ball. We found it necessary to destroy a part of the battery, in order to make a platform strong enough to bear four of our thirty-six pounders. This precaution seemed to me unnecessary, as boats and ships capable of battering walls could not approach near enough to this promontory on account of the rocks and shoals. An attempt would not be made there; and, should the enemy even land, the fortress could not hold out, or even afford a bare security to a magazine, unless lines were constructed in front to defend the approach. It seemed to me the best way [was] to destroy the fortress, fill up the cisterns, and spare the garrison, which would be useless in the absence of the enemy, and which must necessarily yield if the enemy landed.'

References:

No Tomorrow by Vivant Denon, reprinted by New York Review Books, New York, 2009.

The Discovery of Egypt, Vivant Denon's Travels with Napoleon's Army by Terence Russell, Sutton, Stroud, Gloucestershire, 2005.

Travels of Lower and Upper Egypt during the Campaigns of General Bonaparte by Vivant Denon (2 vols. quarto), Taylor, London, 1804. (English translation of the 1802 French publication. The above quotations are taken from this translation.)

Planches du Voyage dans La Basse et La Haute Egypt par Vivant Denon, London, 1802. The quarto plate vol. produced to accompany the original French text.

Vases & Volcanoes, Sir William Hamilton and his Collections by Jenkins and Sloan, British Museum, London, 1996.

The King Ferdinand IV return to Naples Medal

As a semi-commercial venture, Boulton had received a substantial order from Ferdinand IV which ensured its production, but also made it available to market on its own. The involvement of Nelson in securing the throne for the King in Naples ensured interest in Britain for the medal. Nelson was created Duke of Bronte for his efforts in the restoration of the King.

5) The King Ferdinand IV / Nelson & Foudroyant Medal. (MH 489 / BHM 479 / Eimer 908 / Hardy 21)

Description:

Obverse: Bust of the King facing right. FERDINAN IV D:G.SICHLIAR.ET.HIE.REX. (Ferdinand IV, by the Grace of God, King of Sicily and Jerusalem). Signed in the field below the bust C.H.K.

Reverse: View of Naples from the road to Vesuvius, above, Fame carrying a medallion portrait of Nelson, in the foreground, Cardinal Ruffo leading a column of soldiers against the fleeing rebels. In the harbour, the *Foudroyant* and to the right of the castle in the east, the sun is rising. In exergue: PER MEZZO DELLA DIVINA PROVVIDENZA DELLE / DI LVI VIRTV DELLA FEDE & ENERGIA DEL SUO POPOLO / DEL VALORE DE'SVOI ALLEATI ED IN / PARTICOLARE GL' INGLESI GLORIOS / (AMEN) TE / RISTABILITO SUL TRONO / LI 10. JUGLIO . 1799. (Re-established with glory on his throne on 10 July 1799 thanks to Divine Providence, his own virtues, the faith and energy of his own people, the valour of his allies and in particular, the English.) Signed on the fore-plane with K and below right on the exergual line with three dots.

Diameter: 48 mm.

Metals used: Silver RR £1,500; Copper N £650; Copper-gilt RR £900; Tin N £350.

This is a curious medal in that the scene depicted is supposed to be the return of Ferdinand IV to his capital at Naples on board Nelson's flagship, *Foudroyant*. The reality is that the King returned on his own frigate on 10 July 1799 and came on board *Foudroyant* the following day with his entourage and established his headquarters there. Further, the scene depicted shows Cardinal Ruffo personally leading the royal troops as they attack the Republican rabble who are fleeing the scene. One doubts if the Cardinal actually led his troops. But then, a medal may serves as a propaganda device just as a newspaper account would, so in that context the medal is a complete success.

Having said that, the medal is extremely important in telling the story of Nelson and his relationship with Emma, Lady Hamilton and his involvement with the Neapolitan court. One has to return to the aftermath of the Battle of the Nile. Nelson had been severely wounded in the head by a flying piece of wood that had cut a flap of skin from his forehead which caused great pain and terrible bleeding. Nelson had thought he had lost an eye. Having been tended to on board ship, the *Vanguard* and a few other ships sailed to Naples to be replenished and for the wounded to be cared for. Lady Hamilton immediately took charge of Nelson and began to nurse him back to health.

In the meantime, the influence of Republican France was being felt in Naples with a rebel army nearing the city and the Neapolitan army in retreat at which point Nelson evacuated the Royal Family, the Royal Treasure and the Hamiltons on board the *Vanguard* to Palermo in Sicily on Christmas Eve, 1798. While at Sicily, Nelson was joined by Captain Duckworth with four ships sent out by St Vincent, with one of the ships being the *Foudroyant*. Nelson shifted his flag to that ship bringing Captain Thomas Hardy with him from the *Vanguard*.

Nelson returned to Naples on the 25th of June with eighteen sail of the line to find a situation that he was not at all happy with. Cardinal Ruffo had assembled a partisan army of 60,000 who had taken control of Naples and left the remnants of the French stranded in two forts. Captain Foote of HMS *Seahorse*, working in conjunction with Cardinal Ruffo, had negotiated the surrender of the French troops. Nelson, negated the terms of surrender on the basis that no one in Naples had the authority to sign such a surrender.

This led to heated arguments between Nelson and Ruffo and the situation turning from bad to worse. On the 29th, the unfortunate Admiral Caracciolo, who had been in command of the Neapolitan fleet and had sided with the French against the King and used gunboats to fire upon the King's ships, was taken prisoner and brought on board *Foudroyant*. The next day a court was hastily convened on board *Foudroyant*, Carocciolo was found guilty of treason and sentenced to be hanged within two hours. He was transferred to a Neapolitan frigate, hanged and then cut down with his body being thrown into bay. Two weeks later, his body resurfaced with his head and shoulders above water, as it drifted past the anchored *Foudroyant* for all those on board for Sunday service to see. There is a remarkable large oil painting in the History Museum of Naples which recounts this gruesome scene.

As Roger Knight in his *The Pursuit of Victory*, notes that what happened next is unclear, but it appears that Nelson realised that he wasn't in a position to change the arrangements made by Cardinal Ruffo as his men now occupied Naples and were now taking revenge on all those who were thought to support the Republicans. The French troops who had surrendered were embarked on Neapolitan vessels waiting to be transported to a French port as per the terms of surrender. Nelson halted this action, but King Ferdinand finally arrived at Naples on the 10th of July and the last Republican stronghold, Fort Saint Elmo, surrendered. The remaining French troops were then embarked on the waiting transports which sailed for Toulon on the 15th , thus resolving the situation, but leaving Nelson in a very confused state.

This was probably the worst episode in the life of Nelson, but then one has to consider that although a Rear-Admiral and very skilled in most political situations, with the Court of King Ferdinand and the intrigue that engulfed Naples, Nelson was fully out of his depth. His growing fascination with Lady Hamilton and her influence upon him may also have tainted his judgement. This medal, which throws a gloss over this very troubled time, represents the political statement from the King and his dependence upon the English and Nelson for regaining his throne. Although the events don't relate to a major victory at sea, they certainly mark an important passage in the life of Nelson, particularly with regard to his relationship with Emma Hamilton.

Information from Pollard in *The Numismatic Chronicle* and Thomas Hardy's article *Matthew Boulton's Neapolitan Medal* published in *The Nelson Dispatch* of 1984, we learn that the design and intermediary between Ferdinand IV and Matthew Boulton was Thomas Bingham Richards who resided in Naples and was the foreign agent for his father's business as a silversmith and export agent. One wonders if he may have been involved in supplying the glazed copper-gilt cases that were used for the 48 mm Davison Nile medal? Richards notes in his diary: '..Mr Boulton .. suggested that it would be desirable to have a medal made to communicate the first return of the King of Naples to his capital … I drew the designs for one representing the King's head on one side and on the reverse, a view of the city of Naples from the road to Vesuvius with the fleet entering the Bay and Fame carrying a tablet whereon was a portrait of Nelson surrounded with laurel. Of these a number were sent in Silver, bronze, and metal [tin], to Palermo at the King's desire through Sir William Hamilton. The amount [cost] of them was about Two Hundred Pounds.'

Another puzzle! In the design supplied by Richards, there is no sunrise whilst in the finished medal does have a sunrise, this time correctly oriented in the east of the scene depicted. Who decided on that? I really have to think this was just another easy addition to the medal made by Küchler and that he felt it would provide the finishing touch to a dramatic event. With the addition of the sunrise to this medal, I think it adds to my feeling that it was Küchler who decided to add the sunset to the Davison Nile medal, all for dramatic effect.

The first order for the King was 12 silver, 12 copper-gilt, 300 copper-bronzed and 200 tin medals. In the end 24 silver, 12 copper-gilt, 535 copper-bronzed and 344 tin were struck making a total of 915 medals with Boulton using some of this quantity to supply examples to collectors in Britain and elsewhere. Something I find most interesting is the ability for an idea to be conceived in Birmingham and communicated to a distant customer, all resulting in a finished medal within months.

From Tomas Hardy's article in *The Nelson Dispatch*, we have further information regarding Richards:

'T. B. Richards was the eldest son of Theophilus Richards, silversmith of 83 High Street, Birmingham. The family firm had commenced c. 1773, known at 82 High Street as Moody's Toyshop where they traded as silversmith and toymen. They were also known as Richards Marindin & Co., subsequently Theophilus Richards & Co., export merchants, Cannon Street, London. In the latter business Thomas Bingham Richards was employed as agent for his father and also with a view to establishing himself as an export merchant in London. He therefore travelled widely on the Continent and came to be in Naples in 1798. He returned to England in *Le Tigre*, Captain Sir Sidney Smith on January 1799.

'Nelson, being well aware that Boulton was to strike medals regarding the re-conquest of Naples, wrote a letter to Richards dated December 1st 1800, thanking him for the honour. Therein, he mentions Richards' intentions of presenting medals to Sir William and Lady Hamilton and himself. Accordingly, Richards arrived at Nelson's lodgings in Dover Street, Piccadilly, soon after receiving the letter, had breakfast with him and duly presented Nelson with a medal. On this occasion the company present included: Lady Nelson, Mr Nelson senior, Nelson's brother, William and Captain Nisbet. One imagines that the medal presented was silver and is the example known to have been in the Bridport Collection, but the whereabouts of the medal is now unknown.

'In September 1802, Lord Nelson made his only visit to Birmingham in the company of Sir William and Lady Hamilton, which immediately followed their recent visit to the South of Wales. Sir William had written to Matthew Boulton, on 24th August requesting an interview and stating that Nelson was most desirous of making his acquaintance and to visiting the Soho Works. On August 30th *Aris's Birmingham Gazette* reported that the expected visit of the Hero of the Nile was declined, due to Mr Boulton's recent illness and the late regulation not permitting the Soho Works to be shown to anyone. However, an invitation had previously been sent from the High and Low Bailiff, which it was hoped, would now induce his lordship to accept. On September 6 the *Aris's Gazette* reported that Nelson and his party had arrived at Styles's Hotel, Birmingham, on the afternoon of Monday 30th August. On Tuesday morning, Nelson and his party, attended by the High and Low Bailiff and Magistrates, proceeded to view some of the manufactories of the town, which included; Button, Jewellery, Wolley & Deakin's Swords and stained glass, to mention but a few, and last, a visit to Mr Boulton who received them in his bed-chamber. Afterwards, it was reported that they were shown the Mint and had several applicable medals struck in their presence. The party then returned from Soho to their hotel and dinner. On Wednesday September 1st, Nelson and his friends visited amongst other manufactories, Messrs T & T Richards Toy-shop, in the High Street.'

This account just underlines how easy it would have been for almost anything to have been ordered in Birmingham and sent to the fleet, including the copper-gilt glazed cases sent to the ships in the Mediterranean and probably arriving around the time that the Davison Nile medals reached the fleet. This also underlines how networking between Boulton, Richards, the King, Sir William Hamilton and others all worked together. For Hamilton as the British envoy to the King, the medal helped to cement the British relationship with Naples / Palermo and the King, all very important to the Royal Navy and the British government.

As a final note, the dies to this medal passed to Taylor in the late 1840s when Soho closed, and he re-struck the medal and made a mule from the rejected obverse die, containing Nelson's profile, for the Boulton Trafalgar Medal and the reverse of the Ferdinand IV medal.

The British Fleet under Rear Admiral Sir Horatio Nelson KB in the *Vanguard* at anchor in the Bay of Naples, June 17th 1798. Gouache; watercolour painted by Giacomo Guardi circa 1800.
PAG9745 © National Maritime Museum, Greenwich, England

122

Earl St Vincent's Medal of Approbation

Earl St Vincent, Nelson's commander and mentor while he was in the Mediterranean, struck his flag in 1800 and commissioned Matthew Boulton to produce a silver medal that would be distributed to some of his officers and men he served with on board the *Ville de Paris*. Medals were also struck in gold for further distribution by St Vincent to his particular friends. Copper examples appear to have also been struck probably as trial pieces.

6) Earl St Vincent's Medal of Approbation. (MH 456 / BHM 489 / Eimer 919)

Description:

Obverse: Uniformed bust of St Vincent facing left. EARL ST VINCENT'S TESTIMONY OF APPROBATION. 1800 Signed C. H. K.

Reverse: A seaman left shaking hands with a Royal Marine on the right. Behind the figures is the Union Flag, the whole in a laurel wreath. LOYAL AND TRUE Signed below the exergual line K

Diameter: 48 mm. Found in silver with both a thick and thin planchet.

Metals used: Gold RR £10,000; Silver N £800; Silver-gilt RR £1,500, Copper R £500.

You will see in the following that St Vincent originally intended to distribute silver medals to officers and copper-bronzed medals to the men. As the copper examples are rare, I feel they were struck as trial pieces only. That the silver medals are found with both a thick planchet measuring about 2 mm and thin planchet measuring about 1.3 to 1.5 mm, that it was decided not to issue the copper-bronzed medals, but two types of silver medal instead. The rough weight comparison between the thick and thin planchets is 40 grams to 25 grams. In the Catalogue you will see images of the two thicknesses.

The medal was designed by John Flaxman (1755-1826) who was closely associated with Josiah Wedgwood, who was connected to Matthew Boulton. As noted in the Davison Nile medal, John Cleveley worked with Flaxman as well, so Boulton is again using his well trusted associates for the design of another medal. Flaxman was a very fine sculptor and engraver having at times worked with William Blake and Thomas Stothard via his connection with the Royal Academy. Flaxman sculpted the profile bust of Captain Cook for Wedgwood in 1779 and Dr Samuel Johnson in 1784. He was famous for his neo-classical designs with his most famous being the *Apotheosis of Homer* in 1778, which Wedgwood used to decorate a vase in 1786. Sir William Hamilton noted, 'I never saw a bas relief executed in the true and simple antique style half so well.' Flaxman is perhaps best known for his funerary sculpture where his memorials are found in several important locations. He was however criticised for his memorial to Earl Howe in St Paul's cathedral 'having added incorrect pantaloons and putting the ribbon of his order over the wrong shoulder.'

With his portrait of Earl St Vincent, he has captured the likeness very well and the uniform detail is perfect. The images of the marine and sailor on the reverse are also very fine although there is a problem with the Union Flag where St George's Cross for England should superimpose the Scottish St Andrew's Cross. This may have been a Küchler error as I would find it surprising if Flaxman didn't fully appreciate the design of the Union Flag, but then he made important errors in the Earl Howe effigy.

Sir John Jervis, Earl St Vincent (1735-1823) wrote to Countess Spencer, wife to Earl Spencer, First Lord of the Admiralty, from his flagship *Ville de Paris* when cruising off Brest on 15 September, 1800: 'The very uncommon merit of this ship's company in resisting the wiles of the mutinous spirits in the Channel Fleet, and the blandishment and revelings of the courtesans at Plymouth and Portsmouth, calls for some mark of distinction; and I intend to give silver medals to the petty officers, and bronze ones to the seamen and marines; and if your Ladyship will have the goodness to furnish a design and motto adapted to the occasion, I will employ the most eminent engraver to carry the work into execution immediately. I have the honour to be, with the highest respect, your Ladyship's devoted and obedient servant, St Vincent.'

In almost every catalogue that has listed Earl St Vincent's medal is included the reference that it was presented to his men who remained loyal during the Great Mutiny of 1797. I really find this annoying! St Vincent also praises his men for not spending time in the whore houses of Plymouth and Portsmouth and for not letting whores run wild in his ships! Hello! This is St Vincent being playful with Countess Spencer! He didn't reward men for being loyal, instead he hung the disloyal!

On one occasion he did receive criticism for hanging two mutineers on a Sunday. On another an infected mutinous ship joined his fleet at Gibraltar and the captain complained that he couldn't get control of the men. St Vincent made sure the ring leader was identified and tried and sentenced him to be hung the next day. The captain of the ship again told St Vincent that the man couldn't be hung on his ship because the men would then mutiny. The next morning, when that ship's company awoke and came on watch, they found their ship surrounded by the other ships in St Vincent's fleet with their guns run out. And they knew what had to be done and ran the mutineer up the yardarm faster than you could say Billy! Those men knew that St Vincent would not only fire on their ship, but would keep firing until she sank and anybody who didn't understand the meaning of loyalty, went to the bottom with her.

To keep his ships in harmony and kept focused on fighting the enemy, St Vincent sent them off to fight as he did with Nelson and others during 1797. It is St Vincent who characterised Nelson as 'a natural born predator.' He knew Nelson better than any of his commanders. There was no mutiny within St Vincent's command during that terrible year, and the reason there was none is totally down to St Vincent's character and will power.

I really like St Vincent because you knew exactly where you were with him. Although a tough disciplinarian, he would do anything to keep his men well fed and his ships sound. A constant battle ensued between him and the Admiralty and the Navy Office to get for his men what they needed, and he got it. After he struck his flag and returned to England to become First Sea Lord, he commenced a root and branch study of the naval dockyards and victualling facilities. People screamed then, and historians still do, accusing St Vincent of dismantling the Royal Navy.

I'll leave the final word with P. K. Crimmin and her fine assessment from the *Dictionary of National Biography*, but before that remind readers that with better results from the dockyards and victualling office, invasion was thwarted, Trafalgar was won and the fleets of Britain's enemies were never to rise to power over the next 100 years. Britain truly ruled the waves and St Vincent helped to make that happen.

Closing remarks from P. K. Crimmin's account of St Vincent's life in the *DNB*:

'At a critical period his resolution and courage did not falter, yet his authoritarian temper could not tolerate criticism. Careless of wounded feelings when convinced he was right, he could be stubborn and impetuous, inflexible and quick tempered. He possessed a grim [sense of] humour, not always appreciated by its recipients. But he was ungrudging to zeal, skill, and courage, promoting those who showed such qualities, particularly the sons of old officers who lacked influence. In private life he was kind and generous, always ready to help anyone he believed had any claim on him.

'St Vincent was not a great tactician. The battle of St Vincent, the only major battle in which he commanded, was not decisive and gained its fame largely through the nation's relief at the news of a victory during a gloomy period of the war. His importance lies in his being the organizer of victories; the creator of well-equipped, highly efficient fleets; and in training a school of officers as professional, energetic, and devoted to the service as himself. His mind was firm, clear, and decisive. Although his workload was exhausting, no significant detail escaped him and he excelled in the introduction of major improvements in naval health and hygiene. As a reforming administrator St Vincent was well-intentioned but tactless. Dauntless and persevering in his crusade against what he saw as institutionalized corruption in the royal dockyards and civil offices, he impatiently rejected traditional working methods and office practice, and condemned unheard a system often corrupt yet effective, which he did not fully understand. In the short term he alienated the existing naval administration and his reforms resulted in disruption when war was renewed. But St Vincent's term of office at the Admiralty produced important results. By providing a mass of information on working practices in the commission reports, by reducing abuses and promoting greater honesty and efficiency, and by clearing away outdated customs of work and rewards, St Vincent ensured that the navy was better prepared to meet the challenges of the nineteenth century.'

The reverse of this medal shows a marine and sailor shaking hands as peers. St Vincent had a very close regard for the Marines because they played a critical role in ship discipline as well as providing the infantry support needed for the many actions ashore that the ship's companies may be involved in. A problem within the service was that the marine at times lacked the status of Royal Navy officers and men. Further, marine ranks were often supplemented by regular army troops which invariably caused problems, both on board ship and when working together on land. As First Sea Lord in 1802, it was St Vincent who carried out a reorganisation of the Marines and gained the Royal Assent so that henceforth the Marines were known as The Royal Marines. From this point forward, only Royal Marines would be found on board H.M. ships. As St Vincent famously said of the Marines, 'There never was any appeal made to them for honour, courage or loyalty that they did not more than realize my expectations. If ever the hour of real danger should come to England, the Marines will be found the country's sheet-anchor.'

We have seen from the letter to Countess Spencer that St Vincent's plan was to give to his junior and petty officers silver medals and to the men and marines copper bronze medals. Working with David Vice of Format Coins in Birmingham, it appears that St Vincent changed his mind and decided on two grades of silver medal: thick planchet weighing 40 grams and thin planchet weighting 25 grams with probably the thick planchet medals going to petty officers and the thin to the men before the mast and unrated marines. It's possible that the silver-gilt examples may have gone to officers.

Soho records show that 577 silver medals were struck along with 30 gold medals, which would have been contained in red morocco cases. Along with this are 30 silver-gilt medals and some copper-bronzed medals, but very few of the bronze medals, perhaps they were trial pieces.

Commodore Nelson boarding the *San Nicolas* at the Battle of Cape St Vincent.

Admiral Sir John Jervis on board H.M.S. *Victory* raking the Spainish flagship *Salvador del Mundo* at the battle of Cape St Vincent.
Image from Jenkins' *Naval Achievements*, published by Sim Comfort Associates

My view is that the gold medals were distributed to captains, flag officers and other worthy people whom St Vincent admired, which included the King who received a gold example. The silver-gilt medals would most likely have been distributed amongst his lieutenants and other officers on board *Ville de Paris*. We can also see the silver-gilt example which was presented to Joseph Colen of the Hudson Bay Company, so there wasn't a strict order of presentation for either the gold or silver-gilt medals. One problem with this medal is that the 2 mm rim for thick planchet and 1.5 mm for thin doesn't allow much room for engraving. The only other place is in the obverse field and there is one medal named in this way. So, named examples of this medal are very rare indeed.

We then think about the *Ville de Paris*, which had a ship's company of 870 men and marines, but only 577 silver medals were struck. Not everyone on board received a medal. Within the paybook for the *Ville de Paris* there are three lists of men and officers who had left the *Ville de Paris* to join other ships or to come ashore and that they were being found so that they would receive a medal. There is also a List of Marines who received the medal, which all points to St Vincent knowing who he wanted to have his medal and that it wasn't a general distribution. There is no mention of medals going to men on board the *Victory* and although cataloguers continue to note that the medals were distributed to men on board *Victory*, I can't find any proof of it.

I think what I really like about the above comments regarding St Vincent and the distribution of his medal is that it just underlines how close a community it was on board a Royal Navy ship. These men, at least those who received the medal, were almost like family to St Vincent. Although no one makes a point of it, but St Vincent is the only Royal Navy officer ever to make such a presentation to men on board his ship, and that the presentation was an intrinsically valuable silver medal just speaks volumes about the generosity of the man and his close relationship with his ship's company on board the *Ville de Paris*.

HMS *Ville de Paris* was one of the Ville de Paris Class of First Rate 110-gun ships designed by Henslow in 1788 and would have a ship's company of 837 men. She was launched at Chatham Dockyard on 7 July 1795. She was 190 feet in length, 2,332 tons burthen and with 30 x 32 pounders on the Gun Deck, 30 x 24 pounders on the Middle Deck, 32 x 18 pounders on the Upper Deck and 14 x 12 pounders on the Quarterdeck and 4 x 12 pounders in the Forecastle. She was hulked in 1825 and broken up in 1845.

She was named after the French Admiral de Grasse's flagship *Ville de Paris* which was captured by Captain Samuel Hood at Rodney's great victory of The Saints on 12 April 1782. Unfortunately she was lost with all hands, except one seaman named Wilson, when caught by a hurricane on about 19 September 1782 on her voyage from Jamaica to England. The Chatham *Ville de Paris* was the largest warship built in Britain up to that time and she was massive! She was 53ft 2in wide across her beam and drew 14ft 8in of water at the bow and 18ft 4in at the rudder. Her hold, the space between her orlop deck and her bottom was 22ft 2in deep. She was also the most expensive ship built to that date with her construction costing £78,830. As such she was the perfect flagship and hosted St Vincent, who was followed by Admiral William Cornwallis, as he managed the great blockade of Europe's western coast. Lastly she was home to Admiral Cuthbert Collingwood who died on board her on 7 March 1810.

A sailor-made silk picture of the *Ville de Paris* circa 1795.

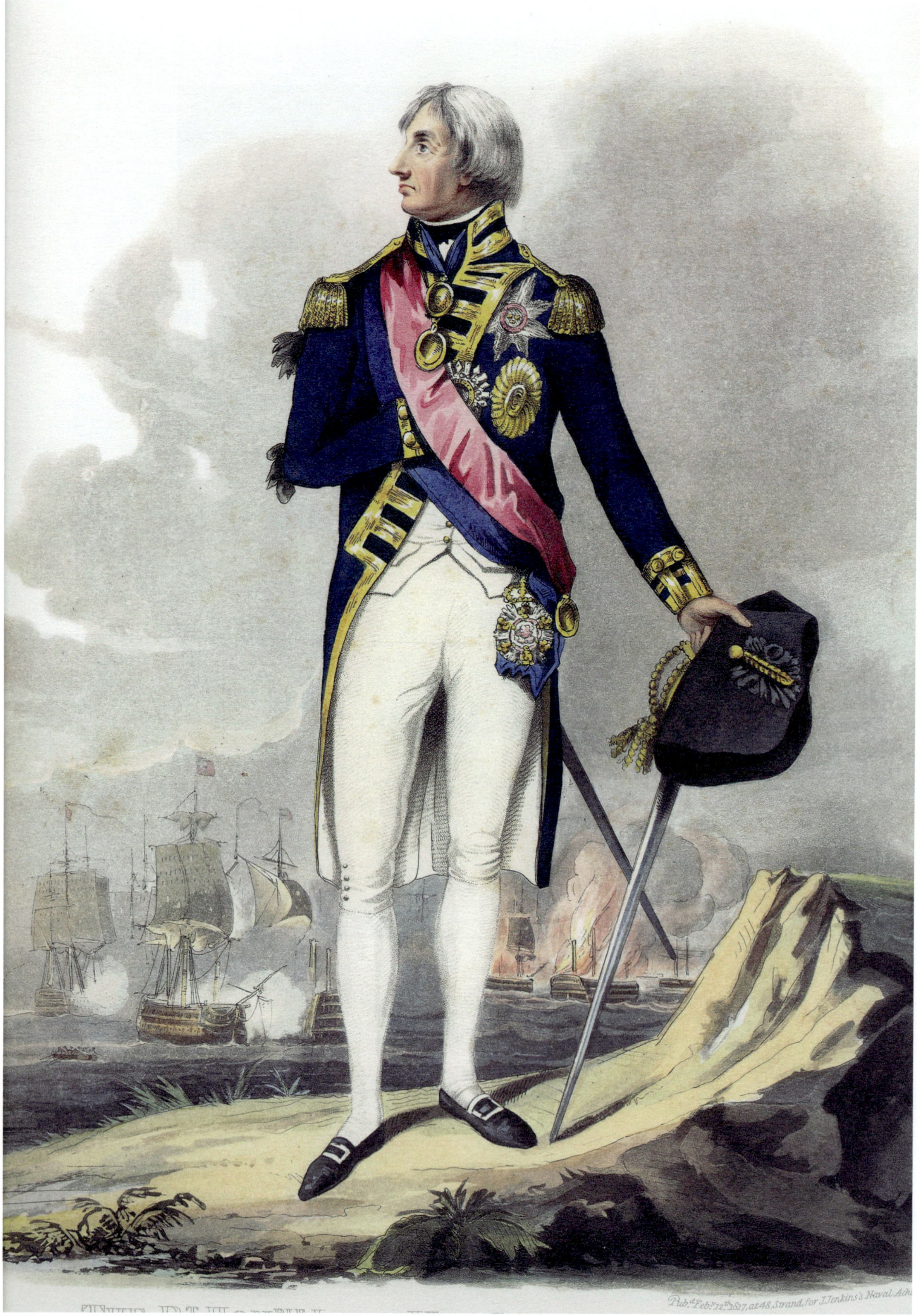
Pub.d Feb.y 12th 1817, at 48, Strand, for J.Jenkins's Naval Achi

Matthew Boulton's Trafalgar Medal

The victory of Trafalgar was reported with emotion throughout the country. Jubilation over the victory mixed with profound sorrow over the death of Lord Nelson. Matthew Boulton simply saw this as an event that he wished to be personally involved with so he had created the Trafalgar medal which was made as a gift to all the men before the mast who took part in the battle. It is with this medal that all of the experience that Boulton and Conrad Küchler had built over the years came together and created arguably the finest of all British naval medals.

7) Matthew Boulton's Trafalgar Medal. (MH 493 / BHM 584 / Eimer 960 / Hardy 40)

Description:

Obverse: Uniformed bust of Nelson, left. HORATIO VISCOUNT NELSON, K.B. DUKE OF BRONTE. & Signed C.H.K. on truncation.

Reverse: View of the Battle of Trafalgar. ENGLAND EXPECTS EVERY MAN WILL DO HIS DUTY. In exergue. TRAFALGAR OCTr 21.1805. Signed in exergue K.

Edge inscribed: TO THE HEROES OF TRAFALGAR FROM M: BOULTON.

Diameter: 48 mm.

Metals used: Fleet distribution: Tin C £500. Contemporarily engraved named medals are worth considerably more, particularly if they are cased and glazed and in EF condition.

Fleet Issue to James Aldridge, Able Seaman on board HMS *Victory*.

131

Presentation distribution as noted by the lump at 11 o'clock on the reverse rim with the features being frosted with mirror fields: Silver RR £2,000, Silver-gilt RRR £3,000, Copper-gilt RR £2,000, Copper-bronzed RR £1,250, Tin RR £1,750; distributed in steel shells.

Restrikes: Gold RR (1905) £2,500, Silver (1870s by Taylor) RR £2,000, 20th century by Pinches Silver R £350, Copper-bronzed (1870s by Taylor) as original medal R £350 and with rejected obverse RR £500, 20 th/ 21st century various copy medals: Copper-gilt C £50, Tin C £50.

Although Trafalgar was the central British naval victory in 1805, one should look at it in the context of several major fleet actions which totally thwarted Napoleon's desire to invade England and gave Britain command of the seas for the next hundred years.

Nelson had been blockading the French fleet at Toulon for over a year while Spanish elements were pinned in at Cadiz. The enemy plan for the summer of 1805 was to break out of Toulon and Cadiz and race to the West Indies hoping that Nelson would pursue the combined French and Spanish squadrons and be left in the West Indies, while the enemy squadron rushed back to Europe and gained control of the English Channel.

The plan seemed to have worked perfectly, but instead of losing Nelson in the West Indies, while the enemy raced back to the English Channel to support an invasion attempt, Nelson clung to the enemy like a limpet. Sir Robert Calder destroyed French invasion hopes off Cape Finisterre 22 July 1805 when he blocked the enemy's approach to the English Channel.

The French and Spanish then consolidated at Cadiz and came out on 21 October, when Nelson and Collingwood took 17 ships of the line and scattered the remaining enemy ships. On November 4, Sir Richard Strachan met four French ships from Trafalgar and captured them all. Later, on February 5, 1806 Sir John Duckworth captured or destroyed the last significant presence of the French fleet in the West Indies.

So, in a period of seven months, the Royal Navy fought four fleet actions which effectively removed French and Spanish fleet activity and left Britain in command of the seas. But with the loss of Nelson and so many others, which was felt deeply throughout the navy and country, the cost was indeed high.

Several people have written fine articles about the Boulton Trafalgar medal. Probably the first of importance was by J. G. Pollard and published in *The Numismatic Chronicle* of 1970 which has proved the mainstay to all those interested in understanding how Boulton and Küchler settled on the final design for the medal. James Hammond of Christie's published in *The Coin and Medal News* of September 1988 a good overview of the medal, but most particularly a list of the known named medals. More recently, Nicholas Goodison in association with Birmingham City Council produced *Matthew Boulton's Trafalgar Medal* as a handsome monograph booklet. To me the finest and most informative is the long article written by David Vice of Format Coins in Birmingham and published in *The Medal News* of May, 1997 and it is with his permission that I reprint David's work.

Boulton's Trafalgar Medal
by David Vice

Nelson's last victory, the Battle of Trafalgar, was fought on October 21, 1805. It was on that fateful day, off Cape Trafalgar, that Nelson finally succeeded in bringing the combined enemy fleets of France and Spain, a total of 33 ships, to battle.

Attacking in two columns, the first under Nelson and the starboard led by Admiral Collingwood, the engagement lasted some seven hours. As a result the enemy suffered a mortal blow having 17 of their ships captured, or burnt and the remainder forced to flee for their lives. It was midway through the battle that Nelson received a bullet in the left shoulder, dying from his wound shortly after. His body was subsequently brought back to England and he was buried in the crypt of St Paul's Cathedral on January 9, 1806.

The flag officers and captains who were present at the engagement were rewarded with the Naval Gold Medal, which had been introduced in the 1794. Lesser ranks, the junior officers and ordinary seamen and marines, who really bore the full brunt of the battle, were ignominiously ignored. They received no badge of any sort from their King or country in acknowledgement of their service on that memorable day. It was against this background that Matthew Boulton decided that at his own expense he would try to rectify this omission. As a result of his endeavours *The Naval Chronicle*, (vol. XV, p.18) was able to report:

'Mr Boulton, the scientific and venerable proprietor of Soho, whose public exertions have so uniformly been distinguished by patriotism the best directed, has solicited the permission of Government that he might be allowed to strike a Medal as his own expense in commemoration of the brilliant victory off Cape

Trafalgar, and to present one to every seaman [and marine] who had served that day on board the British fleet. The permission was immediately granted, with the warmest approbations of so laudable a design. In a short time the Medals will be sent down to the several ports to be distributed amongst the various tars by His Majesty's Commissioner.'

Of all Boulton's medallic ventures none exemplifies better than the Trafalgar Medal, the meticulous care and attention to detail Boulton brought to bear in his striving for perfection. There exists in the Soho Mint Archives a wealth of correspondence with his friend J. Furnel Tuffin, documenting the trials and tribulations of attempting to obtain a lifelike portrait of Nelson for the obverse of the medal. For a full account of their endeavours the reader is referred to an article by J. G. Pollard in *The Numismatic Chronicle*, 1970, entitled *Matthew Boulton and Conrad Heinrich Küchler*. For our purposes suffice it to say that Küchler, in his role as the Soho Mint engraver, initially produced an obverse medal die based on a drawing by Lady Beechey which itself was from a painting of Nelson undertaken by her husband Sir William Beechey for the City of Norwich in 1801. Although Küchler's efforts met with a favourable response from Sir William and Lady Beechey, it was generally disapproved by the Nelson family and Lady Hamilton. Tuffin wrote to Matthew Robinson Boulton on January 17, 1806:

'On shewing them the drawings and proofs [of the medals] I was instantly convinced they all thought the drawing & consequently the proofs unlike the late Lord. Lady Hamilton did not scruple to tell me so & her opinion was confirmed afterwards by the whole family. In this dilemma I was at a loss how to proceed, when she drew from her bosom a gold locket inclosing a small profile placed there by himself with a declaration of its being the best likeness ever taken of him, that she and his brother confirmed in the strongest terms & intreated You would follow no other on your medal.'

This likeness was based upon a drawing of Nelson undertaken by Simon de Koster. The artist was prevailed upon to loan the original drawing to Küchler.

Küchler's second attempt at producing a likeness fared no better than his first. This too was condemned by Lady Hamilton. However, in a desire not to be purely negative, Lady Hamilton loaned a wax portrait by Catherine Andras, which she described in now familiar terms as being the 'most striking likeness' taken of Nelson. This proved more productive. Possibly the likeness of Nelson was better and certainly Küchler, in common with many engravers, appreciated the opportunity to work from a three dimensional model rather than a flat drawing. The result that Küchler's third attempt at producing an obverse die for the Trafalgar Medal met with universal approval.

By comparison the reverse design for the medal proved relatively trouble free. It was based upon a design by the marine artist Richard [Robert?] Cleveley, who wrote to Boulton on Christmas Day 1805:

'Enclosed I send you a design for the Medal you propose presenting to the Seamen and Marines engaged at the Victory off Trafalgar. I have taken it in every point of view and I think this will give the best idea of the general business of the action. I have taken it at the time the *Royal Sovereign* is going into action partly enveloped in smoak, which is said to have been one of the finest sights in the world.'

Despite all the intense activity to find suitable designs and for Küchler to produce satisfactory interpretations of them, the full consignment of Trafalgar Medals were not struck off until October / November 1806.

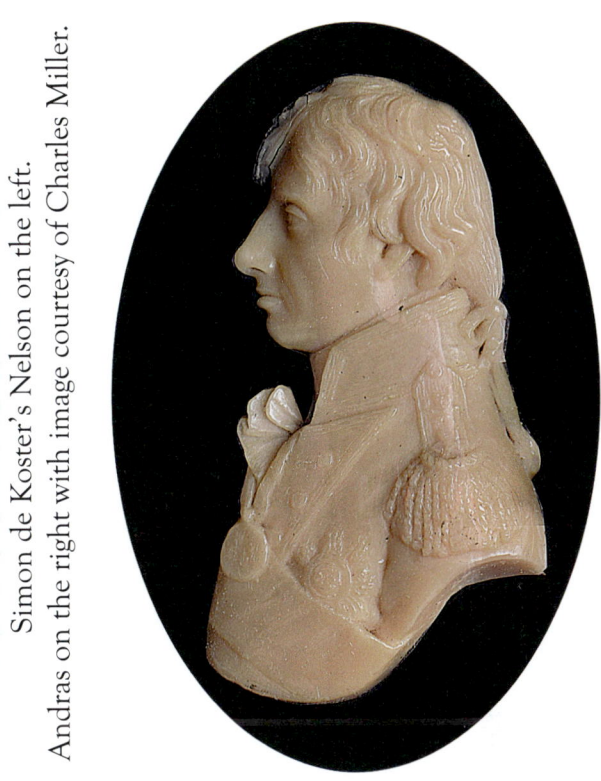

Simon de Koster's Nelson on the left. Andras on the right with image courtesy of Charles Miller.

COMMENCEMENT of the BATTLE of TRAFALGAR — Oct.r 21st 1805.

Plate I.

135

There were several reasons for the considerable delay in completing the medals. The difficulty created by Nelson's portrait obviously provided a contributing factor. However, of far greater significance is that medallions, unlike coins, require several blows to bring them up and are consequently very time consuming. This proved a severe handicap at a period when Soho Mint personnel were heavily engaged on national coinage contracts. Matters were also not helped by the deteriorating health of Matthew Boulton. So severe were his problems that for long periods, his son Matthew Robinson Boulton was obliged to take over the running of the Mint business. The ensuing delays caused practical problems in the distribution of the finished medal. The passing of time increased the likelihood of men being transferred to different vessels, or ships detached from the Home Squadrons and posted to foreign stations. Obviously Boulton was reliant on the Admiralty for this type of information. There exists in the Soho Mint Records an undated holograph, probably prepared at the end of 1807, which records the distribution of the Trafalgar Medal. This source has been instrumental to the author in compiling the following table.

BRITISH SHIPS ENGAGED AT TRAFALGAR, THEIR CASUALTIES and THE NUMBER OF BOULTON TRAFALGAR MEDALS SENT.

Guns	Ship	Killed	Wounded	Distribution of Medals (where stated)	No of Medals to survivors.	Total
74	Ajax	2	9	Lord Collingwood	677	
74	Orion	1	23	Lord Collingwood	543	
74	Swiftsure	9	8	Lord Collingwood	556	
74	Thunderer	4	12	Lord Collingwood	560	
74	Agamemnon	10	7	The Downs	457	
98	Neptune	10	34	Portsmouth	707	
64	Polyphemus	2	4	Portsmouth	461	
64	Africa	18	44	Plymouth	475	
74	Achilles	13	59	Plymouth	608	
74	Bellerophon	27	123	Plymouth	562	
74	Conqueror	3	9	Plymouth	622	
74	Defiance	17	53	Plymouth	575	
74	Mars	29	69	Plymouth	618	
74	Minotaur	3	22	Plymouth	586	
98	Prince	-	-	Plymouth	680	
74	Spartiate	3	20	Plymouth	599	
80	Tonnant	26	69	Plymouth	664	
74	Revenge	28	51	Plymouth	610	
98	Dreadnought	7	26	-	703	
74	Leviathan	4	22	-	592	
100	Victory	57	102	-	782	
(transferred to *Ocean*)						
98	Temeraire	47	76	-	711	
(transferred to *Ganges* and *Captain*)						
74	Defence	7	29	Plymouth	568	
Small contingent of Sailors & Marines from the						
Colossus, Royal Sovereign & *Bellisle* to Sandown (?)					87	————
						14,001

136

Sundry ships not sent up to December 22, 1807 (seamen & Marines transferred to other ships?)

Guns	Ship	Killed	Wounded	No. of Medals Total to Survivors
74	Colossus	40	160	617
100	Royal Sovereign	47	94	809
74	Bellisle	33	93	684
100	Britannia (transferred to Lavinia)	10	42	139
				2.249
	Deduct 87 delivered in the above 14,001			(87)
				2,162

Frigates Etc. – Medals not delivered or struck [because not commited to fighting]

Frigates – *Euryalus, Naiad, Phoebe, Sirius*, Schooner *Pickle*, Cutter *Entreprenant*. 1,101
Total number of men on board ships in action as per the Admiralty Statement: 17,264

* It would appear that there was an error in the Navy Board records or Boulton's interpretation of them. After Trafalgar the men from the *Britannia* which had an entitlement of 749 medals, were transferred to the *Revenge*, based at Plymouth, and the *Lavinia* (subsequently sent on foreign service). Boulton calculated that 139 men were transferred to the *Lavinia* – i.e. *Britannia's* full complement of 749 minus the 610 medals sent to the *Revenge*. This ignores the fact that *Revenge* was present at Trafalgar and entitled to receive 610 medals in her own right.

From the table above it becomes clear that Boulton only struck his Trafalgar Medal for seamen and marines on board ships of the line. Those serving on board the smaller vessels such as frigates, schooners or cutters, did not qualify for the medal and were entitled to feel a little harshly treated. It is still a matter of some debate whether Boulton awarded 14,001 of his medals or 16,163 (i.e. 14,001 + 2,162). According to the Soho Statement, 14,001 of the Trafalgar Medals were sent to Boulton's London Agent, John Woodward, in two separate consignments – the last being made on December 22, 1807. The conjecture surrounds the fate of the 2,162 medals awarded to the four ships which, at this stage of the proceedings, were simply listed as 'not sent'. The inference is that the 2,162 medals had already been struck and were still at Soho awaiting more detailed information from the Admiralty regarding their final destination. It is perhaps no coincidence that the *Colossus, Royal Sovereign* and *Bellisle* suffered particularly heavy casualties, suggesting a fair degree of structural damage to the ships concerned. This may have [actually had] caused them to have been taken out of commission leaving their sailors and marines to be reposted to other vessels throughout the fleet.

The other great controversy regarding Boulton's Trafalgar Medal concerns which rank received medals and in which particular metal. Fortunately the matter is resolved in a letter from M. R. Boulton, dated January 23, 1807, to a Major Timmins of Portsea:

'Sir, I am sorry to perceive from your Letter of the 17th just that there should exist any misconstruction of my intention in regard to the presentation of the Trafalgar medals.

'Soon after the memorable battle of Trafalgar considering that the powers of my Mint Machinery would give facilities in striking of a large quantity of Medals that no other Individual in the Kingdom could command I felt myself called upon to dedicate them to the commemoration of that important event. Accordingly I made an offer to furnish to each of the surviving Seamen & Marines a white metal Medal and with the sanction of Lord Barham & his Successors in Office the whole complement of Medals, executed in conformity to a return furnished by the Navy Office, have been forwarded for distribution Thro' the medium of the board to the several Commanding Officers of the different Stations of His Majesty's Fleets.

'The above proposal you will perceive did not extend to Medals for the Officers of Lord Nelson's Fleet which to have been at all worthy of their acceptance I considered must have been made of the precious Metals, a measure which would have required the possession of wealth to which I have no pretensions.'

To summarise, Boulton's Trafalgar Medal was only presented to ordinary Seamen and Marines in white metal, or grain tin as it was referred to at Soho. As collectors are well aware the Trafalgar Medal exists in a variety of other metals or finishes – what are we to make of these strikings? The answer is that Boulton presented the medal to various of his friends and influential contacts. M.R. Boulton systematically prepared a memorandum detailing who should receive what. This reveals that the son was considerably less generous in this respect than his father. Initially he proposed distributing 47 gilt-silver medals but on second thoughts considered this to be too extravagant and finally settled for six silver specimens, 13 gilt-copper specimens, 54 bronzed copper specimens and 19 examples in tin. Some of the more interesting recipients of the gifts were as follows:

	Gilt-silver	Silver	Gilt-Copper	Bronzed-copper	Tin
His Majesty	1			1	1
Lord Barham	1			1	1
Lady Hamilton	1			1	1
Sir William Beechey			1	1	1
Tuffin			1	1	1
Robert Cleveley	1			1	1
Earl St Vincent			1	1	1
Earl Nelson			1	1	1
Honourable Montagu		1			
Lord Collingwood		1			
Emperor of Russia			1	1	1
M & M.R. Boulton			2	2	2

The total number of presentation strikings quoted above should not be taken as being absolute, for it was the natural order of events for additions to be made and their numbers swell. M.R. Boulton for instance was particularly tardy in his allocation toward His Majesty the King. After a not particularly subtle hint from a member of the Royal Entourage, a further six sets of medals left Soho for the delight of the Court.

Conspicuous for its absence is any contemporary reference to gold strikings of the Trafalgar Medal. There is little doubt that the few specimens known in this medal were produced many years later. Just how many years is where matters become a little complicated since the Trafalgar dies were reused at three different periods. Period 1 covers the activities of the Soho Mint c. 1837 -47. Period 2 refers to the restriking from old Soho Dies by W. J. Taylor c 1860 - 95 and Period 3 relates to the final resurrection of the Trafalgar Dies by John Pinches Ltd in 1966.

Period 1 - Soho Mint c. 1837 - 47

The Soho Mint Order Book covering this time span refers to the following seven Trafalgar Medals being restruck in silver:

1837	2 silver Trafalgar Medals for Captains Pearl and Cappell. each	17/6d
1840	1 silver Trafalgar Medal for Captain Townley.	17/6d
1842	2 silver Trafalgar Medals for Jas Brown. each	17/6d
1843	1 silver Trafalgar medal for Captain Pickernell.	15/-d
1847	1 silver Trafalgar Medal for Lieut. White.	15/-d

In addition there is a suggestion that other precious metal strikings may have been made which escaped the Order Book. There is a letter from an agent, a Mr Langdon, to Chubb of Soho, dated February 24, 1847 which states the following:

'My dear Sir, We have had an application from Mr Paul Harris Nicolas, the Editor of the *Nautical Standard* newspaper and a naval officer present at the Battle of Trafalgar, to know whether you are now prepared to make Nelson Medals in Gold and Silver, the parties of course paying the value of the metal etc. I recollect that a few years since the late Mr Boulton (M.R. Boulton who died in 1842) did this for some friends of our at Woolwich Dockyard.'

Soho's reply to this correspondence has not been traced, but Mr Nicolas appears to have jumped the gun by prematurely printing a paragraph in his newspaper giving the impression that Soho would be prepared to supply gold and silver medals at cost to any officer who could prove his presence at the Battle of Trafalgar. Soho was obliged to admit that a mistake had been made in the above assumption. The small number of Trafalgar medals previously supplied to officers was apparently carried out on an informal basis as a special favour to friends and was not part of a general policy. Even in these rare instances a strict code of ethics still applied. A certificate of presence at the battle had to be supplied and only Captains and Commanders at Trafalgar qualified for the gold medal, the lesser command officers had to make do with silver.

All the Trafalgar Medals struck at the Soho Mint between 1807 and 1847 may be recognised by possessing the lettered edge: TO THE HEROES OF TRAFALGAR FROM M : BOULTON.

[No gold medals have been met with bearing the above edge inscription, so it appears that no gold medals were struck at Soho. My view is that they are Trafalgar Centennial pieces struck in 1905. SC]

Period 2 - W. J. Taylor 1860 -95.

After the closure of the Soho Mint in 1850, the Trafalgar dies remained with the Boulton family. Some years later M. P. W. Boulton commissioned William Joseph Taylor, a London die sinker and manufacturer of coins, medals and tokens, etc., to restrike from the old Soho dies. The Trafalgar Medals so produced were to be sold as collector pieces and were struck from repolished dies resulting in a slight loss of detail, [particularly in the large cloud of cannon smoke on the reverse die]. In addition, they may be recognised by possessing a plain edge.

Period 3 – John Pinches Ltd 1966.

In 1966 restrikes from the original dies of the Trafalgar Medal were made by John Pinches Ltd. These were advertised as being available in hallmarked 22 carat gold (100 specimens) price £96/7/3d inland, £82/-/- overseas and hallmarked sterling silver (2,500 specimens) price £8/10/6d inland, £7/10/- overseas. By this time the obverse die especially had attracted considerable rusting and subsequent repolishing had removed much of the detail of Nelson's uniform. Little remains of the ornamental braid to the collar and jacket, the braided loops of the button holes have almost disappeared as has the fronting on the ruffle at the neck. The pieces are individually numbered and hallmarked for London 1966 on the plain edge.

Notes: A Soho Mint Inventory of 1834 reveals that 214 tin medals of the Trafalgar Medal still held in stock.

The gesture of supplying the tin Trafalgar medals must have cost the Boulton family in the region of £300 - £400. In 1802, Soho supplied the East India Company with similar tin Seringapatam medals and charged them at 6d each.

In conclusion the author would like to gratefully acknowledge the courtesy of the Trustees of the Matthew Boulton Trust, Birmingham, for permission to publish extracts from the Assay Office Collection.

David Vice, *Medal News*, May 1997.

Original Boulton Trafalgar dies auctioned by Woolley and Wallis, 19 January 2016, Lot 446 which made £2,200 hammer. They are in a very rusted condition. The dies had belonged to a Birmingham collector for many years. One of them has an 'H' stamped on the side for the old Heaton Mint. Courtesy Woolly & Wallis.

Lead trial piece without legends. This may have been the sort of example given to Lady Hamilton to see if she approved of the likeness of Nelson.

Silver presentation medal that went to Captain Henry Bayntun of the *Leviathan*. The lunp at 11 o'clock is nearly completely worn away due to the sliding suspension. This medal has the edge inscription.

Silver medal by Taylor that uses the rejected obverse design and the presentation reverse die, which is evident by the remains of the lunp at 11 o'clock being present. Weakness is evident due to polishing the die, amongst the cloud and at the left of the battle scene. There is no edge inscription.

1966 John Pinches restrike which demonstrates the over polishing of the dies, particularly in the cloud of cannon smoke on the reverse. There is no edge inscription.

141

From Nicolas Goodison's *Matthew Boulton's Trafalgar Medal* booklet of 2007, we can see further notes regarding the medals struck:

'In the Birmingham City Archives there is an internal Admiralty note asking an official to estimate for Lord Barham the number of men who served in the ships engaged in the battle. The answer is as near as can be ascertained was 18,414, which seems an amazingly precise number. 423 were killed, which meant that 17,991 medals would be required.'

From looking at the Birmingham City Archives manuscript regarding quantities of Trafalgar medals as detailed by David Vice, one can see that 14,001 medals were struck and sent to London for on shipment to the fleet. One can also see an additional 2,162 medals for ships 'on foreign service' which included *Colossus*, *Royal Sovereign* and *Bellisle*, however as the ships went straight into dock for repairs, the ship's companies were scattered amongst other ships. There is another note which reads: 'Frigates etc., not delivered or Struck' and states 1,101 medals in this class, which brings the grand total to 17,264.

Goodison notes that the reception from the admirals who were to distribute the medals was very positive with Collingwood being particularly pleased. Goodison also notes that 'The distribution took time. As late as February 1808 John Woodward, [Boulton's] London manager still had 1,539 medals on hand and complained that the *Swiftsure* had again sailed without its allocation and that Admiral Young at Plymouth distributed medals indiscriminately as long as supplies lasted.'

So, this is where we have a difference in assessing how many medals were struck and distributed. David Vice is working to the number of 14,001 + 2,162 totalling 16,163, which to me looks to be the best estimate as to the total Fleet medal production. There remains the question regarding Frigates and lesser vessels which are noted at being 1,101 medals, but not delivered or struck. There is a medal listed in the following Catalogue, BT33, to a man on board the *Naiad*, which was a frigate, but checking the ship's logs, *Naiad* was regularly in Plymouth and so with Admiral Young's cavalier approach toward distributing medals, not much of a surprise that a man on board a frigate received a medal. Balance this against the information that in February 1808, 1,539 medals were still with Boulton's London agent awaiting distribution. Who knows where they went in the end? Also sailors were accustomed to trading all sorts of things, so it is very possible that medals went to officers, which they shouldn't have gone to and to frigates which weren't originally destined to receive medals. In the following Catalogue, no less than six fleet tin medals have ended up with Midshipmen which again isn't a surprise as they would have funds available to buy a medal from a willing seller.

There are reports that some of the seamen who received the medal were not pleased because the medal was tin and not bronze, however this is balanced by the care some men took to have their medals engraved with their names and cased and glazed for preservation. These cased Trafalgar medals can be very fine indeed and very valuable.

When one considers the named medals that are known so far, the number of ships represented doesn't total the number of ships of the line present at Trafalgar. James Hammond's list of known Boulton Trafalgar medals, which I helped James to compile, contains many of the medals you will find in the following Catalogue of my collection. The sample isn't extensive, just over thirty medals spread over twenty ships of the line out of 27 present at the battle. There are some conclusions that may be drawn though, such as no medal known to a man on board *Swiftsure*. One wonders if they ever reached the ship. Multiple medals are known to men on board *Victory*, *Conqueror*, *Thunderer*, *Leviathan*, *Spartiate*, *Agamemnon* and *Mars*. The mix of names isn't just to men before the mast. There are named fleet medals to junior officers as well. Captain Henry Bayntun of the *Leviathan* managed to receive a silver presentation medal.

When I think that medals are known to every ship of the line that received the Davison Nile and the way those medals were engraved etc., there is a distinct feeling that the tin Boulton Trafalgar just didn't have the same enthusiastic reception as the bronze and bronze-gilt Nile medals. One does wonder about seven ships at Trafalgar that have no known named Boulton medals and how those men felt about the medal?

When it came to engraving the Fleet issue of the medal with the recipient's name and ship, the Boulton Trafalgar medals appear to have been engraved more by shore based jewellers than on board ship. It is just that the style seems to me to be of a jeweller rather than by a sailor. Where the bronze Davison Nile was typically gilt to improve its appearance, the Boulton Trafalgar was silvered with the process being the same as gilding the medal, except that silver is used. For the Boulton Trafalgar, the silvering of the medal has proved very effective in preserving it from the elements and corrosion.

There appears to have been some strain between father and son in the production of the Trafalgar medal. Matthew Boulton was not a well man and the work at Soho had largely fallen on the shoulders of his son, Matthew Robinson Boulton, who was hard pressed with extensive coinage orders from the British government. That his father decided on such a large personal gift to the men of Trafalgar appears to have created tensions.

There is a curious feature to the medals that were struck as special presentation pieces and that is a lump or sugar loaf located at about 11 o'clock on the reverse die. The presentation specimens are very different from those which went to the fleet. My opinion is that the fleet issues were struck a couple of times to complete them, however the presentation specimens are found normally with mirror fields and frosted devices which indicates striking of several times to bring each medal to a superb finish, whether they be silver, silver-gilt, copper-bronzed, copper-gilt or tin.

I think the lump on the reverse die was created to easily distinguish the special presentation medals and their dies from the fleet issue and it is probable that the minting of these medals as well as to whom they were to be sent, came more under the eye of Matthew Boulton.

It is known that Matthew Boulton wished to see the Trafalgar medal as perfect and above criticism. He certainly achieved his aim with the creation of an iconic medal that will always serve to remember both Nelson and the most important naval victory in the history of the Royal Navy.

Boulton Trafalgar Medal metal analysis

I remember it was a lovely Spring day (6 April 2011), when I arrived at the Royal Observatory at Greenwich to meet Jonathan Betts, Senior Curator of Horology at the National Maritime Museum. We met to carry out tests on Boulton Trafalgar medals to see what they were made of. The device used for the tests is called an X-ray fluorescence gun, XRF for short. When pointed at a metal object, the gun produces a read-out which details the composition of the metal object. I understand the biggest users of the XRF gun are scrap metal dealers, which makes sense!

The Royal Observatory was using the gun in order to analyse a dismantled Harrison H3 Chronometer. Although Lieutenant Commander Gould had worked out how the H3 was assembled, no one knew the actual composition of the metal parts which Harrison had created to withstand extremes of temperature and humidity. The XRF gun would answer those questions.

I brought with me the following medals and here is what was discovered. It is important to keep in mind that the tube within the XRF gun is lined with silver, so all readings will bear a silver trace:

- Tin specimen as sent to the fleet. 97.37% tin, .27% iron, .27% copper, .64% Palladium, .16% lead and traces of arsenic. .64% silver, but most likely an error message. Weight 40.9 grams.

- Tin presentation specimen. 98.7% tin, iron a trace, .17% copper, .62% Palladium, .59% silver with this most likely an error message. Weight 41 grams.

The above analysis says that the tin medals are essentially pure grain tin and that it is unlikely that Boulton added anything to the metal.

The question being asked was did the sodium / salt corrosion which one sees regularly on the fleet strikings, but never on the presentation specimens which are usually found in metal shells, have something to do with the composition of the metal used? It appears not to be the case, i.e. the composition of the two types of tin medal are essentially the same. The difference is that the presentation specimens have been kept in a cabinet or dry place and in shells which has meant that atmospheric agents haven't been able to attack the metal.

The composition of the two types of shells, white metal and copper bronzed used for the tin and copper bronzed presentation medals:

- White metal shell for the tin medal. It appeared to be steel covered in tin and silvered inside.

- Copper metal shells for the bronze medal: 94% copper and 5% zinc (known as gilding metal). There is a 13% reading for silver for the inside of the shell, but this is caused by the inside having been silvered with a silver wash which created the error message.

We then talked about the striking of the two types of tin medals. The fleet medals having only one or two strikes while the presentation medals would have more strikes in order to bring up the mirror fields and frosted devices. This immediately caused a discussion amongst Jonathan's team and consensus was quickly reached by noting that more strikes meant denser metal which in itself would act to protect the surface of the medal from corrosion.

Again, when one compares the fleet medals with no protection provided versus the cased and glazed examples, it is pretty clear that salt in the atmosphere will attack the unprotected fleet specimens and cause corrosion.

- The presentation copper-bronzed specimen had a reading of 99.17% copper with traces of iron, zinc and arsenic. Weight 50.5 grams.

- The presentation copper-gilt specimen couldn't be read past the gilding which showed a very high content of gold at 89%, plus 7.5% copper and 2.4% silver. So it is assumed that because the weight is 50.4 grams, essentially the same as the copper bronzed example, that the medal contains the same 99.17% copper content with the added traces.

I had no silver-gilt example for testing, in fact I don't think I have ever seen a silver-gilt example or perhaps if I did, I thought it was copper-gilt.

Lastly, at the Matthew Boulton conference held on 11 July 2009 at the Birmingham Museum and Art Gallery and sponsored by the British and Royal Numismatic Societies, Dr Richard Doty presented a paper about Boulton's foreign supply of mints and his minting techniques. A question I had always wondered about was did Boulton gild his medals as planchets before striking or after the medals were struck? After a short discussion, there was consensus amongst the attendees and Doty that the planchetes were gilt and then struck. The same would be applicable to the application of bronze colouring to copper planchets to achieve the copper-bronzed effect.

Presentation copper-bronzed medal.

Examples of shells as discussed

The Forger's Detective

Robert Day (1836 – 1914) lived in Cork, Eire and was a leading light of the Cork Historical and Archaeological Society of which he was president for the last twenty years of his life. Robert Day was also a great medal collector and undoubtedly the greatest forger of medals ever! His forgeries specialised in regimental medals, naval medals, gorgets, tobacco boxes and with Franz Tierze in producing fake 17th and 18th century engraved / etched historic glassware.

At times, I feel that the ghost of Robert Day follows me around as I uncover yet another of his fakes and clean up his mess. But here we are, a hundred years after his death and I'm still writing about him!

He had a simple plan. In around 1910 the Hailes Roll for the 1848 Naval General Service Medal (NGS) was published. Robert Day would choose names from the roll and create a Order of Merit or Reward for Gallantry based on that name. He knew the medal would be accepted because he knew the man was at the battle because he was on the NGS medal roll. Simple.

Day was very imaginative and was either an exceptional engraver himself, or he was in league with a very fine engraver. A good example of the engraving skill used is the Plenderleath and Armstrong 49th of Foot Reward for Gallantry at Copenhagen 1801 medal.

The uncovering of this growing list of forgeries is essentially down to statistics. The problem with the Naval General Service medal is that the recipient had to be alive in 1847 in order to apply for the medal distributed in 1849. For a 20 year-old seaman at Trafalgar in 1805, he would be 62 years old in 1847. If one takes the number of men at Trafalgar and the number of NGS medals awarded, the chance of being alive all those years later is 12.5 to 1.

My journey in learning about these fakes began with Captain Hardy's Reward of Merit given to men on board *Victory* at Trafalgar. Four examples are known.

- Midshipman Robert Smith. Killed in action at Trafalgar, but Smith's mother managed to get a posthumous NGS awarded to him. The Hardy medal is silver, Sotheby lot 125, 1 July 1981. Now in the Sim Comfort Collection.

- William Adams, Quarter Master's Mate. Slivered iron? medal. Adams also received the NGS. The Hardy medal is in National Maritime Museum collection, catalogued as MED0006.

- Midshipman John Lyons. Silver Hardy medal and also received the NGS. The Hardy medal is in the National Maritime Museum collection, catalogued as MED0005.

- William Tarrant, Quarter Master. Silvered iron? medal. Also received the NGS. The name is spelled Tarrant on the NGS roll and Terrant on the *Victory* muster roll. Now in the Sim Comfort Collection.

Captain Hardy's Order of Merit to Robert Smith and William Tarrant.

So, we have four medals with one recipient having died in the battle who was certainly not in a position to receive such a medal. All four men received the NGS and the odds against that happening are 12.5 x 12.5 x 12.5 x 12.5 = 24,414 to 1.

We next have the Reward of Merit awarded by Captain Philip Broke of the *Shannon* to his coxswain William Stack, who also received the Naval General Service medal, ergo 24,414 x 12.5 = 305,175 to one.

Also, engraved by the same hand is a tobacco box awarded to J. Johnson of the *Shannon* by Captain Broke. Johnson also received the NGS, so 305,175 x 12.5 = 3,814,697.

With Randy Maffit's discovery of the Plenderleath / Armstrong Reward for Gallantry, which is engraved by the same hand as the copper Captain Hardy medals, we reach new statistical heights as both Plenderleath and Armstrong received the NGS, ergo 3,814,697 x 12.5 x 12.5 = 596,046,447 to 1.

All regimental medal awards to men of the 49th and 95th of Foot at Copenhagen should be viewed with extreme suspicion. The host medal used to create the Plenderleath / Armstrong medal may well have started life as a school medal awarded for the best in Maths, or an agricultural society medal for raising the fattest pig. Creating English hallmarks was child's play for a man like Robert Day, and being Irish he probably took special pleasure in doing it.

There is also a small series of silver Copenhagen badges which were cast from a modified Copenhagen badge, and then engraved with a ship's name. A visitor to Day's house noted that Day had two of these medals one 'a copy'. Probably created before Day had access to the Hailes NGS roll of 1910 which would account for the mistakes in ships present at Copenhagen.

John Hayward in the *Orders and Medals Research Society* journal for March 2003 in his, *Detecting Fakes and Forgeries*, series of articles notes another statistic which indicates just how prolific Robert Day was. Within Hasting Irving's *War Medals and Decorations* published in 1890, are listed 72 volunteer medals over 14 pages and 80 regimental medals over 17 pages. In the 1910 edition, there are now 130 pages of volunteer medals and 58 pages of regimental medals. A very busy Robert Day!

Lastly, the Robert Day collection of medals was auctioned by Sotheby's in April 1913. I've viewed the auction catalogue and it is extraordinary that a number of volunteer and regimental medal lots are illustrated with very fine line drawings. This is really curious as I know Sotheby's would not have employed that effort to illustrate not particularly valuable lots. Then the penny dropped. These line drawings were almost certainly the original artwork for Robert Day's creation of his forgeries. I can imagine this rogue raising a glass of Guinness and having yet another chuckle as to how he cheated the English with fake medals and fooled their greatest auction house and museums!

The only good news regarding Robert Day is that it doesn't appear that he engraved Boulton Trafalgar and Davison Nile medals, but instead created special medals from scratch which is probably because the original Nile and Trafalgar medals may not have been that easy to find. Also, just a named medal would not have been as valuable as a special presentation medal from Hardy or Broke for conspicuous gallantry during a battle! Having said that, a later generation has tampered with both Davison Nile and Boulton Trafalgar medals, so one must be careful and become familiar with contempoary engraving.

Captain Broke's Reward for Merit and the *Shannon* tobacco box. Two examples of the Broke medal are known.. Note that HMS is in the same hand on the box and on Captain Hardy 's Order of Merit to William Tarrant. Also the Copenhagen Badge; the *Tonnant* wasn't at the battle and the style is crude, however a visitor to Day's house saw two examples of this medal, one 'a copy', so his work, probably pre-1910. Lastly the Plenderleath Copenhagen medal.

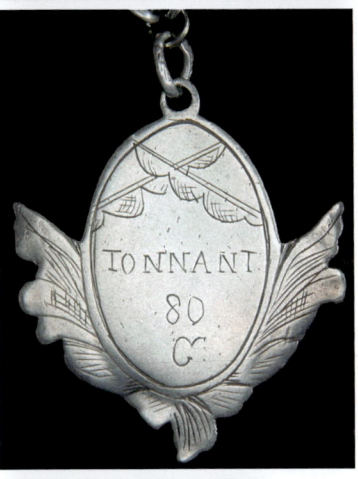

149

Painted by Whitcombe.

T. Sutherland sculp.

BATTLE OF THE NILE, Aug.t 1.st 1798.

London, Pub. March 1 1816, at 48 Strand, for J.Jenkins's Naval Achievements

Plate I.

Part Two

Catalogue of named Earl St Vincent Davison Nile and Boulton Trafalgar medals

The Ville de Paris off Ushant, September 1803. Watercolour by Derek G. M. Gardner, RSMA

SV 01 Isaac Jones, Able Seaman, on board HMS Ville de Paris

Description: The thin planchet silver medal is framed in silver with a silver suspension loop. The frame is engraved both sides with cannon, cannon balls, sponges and etc., near the top and then down the sides with laurel leaves. On the obverse at the bottom of the frame is *Isaac Jones* in script while on the reverse is a broadside view of the hull of *Ville de Paris*. 78 x 62 mm. Weight 58.8 grams. Very fine.

Background: Isaac Jones was clearly a young man of the sea from Whitehaven, which is a small seaport on the west coast of Cumbria, in the north of England. He appears to have been prest into service on board HMS *Sampson* on 4 September 1796, aged 19 years and immediately rated as Ordinary Seaman.

On 10 February 1797, he moved to HMS *Minotaur* for only a few days and then on 14 February 1797 transferred to the *Ville de Paris*. His billet number was 230. Every prest man had the choice of either accepting his fate or fighting it. Isaac Jones certainly accepted it and progressed well in the service. On 17 June 1797 he was promoted to Able Seaman and was most likely a valued topman. He continued in this rating for the rest of his tour with *Ville de Paris*.

On 24 April 1802, he entered Plymouth Hospital suffering from an ulcer and a month later was discharged from hospital and then the Royal Navy which was probably part of the reduction in force created by the Peace of Amiens which commenced on 24 March 1802.

Just looking at the St Vincent medal that Isaac Jones received and the care that was taken in his having a surrounding silver suspension made by a jeweller which includes a hull model of the *Ville de Paris*, is just wonderful and shows how proud he was to have received the medal and to have been part of the before the mast team that St Vincent respected.

This outstanding medal was in Colonel Murray's collection and illustrated for Tancred's book on war medals which catalogued the Murray collection and was published in 1891 by Spink.

As Tancred notes from *The Times*, 21 April 1801: 'Earl St Vincent is having a Medal struck for the officers and seamen of the *Ville de Paris* as a testimony of the high esteem and regard which his lordship entertains for them.'

Provenance: Colonel Murray's collection as illustrated in Tancred.
Spink auction of 23 April 2009, lot 86.

References: ADM36/13632 Muster Book *Ville de Paris*.
ADM35/1981 & 1982 Pay Book *Ville de Paris*.
Historical Record of Medals of Honorary Distinction etc. by George Tancred and including the medals of Colonel Murray of Polmaise. Spink, London, 1891.

SV 02 James Wood, Able Seaman, on board HMS Ville de Paris

Description: The thin planchet silver medal has a silver loop attached for suspension. Engraved in capital letters either side of the portrait is JAMES WOOD. Weight 25.3 grams. Nearly extremely fine.

Left is a thin planchet medal which appears to have been given to seamen and marines befor the mast. Right is a thick planchet medal which may have been presented to officers.

Background: James Wood appears to have been a prime seaman when he accepted the bounty of £2/10/0 to join the Royal Navy on 1 April 1799. He was 21 years old from Croydon, Surrey and his billet number was 410. He was initially rated Ordinary Seaman, but on 16 November of that year, he was promoted to Able Seaman, again a valued topman. Although not checked, it is most likely that he left the service in the Spring of 1802 with the Peace of Amiens.

Provenance: Private purchase.

References: ADM36/13632 Muster Book *Ville de Paris*.
ADM35/1981 & 1982 Pay Book *Ville de Paris*.

SV 03 Thomas Bowden, Ordinary Seaman, on board HMS Ville de Paris

Description: The thin planchet silver medal has been holed to create a place for a ring to be inserted for suspension. Engraved in capital letters on the rim is THOMAS * BOWDEN. Weight 24.2 grams. Nearly very fine.

Background: Thomas Bowden was from Falmouth in Cornwall and entered the *Ville de Paris* on 25 April 1798. He was 30 years old, past the age for being a topman and was rated Ordinary Seaman where he remained during his time on board the ship. He probably left *Ville de Paris* in the Spring of 1802 with the commencement of the Peace of Amiens.

Provenance: Private Purchase.

References: ADM36/13632 Muster Book *Ville de Paris*.
ADM35/1981 & 1982 Pay Book *Ville de Paris*.

SV 04 Joseph Colen, Chief of York Factory, Hudson Bay, Hudson Bay Company

Description: Silver-gilt thick planchet medal which has been cased in gold and glazed. The rim of the case is engraved in script: *Right Hon. Earl of St Vincent to J. Colen*. Weight 60.2 grams including the case. Brilliant proof with frosted devices and mirror fields. Extremely Fine.

With the medal are two miniature portraits with one being on ivory depicting Joseph Colen with powdered hair and in the uniform of the Hudson Bay Company. The miniature is fitted in a gold and glazed case with the reverse containing braided brown hair from the sitter. The miniature portrait was engraved as an aquatint by Daniel Orme entitled *Joseph Colen, Chief of York Factory, Hudson Bay*, and dated 1796.

Background: This medal caused me quite an effort to discover the story behind it. Initially, I was convinced that the name was probably misspelled and should have been Cohen, but I couldn't find any link between a Cohen and Earl St Vincent. Technology, the web and a closer study of the sitter's uniform solved the puzzle. On the epaulette are the letters HBC, so from the Hudson Bay Company website and an email to the librarian, all was revealed. Colen was the correct spelling of the man's name and Joseph Colen was an early explorer and factor in the northern reaches of the Hudson Bay Company, a Canadian hero no less. What is most interesting is that Colen belonged to the Society for the Encouragement of Arts, Manufactures, and Commerce of which Matthew Boulton and Earl St Vincent were also members.

From the *Canadian National Biography*, we have an article about Joseph Colen written by Shirlee Anne Smith:

COLEN, JOSEPH, HBC, Chief Factor; b. c. 1751 in England; d. July 1818 in Cirencester, England.

In April 1785, having had extensive experience in both 'mechanic & mercantile Affairs' and being 'perfect master of his Pen in writing and figures,' Joseph Colen was engaged as a writer by the Hudson's Bay Company for five years at £20 per annum. He was to assist Humphrey Marten, chief at York Factory (Manitoba), and to oversee the rebuilding of the factory, destroyed in 1782 by Jean-François de Galaup, Comte de Lapérouse – a project that was too much of a burden for the gouty Marten.

Marten retired in 1786 and William Tomison, his successor as chief factor, was ordered to reside inland. Consequently, Colen was appointed resident chief at York at £40 per annum plus a premium on made beaver. Though in command at the factory, Colen was subject to the orders of Tomison when the latter visited York. On taking up his new appointment Colen was directed by the HBC's London committee to forward 'the building of a new Factory.' In 1793 the last flanker was covered and two years later the stockade enclosed three acres of ground, one-half of which was 'occupied by buildings – The rest intended for Gardens.'

To meet the competition from the North West Company south and west of York Factory, Colen had sent men inland to establish new posts: in 1790 Charles Thomas Isham settled on Swan River (Man.) and James Spence went to Split Lake, and in 1791 William Hemmings Cook built Chatham House on Wintering Lake. In 1794 Colen tried to organise an expedition to the Athabasca country and ordered boats for use on the inland waterways. That spring he travelled about 109 miles up the Hayes River on the first wooden boat ever to navigate inland from Hudson Bay, and there he selected a site for a provisioning depot which was to be called Gordon House. Its position considerably shortened the route travelled by the inland traders, who now needed to bring their canoes only as far as Gordon House to exchange their furs for supplies brought from York by boat.

Colen's position as resident chief was not an easy one. Tomison did not cooperate on the Athabasca expedition, did not approve of boats, and in general tried to thwart every plan that did not benefit the posts on the Saskatchewan River. In 1794 Colen returned to London to report to the governor and committee on various aspects of the trade. When he arrived back at York the following year he had been appointed Chief Factor at an annual salary of £130 plus £10 for a servant. The change in status was based on the premise that Tomison would be retiring in 1795. The expected retirement did not occur, however, and that year Tomison established Fort Edmonton (Edmonton, Alberta). In 1796, 1797, and 1798 Colen journeyed to Gordon House to hold councils and contract with the inland men. New posts were established and much time devoted to inland transport.

Colen was recalled by the London committee in 1798; his salary was terminated in March 1799. The reasons were not stated, but one was the impatience of the committee with the jealousy and rivalry between Colen and Tomison. In conducting affairs at York, Colen was hampered by his lack of knowledge of inland operations, and he was lax in overseeing the accounting of the York Factory goods and provisions. In fairness to Colen it should be said that he was a man of ideas, an innovator and a thinker, rather than a shrewd businessman. These characteristics are demonstrated by his interests in medicine, tree husbandry, the distilling operation at York, and the collecting of shrubs for London, and by his possessing at York Factory a personal library of some 1,400 volumes.

On his retirement from the company Colen apparently did not return to business life, but he was an active member of the Society for the Encouragement of Arts, Manufactures, and Commerce, in London. Sought out in 1802 by Lord Selkirk [Douglas] for an opinion on his scheme to introduce Scottish emigrants to present-day Manitoba through Hudson Bay, Colen gave a favourable opinion. Colen appears to have spent the last ten years of his life in Cirencester.

Shirlee Anne Smith

The York boat, which was used extensively by Colen and his men on the Hayes and Nelson rivers, was a type of inland boat used by the Hudson Bay Company to carry furs and trade goods along inland waterways in Rupert's Land, the watershed stretching from Hudson Bay to the eastern slopes of the Rocky Mountains. It was named after York Factory, the headquarters of the HBC, and modelled after the Orkney yole, itself a descendant of the Viking long ship.

York boats were preferred as cargo carriers to the canoes used by Northwest Company Voyageurs, because they were larger, carried more cargo, and were more stable in rough water. The boat's heavy wood construction was a significant advantage when travelling waterways where the bottom or sides of the hull were likely to strike rocks or ice. Canoes then were commonly constructed with soft hulls of tree bark or animal hide and were vulnerable to tears and punctures. The solid, all-wood hull of the York boat could simply bounce off or grind past obstacles that could easily inflict fatal damage on a soft-hulled vessel. That advantage became a disadvantage, though, when portaging was necessary. The boat was far too heavy to carry and the crew had to cut a path through the brush, lay poplar rollers, and drag the boat overland.

Regardless of the circumstances, crewing a York boat was an arduous task, and those who chose this life faced 'unending toil broken only by the terror of storms,' according to the explorer Sir John Franklin.

The York boat had a length of about 14 metres (46 ft) and the largest could carry more than 6 tonnes (13,000 lb) of cargo. It had a pointed bow, a flat bottom, and a stern angled upward at 45°, making beaching and launching easier. The boat was propelled both by oars and by a square canvas sail. It was steered by a long steering pole or, when under sail, by a rudder. It had a crew of between six and eight men. The first boat was built in 1749, and by the late 18th century there were boat-building stations from James Bay to Fort Chipewyan. The advent of the steamboat at the beginning of the 19th century signalled the end for the York boat.

The very narrow Echimamish River flows from the Nelson River to the Hayes River, which thus connects Norway House, Manitoba with York Factory on Hudson Bay at the mouth of the Hayes. In some places the Echimamish is so narrow that the oars of the York boats touched the ground on either side. The route included portages around rapids on the Hayes of up to 3 kilometres (1.9 miles). Crews hauled a York boat 15 metres (49 ft) long and up to 12 tonnes (26,000 lb) of supplies or cargo.

Although it doesn't appear that Joseph Colen designed the York boat, he certainly made it famous by pioneering its use on the rivers coming into the Hudson Bay from the west.

Provenance: Earl St Vincent to Joseph Colen late of the Hudson Bay Company. Purchased from Spink in 1986. Upon requesting further information regarding the provenance, a letter from the unnamed seller to Spink notes: 'I inherited the medal and miniatures from my stepfather, Arthur Leslie Moore, son of Leslie Wakefield Moore and Miss? Gibbs. He inherited them from a cousin, Mrs. Alice Nelson, widow of Ernest Nelson, who was living in a flat in St James's Court, London SW1 at the time of his death in the late 1940s. I have an idea that Mrs. Nelson's maiden name was Wakefield and she could have been American. I understand that Joseph Colen was an ancestor of hers.'

References: *Dictionary of Canadian Biography.* http://www.biographi.ca/en/index.php

SV 05 Unattributed thick planchet gold medal

Description: Brilliant gold proof with frosted devices and mirror fields, thick planchet, rim is 2 mm, in its original red morocco leather case. Weight: 60.9 grams. Extremely Fine.

Provenance: Sotheby's 10 March 1989, Lot 265, then Christopher Dixon, purchased 29 November 2004. The name of the original recipient had been written on the inside lid of the leather case, but unfortunately obliterated now.

SV 06 Unattributed thin planchet silver medal with ring suspension.

Description: Silver medal with suspension attached to the rim. Weight: 24.8 grams with ring suspension. Rim is 1.3 / 1.5 mm. Nearly extremely fine.

Provenance: Private purchase.

SV 07 Unattributed thick planchet silver medal with ring suspension.

Description: Silver medal with suspension attached to the rim. Weight: 39.8 grams with ring suspension. Rim is 2 mm. Very fine.

Provenance: Private purchase.

Thin Planchet　　　　　　　　　　　Thick Planchet

ADMIRAL NELSON'S VICTORY
over the French Fleet, near the Mouth of the Nile, August 1st 1798.

DN 01 Lieutenant Thomas Wilks, RN, HMS Goliath, Captain Thomas Foley

Description: Silver medal fitted in a gold case and glazed. The rim of the case is engraved 'LIEUt THOs WILKS RN GOLIATH *first ship in action*.' Proof quality with frosted devices and mirror fields. Extremely fine.

Background: Thomas Wilks was christened on 29 December 1763 at Pebworth, Gloucestershire, the son of John and Margaret Wilks. He volunteered to serve in the Royal Navy on 1 July 1780 at a rendezvous and appeared on board HMS *Assurance*, Captain James Cumming, on 5 July. He was rated as a Captain's Servant which placed him among the young gentleman destined for the quarterdeck.

The American War held no particular adventures for Wilks. However, he undoubtedly learned his seamanship because on 1 November he entered HMS *Ariel*, Captain Fabian, as Able Seaman. In 1783, the *Ariel* was paid off and Wilks saw no more service in the Royal Navy for the next ten years, although when considering his next postings it is quite likely that he saw further service at sea in the merchant marine.

With the commencement of the French Revolutionary War in 1793, Wilks immediately secured a berth on board HMS *Zebra*, Captain Robert Faulknor. Wilks accepted a £5 bounty and was entered on 29 June as Able Seaman and within the week, he was rated Midshipman. He was now 30 years old, which was getting on in age for a Midshipman and the Admiralty required six years service as either a Midshipman or Master's Mate prior to qualifying for a Lieutenant's examination, and Wilks had only three years service from the previous war.

163

The career of Robert Faulknor is of the sort that naval legends are made. Faulknor came from a long line of sea officers and was born in the same year as Thomas Wilks. He attended the Royal Naval College in Portsmouth from 1774 and in 1777 then joined his first ship, HMS *Isis*, Captain Cornwallis. During the American war, Faulknor saw much action and in 1782 he served as Lieutenant on board HMS *Britannia* under the flag of Vice-Admiral Barrington. He took part in the relief of Gibraltar and the action off Cape Spartel. Following the disarmament of 1790, he was promoted to Captain.

HMS *Zebra* was a ship rigged sloop of 314 tons burthen and 98 feet in overall length. She carried 16 x 6 pounders and 12 swivel guns. Her ship's company would have been around 120 men. Captain Robert Faulknor took command of her in June 1793 and after work in the North Sea, she was sent to join Sir John Jervis's fleet off Martinique.

William James provides the detail of the attack on Fort Royal on 20 March 1794:

'The success of Lieutenant Bowen's attack upon the *Bienvenue* [French frigate captured within the harbour of Fort Royal on 17th March, 1794], led to a [plan for an] immediate assault upon the town of Fort Royal. A number of scaling ladders were made of long bamboos connected with strong line, and the *Asia* 64, and *Zebra* sloop [Captain Robert Faulknor], were ordered to hold themselves in readiness to enter the [inner harbour], for the purpose of battering the lower and more exposed part of Fort Louis, the walls of which were not high; also of covering the flat boats, barges and pinnaces, sent in under the direction of Commodore Thompson, and commanded by Captains Nugent of the *Veteran*, and Edward Riou of the *Rose*.

'On the 20th this plan of attack was put into execution, and succeeded in every point, except that the *Asia* was unable to get into her station. ...Observing the *Asia* baffled in her attempt [to enter the inner harbour, and with the wind blowing into the harbour and the *Zebra* now in, Captain Faulknor couldn't turn about and leave!], Captain Faulknor dashed singly on; and, running the *Zebra*, in defiance of the showers of grape that poured upon her, close to the wall of the fort, 'leaped overboard,' says Sir John Jervis in his despatch, 'at the head of her sloop's company, and assailed and took this important post before the boats could get on shore'...

'The boats, already mentioned as commanded by Captains Nugent and Riou, ...pushed across the [inner harbour] before the *Zebra* could get in, and stormed and took possession of Fort Royal, Captain Nugent, with the *Veteran's* people, hauled down the French colours, and hoisted the English in their stead.'

Thus naval arguments are created. There is little doubt of Captain Faulknor's bravery in running the *Zebra* to the fortress wall under heavy fire. He had no choice, either try to battle the wind and be decimated by the Fort's cannon, or board the beast! That is exactly what he and his men did. No doubt that the small flotilla of boats were also doing the same thing, and that the *Veteran's* men broke through first and hauled down the French colours.

Sir John Jervis was so impressed with Captain Faulknor's actions, the he immediately promoted him to

Post-Captain and shortly after gave him command of HMS *Rose*. This appointment was soon followed by the command of HMS *Blanche*, a 12 pounder frigate of 32 guns and a crew of 220 men. She was 129 feet in overall length and 710 tons burthen, over twice the tonnage of *Zebra*.

Fame now stalked Faulknor, but would take him at an awful price. Thomas Wilks transferred to both the *Rose* and *Blanch* and was with Faulknor to the end.

On the morning of 30 December 1794, a large French schooner was sighted and chased into the bottom of a bay of the island of Desirade, near Guadeloupe. Faulknor was determined to cut her out and anchored his ship some 700 yards off shore. The schooner had taken protection under the guns of a small fort which opened fire upon the *Blanche*, who returned fire and silenced the fort whereupon the boats of the *Blanche* boarded and captured the schooner.

Not long after this victory, on the 4th of January 1795, the *Blanche* spied near Guadeloupe, the French 32-gun frigate *Pique*, Captain Conseil. There then followed a cat and mouse set of manoeuvres between the two ships until around 12:30 a.m. on the 5th, when (as William James relates):

'At half past midnight, having got nearly in the wake of her opponent [the *Pique*], the *Blanche* tacked; and at a few minutes past 1 a.m., just as she had arrived within musket shot upon the starboard quarter of the *Pique*, the latter wore, with the intention of crossing her opponent's hawse and raking her ahead. To frustrate this manoeuvre, the *Blanche* wore also; and the frigates became closely engaged, broadside to broadside.

'At about 2:30 a.m., the *Blanche*, having shot ahead, was in the act of luffing up to port to rake the *Pique* ahead, when the former's wounded mizen and main masts, in succession, fell over the side. Almost immediately after this, the *Pique* ran foul of the *Blanche* on her larboard quarter and made several attempts to board. These attempts the British crew successfully resisted, and the larboard quarterdeck guns, and such of the maindeck ones as would bear, were fired with destructive effect into the *Pique*'s starboard bow; she returning the fire from her tops, as well as from some of her quarterdeck guns run in amidships fore and aft.

'At a few minutes before 3 a.m. while assisting his second lieutenant, Mr David Milne, and one or two other of his crew in lashing, with such ropes as were handy, the bowsprit of the *Pique* to the capstan of the *Blanche*, preparatory to a more secure fastening by means of a hawser which was getting up from below, the young and gallant Captain Faulknor fell by a musket ball through his heart.

'At this moment, or very soon afterwards, the lashings broke loose, and the *Pique* crossing the stern of the *Blanche*, who had now begun to pay off for the want of after-sail, fell on board the latter a second time, upon the starboard quarter. In an instant the British crew with the hawser which had just before been got on deck, lashed the bowsprit of the *Pique* to the stump of their own mainmast. In this manner the *Blanche*, commanded now by Lieutenant Frederick Watkins, towed before the wind her resolute opponent: whose repeated attempts to cut away the second lashing were defeated by the quick and well directed fire of the British marines.

'In the mean time, the constant stream of musketry poured upon the quarterdeck of the *Blanche* from the forecastle and tops of the Pique and a well directed fire from the latter's quarterdeck guns pointed forward, gave great annoyance to the *Blanche's* crew, particularly …as the *Blanche* had no stern ports on the main deck [for the placing of cannon]. The carpenters having in vain tried to cut down the upper transom beam, no alternative remained but to blow away a part of it on each side. As soon, therefore, as the firemen with their buckets were assembled in the cabin, the two after guns were pointed against the stern frame. Their discharge made a clear breach on both sides, and the activity of the bucket men quickly extinguished the fire it had occasioned in the woodwork. The two 12 pounders of the *Blanche*, thus brought into use, soon made considerable havoc upon the *Pique's* decks.

'At about 3:15 a.m. the mainmast of the French frigate (her fore and mizzen having previously fallen) fell over the side. In this utterly defenceless state, without a gun which, on account of the wreck of her masts, she could now bring to bear, the *Pique* sustained the raking fire of the *Blanche* until 5:15 a.m. when some of the French crew, from the bowsprit end called for quarter.'

From Second Lieutenant Milne's gazetted letter, he notes that as all of the Blanche's boats were shot through, 'the Second Lieutenant and ten men swam on board and took possession of *La Pique*.'

Out of a crew of around 250, the *Pique* lost her Captain and a further 75 officers and men killed and 110 wounded. The *Blanche*, out of a crew of around 220, also lost her Captain and a further seven men killed and 21 wounded. Thomas Wilks was there throughout the action and appears to not have been wounded.

CAPTURE of LA PICQUE, Jan? 5th 1795.

Following the capture of *La Pique*, Wilks stayed on board *Blanche* which returned to England in October 1796. For a short time he was transferred to HMS *Victory* where he passed his Lieutenant's examination. On 12 December he joined HMS *Goliath* as 5th Lieutenant.

Goliath was one of the Arrogant Class of Third Rate 74-gun ships designed by Sir Thomas Slade in 1758 and would have a ship's company of 550 men. She was launched at Deptford Dockyard on 19 October 1781. She was 168 feet in length, 1604 tons burthen and bore 28 x 32 pounders on the Gun Deck, 28 x 18 pounders on the Upper Deck, 14 x 9 pounders on the Quarterdeck and 4 x 9 pounders in the Forecastle. She was broken up in 1815.

At the Battle of Cape St Vincent, *Goliath* was under the command of Captain Sir Charles Knowles who St Vincent characterised as 'an imbecile, totally incompetent and the *Goliath* of no use whatsoever under his command.' This must have been a trying time for Lieutenant Wilks, but all was corrected when following the battle, St Vincent had Sir Charles replaced by Captain Thomas Foley. Foley had entered the Royal Navy in 1770, was made Lieutenant in 1778 and fought under Rodney at The Saints, 12 April 1782.

By the commencement of the French Revolutionary War in 1793, he had been made Post Captain and was well respected for his organisational skills in that he was Flag-Captain to Admiral John Gell and Sir Hyde Parker where he saw much service. He was again Flag-Captain on board *Britannia* at Cape St Vincent and again at Copenhagen as Flag-Captain on board Nelson's HMS *Elephant*. When Hyde Parker hoisted the recall signal which ordered Nelson to break off the action, Nelson commented, 'You know, Foley, I only have one eye - I have a right to be blind sometimes,' and then holding his telescope to his blind eye remarked, 'I really do not see the signal!' Foley was the essence of Nelson's Band of Brothers and when it came to the Trafalgar campaign, Nelson requested Foley to be his Flag-Captain again, but Foley had to decline due to ill health. He died while serving in command of Portsmouth in 1833.

The Battle of Cape St Vincent had four very important outcomes. First, it humbled the Spanish navy, secondly it regained entry to the Mediterranean for the British, thirdly it achieved instant fame for Commodore Nelson and, lastly, placed John Jervis, the newly created Earl St Vincent to the fore as an effective fleet commander and organiser. It is with St Vincent and Nelson that so much future British success at sea would depend.

By November 1797, Thomas Wilks had been promoted to 3rd Lieutenant of *Goliath*.

Goliath was part of the squadron under the command of Rear-Admiral Nelson that was ordered into the Mediterranean to search out and destroy Napoleon's fleet that threatened Britain's interests in the eastern Mediterranean and possibly India. When finally found anchored in Aboukir Bay, it was the *Goliath* that led the British fleet to battle. From Brian Lavery's excellent book, *Nelson and the Nile*, he notes that Foley had a good French chart which was coupled with the desire of Nelson's to always double the enemy. Foley saw his chance and steered *Goliath* between the shore and the enemy ships. Due to the anchoring of *Goliath* not going to plan, she ended up further along the French line by *Conquerant*.

Goliath's log for 1 and 2 August 1798 reads:

'At 15 minutes past 6, the *Goliath*, being the leading ship, crossed the van of the enemy's line and commenced the action; having crossed, anchored with the sheet-anchor out of the gun-room port, and brought up alongside the 2nd ship. [Lavery cites Lieutenant Wilkes encouraging his men on the Gun Deck, 'Load and Fire, we are too close to miss, warm work my boys.'] About this time a French frigate ran on shore, and was dismasted by our ships as they passed; the *Zealous* followed the *Goliath*, and brought up alongside the first ship. 50 minutes past 6, the *Audacious* crossed the ship we were engaged with, raking her, and having crossed her, brought up on her larboard bow. At half-past 8, ceased firing, the five van ships of the enemy having struck their colours. The *Goliath's* main and mizen masts, with the rigging of those masts, were so much cut in several places that there was much danger of losing them. All of the seamen employed stoppering and repairing the same as fast as possible. At 40 minutes past 8, observed the French Admiral's ship, *l'Orient* of 112 guns on fire; at 10 she blew up. From 11 p.m. to 2 a.m. a very heavy cannonade between the rear of the enemy and H.M. ships *Alexander* and *Majestic*. At 3, the *Majestic's* main and mizen masts went over the side. At daylight, observed that six line-of-battle ship had struck their colours. At 1/2 past 5, the *Artemise*, French frigate, fired her broadside, hauled her colours down, and the crew set her on fire and left her. At 6, cut the cable and run further to leeward to attack the enemy's rear. 1/4 past, anchored with springs on the cable and began to fire on the enemy. About 7 two ship on shore in the SSW struck their colours. They had fired on the *Alexander* and *Theseus*. At noon, the *Theseus* and *Goliath* fired several broadsides at 2 line-of-battle ships and two frigates, which had weighed and stood to the NE.'

Goliath had 21 officers and men killed and 41 wounded.

Following the battle, *Goliath* was employed mainly at Naples and the surrounding sea. Wilks was taken ill in July, 1799 and left *Goliath* for hospital at Port Mahon, Minorca. From here, he was invalided back to England only to appear again for duty on 29 May 1800.

His new ship was HMS *Bellona*, Captain Sir Thomas Boulden Thompson and in less than a year, Thomas Wilks would again be engaged in a major fleet action. With Napoleon's manipulation of the Baltic states, particularly Russian and Sweden, in the creation of an 'Armed Neutrality', which effectively removed Baltic trade from the hands of the British, something had to be done. The Royal Navy couldn't survive without access to the tall pine trees that were used to make the masts and yards of His Majesty's ships, or the Stockholm tar that sealed the seams of ship's decks and hull timbers. Grain was also an important export from the Baltic.

Admiral Sir Hyde Parker was given the task, with Nelson as his second-in-command. Denmark held the key to the Baltic, and Copenhagen was its capital. This was an extremely difficult enterprise due to the shallowness of the harbour and the very considerable defences that guarded Copenhagen. Nelson knew there was no alternative but to manoeuvre his fleet into position and commence a slugging match with the Danes. This was a particularly bitter task because if you were Norfolk born and raised, the links with Denmark, which went all the way back to King Cnut and Danelaw, were very strong. 'Our Brothers the Danes', is how Nelson felt, but the job had to be done.

Bellona was a 74-gun ship with a crew of around 590 men. Although HMS *Leander* and her captain Sir Thomas Boulden Thompson suffered little damage at the Nile, both suffered considerably when the 50-gun *Leander* met *le Genereux* of 74 guns after the battle. The contest was one sided with the French holding the advantage, but only when the *Leander* was completely dismasted and her crew had suffered 25% causalities, including her captain, did she surrender.

Thompson was exchanged and upon his return to England was praised for his defence of *Leander*, knighted and offered a pension of £200 a year.

At Copenhagen, 2 April 1801, *Bellona* suffered a similar fate to *Culloden* at the Nile, i.e. she ran upon the Middle Ground in Copenhagen harbour which saved her from the worst of the enemy's cannon fire. We are most fortunate in that the National Maritime Museum holds a letter written by Lieutenant Thomas Wilks to his father the day after the battle:

'My dear Sir, When you receive this, you will, of course, have received accounts of yesterdays exploits - You are not unacquainted with the share of Battle & Slaughter I have long been accustomed to. But yesterday, I saw and experienced more than ever - my escapes yesterday were more than Miracles. Dreadful was the situation on board the *Bellona* - from the ignorance of the Pilots we got aground very early in the action. Poor Sir Thomas Thompson lost his leg about the same time. I had two Thirty-two Pounders burst at my quarters, & we were obliged to lay in an ungovernable state for upwards of three hours before we could compel our opponents to strike, which I am sure we should have done in 20 minutes if we could have got nearer.

'Three times was I knocked down at my Quarters in the Midst of the killed & wounded, but my Great & Good God shielded me as he has always done to a miracle, and I have escaped all material injuries; black eyes and bruises are my only wounds.

'Our Damages are immense, but we hope to repair them, & expect another attack, if the Danes do not come to terms - then, I apprehend we shall proceed against the Russians at Reval, or elsewhere.

'Shocking was the slaughter on board the captured ships,- it is said with a degree of confidence that one of their ships had 800 men killed. I will do them the credit to say that they fought well, far better than I have ever found the French or Spaniards - not a vessel surrendered till nearly all her men were either killed or wounded, & several of the ships received men from the shore during the battle.

'As far as I can make it out, we have captured six sail of the Line & seven or eight Floating Batteries, carrying from 20 to 30 heavy guns, - & an immense number of prisoners.

'Flags of Truce have been up ever since the conclusion of the Battle and I hope some successful negotiations are going forward, - if not we shall make another attack.

'There are about 13 or 14 fine Ships remaining and the brave Nelson swears he will have them all or destroy them, with the City. I hope he will not be disappointed. The Danes are greatly frightened - the very name of Nelson is a host of strength. Our Chief Sir Hyde Parker - gives him the whole management of the Ships that have and are destined for this Important business. Yesterday, he says, was the first time he ever was in action without being hurt. I saw him at a Distance this morning, he looks in great spirits.

'Our fleet are very much cut up, that is the six or seven ships that were in the height of the Battle. The *Bellona*, the *Russell*, the *Elephant*, the *Defiance* & the *Amazon* all got aground. The *Elephant* & us got off the same evening. I believe the others are now all off, - I forget - the *Desiree* is now on shore & great apprehensions are entertained for her safety, - but you will see all these accounts in the *Gazette*.

'I am very fearful we shall lose poor Sir Thomas Thompson - that is - he will go home if so, I will not on any account stay any longer in the *Bellona*, etc. etc.'

Lieutenant Wilks joined *Bellona* as 5th Lieutenant and following the action was promoted to Second. Although in the above letter, he declared that he suffered no serious wounds, he was discharged the ship on 6 July 1801 and then on 30 May 1802 was engaged to command the signal station at St Anthony's Head at Falmouth, Cornwall where he continued until 1816 when he went on half pay. Signal stations were typically managed by officers who had suffered a disabling wound which would preclude them from service at sea, but not from service ashore. It may well have been that the two exploding cannon damaged Wilks's hearing, although a subsequent letter gives no hint of a disability. It appears that he died on 30 April 1823, aged 60.

Provenance: James Risk, Stack's, New York.
Nimrod Dix.
During the 1980s, business would sometimes take me to New York where I met Jim Risk at Stack's and had first sight of Thomas Wilks's Davison Nile medal. I knew I wanted to buy it, and offered to do so on each visit, but Mr Risk always declined to sell. Then I had a phone call from Nimrod saying that he had purchased a medal that I might want! I couldn't get into town quick enough, and there was Lieutenant Wilks's medal and I immediately accepted the offer price. I had no idea, and neither did Nimrod, of just what a fantastic career Wilks had led. I only hope that the above notes have done him justice.

References: The National Archives, Kew: HMS *Assurance* ADM 36/10252, HMS *Confederate* ADM 34/187, HMS *Ariel* ADM 34/56 & 36/9113, HMS *Zebra* ADM 35/2079 & 36/11502, HMS *Rose* ADM 35/1435 & ADM 36/11317, HMS *Blanche* ADM 35/239 & ADM 36 12177 / 12178 / 12179, HMS *Victory* ADM 35/1995, HMS *Goliath* ADM 35/677 & ADM 36/12993/14816/14817, HMS *Bellona* ADM 35/274 & ADM 36/14353/14354/14355/4356.
ADM 9/6 / 1983 Thomas Wilks's *Memorandum of Service*.
National Maritime Museum, Greenwich: Wilks's Copenhagen letter, NMM AGC/W/2 and MS60/048.
A Social History of the Navy, 1793-1815 by Michael Lewis, George Allen & Unwin, London, 1960.
The Sailing Navy List by David Lyon, Conway, London, 1993.
Dictionary of National Biography, Oxford University Press, 1975.
The Naval History of Great Britain...1793 to 1820 by William James, six vols., Richard Bentley, London, 1837 etc.
The Naval Chronicle, vol. 16, Gold, London, 1806.
Naval Achievements of Great Britain by James Jenkins, London, 1817, reprinted by Sim Comfort Associates, London, 1998.
St Vincent and Camperdown by Christopher Lloyd, Batsford, London, 1963.
Nelson and the Nile by Brian Lavery, Chatham, London, 1998.
Logs of the Great Sea Fights 1794-1805 by Sturges Jackson, Navy Records Society, London, 1899-1900.
The Great Gamble, Nelson at Copenhagen by Dudley Pope, Weidenfeld & Nicolson, London, 1972.

DN 02 Sir William Burnett, Assistant Surgeon, HMS Goliath, Captain Thomas Foley

Description: Soho bronze-gilt medal cased in gold and glazed. The outer rim is engraved: A TRIBUTE OF REGARD FROM ALEXr DAVISON ESQr, St JAMES'S SQUARE, TO MR. BURNETT. GOLIATH. Weight: 57.1 grams. Extremely Fine with the fields chased.

Background: Amongst the Davison Nile medals in this collection and others I have seen, this particular medal stands out. The gilding is original Soho, which is appropriate for an afterguard officer, but the casing and suspension of the medal are identical to the casing of the gold Davison Nile presented to Captain Thomas Foley. As the gold medal would have been shipped in a fine close fitting circular red morocco leather case, the finished glazed and cased medal would have been created by a jeweller. One may suspect that the same jeweller fitted both Captain Foley's and Mr Burnett's medals.

The Trafalgar Roll by Colonel Mackenzie provides a brief, but sufficient sketch of the Life of Sir William Burnett, Kt., K.C.B., K.C.H., F.R.S., M.D.:

'Director-General of the Medical Department of the Navy, was the son of William Burnett, of Montrose, N.B., was born in Montrose in 1779 and entered the service in 1796. Served as Assisstant-Surgeon in the *Goliath* in the battle of St Vincent, 1797; at the bombardment of Cadiz, 1797; and in the battle of the Nile, 1798. Surgeon, 1799. Surgeon of the *Athenian* in the expedition to Egypt, 1801; and the *Blanche* at the capture of Cape Francois, 1803 and in the operations at Curacao, 1804. Surgeon of the *Defiance* in Sir Robert Calder's action and at Trafalgar, 1805. Physician, R.N. 1810. Inspector of Hospitals in the Mediterranean, 1810 - 1813, and to the prisoners of war at Chatham during a dangerous epidemic of fever in 1814. M.D.,

Aberdeen University; L.R.C.P., 1825. Knighted and created K.C.H., 1831. C.B., 1832. Director-General of the Medical Department of the Navy, 1833. Physician in Ordinary to George IV, 1835. F.R.C.P., 1836. In 1841 the Naval Medical Service presented him with his portrait in oils and with a service in plate. He was the author of several scientific publications. Died in Chichester, Sussex, 1861.'

The DNB provides a longer account of his medical career and notes that:

'after Trafalgar Burnett was in charge of the hospitals for prisoners of war at Portsmouth and Foton. His diligence in his most arduous hospital duties recommended Burnett in 1810 to be physician and inspector of hospitals to the Mediterranean Fleet, then including 120 sail of all classes. His health became so much impaired that he returned to England towards the end of 1813, but in March following he was able to undertake the medical charge of the Russian fleet in the Medway, which was suffering severely from fever. He combined with this the charge for the prisoners of war at Chatham, among whom a virulent fever was raging. When he took charge of the hospital ship one surgeon had died, two others were dangerously ill, and fifteen patients had gangrene of the lower limbs. The season was most inclement, snow lay deep, and the prisoners were disorderly; yet Burnett went about his duties fearlessly, going alone among the prisoners and gradually establishing an improved state of things.'

There is another reference to Mr Burnett, which includes one of the best yarns to come out of the battle of Trafalgar.

About noon, on 21st of October, 1805, *Defiance* with Philip Durham as Captain, was closing up behind *Revenge*, in Lord Collingwood's column off Cape Trafalgar. The combined fleets of France and Spain lay before them. Following passing shots with several ships, and now about 2:00 p.m., *Defiance* at last came to the French 74, *Le Aigle*. Dudley Pope relates what happened next:

'Durham had to break off his chase of the *Principe de Austurias* because of damage to the rigging of the *Defiance*, and shortly afterwards met the *Aigle*, fresh from her encounter with the *Revenge* and apparently having been severely handled. She was, however, quite ready for action and defended herself most gallantly for some time; at length her fire began to slacken and Captain Durham, thinking she had surrendered, called up his boarders to take possession. But every one of *Defiance*'s boats was riddled with shot. There was little or no breeze to get the British ship alongside the *Aigle*, and this situation inspired young Midshipman Jack Spratt, described as a 'high-spirited Irishman and one of the handsomest men in the service.'

'Spratt volunteered to swim over to the French ship, and Durham agreed. Sticking an axe in his belt and a cutlass in his teeth, called upon boarders to follow, leapt overboard and swam to the *Aigle*, followed by a few men. Having scrambled up the stern to a gun port, by means of the rudder chains, he quickly discovered that she had not surrendered but, (probably having surprise as an ally) he managed to fight through the decks to get up to the poop.

'Here, three French soldiers with bayonets fixed to their muskets charged him. Grabbing a signal halyard, he swung himself up onto an arms chest and before they could repeat the operation, disabled two of them. Seizing the third soldier, he tried to fling him down the ladder onto the quarterdeck, but the Frenchman grabbed Spratt as he fell. The Frenchman landed on his head, breaking his neck, and Spratt sprawled unhurt on top of him. By this time some other men from the *Defiance* had managed to get aboard and were beginning to fight their way through the ship. Their yells, the clash of cutlasses, the popping of the muskets - sounding like toys against the heavy detonation of the guns of the ships around - echoed across the decks.

'Spratt had just saved the life of a French officer who had surrendered when he saw another French soldier, bayonet fixed to his musket, making a lunge. Spratt parried with his cutlass and the Frenchman immediately aimed his musket at the midshipman's chest and squeezed the trigger. Spratt again struck out with his cutlass and managed to knock the musket barrel down as it fired, but the ball hit his right leg just below the knee, breaking both bones. Managing to avoid falling over, Spratt then hopped between two quarter-deck guns to get his back against the bulwark and thus prevent anyone cutting him down from behind.

'The French soldier made repeated jabs with his bayonet, and he was joined by two more. All three attacked Spratt, but fortunately some of the boarding party arrived and saved him. These men had managed to get lines across to the *Defiance* from the *Aigle*, so that Captain Durham could warp the ships together. One of the first people that he saw through the smoke on the French ship's bulwarks was Spratt, who had dragged himself to the side and, holding his bleeding limb over the rail, called out, 'Captain, poor old Jack Spratt is done up at last!' He was brought on board and taken below to the Surgeon, William Burnett.'

The British boarders in the end had to abandon the fight as the French came back in strength. Durham, then recalled his men, had the *Defiance* stand off to pistol shot, and then poured broadside after broadside into the brave *Aigle*. Finally, she surrendered. Her causalities amounted to nearly all officers dead or wounded, and two thirds of her crew likewise. Aboard *Defiance*, there were 17 killed and 53 wounded, with Jack Spratt amongst them.

'A few days later Burnett went to Durham, asking for a written order to amputate Spratt's leg, saying it could not be saved and the Irishman refused the operation. Durham went below to remonstrate with him. Spratt thereupon held out the other leg and exclaimed, 'Never! If I lose my leg, where shall I find a match for this?' Too crippled to serve at sea again, he was promoted to lieutenant and put in charge of the telegraph station at Dawlish.'

From Douglas - Morris's *NGS Roll*, we find that James Spratt, Master's Mate on board *Defiance* at Trafalgar, and Midshipman on board *Bellona* at Copenhagen 1801, survived and lived to receive his two clasp medal in 1848.

From the same source, we can see that Sir William Burnett also received the NGS with the clasps St Vincent, Nile, Egypt and Trafalgar.

Provenance: Seaby in 1945 for £11. Spink in 1955 for £250. Victory medal fair, 1995..

References: *England Expects* by Dudley Pope, Weidenfeld & Nicolson, London, 1959.
The Naval General Service Medal Roll 1793 - 1840, by Capt. Kenneth Douglas - Morris, published privately, London, 1982.
The Trafalgar Roll, by Colonel Mackenzie, George Allen, London, 1913.
Dictionary of National Biography, Oxford University Press, 1975.

DN 03 Chaplain Edward Southouse, HMS Goliath, Captain Thomas Foley

Description: An original Boulton bronze-gilt medal in company with other family medals for the Crimean War and Chitral Campaign. Extremely fine except for a long test mark on the obverse rim.

Background: That Surgeon Burnett received a bronze gilt medal it also appears that the Chaplain received the same. It is particularly interesting to see the Davison Nile in a family group of 19th century medals.

Michael Lewis tells us about this peculiar post within a King's ship. Lewis refers to the Reverend Edward Mangin of HMS *Gloucester* who

174

left a memoir published by the Navy Record Society, vol XCI, edited by Thursfield, Mangin appears to have taken up a post at sea for barely four months which was 'undertaken partly because he was temporarily hard up and partly out of curiosity as to how other folk lived.'

'If Mangin, then, was not a typical naval chaplain, who was? The answer is curious. It is exceedingly doubtful whether there was such a thing. In several respects these naval clergymen differed markedly from all other naval figures. First in their status. They were not commissioned officers, and though (since Pepys's day) they had been appointed to their posts by Warrant of the Admiralty, they were not really regarded as Warrant Officers either. Nor were they paid as such, receiving up till 1797 the pay of the lowest rating in the ship and, after that date, a pay lower than the lowest - though, as we shall see, they had their allowances. Yet they were not, and were never regarded as Lower Deck, either by the officers or the seamen. That could hardly be because, in the nature of the case, they were educated men with university degrees.'

Although naval regulations required a chaplain to be on board every ship larger than a fifth rate, this is a rule that was regularly not followed mainly because there were so few clergymen who would accept the terms of a naval life. Although the Master taught navigation and the officers and petty officers, seamanship, it was the Chaplain who would teach 'the letters and numbers', to the young gentlemen in the absence of a Schoolmaster as well as assisting the Captain's Clerk. Providing a good Christian service on Sunday was the essential duty and while at action stations, the Chaplain would be found in the cockpit assisting the Surgeon and helping to tend to the wounded and particularly the dying.

The Reverend Cooper Willyams was on board the *Swiftsure* at the Nile and in 1802 published his 'A Voyage up the Mediterranean in His Majesty's Ship the Swiftsure'. One would think that this would be a prime source for the battle, but when it came to it, the Reverend tells us that the detail is so well known, that he won't bore us with it! This is, however, an interesting book as there are details of shipboard life and the places of historic interest that *Swiftsure* visited.

We don't have much information regarding Edward Southouse except that he came on board *Goliath* on 28 March 1797 and remained until 24 April 1799 when he resigned his post. He next appears on board *Foudroyant* on 1 October 1803 at Plymouth, but only stayed until the end of January 1804. He returned to sea at the end of April though on board HMS *Queen*, and remained on board her for nearly a year when he was discharged on 18 April 1805.

He doesn't appear to have returned to the sea. From the web is a note regarding Woolstone, Gloucester where the rector was Edward Southouse from 1795 to 1829. There is a further intriguing document listed on the National Archives website which mentions that in a Memorandum dated 15 September 1813, the Reverend Edward Southouse has returned to Woolstone 'after many years as Chaplain in the Army.' This may well be our man. Perhaps he decided that riding a horse was a better option than riding the waves.

Provenance: OMRS medal fair, 1992.

References: The National Archives, Kew: ADM 35/677 (Goliath), ADM 35/640 (Foudroyant), ADM 35/1396, 2392 (Queen).
The Sea Chaplains by Gordon Taylor, Oxford Illustrated Text, Oxford, 1978.
A Social History of the Navy 1793 - 1815 by Michael Lewis, George Allen and Unwin, London, 1960.

DN 04   Andrew Nicol, Landsman and his 'sea wife' Mary Williams, HMS Goliath, Captain Thomas Foley

Description: Jeweller gilt bronze medal engraved *Andrew Nicol / Mary Williams* in the reverse field. Holed for wearing and in very worn condition. From the condition of the engraving of Andrew Nicol's name, it appears that he wore the medal for some time before Mary Williams's name was added. That her name is inscribed on the Davison Nile certainly would indicate that she took part in the battle, and perhaps some time after the battle the relationship between Andrew and Mary became more permanent which warranted the adding of her name to the medal. All speculation, but that would certainly explain why the two names were engraved in two different hands and at different times. It also appears from the condition of the engraving of her name, that the medal was put aside and no longer worn. Weight: 40 grams.

Background: Andrew Nicol was 28 years old from Dysart on the Firth of Forth when he joined the *Goliath* from HMS *Edgar* on 16 February 1796 and remained on board until 6 December 1799 when he was discharged to the *Royal William*. Therefore he was at both the battles of Cape St Vincent on 14 February 1797 and the Nile on 1 August 1798.

From the *Royal William* (really a receiving and transit ship), he was discharged on 14 January 1800 to HMS *Elephant*, Captain Thomas Foley, where he is noted as being 30 years of age and an Ordinary Seaman. He was on board *Elephant* at the battle of Copenhagen, 2 April 1801 and remained with the ship until she was paid off at Chatham on 3 January 1805. *Elephant* was Lord Nelson's flagship at Copenhagen and full details regarding her at the battle may be found in DN 27, Colonel William Stewart. From the Douglas-Morris medal roll, we can see a number of men who had served with Foley on board *Goliath* also served under him on board *Elephant*, which leads one to think that Captain Foley may well have requested a number of steady men he was used to working with to transfer to his new ship.

But, this particular Davison Nile bears two names with the second certainly being that of a woman. That there were women on board His Majesty's ships is not in dispute. The difficulty is that they weren't entered into the ship's books so we have no information regarding Mary Williams, although it does appear from the engraved medal that she was with Andrew Nicol at the Nile.

From Michael Lewis we learn;

'There certainly was a woman in the *Defiance* at Trafalgar. Her name was Jane Townshend and forty-two years later, she proved her claim to the [Naval] General Service Medal. Further, Queen Victoria herself said that she should have it, though the Admiralty got out of giving it to her on the grounds of dangerous precedent - it would, they alleged, 'leave the Army exposed to innumerable applications.' Likewise, there were certainly two women present at the battle of the Nile - Ann Hopping and Mary Ann Riley - whose claims were not denied, but refused for the same reason. Only those still living in 1847 could claim the medal, and many years - no less than forty-nine in the case of the Nile - had elapsed. How many women were at the Nile? Unfortunately we will never know. Interesting to see the painting by Thomas Stothard of a gun crew in 1798 which depicts a woman dragging a wounded gunner away from the cannon.

The account left by John Nicol is particularly interesting. At the Nile, his action-station was the powder-magazine of the *Goliath*, under direction of the Gunner:

'Any information we got was from the boys and the women who carried the powder. The women behaved as well as the men....I was much indebted to the Gunner's wife who gave her husband and me a drink of wine every now and then....Some of the women were wounded, and one woman belonging to Leith died of her wounds. One woman bore a son in the heat of action; she belonged to Edinburgh.'

There you have it, a first hand account of the women on board *Goliath*. It is interesting that Andrew Nicol and John Nicol both appear to have come from the area around the Firth of Forth and a woman having died during the battle, who came from John Nichol's home town of Leith.

Peter Kemp also tells us:

'Oddly enough, it was also in HMS *Goliath* that four women actually had their names entered in the muster book, entitling them to an official issue of victuals. They were Sarah Bates, Ann Taylor, Elizabeth Moore and Mary French, and they were 'victualled at 2/3 allowance per Captain's order in consideration of their assistance in dressing and attending on the wounded, being wives of men slain in the fight with the enemy on 1st August, 1798.' (National Archives ADM 36/14817 Muster book of HMS *Goliath*.)

From Virginia Medlen's Nile roll, we have John Bates, AB, Killed In Action, 1 August; William Taylor, AB, 'Discharged Dead on 7 August of wounds'; William Moore, Ord., 'DD on 31 August of wounds; William French, Private, KIA 1 August. It all fits.

John Nicol also leaves us with a vivid description of the aftermath of the battle:

'When we ceased firing, I went on deck to view the state of the fleets, and an awful sight it was. The whole bay was covered with dead bodies, mangled, wounded, and scorched, not a bit of clothes on them except their trowsers.'

The *Goliath* continued in the Mediterranean for a while but was found so leaky that she returned to England for a refit. Both John and Andrew Nicol changed ships in December 1799 and went into transit on board the *Royal William*. Andrew joined HMS *Elephant* in January 1800 where John Nicol joined HMS *Ramilies* for a short while and then to HMS *Ajax* and returned to Egypt and took part in the British landings during 1801. With the peace of Amiens in 1802, John Nicol came ashore and having effectively avoided the press gang in the following years, retired from the sea.

As both John and Andrew had served in HMS *Edgar* and *Goliath* together, did they serve in the same crew on other ships? We know that John Nicol was prest out of the Indiaman *Nottingham* into the *Edgar*. He says June 1794, but actually, June 1795. Andrew Nicol volunteered in March 1795 and came on board *Edgar* on 2 May when she was at Sheerness. It looks most likely that John Nicol was prest in the next month to fill out the ship's complement. Both men certainly served together in *Edgar* and *Goliath*, but that appears to be the extent of it. That they would have known each other on board ship is almost certain with their close links with the Firth of Forth and after five years of sailing together.

Provenance: Glenn Stein, 1992.

References: The National Archives, Kew: ADM35/677, ADM 36/14817.
A Social History of the Navy 1793 - 1815 by Michael Lewis, George Allen and Unwin, London, 1960.
The Life and Adventures of John Nicol, Mariner, by himself, Blackwood & Cadell, London, 1822, reprinted Farrar & Rinehart, New York, 1936.
The British Sailor, a social history of the lower deck, by Peter Kemp, Dent, London, 1970.
The Nile Roll, by Virginia Medlen, unpublished mss created during 1995 - 1998.
The Naval General Service Medal Roll, 1793 - 1840 by Captain Douglas-Morris, published privately, London, 1982.

DN 05 John [Josh] Glover, Ordinary Seaman, HMS Zealous, Captain Samuel Hood

Description: Jeweller gilt bronze medal, chased with a hole for suspension. The reverse field engraved 'Jofh Glover, Zealous G.B.' There is a small die break running through C. H. K. with a larger break below at the rim. Weight: 39.6 grams. Very fine.

Background: John Glover was from London and 23 years old when he joined HMS *Zealous* on 22 October 1794. He was rated Ordinary Seaman. Whether he was prest or volunteered for service isn't known, but it does appear that he was a seasoned sailor in 1794 and it is felt that he was probably prest from a merchant ship not long before joining *Zealous*.

HMS *Zealous* was one of the Arrogant Class of Third Rate 74-gun ships designed by Slade in 1758 and would have had a ship's company of 550 men. She was built by Barnard at Deptford and launched on 25 June 1785. She was 168 feet in length, 1604 tons burthen and bore 28 x 32 pounders on the Gun Deck, 28 x 18 pounders on the Upper Deck, 14 x 9 pounders on the Quarterdeck and 4 x 9 pounders in the Forecastle. She was broken up in 1816.

Glover stayed on board *Zealous* until May 1800 when he moved with his captain, Sir Samuel Hood, from *Zealous* to *Courageux*, where he remained until she was paid off in April, 1802.

It is with Hood that *Zealous* really made her name. His commission commenced on board *Zealous* in April 1796. Sir John Jervis was Admiral of the Mediterranean fleet with Commodore Nelson supporting him. Unfortunately, *Zealous* was being refitted at Lisbon when Sir John and Nelson scored their decisive victory over the Spanish at Cape St Vincent on 14 February 1797. Following this victory, Sir John Jervis was elevated to Earl St Vincent and Nelson was made a Rear-Admiral.

In order to keep the pressure on the Spanish, the British mounted several bombardments on their fleet anchored in Cadiz harbour. William James provides the detail, which has been condensed:

'A reinforcement from England having joined St Vincent, and the ships that had suffered in the action [of 14 February], having repaired their damages, Earl St Vincent on 31 March quitted Lisbon with 21 sail of the line and proceeded to Cadiz; where lay the Spanish fleet, 26 ships of the line, all of which, as far as soldiers could supply the deficiency of seamen, were fully manned.

'With the view of provoking Admiral Massaredo to attempt putting to sea, and also perhaps to employ the minds of the seamen and divert them from following the mischievous example of the ships in England [during the mutinies of 1797], St Vincent resolved to bombard the town of Cadiz. On the night of 3 July the *Thunder* bomb-vessel, covered by the gun-boats, launches and barges of the fleet, under the orders of Rear-Admiral Sir Horatio Nelson, who commanded the advance of the in-shore squadron, took her station near the tower of Sans Sebastian, and within 2,500 yards of the wall of the town; then containing a garrison of upwards of 4,000 men and protected on the bay side by 70 pieces of cannon and eight large mortars. The *Thunder* commenced throwing her shells with great precision, but the large 13 1/2 inch mortar was soon discovered to be defective and the *Goliath*, and other ships came forward to screen the removal of the bomb-vessel.

'The retreat of the *Thunder* was the signal for a number of Spanish gun-boats and armed launches to sally forth in hope to capture her. These were met by a similar British force led by Rear-Admiral Nelson. The Spanish commandant, Don Miguel Tyrason, attempted in his barge with a crew of 26 men to carry the comparatively small boat in which Nelson, with 15 hands beside himself, was pushing into the thickest of the fire. A hand-to-hand scuffle ensued, in which both commanders took a conspicuous part. At length, Don Miguel, having had 18 of his men killed and himself and all of the remainder wounded, was compelled to surrender. After this, the Spaniards were driven back and pursued to the walls of Cadiz; leaving in the possession of the British two mortar-vessels and the commandant's launch. Amongst the twenty British killed and wounded was John Sykes, a seaman, severely, in the act of defending the person of the Rear-Admiral, to whom he was coxswain.'

There followed another attempt to bombard Cadiz on 5 July which resulted in another clash between the Spanish and British gun-boats, barges and other ships boats, but it did have the effect of destroying warehouses and some shipping.

Soon after, a rumour circulated that at Santa Cruz, Tenerife was anchored a Manila galleon loaded with riches, enough to divert the attention of any true hearted Jack Tar!

St Vincent detailed a squadron, under the command of Nelson and comprising the *Theseus*, Captain Miller, *Culloden*, Captain Troubridge, *Zealous*, Captain Hood, *Leander*, Captain Thompson and the frigates *Seahorse*, *Emerald*, *Terpsichore* and the *Fox* cutter; which all set sail on 15 July, arriving at Santa Cruz on the 20th.

After several attempts to secure a landing amongst contrary winds and currents, on the 25th at 1:30 a.m., around 1,100 seamen and marines attempted to land in the ships' boats. They were greeted by around 30 or 40 cannon and a strong body of troops. Rear-Admiral Nelson took a shot in the elbow and was returned to his ship. Further desperate fighting cost the life of Captain Richard Bowen and although some objectives were secured, the main body of men had been largely repulsed. By daybreak, in the Prado, or central square of Santa Cruz, Captains Troubridge, Hood and Miller had joined forces which included about 340 men made up of 80 marines, 80 pikemen and 180 seamen with small arms. The situation was hopeless as they were surrounded and the boats they had landed in were largely wrecked.

But, given the circumstances, Troubridge directed Hood to see if he could find a way for an honourable withdrawal. Hood then met with the Spanish Governor, Don Juan Antoine Gutterry and delivered his ultimatum, 'I am come, Sir, from the Commanding Officer of the British troops and seamen now within your walls, and in possession of the principal strutto, to say, that as we are disappointed in the object which we came for (to secure treasure), provided you will furnish us with boats - those we came in being all lost - we will return peaceably to our ships; but, should any means be taken to molest or retard us, we will fire your town in different places, and force our way out of it at the point of the bayonet.'

Don Gutterry was astonished by this proposal by those whom he felt were his prisoners, however upon reflection decided that enough blood had been shed, and accepted Captain Hood's terms. Thus escaped Troubridge, Hood and several hundred seamen and marines from an almost certain death or imprisonment in a Spanish prisoner of war camp. We don't know if John Glover was amongst those men, but he certainly was with the crew of *Zealous* at the time.

Captain Samuel Hood writing to his uncle, Viscount Hood, shortly after the battle of the Nile provides the best account of *Zealous* during the action. Both *Goliath* and *Zealous* were ahead of the rest of Nelson's fleet and the honour of being the first ship to engage the enemy was one which both Foley and Hood would have liked. As noted, Foley had a good French chart of the Bay, so *Zealous* gave way to *Goliath* as they both approached the leading French ship, the *Guerrier*.

'The *Goliath* ahead and *Zealous* following, and as we approached the van ship of the enemy shortened sail gradually; the Admiral allowing the *Orion* to pass ahead of the *Vanguard* as well as the *Audacious* and *Theseus*, we had not increased our distance much from those ships. The van ship of the enemy being in five fathoms water expected the *Goliath* and *Zealous* to stick on the shoal every moment, and did not imagine we should attempt to pass within her.

'The van with mortars, &c, on the island firing regularly at us. Captain Foley of course intended anchoring abreast of the van ship [the *Guerrier*], but his sheet anchor (the cable out the stern port) not dropping the moment he wished it, [he] missed and brought up abreast of the second ship having given the van ship his fire. I saw immediately he had failed of his intention, cut away the *Zealous*' sheet anchor and came to in the exact situation Captain Foley intended to have taken, the van ship of the enemy having his larboard bow toward the *Zealous*; we having received very little damage notwithstanding a fire from the whole van, island &c, as we came in.

'I commenced [such] a well directed fire into her bow within pistol shot a little after six that her fore mast went by the board in about seven minutes, just as the sun was closing the horizon; on which the whole squadron gave three cheers, it happening before the next ship astern of *Zealous* engaged. And in ten minutes more her main and mizen masts [went]; at this time also went the *Goliath* and *Audacious*, but I could not get her commander to strike for three hours, though I hailed him twenty times, and seeing he was totally cut up and only firing a stern gun now and then at the *Goliath* and *Audacious*. At last being tired [of] firing and killing people in that way, I sent my boat on board her, and the lieutenant was allowed with the jolly-boat to hoist a light and haul it down to show his submission. From the time her fore mast fell they had been driven from the upper decks by our canister and musketry; and I assure your Lordship from her bow to her larboard gangway the ports on the main deck are entirely in one, and her gunwale in that part entirely cut away, two of the main deck beams fallen on the guns in consequence. And [she] is so much cut up that we cannot move her without great detention and expense, so I fancy the Admiral will destroy her. [Brian Lavery notes that *Zealous* had only seven men wounded, and that the loses of the *Guerrier* must have been in the hundreds.]

Zealous stayed by *Guerrier* for the rest of the night, but in the morning, Captain Hood recounts:

'The *Theseus*, *Goliath*, *Audacious* and *Zealous* were ordered to the rear [of the enemy line] having little suffered; but as I was going down, the Admiral made my signal to chase the *Diane* frigate, which was under way and attempting to escape. However, she returning and closing with the enemy's ships that had not struck, I was called in and ordered to go to the assistance of the *Bellerophon* who lay at anchor the other side of the Bay; but as I was going down I perceived about 12 o'clock at noon, as I was getting near that ship, the *Guillaume Tell* 80, *Genereux* 74, *Diane* and *Justice* of 40, pressing to make their escape, being the only ships that were not in the least disabled. I immediately directed the *Zealous* to keep close on a wind, in the hope I should be able to bring them to action, and disable them in such a manner as to allow our ships to come to my assistance (there being then none under sail), and that should I disable them at all they could not fetch out of the bay. I just weathered them within musket shot and obliged the *Guillaume Tell* to keep away to prevent my raking her; and through I did them a great deal of damage, they were so well prepared as to cut away every bowline, boom, topmast and standing rigging, sails, &c away. I intended to have boarded the rear frigate, but could not get the ship round for a short space of time; and when I was doing it Sir Horatio called me in by signal, seeing I should only get disabled and not stop them with such a superior force.'

Following the battle of the Nile, Hood and *Zealous* were left in command of a small squadron, which included *Goliath*, to blockade the port of Alexandria. In February 1799, *Zealous* went to Naples where Hood became involved in the fights against the Republicans in both Salerno and Naples. *Zealous* returned to England in December, 1800 and John Glover was discharged in May of that year. Captain Hood was appointed to HMS *Courageux* in that month, and John Glover followed him, which is a good indication that he was a well trusted hand.

The period from May 1800 to April 1802 was spent with *Courageux* being part of the Channel Fleet, which provided little opportunity for adventure. The ship was paid off at Plymouth on 23 April with the Peace of Amiens, and we lose sight of John Glover.

The ever active Sam Hood changed ships to HMS *Venerable* and took part at the battle of Algeciras on 8 July 1801 and in Saumarez's action in the Straits of Gibraltar on 12 July. In the Straits his ship suffered heavily, losing 130 officers and men.

Following the Peace of Amiens, Hood took command of HMS *Centaur* of 74 guns and sailed to the West Indies. Upon the death of the flag officer of the Leeward Islands, Hood succeeded him as Commodore. There followed a very aggressive period where island after island fell to the British. Hood's audacity was marked by the commissioning of HMS *Diamond Rock* which was a pinnacle of stone that rose 600 feet from the sea and stood less than a mile from the shores of Martinique and with British cannon and gunners under the command of Lieutenant Maurice, became a decided thorn in the side of French shipping. It wasn't until May 1805 when the garrison finally surrendered to the French, mainly due to lack of water and supplies.

Hood returned to Europe in the *Centaur* and commanded as Commodore the squadron blockading Rochefort. He lost his arm in an ill fated brush with a squadron of French frigates on 25 September 1806. Staying with *Centaur*, he was promoted to Rear-Admiral and in 1808, in support of the Royal Swedish Navy, captured the Russian 50-gun *Sevolod* following a desperate fight.

In 1814, Hood took command of the East Indies Station at Madras, and unfortunately succumbed to a fever and was buried there. Hood was certainly one of the most brilliant captains of the period and his loss was greatly felt.

Provenance: Medal fair, 1980.

References: The National Archives, Kew: ADM 35/2083, ADM 36/12501, 12502, 12503, 12504, 12505, 12506, 12507, 12508, 12509, 12510 (HMS *Zealous*)
The National Archives: ADM 36/11230, 14108 (HMS *Vengence* and *Victorious*)
The National Archives: ADM 35/355, 356, ADM 36/14635, 14636, 14637 (HMS *Courageux*)
The Naval History of Great Britain...1793 to 1820 by William James, six vols., Richard Bentley, London, 1837 etc.
Nelson and the Nile by Brian Lavery, Chatham, London, 1998.
Logs of the Great Sea Fights 1794-1805 by Sturges Jackson, Navy Records Society, London, 1899-1900.
The Admirals Hood by Dorothy Hood, Hutchinson, London, circa 1941.
The Sailing Navy List by David Lyon, Conway, London, 1993.

Captain Hood's Puzzle Picture

This montage was drawn by Lieutenant George Bell Lawrence of HMS *Centaur* as a celebration of the success of the ship and most particularly the success of her captain, Sir Samuel Hood.

The picture was painted sometime in 1806 and contains a number of items that relate to Hood and *Centaur*, but most intriguing of all are the puzzles which must have been old saws that would always bring much laughter at the captain's table. A wonderful reminder as to how much fun it must have been to be at sea in a winning ship with a great Captain.

- Question: If a woman changes her sex, what religion would she be? Nonconformist!

- Question: Why do we go to bed? Because the bed won't come to you!

- Question: Why is a drawn tooth like a thing forgot? Because it goes completely out of your head!

- Why is an Ugly Woman like the Lord's Prayer? Because she leads you not into temptation!

- Why is the Rock of Gibraltar like a feather bed? Because it's down from head to foot!

- Where was Peter when his candle went out? In the Dark!!

DN 06 Ship's Corporal William Eustace, HMS Zealous, Captain Samuel Hood

Description: Bronze-gilt medal, cased in gold and glazed. This appears be an original Soho gilt medal. The rim of the case is engraved in script: *Mr. W. Eustace. H. M. Ship Zealous. Sir S. Hood Commander.* Weight: 55.5 grams. Extremely Fine.

Background: From Gillian Hughes, there is the following report regarding her discoveries at the National Archives, Kew:

'William Eustace entered HMS *Vengeance* from *Ceres* on 14 May 1794, rated AB. The ship was paid off on 23 October of that year at Chatham. Many of the men were turned over to HMS *Zealous*, Captain Samuel Hood, who entered that vessel on 22 October 1794. William Eustace was listed in the Pay Book as No. 468, born London, aged 23, rated Able Seaman. He was rated Ship's Corporal 24 April 1797 and discharged to HMS *Courageux*, following his Captain, though Hood was superseded on 7 January 1801, and was again listed as Ship's Corporal by her new Captain. He was then promoted to Master-at-Arms with his warrant dated 10 November 1800 which was confirmed in the Succession Books of Inferior Officers. The ship was paid off on 27 April 1802 and at this point no further record of him was found.'

Michael Lewis tells us about the Warrant Officers, of which there were three Standing Officers, i.e. men who were actually part of the ship like standing rigging and always stayed with a particular ship from the day she was launched to the day she was broken up. The Standing Officers were the Gunner, Boatswain and Carpenter. Below the station of the Standing Warrant Officers were the Minor Warrant Officers which included the Sailmaker, Ropemaker, the Armourer, the Caulker, the Cook and the Master-at-Arms, head of the ship's police. The ship's corporals would work for the Master-at-Arms.

185

From Admiral Smyth's *Sailor Word Book*, he tells us the following regarding the Master-at-Arms:

'In former times the Master-at-Arms was an officer appointed to command the police-duty of a ship, to teach the crew the exercise of small arms, to confine by order of superiors any prisoners, and to superintend their confinement. Also, to take care that fires and lights were put out at the proper hour, and no spirituous liquors brought on board. He was assisted by the ship's corporals, who also attended the gangway with the sentinels. Until 1816, the junior lieutenant was nominally lieutenant-at-arms, and drilled the seamen, assisted by the sergeant of marines.'

This was a difficult job on board ship, particularly when it came to being on easy terms with the rest of the crew. But, there is little doubt that being expert in the use of the ship's small arms would mean that Ship's Corporals were most handy in a fight, particularly when boarding an enemy ship, although Michael Lewis notes that the action station for the Master-at-Arms was to manage the Light Room, located by the ship's magazine. That William Eustace excelled in his post and was highly regarded by his captain there is little doubt, particularly as evidenced by his promotion to Master-at-Arms when on board *Courageux*.

Provenance: Medal fair, 1997.

References: The National Archives, Kew: ADM 35/1962 (Vengeance), ADM 35/2083, ADM 36/12508 & 12511 (*Zealous*), ADM 35/356 (*Courageux*), ADM 6/185 Succession Books.
A Social History of the Navy 1793 - 1815 by Michael Lewis, George Allen and Unwin, London, 1960.
The Sailor's Word-Book, by Admiral W. H. Smyth, Blackie, London, 1867.
The Nile Roll, by Virginia Medlen, unpublished mss created during 1995 - 1998.

DN 07   Corporal William Trout, 90th Regiment of Foot & Marine, HMS Audacious, Captain Davidge Gould

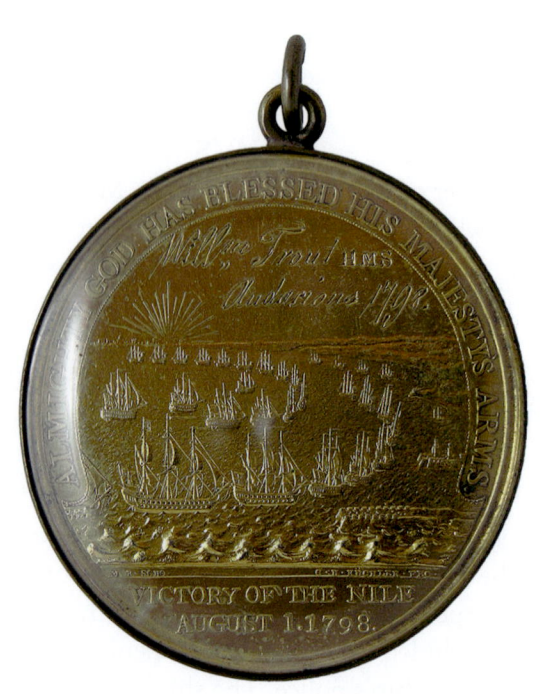

Description: Jeweller gilt bronze medal, cased and glazed. The reverse field is inscribed *Willm Trout HMS /Audacious 1798*. There is a small die break running through C. H. K. with a larger break below at the rim. Weight: 57.7 grams. Extremely Fine.

Background: From Major Lawrence-Archer we learn that the 90th Perthshire Volunteers were raised in 1794 and their first Colonel was Sir Thomas Graham, then Mr Graham, Laird of Balgowan. Graham had served as a volunteer at the siege of Toulon, but as he was an untrained officer, found it difficult to gain a proper commission, so upon his return to Scotland he founded the Perthshire Volunteers which was entered into the British Army as the 90th of Foot.

The regiment comprised 95 Highlanders, 430 Lowlanders, 165 English and 56 Irish soldiers who were ordered to be equipped and trained as Light Infantry. The uniform consisted of a red 'wing jacket and waistcoat faced with buff.' The officers wore 'tights and hessians', while the men appeared in grey trousers. The headdress was a rounded leather helmet of the form peculiar to dragoons of the period.

Soon after the First Battalion of the 90th was raised, a second battalion was formed which ultimately merged with the Marines.

The original battalion served in the Quiberon expedition of 1795 and the occupation of Isle Dieu, afterwards proceeding to Gibraltar. The 90th were at the capture of Minorca in November 1798 and remained a short time in garrison there. During this period it is said that Sir John Moore took a special interest in observing the 90th at drill and subsequently adopted its system, which was introduced at Shorncliffe, and prevailed throughout the Peninsular War.

Under Colonel Richard Hill, afterwards Lord Hill, the regiment particularly distinguished itself in Egypt in 1801 during the advance from Aboukir to Alexandria and at the tower of Mandora, where it appears to have manoeuvred by the 'bugle'. It was at the actions before Alexandria, at Rosetta and in the advance on Cairo.

It appears that Corporal William Trout was amongst the founding members of the Second Battalion of the 90th of Foot as he was entered on the 2nd August 1794. He continued in this capacity until 24 December 1795.

From the muster list of HMS *Audacious* is noted that on 16 April 1795 were entered a group of 'Soldiers belonging to the 90th Regiment serving in lieu of Marines and borne as part of the Complement.' He was discharged on 16 June 1796, but the next day re-entered as a Private Marine until 12 January 1797, when 'By request of Captain [of Marines] James Weir', William Trout was promoted to Corporal. On 4 December 1797, he was broken back to Private and on 2 July 1798 promoted again to Corporal. He was discharged from the *Audacious* on 26 January 1801 at Plymouth.

The records provide the order dated 20 April 1801 (ADM 183/5): 'The under mentioned detachments to march tomorrow morning at 6 o'clock for Woolwich and Deptford to embark on board the vessels hereafter expressed, viz *Mariner*: 1 Sergeant, 1 Corporal and 12 Men.'

On 23 April 1801, Trout was entered on the books of HM Gun Brig *Mariner*, Captain David Williams, as a Sergeant Marine. *Mariner* appears to have been part of the coastal defence for the Thames estuary and Kent coast. Unfortunately for William Trout, on the 16th of June 1801, while exercising his men on shore, he lost two fingers while loading his musket. He was subsequently discharged to hospital and ultimately pensioned off.

HMS *Audacious* was one of the Arrogant Class of Third Rate 74-gun ships designed by Slade in 1758 and would have had a ship's company of 550 men. She was built by Randall at Rotherhithe and launched on 23 July 1785. She was 168 feet in length, 1604 tons burthen and bore 28 x 32 pounders on the Gun Deck, 28 x 18 pounders on the Upper Deck, 14 x 9 pounders on the Quarterdeck and 4 x 9 pounders in the Forecastle. She was broken up in 1815.

The log of *Audacious* tells us that she didn't take part in the battle of Cape St Vincent, 14 February 1797, but maintained station at Gibraltar.

A letter from her Captain, Davidge Gould, to his uncle best describes the events of 1 August 1798:

'My dear Uncle, I did myself the pleasure to write to you from the mouth of the Nile by the *Leander*, but as that ship is unfortunately captured by the enemy, I cannot expect that you will ever receive my letter. I am therefore induced to avail myself of opportunity I now have to acquaint you of my health, which I am convinced you will be glad to hear, after all my fatigue of the summer in search of Bonaparte. etc. etc.

'I was particularly fortunate with le *Conquerant* which struck to the *Audacious*, and whose captain's sword was delivered unto one of my lieutenants. I brought my ship to an anchor so very near him and on the opposite side from what he expected, that the slaughter became so dreadful it was impossible to make their men stand to their guns.

'We are now cruising before Malta [2 December 1798], to prevent the enemy from getting any supplies, as well as to prevent the escape of the *Guillaume Tell*, which escaped us at the Nile. The French have only the garrison of Valetta, the whole of the rest of the island being in the possession of the Maltese; and, from the great discontent prevailing in the garrison, having already nothing but bread and water to subsist on, we are in great hopes to put the island in the possession of the Maltese again before long. Your affectionate nephew, D. Gould'.

John Marshall tells us that the loss to *Audacious* was one man killed and 35 wounded. Captain Gould then assisted in operations in the Mediterranean and returned to England early in 1801, which is when William Trout left the ship.

Davidge Gould then advanced through the lists to become a Vice-Admiral in 1810 and was awarded the KCB. in 1815. He wasn't amongst the brilliant officers of the period, but considered reliable and a good administrator, however his contribution at the Nile was certainly not impressive.

Provenance: Medal fair, 1985.

References: The National Archives, Kew: ADM 35/99, ADM 36/11737, 11738, 13754, 13755, 13756, 13757, 13758, 13759 (HMS *Audacious* logs and musters)

ADM 96/194, 197, 200 (Marine Effective & subsistence List, Chatham Division)
WO 12/9238 (Musters for the 90th of Foot)
The British Army by Major Lawrence - Archer, George Bell, London, 1888.
Nelson and the Nile by Brian Lavery, Chatham, London, 1998.
Logs of the Great Sea Fights 1794-1805 by Sturges Jackson, Navy Records Society, London, 1899-1900.
Royal Naval Biography by Lieut John Marshall, R.N., Longman, London, 1822-1830, (12 vols.)
The Sailing Navy List by David Lyon, Conway, London, 1993.

DN 08   Joseph Hollingrick [Allendrake], Ordinary Seaman, HMS Orion, Captain Sir James Saumarez

Description: Jeweller gilt bronze medal engraved *Joseph Hollingrick* in script. On the obverse there is a small die break running through C. H. K. with a larger break below at the rim. Weight: 39.9 grams. Nearly extremely fine. The medal may have been previously cased and glazed and at sometime the case was removed to be melted down for its bullion value.

Background: Working out a man's name can be a bit of a challenge. With the assistance of Virginia Medlen's *Nile Muster Roll*, the only man at the Nile with a name that phonetically could represent Hollingrick is Joseph Allendrake of HMS *Orion*. He was a Quota Man aged 21 from Bingley in Yorkshire and was entered in the muster of *Orion* on 19 April 1795. Gillian Hughes notes that from genealogical sources, she can see the surnames Hollindrakes and Hollingrackes located in Bingley, but no Allendrakes. As the Nile medal appears to bear the near correct spelling of a Bingley surname, it is probable that the use of Allendrake as the man's entered name may be less a mistake and more a device which may have been useful in the event of Joseph Hollingrick deciding to Run!

Michael Lewis tells us of the predicament that Mr Pitt faced in securing enough men to man the fleet. The normal method was the Press Gang which worked to secure seamen from the merchant marine, but this was a limited resource. If the Press was too aggressive, then the merchant marine would suffer which in turn would cripple trade which was even more important as the government needed the taxes that trade produced.

The solution was the Quota System wherein towns and counties were given a quota of men that their local administrations should secure for service at sea. There was no requirement for the men to have had any maritime experience, what the government wanted was raw manpower that could be trained at sea.

Michael Lewis continues: 'What the scheme was in fact, if we would tie a modern label on it, was 'Selective National Service'. And it failed - for fail it did - because those important people, the Selectors, being the wrong selectors, selected the wrong people.

'It was perhaps inevitable. These selectors, in practice the town and county authorities, were being asked to perform a perfectly new kind of duty, and were not qualified to do it. ...The scheme soon degenerated into a sort of minor gaol delivery. The counties tended to select their 'bad boys', their vagrants, tramps, and idlers. It suited the Justices of the Peace to conclude that the local poacher would be as destructive to French sailors as he was to English birds - and possibly they were right, though there was no shred of evidence to prove it.'

As one would imagine, Quota Men were viewed with suspicion by the ship's company which may have made their assimilation on board ship that much more difficult. Sink or Swim. As far as Joseph Hollingrick was concerned, he came on board as a Landsman, but by June 1797, he was rated Ordinary Seaman which means he accepted his life on board ship and progressed. He continued on board *Orion* until 6 January 1799 when she was paid off. He next served on HMS *Lowestoffe*, mainly cruising in the West Indies, until she was paid off on 6 September 1801.

HMS *Orion* was one of the Canada Class of Third Rate 74-gun ships designed by Bately in 1759 and would have had a ship's company of 550 men. She was built by Adams & Barnard at Deptford and launched on 1 June 1787. She was 170 feet in length, 1632 tons burthen and bore 28 x 32 pounders on the Gun Deck, 28 x 18 pounders on the Upper Deck, 14 x 9 pounders on the Quarterdeck and 4 x 9 pounders in the Forecastle. She was broken up in 1814.

Peter Shuyler Bruff was the Master of *Orion*, under the command of Captain Sir James Saumarez, and it is from the Master's Log that we have the following:

'*Zealous* and *Goliath* anchored opposite the first and second ships of the enemy and opened their fire. In our passing the enemy's van gave them our fire. The Admiral passed the starboard side of the enemy's van and anchored abreast of the third ship, as also did a number of ships who took their stations in the rear of our Admiral. In our passing the third ship of the line a frigate began to fire on us; got the starboard guns to bear on her which totally dismasted her, and some little time after sunk in shoal water, with her upper works above water. At 45 minutes past 6, we let go our best bower anchor and veered till abreast of the fourth ship in the enemy's van; opened our fire. As we tended on two of the ships in the rear, the one a three-deck ship, and when brought up continued a heavy and well directed fire on the ships abreast of us.

'Observed a fire raft coming down on us from one of the enemy's headmost ships. The boat over the stern shot through. Prepared to boom her off; a little time after she drifted clear of our larboard bow about 25 yards and passed on our lee quarter. 55 minutes past 6, the action became general from van to centre. At 7, observed 2 of the enemy's ships in the van dismasted and several others much disabled. The fire heavy on both sides. Hoisted 4 lights horizontally, the night signal. 1/4 past ten, perceived the 3 deck ship on fire abaft. At 10, ceased firing on account of the *Leander* being in the direction of our guns. Five of the enemy's van ships had been silenced some time. The fire having communicated fore and aft of the three-deck ship [*L'Orient*], secured the magazine, lowered down the ports, handed the sails, expecting every moment she would blow up. 1/2 past 11, she blew up.'

Sir James Saumarez came from a very old Guernsey family which dated itself back to William the Conqueror and was much associated with the sea. Captain Philip Saumarez, uncle to Sir James, sailed with Anson on his circumnavigation and the capture of the Manila Galleon.

Saumarez joined the Royal Navy in 1770 as a Midshipman, aged 13, and was very active during the American Revolutionary War, particularly on board HMS *Bristol* and then as a Lieutenant in command of the *Spitfire* galley, were he worked along the American coast searching out privateers and in assisting the Army. He took part in the ill fated action against the Dutch at Dogger Bank in 1781 against Admiral Zootman.

Following this action, Saumarez went to the West Indies with dispatches for Sir Samuel Hood, later Lord Hood, and having been promoted to Post Captain was given command at age 25 of HMS *Russell* of 74 guns and fought her at The Saints, 12 April 1782.

With the commencement of the French Revolutionary War in 1793, Saumarez was given command of HMS *Crescent*, a fine frigate of 36 guns. In October she met *le Reunion* of 36 guns off Cherbourg and after coming upon the enemy, sailing past her on the opposite tack, placed the helm hard a starboard and brought her larboard guns to bear on her stern. The result was a deadly raking fire, which caused her surrender shortly after. The loss to the enemy was estimated at around 120 killed and wounded, where Saumarez lost not a man and no man was wounded. For this success he was knighted.

CAPTURE OF LA REUNION — Oct.r 21st 1793.

It appears that Joseph Hollingrick and Sir James Saumarez both joined HMS *Orion* in the spring of 1795. At Lord Howe's great victory of 1st June 1794 she was commanded by J. T. Duckworth and fought with great distinction during the action. It is after a refit at Portsmouth, that Hollingrick and Saumarez came on board.

With *Orion* attached to Lord Bridport's squadron, she joined in the chase on 24 June 1795 of a very strong French squadron which was headed toward L'Orient. Bridport ordered his fastest ships to chase, and *Orion* was amongst them. The day ended with three enemy ships taken which included the *Alexander*, 74, which was a previously captured British ship that would prove her worth at the Nile.

The *Orion* was then detached along with two frigates to keep a watch over the French port of Rochfort. This duty continued over the next six months of hard sailing, often in the midst of storm weather. Saumarez was next ordered to join the fleet off Brest, and from there to join Sir John Jervis, which he did just five days before the battle of Cape St Vincent.

John Marshall tells us, 'the *Orion* was one of six ships that attacked the main body of the enemy's fleet, and afterwards joined in the attack on the huge *Santissima Trinidada* of four decks and 130 guns, which according to the *Orion's* log book, hauled down her colours and hoisted English ones, but was rescued by several of the enemy's fresh ships. In this engagement the *Orion* had only nine men wounded.'

Although *Orion* played her part in the action, the glory really went to Commodore Nelson and his boarding and capture of two Spanish ships of the line.

Following Cape St Vincent, *Orion* took part in the blockade of Cadiz and then in late April 1798 formed part of Rear-Admiral Nelson's squadron with Saumarez as second in command, entering the Mediterranean which culminated in the battle of 1 August 1798. *Orion* had 13 killed and 29 wounded which included Sir James who had received a severe contusion to the side, but refused to leave the quarterdeck.

After the battle, Saumarez was ordered to take the French prizes to Gibraltar and from there back to England. She arrived in Plymouth in November and with *Orion* being found in a very weak condition, the ship was paid off in January 1799.

For Joseph Hollingrick this meant being posted to HMS *Lowestoffe* on 22 January 1800 and then cruising in the West Indies with Port Royal, Jamaica as her home base. He continued in her until September 1801 when it appears the ship was paid off at Plymouth.

For Sir James, he next had command of HMS *Caesar*, 80 guns, and spent the winters of 1799 and 1800 blockading the port of Brest. In 1801 he was promoted to Rear-Admiral and the command of a small squadron watching the movements of the Spanish fleet at Cadiz. On the night of 12 July 1801 in the Gut of Gibraltar, Sir James on board *Caesar* formed his squadron in chase of the enemy. W. H. Long tells us: 'the *Superb* [74 guns, Captain R.G. Keats], being the best sailer, was ordered to crowd all sail and attack the first ship of the enemy he came up with.

'By eleven p.m. the *Superb* was nearly four miles ahead of the *Caesar* and soon after came up with the *Real Carlos*, 112 guns and another three decker, the *Hermangildo* nearly abreast of her. Captain Keats opened fire on both of them at about three cables distance, shot away the fore topmast of the *Real Carlos* and put crews of both ships into such confusion, that they fired at each other, as well as the *Superb*.

'In about a quarter of an hour, Captain Keats saw that the ship which had lost her fore topmast was on fire, upon which he ceased to molest her and stood after the *San Antonio*, 74 guns, which ship after an action of about half an hour, hailed to say she had surrendered, just as the *Caesar* and *Venerable* came up. Meanwhile the *Real Carlos* and *Hermangildo* ran foul of each other, both were soon in flames fore and aft, and shortly after midnight blew up with the greater part of their crews.'

The battle became known as the Battle of Cabareta Point or Saumarez's Action and along with the thanks of Parliament to him and his officers, he received the Knight of the Bath and a pension of £1,200 per annum.

When war broke out with Russia in 1809, Saumarez was to take HMS *Victory* to the Baltic in support of Sweden who recognised him by the award of the Order of the Sword. Following the final fall of Napoleon, Sir James continued to gain titles and became Baron de Saumarez in 1831. He died at Guernsey in 1836.

Provenance: Medal fair, 1989.

References: The National Archives, Kew: ADM 35/1212, 1213, ADM 36/11856, 11857, 11858, 11859, 11860. (Logs and Muster Roll for HMS *Orion*)
ADM 35/950, ADM 36/13940, 13941. (Log and Muster Roll for HMS *Lowestoffe*)
The Nile Roll, by Virginia Medlen, unpublished mss created during 1995 - 1998.
A Social History of the Navy 1793 - 1815 by Michael Lewis, George Allen and Unwin, London, 1960.
Nelson and the Nile by Brian Lavery, Chatham, London, 1998.
Logs of the Great Sea Fights 1794-1805 by Sturges Jackson, Navy Records Society, London, 1899-1900.
Royal Naval Biography by Lieut John Marshall, R.N., Longman, London, 1822-1830, (12 vols.)
Naval Achievements of Great Britain by James Jenkins, London, 1817, reprinted by Sim Comfort Associates, London, 1998.
Medals of the British Navy and How they were won by W. H. Long, Norie & Wilson, London, 1895.
The Sailing Navy List by David Lyon, Conway, London, 1993.

DN 09 Quarter Master Andrew Craigie, HMS Theseus, Captain Ralph Willett Miller

Description: Jeweller silvered bronze medal engraved *Theseus* 74 with a monogram for AC. There is a small break running through C. H. K. with a larger break below at the rim. This medal weighs 40.9 grams where a silver example (James Keltie, Master of the *Minotaur*) weighs 47 grams, therefore the medal to Andrew Craigie is a bronze medal that has been silver plated by a jeweller. Very fine.

Background: It is fortunate that on board *Theseus* at the battle of the Nile there was only one man with the initials AC and that was Andrew Craigie. He was a Scot from Gordon, Kincairn on the Scottish Borders near Berwick upon Tweed. Craigie was 26 years old when he appeared on board *Theseus* in February 1794 as a Volunteer and rated Able Seaman. I would think that his status as a Volunteer was simply the result that after having been prest into the service, when offered the Bounty, he knew his fate was sealed and took the only option. That he was a skilled seaman, there is no doubt and in a little more than a year from his coming on board, he was advanced to Quarter Master.

According to Smyth, the Quarter Master was, 'A petty officer appointed to assist the Master and Master's Mates in their several duties such as stowing the hold, coiling the cables, attending the binnacle and steerage, keeping time by the watch-glasses, assisting in hoisting the signals and keeping an eye on general quaterdeck movements.' In fact, this author thinks to have been a Quarter Master was one of the best jobs on board ship, there can't be a better thrill that steering a 74-gun ship when she is on a fine tack, or taking her into battle, even though you know that every enemy gun that can bear will want to blast the ship's wheel and those who steer her.

Andrew Craigie stayed with *Theseus* until November 1800 when she had returned to Chatham for refit. He then transferred to HMS *Zealand*, a transit ship at Chatham, and was discharged from her on 22 December to HMS *Texel*, which was one of the Dutch ship's surrendered in 1799 and stood duty as a floating battery to protect the naval base at Chatham. He remained on board *Texel* until 24 April 1802 when the ship was paid off and we lose site of Andrew Craigie.

HMS *Theseus* was one of the Culloden / Thunderer Class of Third Rate 74-gun ships designed by Slade in 1769 and would have a ship's company of 550 to 600 men. She was built by Perry of Blackwall and launched on 25 September 1786. She was 170 feet in length, 1652 tons burthen and bore 28 x 32 pounders on the Gun Deck, 28 x 18 pounders on the Upper Deck, 14 x 9 pounders on the Quarterdeck and 4 x 9 pounders in the Forecastle. She was broken up in 1814. She came out of Ordinary Reserve in 1793, but didn't join the Channel Fleet until early 1794 which is when Andrew Craigie joined her. Robert Calder was her captain and time was spent in convoy duty to the West Indies.

Early in 1797 command passed to Captain Frederick Aylmer and *Theseus* joined Sir John Jervis's fleet at Lisbon. Jervis felt that *Theseus* was neither an efficient nor happy ship and ordered in late May, the newly created Rear-Admiral Sir Horatio Nelson to move his flag to her. Nelson took with him the American, Ralph Willett Miller as Flag Captain.

Brian Lavery relates that a few weeks after Nelson and Miller took command of *Theseus*, a note was dropped on the quaterdeck that read: 'Success attend Admiral Nelson! God bless Captain Miller! We thank them for the officers they have placed over us. We are happy and comfortable, and will shed every drop of blood in our veins to support them and the name of the *Theseus* will be immortalised as high as the Captain's.' The note was signed, 'Ship's Company.' Truly a remarkable testimony to the affection these two men generated.

Ralph Miller was born in New York in 1762 and sent to England for his education. His parents were strong supporters of the British Crown which resulted in the loss of their property upon the success of the Revolutionaries. He entered the Royal Navy in 1778 and is 'said to have fought in all the actions of Admirals Barrington, Hood, Rodney and Graves, and was three times wounded.' Miller was certainly recognised as capable and received promotion to Lieutenant from Lord Rodney in 1781 and appointed to HMS *Terrible*. In the action off Cape Henry in September 1781, she received such damage that she had to be abandoned and burnt.

With the new war in 1793, Miller was at Toulon with Hood and was placed under the orders of Sir Sidney Smith and no doubt took pleasure from creating as much havoc as possible amongst the anchored French shipping when the British withdrew from Toulon. Lord Hood next placed Miller on board *Victory* where he did good service in the ship's boats and on shore, assisting in the reduction of San Fiorenzo, Bastia and Calvi.

He was then given in succession, command of HMS *Mignonne* and *Unite* with the last appointment being made by Sir John Jervis early in 1796. In June, Commodore Nelson was given HMS *Captain*, Captain Ralph Miller, who was selected as his Flag Captain. Subsequently, at the Battle of Cape St Vincent, 14 February 1797, it was Berry, then a newly appointed Commander and visitor on board the *Captain*, and Nelson who boarded the Spanish ships while Miller was asked to stay on board *Captain* and keep men flowing into the enemy ships.

Following Cape St Vincent, Miller and Nelson transferred to the unhappy *Theseus* and such was their effect upon the ship's company that *Theseus* played an important role during the blockade of Cadiz and the ill fated attack upon Santa Cruz, please see DN 04 / Samuel Hood for more detail.

In Sturgis Jackson is the letter written by Ralph Miller to his wife on 19 October 1798 as *Theseus* and *Orion* neared Gibraltar with their prizes. There is no doubt that the letter is based upon discussions with other Nile captains in an effort to try to piece together the events of all the ships involved. When compared to recent research, this letter still remains quite valid as an accurate account of the battle and for this reason the whole of it has been employed as the description of the action, so please refer to the Davison Nile Medal section of this book to learn more about HMS *Theseus* and the battle.

However, in order to follow the attack of the British ships upon the French, *Theseus* followed *Orion* into action and produced yet another devastating blow to the *Guerrier* as she passed the head of the French line. Miller wrote: 'I closed them suddenly, and, running under the arch of their shot, reserved my fire, every gun loaded with two and some with three round shot, until I had the *Guerrier's* masts in a line, and her jib-boom about six feet clear of our rigging, we then opened with such effect that a second breath could not be drawn before her main and mizzen mast were also gone.' For the rest of Ralph Miller's account, please read all of his exciting letter to his wife.

Following *Theseus* escorting the Nile prizes to Gibraltar, she was deployed in the Eastern Mediterranean off Alexandria to increase the pressure on Napoleon's forces in Egypt. With the arrival of Sir Sidney Smith in HMS *Tigre*, Miller and *Theseus* joined forces and sailed to the fortress port of St Jean d'Acre. What followed was a defence of great heroism as Sidney Smith and his men held off the might of Napoleon's army.

Sadly, Ralph Miller was to pay the ultimate price. From the *DNB* we have:

'Miller was killed on board his ship during the defence of St Jean d'Acre by the accidental explosion of some shells on 14 May 1799. 'He had long', wrote Smith to Lord St Vincent, 'been in the practice of collecting such of the enemy's shells as fell in the town without bursting and sending them back to the enemy better prepared and with evident effect. He had a deposit on board *Theseus* ready for service, and many more preparing, when by an accident for which nobody can account they exploded at short intervals,' killing and wounding nearly eighty men, wrecking the poop and the after part of the quarter-deck, and setting fire to the ship. The monument in St Paul's [Cathedral, London], by Flaxman was erected to Miller's memory by subscription among his fellow officers who fought with him at the Nile and St Vincent. He left a widow and two daughters.'

Provenance: Medal fair, 1978.

References: The National Archives, Kew: ADM 36/11666, 11667, 11668, 11669, 12647, 12648, 12649, 13640, 13641, 13642 (*Theseus*), 14283 (*Zealand*), ADM 35/1919 and 1920 (*Texel*).
The Sailor's Word-Book by Admiral Smyth, Blackie, London, 1867.
Dictionary of National Biography, Oxford University Press, 1975.
Logs of the Great Sea Fights 1794-1805 by Sturges Jackson, Navy Records Society, London, 1899-1900.
Nelson and the Nile by Brian Lavery, Chatham, London, 1998.
The Sailing Navy List by David Lyon, Conway, London, 1993.

DN 10 Captain Edward Berry, HMS Vanguard, Rear-Admiral Nelson's flagship

Description: Bronze-gilt medal with loop suspension. Weight: 41.1 grams. Very fine condition although it has suffered from some corrosion which may have been caused by salty sea air, i.e. it is quite possible that Captain Berry wore this medal regularly while at sea.

Background: When I purchased the letter from Alexander Davison to Captain Berry, which acted as a cover note for the presentation of the gold Davison Nile medal, this gilt bronze medal was included. The gold medal is now in the National Maritime Museum collection, MED 0971, and is a bit of a shock to find a hole has been drilled at 12 o'clock and fitted with a large gilt ring for suspension. The Museum also has a silver example that belonged to Berry, MED 0972.

The correspondence from Davison was contained in an envelope with a circa 1900 label pasted to the outside that described the contents which included the 'original medal presented to Captain Berry.' At the time, I didn't give the gilt-bronze medal that much attention as it clearly wasn't the gold medal presented to Berry and may well have been a medal inserted with the correspondence by some unknown third party. But then the catalogue description doesn't say the medal is gold, and if it was, most likely it would have. The description does provide a firm provenance to Captain Berry.

Battle of the Nile.
Original Medal and Documents.

Admiral Sir Edward Berry. Original letter of Lord Charles Spencer (Lord of the Admiralty) to Sir Edward Berry, two pages folio, 1799, presenting his correspondent, on behalf of the King, with a medal to commemorate the Battle of the Nile; also a letter from Alexander Darwin to the same, and directions for wearing the medal, together with the original medal presented to Sir Edward Berry.

∴ Sir Edward Berry was Lord Nelson's Flag-Captain at the Battle. On one side is a portrait of Nelson, and on the reverse a view of the battle.

197

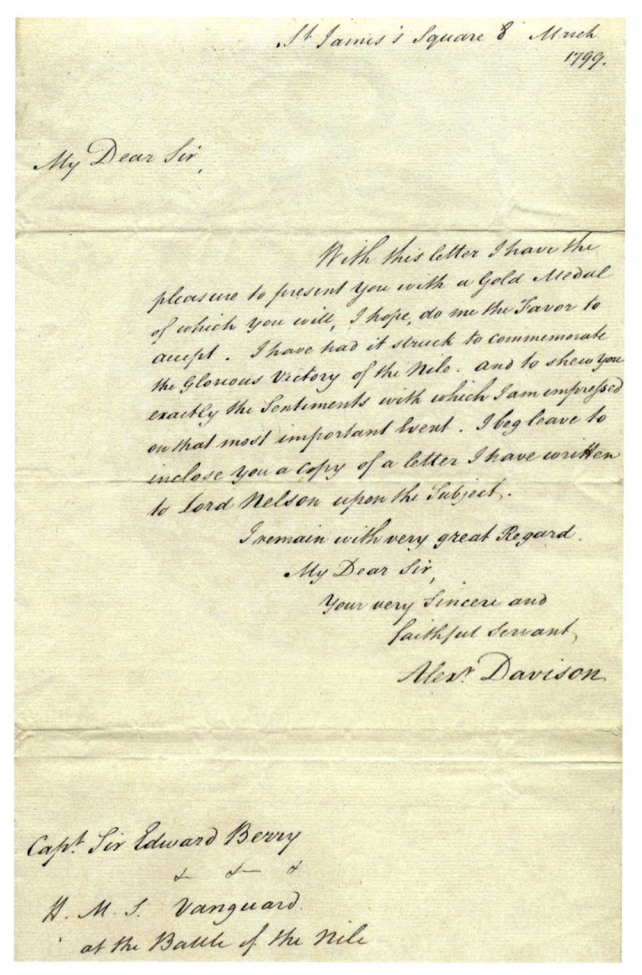

However, as the letter clearly came from Captain Berry's family and with the knowledge that Berry also had a silver example, it may well have been that he wished to have one of each type of Davison Nile medals, which would include a gilt-bronze specimen. Due to the weight of the gold medal, the gilt-bronze medal would be useful for regular wearing. The corrosion of the medal, possibly caused by sea air, also looks right to me as Berry was the sort of captain who may have liked to regularly wear his Nile medal at sea. One may also reflect that the Nelson effigy in Westminster Abbey has Nelson wearing a gilt bronze Davison Nile medal.

Rear-Admiral Sir Edward Berry, 1st Baronet, KCB (1768 - 1831) was perhaps characterised as a fine seaman and born fighter that never rose to the higher levels of command at sea. A slight, rather delicate man with fair hair and piercing blue eyes, Berry was quick-witted, impulsive and aggressive to the point of recklessness. He did, however, receive from the King three Naval Small Gold medals (Nile, Trafalgar and St Domingo), and was the only captain to do so. Born in London with the misfortune of his father passing away when Edward was still quite young, he was put to sea at the age of ten on board HMS *Burford* in the East Indies.

He was promoted lieutenant in 1794 for boarding a French man-of-war and was present at Lord Howe's victory of 1st June 1794. It is, however, when he joined HMS *Agamemnon* in May 1796 with Nelson as his captain, that his talents as a seaman were fully recognised. Nelson and Berry formed a bond that would remain during the rest of Nelson's life. When Nelson shifted his commodore's pennant to HMS *Captain* in June 1796, under the command of Ralph Miller, Berry moved as well and in November was promoted to Commander, but without an immediate ship to command, remained on board *Captain* as a passenger.

At the battle of Cape St Vincent, 14 February 1797, when Nelson boarded the *San Nicolas*, 80 guns, through the upper quarter gallery windows, Commander Berry and those who followed him jumped into the ship's mizen chains and swept all before them. When Nelson came topside, Berry was lowering the Spanish colours. The two of them together then boarded the *San Josef*, 112 guns, from her main chains and such was the fury of these two officers and those who followed them, that the Spanish immediately surrendered the ship. Never was a finer feat of boarding first rates seen before or since.

When both Nelson and Berry were again in England in October, Nelson invited Berry to accompany him to Court and to meet King George III. The King remarked on Nelson being without his right arm, wherein Nelson commented that with Berry, he had his right hand.

It was agreed between Nelson and Berry that when Nelson was next given a ship, Berry would be his flag captain. Upon Nelson writing to Berry, who was contemplating marriage, that if he wished to marry he should set about it as Nelson expected to be appointed to a new ship shortly. Berry did move quickly and on 12 December he married his cousin, Louisa. On 19 December, Berry and Nelson were appointed to the *Vanguard*, however the ship didn't leave England until April 1798.

HMS *Vanguard* was one of the Arrogant Class of Third Rate 74-gun ships designed by Slade in 1758 and would have a ship's company of 550 men. She was launched at Deptford Dockyard on 6 March 1787. She was 168 feet in length and 1604 tons burthen and bore 28 x 32 pounders on the Gun Deck, 28 x 18 pounders on the Upper Deck, 14 x 9 pounders on the Quarterdeck and 4 x 9 pounders in the Forecastle. She was hulked in 1813.

As Brian Lavery recounts Nelson: 'was fond of the open gallery on the stern of the ship, where he could walk in the fresh air unobserved by officers and crew. When the *Vanguard* was refitted at Chatham he had insisted on it being extended [in depth] by a foot, by moving the bulkhead forward and reducing the size of the cabin.'

This was much to the displeasure of the Navy Board who were trying to do away with these walkways, however Nelson was Nelson and they bowed to his demands.

Lavery further details how Berry and Nelson worked toward improving the Admiral's quarters: 'His furniture had been sent to Chatham to be put on board the ship and Berry advised him on making his cabin more comfortable. A floor covering of kersey cloth, probably painted in a black and white chequer pattern, and some curtains for the windows were provided by Chatham Dockyard, but it seems they were not suitable. Berry suggested that: 'if a floor cloth would not be too expensive and you thought it worthwhile, I think that one in the dining room would be comfortable where the table stands - 16ft in length and 13ft 5, 6 or 7ins broad. Also a carpet for the side of your cot if you use one. A looking glass I believe I mentioned, about two ft long in a gold frame.' He strongly recommended curtains for the quarter galleries which, he joked, were 'very necessary' - one of these galleries would have served as the admiral's toilet, or 'necessary house' and privacy was important. Nelson wrote to his wife before sailing: 'My place is tolerably comfortable, but I do not shine in servants.'

Having joined Earl St Vincent off Cadiz at the end of April, *Vanguard* was ordered into the Mediterranean and towards the end of May suffered terribly in a storm in the Gulf of Lyon. Intelligence told of Napoleon's fleet leaving Toulon and the great search began which was only resolved on 28 July with news that the enemy were at Alexandria. Nelson immediately gathered together his squadron and headed south.

With *Goliath*, *Zealous*, *Audacious*, *Orion* and *Theseus* all having rounded the van of the enemy and taken position on the shore side, Nelson had *Vanguard* placed beside *Spartiate*, the third ship in the French line, in an effort to complete the doubling of the enemy van. Nelson could see that the first two French ships were already beaten, so with his position on the third ship he set the stage for the rest of his squadron to place themselves against the remaining French ships in the middle and rear of their line.

Brian Lavery recounts: 'A little before 8:30 that evening, Nelson was with Berry on the quarterdeck of the *Vanguard*. Amid the flashes of gunfire, noise and danger of shot he was looking over a sketch of the bay 'which had been taken from a French ship captured a few days earlier. While he was doing this a piece of langridge shot fired from the *Spartiate* struck him on the forehead causing a 'wound ...over the right eye. The cranium bared for more than an inch, the wound three inches long.' Nelson fell into Berry's arms, his blood staining the sketch in his hands. He could see nothing with his good eye ... and with his typical morbidity he called out, 'I am killed; remember me to my wife.' Nelson recovered, but remained in great pain for weeks to come until the nursing by Lady Hamilton in Naples would restore the full Nelson.'

The *Spartiate* was the first ship to be doubled and while faced by *Theseus*, she fought with great determination, but when *Vanguard* commenced to attack her on the starboard side, her fire slackened and she quickly lost her main and mizen masts. She had more than 200 killed and wounded and after two hours, hauled down her French colours. Brian Lavery further details: 'Berry sent Lieutenant Galwey over [to *Spartiate*] in a boat with a party of marines and the French captain's sword was handed over to him as a token of surrender. He returned to *Vanguard* and Berry took it below to show the sword to Nelson, now wounded in the cockpit.'

Following the securing of prizes, Nelson completed his dispatch of the action and gave to Berry the pleasant duty of taking one set to Earl St Vincent at Gibraltar. Another set would go overland via Naples. Berry then joined HMS *Leander*, 50 guns, Captain Thomas Boulden Thompson. *Leander* set sail on 6 August with up to 80 of her ship's company being left with the main squadron to assist in restoring the prizes. On the 18th, five or six mile west of Goza di Candia, Crete there was sighted a strange sail which proved to be the French *Genéréux* of 74 guns, which was one of two capital ships that escaped surrender at the Nile. A furious action of some six hours ensued which resulted in Berry being badly wounded in the arm by a fragment of another man's skull and the surrender of *Leander* with a total of 35 killed and 57 wounded. For a full account of the action please refer to DN 32 which recounts the plight of the *Leander*.

Berry, along with Thompson, were exchanged for captive French officers apparently in November and arrived back in England in early December. Although Berry was disappointed in not bringing the news of the victory at the Nile, the country ignored the fact and he was knighted on 12 December, given the Freedom of the City of London and other honours.

In June 1799 Berry was sent out to join Nelson in the newly built HMS *Foudroyant*. During the remainder of the year he was largely employed with Nelson on board at the blockade of Malta and other duties around Naples.

The following is mainly from Midshipman George Parsons's recollections of serving with Berry and Nelson on board *Foudroyant*. Off Cape Passaro during February 1800, the *Foudroyant*, *Northumberland*, *Audacious* and *Success* fell in with a French squadron under Rear-Admiral Perree in *Le Genéréux*....After four days of groping about in heavy sea, interspersed with fog, Nelson heard the sound of firing, and steered towards it. When it was apparent that it was *Le Genéréux* which was being chased, Nelson said: 'Make the *Foudroyant* fly!.....This will not do, Sir Ed'ard, it is certainly *Le Genéréux* and to my flagship she can alone surrender. Sir Ed'ard, we must and shall beat the *Northumberland*.'

'I will do my utmost, my lord,' said Berry, 'Get the engine [fire pump to wet the sails to improve draw in light airs], to work on the sails - hand butts of water to the stays - pipe the hammocks down, and each man place shot in them - slack the stays, knock up the wedges, and give the masts play. Start off the water, Mr James, and pump the ship.' The *Foudroyant* drew ahead, and at last took the lead. 'The Admiral is working his fin' (stump of his right arm): [and calls to the helmsman to keep his bearing, so as not to tack], 'do not cross hawse, I advise you.' Such were Parsons's thoughts at the time and how right he was because he soon saw Nelson turning furiously on the petty officer who was conning the ship.

'I'll knock you off your perch, you rascal,' he said, 'if you are so inattentive [and force me to tack]! Sir Ed'ard, send your best Quarter Master to the weather wheel.'
'A strange sail ahead of the chase,' called the look-out man.
'Youngster, to the mast-head! What - going without your glass and be damned to you! Let me know what she is immediately.'
'A sloop of war or frigate, my lord.'
'Demand her number.'
'The *Success*, my lord.'
'Signal her to cut off the flying enemy. Great odds, though! Thirty-two small guns to eighty large ones.'
'The *Success*, my lord, has hove to athwart-hawse of *Le Genéréux* and is firing her larboard broadside. The Frenchman has hoisted the tricolour with a Rear-Admiral's flag.'
'Bravo, *Success*, at her again!'
'She has wore, my lord, and is firing her starboard broadside. It has winged the chase, my lord. Her flying kites are flying all together.'
'*Le Genéréux* now opened fire on the frigate and everyone stood aghast, fearing the consequences. But when the smoke cleared there was the *Success*, crippled it is true, but bull-dog like, bearing up for the enemy.'
'Signal the *Success* to discontinue the action and come under my stern,' said Nelson. 'She has done well for her size. Try a shot from the lower deck at her, Sir Ed'ard.'
'It goes over her.'
'Beat to quarters and fire coolly and deliberately at her masts and yards.'

'*Le Genéréux* at this moment opened her fire on us,' continued Parsons, 'and, as a shot passed through the mizzen stay-sail, Lord Nelson, patting one of the youngsters on the head, asked him jocularly how he relished the music; and observing something like alarm depicted on his continence, consoled him with the information that Charles XII ran away from the first shot he heard, though afterwards he was called 'The Great', and deservedly, from his bravery. 'I therefore,' said Nelson, 'hope much from you in the future.'

Here the *Northumberland* opened her fire and down came the tricoloured ensign, amidst the thunders of our united cannon. Berry boarded the prize and received the sword of Rear-Admiral Perree, who was dying of wounds. The date was 18 February 1800 and Sir Edward Berry had claimed the ship that had defeated him and Captain Thompson.

This success was made the sweeter when on 31 March was sighted the *Guillaume Tell*, the last of the capital ships to escape from the Nile.

W.H. Long, who is quoting a 'Letter from an officer of the *Foudroyant*, at Syracuse', picks up the narrative following the outstanding effort displayed by Captain Henry Blackwood of the 32-gun frigate *Penelope* that caused the *Guillaume Tell* to lose speed and allow *Lion* and *Foudroyant* to come up.

Penelope attacking *Guillaume Tell* with *Foudroyant* and *Lion* coming up, aquatint by N. Pocock.

'Sir E. Berry, laying the *Foudroyant* alongside, so close that her spare anchor was just clear of the *Guillaume Tell's* mizzen chains, hailed her commander, and ordered him to strike. He answered by brandishing a sword over his head, and then discharged a musket at Sir Edward; this was followed by a broadside which nearly unrigged the *Foudroyant*, whose guns however being prepared with three round shots in each, she poured in a most tremendous and effectual discharge crashing through and through the enemy; but she fired another broadside, when down came *Guillaume Tell's* main and mizzen masts, and at the same time the *Foudroyant's* foretopmast, jib-boom, spritsail, main topsail yard, stay sails, fore sail and mainsail all in tatters. The combatants then separated. Sir E. Berry called his men from the main deck, and cutting away the wreck, got the ship manageable, and again close alongside her determined opponent, who nailed his colours to the stump of his mast, and displayed his flag on a pole over them. Sir Edward then commenced a most heavy and well directed fire, his men firing every gun two or three times a minute, and musketry was occasionally used, but latterly the mizzen mast being almost in two, Sir Edward called the marines from the poop, and put them to the great guns. At a few minutes past eight the *Guillaume Tell's* foremast was shot away, and becoming a mere log, she struck her colours.'

The *Foudroyant* had eight men killed and wounded; her captain, lieutenant, boatswain, three midshipmen and 53 seamen and marines.

From Colin White's *Trafalgar Captains* we have: 'Nelson left the Mediterranean in the summer of 1800 and Berry took the *Foudroyant* home to England, where he remained until the summer of 1805, when he was appointed to HMS *Agamemnon* and joined Nelson in time for Trafalgar. *Agamemnon* was towards the rear of Nelson's line and so she did not get into action until nearly 2pm. She joined *Neptune* and *Conqueror* in pounding the mighty four-decked Spanish battleship *Santissima Trinidad* until she was forced to surrender. In the closing stages, when the enemy van, under Dumanoir, threatened an attack on the badly damaged British ships, *Agamemnon* was part of the hastily formed line of battle that drove them away. As the smoke of battle began to clear away, Berry felt a premonition that something was wrong on board the *Victory* and, calling for his boat, he had himself rowed across to the stricken flagship. But he arrived too late to bid farewell to the dying Nelson.

'The following year, Berry, still commanding the *Agamemnon*, took part in the Battle of San Domingo (6 February 1806) and was made a baronet. He remained in active service until 1813 when he was placed in command of one of the royal yachts, but his health was broken and, although he became a Rear-Admiral in 1821, he never hoisted his flag. He died at Bath on 13 February 1831 and was buried in the graveyard of Walcot church.'

Provenance: Captain Edward Berry?
Christie's London catalogue for 20 June 1990, Edwin Wolf Collection of Nelson and Hamilton papers, part 2, lot 276 which included the Alexander Davison letter to Captain Berry and the bronze gilt Davison Nile medal.

References: *Naval Medals, 1793-1856* by Kenneth Douglas-Morris, published privately, London, 1987.
Dictionary of National Biography, Oxford University Press, 1975.
St Vincent and Camperdown by Christopher Lloyd, Batsford, London, 1963.
The Battle of the Nile by Oliver Warner, Batsford, London, 1960.
Nelson and the Nile by Brian Lavery, Chatham, London, 1998.
Royal Naval Biography by Lieut John Marshall, R.N., Longman, London, 1822-1830, (12 vols.)
The Naval History of Great Britain...1793 to 1820 by William James, six vols., Richard Bentley, London, 1837, etc.
Medals of the British Navy and How they were won by W. H. Long, Norie & Wilson, London, 1895.
Nelsonian Reminiscences by Lieutenant G. S. Parsons, Gibbings, London, 1905.
The Trafalgar Captains, edited by Colin White, Chatham, London, 2005.
The Sailing Navy List by David Lyon, Conway, London, 1993.

DN 11 Sergeant Samuel Plant, Marine, HMS Vanguard, Captain Edward Berry

Description: Gilt-bronze medal engraved in the reverse field: *SP Sergt / H M S / Van* [Masonic square rule and compass] *guard*. Weight: 39.1 grams. Fair, much worn and used as a pocket piece for many years.

Background: Although this medal is much worn, it is quite stellar as a relic that belonged to a senior non-commissioned Marine on board Rear-Admiral Nelson's flagship at the Nile. That this marine was also a Mason just adds more interest to the medal and harks back to the essay by Martyn Downer as he described the relationship between Masons and men on board *Vanguard*. We are also fortunate that on board *Vanguard*, there was only one Sergeant of Marines with the initials SP, and that was Samuel Plant.

He came from Ashburn in Derbyshire, stood 5 foot 6 1/2 inches tall, light brown hair and a fresh complexion. His trade was a farm labourer, but he must have had military training before the commencement of the war because when he joined the Marines on 28 January 1793 and then HMS *Thames* on 20 May, aged 23, he was quickly rated Corporal. He clearly had natural leadership abilities as evidenced by his having been made Sergeant on 3 October 1795.

He was stationed at Chatham as part of the 86th company and his first ship was the *Thames*, a frigate of 32 guns (12 pounders), Captain Thomas Cotes. Her compliment was 220 men, but she never achieved a ship's company more than 184 men.

William James tells us of the plight of the *Thames* when she met the French national frigate *Uranie* of 44 guns and ship's company of 320, some miles west of La Hogue on 24 October 1793. A strange sail was sighted at 9:30 am, but then the weather turned thick and at 10: 15 am, the stranger proved to be an enemy frigate and the *Thames* was immediately cleared for action.

'The two ships, having the same object in view, soon passed very near each other on contrary tacks; at which time the *Uranie* fired her broadside, and wore round on the opposite tack. An action now commenced, and was continued, with great spirit on both sides, until 2:20 pm; when the *Uranie*, getting under the stern of the *Thames*, gave her two or three raking broadsides, and then attempted to board on the starboard quarter; but, on receiving through her bows a well directed fire from six or seven of the *Thames'* maindeck guns, double-shotted, the *Uranie* threw all her sails aback, and hauled off to the southward. The British crew, on seeing this, gave three hearty cheers; but the *Thames* was in too crippled a condition to make sail in pursuit.

'Her loss in the action, out of a crew of 184 men and boys, amounted to ten seamen and one marine killed and four officers, 22 seamen and one marine wounded. Her three lower masts and bowsprit were shot through in several places; all her stays were shot away, as was all the main rigging, except a few shrouds, and they were rendered useless. The maintopmast rigging was even worse than the main rigging, and the topmast was shot through in three places. The maintopsail yard was shot away in the slings by a double-headed shot, and the yard-arms came down in front of the main yard; the slings, both iron and rope, and the jeers of the main yard were shot away, so that the yard hung by the tresses, about a third of the mast down; and the mainsail was cut to pieces, particularly the leech-ropes.

'The hull of the *Thames* had received innumerable shots, the chief part of the gangways was shot away; the main deck in front of the mainmast was torn up from the waterway to the hatchways, and the bits were shot away and unshipped. Six shots had passed between wind and water on the starboard, and three on the larboard side. One gun on the quarterdeck, and two on the main deck were dismounted; and almost all the tackles, and breechings were cut away. The surprise is that, after being so terribly mauled by shot, her loss in men was not treble what it proved.

'The *Thames* could steer but one course, and that was right before the wind. Soon afterwards, four sail made their appearance, and came up fast, under [false] English colours. The wind had by this time freshened from the south-west; and the *Thames*, being without any after-sail, and having her runners all carried forward and crossed, to serve both as stays and shrouds, was not able to haul upon a wind. On this, one of the frigates ranged up under her stern and gave her a broadside. The *Thames* then brought to, hailed that she was in a defenceless state from a previous action, and struck her colours to the French 40-gun Frigate *Carmagnole*, Captain Allemand.'

James notes that initially, because the *Uranie* didn't push her clear advantage and that it was seen men working to plug shot holes in her hull, that she may have gone down when the wind freshened, however it was later learned that she did make it back to Brest but that her name was changed to *Tortue*. The *Thames* was taken to Brest as well and it appears that her officers and crew were later exchanged as we find Samuel Plant being formally discharged from the accounts on HMS *Thames* on 11 June 1795. He was promoted to Sergeant in October and appears to have remained at Chatham for a couple of years before joining HMS *Vanguard* on 31 December 1797.

Please see DN 10 for an account of the *Vanguard* at the Nile. From the complement of marines, she had Lieutenant William Faddy (Taddy?) with six other marines killed in the battle.

With Captain Berry having been sent with dispatches, Captain Thomas Hardy was promoted from the *Mutine* brig to command *Vanguard*. In the Captain's log it notes that on 16 November, the crew of Captain Thompson's ill fated *Leander* were repatriated to *Vanguard* at Naples and that over the next few months these men were discharged to various ships.

There followed what some would call Nelson's Neapolitan mess, wherein he became immersed in the plight and requirements of the King and Queen of Naples. *Vanguard* departed at the end of December with the Royal Family and their entourage for Palermo and more or less remained at Palermo during the first half of 1799. She then sailed to Mahon where Samuel Plant spent most of July and August on shore.

Vanguard then cruised until 17 February when she returned to Portsmouth and was paid off.

Provenance: Medal fair, 1989.

References: The National Archives, Kew: ADM 96/155 Effective & Subsistence Lists, Chatham Division. ADM 35/1865 and ADM 36/1132 (HMS *Thames*), ADM 35/1990 & ADM 36/15356, 15357, 15358 (HMS *Vanguard*).

The Naval History of Great Britain...1793 to 1820 by William James, six vols., Richard Bentley, London, 1837, etc.

DN 12 Ebenezer Battison, Able Seaman, HMS Minotaur, Captain Thomas Louis

Description: Soho gilt-bronze medal which has been chased in the fields and high points by a jeweller and then cased in gold and glazed. Engraved in the reverse field is *Ebenezer Battison / Minotaur*. Weight: 65 grams. Extremely fine.

Background: Ebenezer Battison was christened at Saint Ninian's church in Stirling, Scotland on 29 April 1770. His parents were Thomas Battison and Mary Christie. He was 23 years old when he volunteered on 23 March 1794 on board HMS *Minotaur* and was rated Quarter Gunner which indicates that he had previous service or was trained as a gunner in the merchant marine. On 1 April 1797, Battison lost his petty officer status and was re-rated as Able Seaman. He was with *Minotaur* during the whole of the time that Captain Thomas Louis was in command, so with the telling of the Captain's story, that of Battison shall also be told. With the Peace of Amiens, the *Minotaur* was paid off and Battison was transferred to the receiving ship *New Zealand* and from there discharged. We have no further record of him, although he may well have served again following the resumption of hostilities in 1803. As a note, his Davison Nile medal is the original gilt-bronze medal struck at Soho and would have gone to a petty officer, so his status on board *Minotaur* may well have been more than Able Seaman.

HMS *Minotaur* was built at Woolwich Dockyard with lines based on the captured French 74-gun ship *Courageux*. She was much larger than a normal British 74-gun ship which was typically 1600 to 1650 tons burthen, where *Minotaur* and her sister ship *Leviathan* were of 1703 tons. This meant that the size of the ship's company, which was normally 550 officers and men, was increased to 650 when under Captain Louis's command at the Nile. She carried 28 x 32 pounders on the Gun Deck, 28 x 18 pounders on the

Upper Deck, 14 x 9 pounders on the Quarter Deck and 4 x 9 pounders in the Forecastle. The keel was laid in 1788 and she was launched in November, 1793. When under the command of Captain John Barrett, she was wrecked on 22 December 1810. In a fierce gale, she stuck the Haak Sands off the Texel and lost 370 hands including her captain.

Sir Thomas Louis (1759 - 1807) was born in Exeter, Devon and entered the navy at the age of 11 in 1770. He was continually at sea on board various ships, passed for lieutenant in July 1777 and posted on board HMS *Bienfaisant*, Captain John Macbride. During this cruise he took part in the action off Ushant, 1778, the Channel cruise of 1779, the defeat of Langara off Cape St Vincent in January 1780, and the consequent relief of Gibraltar. In August 1780, the *Bienfaisant* captured the *Comte d'Artois* off the Old Head of Kinsale, Ireland. He then followed Captain Macbride to the *Artois* frigate and was given command of the gun-ship *Mackworth*, but then came ashore as a regulating officer of the Impress Service during which he was promoted to Post Captain. With the end of the American war, Captain Louis resided in Torquay on half-pay.

With the commencement of war with France in 1793, his old friend John Macbride, now a Rear-Admiral, appointed him flag captain of HMS *Quebec*, but then briefly to the *Cumberland* and finally in the spring of 1794, to the *Minotaur*. She formed part of the Channel Squadron and spent her time chiefly off the coast of France. In 1796, *Minotaur* escorted a convoy to the West Indies and returned to England shortly after and rejoined the Channel Fleet. It is noted that due to Captain Louis being held in high regard by the lower deck, he had little trouble in gaining volunteers to man his ships, which may well have had a bearing on Ebenezer Battison joining *Minotaur*.

Trouble, however, lay ahead with the fleet at Spithead under the command of Admiral Lord Bridport. Complaints came forward in February and March from several of the ship's company that asked for consideration of increasing the pay and provisions allowed to the lower deck. It may have been that Ebenezer Battison was involved and that this cost him his post as a petty officer. From *The Floating Republic*, we have: 'Bridport, as a supremely sensible man, asked for complaints; at least the *Minotaur*, in sending some in on 24th April, said they were 'informed by the Delegates of the Fleet that your Lordship will receive any grievances from any of the ships under your command.' Their objections sound well justified, and in one part reveal a further piece of maladministration. In this they arraigned their surgeon, Bell, 'for inattention and ill-treatment of the sick and wounded and not being qualified, as we can judge by several accidents happening in the ship… And for not visiting the sick for two or three months together, and when visiting has often been observed in liquor, and not serving to the sick such nourishments as is allowed by Government, and for the want of which many men has died in this ship. There has been men went down to him for relief when sick, and he has told them that a flogging would do them most good.'

One can only imagine that Surgeon Bell was forced to leave the ship as he certainly wasn't on board *Minotaur* at the Nile. The Spithead Mutiny was resolved by Admiral 'Black Dick' Howe becoming the mediator between the delegates, the King and the Admiralty. All of the complaints were adjudged and largely agreed to. The later Mutiny at the Nore, was quite different and ended with the ringleader dangling from a yard-arm.

Late in 1797, *Minotaur* was ordered to join Sir John Jervis off Cadiz. As part of a squadron commanded by Thomas Troubridge, *Minotaur* then joined Rear-Admiral Nelson's squadron in June 1798 to cruise in the Mediterranean. When the French fleet was finally sighted on 1 August 1798, the *Minotaur* became the seventh ship in action steering just past the *Vanguard* and taking station beside the French *Aquilon* of 74 guns. From the *Naval Chronicle* we have: 'When the *Vanguard* came alongside the *Spartiate*, she became exposed to the raking fire of *l'Aquilon*, the next ship in the enemy's line; by which the *Vanguard* had between fifty and sixty-five men disabled in the space of ten minutes. Owing, however, to the gallant and judicious manner in which Captain Louis took his station ahead of the *Vanguard*, the *Minotaur* not only effectually relieved her from this distressing situation, but overpowered her opponent. Admiral Nelson felt so grateful to Captain Louis for his conduct on this important occasion, that at nine o'clock, while yet the combat was raging with utmost fury, and he himself was suffering most severely in the cockpit from a dreadful wound in the head, he requested Captain Berry to hail the *Minotaur*, and desire Captain Louis to come to him, as he could not have a moment's peace until he had thanked him for his conduct; adding, 'this was the hundred and twenty-fourth time I have been engaged, but I believe it is now nearly over with me.'

'The subsequent meeting which took place between the Admiral and Captain Louis was affecting in the extreme. The latter hung over his bleeding friend in silent sorrow. – 'Farewell, dear Louis,' said the Admiral, 'I shall never forget the obligation I am under to you for your brave and generous conduct; and now, whatever may come of me, my mind is at peace.'

From Brian Lavery we have the following. 'The *Aquilon*, fourth in line, was unscathed in the early stages, after the *Orion* failed to anchor on her inside. Later, she was attacked on the outside by Thomas Louis's *Minotaur* and received some of the fire of Miller in the *Theseus*. Her officers claimed to be under fire from three vessels but it is difficult to see what the third one was [*Vanguard*?], except for stray shots. However, her men were driven from the quarterdeck and forecastle and then abandoned the 18-pounder guns on the upper deck to concentrate on the 36-pounders below - a cost-effective way of fighting with a reduced crew and opponents on both sides. After two hours of battle *Aquilon's* three masts fell in quick succession and half an hour later virtually all her guns had been dismounted. She had 87 men killed and 213 wounded when she surrendered to the *Minotaur*.' The *Minotaur* suffered 23 killed and 64 wounded.

From the *Naval Chronicle* we have the following wherein Admiral Nelson has dispatched Captains Louis and Troubridge to take possession of the Roman territories in the summer of 1799. 'Having entered into articles of capitulation with the French General, Grenier, a detachment of 200 seamen and marines was landed from the *Minotaur* and *Culloden*, for the purpose of taking possession of Civita Vecchia, Cornatto, and Tolfa; while Captain Louis, and General Bonehard, proceeded to take possession of Rome on the same terms. For this service, Captain Louis was afterwards presented with the insignia of the Sicilian Order of St. Ferdinand and of Merit.'

Captain Louis continued to work in the Mediterranean and *Minotaur* became Lord Keith's flagship during the siege of Genoa. *Minotaur* was also part of Lord Keith's force during the landings in Egypt in 1801. With the peace, Captain Louis brought *Minotaur* back to England where she was paid off, and he went on half-pay.

Further from the *Naval Chronicle*: 'At the commencement of the present war [in 1803], his services were again called upon, and he was appointed to the *Conqueror*, another new 74; in which ship he remained until his promotion to the rank of Rear-Admiral of the White Squadron, which took place on the 2nd of April 1804. He then hoisted his flag in the *Leopard*, of 50 guns, and commanded on the Boulogne station during the whole of that year.

'In the month of March 1805, the Rear-Admiral was particularly applied for by the much-esteemed, and much-lamented friend, Lord Nelson; and was appointed to serve under him, in the *Canopus* of 80 guns, one of the prizes at the battle of the Nile, on the Mediterranean station. Rear-Admiral Louis was a companion of Lord Nelson in the arduous task of chasing the French fleet to the West Indies and back; after which he was detached by his Lordship, with seven sail of the line, to Tetuan Bay, on a service [to replenish water and provisions.]'

The night before Louis left, he dined with Lord Nelson on board *Victory* and complained that surely while he was away the French would come out of Cadiz and he would miss the battle, to which Nelson responded, 'My dear Louis, I have no other means of keeping my fleet complete in provisions and water but by sending them in detachments to Gibraltar. The enemy will come out, and we shall fight them, but there will be time for you to get back first. I look upon *Canopus* as my right hand, and I send you first to ensure your being here to help to beat them.' Apparently Villeneuve learned of the seven ships leaving Nelson's fleet on 18 October, which was a prime reason for his putting to sea on the 19th. The rest is history, but poor Louis forever regretted not being with his dear Nelson at his most glorious triumph.

In November 1805, *Canopus* joined Sir Thomas Duckworth in the blockade of Cadiz but then departed with Duckworth's fleet for the West Indies where was fought the Battle of Saint Domingo on 6 February 1806. Duckworth's flag was on board HMS *Superb*, 74 guns. He was supported by Rear-Admiral Alexander Cochrane in HMS *Northumberland* and Rear-Admiral Louis on board *Canopus*, whose captain was F. W.

Austen, Jane Austen's brother. Also present was Sir Edward Berry in the *Agamemnon* plus three other 74s. They caught the French squadron at anchor off Santa Domingo. The French slipped their cables and quickly left the bay but Duckworth 'at once made the signal to attack, and with a portrait of Nelson suspended from the mizen stay of the *Superb*, and the band playing *God Save the King* and *Nelson of the Nile*, bore down on the leading French ship *L'Alexandre* and engaged her at close quarters.'

After a severe action of two hours, the French admiral's ship, *L'Imperiale*, 138 guns, being heavily engaged by the *Northumberland*, was run ashore and set on fire. Another French ship, *Le Diomede* of 84 guns also joined her admiral on shore and was set alight. Captain Berry in the *Agamemnon* maintained fire on her until he had to bear off due to the shallowness of the water. Two other ships of the line were captured, with *L'Alexandre* surrendering to Captain Louis. The British lost 74 killed and 264 wounded while it is estimated that the French lost nearly fifteen hundred. For this success, Thomas Louis was made a baronet and awarded, from the Patriotic Fund, a vase valued at £300.

Following this action, *Canopus* returned to the Mediterranean and ultimately joined Sir Thomas Duckworth in his attempt to force a passage through the Dardanelles in February 1807. The operation was a success, however, 'On the return through the Strait on 3 March the *Canopus* was struck by some of the huge stone shot fired by the Turks; her wheel was carried away and her hull much damaged, but she had only three men wounded. The squadron afterwards went to the coast of Egypt, and was left by Duckworth under the command of Louis. But Sir Thomas Louis died [of a severe fever] on board the *Canopus* on 17 May 1807.'

Provenance: Christie's King Street, lot 273, 12 November 1985.

References: The National Archives, Kew: ADM 36 / 11815-11818, 12829-18230, 14416-14423, 14287, 15723 Muster Rolls.
ADM 35 / 2075-2076 Pay Lists.
www.familysearch.org for christing date and parental information.
The Foating Republic by Manwaring and Dobree, Geoffrey Bles, London, 1935.
Nelson and the Nile by Brian Lavery, Chatham, London, 1998.
The Naval Chronicle, edited and published by Joyce Gold, London, 1799-1819 in 40 vols.
The Sailing Navy List by David Lyon, Conway, London, 1993.
Naval Achievements of Great Britain by James Jenkins, London, 1817, reprinted by Sim Comfort Associates, London, 1998.
Dictionary of National Biography, Oxford University Press, 1975.
Medals of the British Navy and How they were won by W. H. Long, Norie & Wilson, London, 1895.
One of Nelson's Band of Brothers, Admiral Sir Thomas Louis, Bart. by Henry Brakenbury Louis, St Edward's School, Malta, 1951.

The Coat of Arms awarded to Sir Thomas Louis for his success at San Domingo in 1806.

DN 13 James Keltie, Master, HMS Minotaur, Captain Thomas Louis

Description: Silver with a jeweller's gold wash and engraved in script: *Minotaur / Ja s Keltie / Master*. Weight 47 grams. Well worn and has served as a pocket piece for many years. Fine.

Background: Michael Lewis provides an interesting insight as to how the Captain and Master of a ship split their responsibilities. When referring to a Post Captain: 'Post is the operative word. It is a strange story. Very soon after we began fighting at sea we discovered that there were two posts on board that must be filled by competent persons - that of Master, the expert in navigation, and that of Captain, who from the first had directed the fighting but soon came to direct the whole: for we also quickly discovered the elementary truth that a double command is fatal. So the Captain became, and remained, more important than the Master. Yet the Master remained essential too, since the ship lost all value if cast away. So every ship of any size had to have both posts filled, the Captain's and - now under him but still as essential as ever - the Master's. Such ships were Post Ships and their Captains were Post Captains.'

On board ship, the Master wore a plain blue frock coat as did his Master's Mate, which was the highest post that a man before the mast could achieve within the Royal Navy.

Smyth also provides more information: 'An officer appointed by the commissioners of the navy to attend to the navigating a ship under the direction of the captain, the working of a ship into her station in the order of battle, and in other circumstances of danger, but he reports to the first lieutenant, who carries out any necessary evolution. It is likewise his duty, in concert with lieutenants to survey, to examine and report on the provisions. He is moreover charged with their stowage [i.e. to ensure the stowing of provisions is done in a manner that will keep the ship in trim and not create a ship that would handle awkwardly under sail.]

As a further note, it was the Master who would train the young Midshipmen in the art of navigation and understanding the various states of the sea and wind. He is often portrayed as a dourer husbander of his ship, always in abeyance to his captain, but could well be at loggerheads with captains that showed a lack of prudence.

Unfortunately, the muster rolls for the post 1793 period don't provide the age and birthplace of Commissioned and Warrant officers, so James Keltie's origins remain a mystery. However, with his surname spelled as Keltie (often misspelled Kelty by other sources) we have a fair indication that he was a Scot. From www.familysearch.org there are listed six James Kelties, all Scots and all born between 1743 and 1759. The National Archives does have a note stating that on 10 June 1802, James Keltie was 44 years old. From the above six names is James Keltie baptised 1 April 1757 at Saint Cuthberts, Edinburgh, Midlothian, which really does look like our man whose record at sea is both extensive and important.

We first meet James Keltie on board HMS *Salisbury*, a fourth rate of 50 guns, at Chatham where he volunteered as an Able Seaman on 13 August 1778. He was quickly re-rated as a Midshipman on 2 November. Early in 1779, the *Salisbury* sailed to the West Indies where she remained cruising out of Port Royal, Jamaica until August 1780 when she returned to Plymouth and was paid off.

Keltie was immediately transferred as a Midshipman to HMS *Queen*, a second rate of 90 guns. The *Queen* cruised in the English Channel and fought at the Second Battle of Ushant on 12 December 1781. 'A French convoy had sailed from Brest on 10 December with reinforcements and stores for the East and West Indies, protected by a fleet of 19 ships of the line commanded by Comte de Guichen. The British squadron of 13 ships of the line, commanded by Rear-Admiral Richard Kempenfelt in HMS *Victory*, which had been ordered to sea to intercept the expected convoy, sighted the French on 12 December, discovering only then that the protective escort had been strengthened. De Guichen's fleet was downwind of the convoy, which let the British ships sweep down to capture 18 ships carrying troops and supplies, before the French ships could intervene.'

With the ending of the American War, it appears that James Keltie had decided to make navigation his speciality and passed the examination for ship's Master. He was appointed in January 1783 to the frigate *Hyaena*, a sixth rate of 24 guns, which spent her time cruising in the Irish Sea. Keltie remained on board until 6 March 1786 when he came ashore after eight years of being continually employed at sea.

There is little doubt that Keltie heard of the newly conceived expedition to New South Wales to establish a penal colony. As background, the British had been shipping miscreants during much of the 18th century to the American colonies. It is estimated that something around fifty thousand convicts made the trip. With the American war, this practice obviously was no longer an option to the British government. The gaols and prison hulks in Britain were full to overflowing and a continuing cry from the public outlined the dreadful state of the prison system. A new destination had to be found.

With the discoveries of Captain Cook and more importantly the enthusiastic descriptions from Joseph Banks as to the suitability for the establishment of a colony in Botany Bay on the east coast of Australia, just a few miles south of what is now Sydney, the British government agreed to pursue a new colonial venture in New South Wales.

The First Fleet to Australia comprised the flagship, HMS *Sirius*, with Arthur Phillip as the overall commander of the expedition and governor designate for the new colony, Captain John Hunter, RN in command of the ship and Micah Morton as ship's Master. HMS *Supply* was the only other Royal Navy ship, while there were six private contract ships for conveying the 750 convicts (both men and women) and three further store ships which also carried passengers.

Taking into account the ship's crews and just over two hundred marines, in all, nearly 1,500 souls would set off on this great adventure.

The Royal Navy and marine contingents were largely volunteers for the voyage. The sailors expected to return to England once they had delivered the cargo, and the marine contingent understood that they would be posted for some time in New South Wales to both maintain order and defend the new colony. The convict men and women, however, were not selected as pioneers. Although their period of transportation was typically seven or fourteen years, they realised that this was a one way trip and that they would never see their families again.

David Hill notes, 'The preparation for the First Fleet's departure from Portsmouth was characterised by chaos, disease, promiscuity and death. It would take nine months to prepare and load the two navy ships, six convict transports and three supply ships with fifteen hundred people and two years' provisions and equipment.'

Although Keltie was a warranted Master in the Royal Navy, it appears that he was only able to secure a post as Master's Mate on board the private supply ship *Fishburn*, whose Master / Captain was Robert Brown. She carried twenty eight passengers and a crew of about fifty, but had no convicts on board. By coincidence, Keltie's last ship, HMS *Hyaena*, was the escort for the First Fleet during the sail down channel. I don't have from the Muster Rolls a direct transfer for Keltie from the *Hyaena* to the *Fishburn*, but it is possible, the Muster for the *Fishburn* has not survived.

The fleet of eleven ships finally set sail from Portsmouth on 13 May 1787. The route was south to Santa Cruz, Tenerife, then Port Praya, Cape Verde Islands before westing across the Atlantic to Rio de Janerio. The state of the holds of the ships where the convicts were kept was a constant worry and Phillip and his Surgeon, John White, continued to improve conditions. David Hill provides a note which describes a refusal to work by the crew of the *Friendship* where the crew wanted extra provisions of meat 'to give to the damned whores the convict women of whom they have found since they [the crew] broke through the bulk head and had made connections with them.'

The period in the doldrums was particularly bad as the convict hulks had no port holes and there was no circulation of air in the foul holds. On 6 August, the fleet finally arrived in Rio. On 31 August, Lieutenant Bradley notes in his journal, 'Mr Morton, Master of the *Sirius* was invalided, having received a hurt on the passage from Tenerife which rendered him for a time of incapable of duty....Mr Seally & Mr Rotton two of the Master's Mates were also invalided their health being in so bad a state as to make it necessary & there being an English ship boarded to London. ...Mr Kelty a Master in the Navy & serving as mate on board one of the store ships was appointed Master of the *Sirius*.'

Many of the crew and passengers in the fleet were suffering from malnutrition by the time they arrived at Rio, with twenty brought low with scurvy. The Portuguese governor of Rio and his staff couldn't do enough for supplying the fleet with all their needs.

The trip to Cape Town was hard with contrary winds and then upon arrival the Dutch were far less welcoming than the officials of Rio, however on 13 November the fleet set off on the final leg of their journey. Taken on board at the Cape were many species of fruit and other useful plants along with a very considerable selection of livestock to be used to establish herds in Australia. As one would imagine, with the livestock on deck and the convicts directly below, this was not an arrangement for maintaining a healthy ship.

The fleet struggled against head winds after leaving Cape Town. Phillip decided to split the fleet and move his command to HMS *Supply*, which although small was fast. The three fastest transports were also added to the squadron, the *Alexander*, *Scarborough* and *Friendship*.

On 25 November, the two squadrons separated with the *Sirius* and slow transports under the overall command of John Hunter, Captain of the *Sirius*. As soon as Hunter felt he was fully on his own, he changed course to a much more southerly direction. He had long felt that to gain real speed in the Southern Ocean, one had to be well south, and he was right.

With both squadrons following the southern coast of Australia and rounding Van Diemen's Land to then beat up the east coast of Australia, it was Arthur Phillip in the *Supply* who won the race having reached Botany Bay on 18 January 1788. The other three ships in the fast squadron arrived the next day and to everybody's surprise, the slow squadron arrived the following day, 20 January. This must have brought a wide grin to both Captain Hunter and James Keltie, his Master.

All of the ships were now in Botany Bay. Although the conditions on board had often been horrendous, the reality was that all eleven ships made the trip and only sixty-nine deaths had occurred out of nearly 1,500 crew and passengers, and that most of those who had died were the very infirm who passed away either in Portsmouth or during the first few weeks at sea. It took only a day in Botany Bay for Arthur Phillip to decide that this was not the place to establish the colony. Water was scarce, the trees weren't suitable for building and the soil was sandy. Worse was the exposure of the anchorage to an east wind and with the sea in the bay being quite rough at the time, a new site had to be found quickly.

The next day, 21 January, David Hill relates, 'With the fleet in Botany Bay and the convicts and cargo still aboard, Phillip departed [in three small boats] with John Hunter, James Keltie, Judge David Collins and a number of other officers to examine Port Jackson, twelve kilometres to the north. They had very little idea what to expect at Port Jackson, as the only information about it was a brief mention in Cook's journal from eighteen years ago. Cook had made only a passing observation about what he named Port Jackson as they sailed past several miles at sea.

'Phillip's three boats reached the mouth of Port Jackson in the early afternoon and rowed through the one and a half kilometre gap between the north and south headlands into the harbour. That night they pitched tents in the small inlet on the south side, which is still called Camp Cove.

'Mindful that more than fourteen hundred people and many starving animals were still aboard ships in Botany Bay awaiting instructions, Phillip quickly explored a number of coves that might be suitable. Later on the second day and some six kilometres deeper into Port Jackson, Phillip discovered a sheltered bay about eight hundred metres long and four hundred metres wide, which had fresh water running into it. He decided it was here, and not Botany Bay, that the settlers would found the new colony. He was to describe Port Jackson as the 'finest harbour in the world' and name the site of the proposed settlement Sydney Cove after the Home Secretary, Lord Sydney.'

So, James Keltie was there probably in charge of taking soundings in Sydney Cove. The American, Jacob Nagle, was also there as he was part of Phillip's boat crew. It wasn't until 26 January that the rest of the fleet joined Phillip at Sydney Cove and it is this day that is celebrated as Australia Day.

Keltie was regularly part of any exploration team led by either Arthur Phillip or John Hunter at Port Jackson and later Botany Bay. Lieutenant Bradley relates an incident during a trip up Sydney harbour when Keltie, 'shot a fish in a branch of a high tree which we got and ate, the fish was in the claws of a large hawk when fired at, dropped it and flew away.' This was such a good joke that Lieutenant Bradley painted a watercolour of 'A view of the upper part of Port Jackson; where the fish was shot.'

With time, the situation at Sydney Cove grew more and more desperate due to lack of food. On the 2nd of October 1788, Captain John Hunter, James Keltie and the rest of the crew of HMS *Sirius* set sail for Cape Town by sailing the Southern Ocean south past New Zealand, south east past Cape Horn and east to Cape Town. Almost immediately after departing Port Jackson, the *Sirius* sprang a serious leak which was to tax the crew during the whole of the voyage. Lieutenant William Bradley recorded in his journal on 21 December, 'We first were with Ice Islands November 25, so that we were 28 days floating with these lumps of misery in sight & near 836 leagues [2,500 miles] through be-

Lieutenant William Bradley's view of shooting the fish.
Image courtesy of the State Library, New South Wales.

tween them, which was frequently rendered very dangerous from the thick fogs which we had much of after passing Cape Horn.....No particular occurrence happened till the ever memorable 25th on which day at Noon we arrived at the Meridian of Greenwich having since last passing it, sailed East round the South Pole: we therefore drop 360 degrees of Longitude & begin East Longitude again, repeating Thursday 25th December to make our time correspond with that at Greenwich. In this voyage we have had two Christmas Days & it being leap year 367 in the year; what few of any Navigators can boast of. ' On the second of January 1789, the *Sirius* arrived at Table Bay, a really remarkable run for two months and a fine feat of navigation for Master James Keltie.

216

Jacob Nagle reported that at one point they had passed amongst whales with numbers so thick that they could not count them and that their spouting soaked all the crew on deck with spray.

Scurvy had beset the crew and when they arrived at Table Bay, Captain Hunter wrote in his log, 'we had just twelve men in each watch, and half that number, from scorbutic contractions of their limbs, were not able to go aloft.' Fresh fruit was immediately brought on board. Jacob Nagle wrote that when 'biting an apple, peach or pear the blood would run out of our mouth from our gums.'

Captain Hunter stayed in Cape Town only long enough for his crew to revive and to load supplies for Sydney Cove. *Sirius* departed Cape Town on 20 February and arrived at Sydney Cove on 2 May. Both legs of this trip were remarkably fast and one can imagine that both Hunter and Keltie were stretched to the limit to achieve such success.

Governor Phillip was greatly relieved, but no other help from England had arrived. Unknown to Arthur Philip was the loss of the *Guardian* relief ship which was captained by Lieutenant Edward Riou, RN, who had sailed on Cook's third voyage. Riou had decided to sail deep into the Southern Ocean following departure from Cape Town, but on Christmas Eve hit a large iceberg. The thought of reaching Port Jackson was abandoned and livestock, plants and stores were thrown overboard in a desperate attempt to save the ship and the crew. Those who wished could take the ship's boats and fare for themselves, of these only one boat made it back to Cape Town. For the remainder of the crew, they were rescued by a Dutch vessel off the east coast of Africa, and the *Guardian* was assisted all the way to Cape Town, where she was in such bad shape, that she was broken up. Riou would suffer further misfortune by being killed in action as Captain of HMS *Amazon* at the battle of Copenhagen, 2 April 1801.

Arthur Phillip learning of good harvests on Norfolk Island and in an effort to reduce the strain on the ever diminishing store of food at Sydney Cove, on 5 March 1789 sent 200 convicts and a number of marines on board the *Supply* and *Sirius* to Norfolk Island. On 19 March, while unloading the convicts and supplies at Norfolk Island, the *Sirius* dragged her anchor and was quickly caught in the pounding surf of the reef. Every effort was made to rescue as much of the supplies as possible from the doomed ship. Thus Captain Hunter and James Keltie and the rest of the crew of the *Sirius* were marooned on Norfolk Island until 27 March 1791, when the hired Dutch vessel *Waaksamheyd* picked them up for the journey back to England where they arrived in April, 1792. Both Captain Hunter and James Keltie were tried by court martial for the loss of the *Sirius*, and both acquitted as were the rest of the ship's company. John Hunter was to return to New South Wales to become the second Governor of the colony.

James Keltie was discharged from the service on 4 May 1792, undoubtedly in need of a rest. The cruise of the *Sirius* has to stand as one of the greatest voyages of any Royal Navy ship. However with the commencement of the French wars, he returned to sea on 1 February 1793 as Master of HMS *Beaulieu* and sailed in the West Indies and North American stations. He then transferred to HMS *Assurance* in the West Indies on 23 March 1795. He was subsequently on board HMS *Canada* and *Malabar*, again making trips to the West Indies.

The *Malabar*! David Hepper tells the story: 'The *Malabar* (1,252 tons, Captain Thomas Parr), sailed from Jamaica in July 1796 with a homeward bound convoy, but she became separated in poor weather about eight hundred miles west of Land's End. By 5 October the weather had deteriorated into a full Atlantic storm, the *Malabar* suffering badly. She was a former East Indiaman and was a slow, sluggish sailor, difficult to handle. She rolled very deeply, the bowsprit becoming unseated, which led to its loss, and in two days all three masts had been rolled overboard, the rudder unshipped and the tiller broken. She had been given iron knees rather than the traditional oak and these soon pulled out, allowing the beams to work loose. When the securing bolts for the carronades pulled out of the bulwarks, four of the guns came loose, crashing across the waist, smashing the booms and the boats on them, killing one man and injuring four until they were tumbled down a hatchway. All the guns were heaved overboard after this and jury masts rigged as the winds moderated, although the ship continued to work her timbers. On 8 October the merchant brig *Martha* of Whitby came in sight and stood by the *Malabar* until the crew could be taken off, she was abandoned three days later [11 October 1796]. Lieutenant Richard Crocombe was dismissed the service afterwards for 'reprehensible conduct', as he seemed to have spent most of the time in the wardroom getting drunk. Also criticized was the Master, James Keltie, who was seen on the quarterdeck with Crocombe drinking, and later, when a party of seamen went to check the broken rudder, he was so drunk that he 'tumbled out of his cabin, almost puked.....and tumbled over to leeward and disabled himself.' He was ordered to be reprimanded.'

James Keltie certainly wasn't the first, nor would he be the last sailor who decided that being dead drunk was the way to meet Davey Jones when stuck with a doomed ship. But unlike Conrad's Lord Jim and the S.S. *Jeddah*, the *Malabar* was doomed, although not the officers and crew, so Keltie had to face the discredit linked with his conduct.

Following a few months rest, it appears that Keltie managed to recoup and on 21 February 1797, he came on board HMS *Minotaur* as ship's Master. For details of the *Minotaur* at the Nile and her subsequent cruise, please see DN 12. However, keeping the role of the Master during the battle in mind as noted by Smyth, once Captain Louis had decided where he wanted *Minotaur* stationed, it was up to James Keltie to get her there and anchor her beside the French 74-gun ship *Aquilon*. On 15 August 1800, Keltie transferred to HMS *Regulus* at Port Mahon and took part in Lord Keith's landing of troops at Aboukir Bay in 1801. He then transferred on 17 October 1801 to HMS *Dictator* from which he was discharged on 9 February 1802 to Haslar Hospital, Gosport.

There is a letter (ADM 106/ 2928) written on 12 June 1802 to an unknown addressee from Captain John Hunter which reads, 'You will, I am sure, excuse the liberty I take in recommending to your kindness Mr James Keltie, late Master of the *Minotaur*. He sailed formerly with me in the *Sirius*, was wrecked with me on Norfolk Island, & has been at this War employed on Arduous and Active Service. When I returned from New South Wales the first time, Sir Henry Martin gave him a Division at Deptford, but the Service requiring that he should serve afloat again, he held that situation only about six months & was promised that he should again have the Chance of returning to it when the Service would admit, from these Considerations, I am induced to trouble you in his favour, for which I will not venture any other Apology than this short Statement of his Service. [signed] John Hunter.'

After a year's absence, James Keltie was again appointed as Master, this time to HMS *Spartiate* on 24 March 1803 where he remained until 27 March 1804. From Mackaness, we learn that his next appointment was in July 1804 to HMS *Warrior*, Captain William Bligh. This was a short cruise with *Warrior* returning to Portsmouth in November. Bligh behaved true to form and a court martial was required by Lieutenant John Frazier where he accused Bligh on charges of 'tyranny, unofficer-like conduct and ungentlemanly behaviour.' The trial was a turgid affair with lots of name calling which included Bligh naming James Keltie as 'a damned old rascal and a villain.'

One can only imagine what James Keltie thought of all this. The result of the court martial was that Bligh was admonished, but continued in the service, and Lieutenant John Frazier is heard of no more. Perhaps the knowledge that Bligh would himself become Governor of New South Wales and the subject of the only military coup in Australian history is particularly apt.

Further records in the National Archives show that Keltie continued to serve in ships, but for only short periods. We then have a document dated 20 November 1810 (ADM 106/2928) which details a medical survey of Master, James Keltie, currently employed on board HMS *Namur* at the Nore, 'and do find him aged, and labouring under Chronic Rheumatism, Piles and Debility:- after a long period of arduous and active Service and we do consider him totally unfit to serve in any Active Situation, etc. etc.'

Although, James Keltie was not to go to sea again, he was posted on 17 January 1811 to the *Sampson*, a prison ship anchored off Chatham. The *Sampson* was effectively the Colditz of its day where the prisoners of war who attempted to escape were kept. On 31 May, there was a demonstration by the prisoners over food. Upon being ordered to return below deck, the prisoners refused and the commander, Lieutenant Monnier, ordered the marines to open fire. The log records three prisoners killed and six seriously wounded. A French account has the killed and wounded at twenty. Three days later, 263 pounds of fresh beef was brought on board. We don't know Keltie's role during this action, but I have to think that shooting men in cold blood was not what he had signed up for.

On 28 July 1812, Keltie was ordered 'to superintend the raising of the mud from the river before Woolwich Yard and the Storehouse at Deptford', which was a job for the convict ship *Censor*. Not very glamorous, but one would sleep ashore each night.

And so passes a truly great man of the sea after thirty years of near continuous service. I can well imagine James Keltie sitting by the fire and drawing this medal from his pocket just to reflect on much better times with adventures enough for any man.

The engraved coins for Sirius, Sampson and Censor are all from this author's
Forget Me Not, a study of naval and maritime engraved coins.

219

Provenance: Medal fair, 1982.

References: The National Archives, Kew: ADM 36 / 7989, 7990, 8700 - 8703, 8708, 8712, 10315, 10341, 10692, 10917, 10968, 10978, 11031, 11151, 11248, 11779, 11919, 11957, 12829, 14416 - 14418, 14420, 15106, 15107, 15340, 15999 Muster Rolls. ADM 102 vol. 287 Haslar Hospital Muster Roll. ADM 106 vol. 2928 & Index, Master's Papers. ADM 37/2853 (Muster, *Sampson*), ADM 52/4601 (Master's log, *Sampson*), ADM 51/2843 (Capt's Log, *Sampson*).
A Social History of the Navy 1793 - 1815 by Michael Lewis, George Allen and Unwin, London, 1960.
The Sailor's Word-Book, by Admiral W. H. Smyth, Blackie, London, 1867.
www.wikipedia.com (Battle of Ushant).
The Sailing Navy List by David Lyon, Conway, London, 1993.
British Warship Names, by Manning & Walker, Putnam, London, 1959.
1788, the Brutal Truth of the First Fleet, by David Hill, Heineman, Sydney, 2008.
A Voyage to New South Wales, by Lieut. William Bradley of HMS Sirius, Ure Smith, Sydney, 1969.
The Nagle Journal, edited by John Dann, Weidenfeld & Nicolson, New York, 1988.
The life of Vice Admiral William Bligh, by George Mackaness, Angus & Robertson, London, 1951.
British Warship Losses in the Age of Sail (1650-1859) by David J Hepper, Boudriot, Rotherfield, East Sussex, 1994.
The English Prison Hulks by W. Branch Johnson, Phillimore, London, 1970.
Forget Me Not, by Sim Comfort, Sim Comfort Associates, London, 2004.

DN 14 William Stonelake, Ordinary Seaman and Cook, HMS Minotaur, Captain Thomas Louis and HMS Tonnant, Captain Charles Tyler

Description: The bronze Davison Nile is jeweller gilt and engraved *William Stonelike / Minotaur & / Tonnant*. The medal had added a device for suspension which was later removed and then fitted in a gilt glazed case which is housed in a leather case. Weight, medal only: 39.9 grams. Medal and glazed case: 67 grams. Extremely fine.

The Naval General Service medal, with its original ribbon, has both the Nile and Trafalgar clasps and is impressed on the rim William Stonelake. Very fine.

Background: This is a case of serendipity at work. When Gillian Hughes was researching the Davison Nile medal to William Stonelake at the National Archives, she let me know that she had met an employee at the National Army Museum who had asked her to have a look in the Archives for William Stonelake's service as he had his Naval General Service medal. Money changed hands and the group were once again united!

I am always particularly careful when there is a Davison Nile or a Boulton Trafalgar medal to a man who also received the Naval General Service medal. The desire to create a group is very great for the collector. So the question is: Was this Davison Nile engraved at the time that the NGS was awarded in 1848 or is the engraving of an earlier date? Or was the engraving carried out in the 20th century in an effort to enhance the value of the NGS by creating a group of two medals?

First, the Nile medal is in two states, i.e. it had a suspension device added early in its life. This was subsequently removed so that the medal could be cased and glazed for safe keeping. As William Stonelake lived to 1848, fifty years after the Battle of the Nile, this change to the medal could have been carried out by him. The engraving in the reverse field is in the same hand and as it cites both the *Minotaur* and *Tonnant*, then it had to have been carried out post Trafalgar. That the engraver misspells Stonelake is strange, but then it is an unusual name and to me harks to a 19th century error as opposed to a 20th century mistake. If the name was copied from the NGS roll post 1910, then it would have been spelled correctly as it is correct in the roll.

So, for what it is worth, I think the medal was William Stonelake's Davison Nile and that he had a suspension added so that he could wear it on the anniversary of the Nile. Sometime, much later, he decided to retire his medal and have it engraved with the names of his two most important ships, the *Minotaur* and the *Tonnant*, which he was on board at Trafalgar. I think the medal was gilt, cased and glazed at that time and that the case was most likely gold. There is evidence on the rim which indicates the medal had been tightly inset into a case. The medal then, some years later, went to a pawn broker or a general jeweller who removed the medal from its case on the basis that the gold of the case was worth more than the medal. From here it drifted into the medal collecting world and ultimately to myself. I have supplied the glazed casing that the medal is now kept in. The NGS medal went through a similar fate, ultimately going to a medal collector and hence to myself which has reunited the two medals. And what a wonderful pair they are!

William Stonelake gave his age as 20 years old from Teignmouth, Devon when he appeared on board HMS *Cumberland* as a volunteer on 8 March 1793. From the International Genealogical Index, there is a record of the christening at West Teignmouth, Devon on 6 January 1776 of William Stonelake whose father was James and mother Elizabeth. Further searches show no other candidates, so William has increased his age upon joining the Royal Navy by four or five years. As he was immediately rated Ordinary Seaman, then he was certainly a lad who had spent time at sea, probably in the merchant marine and may well have been at sea from the age of twelve or thirteen. On 22 March 1794, he transferred to HMS *Minotaur* along with his Captain, Thomas Louis and nearly all of the ship's company of the *Cumberland*. For the history of the *Minotaur* at the Battle of the Nile, please review DN 12.

Something happened to William Stonelake at either the battle or sometime not long after as he was transferred to HMS *Colossus* on 5 October 1798 as a supernumerary passenger along with other wounded men from the Nile. Although we have no firm information as to what ailed him, it is most likely that he suffered the loss of a foot, a leg or an arm and was being sent back to England to recuperate.

Stonelake's adventures certainly weren't over. *Colossus* was to be the ship that would take the fabulous collection of Greek and Roman ceramics that had been assembled by the great antiquarian Sir William Hamilton, the British envoy at Naples and husband to Emma. *Colossus* departed from Naples with William Stonelake and Sir William Hamilton's treasure on board in October and called at Algiers and later Lisbon. She arrived in England and anchored off St Mary's in the Scilly Isles on 7 December as a storm was coming. The wind increased and even though additional anchors were employed and masts struck, the ship continued to drift until during the night of the tenth, she hit hard on the reef. By morning, *Colossus* was breaking up. Local boats came out to bring the ship's company and passengers ashore, only one man drowned. But Sir William Hamilton's vast collection was lost to the deep.

As a note, the Cornish treasure hunter, Roland Morris in the 1970s found the wreck and was able to recover much of Sir William's collection of vases, but after nearly two hundred years thrashing about in the sea, they had been smashed into a million shards. Some were able to be reconstructed by the British Museum and are on display.

Stonelake was first taken on board the gun boat *Hecate* on 16 December and then on the 20th to HMS *Cambridge* and from her to Plymouth Hospital. It is noted that there were six invalids from the *Hecate* (late *Colossus*) of which four had previously been on board *Minotaur*. It appears that after 21 days in hospital Stonelake was discharged, but he hadn't finished with the sea yet.

On 2 July 1799 he appeared on board HMS *Fisgard*, Captain Thomas Byam Martin, and was rated Cook. Michael Lewis tells us that the cook, 'was a pensioner seldom in possession at once of both arms, both legs and both eyes.' During action stations, the cook would first ensure that the fire of the ship's stove was fully extinguished and then reside with the Master-at-Arms in the Light Room keeping track of the powder coming from the Magazine.'

John Masefield tells us, 'An important member of the ship's crew was the cook. This warrant officer was appointed by the Commissioners of the Navy, who invariably chose him from the Greenwich pensioners. He was seldom blessed with all his limbs, and never rose beyond the making of pea-soup and the boiling of junk. His duty was very simple. He had to steep the salt junk served out to him in a barrel of salt water, known as the steep tub. When the meat had become a little soft and pliable, through the dissolution of the salt, he took it and boiled it for several hours, or until the boatswain piped to dinner. It was then served out to the different messes. Directly the last piece had been handed out the coppers were skimmed. The salt fat or slush, the cook's perquisite, was scraped out and placed in the slush tub. Half of all the slush went to the cook. The other half went to the ship, for the greasing of the bottom and running rigging. The coppers were then scoured, and made ready for the cooking of the next meal. A cook was not allowed to give the slush or melted fat to the men, as they used it in making their private duffs or puddings, and scarcely anything more unwholesome, or more likely to produce scurvy, can be eaten. A cook was expected to be frugal with his firewood, except after a battle, when he had generally a stack of splinters to eke out his store. He was expected to keep the galley clean, and usually had a mate or assistant, with the full complement of limbs, to help him in his work. His pay was very small, being only about thirty-five shillings a month, but as he was always a Greenwich pensioner, in receipt of 11s 8d. a month relief, and as he generally cleared a handsome sum from his slush, the pay was sufficient. He wore no uniform, kept no watch, seldom strayed very far from his galley, and slept at nights on the lower gun-deck, in a favoured place, with the ship's corporal for his neighbour.'

From *Jack Tar* we have, 'The stove comprised chain-driven spits, coppers with lids for boiling, ovens and hot plates. Cooking was done mainly by boiling in the coppers. The meals of the officers were cooked here as well, mostly by their servants, using more elaborate techniques. Further, drawing on Robert Wilson, the ship's cook assisted by his mates dresses the victuals for the ship's company, i.e. for all those under the denomination of officers. The cook's mate does all the drudgery work, the cook inspects him. Every article into which the provisions are put is perfectly clean. The serving out of the provisions out of the boilers or coppers is managed entirely by the cook himself, for if there is any deficiency, he is answerable for it. When he receives the meat from the Ship's Steward he has to count the number of pieces he receives, and to provide himself with a list of those messes which have received any raw meat so as to know what quantity of dressed meat to give them. As the cooks in general are not over and above stocked with learning, the manner in which they serve out the provisions by the list is by making a mark with a pin on the paper opposite the number of the messes issued out to.

'The post of cook was not a laborious one and was usually given to a disabled seaman: The cooks are in most ships men that have lost a precious limb, or otherwise maimed in the defence of their King and Country, so as a compensation they receive a warrant as cooks. At the same time most of them are entitled to pensions, so that with their wages and perquisites, of fat [slush] etc., and their pensions together, they make it out pretty well. They are for the most part of them elderly men who have seen much of seafaring life, and when their work is finished for the day they'll take their pipes, seat themselves in Copper Alley, and spin you a long yard [yarn]...about what they have seen and done.'

As a further note, it is recorded that Admiral Collingwood often served his officers the same fare of Salt Junk that the ship's company ate. Midshipman Parsons related that, 'Sir Sidney [Smith] asserted that rats fed cleaner and were better eating than pigs or ducks; and, agreeably to his wish, a dish of these beautiful vermin were caught daily with fish hooks, well baited, in the provision hold, and served up at the captain's table.'

HMS *Fisgard* was the captured French *La Resistance* taken by the *San Fiorenzo* and others on the 9th of March 1797. She was 160 feet in length and 1182 tons burthen with a ship's company of 280 men. In the Royal Navy her armament was 28 x 18 pounders (later 32 pounder Carronades) on the Upper Deck, 4 x 9 pounders and 10 x 32 pounder Carronades on the Quarterdeck and 4 x 32 pounder Carronades in the Forecastle. She was a quite powerful fifth rate frigate of 44 / 46 guns.

T. B. Martin was a man of intellect, energy and fire! His ship, the *Fisgard* was one of the most powerful frigates in the Royal Navy and he put her to good use. John Marshall notes in his biographical sketch of Martin that on the 20th of October 1798, the *Fisgard* off Brest met with the equally powerful French frigate, *l'Immortalite*. After an hour's action, the *Fisgard* had suffered greatly in her running rigging and so fell away to repair damage while the enemy endeavoured to flee. Having made repairs, the *Fisgard* commenced the chase and after an hour and fifty minutes of further action secured the prize. William Stonelake wasn't present for this action, but was for the next.

Captain Martin's working under the orders of Commodore Sir John Bolase Warren off the west coast of France, demonstrated his willingness to attack. On the morning of 23 June 1800, it was determined that the boats of the squadron, under the immediate command of Captain Martin should attack some armed and other vessels up the Quimper river. 'Two parties of marines were landed, one on each bank of the river, in order to protect the boats in the execution of the service, which were going on with the expedition to the attack; but it was then found that the enemy had removed the vessels higher up the river. The British then immediately landed, and stormed and blew up three batteries, on which were mounted seven 24 pounders, together with their magazines.'

'On the 1st of the following month, the Commodore having been informed that a ship of war and a number of merchant vessels were lying within the island of Noirmoutier, destined for Brest, resolved to attempt their destruction. Captain Martin was appointed to head and direct the enterprise. As the enemy never conceived themselves free from danger, they had used every means in their power to defend and protect the vessels which were lying within the sands of Bourneuf Bay, moored in a strong position, under the protection of six heavy batteries, besides flanking guns on every projecting point.

'The boats destined for the attack were formed into three divisions...and sent from the *Fisgard* soon after dark. By midnight, they reached their destination; immediately boarded, and after experiencing a very formidable resistance, succeeded in obtaining possession of the ship of war, four armed vessels, and fifteen merchantmen, but as they found it impracticable to bring them out, the whole were burnt.

'The most arduous and dangerous part of the business was still to be performed. [The tide had run out which left the British stranded on an extended beach.] In this unfortunate and unexpected situation, they were exposed to a continued fire from the forts; and besides this, a body of 400 French soldiers drew up in their rear, and fired on them with great effect. In this critical state of their affairs, they resolved to make an attempt, so very singularly daring, that none but British seamen could have either executed or conceived it; they determined to make an attack on some other vessels of the enemy, for the purpose of securing one sufficiently large to carry off the whole party, as there was no chance of their succeeding in getting off all their boats. They according set out, and succeeded in gaining possession of a vessel suited for their purpose; but she lay on the opposite side of the bay, and before she could be of service to them, it was necessary to drag her upwards of two miles over the sands.'

In the end, out of 192 officers and men employed, 100 secured their retreat and the remainder were made prisoners of the French. Cook William Stonelake certainly wasn't amongst them, but I would hope that he had a pot of hot grog waiting for the survivors!

Marshall concludes the service of Captain Martin on board *Fisgard* with the Peace of Amiens, 'in addition to the above services, either took, or assisted at the capture, of the following French and Spanish armed vessels:-*La Venus* of 32 guns and 200 men; *Dragon* corvette of 14 guns; *la Gironde* privateer of 16 guns and 141 men; *l'Alerte* privateer of 14 guns and 84 men; *El Vivo* national vessel of 14 guns and 100 men; and three others mounting 18 guns.' As Cook, Stonelake would have received his share of prize money as an 'inferior officer', so this cruise would have produced quite a nest egg.

Stonelake stayed on board *Fisgard* as she cruised in the approaches to the Channel and regularly put into Plymouth. It appears he left the ship in June 1802 when the ship went into dock for repairs. We lose track of him until 1 April 1803 when he was entered on board HMS *Tonnant* as her Cook. William Stonelake was to remain on board *Tonnant* until 7 September 1815, a little over twelve years and under the command of fifteen different captains, two of whom were to die on board.

HMS *Tonnant* was the last of the ships captured at the Nile and was most likely dismasted by Lieutenant Robert Cuthbert commanding the *Majestic*. Within the Royal Navy she was classed as a Large Two-Decker (Third Rate), and she was indeed large and powerful. *Tonnant* was 194 feet in length and 2,281 tons. She mounted 84 guns arranged as 32 x 32 pounders on the Gun Deck, 32 x 18 pounders on the Upper Deck, 2 x 18 pounders and 14 x 32 pounder Carronades on the Quarterdeck and 4 x 32 pounder Carronades in the Forecastle. Her ship's company would be around 700 officers and men. She was broken up in 1821.

Tonnant made up part of the vast fleet under the command of Admiral Cornwallis which stretched from the Danish coast to Gibraltar in an effort to totally blockade the French ports and keep their fighting ships within and deter the supply of provisions. This was hard sailing in keeping so many ships on station.

In the spring of 1803, *Tonnant* was commanded by Sir Edward Pellew and then in April 1804 by Captain William Jervis, who was a nephew of Earl St Vincent. The *Naval Chronicle* relates that in January 1805 it was discovered that the French squadron at Rochfort had escaped port and in an effort to communicate this information to Vice-Admiral Sir Charles Cotton, who commanded that section of Cornwallis's fleet, Captain Jervis set out in a boat from the *Tonnant* to the Admiral's ship. 'Unfortunately, when she got about half way, a sea broke into the boat; and, before the crew could extricate her, another sea broke; she upset, and Captain Jervis and one of the boat's crew were drowned.'

Sir Charles Tyler (1760 - 1835) was appointed as captain of *Tonnant* in February 1805. Tyler had a long and eventful career. He joined the navy aged 11 and mainly served in large gun ships of the line. While on the North American station in 1777, he suffered an injury to his leg which resulted 'in the removal of a small bone', which caused him to convalesce for two years and left him lame for the rest of this life. He was promoted to Lieutenant in 1779 and continued to serve in large ships, mainly in the Channel. From 1784 to 1789, he commanded HMS *Trimmer*, mainly out of Milford in an effort to suppress smuggling. In 1790, Tyler was promoted to Post-Captain and in March 1793 given command of the *Meleager* frigate and went out to the Mediterranean with Lord Hood and took part in the reduction of Calvi. He was given command of the *San Fiorenzo*, one of the prizes, and in February 1794 to the *Diadem* of 64 guns. While in this command an event occurred that would have a lasting impact upon Britain's naval forces. Stationed on board *Diadem* was a detachment of the 11th Regiment of Foot, acting in the role of marines and under the command of Lieutenant Fitzgerald. Fitzgerald felt that as a military officer, he was independent of Captain Tyler's command and acted with contempt toward Tyler, who recorded the event and called for a court-martial to clarify his command.

Fitzgerald was found guilty of contempt and cashiered from the service. The Duke of York took up the matter and declared that military officers were independent, however it was proved that this contravened an Act of Parliament and as a result all military personnel were put ashore from His Majesty's Ships and fully replaced by marines. With the involvement of Earl St Vincent in 1802, the marines were given a Royal Warrant by King George III and were known thereafter as Royal Marines.

During 1795 and 1796, the *Diadem* was frequently under the command of Commodore Nelson operating in the Gulf of Genoa. Later, Tyler was given command of the *Aigle* frigate, but unfortunately wrecked her off the coast of Tunis in July 1798 which meant he missed the Nile. In February 1799 he was appointed to the *Warrior* and joined Hyde Parker's fleet for Copenhagen in 1801, but was held in reserve and saw no action on 2 April. This was followed by a cruise to the West Indies and then home with the *Warrior* being paid off due to the Peace of Amiens.

When the war resumed in 1803, Tyler was given command of a district of Sea Fencibles, however as noted, in early 1805 he took command of the *Tonnant*. She was initially assigned as part of the Channel Fleet, but with the likelihood of action by Nelson's fleet off Cadiz, she sailed to join him. On 21 October, *Tonnant* was stationed fourth behind the *Royal Sovereign*, located between *Mars* and *Bellerophon*, as the leeward column sailed into the wall of fire created by the broadsides of the enemy fleet. By the time *Tonnant* broke through the line, the *Royal Sovereign* was hotly engaged with the *Santa Anna*, the *Belleisle* with the *Fougeux* and the *Mars* was being raked by both the *Santa Anna* and the *Pluton*.

As the *Tonnant* approached, the *Fougeux* broke free from the *Belleisle*, who just lost her mizzen mast, and turned her attention toward the *Mars*. Captain George Duff of the *Mars* and his officers where having great difficulty distinguishing friend from foe due to the cloud of cannon smoke that surround the field of battle. Duff went to the rail for a better look just as the *Fougeux* unleashed her broadside. Duff died instantly with the loss of his head and the quarterdeck of the *Mars* was decimated. Lieutenant William Hennah took command and fought the ship during the rest of the battle.

Tonnant cut the enemy line between the *Monarca* and *Algesiras*, 'so close that a biscuit might have been thrown on board either of them.' With double shotted guns she poured fire into the hulls of both ships. The third broadside from the *Tonnant* into the *Monarca* silenced her for a while and then she drifted astern and hauled down her colours. Seeing the *Pluton* ahead pouring broadside after broadside into the helpless *Mars*, Captain Tyler directed his ship toward her and while still engaging the *Algesiras* on the starboard side, poured his larboard broadside into the *Pluton*. This was the chance that the *Algesiras* was waiting for and passed down the starboard side of *Tonnant* in an attempt to rake her stern. Tyler saw the danger and turned to starboard which resulted in the *Algesiras's* bow crashing into *Tonnant's* starboard side with her bowsprit tangled in the *Tonnant's* main rigging which held her there and at the mercy of *Tonnant's* raking broadsides.

Captain Magon of the *Algesiras* immediately ordered the boarding of the *Tonnant*. The boarding party rushed to the bows, but the *Tonnant's* were ready with their quarterdeck carronades loaded with grape shot. Few of the French boarding party survived the initial blast from *Tonnant*. The fight between *Tonnant* and *Algesiras* continued for more than an hour. With the cannonade being at point blank range it was only a matter of time before both ships caught fire which both sides were able to contain, however the constant cannonade coming from *Tonnant* began to give the British the upper hand. Captain Tyler had been taken below with a musket shot in his right thigh. Lieutenant John Bedford took command of the ship. Not long after, the *Algesiras* was left wallowing in the swell with all three of her masts over the side. Lieutenant Bedford immediately called for boarders and sixty *Tonnants* roared over the side with cutlasses, pikes and tomahawks. They met little resistance and soon had the *Algesiras* under their command.

The *Algesiras* now drifted away, but the *San Juan Nepomuceno* came into view, and the *Tonnant* was able to give the enemy her full starboard broadside. Her foremast fell, the *Tonnants* cheered and gave her another, which resulted in the Spaniard hauling down her colours, but the attempt to get boarders over to the enemy failed and the *San Juan Nepomuceno* drifted away leaving the *Tonnant* in a fairly shattered state herself. *Tonnant's* ship's company lost 26 killed and 50 wounded where the loss of the *Monarca*, *Algesiras* and *San Juan Nepomuceno* had a combined butcher's bill of over seven hundred men.

Sir Charles Tyler's Lloyd's Patriotic Fund Trafalgar sword. Image courtesy of Bonham's.

When one considers the plight of Collingwood's supporting ships: *Mars*, Captain Duff killed; *Tonnant*, Captain Tyler badly wounded; *Bellerophon*, Captain Cooke killed; one may appreciate that this section of the enemy's fleet appears to have offered stiffer resistance than the section that Nelson and *Victory* broke through.

Trafalgar saw the end of fighting at sea for Charles Tyler who was promoted to Rear-Admiral in 1808 and stationed as second-in-command at Portsmouth. This was followed by other shore-based postings with the last being commander-in-chief at the Cape of Good Hope, which was followed by his return to England in 1816. The usual honours followed and he died at Gloucester in 1835.

For William Stonelake we know that he survived Trafalgar and that by 1 April 1806 he was a married man as he signed a Power of Attorney in favour of his wife Martha who resided at 6 George Street, Stonehouse, Devon. He stayed on board *Tonnant* cruising in the Channel. In 1809 she assisted in the evacuation of British troops from Corunna and later maintained blockade off Basque Roads. Through to July 1812, when the ship was paid off at Plymouth, *Tonnant* was regularly cruising between England and Portugal.

Stonelake, as cook, stayed with the ship while she was in ordinary at Plymouth, then early in 1814 she was ordered to Chatham Dockyard in the Thames for repairs. On 21 June, *Tonnant* set sail with Admiral Sir Alexander Cochrane flying his flag and Captain John Wainwright in command, destination Bermuda and the American War. *Tonnant* was present at the bombardment of Fort McHenry, and it was on board her that Francis Scott Key came before the battle with a flag of truce to secure the release of a fellow American, Dr William Beanes. Beanes was released, but the sloop that Key came in was held by the British until the action was over. It was thus that Francis Scott Key saw the bombardment which was the inspiration for his *Star Spangled Banner*, the American National Anthem.

In December, men from *Tonnant* manned her boats to assist in the capture of American gun boats at Lake Borgne near New Orleans. In September 1815, *Tonnant* was back in Plymouth and again paid off.

The next twelve years of William Stonelake's time in the Royal Navy would have been considered a choice billet. He remained cook on board HMS *Mulgrave* and HMS *Circe*, both ships in ordinary and enjoying a well deserved rest while they tugged at their anchors in Plymouth Harbour. His wife was nearby and she may well have moved in with him while he kept the skeleton crew of his ship in good grub. In 1828, the Admiralty received notice that William Stonelake, Cook, had applied for superannuation, 'being unable to discharge his duty from bodily infirmity.' After thirty four years afloat, taking part in two major fleet actions and acting on board Cochrane's flagship on the American coast and getting on toward sixty years of age, it was time for William Stonelake to come ashore. He certainly lived another twenty years, as he was able to claim the Naval General Service medal with clasps for the Nile and Trafalgar, but we have no record of him after that. According to Douglas-Morris, Stonelake was one of only twenty-two men who were able to claim both the Nile and Trafalgar clasps.

Provenance: Medal fair, 1992. Case supplied by Chris Dixon.

References: The National Archives, Kew: ADM 35/306 (*Cumberland*), ADM 35/1055-1058 (*Minotaur*), ADM 36/12119 (*Colossus*), ADM 36/12450 (*Hecate*), ADM 36/15452 (*Cambridge*), ADM 102/608 & 609 (Plymouth Hospital), ADM 36/15396 - 15398 (*Fisgard*), ADM 35/1933 - 1934, 2479 - 2480, 3149 - 3151, ADM 36/16227 - 16233,

ADM 37/81-86, 1205 - 1207, 2254 -2256, 2861 - 2862, 3472, 5165 - 5168 (*Tonnant*), ADM 106/2293 (Navy Board In Letters 1828), ADM 37/82 (Power of Attorney).

Treasure Trove Islands, the Scilly Isles by Roland Morris, Roland Morris, St. Ives, Cornwall, no date.

British Warship Losses in the Age of Sail (1650-1859) by David J Hepper, Boudriot, Rotherfield, East Sussex, 1994.

A Social History of the Navy 1793 - 1815 by Michael Lewis, George Allen and Unwin, London, 1960.

The Sailing Navy List by David Lyon, Conway, London, 1993.

www.familysearch.org for christening date and parental information.

Dictionary of National Biography, Oxford University Press, 1975.

The Naval General Service Medal Roll 1793 - 1840, by Capt. Kenneth Douglas - Morris, published privately, London, 1982.

Royal Naval Biography by Lieutenant John Marshall, R.N., Longman, London, 1822-1830, (12 vols.)

Jack Tar by Roy & Lesley Adkins, Little Brown, London, 2008.

Sea Life in Nelson's Time by John Masefield, Methuen, London, 1905.

Nelsonian Reminiscences by G. F. Parsons, Giggings, London, 1905.

England Expects by Dudley Pope, Weidenfeld & Nicolson, London, 1959.

The Dawn's Early Light by Walter Lord, Norton, New York, 1972.

DN 15 George Knighton, Captain of the Main Top, HMS Minotaur, Captain Thomas Louis

Description: The Davison Nile was gilt and engraved on board *Minotaur* with the 48 mm glazed case being purchased on shore or from a trader's boat while in harbour. Engraved in the reverse field is *Geo e Knighton / Minotaur*. Weight, medal only: 39.1 grams. Medal and case: 64.7 grams. Extremely fine for the medal. The case has lost its suspension loop.

Background: This medal to George Knighton and the next two medals to Thomas Turner and Robert [William] Lewis were all done by the same ship board jeweller. The engraving is quite distinctive and the style is only found to men on board the *Minotaur*, so I have named him the *Minotaur* engraver. That an engraver would be found on board ship should be no surprise as with a ship's company of 550 men

229

from all walks of life, I would expect an engraver to be amongst them somewhere. That sailors themselves enjoyed engraving coins is described in this author's *Forget Me Not*, which is a study of sailor and jeweller engraved coins and plate during the 18th century and later. Please see pages 74-75 to see examples of sailor engraved coins and plate.

From Erik Goldstein, Curator at Colonial Williamsburg, comes the insight that the coin to be engraved would have been placed in a 'pitch block' to be held secure for engraving. A 'pitch block' is a square or round shallow frame filled with pitch or pine tar. The pine tar or Stockholm Tar would readily be available on ship as this was the main ingredient used to seal the seams between timbers. Our drawing of the old salt holding a frame and engraving a coin looks to be pretty much what one would have seen.

The tool used for engraving is called a 'graver' which is really a four sided steel awl with a specially finished point for engraving which could have been fashioned by any jeweller in a seaport or on board ship if someone knew how to do it. The steel awl would have been found regularly on board ship as the cobbler, sail maker, boatswain and probably the armourer and all their mates would use them. Sailor-made engraved coins of the period attest to this skill as not being uncommon amongst seamen. The gilding of the medal on board ship is discussed on pages 71 - 72. The 48 mm glazed case would have been supplied by a jeweller who speculated that the Davison Nile medal recipients would want a case for the medal. The cases would have been supplied by a jeweller either from his shop or from one of the trader's boats in port. Please see page 73.

From Geoffrey Green who wrote a wonderful book about the relationship between the Jewish community in Britain and abroad and the men of the Royal Navy: 'The Jewish pedlars, of the mid-eighteenth century soon found a virtual captive customer in the men-of-war as they plied their wares from boats that came alongside the great fighting ships. Then later as slopsellers, jewellers and silversmiths became established ashore with their own shops. These traders supplied the goods in which the seamen delighted.'

The shore based Jewish community acted as the main source for both officers and men to handle their financial affairs as well as providing general supply to the fleet. One could remark that the Royal Navy at the time of Nelson couldn't function without the support of the Jewish community located in the ports around Britain, the Mediterranean and elsewhere. As the *Minotaur* stayed in the Mediterranean throughout 1799, during which the Davison Nile medals would have arrived on board for distribution to the ship's company, the jeweller who supplied the glazed cases may have been located in Gibraltar, Naples, Palermo, Port Mahon, Genoa or Leghorn, which were all regularly visited. The *Minotaur* engraver's medals remain a bit of a mystery, but are amongst the finest engraved Davison Nile medals encountered.

I know of a fourth Davison Nile that has been engraved by the *Minotaur* engraver. That medal was to Nathaniel Kinsman who also joined the *Cumberland* in March of 1793 as a volunteer. He came from Plymouth, Devon and was paid a bounty of £2/10/0 as he was rated Ordinary Seaman. All four of the men, that I'm aware of, who had medals engraved by the *Minotaur* engraver, were Devon men. I don't know the significance of this, but it certainly was the case that on board ship the men from the same locality tended to club together. One reason would be language which contained much more dialect than the language of Britain today. That these men knew each other and worked together to get their medals gilt, engraved and cased may have been what happened.

John Masefield painted the most lurid and brutal image of the life of a topman: 'Having picked his forecastlemen [the best of the Able Seamen], a lieutenant had to select his 'topmen'. There were three divisions of topmen, one for each mast - fore, main and mizen. The topmen had to work the three masts above the lower yards. The lieutenant chose for the topmen all the young, active seamen who had been to sea for three or four years. Their work was very arduous, and very exacting. It was the hardest work of the ship, and demanded the smartest men, yet no men were more bullied than those to whom the duty fell. A topman lived in continual terror. He was at all times under the eye of the officer of the watch. His days were passed in an agony of apprehension lest something should go wrong aloft to bring him to the gangway. Smartness aloft was, to many captains, the one thing essential aboard a man-of-war. A topman had to be smart, and more than smart. He had to fly up aloft at the order, lay out on the yard, reef or furl, lay in, and be down on deck again, before the boatswain's mate could draw his colt. [a knotted rope end] The sailors raced 'mast against mast' whenever sail was made or shortened, and whenever a spar was struck or sent aloft. They were not only smart, they were acrobatic. They were known to run aloft and to run along the yard to the yard-arms, and this in blowing weather, and with the ship rolling. But, no matter how swift they were, the captain and lieutenant, who watched from the deck, wished them to be swifter. It did not matter to these two flinty ones whether the men were doing their best, and breaking their hearts to do better. All they cared for was the honour of the ship, and perhaps a word from the admiral.'

Masefield continued to describe the injustice of the officers leading to topmen rushing too much with fatal results, as falling to the deck or into the sea from aloft was not an uncommon occurrence.

N.A.M. Rodger felt that Masefield's account of life at sea in the Royal Navy was overly harsh and this led him to write about topmen in his *The Wooden World*. Here we see the balance and common sense comes forward. If one were to beat your skilled seamen every time they carried out a task, the inevitable result would be sullenness and an unhappy ship. There were certainly captains and lieutenants who felt that harsh treatment was the only way to get what they wished from the men, but they were not the true leaders of the King's ships.

Rodger notes that the single most important difference between the ship's company of the Royal Navy and those of her enemies was the skill of her topmen which allowed the British vessels to manoeuvre more quickly and take advantage of every change in the wind which meant they could most likely gain a position of advantage before the enemy could react. When one considers that during the 1793 - 1815 period, the primary role of the British was to blockade the enemy in their ports, which denied the enemy time at sea to keep their topmen's skills at peak performance, while the British blockading squadrons and fleets stayed on station through all weather and thus became most expert at seamanship.

The other aspect is the role of the extensive merchant marine that the British enjoyed. The merchant marine was the school for Royal Navy seaman. It was indeed a harsh custom for men on board, say, an East Indiaman which had just completed a nine month voyage to the Orient and back, to arrive at the mouth of the Thames only to be boarded by a Royal Naval officer who prest their best seamen into His Majesty's Service. Harsh, certainly, but it was something that all who went to sea in those days knew could happen. And because it did happen, the British had a constant pool of skilled seamen to replenish the fleet, which was yet another contributing factor toward Britain's dominance of the oceans.

Captain of the Main Top was truly the King of the Hill! He was a seaman's seaman and had the job because the First Lieutenant knew that he could be trusted in all circumstances to get the best of his men aloft. One wonders just what it would be like to sit in a pub with a pint and in company of George Knighton and hear what he had to say about his years in the Royal Navy. A man-of-war's man who must have been most impressive in his day.

A good example of how a star frigate captain worked with his crew to get the very best through leadership is found with Thomas, Lord Cochrane and his men of the flying *Pallas* in 1805. Donald Thomas tells the story: 'By the end of March, the *Pallas* had sent home four captured vessels with prize crews on board and was herself heavily weighted down by plunder. As the laden frigate prepared to turn for home the sea off the Azores was covered in a low heat-mist, the mastheads of the *Pallas* standing clear of it. Though Cochrane could see nothing from the quarterdeck, the look-out [in the tops], suddenly called out, reporting the main-topgallant masts of three ships of the line closing upon the *Pallas*. Cochrane altered course immediately, but as he strained to make out the shapes of the approaching battleships through the bright dazzle of the haze he identified them clearly as French. The weeks of happy plundering had come to an end.

'As *Pallas* altered course, the wind freshened and a heavy sea began to run. The ports were closed across the main-deck guns, which were otherwise under water, and even the guns of the quarterdeck, where Cochrane stood, dipped into the waves as the frigate heeled over in the rising sea. The heavy surges also made it impossible for the three battleships to use their guns at this stage, but they were coming up fast on the *Pallas*.

'To hoist more sail in the face of the storm was contrary to most rules of safety, but it was Cochrane's only chance of getting clear. He ordered the *Pallas's* hawsers to be got to the mastheads and hove taut, securing the masts as firmly as possible, and then for every stitch of canvas to be spread. The lumbering frigate ploughed into the sea which burst in plumes of spray over her bows as the forecastle plunged underwater and sent the waves sluicing back along the deck as it rose again. But still the battleships were gaining and, looking back, Cochrane logged several yellow flashes of the priming pans as the French gunners tried unavailingly to get a steady aim at their target.

'Until there was a lull in the storm, it would be difficult for the French to take advantage of their broadsides, but the battleships drew level with the *Pallas*, one on either bow at a distance of less than half a mile, while the third was more remote. Their guns were in position and they had only to wait for the sea to grow calmer in order to confront Cochrane with the choice of annihilation or surrender. For the time being, the storm was Cochrane's ally as the four ships plunged along with sails taut under the full force of the gale.

'In the two months of the cruise he had trained his men to perfection to do things which some of them saw little use in. He now ordered them to man the rigging and, at a given signal, to haul down every sail at precisely the same moment. As he gave the signal, the helm of the *Pallas* was to be put hard over and the frigate turned across the path of the storm. The effect of this manoeuvre, and of the lowering of sails, was that she was 'suddenly brought up' and, as Cochrane felt, 'shook from stem to stern.'

'The three French battleships, with the wind in their sails, shot past at full speed, quite unprepared for anything of this kind. Indeed they were several miles farther on before they could shorten sail or trim on the opposite tack. Meanwhile it was the *Pallas* which spread full sail and again set off in the opposite direction at a speed of more than thirteen knots.'

Needless to say, a week or so later the *Pallas* arrived safe in Plymouth Harbour. Cochrane had lashed to her masts three enormous gold candlesticks as a sign of triumph. He became an instant hero as did all of the ship's company of the flying *Pallas* and they all shared in the prize money.

George Knighton came from the small fishing port of Dawlish in Devon. He was twenty years old when he joined the Royal Navy as a volunteer at the Exeter Rendezvous in March 1793 and received £2/10/0 as a bounty. On 21 March, he appeared on board HMS *Cumberland*, Captain Thomas Louis, and was immediately rated Ordinary Seaman, so he had probably spent some years in the local fishing smacks or elsewhere in the merchant marine.

The *Cumberland* mainly cruised in the Channel during 1793, but then in March 1794 nearly all of the ship's company, including her captain, were transferred to the newly commissioned HMS *Minotaur*. For the history of the *Minotaur* at the Battle of the Nile, please review DN 12.

There is no doubt that George Knighton applied himself to gain added skills while on board *Minotaur*. He joined the navy as an Ordinary Seaman in 1793, promoted to Able Seaman in March 1795 and then Captain of the Main Top in August of 1799. The muster roll doesn't note any demotions, so he was a fully squared away man-of-war topman. He was paid off in March 1802 at Chatham when *Minotaur* was placed in ordinary, and we lose sight of him. Such a skilled seaman would have easily found a berth on a merchantman, and he may well have joined the East India Company for trips out East.

As a note, on board HMS *Leviathan* was Lieutenant Charles Knighton who was also from Dawlish. He was invalided from the service in January 1805 and missed Trafalgar. He may well have been a relation to George Knighton.

Provenance: Medal fair, 1992.

References: The National Archives, Kew: ADM 35/306. ADM 36/11203 (*Cumberland*). ADM 35/1055-1058. ADM 36/11816 - 11818, 12829 - 12830, 14416-14423 (*Minotaur*).
Sea Life in Nelson's Time by John Masefield, Methuen, London, 1905.
The Wooden World, by N.A.M Rodger, Collins, London, 1986.
Cochrane, Britannia's Last Sea-King, by Donald Thomas, Viking, New York, 1978.
Forget Me Not, by Sim Comfort, Sim Comfort Associates, London, 2004.

DN 16 Thomas Turner, Quarter Gunner, HMS Minotaur, Captain Thomas Louis

Description: The Davison Nile medal is ship board gilt and engraved. The medal was probably cased and glazed. Engraved in the reverse field is *Tho s Turner / Minotaur*. Weight: 39.5 grams. Extremely fine.

Background: This is another of the *Minotaur* engraver's medals. Please see DN 15 for further details regarding this engraver.

N.A.M. Rodger notes: 'There were among the seamen one quarter gunner to every four guns, who assisted the gunner's mates in looking after them, and one captain of each gun, who was in charge of the gun's crew in action. Quarter gunners were officially established, and paid two shillings a month more than able seamen, but captains of guns, like captains of the tops, received no official recognition.'

Masefield also notes that ranking amongst the standing officers were the boatswain, the purser and the gunner. A most important officer who gained his post only after a rigorous examination in the art of gunnery, which was the whole reason for a naval ship to be sent to sea. The extent of responsibilities of the gunner were great and encompassed everything that had to do with the supply of powder and shot and its maintenance, to ensuring each and every gun was properly situated and served. To provide support to the gunner were a number of gunner's mates and quarter gunners which on board a large ship produced a hierarchy of their own within the ship's company.

Thomas Turner came from Torquay in Devon, just up the coast from Dawlish. He was entered on board the *Cumberland* on 8 March 1793 and was recruited at Exeter. As he was rated Able Seaman, his bounty was £5/-/-, twice as much as the bounty paid to George Knighton who was rated Ordinary Seaman.

Having come on board the *Cumberland* rated as Able Seaman and then in October he was advanced to Quarter Gunner. Like most of the *Cumberlands*, he transferred to the *Minotaur* in March of 1794. It seems he met with some bad company as in the Spring of 1794, shortly after coming on board the *Minotaur*, he was docked 15/- for treatment of the venerals. At this time it also looks like he lost his rank as Quarter Gunner and was returned to being Able Seaman.

He served right through the Mediterranean cruise of the *Minotaur*. Please see DN 12 for a full account which includes the *Minotaur* at the Nile. When *Minotaur* returned to Portsmouth in March 1802, the ship was in the main paid off, but there is a comment beside Turner's name, 'Unsble' for Unserviceable. The hard years at sea had certainly taken their toll on Thomas Turner and the navy didn't want him anymore, however he did live to 1848 and received the NGS with Nile clasp.

Provenance: James Hammond, 1988.

References: The National Archives, Kew: ADM 35/306. ADM 36/11203 (Cumberland). ADM 35/1055-1058. ADM 36/11816 - 11818, 12829 - 12830, 14416-14423 (*Minotaur*).
Sea Life in Nelson's Time by John Masefield, Methuen, London, 1905.
The Wooden World, by N.A.M Rodger, Collins, London, 1986.

DN 17 Robert [William] Lewis, Landsman, HMS Minotaur, Captain Thomas Louis

Description: The Davison Nile medal is ship board gilt and engraved. The medal has a silver case with suspension. Engraved in the reverse field is *Rob t Lewis / Minotaur*. Weight, medal with silver case: 46.2 grams. Good very fine.

Background: The Davison Nile is another of the *Minotaur* engraver's medals. Please see DN 15 for further details regarding this engraver.

The Landsman was the backbone and muscle of the ship. With no power lifting or hauling winches during this period, all heavy work was carried out by Landsmen. The capstan for lifting anchors may have a hundred men at the capstan bars. There were no qualifications for being a Landsman, however there was skill involved, i.e. every man would have to learn very quickly which line in the running rigging required hauling or trimming in order to fulfil the order of the boatswain's mate or the new recruit would pretty soon feel the strike of the mate's 'starter'.

Julian Stockwin's Thomas Kydd novels certainly describe the plight of a man prest from the streets of England and the awful change that suddenly being on board one of His Majesty's Ships meant for the man. But, as Thomas Kydd learned, there were opportunities to be taken. A Landsman who was willing and paid attention to the work on board ship could be promoted to Ordinary Seaman and from there to Able Seaman and from there to Master's Mate or Mate to one of the other standing officers. And there was the chance of prize money, lots of travel and hopefully success when your ship was brought to action. Certainly it was a more eventful life than staying on the farm or competing for some drudge of a job in one of Britain's cities.

This is another of the *Minotaur* engraver medals, but there is some mystery surrounding Robert Lewis, because in the Muster Roll for the *Minotaur* there is no Robert Lewis listed. We do, however, have a William Lewis listed. He volunteered in 1794, aged 24, and came on board the *Minotaur* on 16 March from the *Sandwich* receiving ship, which means he joined up in London or somewhere along the Thames. As a man with no sea qualification, he was rated a Landsman and paid the bounty of £1/1/-. When he originally volunteered he said he was born in London, but later this was changed to Biddeford, Devon! Here was another one of the Devon lads with a medal engraved by the *Minotaur* engraver. From his service record one can see that for the eight years he served on board the *Minotaur*, he remained a Landsman which could mean that he wasn't the brightest spark on board ship.

However, with the medal named Robert and his name in the muster being William, this could very well indicate that he joined the Royal Navy to leave a past behind him and a new name may have proved useful for several reasons. First, if people were looking for Robert Lewis, he wouldn't be found on board the *Minotaur*. Secondly, if he decided to Run, then the navy would be looking for William when he was actually Robert.

Robert (William) Lewis remained with the *Minotaur* during her whole time in the Mediterranean and was discharged at Portsmouth on 2 March 1802. Gillian Hughes noted that the Muster Roll for the *Minotaur* shows that Lewis was discharged to HMS *Haughty*, almost certainly as transport from Portsmouth to HMS *Zealand*, which was a receiving ship at Plymouth. Gillian wasn't able to find Lewis as a passenger on board the *Haughty* and there is no reference to his having appeared on board HMS *Zealand*. I think William became Robert Lewis again and set course for a life without the Royal Navy!

Provenance: James Hammond, 1988.

References: The National Archives, Kew: ADM 35/1055-1058. ADM 36/11816 - 11818, 12829 - 12830, 14416-14423 (*Minotaur*).
Kydd (and other titles with Thomas Kydd as the main character), by Julian Stockwin, Hodder and Stoughton, London, 2001.

DN 18 Benjamin Corbett, Landsman, HMS Minotaur, Captain Thomas Louis, Sergeant Benjamin Corbett, 88th Foot, The Connaught Rangers

Description: 2nd Class Regimental medal for the 88th Foot named on the edge to Serjt. Benjn. Corbet. In the field of the reverse are engraved the battle honours for Orthes, Busaco, Badajoz, Vittoria, Salamanca, Fuentes d'Onor, Ciudad Rodrigo, Pyrenees, Toulouse, Nivelle and Nive. The medal has a suspension bar engraved PENINSULA. The Military General Service medal has impressed naming on the edge to B. Corbett, Serjt. 88th Foot., with clasps for Busaco, Salamanca, Vittoria, Orthes and Toulouse. An unnamed gilt-bronze Davison Nile medal with ring suspension at 12 o'clock has been added to the group. Very fine the group.

Background: From John Hayward's catalogue of December 1975: 'Sergeant Benjamin Corbett, Royal Navy, later 88th Foot, M.G.S. five clasps, Busaco, Salamanca, Vittoria, Orthes, Toulouse (Sergt. 88th Foot), 88th Foot silver Regimental Medal, reverse listing eleven battles, edge named.

'The recipient of these two awards for his service in the ARMY had served previously in the BRITISH NAVY, when he qualified in every respect to claim the Naval War Medal with clasps NILE and EGYPT.

'He was born in 1780 at Ross, Co. Wexford, Ireland, and in his youth had taken the trade of Hosier. On 8th May 1795 he presented himself as a volunteer at his nearest Naval rendezvous (probably a tavern serving as a recruiting station) in Waterford. From here he was transferred to the main rendezvous and staging centre a little further west at the Cove of Cork - here he was placed on board the hired tender *Bloom* which took him, other volunteers and prest men to Spithead.

'On 29th May 1795 he was signed on at the capstan of a British man-of-war for the first time, as a supernumerary landsman, the lowest rank for an ex-landlubber of his age, aboard HMS *Terpsichore*. On 6th June 1795 he was transferred to HMS *Glory*, there to receive agreeably his hammock and bedding for which he was charged 13s. deducted from his bounty of 30s. Later that year he was moved once more, this time to HMS *Prince George* on 24th November, and again drafted to another ship, but this time to a fully commissioned fighting ship of the Fleet, HMS *Minotaur*.

'He joined her as a Landsman on 8th March 1796 as a supernumerary, but became a member of her Ship's Company (No. 922) on 23rd April 1796. For 6 years he served on board *Minotaur*, rising to the rate of Ordinary Seaman on 1st August 1801. During his time on board he served during the historic Battle of the Nile when he was wounded, leaving him with a 'scar on left side from explosion of shell', furthermore he was wounded for a second time in 1801 'in right side whilst landing troops in Aboukir Bay' during the Egypt Campaign.

'He continued to serve as an Ordinary Seaman in *Minotaur* until she was paid off on 2nd March 1802, when he was sent that day to HMS *Zealand* to be discharged from the service. This was the time of the phoney peace following the so-called end of the Revolutionary War by the Treaty of Amiens, and a period when the Navy was cut to one-third of its former size, before rising again.

'No details of Corbett's life between 1802 and 1809 are known, except that he returned to the trade of being a Hosier back in Ireland, and that his desire to serve once more made him volunteer, but this time in a different service - the Army.

'On 3rd May 1809 he enlisted in the 88th Regiment at Ballina, Co. Mayo, and later joined the 7th Company, 1st Battalion, as a Private on 25th October 1809 in Portugal. Whilst he does not appear to have been wounded in any of the Actions portrayed on his M.G.S. Medal, he would not seem to have enjoyed robust health. He spent much time being Absent Sick in the General, Regimental and Detachment Hospitals - for Sept. 1810, Oct. 1811, April - June 1812, Nov. and Dec. 1812 and Sept. 1813 to Feb. 1814 while serving in Portugal, Spain and France.

'On 28th February 1814 he was promoted to Corporal, and then soon made a Sergeant on 25th August 1814. His service took him to St. John's, Canada, in early 1815 and to Paris in the Autumn of that year. He was discharged from the Army whilst he was stationed at Chester Castle, on 6th February 1821, with a combined R.N. and Army time of 18 years and 319 days.'

Sergeant Corbett's discharge paper from the Army (WO 97/968) also notes that he stood 5 feet 7 1/2 inches tall, had sandy hair, grey eyes and a fresh complexion. His general conduct is noted as Very Good and Exemplary. He was discharged with a pension for 'Being Worn Out due to length of Service.'

On board ship, it has been said, that the Irish sailors were the heart and soul of the ship's company. With their music and happy nature, the Irish were simply fun to have on board. Drink was too often a problem, but life is never perfect. One has to remember that Irishmen made up a third of Lord Nelson's fleet at Trafalgar and without them, Britain would never have won the day or gained command of the seas.

Ian Fletcher describes the 88th Foot / Connaught Rangers as part of Wellington's army in the Peninsular.

'In February 1810 the 3rd Division in which the 88th was brigaded, came under the command of Thomas Picton, under whose leadership the 88th was to establish a reputation as one of the most fearsome battalions in Wellington's army. On September 27th 1810 the 88th fought at Busaco where, under the command of Lieutenant Colonel Wallace, the battalion distinguished itself with a fierce bayonet charge, prompting Wellington to say, 'Wallace, I never saw a more gallant charge than that just made by your regiment.'

Although Wellington was to refer to the Connaught Rangers as the Connaught Footpads, it was the willingness of the Connaughts to get in close with the bayonet that made them so unstoppable. Again and again, they saved the day for Wellington. At Ciudad Rodrigo, General Picton addressed the Connaughts that were to assail the breach, 'Rangers of Connaught! It is not my intention to expend any powder this evening. We'll do this business with the could [cold] iron.' Needless to say the Connaughts secured their position, but not after a bloody defence by the French.

Further, from Ian Fletcher, 'On July 22nd 1812, at Salamanca, the 88th achieved a notable feat when it captured the 'Jingling Johnny' of the French 101st Regiment. The instrument was carried in triumph for the rest of the war.' The Jingling Johnny now resides at the National Army Museum in Chelsea. Originally a Turkish military instrument, it consists of a canopy and a crescent frame from which bells and various other jingling objects are hung. Very probably, the Jingling Johnny was originally captured in Egypt by Napoleon's troops.

The discrepancy between the list of battles on the Regimental medal and the clasps of the MGS is a situation frequently met with. One may be sure that the MGS clasps represent battles the recipient took part in and the Regimental medal may well contain battle honours due to him that have not been recognised by the MGS. The Regimental medal was issued in 1818 and the MGS thirty years later in 1848. It will always remain a mystery why Corbett didn't also apply for the Naval General Service medal which would have had the Nile and Egypt clasps, but at an age nearing seventy, he may have thought you were only entitled to one medal?

Painting of the Connaughts by Simon McCouaig showing the men with their fierce beards and celebrating the capture of the Jingling Johnny after Salamanca, 22 July 1812.

I think this group of three medals says so much. Here's a man who spent a number of years in the Royal Navy, twice wounded and then discharged. Probably bored with life, when he learned the Connaughts were recruiting. Ben Corbett was looking for another adventure, joined up and fought right through the Peninsular War with Wellington. Wonderful.

For the history of the *Minotaur* at the Battle of the Nile, please review DN 12.

Provenance: The MGS and Regimental medal:
Sotheby's 27 November 1907.
Birkin at Glendinning 17 March 1921.
Needes 1940.
Moutray 1954.
Hayward 1975.
Captain E. Gale Hawkes.
Peter Power-Hynes at Spink, 16 July 1996.
Unnamed Davison Nile added to the group, August 1996.

References: John Hayward catalogue, December 1975.
The National Archives, Kew: WO 97/968 for the 88th of Foot. This document details the two wounds Corbett received whilst on board HMS *Minotaur*.
ADM 35/1056-1058 details Benjamin Corbett as being on board *Minotaur* from 1796 to 1802.
Adventures with the Connaught Rangers (1809-1814) by William Grattan, reprinted by Edward Arnold, London, 1902.
Wellington's Regiments by Ian Fletcher, Spellmount, Staplehurst, Kent, 1994.

DN 19, Midshipmahn George Thompson

DN 19 Midshipman George Thompson, HMS Defence, Captain John Peyton

Description: Soho gilt bronze medal cased, glazed and contained in its original dark green leather case with watered green silk interior. The medal is engraved in the reverse field *George Thompson / 1798 / H. M. S. / Defence*. The obverse and reverse fields are chased. There is a small die break running through C. H. K. with a larger break below at the rim. Weight of the medal in its glazed case: 68.9 grams. Extremely fine.

Background: This Davison Nile to George Thompson was bought in 1970 from Nimrod Dix and was the first named example that I was able to buy, i.e. it wasn't that I was turning down any medals, this was the first time that I saw one for sale. £25 was the cost and the medal remains one of the finest I have ever seen and it set me on the road toward collecting named Davison Nile, Earl St Vincent and Boulton Trafalgar medals. I had to wait until 1975 before I found another named Davison Nile. In that year I also found my first named Boulton Trafalgar medal, which was named to Thomas Randall of HMS *Victory*. I think that these named pieces are much more scarce than the Naval General Service medal with clasps to either the Nile (326) or Trafalgar (1,611).

HMS *Defence* was one of the most involved third rates during the great wars with France. Her first commission during the American Revolution saw her at the battle of Cape St Vincent, 1780, and then to the Indian Ocean and Cuddalore in 1783. During her second commission between 1793 and 1802, she took part in the Glorious First of June, 1794, the battle of the Nile, 1798, and was with Hyde-Parker's reserve fleet at Copenhagen in 1801. George Thompson was on board during the whole of this second commission, but we lose sight of him after *Defence* was paid off in July 1802. With the war starting again in 1803, *Defence* returned to service with a new ship's company and fought at Trafalgar in 1805. She was wrecked off the coast of Jutland during a fierce gale on Christmas Eve, 1811. All but a few of the ship's company were lost.

Defence was built at Plymouth Dockyard to the Slade design, Arrogant Class of 1758. She was launched in 1763 and was 1,604 tons burthen and 168 feet in length. She carried 28 x 32 pounders on her Gundeck, 28 x 18 pounders on the Upperdeck, 14 x 9 pounders on the Quarterdeck and 4 x 9 pounders in the Forecastle. It is possible that some of these lighter guns were exchanged for carronades in the 1790s.

George Thompson was from Beverley, East Yorkshire which is about ten miles from Hull located at the mouth of the Humber and noted as a major shipping and fishing port serving the North Sea. He was 21 years old when he volunteered in January 1793 and joined *Defence* on 11 September of that year. Thompson was immediately rated as Able Seaman and was promoted to Midshipman on 1 June 1796. He continued in this station to 12 June 1800 when he was made Yeoman of the Sheets and stayed as such until *Defence* was paid off on 3 July 1802. He never passed his lieutenant's examination, so we have no record of him in the *List of Sea Officers*.

The above detail of George Thompson's career in the Royal Navy does pose a few questions. As Michael Lewis tells us, 'thirty-nine out of forty naval officers entered the Service without any Admiralty sanction....The Captain could take into his ship when he commissioned her anyone he liked; and the only posts he could not fill with his own untrammelled choices were those of officers, commissioned and warrant. These, then as now, were appointed to the ship by the Admiralty.' Lewis continues and tells us of various posts that the Captain could fill with his protégés, e.g. Captain's Servants, Boys, 1st Class Volunteers and Midshipmen.

Apparently after an Order in Council in 1794, the term Captain's Servants was abolished and two classes of young gentlemen were formed, i.e. Boys and 1st Class Volunteers. Having said that, Michael Lewis comments that young gentlemen may be borne on the ship's books as Able Seamen with 'The fact that they started in an apparently lower deck rating, however, does not mean that they were necessarily lower deck types. Most of them, probably, were lads bound for the Quarter-deck but fitted, pro tempore, and for the Captain's immediate convenience, into an ordinary rating.

Michael Lewis carried out an extensive analysis of volunteers / captain's protégés and the various billets they occupied. In a section of his book called 'Irregularities', which includes various petty officer posts with Yeoman of the Powder Room being one, Lewis notes ten men who held this post with nine of them becoming lieutenants and one a captain. He doesn't note any officer who had served as Yeoman of the Sheets. When Lewis describes the various posts within the lower deck, he says, 'There were dozens of these Petty Officers [which included the Yeomen of the Sheets], but they were socially little above 'common men' and, navally, regarded as the most trustworthy specimens of the breed. ... These men had their messes on the Lower Deck, and slept either there or in the cable-tier below, their superior standing securing for them the more favoured corners.'

When I look at George Thompson and compare him to the normal range of captain's protégés, I can see some differences. Thompson volunteered at age 21. Most of the 1st Class Volunteers and ship's boys were quite a bit younger, perhaps five to eight years younger. Nelson first went to sea at age twelve. With Thompson having been rated Able Seaman upon joining, this could mean that he was indeed a seasoned mariner or that as a protégé, there was no spare midshipman's billet available, so he was given a lower posting until a Midshipman's berth was free. He was promoted to Midshipman three years after joining the *Defence*, which seems quite a long time to wait for a billet to become vacant, however if he was actually a lower deck man, then this could be viewed as a very impressive promotion to the Quarterdeck in a relatively short period of time. As noted, the *Defence* had fought at the 1st of June, and it may well have been that George Thompson made his mark during the battle.

We then have his being made Yeoman of the Sheets four years after he was promoted to Midshipman, which really does look to me to be a post for an Able Seaman as opposed to a Midshipman. The job was essentially that of a storeman who didn't stand watches, but worked the day shift and kept track of the vast quantity of cordage that was used for the ship's rigging. This role would be quite different from that of a Midshipman who was in training to command gunnery, working aloft, navigation, etc. all of the skills needed to pass the examination for lieutenant.

That Michael Lewis doesn't mention any Yeoman of the Sheets that had advanced to a King's commission may well be evidence of this. It is quite possible that George Thompson was actually lower deck and that with his promotion to Midshipman found that the change in society just didn't suit him and that this was noted by his officers and he reverted back to being before the mast with the rest of his mates. That he never passed for lieutenant may also give weight to this view. Having said that, there is no doubt that he cherished his time on board *Defence* and particularly being on board her at the Nile, which is evidenced by the money spent in creating such fine casing for his Davison Nile medal.

HMS *Defence* formed part of the Channel Fleet. As Oliver Warner notes, 'By common consent, none of the 74's did better service on the 1st of June [1794], than the thirty-year old *Defence*, Captain James Gambier.'

'Preaching Jemmy' Gambier (1756-1833) was an officer with very set ways. He believed that maintaining a Christian enthusiasm within a ship's company created a happy ship, and I have to think he was right in this respect. There is nothing like some solid hymns on a Sunday to raise the spirits. It may, however, have been sermons that were both too long and too full of fire and brimstone that gained for James Gambier the sobriquet of 'Preaching Jemmy'. That Gambier wasn't afraid of a fight is best described by William Dillon who was on board *Defence* during the three days of battle in June 1794. On the second day, Dillon records, 'One or two shots passed so close to the Captain that I thought he was hit. He clapped both hands upon his thighs with some emotion; then, recovering himself, he took out of his pocket a piece of biscuit, and began eating it as if nothing had happened. He had evidently been shook by the wind of a shot. He had on a cocked hat, and kept walking the deck, cheering up the seamen with the greatest coolness.'

Dillon soon saw a man killed, blood and brains spattering the deck, with men around him wounded. Further shots made havoc on the poop, cutting away the main brace. 'Some of the men could not help showing symptoms of alarm', said Dillon, 'which the Captain noticing, he instantly went up, and calling the seamen together, led them to set the brace to rights.' Oliver Warner considered Gambier, 'had all the best ideas; coolness, setting example, activity in leadership.'

Oliver Warner relates that on the 1st of June, *Defence* was the first of the British ships to break the French line, 'Gambier took the *Defence* down upon the enemy in bold fashion. She was the only ship in Howe's line to have her main topgallant sails set. 'Look at the *Defence*,' said Admiral Howe, 'See how nobly she is going into action!' At 10:30 *Defence* lost her mizenmast and at 11:30 her mainmast went by the board, but she kept pounding her opponents with broadside after broadside. Dillon records, 'They reported the upper and the quarterdeck to be dreadfully shattered. The lower deck was at time so completely filled with smoke that we could scarcely distinguish each other, and the guns were so heated that, when fired, they nearly kicked the upper deck beams. The metal became so hot that fearing some accident, we reduced the quantity of powder, allowing also more time to elapse between the loading and firing of them.'

Warner continues, 'When the action seemed almost over, orders came from the quarterdeck for all hands to lie down. An enemy three-decker was approaching, and as the *Defence* could not steer, her helm being lashed a-lee, it seemed likely that she would be raked, with dire effects. A lieutenant struck with a kind of momentary panic, ran up to the quarterdeck and addressing the Captain with great eagerness exclaimed: 'Damn my eyes, Sir, but here is a whole mountain coming down on us; what shall we do?' Captain Gambier, unmoved, and looking gravely at him, said in a solemn tone: 'How dare you, Sir, at this awful moment, come to me with an oath in your mouth? Go down, Sir, and encourage your men to stand to their guns, like brave British seamen.'

The three-decker passed astern, but only fired a few random shot, one of which brought down the foremast. *Defence* finished the battle with 18 killed and 39 wounded. This was the first contest between the British and French fleets during the French Revolutionary War. At the end of the day, the British had secured seven prizes and lost no ships, however the British fleet was much damaged and an estimated 1,200 British seamen were either killed or wounded.

Gambier received the King's Naval Small Gold Medal and the compliments of Lord Howe. Not long after the battle he was promoted and served as a Lord of the Admiralty until 1806. In 1807 he commanded the fleet that bombarded Copenhagen although a brutal attack, it did achieve its purpose which was to restore access to the Baltic by the British, and this success with very few British casualties. Later in 1809, he was again in command at Basque Roads which led to a fierce argument with Thomas, Lord Cochran as to whether the big 74-gun ships could have entered the shallow estuary to destroy the remaining French ships. My opinion is that Gambier acted quite correctly and that Cochran's attack on Gambier was unjustified, there just wasn't enough sea room for Gambier to commit his heavy ships.

HMS *Defence*, now under the command of Captain Thomas Wells formed part of Vice-Admiral Hotham's fleet in the Mediterranean and on 13 July 1795 was present at the action against Admiral Renaudin's squadron which resulted in the loss of one French ship. There then followed the expulsion of the British from the Mediterranean with *Defence* returning to the Channel Fleet.

Defence missed the battle of Cape St Vincent, 14 February 1797, which unlocked the door to the Mediterranean. On 24 May 1798, she sailed, with John Peyton as her commander, as part of the squadron that Troubridge had assembled from St Vincent's fleet. They sailed east to join the few ships that Nelson had in the Mediterranean.

Of Captain John Peyton, all that appears to be known of him is that he came from a well established naval family, but other than that, just the bare bones on his naval career. He was made Lieutenant on 17 February 1772, Commander on 27 March 1782, Captain on 21 January 1783, Rear-Admiral of the Blue on 9 November 1805, Rear-Admiral of the Red on 29 April 1808 and he died on 2 August 1809. The silhouette by William Williams, is inscribed on the reverse, 'Capt. Peyton / *Hite* Sloop, 1782'. The picture was auctioned at Bonham's, lot 263, 24 November 1994. Image is courtesy of Bonham's.

Brian Lavery notes that Peyton had written to Nelson on 3 July 1798, shortly after joining him, complaining that his health was not at all good and that the hot weather made him feel worse. He was concerned that he wouldn't be up to the contest ahead and asked to be replaced as soon as was convenient. Peyton clung onto such strength that he had. On the 1st of August at the Nile, following in the wake of HMS *Minotaur*, the *Defence* was the eighth ship to engage the enemy. She passed the *Minotaur*, who had anchored alongside the *Aquilon*, and anchored gun to gun with the *Peuple Souverin* of 74 guns which the *Orion* had been attacking for some time. The *Peuple Souverin* then became dismasted and drifted out of the line which allowed the *Defence* to move forward and attack the 80-gun *Franklin* in the bows.

The best account of her movements comes from Captain John Peyton's official log: 'August 1st. PM- Moderate breezes and fair. Alexandria SE 1/2 S 7 leagues. The *Zealous* made the signal for 16 sail of the line east. The Admiral made the signal to prepare for battle. At 4, the body of the enemy's squadron SE by E 9 or 10 miles. At 20 minutes past 4, the Admiral made the general signal to prepare for battle and to anchor. Admiral made the signal to engage the van and centre of the enemy. At 20 minutes past 6, made sail for the enemy's fleet in the line of battle at anchor; the enemy opened their fire upon us. The *Goliath*, our leading ship, began to engage the van of the enemy. At 1/2 past 6, Admiral made the signal to engage close. At 10 minutes before 7, the *Culloden* made the signal for being aground. At 7, came to an anchor with the sheet cable out of the gun-room port, and engaged our opponent [the *Peuple Souverin*], until 10 o'clock, when she ceased firing, being totally dismasted. At the same time, our fore topmast went over the side. At 5 minutes past 10, veered away on the sheet cable, in order to get alongside the next ship of 80 guns [the *Franklin*]. At 1/2 past 10, the *Orient* of 120 guns, the French commander-in-chief's ship, took fire; at 1/4 past 11, she blew up. At 20 minutes past 11, the 80-gun ship hailed us to say she had struck. Sent the 1st lieutenant on board and took possession of her.' Amazingly enough, *Defence* lost only four killed and eleven wounded during the action.

Following the battle, there were emergency repairs to be made both to the *Defence* and the prizes. *Defence* then sailed to Gibraltar in company with the *Orion* and prizes. She was there on 20 October when the seriously wounded were transferred to Gibraltar Hospital. It appears that *Defence* stayed with St Vincent's fleet on the Atlantic side of Gibraltar and cruised as required. In December 1799 she was at Plymouth, February 1800 at the Nore, and in June at Spithead.

Early in 1801, the *Defence* came under the command of Lord Harry Paulet, son of the Marquis of Winchester and 'one of the Navy's more eccentric and colourful captains.' When he was denied leave by his Admiral to travel to London and was told he could go as far as his barge would take him, he loaded his barge on a carriage and set off for Town! *Defence* sailed with Hyde Parker and Nelson for Copenhagen in March, but she was held in reserve by Hyde Parker and played no part in the battle, which I can only imagine a number of the ship's company were not that disappointed with following what they went through at both the 1st of June and the Nile. On 3 July 1802, *Defence* was paid off at Chatham. So, ended nine years of being at sea for George Thompson with nearly all of it spent on board HMS *Defence*.

Provenance: Nimrod Dix, 1970.

References: The National Archives, Kew: ADM 36/11157 (Thetis); ADM 36/12568 - 12569, 13991 - 13993, 14342 - 14351, 15938, ADM 35/ 15938 (*Defence*).
The British Library: BL Addit 34907, 3/7/1798 (Peyton letter to Nelson.)
A Social History of the Navy 1793 - 1815 by Michael Lewis, George Allen and Unwin, London, 1960.
The Sailing Navy List by David Lyon, Conway, London, 1993.
The Wooden World, by N.A.M Rodger, Collins, London, 1986.
The Sailor's Word-Book, by Admiral W. H. Smyth, Blackie, London, 1867.
The Glorious First of June by Oliver Warner, Batsford, London, 1961.
A Narrative of my Professional Adventures (1790-1839), by Sir William Henry Dillion, edited by Michael Lewis, Navy Records Society, 2 vols, 1953 & 1956.
The Commissioned Sea Officers of the Royal Navy, edited by Syrett and DiNardo, Scolar for the Navy Records Society, Aldershot, 1994.
Nelson and the Nile by Brian Lavery, Chatham, London, 1998.
Logs of the Great Sea Fights 1794-1805 by Sturges Jackson, Navy Records Society, London, 1899-1900.
Dictionary of National Biography, Oxford University Press, 1975.
The Great Gamble, Nelson at Copenhagen by Dudley Pope, Weidenfeld & Nicolson, London, 1972.

DN 20 James Watts, Quarter Master's Mate, HMS Defence, Captain John Peyton

Description: Soho? or jeweller? gilt bronze medal cased and glazed with a loop suspension. Engraved in the obverse fields are *James Watts* and in the reverse field, *Defence*. The medal is illustrated on page 62 of Tancred's, *Historical Record of Medals*. Weight of the medal in its glazed case: 70.7 grams. Extremely fine.

Background: In the *Historical Record of MEDALS and Honorary Distinctions etc.* by George Tancred, which contains a catalogue of the collection of medals formed by Colonel Murray of Polmaise and was published by Spink in 1891 is found a most interesting Davison Nile Medal to James Watts of HMS *Defence*. Like many collectors, when you see something that was published over 100 years ago, there is a certain amount of lusting that takes place. When I saw the medal offered in a Dix Nooan and Webb sale in 1992, I knew I would be there and I also knew that added financial reserves may have to be called upon to secure this treasure. In the end, the medal fell to my bid at a quite reasonable price.

246

It is magnificent to hold. I can't make up my mind as to whether or not the gilt is original Soho or done by a jeweller, either way, it is of the highest quality and the case and glazing are well above normal quality.

James Watts joined HMS *Defence* on 23 July 1794 from the *Royal William* which was a receiving hulk located at Portsmouth. He came from North Britten (sic) and was 23 years old and was immediately rated Able Seaman and may well have been taken on board to replace losses the *Defence* suffered on 1 June.

There is no doubt that he was a prime seaman although he and 39 other men from *Defence* met with some ailment which caused them all to be discharged to Falmouth Hospital on 6 January 1797. He was in hospital for 25 days and then sent to St Maws Castle to further recover. He finally returned to duty on board *Defence* 7 April. The cause may have been food poisoning or a severe form of flu, but whatever it was, it took ninety days for him to fully recover.

Once back on board, his career progressed with his becoming Quarter Gunner on 1 August 1797 and then shortly after on 1 October to Quarter Master's Mate. He continued in this post until 20 June 1799 when he probably committed some error and was broken back to Able Seaman, but quickly regained his rating of Quarter Master's Mate. James Watts continued in this post until 2 September 1800 when he was named Coxswain, in charge of the captain's barge and one of the most highly regarded ratings for a seaman on board ship.

Smyth notes that the Quarter Master is a 'Petty Officer, appointed to assist the Master and his Mates in their several duties, as stowing the hold, coiling the cables, attending the binnacle and steerage, keeping time by the watch glasses, assisting in hoisting the signals, and keeping an eye on general quarterdeck movements.' So a Quarter Master's Mate is very much under the eye of the Captain and his officers. No doubt that James Watts cut a fine figure as he carried out his duties and that the Captain appointed him his Coxswain. The Coxswain and the other bargemen were often placed in the role of being the personal bodyguard / servants of the Captain. At the battle of Cape St Vincent, it appears that Nelson's boat's crew boarded the Spanish ships with Nelson and that with the end of the action and the surrender of the Spanish captains who offered up their swords, 'which as I received, I gave to William Fearney, one of my bargemen, who put them with the greatest sangfroid under his arm.'

For details of HMS *Defence* at the battle of the Nile, please refer to DN 19. From the Muster Roll of HMS *Defence*, we can see that following the battle James Watts was loaned to the prize *Franklyn* until February 1799. Following that, he was loaned to HMS *Canopus* until October 1799. He then returned to HMS *Defence* and served in her during the landing of the British Army in Egypt in 1801. He remained on board until *Defence* was paid off at Chatham on 3 July 1802.

Provenance: Dix, Noonan & Web, lot 4, 29 July 1992.

References: The National Archives, Kew: ADM 35/504-507; ADM 36/14346-14347 & 14351 (*Defence*); ADM 102/223 (Falmouth Hospital).
Historical Record of MEDALS and Honorary Distinctions etc. by George Tancred, Spink, London, 1891.
The Sailor's Word-Book, by Admiral W. H. Smyth, Blackie, London, 1867.
The Pursuit of Victory, by Roger Knight, Penguin, London, 2005.
St Vincent and Camperdown by Christopher Lloyd, Batsford, London, 1963.

DN 21 John Dean, Landsman, HMS Defence, Captain John Peyton

Description: Bronze medal glazed and cased in silver with a ring suspension. Inscribed in the obverse field *John Dean* and in the reverse field *Defence*. Weight of the medal in its glazed case: 66.3 grams. Extremely fine.

Background: This is one of the most poignant medals that I have encountered. You'll notice that this medal is unlike all of the rest of the named bronze Davison Niles in that it hasn't been gilt. I think the reason for this is explained when you learn the fate of John Dean, Landsman.

John Dean was from Newcastle and not a skilled seaman as he was rated Landsman upon his joining HMS *Defence* on 21 August 1794. He was 21 years old. As with James Watts, he was probably taken on board to replace casualties from the battle of 1st June 1794.

He served on board *Defence* at the battle of the Nile, please see DN 19 for details of the battle. He was however wounded during the engagement with a compound fracture of the leg. The Muster Roll for Gibraltar Hospital (ADM 102/229) notes that he, and sixteen other men from *Defence* were admitted to the hospital on 20 October 1798.

Within the muster rolls of the Royal Navy, there are only three ways that a man can leave the service. R = Run. D = Discharged. DD = Discharged Dead. John Dean was DD / Discharged Dead on 12 December 1798 and interred at the hospital cemetery. I would have thought that his shattered leg probably turned gangrenous which ultimately cost him his life.

He was noted in Steel's *Navy List* of 1803 in a special section inserted by the Patriotic Fund. The first page contains a letter printed on blue paper from Lloyd's Coffee-House, March 10, 1803: 'At a Meeting of the Committee appointed to manage the Subscriptions raised for the Benefit of the Wounded, and the families or Relatives of such as were Killed, in the ever memorable Action of the 1st of August, 1798, JOHN JULIUS ANGERSTEIN, in the chair,

Resolved, - That the following advertisement be published in Steel's *Navy List*.

Resolved, - That the families or next of kin to the following Officers, Seamen and Marines killed in the memorable action, be desired to send to Mr White, the Secretary, at this house, an account, in writing, of their consanguinity, or relationship, to the deceased, together with a statement of the number and situation of their families; of the places to which the parties so applying respectively belong, in order that this committee may be enabled to transmit to them, free of all expense, such gratuities as may be found expedient, without the necessity of an agent, or of the parties coming up to town. etc. etc.

In the list of Wounded men on board HMS *Defence* is noted 'JOHN DEAN, LM (since dead)'.

The Muster Roll for *Defence* also notes that £20 was paid at the Nore on 14 February 1800 to John Dean's sister, Margaret Darling. I would think that Margaret was delivered his bronze Davison Nile medal and that she, not being aware of the universal custom of unrated lower deck sailors having their bronze medals gilt, simply had a modest inscription made and the whole of the medal cased in silver and glazed as a memorial to her departed brother, who had fought with Nelson at the Nile. She probably would have received an annuity from the Patriotic Fund if she made application to them.

The Patriotic Fund at Lloyds, now moved from the Coffee-House, is still in operation and offers support for the families of British men and women killed or wounded in action just as they did in 1803. It is a testimony to the insurers at Lloyd's who felt a need to support those who had either died or suffered in the removal of an enemy threat; which would have a direct impact on the improved safety of shipping, which was what Lloyd's of London was all about.

Provenance: Glenn Stein, 1992.

References: The National Archives, Kew: ADM 35/505. ADM 36/13993, 14342 - 14346 (*Defence*). ADM 102/229 (Gibraltar Hospital).

DN 22   Joseph Chatterton, Yeoman of the Sheets, HMS Bellerophon, Captain Henry D'Esterre Darby

Description: Ship-board gilt bronze medal cased and glazed. The obverse and reverse fields are chased with the reverse field engraved JOSEPH / CHATTERTON. Attached to the ring suspension is a blue ribbon that is 3.5cms wide and approximately 56cms long. The engraving is by 'The *Bellerophon* engraver', please see DN 23 for more information. There is a small die break running through C. H. K. with a larger break below at the rim. The weight of the medal only is 38.9 grams and cased with ribbon is 73.8 grams.

Background: HMS *Bellerophon*, better known as the *Billy Ruffian* within Nelson's fleet, was a hard fighting 74-gun ship that had a knack for being in the worst possible place during a battle. She anchored alongside *L'Orient* of 120 guns at the Nile and suffered terribly for it. At Trafalgar, she was surrounded by five enemy ships and again suffered heavily. However, *Bellerophon* gained ever lasting fame when, under the command of Captain Frederick Maitland following Waterloo, he negotiated the surrender of Napoleon Bonaparte and *Bellerophon* had the privilege of bringing Napoleon to Plymouth where he awaited to learn his fate.

She was built to the Slade design of the Arrogant Class of 1758 at the private shipyard of Mr Edward Greaves [Pengelly states 'Messrs Graves & Nicholson'], at Frinsbury on the River Medway, near Rochester. *Bellerophon* was 168 feet in overall length and 1604 tons burthen. She carried 28 x 32 pounders on her Gundeck, 28 x 18 pounders on the Upper Deck, 14 x 9 pounders on the Quarterdeck and 4 x 9 pounders in the Forecastle. Some of these lighter guns may have been exchanged for carronades in the 1790s. She was launched on 6 October 1786 and her ship's company would have been around 550. She remained in ordinary until 1790 when there was a possibility of war with the Spanish, which quickly blew over, but during this time *Bellerophon* acquired her first Captain, Thomas Pasley.

David Cordingly notes: 'Captain Pasley was aged fifty-two (considerably older than any of the other captains who would succeed him). For the past three years he had been commander-in-chief of the ships in the Medway with the title of commodore. And, until his appointment to the *Bellerophon*, he had been in command of the 60-gun *Scipio*, the guardship on the Medway.

'Thomas Pasley was a Scotsman and a veteran seaman who had served on ships in the West Indies, on the Guinea coast of Africa and on the Newfoundland station. He had been present at several minor engagements during the Seven Years War but had yet to take part in a major fleet action. In 1774 he married Mary Heywood, daughter of the Chief Justice of the Isle of Man. He later described her as 'my beloved Mary, my wife, friend and companion'. They had two daughters to whom he was devoted. For several years he kept a personal journal recording his daily experiences as a captain in command of frigates, and his writings reveal a man of intelligence and sensibility. He was strict but fair with his crew, and seems to have inspired their loyalty and trust. Contemporary observations on his character stress his warmth and his 'unbounded benevolence' and this is borne out in [his] portrait which shows a man with a strong but kindly face.'

Captain Thomas Pasley

Although the tensions with Spain eased by the end of 1790, the events of the French Revolution were now gaining more attention in Whitehall and the British fleet in the Channel was kept on alert. Finally, at the beginning of 1793, the French executed their King, Louis XVI, and the call to war was inevitable with the French making the declaration at the end of February. *Bellerophon* was attached to Lord Howe's Channel Fleet with the object being to keep an eye on the French fleet at Brest.

Joseph Chatterton, whose medal this is, was born in York and volunteered to join the Royal Navy at the time of war being declared, 27 February 1793. He was immediately rated as an Able Seaman which could mean that he was either a very seasoned mariner or a captain's protégé. He was given £2/5/4 as advanced pay from which was deducted 15/- for treating 'the venereals'. A nasty process which required a long syringe to be inserted into the penis and mercury injected. His record shows no repeat occurrence, so he probably found a better class of women! He remained an Able Seaman until 1 February 1797 when he was promoted to Yeoman of the Sheets (please see DN 19 for more information regarding this station). He continued on board *Bellerophon* until she was paid off on 30 April 1800. He then followed his captain, Henry Darby, to his next ship, the newly launched HMS *Spencer*, and joined her as a Midshipman, so one would reckon that both Pasley and Darby saw merit in this young man. Chatterton, however, didn't pass his lieutenant's examination and we lose sight of him after the *Spencer* was paid off on 15 September 1802.

During the rest of 1793, Lord Howe spent his time exercising the Channel Fleet so that they would start to work as a unit. It had been ten years since Britain had been at war, and during most of this time the navy had been in ordinary and the skills needed to handle the big ships of the line and fight a fleet action had to be relearned. During this period, Howe was most interested in the sailing qualities of each of his ships and speed trials were performed. The *Bellerophon* was without question the fastest big gun ship in the fleet. 12 knots was her top speed and it is interesting to note that in 1811 she was tested again and 12 knots remained her top speed and was noted as 'being well built, and very weatherly. She steered very well, and in the trough of the sea she rolls deep, but very easy.' It really must have been a thrill to have been a topman on board *Bellerophon* when she was running with all sail set on her best point of sailing!

January 1794 saw Captain Pasley promoted to Commodore and Captain William Johnstone Hope taking command of the *Bellerophon* with Pasley staying on board and flying his pennant. Hope was only 28 years old, however he had joined the navy age ten and had served under Nelson on board *Boreas* in the West Indies.

The early Spring was passed with the Howe's fleet cruising off the coast of France. Horace Walpole noted that Lord Howe 'was a man of few words, as unshakeable as a rock, and as silent.' Cordingly continues, 'His dour manner, his rugged, impassive features, his dark eyes and heavy black eyebrows had earned him the name of Black Dick.' Stern he may have been, but the sailors all trusted him and when it came to mutiny at Spithead in 1797, the King turned to 'Black Dick' to resolve the issues, which Howe did by listening to the complaints and putting them to right. There was no hanging of mutineers at Spithead.

Pasley was promoted to Rear-Admiral and put in charge of the four fastest ships in Howe's fleet, thus creating The Flying Squadron. On 28 May, the French fleet of 26 ships of the line was sighted and the chase was on. *Bellerophon* was the first to make contact with the rear-most ship which was the 110-gun *Revolutionaire*. An unequal contest, and although supported by the other British ships that came up, the *Revolutionaire* was able to escape, but so damaged that she headed for port and was out of the action for the coming days. *Bellerophon* did not escape unscathed and suffered damage as well, which was quickly repaired.

On the 29th, Howe, on board the *Queen Charlotte*, led his fleet toward the enemy, but due to the lack of effort by some of his ships, it was only the *Queen Charlotte*, *Bellerophon* and *Leviathan* that broke the rear of the French line and cut off three French ships. The French doubled back and were able to rescue their stricken friends, however the damage they received was such that they, like the *Revolutionaire*, headed for port and were out of the subsequent day's fight.

May 30 and 31 were marked by fog and very poor visibility, but the two contesting fleets remained relatively close to one another. The 1st of June saw the sun and the enemy as the British mounted the final attack. After some manoeuvring of the opposing fleets and around 11 a.m., Lord Howe made the decisive signal and ordered his fleet to attack in line abreast. *Bellerophon* was near the end of the British line and was faced with three or four French ships who poured in shot as she approached. An 18 pound cannon ball swept across the quarterdeck hitting Admiral Pasley in the leg. Pasley seeing the distress of those around him replied, 'Thank you, but never mind my leg, take care of my flag.'

Bellerophon continued to strike out at her enemies on both sides until she was quite unmanageable due to loss of her upper masts and much of her rigging. The frigate *Latona* came to tow her clear of the devastation. Her strong sides had offered some protection to the ship's company and she suffered only four men killed and 30 wounded after several hours action. The Glorious First of June was the first encounter of the British and French fleets during the French Revolutionary War. The result was that the British lost no ships while the French had captured two 80-gun ships, four 74-gun ships and one 74-gun ship sunk.

Following the battle, both Admiral Pasley and Captain Hope left *Bellerophon* with Captain James, Baron Cranston taking command. He had gained much experience during the American War and was Rodney's flag captain at the Battle of the Saints, 1782, and boarded the French flagship *Ville de Paris* to receive the sword of surrender from Comte de Grasse on behalf of Rodney. When Cranston came on board *Bellerophon* he brought his own midshipmen, several warrant officers and thirty able seamen, who were particularly loyal to him, which was not an uncommon occurrence with a change in command.

Bellerophon was not a happy ship and spent the winter months at anchor in the Solent with the tedium being broken only by bad weather and frequent floggings. At last in late May 1795, she was directed to join Admiral Cornwallis, old 'Billy Blue', and his squadron of the *Royal Sovereign* of 100 guns, and four 74-gun ships which included *Bellerophon*. Cruising in the Bay of Biscay yielded a number of merchant ships as prizes but then on 16 June fourteen French ships of the line came out to remove the British annoyance. The wind dropped and during the night all waited to see what would happen. *Bellerophon* was at the rear of the British line and let go her best bower anchors to lighten the ship.

With the dawn, the French were seen coming up very fast in three divisions. *Bellerophon* jettisoned sixteen tons of water to lighten ship and then cleared for action. Cornwallis in the *Royal Sovereign* ordered his and the other ships to slow their speed to allow *Bellerophon* and *Brunswick* to take the lead of the squadron. When the *Bellerophon* passed Cornwallis, the 'Billy Ruffians' cheered the Admiral. The last ship in the line was the *Mars* which the French started to harass. Seeing this Cornwallis hauled the *Royal Sovereign* around to sail back and protect the *Mars*. Upon arriving, Cornwallis unleashed a devastating broadside against the French who immediately checked their progress.

Cornwallis then resorted to a 'ruse de guerre' by having one of his frigates race ahead of the squadron and towards dusk to commence signalling the flagship that a large friendly fleet was approaching. The French worked out that the tables would soon be turned and sailed back to port, leaving Cornwallis and his squadron to complete 'Cornwallis's Retreat.'

The rest of the year was spent either at anchor, dry dock or routine cruising. April 1796 saw Lord Cranston retire from the ship due to ill health, he would die not long after. John Loring briefly became captain but then handed over command on 10 September to Henry D'Esterre Darby (1749 - 1823), who would fix *Bellerophon* in the public eye. Cordingly notes that Darby was from Irish landed gentry and had an uncle who was his patron and a Vice-Admiral. He joined the navy when he was thirteen, became a lieutenant when twenty-seven and a captain at age thirty-four in 1783, which was not a particularly brilliant career. He was forty-seven when he took command of *Bellerophon*.

Initially the *Bellerophon* patrolled the Irish Sea, but then in March was ordered to join Earl St Vincent's fleet and assist in the blockade of Cadiz. Nelson came on board the ship on 1 June to muster the ship's company, perhaps as part of the anniversary of the Glorious First of June. Weeks were spent off Cadiz until news arrived that Napoleon and the Toulon fleet were out in the Mediterranean. Troubridge and a squadron, which included *Bellerophon*, were dispatched to join up with Nelson and find the French fleet.

Bellerophon was the ninth ship to approach the anchored French fleet in Aboukir Bay. The log of the Master, Edward Kirby, tells us of the plight she went through: 'Wednesday, August 1st. P.M. Moderate and clear. The *Zealous* made the signal for a strange fleet east. At 2, saw the enemy, 13 sail of the line and 3 frigates at anchor. Got the best bower cable out by the stern, and got springs upon the cables. 1/2 past 6, the enemy hoisted the French national colours. 3/4 past. began engaging, running down the enemy's line. At 7, let go the best bower-anchor alongside *l'Orient*, and brought up the stern to the wind. At 8, the mizen mast was shot away and shortly after the main mast, which fell along the booms on the starboard side of the forecastle. At 9, observing our antagonist on fire on the middle-gun deck, cut the stern cable, and wore clear of her by loosing the spiritsail. Shortly the fore mast went over the larboard bow. At 10, *l'Orient* blew up. Picked up two of *l'Orient*'s men who escaped the fire. Employed clearing the wrecks and putting out the fire, which had caught in several places of the ship.'

Just the bare bones of the awful contest the 74-gun *Bellerophon* fought against the 120-gun *l'Orient*. *Bellerophon* was pretty much a shattered wreck when she drifted clear of the battle and finally came to rest some five or six miles to the east, up the coast. David Cordingly describes the carnage on board the ship: 'Whether Captain Darby intended to lie alongside *Le Franklin*, [which was the next position after the *Defence's* opponent *Peuple Souverin*], which was the ship anchored ahead of the French flagship, or hoped to position the *Bellerophon* so that she could fire her broadsides at the vulnerable bows of *L'Orient* is not clear and was never explained. What subsequently happened was disastrous. At 7 o'clock she let go her best bower anchor which splashed into the water, hauling the anchor cable down and along the ship's sides until it was stretching out in a long line from one of the stern ports. The sailors out on the yards heaved the topsails as the anchor cable streamed out astern. The ship began to swing stern into the wind but continued forward progress. Either the anchor was dragging on the seabed or the sailors failed to check the cable and let out too much. When the anchor finally brought the ship to a halt she found herself, not at the bows of the enormous French flagship, but exactly alongside her, facing the entire weight of her broadside guns.

'Every time *L'Orient* fired her upper deck broadside she wrecked more of the *Bellerophon*. The boats stored on the booms in the waist of the ship were smashed to pieces, most of the guns on the quarterdeck were dismounted and the standing rigging was so shot through that the masts were increasingly precarious. The first of the officers to be hit was Captain Darby who received a head wound which knocked him to the deck unconscious. He was carried below to the surgeons. Lieutenant Daniel, the first lieutenant, and Lieutenant Launder, the second, were both wounded but were able to remain at their posts for a while. Then Daniel was hit by a cannon ball which took off his right leg. As he was being carried towards the cockpit he was hit again, this time by a lethal round of grapeshot which killed him and also killed the seaman who was carrying him. John Hadaway, the fourth lieutenant, was hit and had to be taken below. George Jolliffe, the fifth lieutenant, was killed outright.'

Captain Darby survived and his account of the action showed that *Bellerophon* lost 49 in killed and 149 wounded with more of the wounded to die in the following days. On the 14th of August, *Bellerophon* joined the British ships and their prizes that Saumarez commanded for the trip to Gibraltar where repairs could be made. When St Vincent saw *Bellerophon* upon her arrival at Gibraltar, he remarked that he had never seen a ship so mauled.

Captain Darby, and his ship's company were looking forward to returning to England to have *Bellerophon* repaired. There was utter dismay when St Vincent ordered Saumarez to proceed home with the prizes, but for the British ships to remain at Gibraltar for repairs. Darby's hot Irish temper got the better of him as he put it about that the shipwrights at Gibraltar weren't up to effectively repairing *Bellerophon*, which he could drive a post-chaise through the holes in her sides. It wasn't long before Darby's discontent reached St Vincent's ears and he decided to take some action, but of a gentle sort considering what Darby had been through at the Nile.

Colin Pengelly tells the story: 'One night after a long party at which both St Vincent and Darby were present, St Vincent called round to the house where Darby was staying. Darby had just retired to bed when he heard a knocking on his window. Feeling rather annoyed, he asked who the blazes was there at that time of night! He was much surprised to recognise St Vincent's voice saying, 'Open up! Open up, Darby! Tis I! I have something which I must say to you.' Darby opened the window and there below was the Commander-in-Chief in full-dress uniform. He told Darby that he had a dream which he felt he must recount to him. He said he dreamed he was watching the battle of the Nile and was much struck by the noble part played by the *Bellerophon*, contending alone against the mighty *l'Orient*. The scene of his dream then changed to the Rock [Gibraltar], where people were saying what a fine fellow that Darby was and what a great fight he put up. But, said St Vincent, he dreamed that Darby himself was saying that the Rock lacked the shipwrights to repair his ship, and that there would be a dreadful catastrophe when the ship next put to sea. St Vincent said to himself that this surely could not be the same Darby he had seen fighting so nobly at the Nile; he must have turned chicken-hearted!

Captain Henry Darby

'A rather exasperated Darby burst in at this point, and asked what he meant by such a term, but St Vincent continued calmly and said that in his dream the reports of the bad condition of the *Bellerophon* were soon all over the Rock. Then the scene of the dream changed to a court martial and the officer being tried was Darby, and the blade of his sword was pointed towards him. St Vincent finished the story with these words: 'Now remember, this was only a dream, Darby; but now I have told you I hope I shall be able to rest, so good night!' He then strode away leaving Darby to spend a rather restless night! To speed repairs on the *Bellerophon* and the other badly damaged ships, St Vincent gave orders for every ship at Lisbon to send a carpenter and shipwright to the Rock to aid in the repair of the remaining ships.'

On the 8th of January, *Bellerophon* set sail for Port Mahon as escort for a convoy which was to characterise her deployment during the rest of 1799 and the early part of 1800 when she at last reached Portsmouth and was taken in for a refit. Her ship's company were paid off on 3 May 1800.

Captain Darby was given command of the recently launched HMS *Spencer*, named after Earl Spencer, First Lord of the Admiralty. She was an 80-gun two decker designed by the French émigré Barralier and built by Adams at Bucklers Hard. Her dimensions were impressive, 181 feet in overall length and 1,901 tons burthen. She carried 30 x 32 pounders on the Gun Deck, 30 x 18 pounders on the Upper Deck, 4 x 18 pounders and 10 x 32 pound carronades on the Quarterdeck, 2 x 18 pounders and 2 x 32 pound carronades in the Forecastle, and finally 6 x 18 pounders on the Poop Deck.

Her ship's company numbered 650. There is little doubt that Joseph Chatterton had made an impression on Captain Darby as he not only transferred from the old *Bellerophon* to the *Spencer*, but was entered onto the books as a Midshipman in May 1800.

Darby took her to the Mediterranean and, although there were several scares involving the excursions of the French and Spanish fleets, things came to a head when *Spencer* was part of Sir James Saumarez's squadron operating near Algesiras and Gibraltar. W. H. Long gives us the detail surrounding Saumarez's victory and the destruction of two Spanish first rates. 'On July 6th 1801, the British squadron under the command of Sir J. Saumarez, made an attack on three French ships of the line, and a frigate, moored under the batteries in Algesiras Bay. After a well fought action of four hours duration, the British ships retired to Gibraltar to repair damages, leaving the *Hannibal* seventy-four, Captain Ferris, which had run aground, in the possession of the enemy. [The *Spencer* suffered six men killed and 27 wounded. Amongst the wounded was Midshipman Joseph Chatterton, although it is thought that his wound wasn't serious as he remained on board for the action of 12 July.] Two of the French ships ran ashore, but were got afloat the next day. The French Admiral Linois, apprehensive of another attack, sent to Cadiz for assistance, and on July 9th, Vice-Admiral de Moreno, with six sail of the line and some frigates, stood into Algesiras Bay, with the intention of removing the French ships and their prize to Cadiz, for safety. The combined fleet then consisted of nine ships of the line, two of one hundred and twelve guns, one of ninety-six, three of eighty, and three of seventy-four guns, besides frigates.

'The [British] ships were removing their wounded and repairing their damages, which were very considerable; the *Pompee* seventy-four, being so shattered, that her crew was employed in refitting the other ships. The *Caesar*, flag ship, was in such an unserviceable state, that the Admiral shifted his flag to the *Audacious*, but her crew declared they would work night and day to get the ship ready to meet the enemy. [Long has a note that when the *Caesar* was ready, and lying off Europa Point with the 'Prepare For Action' signal flying, the Officer of the Watch was surprised to see a small boat with two men coming out to the flag ship. Upon the boat coming in close, the two men called up that they were from the *Caesar*, wounded in the last action, escaped from hospital and ready to fight some more. They were let on board. Long also notes that two men from the *Pompee*, which wasn't ready for sea, stowed away on board the *Caesar* so that they wouldn't miss the fight. After the action it took some doing to have 'Run' removed from their names on the *Pompee's* muster roll.]

'About noon on July 12th, the combined fleet began to move; and the *Caesar* warped out of the mole, with her band playing *Come cheer up my lads, 'tis to glory we steer*, which was answered by the military bands on the mole head, with *Britons strike home*. The flag of Sir J. Saumarez was re-hoisted, and the squadron signalled to prepare for action. The British ships comprised the *Caesar* eighty, Rear-Admiral Sir J. Saumarez, Captain J. Brenton, *Venerable* seventy-four, Captain S. Hood, *Spencer* seventy-four, Captain H. D. Darby, *Superb* seventy-four Captain R. G. Keats, *Audacious* seventy-four Captain S. Peard, *Thames* thirty-two Captain A.

P. Holles, *Calpe* sloop Captain the Hon. G. H. Dundas, *Louisa* brig, and the Portuguese frigate *Carlotta* Captain C. Duncan.

'About eight p.m. Sir J. Saumarez stood after the combined fleet, then almost out of sight, and the *Superb* being the best sailer, Captain Keats was ordered to crowd on all sail, and attack the first ship of the enemy he came up with. By eleven p.m. the *Superb* was nearly four miles ahead of the *Caesar* and soon after came up with the *Real Carlos*, one hundred and twelve guns, on the larboard beam, and another three decker, the *Hermangildo* nearly abreast of her. Captain Keats opened fire on both of them at about three cables distance, shot away the fore topmast of the *Real Carlos* and put the crews of both ships into such confusion, that they fired at each other, as well as at the *Superb*.

'In about a quarter of an hour, Captain Keats saw that the ship which had lost her fore topmast was on fire, upon which he ceased to molest her, and stood after the *San Antonio* seventy-four, which ship, after an action of about half an hour, hailed to say she had surrendered, just as the *Caesar* and *Venerable* came up. Meanwhile the *Real Carlos* and *Hermangildo* ran foul of each other, both were soon in flames fore and aft, and shortly after midnight blew up, with the greater part of their crews. The *Superb* and *Calpe* were left to secure the prize, and remove the prisoners, while the *Caesar* and other ships pursued the flying enemy. About five in the morning the *Venerable* came up with the *Formidable*, eighty, and engaged her for an hour and an half, till her own main mast went by the board, and her opponent made off for Cadiz. About the same time her mizzen mast fell, and the remainder of the enemy's ships, five sail of the line and four frigates, seemed inclined to bear down and attack her, but observing the *Caesar*, *Superb* and *Audacious* approaching, they hauled up, and entered Cadiz.

An engraved 8 real celebrating Saumarez's victory.

'At two p.m. the *Venerable* by the assistance of the *Thames* and boats of the squadron was hove off, and the *Thames* took her in tow. Before sunset she was off Cape Trafalgar, under jury masts, and fit for action, had any enemy appeared. Her loss was heavy; her Master, and 17 men were killed, and four officers and 83 men wounded. The *Superb* had Lieutenant Waller, and 14 men wounded. On board the two Spanish three deckers nearly two thousand men perished. The Captains, Officers, and crews of the squadron, received the thanks of Parliament, Sir J. Saumarez was created a Knight of Bath, and granted a pension of £1,200 per annum.'

Although Darby and the *Spencer* didn't play an important part in this action, they were there and I'm sure that if the enemy wished to have a broader battle, Darby would have certainly obliged. *Spencer* returned to Plymouth in September 1802 when she was paid off and we lose sight of Joseph Chatterton.

Provenance: Medal fair, 1990.

References: The National Archives, Kew: ADM 35/224-226. ADM 36/11904-11907, 12455-12460 (*Bellerophon*). ADM 35/1804. ADM 36/14401-14403. ADM 1/404 (*Spencer* with the last being killed and wounded on 6 July 1801.)
The Sailing Navy List by David Lyon, Conway, London, 1993.
Billy Ruffian by David Cordingly, Bloomsbury, London, 2003.
The First Bellerophon by Colin Pengelly, John Baker, London, 1966.
The Naval Chronicle, vol 4, Gold, London, 1801.
Forget Me Not by Sim Comfort, Sim Comfort Associates, London, 2004.
Medals of the British Navy and How they were won by W. H. Long, Norie & Wilson, London, 1895.
Logs of the Great Sea Fights 1794-1805 by Sturges Jackson, Navy Records Society, London, 1899-1900.

DN 23 Oliver Aunger, Able Seaman, HMS Bellerophon, Captain Henry D'Esterre Darby

Description: Soho gilt bronze medal cased and glazed. The obverse and reverse fields are chased with the reverse field engraved O. *Aunger*. There is a small die break running through C. H. K. with a larger break below at the rim. The weight of the medal only is 40 grams and cased is 71.5 grams. Extremely fine.

Background: Oliver Aunger joined the Royal Navy on board HMS *Perseus* on 2 January 1792. He was 25 years old and from Plymouth and was immediately rated as Able Seaman, so another seasoned hand. *Perseus* cruised in the West Indies during the summer of 1792 calling at Barbados, Granada, Antigua, St Kitts etc. She returned to Plymouth in late March 1793 and Oliver Aunger was paid off, however on 29 June 1793 he joined HMS *Bellerophon* 'per order of Earl Howe'. He was again rated Able Seaman and remained as such until the *Bellerophon* was paid off on 3 May 1800. On 13 May 1800 he joined HMS *Eurus* as an Able Seaman, now aged 32. *Eurus* was a Dutch built 32-gun frigate that was captured by the British in 1796. She was converted to carry troops in 1799 and carried out the transport of troops for both the landings at Malta in late 1800 and with Lord Keith's invasion of Egypt at Aboukir Bay in March of 1801. On 14 September 1801 he was advanced to Acting Armourer for the ship which meant that he was particularly skilled in the maintenance and use of the ship's small arms. She returned to Portsmouth in the next year and was paid off on 3 September 1802, when we lose sight of Oliver Aunger.

There's no doubt that Aunger was a very useful man. It is interesting that his Davison Nile medal is one that was originally gilt at Boulton's works at Soho, which meant the medal should have gone to a petty officer who had been on board *Bellerophon* at the Nile. That Aunger wasn't a petty officer, at least according to the ship's muster, leads one to think that he did a deal with a shipmate petty officer for the bronze gilt example, or that it was simply awarded to him for good service by Captain Darby as, due to the long list of killed, there were spare gilt medals. One remembers that Nelson made use of 'Poor dear' Captain Ralph Miller's gold medal after he had given to Captain Hardy the gold Davison originally intended for himself. For a full description of Oliver Aunger's time on board HMS *Bellerophon*, please refer to DN 22.

When I examine the engraving of the Davison Nile medals given to Joseph Chatterton, John Stewart and W.G. Cocker, there is no doubt that all three were engraved by the same hand. So, like the *Minotaur* engraver, this man I term the '*Bellerophon* engraver' because the style is unique amongst engraved Davison Nile medals. Oliver Aunger's medal may also be by the same hand although because the reverse field was chased after the engraving of the name, which has thinned out the letters, it is hard to be sure. What is certain is that the setting sun has been erased from Aunger's, Stewart's and Cocker's Davison Nile medals. The removal of the setting sun from the battle scene is only found amongst these medals given to men on board *Bellerophon*. I think the removal of the setting sun was intentional because these men figured out that it shouldn't have been part of the battle scene.

Provenance: Medal fair, 1982.

References: The National Archives, Kew: ADM 35/1292-1293. ADM 36/11318-11319. (*Perseus*). As DN 22 for *Bellerophon*. ADM 36/13638 (*Royal William*). ADM 35/567. ADM 36 14770-14771. (*Eurus*).

Tubular grip double-disc cutlass circa 1770 - 1803. The type of cutlass that Oliver Aunger as Acting Armourer would have been very familiar with both in terms of maintenance and use. Image from *Naval Swords and Dirks* by this author.

DN 24   John [Archibald] Stewart, Able Seaman, HMS Bellerophon, Captain Henry D'Esterre Darby

Description: Ship board gilt bronze medal with the reverse field engraved *John Stewart* / BELEROPHON (sic). Engraving by the *Bellerophon* engraver. There is a small die break running through C. H. K. with a larger break below at the rim. Weight: 39.9 grams. Near extremely fine.

Background: In the muster roll of the *Bellerophon* there is only one man with a surname of Stewart and that is Archibald Stewart who was a twenty year old Scot when he joined the ship on 13 September 1795. Where he came from to join the ship was a 'French Cartel' which means that he was a British prisoner of war that had been exchanged for a French prisoner of war. He may have been a merchant seaman or in the Royal Navy, the British lost a number of naval ships to the French in the early years of the war. If he had been a merchant seaman, it appears that upon his release he decided that fighting the French was now a personal matter and joined the Royal Navy, or if he had been in the navy, then with release he simply returned to duty, but this time on HMS *Bellerophon*. He was immediately rated as Able Seaman and served on board *Bellerophon* continuously until she was paid off on 30 April 1800 at Portsmouth.

As a note, the French and British maintained this system of exchange of prisoners of war during the Revolutionary War. With the recommencement of war in 1803 and Napoleon now firmly in control, he decided this system didn't make any sense if one was going to weaken the manpower of the Royal Navy, so captured British sailors went into Prisoner of War camps and stayed there until the fall of Napoleon in 1815. Naturally the British held onto their French prisoners as well which resulted in a wide range of French Prisoner of War craft ware, with the most impressive being the bone models of naval ships.

Why was the medal engraved with the name John instead of Archibald? Well, one reason could be, taking note that *Bellerophon* is misspelled on this particular medal, that the engraver just couldn't get his mind around spelling Archibald. To me, the more likely reason is that Archibald wasn't that happy with being an Archibald and that he was known to his shipmates as John and as the *Bellerophon* engraver appears to have been on board the ship, he may have only known him as John Stewart and engraved his name that way. Also, as with Robert Lewis of the *Minotaur*, there could have been the use of a *nom de guerre*, i.e. if he decided to Run, then the authorities would be looking for John and not Archibald. As he didn't Run, it really seems to me that this piece reflects a more innocent use of John simply because he didn't want to be known as Archibald! Just my opinion though. Interesting to see that the setting sun has been erased from the reverse field which you only find on *Bellerophon* medals.

For details regarding his time on board *Bellerophon*, please refer to DN 22.

Provenance: Ex A. A. Payne Collection, circa 1911.
Medal fair, 1989.

References: The National Archives, Kew: As DN 22 for *Bellerophon*.
The History of Napoleonic and American Prisoners of War 1756-1815 by Clive Lloyd, Antique Collectors' Club, Woodbridge, Suffolk, 2007.
The Arts and Crafts of Napoleonic and American Prisoners of War 1756-1816 by Clive Lloyd, Antique Collectors' Club, Woodbridge, Suffolk, 2007.
A Handbook of British and Foreign Orders, War Medals and Decorations awarded to the Army and Navy by A. A. Payne, reprinted by Hayward, Polstead, Suffolk, 1981.

DN 25   Boy, 3rd Class William George Cocker, HMS Bellerophon, Captain Henry D'Esterre Darby

Description: Soho gilt bronze medal. The obverse and reverse fields are chased with the reverse field engraved W.G. / COCKER / BELLEROPHON, by the '*Bellerophon* engraver'. There is small die break running through C. H. K. with a larger break below at the rim on the obverse. The weight of the medal only is 39.8 grams and cased is 66.7 grams. Extremely fine. Subsequent to the purchase of this medal, the 48 mm glazed case was found to offer protection.

Background: This is a particularly interesting medal. The original Soho gilding means that the award went to a petty officer on board the *Bellerophon*, but when one considers who William George Cocker was, you quickly realise that something is amiss.

W. G. Cocker was from London and joined *Bellerophon* on 17 May 1797 as a Boy, 3rd Class aged 13 years old. He served on board at the battle of the Nile and continued until 30 April 1800 when the ship was paid off at Portsmouth and he transferred to the *Royal William* receiving ship. From there he was lent to HMS *Gladiator* for a short period in early June until he transferred to HMS *Spencer* on 10 June. He stayed with *Spencer* until 15 September 1802 when the ship was paid off. (Please see DN 29 for information regarding 1st to 3rd Class Boys and their placement in the Royal Navy.)

What is interesting is that also on board *Bellerophon* was William Cocker, also from London and who had joined the ship as part of her original complement on 6 June 1793. He was aged twenty at the time and was rated Ordinary Seaman. On 22 July 1796 he was promoted to Armour's Mate, a petty officer posting. He was present at the battle of the Nile and continued to serve until 30 April 1800 when he too transferred to the *Royal William*. He also was lent to HMS *Gladiator* in early June and then on 10 June transferred to HMS *Spencer* and continued in her until she was paid off on 15 September 1802.

Both of these young men followed Captain Darby to the *Spencer* and were most likely known to him and considered valuable hands. That the two Cockers were related is also a distinct possibility, in fact with only eleven years age difference, they could have been brothers and very certainly stuck together during their time in the *Bellerophon* and *Spencer*. As the medal owned by the younger of the two is a Soho gilt medal that would have been presented to a petty officer and as the elder William would have received such a medal, it may well be that he gave his medal to the youngster for engraving. Speculation, but it may well be what has happened.

From Smyth we have the following about the Armourer: 'In a man-of-war, is a person appointed by Warrant [from the Board of Ordnance], to keep the small arms in complete condition for service. As he is also the ship's blacksmith, a mate is allowed to assist at the forge.'

In *Jack Tar* is a quote from Basil Hall which is of interest and relates to the ship's forge: 'The circumstance which most distinctly marks the afternoon of Sunday on board a man-of-war, even more than on land, is the absence of all the usual stir caused by the multifarious occupations of the artificers and crew. The fire in the armourer's [portable] forge, abreast of the fore-hatchway being extinguished, the rattle of his hammer, and the gritting of his rasp, are no more heard.'

In the case that the Armourer was not able to take care of all of the ship's blacksmith needs on board ship, these would have been carried out in the port workshops when the ship was in British waters. The *Naval Instructions* allow that, 'When the Ship is in Foreign Parts, and the Small Arms want such cleaning or Repairs as cannot be performed aboard, ... the Captain may order them ashore, to be repaired by the Workmen, of the Country; but the Armourer or Gunsmith is to be present while those Repairs are performing, to see the same well executed, and the Abuses they are liable to, in the Hands of the Country Workmen, prevented.'

This is the other aspect of these two Cockers. The most likely person on board ship to have carried out the gilding of Davison Nile medals is the Armourer or his Mate as they were in charge of the ship's forge and were skilled in working with hot metal. The note from the *Naval Instructions* also provides scope for the operation to have taken place on shore either at Gibraltar of one of the foreign ports in the Mediterranean. It really does look like the Armourer or his Mate may have assisted in the gilding of Davison Nile medals on board ship.

For a full discussion regarding the gilding process, please refer to the special article on pages 71-72. For details regarding the commissions of the *Bellerophon* and *Spencer*, please refer to DN 22.

Provenance: The Roy Butler Collection, Wallis & Wallis Nelson Sale, 19 July 2005, Lot 13.

References: The National Archives, Kew: As DN 22 for *Bellerophon* and *Spencer*.
The Sailor's Word-Book, by Admiral W. H. Smyth, Blackie, London, 1867.
Jack Tar by Roy & Lesley Adkins, Little Brown, London, 2008.
Regulation and Instructions relating to His Majesty's Service at Sea, Admiralty, London, 1790 (13th edition).

DN 26 John Glass, Able Seaman, HMS Majestic, Captain George Blagdon Westcott and Lieutenant Robert Cuthbert

Description: Jeweller gilt and engraved bronze medal inscribed in the reverse field *John Glass / Majestic 74*. Because of the condition of the medal, I would imagine that it had been cased and glazed. There is a small die break running through C. H. K. with a larger break below at the rim. Weight: 40.1 grams. Extremely fine.

Background: When one reads the biographical sketch of George Blagdon Westcott (1745?-1798), by J. K. Laughton in the *DNB*, there is a curious note at the end which reads: 'There is no record of Westcott's life beyond the logs and pay-books of the ships in which he served in the Public Records Office [National Archives]. So far as it can be tested, the traditional anecdote (*Naval Chronicle*, vol. XII, pp 453) is unworthy

263

of credit; but it seems probable that, whether in a ship of war or a merchantman, Westcott's beginnings were very humble.'

Well, I just can't resist reading the reference in the *Naval Chronicle* and as it is such a good story, I include it here: 'THE LATE CAPTAIN WESTCOTT: This respected Officer, who closed his mortal career in the memorable battle of the Nile, was the son of a baker, at Honiton, in Devonshire. Being led by his profession to a connexion with the millers, young Westcott used frequently to be sent to the mill. It happened in one of his visits, that by the accidental breaking of a rope, the machine was disordered; and neither the owner nor his men being equal to repairing it, Westcott offered to use his skill in splicing it, although attended with danger and difficulty. The miller complied, and the job was executed with such nicety, that he told him 'he was fit for a Sailor, since he could splice so well; and if he ever should have an inclination to go to sea, he would get him a berth.' Accordingly so, opportunity presented itself, of which the lad accepted; and he began his naval career in the humble capacity of a cabin-boy; a situation the most common in the Ship, and not much calculated to afford vent to the expansion of genius. But he contrived to exercise his abilities to such good purpose, and discovered such an acuteness of understanding, that he was, in a very short time, introduced among the Midshipmen; in which rank his behaviour was so conciliating and prudent, that further advancement followed, since that time he became so signally conspicuous, both for his skill and bravery, that he gradually, or rather hastily, continued to be promoted, until he reached the honourable station in which he lost his life. Had he survived the battle, his seniority of appointment would have obtained him an Admiral's Flag; but, alas! human expectations end in the grave!'

From the *DNB* we can see that his first posting in the Royal Navy was as Master's Mate on HMS *Solebay*, Captain Lucius O'Bryen in 1768. Westcott would have been about 23 years of age then, and may well have been at sea for the previous ten years. For his having been rated Master's Mate certainly indicates that he was a most skilled seaman and navigator by the time that he joined the *Solebay*. He passed his lieutenant's examination in 1776 with a note added to his certificate stating that he was 'more than twenty-two years of age'. Laughton comments that he was certainly over thirty by that time. He served in several ships early in the American war and had his big break in November 1781 when he was posted as lieutenant on board HMS *Victory* which carried Admiral Richard Kempenfelt's flag and took part in his 'brilliant attack' on a French convoy on 12 December. Not long after this, Richard, Lord Howe flew his flag from *Victory* and carried out the relief of Gibraltar and the action off Cape Spartel in October 1782.

Westcott continued to gain good postings and finally his own command and was made post-captain in 1790. There followed a period ashore on half-pay, but then with the French war commencing in early 1793, he was appointed as flag-captain to Rear-Admiral Benjamin Caldwell on board HMS *Impregnable* of 98 guns and fought with Lord Howe at the Glorious First of June. Caldwell and Westcott were not to receive the King's gold medal for the action, although they were not marked out suffering from shyness, as some other ship's officers were. It just was that Lord Howe expected more from his big three-deckers. There is little doubt that this snub did not settle easily with George Westcott.

Afterwards, both Admiral Caldwell and Westcott moved to HMS *Majestic* of 74 guns. She was built by Adams & Barnard of Deptford as part of the Canada Class of 1759 by Bately. She was 170 feet in overall length and 1,632 tons burthen and launched in 1785. Her armament was 28 x 32 pounders on the Gun Deck, 28 x 18 pounders on the Upper Deck, 14 x 9 pounders on the Quarterdeck and 4 x 9 pounders in the Forecastle. Her ship's company would be around 550 men and officers. She was broken up in 1816. Caldwell cruised in the West Indies, but then returned to England in June 1796 and joined the Channel Fleet. They went through the Mutiny at Spithead in '97 without any apparent difficulty. Towards the end on 1797, *Majestic*, without Admiral Caldwell, joined Earl St Vincent at Gibraltar and then in May 1798 moved into the Mediterranean with Troubridge's squadron to reinforce Nelson.

John Glass was from Perth, Scotland. He was a twenty years old volunteer and immediately rated Able Seaman when he joined *Majestic* on 24 June 1793. He was at the Glorious First of June with Charles Cotton as captain. Cotton also didn't receive the King's gold medal even though *Majestic* lost three men killed and five wounded. Glass was present at the battle of the Nile and stayed with the ship until 28 November 1799 when he was moved to HMS *Renown*, 74 guns, again as Able Seaman. On 1 May 1800 he was appointed Quarter Gunner in which post he remained until 28 May 1805. He then moved to HMS *Thunderer*, 74 guns, as a Quarter Gunner, but missed Trafalgar due to his being Discharged as Unserviceable on 3 June 1805. Twelve years of being constantly employed by the Royal Navy had just worn this man out.

Robert Cuthbert (1755?-1821), was First Lieutenant on board the *Majestic*. He came from the Suffolk town of Chelsworth and his family were involved in processing malt for making beer, a profession that held some status in society. Cuthbert's first ship was HMS *Invincible* of 74 guns, Captain Hyde Parker, which he joined on 9 February 1777 and was rated Able Seaman. Being twenty-two years old, one would imagine that he had previous experience at sea. Hyde Parker certainly considered Robert Cuthbert skilled as a seaman because shortly after he was advanced to the quarterdeck as a Midshipman.

A year later Cuthbert moved to HMS *Minerva*, a 32-gun frigate, Captain John Stott. He was again rated as Midshipman, but the cruise was short lived as the *Minerva* was captured by the French frigate *Concorde* off Puerto Plata, Hispaniola in the West Indies on 22 August 1778. France had just entered the American Revolutionary War, and Captain Stott was caught unaware of the event which allowed *Concorde* to fire a couple of broadsides before the *Minerva* was fully at quarters. A lucky shot from the French ship blew up a cask of gunpowder below decks which dismounted three of *Minerva's* guns. Nevertheless, two and a half hours were needed before she finally surrendered. Both Captain Stott and his First Lieutenant were killed, the mizen mast had gone by the board, the wheel shot away and the ship totally unmanageable. *Minerva* lost 14 killed and 30 wounded.

Robert Cuthbert was exchanged for French prisoners in 1779, returned to England and then back to the West Indies to join Sir George Rodney's flagship, HMS *Sandwich*. He was on board for Rodney's two actions against Admiral de Guichen on 7 April and 19 May 1780. He then transferred to HMS *Montagu*, 3rd rate of 74 guns, as Fifth Lieutenant 'by order of Admiral Rodney', which strongly suggests that Rodney was quite impressed with him by granting this temporary promotion. *Montagu* was commanded by George Bowen and fought her against Admiral de Grasse at both the action off the Chesapeake on 5 September 1781 and later at Rodney's greatest victory at the battle of the Saintes, 12 April 1782.

From here, Acting Lieutenant Cuthbert was transferred in July 1782 to HMS *Lively*, a brig sloop of 12 guns commanded by Lieutenant Michael Stanhope. David Hepper tells us what happened on 9 December 1782: 'Cruising off the Florida coast in company with the *Jupiter*, 50 guns, the pair had taken several American prizes. The sloop was ordered to investigate the small islands around the Double Headed Shot Keys and Cay Sal for water. The brig had forty-four American prisoners on board from the prizes, and her complement had been reduced to only forty-eight by manning prizes. Having anchored off Cay Sal, the crew was reduced still further by sending the Gunner and ten men ashore to fill water casks. At two o'clock in the afternoon, when Lieutenant Stanhope and the Master went below for dinner, one of the American prisoners, called Whitmore, who had been allowed on deck to exercise, suddenly produced a cutlass and shouted, 'Now, now is the time!' This was the signal for the Americans below to charge up on to the upper deck, which they soon commanded, and opened an arms chest to hand out cutlasses and muskets.

'Stanhope found himself trapped in his cabin, and the only other officer, Lieutenant Walton, the Officer of the Watch, was in the fo'c'sle and soon taken prisoner. The Americans took the sloop to Havana where it was turned over to the Spanish. The court martial revealed the very lax routine on board the *Lively*. Little was done to prevent the prisoners conversing with the crew, at least one of whom was an American, who joined them. Stanhope also kept a woman on board, referred to as 'the Captain's girl', who was also an American.' Both Stanhope and Walton were dismissed the service. Robert Cuthbert was sent to New York as a prisoner of war for a second time. In October 1782, Cuthbert was released and gained passage to Antigua and thence back to England in early 1783. The war was over and Robert Cuthbert stayed ashore, but without a lieutenant's commission, as his previous appointments had been temporary.

With the war scare of Nootka Sound in 1790, Cuthbert again went to sea on board HMS *Juno*, Captain Samuel Hood. It was Hood who, in October 1793, sat on the board for Robert Cuthbert's examination for Lieutenant and passed him. Although Cuthbert had experienced a strong mix of both good and bad luck, there is no doubt that men like Rodney and Hood saw a man who would make a fine naval officer.

With the commencement of the French Revolutionary War in early 1793, he served on a couple of ships and then with his fresh lieutenant's commission was appointed to the 14-gun sloop, HMS *Thorn*, in which he served in the North Sea and West Indies. On 7 March 1796, he transferred to HMS *Majestic* when she was in the West Indies with George Westcott as captain. Both Westcott and Cuthbert were the sons of tradesmen, and made their mark by merit. Their ages were quite close with Westcott being forty-three and Cuthbert forty-one. Advancing Robert Cuthbert to First Lieutenant of *Majestic* looks a very natural progression amongst two men who had so much in common.

We are now at the point where three men, Captain George Westcott, First Lieutenant Robert Cuthbert and Able Seaman John Glass are all on board HMS *Majestic* of 74 guns. The sun was setting on 1 August 1798 as the ship followed the line of battle and prepared to engage the anchored French fleet. Brian Lavery describes the plight of the *Majestic* which, 'was the last ship of the main group to reach the action. Just before 7pm, less than half an hour after the *Goliath* had first opened fire, she sailed past the *Vanguard* in darkness and thick smoke. Possibly Captain Westcott had intended to anchor opposite *L'Orient* to give support to the *Bellerophon*, or perhaps opposite the 80-gun *Tonnant*, the next unengaged ship. But yet again there was trouble with the anchor cable and she ran on, and into the next ship, the 74-gun *Heureux*. Her bowsprit became entangled with the rigging of her opponent and she found herself in a dangerous position, with her main guns unable to bear and subject to musket fire [and raking broadsides], from the enemy. Captain Westcott was killed [by a musket ball through the throat], before the ship could extricate herself.'

Pause for a moment to reflect on what Robert Cuthbert was faced with. It was pitch dark with the only illumination being from the cannon flash of an enemy pouring double shotted broadsides into the bows of your ship. His friend and mentor, George Westcott, was dead along with others on the quarterdeck. Cuthbert put panic aside and focused on getting *Majestic* out of this awful predicament by swinging the ship so the bowsprit broke and Cuthbert was able to bring *Majestic's* starboard broadside to bear fully on the *Heureux* with devastating effect. Brian Lavery continues, 'She [*Majestic*], tried to slip astern of the *Heureux*, where she fell foul of the cable run out between that ship and the *Mercure*. Nevertheless she found herself a good position between two French ships, being held in place by an anchor out of one of her stern gunports. She was able to fire on the port bow of the *Mercure* and the stern of the *Heureux*, having revenge on her former tormentor and wounding Captain Etienne.'

On the second of October 1799, Robert Cuthbert wrote to Evan Nepean at the Admiralty, as part of Cuthbert's claim for the Naval Small Gold Medal for the Nile, to describe what happened on board *Majestic* on the nights of 1st and 2nd August 1798, 'Captain Westcott of the *Majestic* having fallen within a few minutes after the commencement of the action, the Ship was continued to be fought by me as First Lieutenant, without intermission until half past three on the morning of the 2nd with an interval of only 10 minutes, which was occasioned by the *La Orient*, blowing up at 10 O'Clock on the night of the first, after which time [3:30 am on the 2nd], I beg to observe that none other of His Majs. Ships were engaged (except the *Alexander* who very gallantly came down to our assistance), until five O'Clock in the morning of the second, when we again commenced our fire on the retreating Ships of the Enemy. That in shifting the Berth of the *Majestic*, which I was under the necessity of doing we let go an Anchor athwart hawse of *La Heureux* with her Jib Boom in our Mizen Rigging, where we lay for an hour or more constantly raking her, when they or we cut her Cable, and she was driven on shore, with the *La Mercure*, the ship immediately astern of her. I have also the honour to claim the merit of dismasting the *La Tonnant*, at half past one in the Morning of the 2nd., no other ship but the *Majestic* having been engaged with her during the Night, by which means she was perfectly secured from making her escape.'

In the end, Robert Cuthbert and the ship's company of *Majestic* accounted for two French 74s, the *Heureux* and *Mercure*, as both had cut their cables and gone ashore to escape *Majestic's* devastating broadsides, and played a large part is securing the capture of *Tonnant* of 80 guns. The men of the *Majestic* suffered terribly though. Their Captain and two other officers, 33 seamen and 14 Marines were killed; five officers, 126 seamen and 17 Marines were wounded which totalled 198 casualties or 36% of the ship's company which was the highest at the Nile. It is a miracle that Robert Cuthbert made it through the night unscathed although his subsequent career may indicate that he suffered greatly from an unrecorded physical or mental wound.

Oliver Warner notes, 'Speaking of the trials of the *Majestic*, [Captain Samuel] Hood referred in generous terms to her First Lieutenant, who was promoted immediately after the battle, 'Captain Westcott', he said, 'was killed by a musket ball early in the action, but the loss was not felt; his First Lieutenant, Cuthbert, who was in the *Montagu* in the West Indies, fought the *Majestic* most gallantly during the remainder of the action.'

Robert Cuthbert was immediately promoted by Nelson to the command of *Majestic* and after securing the prizes and a week's worth of repairs, *Majestic* joined Troubridge's squadron for the return to Gibraltar. Cuthbert stayed with *Majestic* until 21 March 1799 when he returned to England and remained ashore until January 1801 which makes me think that although he may not have received a physical wound from the action, perhaps he was hurt in some other way. During this period he received the gift of a crocodile hilted sword, as did Captain Hardy of the *Mutine* (neither officer received the King's Naval Small Gold Medal for the Nile), probably from the Duke of Clarence. This occasioned the painting of the fine portrait by John Berridge, R.A. That Robert Cuthbert isn't wearing a silver Davison Nile medal in his portrait is probably due to Davison having sent the medals to Nelson, who received them at Palermo in the middle of August 1799.

His next ship was the old *Montagu* which he had served on board as a Midshipman. Attached to the Channel Fleet, she was caught in the Bay of Biscay in a particularly bad storm during the middle of February 1801. By the 15th, *Montagu* had lost her main and mizen masts and the shroud bolts were being drawn by the strength of the wind and the rottenness of her bulwarks. Fortunately a frigate appeared on the scene and was able to tow *Montagu* to Lisbon. Not a happy result for Robert Cuthbert's first full command.

He was then without a ship from July to November 1801, but finally gained command of HMS *Orion* and returned to cruising in and around the Bay of Biscay, which continued until July 1802 when she returned to port and was paid off. Cuthbert was now 47 years old, and I think he had had enough of the sea. Finding a wife and raising a family became his priority. Elizabeth Willock of Bedford Square, London became his wife and the couple had three children who all survived. Robert and Elizabeth later lived in Great Bedford Street, Bath, where he died in 1821.

Provenance: Medal fair, 1984.

References: The National Archives, Kew: ADM 36/11790, 12317-12319 (*Majestic*). ADM 36/14812-14815, 15653-15656 (*Renown*). ADM 36/15676 & ADM 37/192 (*Thunderer*).
The Sailing Navy List by David Lyon, Conway, London, 1993.
Logs of the Great Sea Fights 1794-1805 by Sturges Jackson, Navy Records Society, London, 1899-1900.
Nelson and the Nile by Brian Lavery, Chatham, London, 1998.
Naval Swords and Dirks by Sim Comfort, Sim Comfort Associates, London, 2008.

DN 27 Charles Tippett, Ordinary Seaman, HMS Culloden, Captain Thomas Troubridge

Description: Jeweller gilt with the reverse field engraved *C. Tippett*. The medal is holed at 12 o'clock and has a two ring suspension with a blue ribbon attached. As *Culloden* returned to England in August 1800, it is probable that the gilding and engraving of this medal wasn't done on board ship, but by a Plymouth jeweller. There is a small die break running through C. H. K. with a larger break below at the rim. The weight of the medal and ribbon suspension is 42.4 grams. Extremely fine.

Background: HMS *Culloden* was based on the Ganges / Culloden Class of 1778 design by Hunt. She was built by Randall of Rotherhithe and launched in March 1782. Her overall length was 169 feet and she displaced 1,656 tons burthen. Armament consisted of 28 x 32 pounders on the Gun Deck, 28 x 18 pounders on the Upper Deck, 14 x 9 pounders on the Quarterdeck and 4 x 9 pounders at the Forecastle. Ship's company was between 550 and 600 officers and men. She was broken up in 1813.

From the *DNB* we learn that Captain Thomas Troubridge (1758? - 1807), was born in London and entered the Royal Navy on board the frigate HMS *Seahorse* on 8 October 1773 aged 18. Troubridge was actually only 15 years of age and was rated Able Seaman, which may have been nominal as he was clearly headed for the Quarterdeck. A few days after Troubridge joined the ship, Horatio Nelson also came on board and his age was noted as being 18. Nelson was rated as Midshipman.

Seahorse made a cruise to the East Indies and in March 1774, Troubridge was duly advanced to Midshipman. Both Troubridge and Nelson shared the Midshipman's berth on board *Seahorse* until March 1776 when Nelson started his trip back to England on board HMS *Dolphin*. He had almost certainly contracted malaria during his time spent ashore and was seriously ill. Troubridge had faired better and on 13 May 1780 moved to HMS *Superb*, the flagship of Sir Edward Hughes. On New Year's Day, 1781, Troubridge passed his lieutenant's examination and returned to the *Seahorse* where he was present at the battles off Sadras and Trincomalee in early 1782. On the 13th of April, he returned to the *Superb* as a junior lieutenant and took part in Hughes's third and fourth actions. Admiral Hughes evidently thought quite highly of Troubridge as he was given command of a sloop and then a frigate and ultimately to HMS *Sultan*, as flag-captain to Hughes's flagship, returning to England in this post with the Admiral in 1785.

Further from the *DNB*: 'In 1790 [Troubridge] went out again to the East Indies in the *Thames* frigate, and on his return to England was appointed to the *Castor* frigate of 32 guns, which in May 1794, had the ill luck to fall in with a division of the Brest fleet and to be captured. Troubridge, as a prisoner, was moved into the French 80-gun ship *Sanspareil*, and in her was bodily present at the battle of 1 June, [Lord Howe's victory]. The *Sanspareil* was captured, and Troubridge, on his return in her to England, was appointed to the 74 gun ship *Culloden* on 8 November.' As noted by Oliver Warner, *Culloden* was far from being a happy ship and with the very strict Troubridge as captain, the crew mutinied on 5 December. Their claim was that the ship wasn't fit for service and required urgent repairs, therefore they refused to put to sea. A hasty court martial was held and of the ten ringleaders, two were acquitted. Of the remaining eight charged, all were sentenced to death, with three later pardoned. Thus five men were hung on board *Culloden* on 13 January, 1795. She then set sail for the Mediterranean and was present at the unsatisfactory action off Hyeres on 13 July.

The Mediterranean Fleet now came under the command of John Jervis, later Earl St Vincent and with the leadership of 'Old Jarvie', the scene was set for Nelson and his brother officers to really excel. By the end of 1796, the British had been closed out of the Mediterranean and Spain had joined the French in the war against Britain. Admiral Jervis had recently been reinforced by Rear-Admiral Sir William Parker who provided intelligence that the Spanish may try to join the French so he positioned his fleet off Cape St Vincent, the most westerly point in Europe, and waited. On 14 February, the wait was over with the sighting of the Spanish fleet heading north. Jervis formed line of battle with the *Culloden* leading the British fleet southward toward the enemy. The two fleets were now passing each other on opposite tacks with *Culloden* having reversed course and heading for the van of the Spanish fleet. At this point, Commodore Nelson saw that if he waited his turn to change course, he would miss the enemy, so he wore directly into them from his current position.

Christopher Lloyd tells us the story from the point when it became essential for the British to tack into the enemy fleet. 'So intelligently did Troubridge anticipate Jervis's signal to tack in succession that before the flags fluttered out on board the flagship his own acknowledgement signal was ready to be broken at the top-gallant mast of the *Culloden*. 'Break the stop - down the helm!', he shouted, and the ship swung round on the opposite tack. Accustomed as he was to the highest standards of seamanship, Jervis could not restrain his delight with Troubridge's virtuosity. 'Look', he cried to the Master of *Victory*, 'Look at Troubridge there! He tacks his ship in battle as if the eyes of England were upon him; and would to God they were, for they would see him to be, what I know him to be, and, by Heaven, sir, as the Dons will soon feel him to be!'

Jervis continued to pace the Quarterdeck of his flagship, HMS *Victory*, as the ships before him continued to tack in succession and the Spanish shot grew warmer by the minute. Suddenly, 'a shot took off the head of a marine standing beside Jervis covering the admiral from head to foot with the man's blood and brains. Fearing that the admiral was wounded, the captain of marines ran up. 'I am not at all hurt', replied Jervis, wiping the blood off his face, 'but do, George, try if you can get me an orange.' A midshipman ran up with one from the cockpit and Jervis rinsed his mouth with it.'

We now move to the point where Nelson tacked on his own to cut off the Spanish van. Christopher Lloyd again takes up the narrative: 'It was thus that a comparatively obscure commodore sailed into history. The ships which the *Captain* [Nelson's 74 gun ship], now engaged were the *Santissima Trinidada* of 136 guns, the biggest ship at that time afloat, closely supported by the *San Josef* of 112 guns, the *Salvador del Mundo* of 112 guns and the *San Nicolas* of 80. Fortunately, the *Culloden* was nearly up with the latter, having fought her way through the ships astern, and Collingwood's *Excellent* [74 guns], the rearmost ship in the British line, was prompt to follow his friend's example in wearing out of the line. Within a few moments of the preposterous spectacle of a two-decker engaging a four-decker, there were three ships in support of her - *Culloden, Excellent, Blenheim* - and the rest of Rear-Admiral Parker's ships were not far away. For the next hour the battle was a melee. According to Parker, 'we sometimes had the fire of two or three ships together; yet from their disordered state, our fire had great effect upon them, for it could not be lost; they were generally so huddled together in a very irregular manner, and I have no doubt but that they did each other a great deal of injury.'

The *Culloden* suffered ten killed and 47 wounded with the whole of the British fleet having around three hundred causalities which was quite a small price to pay for the capture of four large Spanish ships and having access to the Mediterranean once again. Two of prizes were captured by Nelson and his men who first boarded the *San Nicolas* and then from the *San Nicolas* to the *San Josef*, making him an instant naval hero. (Please see DN 10, Captain Edward Berry for more detail.)

In July 1797, it was decided to make an attempt to capture the Spanish port of Santa Cruz in Tenerife which rapidly deteriorated into a near disaster. Troubridge was in charge of the landing party of around 1,100 seamen and troops which, over two attempts to secure the town, were sharply rebuffed by the Spanish, and it was through the quick thinking of Hood that they all didn't end up as Spanish prisoners of war. It was also at Santa Cruz that Nelson took a musket ball in the elbow, which cost him his right arm. (Please see DN 5, Sir Samuel Hood, for more information.)

April and May 1798 were wild with rumours of Napoleon about to embark on a Mediterranean adventure, the destination unknown. Troubridge had been commanding the small inshore squadron that St Vincent used to keep an eye on the Spanish at Cadiz. There was high regard between Troubridge and St Vincent and it is because of this that Troubridge was chosen to take his squadron to support Nelson who was keeping an eye on the French based at Toulon. In fact it was the intent of both St Vincent and Nelson to have Troubridge as second-in-command to Nelson, however, due to the more senior and somewhat aloof Sir James Saumarez being captain of the *Orion* and part of Nelson's squadron, the privilege fell to him.

Brian Lavery has more to say regarding Thomas Troubridge, 'If St Vincent was forthright, Troubridge was more so. When the two men took office at the Board of Admiralty in 1800 they began a programme of dockyard reform. When St Vincent commented, 'The artificers are all thieves', Troubridge went further and said, 'All the master shipwrights should be hanged, every one of them, without exception.' As a captain his views were equally derisive. When asked how to spot a potential mutineer, he replied, 'Whenever I see a fellow look as if he was thinking, I say that's mutiny.' Troubridge was a highly effective leader, seaman and fighter. St Vincent considered him to be 'the greatest man in that walk that the English Navy has ever produced.' When Nelson sent Troubridge to Naples to meet Sir William Hamilton, he included a note of introduction which said, 'Captain Troubridge is in full possession of my confidence....my honoured acquaintance of 25 years, and the very best sea officer in His Majesty's Service.' The regard was fully reciprocated by Troubridge at the time.'

On 24 May St Vincent sent Troubridge in the *Culloden* into the Mediterranean. As luck would have it and with a favouring wind, the French escaped from Toulon on the 19th. The next day a fierce wind

Sir Thomas Troubridge

caught Nelson's small group of ships and greatly damaged his flagship, the *Vanguard*, which resulted in delay in assembling the combined squadrons and starting the search for Napoleon's fleet which had been sped south by the same wind.

June and July were spent scouring the Mediterranean until the intelligence was learned that Napoleon had landed in Egypt. On the 28th of July, Nelson's fleet arrived at the Gulf of Coron [Koroni], on the southwest corner of the Greek mainland. Troubridge and the *Culloden* were sent into the bay to consult with the Turkish governor who related that the French were in Egypt. Troubridge also took the opportunity of having his men board a French brig and bring her out under tow. The news electrified the British fleet and they immediately turn south.

As the British came into sight of the anchored French fleet in the late afternoon of the 1st of August, the *Majestic* and *Leander* were bringing up the rear of the main body of ships with the *Leander* well behind the *Majestic*. The *Culloden* was seven miles to the north-east of Aboukir Bay and the *Alexander* and *Swiftsure* were two or three miles to the west of Aboukir Bay, having looked into Alexandria harbour. The wind favoured *Culloden* and as she approached, Nelson ordered that she cast off her prize.

From the log of *Culloden's* Master, John Rose, we have, 'Beat to quarters and cleared ship for action, cast off the tow. Observed the enemy's fleet to an anchor in Aboukir Roads about 5 leagues east of Alexandria.

Made all possible sail. ...At 5, moderate breezes and cloudy. 1/2 past 6 bore up, *Goliath* leading ahead. 3/4 past 6, the 1st, 2nd, 3rd of the enemy's line began to engage. Up mainsail, staysail, and spanker, hauled up to clear the *Leander*. 40 minutes past 6, struck on a rock and made the signal No. 43 tabular. [Striking and sticking on a shoal, with guns firing until observed]. *Swiftsure* and *Alexander* astern of us hauled their wind to clear the reef. The island of Aboukir WSW 1/4W, distance 2 miles and 3/4. The enemy on the island threw several shell at us, but none reached. Found the most water a cable's length astern and on the starboard quarter. Put the stream anchor and cable into the launch and carried it out one cable's length from the ship and dropped in eleven fathoms water. Sent the launch to the *Mutine*, who anchored 3 cables length to the ship. Took the end in at the ward-room window. Hove taut on both cables and began to start [throw overboard], water in the fore and main holds, and threw the empty casks of the upper and middle tier overboard. Found the ship struck very heavy abaft and eased a little forward. Started the wine in the coal hold and threw a quantity of bread and provisions of different sorts and empty wine pipes overboard as per certificates, and also a great quantity of shot. Also boats carrying shot, bread, &c, on board the *Mutine* brig. The swell increasing and the ship striking very heavy, which knocked her rudder off, which sunk immediately, and from the violent sending of the ship it carried away the pintles [and braces; the hardware that secures the rudder to the ship's stern-post], and everything that was fast to it. Found the ship made 3 feet water per hour.

'August 2nd, A.M. - People employed throwing shot and provisions of all sorts overboard and sending some on board the *Mutine*. Found the ship make more water. Sent all hands to the pumps. Found the leak increasing. At this time, 5 feet water per hour. At 1/2 past 2, found the ship's head swinging to the westward and the NE. Parted the stream cable close to the end and lost both anchor and cable. Veered away on the brig's cables, her head being NE by E. At 3, the ship struck 3 or 4 times very hard. Swung off the rock into 5 fathoms water, making at this time 7 feet water per hour. Veered away and slipped the brig's cable, which she took on board. 1/4 past 3, came to with the small bower in 10 fathoms water, fine sand. The ship leaking so much that all hands were continually employed at the pumps. Came on board the brig's people to spell [give a break to], ours to get breakfast. Sailmakers employed thrumming the fore, topgallant sail to put under the bottom. Carpenters employed making a rudder out of a spare topmast, &c. &c.

'All hands employed at the pumps. Observed 6 of the enemy's ships had struck and one to leeward totally dismasted. Observed the *Bellerophon* to an anchor east 8 or 9 miles totally dismasted, also the *Majestic* with only her fore mast standing; *Alexander*, *Defence*, and *Swiftsure* very much disabled in the rigging and hulls, but *Alexander*, *Majestic* and *Goliath* in action. One of the enemy's frigates was dismasted and sunk in the action. One of the enemy's frigates showed her colours, hoisted an English jack, fired a broadside at the *Orion*, set fire to her and left her. At noon, the frigate blew up. Carpenters employed making the rudder, &c. Sailmakers about the sail for her bottom. People employed picking oakum. People continually at the pumps.'

From Smyth, 'Thrum, any course woollen or hempen yarn. It is used for making mops and mats. A vessel, when leaky, is thrummed by working some heavy spare sail, as the spiritsail, into a thrummed mat, greasing and tarring it well, passing it under the bottom, and heaving all parts tight. The pressure forces the tarred oakum into the openings, and thus, in part, arrests the ingress of water.'

What an awful situation to be in and one can easily imagine that for Thomas Troubridge, on the verge of again striking the enemy with everything that he and the *Culloden's* ship's company could throw at them, he and his ship were stuck on a reef unable to assist his brother captains in what would prove to be probably the most decisive victory the Royal Navy was to ever achieve. And for John Rose, the Master of *Culloden*, who was responsible for placing the ship in her station for battle, the result would be truly mortifying; however, from his journal, he just continued to assist in what could be done to save the ship. It does appear that the fault really rests with Troubridge though. He wanted to pass inside the French line as opposed to following the other ships and attacking from the seaward side. Inadequate charts and taking a bet that safe water was available all ended in near disaster. The only good news was that both *Alexander* and *Swiftsure* were able to steer clear of *Culloden* and adjust course to attack the French on the seaward side.

There was a potential slight to Troubridge that Nelson felt most deeply. The King, it was feared, would not award Troubridge the Naval Small Gold Medal for the Nile because Troubridge hadn't actually fought the enemy. Nelson wrote on Troubridge's behalf and the medal was awarded, however both Hardy of the *Mutine* and Cuthbert of the *Majestic* didn't receive the medal, although both had certainly earned it, particularly Cuthbert of the *Majestic*.

While most of the damaged British ships and their prizes made repairs and then sailed for Gibraltar under the command of Saumarez, the *Culloden*, along with Nelson's *Vanguard* and a few other ships headed for Naples, only to arrive on 22 September after a long tedious voyage during which the *Culloden* required constant tending to.

From the *DNB* we have the subsequent events, 'At Naples and off Malta, Troubridge's services were closely mixed up with those of Nelson. In the end of 1798 he was sent to command a small squadron off the coast of Egypt, but rejoined Nelson in March 1799, when he was again detached to take possession of Ischia, Procida, and Capri, and maintain the blockade in the Bay of Naples. In June he was landed at Naples for the siege of St. Elmo, which he reduced, as he afterwards did Capua, and Gaeta, and Civita Vecchia, securing the evacuation of the Roman territory by the French.'

For these services, Troubridge was awarded by the King of Naples, the Order of St Ferdinand and created a baronet. He then took over command of the blockade of Malta until May, 1800 when the *Culloden* was ordered to return to England. Following the Peace of Amiens and promotion to Rear-Admiral, Troubridge was ordered to the East Indies in the worn out HMS *Blenheim* of 74 guns. Once at Madras, he shared an uncomfortable command of the station with Pellew. Finally, in January 1807, Troubridge, still in the *Blenheim*, was given command of the Cape of Good Hope and set sail with an old Dutch prize, the *Java*, and the brig *Harrier*. On 1 February, the little squadron was caught in a cyclone off Madagascar. When the storm finally abated, it was clear that only the *Harrier* survived and that Sir Thomas Troubridge was no more.

Sir Thomas Troubridge

This just leaves the story of Charles Tippett, whose medal this is. He joined the *Culloden* as a young lad of 14 as Captain's Servant to Captain Thomas Rich, Bt, on 26 December 1792. He was noted in the muster book as born at Plymouth Dock, as were two other boys who joined at the same time. In April 1793, Captain Isaac Schomberg took command and retained the servants of Captain Rich. *Culloden* formed part of Earl Howe's Channel Fleet and took part in the Glorious First of June, 1794 although Schomberg didn't display the effort to engage the enemy that Earl Howe expected and he didn't receive the King's Naval Gold Medal for the action. Oliver Warner notes that Schomberg was certainly not a lucky captain and that *Culloden* was far from a happy ship.

With Troubridge in command of *Culloden* from 8 November and the mutiny and subsequent execution on men on board the ship, one wonders what effect this had on young Tippett. He had earlier, on 10 July, experienced another set back wherein his rating as Captain's Servant was changed to Boy 3rd Class, which effectively removed any hope of his reaching the quarterdeck. In June, 1797, Tippett was rated as Boy 2nd Class, but then on 1 July 1798, his position as part of the lower deck was confirmed with his being rated Ordinary Seaman. He was now twenty years old and no doubt played his part during the Battle of the Nile and the subsequent activities of the ship's company under Troubridge's command.

Culloden returned to Plymouth in early August 1800 when her men were, in the main, transferred to HMS *Princess Royal* on 15 August, Captain Thomas Macnamarra Russell who was superseded by Captain David Atkins on 1 January 1801. This was a rather uneventful period with *Princess Royal* cruising in the Channel. She was paid off at Portsmouth on 17 April 1802 with the Peace of Amiens coming into force.

We lose sight of Charles Tippett for a while. He probably signed on as a merchant seaman and gained more experience. We do know that by 26 May 1808 he had been 'prest' and entered onto the books of HMS *Growler*, Lt. and Commander Richard Crossman who was replaced by Lt. and Commander John Weeks on 16 November 1809. *Growler* was an Archer Class of 1800 gunboat which was typically armed with twelve 32 or 18 pounder carronades. Her ship's company would have been only fifty men. *Growler* was built at Buckler's Hard and 80 feet in overall length. She displaced 177 tons burthen.

So a small ship with a ship's company that could really work as a specialised team, that could take her into any enemy creek and cut out all manner of merchant and small naval vessels. When Charles Tippett came on board, he was rated Ordinary Seaman, probably based on his last post in the Royal Navy. This was quickly corrected with his advancement to Able Seaman on 1 July 1808. On 1 August 1810 he was further advanced to Captain of the Forecastle, which meant that he played a leading role amongst the lower deck.

From the ship's logbooks, one can see that *Growler* was constantly employed along the coasts of France, Spain and Portugal. She played an important role at the action of Basque Roads on 12 April 1809, where in company with a swarm of other shallow draft ships, she attacked the three-decker *Ocean* and other French ships for nearly five hours until the falling tide required them to break off the fight.

On June 16 1811, from the Master's log it appears that *Growler* was cruising off San Sebastian in north-west Spain. She sent the cutter, 'manned and armed' in shore, but it didn't return. Not until the 27th of June was information received from a local fishing boat that the cutter 'with the officers and men were captured off Gataria.' Gataria Castle appears to be located nine miles west of San Sebastian.

We again lose sight of Charles Tippett as he remained in a French prisoner of war camp until an Admiralty record notes 'Men returned from French prison', which includes Charles Tippett. He was then paid off at Portsmouth on 11 January 1815. It appears that Charles married Joanna Bynon of Stoke Damerel, Devon on 14 March 1804. From the 1841 census, there is noted Joanna living in Clowance Lane, Stoke Damerel, a charwoman aged 55, with probably a son, John, aged 20 and in the Royal Navy. Also, noted is a daughter aged 35 who is a fishwoman. On 20 August 1845, Charles Tippett (or Tipper as both names are now used at Greenwich), was entered into Greenwich Hospital as a widower aged 59 and that he had served 15 years and 9 months in the Royal Navy. He was given number 8822 and remained at Greenwich until his death on 20 April 1858 aged 71. He was buried in the grounds of the Hospital on 23 April, possibly in the East Greenwich Pleasance.

It appears that Charles Tippett didn't make application for the Naval General Service Medal in 1847. He certainly qualified for the clasps St. Vincent, 1st of June, 1794, Nile and Basque Roads. One wonders if he felt that his Davison Nile medal was what really counted and that this latter day award just wasn't worth the bother! Or was there some other reason, because looking at the Douglas-Morris NGS Medal Roll, there was no clasp awarded to any man on board *Growler*, although she was certainly at Basque Roads and earned the clasp.

Provenance: Dix Noonan and Webb, Lot 265, 28 March 2002.

References: The National Archives, Kew: ADM 35/362 - 363, ADM 36/12166 - 12175, 13690 - 13692 (*Culloden*); ADM 35/1231, ADM 36/13805 - 13807 (*Princess Royal*); ADM 35/2826, 3483, ADM 37/340, ADM 36/994, ADM 37/2319 - 2320, 2908 (*Growler*); Greenwich Hospital Records: TNA, ADM 73/30 (Admission to GH), ADM 73/46 (General Register of Pensioners and their families), TNA, ADM 73/48 (Alphabetical List of General Register notes Tippett DD), TNA, ADM 73/460 (Register of Burials at Greenwich).
IGI for marriage / birth details, data not always reliable.
A contemporary manuscript signal book that is believed to have been used at both Cape St Vincent and the Nile used to decode the Tabular messages. Sim Comfort Collection.
The Sailing Navy List by David Lyon, Conway, London, 1993.
Logs of the Great Sea Fights 1794-1805 by Sturges Jackson, Navy Records Society, London, 1899-1900.
The Glorious First of June by Oliver Warner, Batsford, London, 1961.
Nelson and the Nile by Brian Lavery, Chatham, London, 1998.
Dictionary of National Biography, Oxford University Press, 1975.
The Sailor's Word-Book, by Admiral W. H. Smyth, Blackie, London, 1867.
St Vincent and Camperdown by Christopher Lloyd, Batsford, London, 1963.
The Pursuit of Victory, by Roger Knight, Penguin, London, 2005.
The Naval General Service Medal Roll by Captain K. Douglas Morris, privately printed, London, 1982.
Forget Me Not by Sim Comfort, Sim Comfort Associates, London, 2004.

DN 28 Captain Thomas Masterman Hardy, HMS Mutine and Nelson's gold Davison Nile medal

Description: Lot 12, Christie's, *Trafalgar Bicentenary* Auction, 19 October 2005: Gold medal cased in copper [actually gold] and glazed with ring suspension, fitted in a red morocco case. The edge of the case is engraved: A TRIBUTE OF REGARD FROM ALEXR. DAVISON, ST. JAMES'S SQUARE TO CAPT. HARDY MUTINE. No weight given, Extremely fine. Made £65,000 hammer, circa £80,000 all in.

Lot 8, Sotheby's, *Alexander Davison Collection* auction, 21 October 2002: Gold medal set in a glazed gold mount with the mount engraved 'A TRIBUTE OF REGARD FROM ALEXr DAVISON ESQr St JAMES'S SQUARE'. Weight 100.84 grams, Extremely fine. Made £22,000 hammer, circa £28,000 all in.

The Hardy example sold by Christie's is described as fitted with a 'copper band' and no weight is given in the catalogue description. The copper band is almost certainly a mistake for low grade gold.

Background: The bicentennial of Trafalgar, 2005, brought forward major collections relating to Lord Nelson for auction by the main London houses. It was really incredible to see so much important material come onto the market in one year, and it all sold and sold very well indeed!

Amongst the vendors was the descendant of Captain Thomas Masterman Hardy via his youngest daughter, Mary Charlotte, and hence to the family MacGregor of MacGregor, who exhibited Hardy's relics at the great Chelsea naval exhibition of 1891. As a note, in the Chelsea exhibition catalogue, there are listed two gold Davison Nile medals as belonging to Hardy, but as there are also listed two Trafalgar Naval Small Gold medals presented to Hardy, one may conclude that the duplicates are catalogue errors. Both the Davison Nile and Trafalgar Naval Small Gold medals were offered at Christie's auction on 19 October 2005.

When it came to the distribution by the King of the Naval Small Gold Medal for Nelson's victory of the Nile, every surviving captain of a ship of the line that was engaged on the 1st of August 1798 would be a recipient. This meant that the family of Captain Westcott, who died on board *Majestic*, would receive no medal to mark his sacrifice. Robert Cuthbert, who took command upon the death of his captain, also received no medal because he was a lieutenant and not a captain. Captain Hardy didn't receive the medal because the *Mutine* wasn't a ship of the line, and Troubridge of the *Culloden* wasn't to receive the medal because his ship was aground and not able to engage the enemy. Nelson protested this last decision and eventually won the medal for Troubridge. This neglect of recognition to both Hardy and Robert Cuthbert by the King, appears to have been addressed by the presentation of a fine crocodile hilted sword by his son, the Duke of Clarence, to Hardy and Cuthbert. Hardy's Nile sword is currently on display at the Keep Museum, Dorchester, Dorset and the Cuthbert sword is with an English collector. Please see *Lord Nelson's Swords* by this author for more information.

8 obverse   8 reverse

From Martyn Downer's *Nelson's Purse* we have the following:

'The first of neat oak packing cases [containing Nile medals] from Birmingham arrived towards the end of March 1799. In a state of high excitement, Davison called for his carriage to drive the short distance to the Queen's House (now Buckingham Palace). In his pocket were one gold and one silver medal. The medals were received 'with much Joy & Pleaseur'. 'I was alone with the King a full hour,' he breathlessly recalled in his next letter to Nelson, 'when much of the conversation was about you. It is impossible to express how warmly he spoke of you and asked me a thousand questions about you.' He returned the next month to present one of his prints of Nelson to the king, who 'speaks of you with the tenderness of a father'. And, like a concerned father, the king quizzed Davison on the hero's whereabouts. 'I said a great deal (but not

279

too much) regarding my idea of your situation,' Davison reported archly. The next gold medal was given to Earl St Vincent, who had returned early from the Mediterranean suffering from ill-health. Two years later the earl reciprocated Davison's gift with a gold medal of his own, struck by him as a 'testimony of approbation' to his brother officers. Below the motto 'Loyal and True' a seaman and marine make what could be a Masonic handshake. Davison sent another medal which was almost certainly not gold but bronze gilt by express to [Nelson's wife in] Bath. (ref: Christie's South Kensington, lot 1 of 2 July 2012 auction with bronze gilt, silver and bronze medals, provenanced to descendent of Josiah Nisbet.) Fanny thought it 'elegant' and 'an heirloom to my son'. She sent it out to Josiah at Naples with a letter for her husband, asking her son to deliver it to his stepfather in person, 'fearing it might fall into other hands'. 'I never had a secret from him,' she wrote desolately.

'Davison was hoping to present Nelson with his medal in person. So he was 'truly mortified' to learn, on 6 April, that Nelson was marooned at Palermo, having committed himself to the restoring Ferdinand to his throne. An alternative plan was hurriedly put into action. A box of the medals, '15 inches long, 11 inches wide and 1 ½ inches Deep', was despatched to Portsmouth after a tip-off from Evan Nepean that the *Queen Charlotte* was about to sail for the Mediterranean. Admiral Sir Peter Parker, the shore-based commander-in-chief at Portsmouth and an old friend of Nelson's from the West Indies, ensured that the medals safely reached the ship before she sailed. In return for this help (and, no doubt, because he was the Deputy Master of the Freemasons in England), Sir Peter received a silver medal.

'The box held twenty-two medals. Eleven of them were gold: two for Nelson and nine for the Egyptian Club captains remaining in the Mediterranean. John Campbell, Nelson's former secretary in *Vanguard* and a partner in the prize business, was recruited to distribute the gold medals from Gibraltar, The other eleven medals were in silver, including one for Campbell himself and ten for Nelson, 'to be given to whom you please.' Each of the medals was cased in its own red morocco box and arrived with a short printed testimonial from Davison.'

As a note, it would appear that Campbell kept the medals to be handed out to ships at Gibraltar or cruising nearby. It looks like Nelson received two medals for himself, a medal for Berry who was with him on board *Foudroyant* and the medal that would have gone to Miller, who was blown up on board his ship on 14 May 1799. This author thinks that other medals for Nile ships were also sent to Nelson.

From the letter recorded by Nicolas to Alexander Davison from Nelson:

'My dear friend,   Palermo, August 15, 1799

Yesterday brought me your letters of the beginning of April, together with your elegant Medals, which cannot fail to be as highly grateful to all the brethren of the Nile, as they are to your old friend. The spare gold Medal which you was so good as to send me, I presented to the man that all Europe is obliged to for his encouragement of the Arts, as well as many other acts of public benefit. You will know this person can only be Sir William Hamilton. I have also sent all the boxes as directed. In your postscript I see you intend gold Medals for all the Captains. I have presented the other gold one to Captain Hardy in your name, as I am confident it was not your intention to exclude Captain Hardy, who dear friend, it hurt me to part with your kind and invaluable present, but I considered you before myself. A silver or even a copper one I shall esteem as equally valuable. Etc., etc.

P.S. August 24th. - Poor dear Miller is dead, so will be your Nelson, but I trust till death that your friend longs to wear your present: therefore I have kept Miller's and hope you send another to his family. If that cannot be, they shall have this which I have unjustly kept. Adieu, probably for ever!

Nelson.'

I think that Davison would have immediately complied with Nelson's request and sent to Miller's widow one of his spare gold medals.

The key piece of information from the above is 'I have also sent all the boxes as directed', which has to mean that Nelson received a number of boxes intended for various Nile ships and that one box was intended and labelled for himself. In that box were the two gold medals, one he gave to Sir William Hamilton and the other to Captain Hardy. Then after making his generous gift to Hardy, Nelson realised that he really did want a gold medal and used the medal from the *Theseus* box which was intended for Ralph Miller.

One should keep in mind that the Davison Nile medals weren't named, so the only indication as to which gold medal belonged to whom, would have been the labelled box that contained the medals. It is possible that because Davison didn't include a gold medal for Hardy of the *Mutine*, or indeed any medals for the ship's company of the *Mutine*, that he also didn't include a gold medal for the deceased Captain Westcott of the *Majestic*, as his memory wasn't recognised by the King with the gift to his widow of a Naval Small Gold Medal. It also appears the Lieutenant Cuthbert of the *Majestic* didn't receive a Davison gold medal.

Captain T. M. Hardy by Abbott, image courtesy of the Britannia Royal Naval College.

It seems that the medals that belonged to Thomas Troubridge were lost with him when the *Blenheim* went down. Nelson was only able to convince the Admiralty / King that Troubridge deserved the Naval Small Gold Medal for the Nile in 1799, so did Davison have a medal for him? There is a named Davison Nile to a man on board the *Culloden* which is a strong indication that Davison had medals struck for the ship and so this author feels pretty sure that Troubridge did receive a Davison gold medal.

As mentioned, this author doesn't think that there were any Davison Nile medals distributed amongst the ship's company of the *Mutine*, or if there were, he hasn't encountered a named example to a man on board the ship. The surviving men of the *Mutine* were finally recognised by Queen Victoria when in 1848 the Naval General Service Medal with Nile clasp was distributed, but by that date there were only one officer and five men still living who made an application for the medal.

From the *DNB* biography of Captain George Westcott, who died on board *Majestic* and who appears to have received neither the Naval Small Gold or gold Davison Nile medals, there is the following note: 'In January 1801, while passing through Honiton, Nelson invited them [Westcott's wife and daughter], to breakfast, and presented Westcott's widow with his own Nile medal, saying, 'You will not value it less because Nelson has worn it'. On 17 January 1801 he wrote to Lady Hamilton: 'At Honiton I visited Captain Westcott's mother—poor thing, except from the bounty of government and Lloyd's, in very low circumstances. The brother is a tailor, but had they been chimney-sweepers it was my duty to show them respect.' It appears that Nelson gave away his gold Davison Nile medal twice, however I rather think that he gave Westcott's widow a copper gilt example. Another copper gilt Davison medal was used to adorn the effigy of Nelson at Westminster Abbey and that medal is presumed to have come from Lady Hamilton.

The Sotheby's catalogue for the sale of the Alexander Davison Collection on 21 October 2002, notes that lot 3 is a gold example of the medal, which weighs 79.64 grams. The catalogue further states that 25 gold examples were ordered by Davison from Boulton and that they should be supplied 'in red morocco cases'. Also in this sale is lot 8 which is another gold Davison Nile, but this example is cased and glazed and with a ring suspension very similar to the example that Nelson gave to Hardy. In the auction lot 3 made £24,000 and lot 8 made £22,000 hammer.

If one considers the ring suspension of both the Hardy medal sold at Christie's, and the cased and glazed lot 8 from the Sotheby's Davison Collection sale, there is a distinct similarity. My view is that both medals were cased and glazed by the same jeweller in Palermo. The design of the ring used for suspension is unlike any ring suspension that I have seen on any English cased medals and has a certain Italian flare about it.

That similarity of casing between these two medals really is a compelling reason to consider the cased and glazed lot 8 from the Davison Collection as being the original Ralph Miller medal that Nelson decided to make use of. How it came back into Davison's possession, we don't know, but we do know that he was very involved with assisting Lady Hamilton following the chaos created for her by the death of her 'dear Nelson'. One can easily imagine that Davison would like to have had the medal back and very likely managed to secure it.

Having said that, there are other opinions as to where Nelson's Davison Nile gold medal might be. From Rina Prentice we have:

'The question of the fate of Nelson's own Davison Nile medal is particularly complex. In September 1901, the Connoisseur reported that 'the gold medal given to Horatio Lord Nelson by Alexander Davison, etc... fetched £180 at Messrs Debenham's. This medal was formerly in Viscount Bridport's collection of Nelson relics.' Rina then charts the sale of several other gold Davison Nile medals which may or may not have been Nelson's, but most importantly notes that some of these medals may have been bronze gilt and not gold. Rina concludes by saying, 'It is now impossible to be sure which was Nelson's personal one.'

Martyn Downer has created a list of recipients of the Davison Nile in gold. 25 medals were struck and Martyn had identified 20 of them: King George III, Earl St Vincent, Sir William Hamilton, Emperor of Russia, Emperor of Germany, Grand Signior Selim III, and the King of Naples. Captains Hardy, Troubridge, Darby, Louis, Peyton, Ball, Hood, Gould, Foley and Hallowell. Captain Miller's medal to Nelson and a spare medal from Davison to Miller's widow. To Captain Westcott's widow, a bronze gilt medal and not a gold. Davison's own medal lot 3 from Sotheby's 21 Oct. 2002.

Martyn further notes that the Küchler dies for the Nile medal were given to Davison who had them destroyed, so there were no restrikes of the issued medal.

When one also considers that the effigy of Nelson in Westminster Abbey, which includes a bronze gilt Davison Nile probably presented by Lady Hamilton, and the gift of the bronze gilt example to Colonel William Stewart at Copenhagen (DN 33), and lastly how much Nelson enjoyed the medal, then there will continue to be multiple claims put forward as being 'Nelson's personal Davison Nile medal.' He certainly cherished the medal and used it regularly to present as a token of respect for the rest of his life. This author feels fairly certain that the Davison Nile that Nelson wore suspended from a ribbon around his neck, that this medal would most likely have been a bronze gilt example. My reasoning is first, the gold medal was both heavy and valuable and could well become detached when one reckons the movements of a ship or a carriage. Secondly, the bronze gilt medal would serve the same function as the embroidered orders sewn to Nelson's uniform coat. One would keep the gold medals and jewelled orders in a safe place and wear the replicas.

One thing, however, is certain and that is this gold example which belonged to Hardy was given to him by Nelson and for that reason has to make it the most interesting of the surviving gold examples, if not the most interesting of all Davison Nile medals.

HMS *Mutine* was a brig sloop of 18 guns cut out at Teneriffe by the boats of HMS *Lively* on 12 June 1797. She was French built in 1794 and measured 108 feet in overall length and appears to have been about 350 tons burthen. She carried 18 x 6 pounders and her ship's company was 121 officers and men. She was sold from the service in 1807.

There is no surviving log for the *Mutine* at the Nile, however one can see that upon the *Culloden* going aground, Captain Hardy immediately placed *Mutine* near *Culloden* in an effort to haul her off the reef and also to transfer stores from *Culloden* to lighten the ship.

For a biographical sketch of Vice-Admiral Sir Thomas Masterman Hardy, GCB (1769-1839), I find that provided in the Christie's catalogue of 19 October 2005, particularly fine and present an abridged version here:

'In addition to participating in the battle of Cape St Vincent, the action at which Nelson's tactical brilliance was first recognised, Thomas Hardy was the only officer of rank in the entire fleet to have fought at all three of Nelson's great victories at the Nile, Copenhagen and Trafalgar.

'Sir Thomas was the second son of Joseph Hardy of Dorset and his wife Nanny, daughter of Thomas Masterman, of Kingston, Dorset. He was born at Martin's Town near Dorchester on 5 April 1769. At the age of twelve he entered the navy on the brig *Helena*, and with intervals to attend school was noted on the books of two guardships. He entered the merchant service and was afterwards appointed to various ships until he was promoted lieutenant of the frigate *Meleager* under Captain Charles Tyler, serving in the Mediterranean as part of a squadron under Nelson's command. Although no meeting is specifically recorded, it is generally believed that it was during this period (July 1795 - August 1796) that Nelson and Hardy first became acquainted. Transferring into the frigate *Minerve* in August 1796, Hardy was still in her when Nelson, by now promoted Commodore, hoisted his flag in her that December. Nelson acquired a healthy respect for Hardy's dependability and sound judgement, and the ship's company witnessed a remarkable demonstration of his respect for Hardy on 10 February 1797. The *Minerve* was passing through the Straits of Gibraltar pursued by several Spanish warships. A seaman fell overboard and Hardy immediately launched the jolly-boat to effect a rescue. Once over the frigate's side, the boat was carried by the current towards the leading enemy ship and was in danger of being taken. Nelson, on the quarterdeck, saw the danger at once and famously bellowed, 'By God, I'll not lose Hardy! Back the mizzentopsail!' This bold and unexpected action caused the Spaniards to hesitate and shorten sail, thereby allowing Hardy's boat to return safely. It had been a risky manoeuvre and one which typified Nelson's daring.

'Hardy's conduct at St Vincent brought him promotion and he commanded the brig *Mutine* at the Nile which took the first dispatches announcing the victory. The esteem in which he was held by Nelson would again be shown by Nelson's presentation of his own [Davison gold] Nile medal to Hardy at Palermo in 1799. Nelson transferred Hardy into the *Vanguard* as flag-captain in August 1798 [following the departure of Captain Berry to England with duplicate dispatches], and the two men were rarely separated in the ensuing years. On the expedition to the Baltic in 1801, Hardy was again flag-captain, on the *St George*, and when her draught proved too deep for the attack on Copenhagen and Nelson was forced to transfer his flag into *Elephant*, Hardy joined him as a volunteer. When the war with France resumed after the collapse of the Peace of Amiens, Nelson was given command in the Mediterranean and hoisted his flag in *Victory* in July 1803. Hardy was reappointed as his flag-captain and the bond between the two men grew ever stronger as they embarked on their final campaign together, beginning with the long blockade of Toulon, continuing throughout the pursuit of the combined enemy fleet to the West Indies and back, and culminating in the battle of Trafalgar where Hardy was Captain of the Fleet on the *Victory*. With Nelson when he was shot, Hardy attended Nelson as he lay dying in the cramped 'tween deck of the *Victory*, where he received Nelson's famous dying utterance, 'Kiss me Hardy'.

'On 4 February 1806 Hardy was appointed a baronet, and subsequently set out for the North American stations under Sir George Berkeley, whose daughter Anne Louisa Emily he married at Halifax, Nova Scotia, in 1807; they had three daughters. After a sojourn at Lisbon he returned to North America where he remained until nominated KCB in January 1815. He returned to England in 1816. In 1819 Hardy was appointed commodore and commander-in-chief in South America, returning to England in 1824. A year later he was made rear-admiral, and on 21 October 1827 retired from life at sea to join the Admiralty board as First Sea Lord under Sir James Graham. In September 1831 he was appointed GCB. His interests at the

Admiralty were expressed as professional, rather than political, and he refused to adopt a party political line on naval expenditure, preferring to absent himself from Parliament and devote his energies to increasing the sailing performance and fighting strength of the vessels in the battle fleet. In April 1834 he was made governor of the Royal Naval Hospital at Greenwich where he died on 20 September 1839.'

Following the Battle of Copenhagen, 2 April 1801, the government decided not to support the issuance of Naval Gold Medals to the captains and Nelson. This became such an issue that Nelson declared to Foley, who was his Flag-Captain on board the *Elephant* at the battle, that 'he would never wear his other [King's Naval Gold] medals till that for Copenhagen was granted.' (Ref: Nicolas vol. VI page 527) Does this mean that the effigy in Westminster Abbey showing Nelson wearing just the Davison Nile medal, which is bronze gilt, presents Nelson as he would have been seen after Copenhagen? Very possibly so.

Provenance: Descendent of Captain Thomas Hardy.
Christie's King Street, London, 19 October 2005, lot 12 which made £65,000 hammer.

Alexander Davison Collection.
Sotheby's Bond Street, London, 21 October 2002, lot 8 which made £22,000 hammer.

References: *Trafalgar Bicentenary* auction catalogue for 19 October 2005, Christie's, London.
The Alexander Davison Collection auction catalogue for 21 October 2002, Sotheby's, London.
British Battles and Medals by Hayward, Birch and Bishop, Spink, London, 2006.
The Authentic Nelson by Rina Prentice, National Maritime Museum, Greenwich, 2005.
Dictionary of National Biography, Oxford University Press, 1975.
Royal Naval Exhibition at Chelsea catalogue, by anon, Griffith, London, 1891.
Naval Swords and Dirks by Sim Comfort, Sim Comfort Associates, London, 2008.
Lord Nelson's Swords by Sim Comfort, Sim Comfort Associates, London, 2014.
Nelson's Purse by Martyn Downer, Bantam Press, London, 2004.
Dispatches and Letters of Vice-Admiral Viscount Horatio Nelson by Sir Nicholas Harris Nicolas, seven vols. Henry Colburn, London, 1844-6.
Nelson's Band of Brothers, Lives and Memorials by Peter Hore, Seaforth, Barnsley, South Yorkshire, 2015.
Nelson, Britannia's God of War by Andrew Lambert, Faber & Faber, London, 2014.

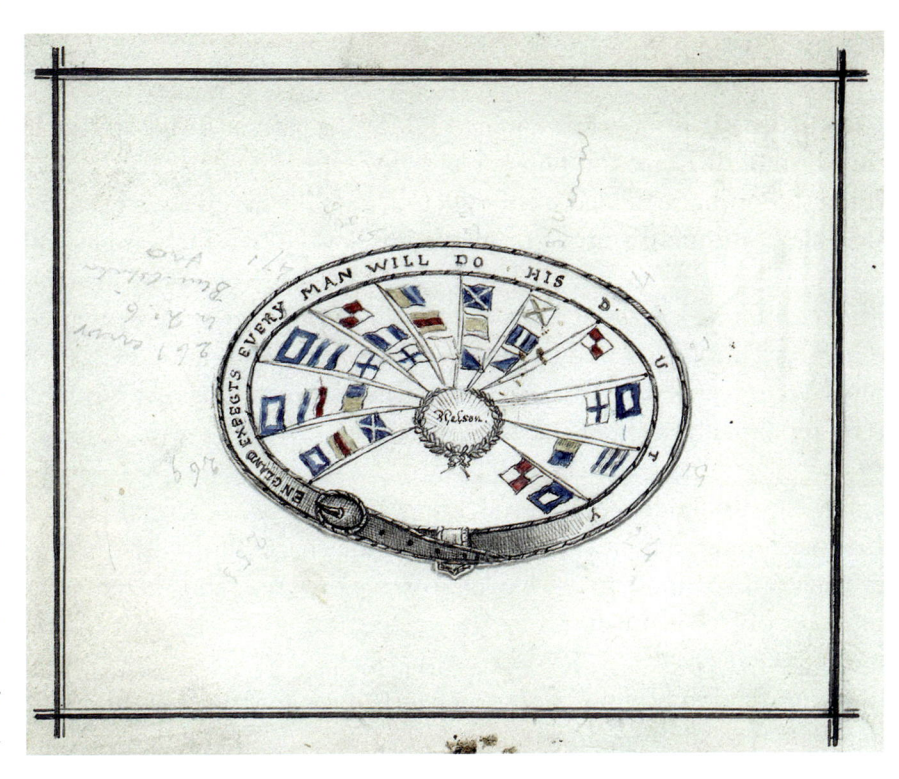

DN 29 Robert Rowe, Steward's Mate, HMS Alexander, Captain Alexander Ball

Description: Jeweller gilt and chased with the reverse field engraved *Rob t Rowe*. There is a small die break running through C. H. K. with a larger break below at the rim. The weight of the medal only is 40.7 grams and cased is 70.5 grams. Extremely fine.

Background: Robert Rowe joined HMS *Alexander* at Plymouth on 18 May 1796. He was 15 years old from Plymouth Dock and entered as a Boy, 3rd Class. On 12 October he was rated Steward's Mate in which station he remained until 6 October 1800 when he was reassigned as a Landsman. He served on *Alexander* continuously until 26 August 1802, when the ship was paid off at Portsmouth.

From *Jack Tar* we learn that a Boy was a volunteer under the age of eighteen. 'Those under the age of fifteen were Boys Third Class, and those over fifteen were Boys Second Class. The Boys First Class, more usually called Volunteers First Class, were literally a class apart, as they were training to be officers and expected to be appointed midshipmen.'

Smyth tells us about the duties of a Steward, 'There are several persons under this appellation in most ships, according to their size, appointed to the charge of the sea-stores of the various grades. The paymaster's steward has most to do, having to serve the crew, and therefore has assistants, distinguished by the sobriquet of Jack-of-the-dust.'

So, there shouldn't be any confusion between a Captain's Servant / Volunteers First Class as these young men were typically appointments made by the Captain and destined for the quarterdeck. The Boy Third Class rated as a Steward's Mate was essentially a very young person serving before the mast who may have a responsible job or was probably acting as a domestic servant to a Warrant or Petty Officer.

HMS *Alexander* was built Deptford Dockyard to the Alfred Class of 1772 design by Williams. She was launched in October 1778. Her overall length was 169 feet and she displaced 1,620 tons burthen. Armament consisted of 28 x 32 pounders on the Gun Deck, 28 x 18 pounders on the Upper Deck, 14 x 9 pounders on the Quarterdeck and 4 x 9 pounders at the Forecastle. Ship's company was between 550 and 600 officers and men. She was hulked in 1805 and used as a lazaretto or quarantine holding area at Portsmouth. She was finally broken up in 1819.

In the early hours of 6 November 1794 off the Scilly Isles, the *Alexander* in company with HMS *Canada* of 74 guns, after successfully seeing a convoy bound to Lisbon safe on its way, found a strange squadron of ships headed toward them. The ships proved to be French and under the command of Rear-Admiral Nielly and comprised five 74-gun ships plus frigates. The two British ships struck north toward home, but the French were able to come up to them. The *Canada* was able to make a break from the action while the *Alexander* was surrounded by three of the French ships. After a furious fight, with her masts, rigging and sails much damaged and 40 killed and wounded, Captain Richard Rodney Bligh hauled down his colours.

The *Alexander* was entered into the French navy as *Alexandre* and formed part of the Brest fleet which was the counter to the English Channel Fleet. In late June 1795, a British expedition was mounted to support French Royalists in the area of Quiberon Bay. The Channel Fleet, now under the command of Lord Bridport, provided support for this expedition and had taken station near Belle-Isle [Isle de Groix], where a squadron from the Brest fleet had taken shelter from a recent storm. On the 22nd of June the French came out and met the British in a hot, but not conclusive action which resulted in Bridport's ships capturing three of the French ships, the *Alexandre*, the *Formidable* and the *Tigre*. As William James notes, 'Of the three prizes, the *Alexandre*, or *Alexander*, as now again entitled to be called, was scarcely worth anything; but the *Tigre* and *Formidable* were fine new 74s. The *Tigre* was allowed to retain her name; but there being a *Formidable* 98 already in the service, the name of the *Formidable* 74, was changed to *Belle-Isle*.' Both the *Tigre*, which became Sir Sidney Smith's flagship at Acre in 1799, and *Belleisle*, which fought so bravely at Trafalgar, would serve the British very well.

Considering that the *Alexander* was pretty well shattered by the French in 1794, and again mauled by the British, which resulted in her French crew suffering around 300 killed and wounded, and then hulked in 1805, really confirms the remarks by William James. That she served well at the Nile is remarkable and also has a lot to say about how strong and easily repaired these great wooden ships were.

As Brian Lavery notes, Alexander John Ball (1757-1809), 'had intellectual interests far beyond the range of the average naval officer. Most had been 'round the world but never in it'; they knew the winds, tides and currents, whereas Ball could understand societies and cultures on land….Ball could understand and work with the aspirations and desires of people on shore. He wrote intelligently about the economy and society of Egypt and later became a great colonial administrator as governor of Malta, where his name was revered at the time and is still respected.'

I don't have any information regarding Ball's early career in the Royal Navy. He was promoted to lieutenant in 1780 and in April 1781 had the good fortune to move to HMS *Sandwich* which was Rodney's flagship. While on board he took part in The Battle of the Saints, 12 April 1782 and was promoted to commander shortly after, and then to post-captain in 1783 at the end of the American War. Ball, like Nelson, took advantage of the peace to spend time in France. Nelson commented in a letter to Captain Locker, in November 1783 from Saint Omer, 'Two noble captains are here, Ball and Shepherd: they wear fine epaulettes, for which I think them great coxcombs.' The wearing of epaulettes, at this time, was a sole French fashion which Nelson didn't approve of.

Alexander Ball had good interest behind him as he was appointed captain of the frigate *Nemesis* of 28 guns in 1790 and served in her for three years. He then moved to HMS *Cleopatra* of 32 guns and stayed with her also for three years mainly cruising off Canadian shores. He returned to England in August 1796 and was appointed to HMS *Alexander* of 74 guns in which he spent the winter cruising off Brest, but then was ordered to join Sir John Jervis off Cadiz and from there in May 1798, to serve under the orders of Commodore Nelson in the Mediterranean.

There must have been something of a question mark regarding Alexander Ball and his capacity as a warrior. He missed the First of June and Cape St Vincent. He didn't take part in the Nelson actions at Tenerife or along the coast of Spain. But it was fate that kept him away from the fight. So it was that during the night of 8 May, Nelson and Berry in the *Vanguard*, Saumarez in the *Orion* and Ball in the *Alexander* set sail and entered the Mediterranean to carry out a scouting mission around Toulon.

In the afternoon of 20 May, the squadron was about 75 miles south of Toulon. The weather was mild so the crew of the *Vanguard* hauled up the upper masts and yards to fly the topgallant and royal sails in preparation for easy cruising. Then the wind started to strengthen. By 10 pm there were heavy squalls and the ships started to reduce sail. At around 1 am on the 21st, the wind had now reached a full gale and storm sails on board the *Orion* had been blown out. At 1:30 am, the main topmast of the *Vanguard* gave a heavy groan, a resounding crack and went over the side. The topsail yard was fully manned at the time, but fortunately only two men were lost, one fell to the deck and the other overboard while the rest managed to cling to the wreckage and scramble back onto the ship.

As Brian Lavery notes, 'By this time the ships were in conditions which Admiral Beaufort in his famous scale would have described as 'the air completely filled with foam and spray. Sea completely white and driving spray; visibility very seriously affected.' This translates to Hurricane Strength, Force 12.

Worse was to come as on board the *Vanguard* as her fore topmast went by the board half an hour after the main topmast. The rolling of the ship placed her in a perilous state and at around 4:00 am, the 'foremast broke just above the deck, damaging the bowsprit as it fell.' *Vanguard* was now more or less in an unmanageable condition with the relentless wind pushing her nearer and nearer to the coast of Corsica. Through great seamanship, Nelson and Berry managed to get a scrap of sail to act as a spiritsail under the bowsprit so they could get the head of the ship to respond as they attempted to wear ship.

The manoeuvre was successful which removed the crisis. The gale continued while the *Vanguard's* men set to work repairing the ship which was made most difficult due to the continual rolling of the vessel. At 4:00 am on the 22nd the wind began to moderate and at 6:45, Nelson signalled Captain Ball in the *Alexander* to take the *Vanguard* in tow which proved both difficult and dangerous to do, however at 3:00 in the afternoon, the task was completed and *Vanguard* was tethered astern of *Alexander*.

As the afternoon wore on, the wind dropped to practically nothing, but a tremendous swell continued as the ships edged south along the coast of Sardinia. Closer and closer to the coast both *Alexander* and *Vanguard* were driven. Brian Lavery quotes Captain Berry, 'All this time there was a heavy swell driving in towards the shore, so that at midnight we were completely embayed. You may easily figure to yourself our situation and the feelings of those who knew the dangers when I tell you I could only distinguish the surf breaking on the rocky shore; still there was hope anchorage might be found, though we knew of none.'

Lavery continues, 'Nelson hailed Ball in the *Alexander* and ordered him to cast off the tow, so that his ship at least might be saved. Ball refused and Nelson, already perhaps feeling the stress of command, 'became impetuous and enforced his demand with passionate threats.'

Captain Alexander Ball painted by Gaetano Calleja, BHC2527©National Maritime Museum, Greenwich, London.

Ball remained calm and replied in his rather pompous manner: 'I feel confident that I can bring you in safe. I therefore must not and by the help of the almighty God will not leave you.'

And he didn't and Nelson now knew the metal of Alexander Ball and when the two ships had rounded the coast and come to safe anchor, Nelson went on board the *Alexander* and embraced Ball saying 'A friend in need is a friend indeed.' Nelson never forgot the steadfastness of Ball and his certainly saving *Vanguard* and her ship's company from a watery grave.

While Nelson's squadron were repairing damage to their ship to the south of Sardinia, Napoleon and his fleet left Toulon and began their great adventure to invade Egypt. Following Nelson's desperate attempts to gain intelligence as to the location of the French, they were finally discovered in Aboukir Bay on 1 August. Both the *Alexander* and *Swiftsure* were late in coming into action, having been detached to look into Alexandria. Both ships benefited from the *Culloden* having been grounded upon the reef ahead of the anchored French line of battle, steered clear of the hazard and continued down the seaward side of the enemy line. The log of the *Alexander's* Master, W. Lawson, relates the following which shows the problem of getting into action in light and contrary winds:

'At 1/2 past 2, saw the French fleet at anchor inside the Isle of Aboukir, amounting to 13 sail of the line and 4 frigates. Took the small bower cable out of the gun-room port and bent it to the anchor again. Made all sail possible towards them. At 1/2 past 5, tacked in 15 fathoms water, not being able to weather the reef that extends to the eastwards from the island. At 6, tacked in 20 fathoms. At 38 past 6, the headmost of our ships commenced the action with the enemy's van. At 25 minutes past 8, came to with the small bower and commenced firing on one of the enemy's ships, a three-decker [*L' Orient*]. At 1/2 past 8, let go the best bower, our ship being then on the larboard quarter of the enemy. At 25 minutes past 9, the ship we were engaged took fire. At half past 9, cut the stern cable, ceased firing, veered away the best bower, and got alongside another of the enemy's ships [*Tonnant*], commenced firing. At 50 minutes past 9, cut away the best bower cable to prevent the ship on fire falling on board us. At 10, the enemy's ship that was on fire blew up; with the explosion of the enemy's ship our jib and main royal was set on fire; by cutting away the jib boom and heaving the royal overboard, the fire was luckily extinguished.

'At 1/4 past 12 [August 2nd], came to with the sheet anchor and commenced firing upon three of the enemy's ships. [*Tonnant*, *Hereux* frigate and *le Mercure*, 74 guns] At 1/4 past 3, ceased firing. Cut away and threw overboard to prevent their taking fire, main topsail, fore and main topgallant sails. At daylight, commenced the action. At 6, one of the enemy's frigates struck to us. [*Hereux*] At 1/4 past 6, one of their frigates took fire and blew up. Took possession of the line of battle ship, ceased firing. She proved to be *le Mercure* of 74 guns. Killed during the action; Lieutenant John Collins and 13 seamen. Wounded: Alexander John Ball, Esq. captain, W. Lawson, Master, Messrs. Anderson and Bulley, midshipmen, Captain Creswell of marines, 48 seamen and 5 marines. The masts shot through in several places [etc. etc.].'

Having made repairs at Naples, Ball and the *Alexander* were ordered in October to take up station at Malta and support the siege of the French garrison at Valetta. The British force was very small comprising 500 marines and some 1,500 Maltese. It took two years to finally overcome the French, who by that time were starving having eaten every cat, dog and anything else that was catchable. The Maltese suffered as well and it was really down to Ball who secured provisions, not actually authorised, that kept the civilian population from slipping into famine. The Maltese never forgot his kindness.

Following the reduction of Malta in 1800, Captain Ball was made commissioner of the navy at Gibraltar. Nelson wrote to Ball from the Baltic in June 1801, saying: 'I pity the poor Maltese; they have sustained an irreparable loss in your friendly counsel and an able director in their public concerns; you were truly their father, and, like you, they may not like stepfathers...' Although a difficult time passed, in the end the right decisions were made primarily because Whitehall finally appreciated the importance of Malta to British interests. Sir Alexander Ball was ordered on 24 June 1801 to return to Malta and then ultimately as Governor of Malta where he remained until his death on 25 October 1809. Although he had been promoted to Rear-Admiral while serving at Malta, he never raised his flag and traded his sea experience for those of a diplomat and servant to the people of Malta. He was buried in Malta and a substantial monument was built in his honour at Valletta and is revered to this day.

Robert Rowe and HMS *Alexander* continued to support Malta during the remainder of the first French war, and with the Peace of Amiens, returned to Portsmouth in August 1802 where the ship's company was paid off.

Provenance: Medal fair, 1983.

References: The National Archives, Kew: ADM 35/163 - 164, ADM 36/14331 - 14339. (*Alexander* musters and logs).
The Sailing Navy List by David Lyon, Conway, London, 1993.
Logs of the Great Sea Fights 1794-1805 by Sturges Jackson, Navy Records Society, London, 1899-1900.
Nelson and the Nile by Brian Lavery, Chatham, London, 1998.
Dictionary of National Biography, Oxford University Press, 1975.
A Social History of the Navy 1793 - 1815 by Michael Lewis, George Allen and Unwin, London, 1960.
The Naval History of Great Britain...1793 to 1820 by William James, six vols., Richard Bentley, London, 1837 etc.
Jack Tar by Roy and Lesley Adkins, Little Brown, London, 2008.
The Sailor's Word-Book, by Admiral W. H. Smyth, Blackie, London, 1867.

The Alexander Ball monument at Valletta, Malta.

DN 30   Private William Flinn & Ann Crumwich, HMS Alexander, Captain Alexander Ball

Description: Jeweller gilt bronze medal engraved in the reverse field *Will m Flin, / & Ann / Crumwich*. Attached at 12 o'clock is a loop suspension with two rings and a blue ribbon. There is a small die break running through C. H. K. with a larger break below at the rim. Weight of the medal and ribbon is 41.2 grams. Very fine.

Background: William Flinn or William Flynn, was a labourer from Audians, in County Dublin. He became a private in the marines as opposed to being one of the many British Army enlisted men found amongst Nelson's Nile fleet. He was part of the Plymouth Division, 54th Company and joined as a private on 25 January 1796 and joined the *Alexander* on the 9th of April of that year. He was advanced to corporal on 4 July 1801, but reverted back to the rank of private when he joined the *Bittern* in 1803. When *Alexander* was paid off on 26 August 1802, his record states that his residence was St Luke's Parish in Dublin and that his wife's name was Elizabeth and he had deducted from his monthly wages an allowance that was sent to Elizabeth. He was discharged from the Royal Marines on 28 December 1812 due to a 'diseased foot'.

As you can see from the reverse of the medal, William Flinn formed a relationship with Ann Crumwich when on board *Alexander*. Please see DN 04, Landsman Andrew Nicol and his 'sea wife' Mary Williams, for more information about women on board Nelson's ships. During the time on board *Alexander*, Flinn would have most likely assisted on shore at Malta in securing the surrender of the French garrison at Valetta. For more information regarding his time on board *Alexander* and particularly during the battle of the Nile, please see DN 28.

What most interests me about this man is the next ship he served on, HMS *Bittern*, Captain Robert Corbett or Corbet. Flinn joined her on 1 January 1803 as a private and stayed on board until 2 August 1808. There couldn't have been a captain in the Royal Navy that is more controversial than Robert Corbett. J. K. Laughton wrote in 1887 the following for the *DNB*:

'Corbet, Robert (d 1810), captain in the navy, of an old Shropshire family, attained the rank of lieutenant on 22 December 1796; and having served with distinction during the operations on the coast of Egypt in 1801, in command of the *Fulminette* cutter, was promoted to be commander on 29 April 1802. On renewal of the war he was appointed to the *Bittern* brig, and sent to the Mediterranean, where he won high praise from Nelson, then commander-in-chief of the station. April 1805 he was appointed, by Nelson, acting captain of the *Amphitrite*, but he was not confirmed in the rank until 24 May 1806. Shortly afterwards he commissioned the *Nereide* frigate, and in her took part in the operation in Rio de la Plata. He then passed on to the Cape of Good Hope, and in August 1808 was sent to Bombay to refit. His conduct at Bombay, in taking on himself the duties of senior officer and breaking through the routine of the station, drew on him the displeasure of the commander-in-chief, Sir Edward Pellew, afterwards Viscount Exmouth, who represented that Corbet's letters and actions were unbecoming.

'The ship's company of the *Nereide* also proffered a complaint against him of cruelty and oppression. Corbet, in reply, demanded a court-martial; and Pellew, not being able to form a court at Bombay, ordered the ship to return to the Cape of Good Hope, in order that he might be tried there. This was, unfortunately, not explained to the men, who, conceiving that their temperate complaint had been unheeded, broke out into open mutiny. The mutiny was quelled, and when the ship arrived at the Cape, ten of the ringleaders was tried, found guilty, and sentenced to death, protesting their innocence of any evil design, beyond the wish for the ship to return to the Cape so that their grievances might be inquired into. One of the ten was left for execution, but the other nine were pardoned.

'When this trial was over, that on Corbet began. No charges of diabolical cruelty were ever more simply put, or more clearly proved, even if they were not admitted. In was acknowledged that the number of men flogged was very great; that the cat in ordinary use had knots on the tails, and that the backs of the sufferers were habitually pickled; that the boatswain's mates and other petty officers were encouraged to thrash the men without any formality - an irregular punishment known as 'starting', and that these startings were administered with thick sticks. There were numerous other minor charges, and Corbet, making no attempt to refute the evidence, based his defence on the necessities of his position and the custom of the service.

'The ship's company, he urged, was exceptionally bad; drunkenness, malingering, and skulking were everyday offences; desertion was frequent; the petty officers were as bad as or worse than the men; 'severity was necessary to reform their conduct, and perhaps it was used.' The prisoner was, strangely, acquitted on all the counts except on that of having caused men to be punished 'with sticks of an improper size and such as are not usual in his majesty's service', and for this he was reprimanded. The admiralty, however, wrote (4 August 1809) to express high disapproval 'of the manifest want of management, good order, and discipline' in the ship, and strongly condemned and prohibited 'starting', which they pronounced 'unjustifiable', and 'extremely disgusting to the feelings of British seamen.'

'After the court-martial, however, Corbet resumed the command of the *Nereide*, and on 21 August 1809 had an important share in the capture of the *Caroline* frigate and other vessels in St Paul's Bay in the Isle of

Bourbon. The *Caroline* was received into the service as the *Bourbonnaise*, and Corbet appointed to command her for the voyage to England. He arrived at Plymouth in the spring of 1810, and was immediately appointed to the *Africaine*, under orders to go out to the station from which he had just come, [the East Indies].'

Leaving Laughton for the moment, there was another personality on the East Indies Station that had a bearing upon Corbet and his conduct, this was Nesbit Willoughby, captain of the 16-gun sloop *Otter*. Willoughby was tall, lean and an aristocrat who approached life with a distinct haughtiness, but also had a theatrical streak which made himself popular with his crew. This in spite of his also being a ferocious flogger. It was said of Willoughby that, 'it was as much pleasure to him to punish a man when he comes to the gangway as it was to go to his breakfast.' It was Willoughby who would follow Corbet in command of the *Nereide* and who, in company with the *Magicienne* and *Sirius*, fought a reckless action against the French at Grand Port, Ile de France on 23 August 1810. Willoughby was proud to boast that the *Nereide*, 'lost as great a number of officers and men as ever were lost in a British frigate.' Of the 281 men on board when she went into action, no fewer that 230 were casualties, with 92 dead and the balance wounded. Many of those men who had suffered under Corbet were only to find an even more fierce devil awaiting them. The *Nereide* was so torn apart, she never saw service again and both the *Magicienne* and *Sirius* were burned to escape their capture by the French.

Laughton continues, 'The *Africaine* had been some time in commission, and her men were extremely averse to receiving their new captain, who was reported to be a monster of cruelty. They forwarded a round-robin to the admiralty, expressing their determination not to let Corbet come on board. But the ship was in Plymouth Sound, and the *Menelaus* dropped alongside ready to fire into her. The mutiny was thus repressed almost before it broke out, and Corbet, going on board read his commission and assumed the command. Some further display of ill-will was repressed without undue severity, and during the passage out to Mauritius, the ship's company seem to have been well satisfied with their lot.

'On 11 September 1810 they sighted Mauritius. During the previous month things had gone badly with the English squadron. The *Sirius*, *Magicienne*, and *Nereide* had been destroyed, and the *Iphigenia* had been captured. Corbet learned at the same time that two sail seen in the distance were the French frigates *Astree* and *Iphigenie* (the former *Iphigenia*). He stood toward them; was joined by Commodore Rowley in the *Boadicea* frigate, together with the *Otter* and the *Staunch*; the capture of the French ships appeared probable.

'It was not till the morning of the 13th that the *Africaine* was close up with the French ships; they were then within two or three hours' sail of Port Louis, and the *Boadicea* was some five miles dead to leeward. Corbet, fearing they might escape, opened fire on the *Astree*, which immediately returned it. In her second broadside a round-shot took off Corbet's right foot, and a splinter smashed his right thigh. He was carried below, and died a few hours afterwards. But meantime the *Africaine*, overpowered by the two French ships, all her officers being killed or wounded, having sustained a total loss of 163 killed and wounded out of a complement of 295, and being dismasted and helpless, struck her flag and was taken possession of. In the afternoon, when the *Boadicea* with the *Otter* and *Staunch* came up, the French fled, leaving their prize, which was captured without difficulty.'

Laughton finishes with Corbet by noting several rumours then still current when he wrote the above that Corbet was shot by one of his men which was disproved when compared with his wounds. Also that the men refused to fight and thus were cut down in droves by the enemy, also hard to prove, although the source of this statement is from Marshall who wrote in the 1820s and states, 'Not only was her shot-locker nearly full, but even the racks around the hatchways still contained many shot, blackened as they were before the action. Our informant, now a captain in the navy, is of opinion, as are many other persons, that the *Africaine's* crew, disgusted with their captain's tyrannical conduct, did not shot the guns at all after the second or third broadside.' However Laughton does finish by stating, 'It seems certain, however, that ... the fire of the *Africaine* was wild and ineffective; that she fired away all her shot without inflicting any serious loss on either of her opponents, whose return, on the contrary, was deadly and effective. Of Corbet's courage there can be no doubt; but his judgement in engaging may be questioned, his neglect of the essential training of his men must be blamed, and the brutal severity of his punishments has left a stain on his character which even his gallant death cannot wipe away.'

Stephen Taylor's work has delved deeper than the *DNB*. He remarks: 'The early life and background of Robert Corbet are as much an enigma as everything else about the man. Even the year of his birth is unknown. Although it was long believed that he came from an old Shropshire family, recent research points to an obscure line of Irish clergy from Wexford. Either way, he lacked glittering connections.

'There is no known portrait of him. By all accounts he was short and dark, and it is tempting to imagine him as a sizzling tinderbox, a furious black-browed figure beneath a cocked hat. But the legends that attached to him are as suggestive of an icy and obsessive rigour as they are of rage. ... Certainly there was more to him than mere anger. Corbet lusted for honour as some men lusted for women, blindly and destructively. If he was hated by a great many, he was esteemed by a few, for he seemed to incarnate the virtue prized above all others by the Navy - zeal. A zealous officer, it goes without saying, was brave, he was also able, energetic and devoted to the Service body and soul. All these qualities Corbet possessed.

'Essentially, however, Corbet was remote from the real values of Nelson's Navy. To the elements that won great battles, gunnery and teamwork, he was seemingly blind. And here perhaps lies one of the keys to an understanding of him. He had never participated in a major action and, in the absence of a reactive foe, had never had his obsessive assumptions tested. This may account for his neglect of gunnery. One can scan, week by week, the pages of *Nereide's* log without a hint of the great guns being exercised, let alone fired at targets. As for teamwork, the kind of fond male companionship on which the Navy thrived, Corbet had no truck with it. An aloof, solitary figure, he almost invariably ate alone in his cabin while his officers messed together. He was equally reluctant to mix with his officers, rarely leaving the ship to dine or receiving other captains on board.'

This is the man that held in balance the life and welfare of Private William Flinn.

HMS *Bittern* was a ship sloop built by Adams of Buckler's Hard and launched in 1796. She was of the Brazen / Termangant Class of 1795 with an overall length of 110 feet and displaced 419 tons burthen. She carried 18 x 6 pounders on the Upper Deck, 6 x 12 pound carronades on the Quarterdeck, and 2 x 12 pound carronades in the Forecastle. Her ship's complement was 121 officers and men.

During part of the cruise of the *Bittern* in the Mediterranean in 1804, it appears that she formed part of the command of Captain Cracraft of HMS *Anson*. The Nelson correspondence that relates to Corbet is of interest.

Nelson wrote to Cracraft in January 1804, 'I have this day received your letter of the 13th ultimo with a copy [of a letter] from Captain Corbett of his Majesty's Sloop *Bittern*, giving an account of his having run on shore a large Ship near Brindisi, and of his having set fire to her, owing to his not being able to get her off. In answer thereto, from the circumstances mentioned in Captain Corbett's said letter, his conduct appears to have been perfectly correct, and that the Ship in question, from her suspicious manoeuvres, was, most probably, Enemy's property.'

There followed in June, a stunning success for Corbet with his capture of the French Privateer *L'Hirondelle* and her two prizes. The capture apparently only came about after Corbet had pushed his men to man the sweeps and row *Bittern* for thirty-six hours across a dead calm sea to get at his quarry.

Then in June, Nelson wrote directly to Corbet: 'Captain Schomberg of His Majesty's Ship *Madras* has transmitted to me your letter ..giving an account of your having captured the *Hirondelle* French Privateer, and re-captured the two English Merchantmen named in the margin, her prizes; I therefore beg to assure you, that your conduct and perseverance in the capture of the said Privateer, and her Prizes, merit my entire approbation, and I must request that you will be pleased to receive, and to express my thanks to the Officers and Company of the *Bittern*, for their great exertions on this occasion.'

It also appears that in the letter from Corbet to Schomberg, that Corbet requested a court-martial for five men who had Run and had been retaken in March, but had assisted in the capture of *L'Hirondelle*. Nelson wrote to Schomberg: 'But I am inclined to think that Captain Corbet, from the said men's long confinement, and their late exertions in capturing *L'Hirondelle*, French Privateer, may be inclined to forgive them. You will, therefore, signify the purport of this letter to Captain Corbet, that if he is disposed to forgive them, I have no objections, under the present circumstances.'

Then on the 4th of October, Nelson again acknowledged a letter from Cracraft wherein Nelson notes that the five Run men have been forgiven by Corbet.

I have to think that the character of Corbet was certainly known to Nelson, as he would be very aware of every captain within his command. Corbet and the men of the *Bittern* were certainly active and successful however, reading between the lines, Nelson's letter to Corbet congratulating him on the capture of *L'Hirondelle* also includes the direct command that he share this news with the officers and men of the *Bittern*. Further, with regard to the 'hint' that the five Run men who Corbet wanted to court-martial and ideally see hanged, that the hint was taken by Corbet and that the letter from Cracraft to Nelson indicates that Nelson checked up on the matter to ensure his feelings were carried out.

I can't imagine Nelson feeling an affinity toward Corbet, but from the professional relationship, he would certainly congratulate success and if possible, moderate the actions of Corbet upon his ship's company.

I think that William Flinn was lucky being a Royal Marine. As part of the after guard, he was less likely to be a focus for punishment, however, he may well have had the unpleasant task of enforcement. Fortunately, Corbet left the ship early in 1806. *Bittern* continued to cruise in the Mediterranean, mainly working out of Malta. She returned to Plymouth in August 1808 and was paid off. We don't have the subsequent service of William Flinn, but, as noted above, we do know that he was discharged from the Royal Marines on 28 December 1812 due to a 'diseased foot'.

Provenance: Bonham's, lot 14, 19 October 1993.

References: The National Archives, Kew: ADM 35/163 - 164, ADM 36/14331 - 14339. (*Alexander* musters and logs). ADM 27/1 (Allotment by Flinn to his wife Elizabeth and that they have a daughter. Total paid to 26 August 1802 was £33.0.4d) ADM 96/219 & 221 (Effective and Subsistence List) ADM 35/2145, ADM 36/17027 - 17029, ADM 37/190 - 191 (HMS Bittern)
The Dispatches and Letters of Vice Admiral Lord Viscount Nelson edited by Sir N. H. Nicolas, Colburn in six vols., London, circa 1835.
Dictionary of National Biography, Oxford University Press, 1975.
Royal Naval Biography, 12 vols, by Lieuteant John Marshall, R.N., Longman, London, 1823 - 1835.
Storm & Conquest, The Battle for the Indian Ocean, 1809, by Stephen Taylor, Faber and Faber, London, 2007. Willoughby flogging and breakfast, note from *Storm & Conquest*, ADM 1/60 enclosure of a petition dated 30 September 1808.

DN 31 William Neads [Navel], Landsman, HMS Swiftsure, Captain Benjamin Hallowell

Description: Jeweller gilt bronze medal engraved in the reverse field *William Neads / Swiftsure / 74*. At 12 o'clock is a small silver ring for suspension. There is a small die break running through C. H. K. with a larger break below at the rim. Weight: 39.6 grams. Near extremely fine.

Background: William Neads is a mystery. In the *Swiftsure's* pay book there is no William Neads, however in Surgeon James Dalziel's journal we have two entries: 'Wm Neads / Aged 20 Ordy / July 14 / 1797 / off Cadiz / Symptoms / Great pain in his bowels, frequent inclination to go to stool, sometimes purged strongly without receiving relief. / Treatment / A sample of Rhubarb with five grains of Calomel to be made into pills and given Barley water to be drunk freely or when it begins to operate. Rice to be used for food. / Discharged to duty / July 21 / Remarks / These are the first cases of a purging attended with Dysentery Symptoms I have observed on this station. The weather is extremely hot and sultry and grapes and other fruit are brought alongside by the Portuguese, which in some measure may account for this perdition.'

There is a new entry on 30 September 1798. 'William Needs / Aged 20 Ordy / 30th Sept / At Sea / Symptoms / Fractured Clavicle of the right side by a fall down the Main Hatchway / Treatment / The bone being fractured very obliquely: had suffered great pain 'till it was reduced, is now easy, the dressings to be kept wet with a weak solution of Cerupa Scetata. / Discharged to Duty 6 Novr.'

Yet William Neads or Needs is not on the *Swiftsure's* books, although from the surgeon's journal he was clearly on board between 14 July 1797 and 30 September 1798 which is also evidenced by his engraved Davison Nile medal. There is, however, another man. William Nave who was entered on 19 November 1796 but didn't appear until 23 February 1797. He was a Quota Man from HMS *Cambridge*. Although he was originally rated as Boy, 3rd Class, he was quickly re-rated as Ordinary Seaman. He came from Gloucester, was 19 years old upon signing and was most likely 20 in July 1797.

So, two men of the same age, the same rating and somewhat similar names on board *Swiftsure*. I think the clue to this mystery is that William Nave was a Quota Man. As Michael Lewis tells us, in addition to the hot press of merchant seaman to keep the fleets manned, something else was needed as the numbers prest just weren't meeting the requirements of the Admiralty. The Quota System was introduced in 1795, wherein, counties, and cities were given quotas of men to supply to the navy. On paper this should have been something like conscription, but as the power to select what men filled the quota was left with the local county and town authorities, it was quickly worked out that this was an ideal method for ridding their community of all their miscreants.

If that was the case with William Neads, then I would think that William Nave was his *nom de guerre*, used in case he decided to Run. Perhaps another clue is that he was initially rated as a Boy, 3rd class, e.g. a landsman servant, but then very quickly re-rated Ordinary Seaman. I wonder if William Neads had already Run from the service, was hiding out in Gloucester under an alias, got into trouble and perhaps gaol, and then shipped back to the Navy under his alias. Under his real name, he would be a deserter and liable for the long drop from the yard-arm!

If this is what happened, then why would the surgeon know his true name. Well, Neads, 'who was in great pain' may have just blurted it out and the Hippocratic Oath meant that Surgeon Dalziel would keep his secret. Or, perhaps he was entered on the ship's books under an alias and nobody bothered to change it even when his real name and quality as a seaman became known. We will never know the truth of it, but this really does make a good sea story and it all fits!

He remained on board until 24 June 1801 when *Swiftsure* was captured by the French. We lose sight of him as a prisoner of war, however prior to the full control of France by Napoleon, it was the custom to exchange prisoners at fairly regular intervals, so Neads / Nave may well have returned to the Royal Navy not long after his capture. He is shown as officially discharged from *Swiftsure* on 20 October 1801, but this looks to be the Admiralty notation that he had become a prisoner of war.

HMS *Swiftsure* was one of the Elizabeth Class of Third Rate 74-gun ships designed by Slade in 1766 and would have a ship's company of 550 / 600 men. She was built by Wells at Depthford or Rotherhithe and launched on 4 April 1787. She was 168 feet in length and 1612 tons burthen and bore 28 x 32 pounders on the Gun Deck, 28 x 18 pounders on the Upper Deck, 14 x 9 pounders on the Quarterdeck and 4 x 9 pounders in the Forecastle. She was taken by the French in 1801, but recaptured at Trafalgar in 1805, renamed *Irresistible* and finally broken up in 1816.

This author has benefited greatly from two recently published books by Benjamin Carp and Bryan Elson. Sir Benjamin Hallowell was born on New Year's Day, 1761 at Boston, Massachusetts. From Bryon Elson we have, 'The first Hallowells had emigrated from Devonshire in 1643, seeking freedom to practice their Dissenter beliefs in the New World. By the 1760s they had become a family of substance. Our Benjamin's Grandfather Hallowell possessed extensive property in the city [of Boston], including water frontage and a shipyard on Batterymarch. He traded with the West Indies, was involved in the Newfoundland fishery, and became a shareholder in a tract of land along the Kennebec River, including most of the present town of Hallowell, Maine.

'When our Benjamin was born, his father [also a Benjamin], was captain of the *King George*, a 20-gun brig belonging to the province [of Massachusetts]. [The French and Indian] War between Britain and France had been raging for six years. Each year the *King George* had patrolled the waters between Boston and Halifax, protecting trade against French privateers or, as his orders stated, 'cleansing the sea of those vermin from Louisbourg.' After Louisbourg fell in 1758 he carried dispatches and troops between there and Halifax, and in 1762 he served under Admiral Colville in the expedition that retook St John's, Newfoundland from the French.

'When the war ended in 1763 his services were rewarded by a grant of 20,000 acres in a location of his choice. In the autumn of 1759 he had unsuccessfully chased a privateer into a broad inlet in northeastern Nova Scotia - Chedabucto Bay, whose forested and deserted shores gradually narrowed to a sheltered harbour at its western head. The sight had remained with him, and when the opportunity arose he chose 'a tract of land situate, lying and being on the east side of Chedabucto Harbour, just entering into the Second Basin.' At the time the undeveloped land in an empty colony was practically valueless.

'With the end of the war the *King George* was paid off. Rather than returning to his mercantile life in Boston, her former captain travelled to London to lobby for a position in colonial administration. With the help of Admiral Colville, Hallowell senior gained access to Lord North, and a suitable position was soon identified. As a former merchant captain, Hallowell also possessed excellent qualifications for his new post, Comptroller of Customs for the Port of Boston. He was sworn in on 18 July 1764, when young Benjamin was three years old.'

The Hallowell family certainly looked secure within the community of Boston, with Hallowell senior now able to spend his time ashore with his family and execute the duties of his important post. His brother Robert also joined the Customs as Deputy Comptroller. But the settled family life, that a man of the sea would so much yearn for, was to be shattered by the growing discontent of the colonists.

In 1765 the Stamp Act was passed wherein the British government imposed a tax on all sale of goods in the American Colonies. The reason for the tax was certainly justified, i.e. to pay for the war with France which had secured all of Canada and the territory east of the Mississippi for the Crown. The tax would also assist in the continued employment of the Royal Navy to protect trade between the colonies and Britain. With the introduction of the tax smuggling became rampant and at one stage in June 1768, Hallowell seized John Hancock's ship *Liberty*. Upon Hallowell's returning to his house that evening, he was 'surrounded by a mob and pelted with dirt and stones, ...he might well have been murdered had some passersby not come to his aid. That night the mob surrounded his home but withdrew after breaking a few windows.'

Bryon Elson continues, 'Rioting continued, forcing the members of the Board of Customs to flee to Castle William. Virtual prisoners and quite unable to carry out their duties, they decided to send an emissary to London to report on the situation and seek guidance. The choice fell on Hallowell, partly no doubt to remove him from the situation of personal danger his diligence had created.'

Hallowell decided to take his young son, Benjamin, with him probably to avoid the young man being the object of bullying due to his father's, now infamous, attack on a Boston shipowner of high repute, albiet a suspected smuggler!

Further from Bryon Elson, 'On their arrival in England father and son [aged seven], were welcomed into the home of Samuel Vaughan and his wife Sarah, the elder Hallowell's sister. Samuel Vaughan had prospered in the three-way trade between Britain, the West Indies, and the Thirteen Colonies, and had built a large residence at Wanstead near London. The couple had seven children ranging in age from seventeen year old Benjamin to two year old Rebecca. Three of the cousins - Charles, Sarah and Samuel Junior - were near the young Ben's age, ideal playmates to help him adjust to his new surroundings. In the ensuing years the Vaughans were to treat Benjamin as one of their sons, and their home was to offer the nearest approach to a family circle that he was to know as a child.'

Young Ben was enrolled at the school of Mr. John Morrice located in Chestnut, a village about fifteen miles north of London. He studied mathematics, French, Latin and Greek. It was said that after two years of tuition, he spoke classical Greek. No doubt the study of mathematics greatly assisted his later study of navigation.

Benjamin senior's work in London resulted in his promotion to becoming one of the five Commissioners of the American Board of Customs which allowed his brother, Robert, to take his old job of Comptroller of Customs at Boston. When Benjamin returned to Boston in September, 1770, the political situation had worsened, mainly due to a sequence of bad decisions made in England which did nothing but to further infuriate the local colonists. Benjamin Carp's book about the Boston Tea Party provides the full background to the hardening of colonial opinion against the British. The Boston Tea Party, which took place on 16 December 1773, followed the refusal of Customs officials in Boston to allow three shiploads of tea to leave port because the colonial importers refused to pay the duty levied on the cargo. A group of colonists boarded the ships and destroyed the tea by throwing it into Boston Harbour. The incident remains as one of the important initial protests based on 'no taxation without representation', which was to culminate in the American Revolution.

Following further acts of independence by the people of Massachusetts, General Gage began dispatching troops to key New England towns to secure stores of arms and powder. On 2 September 1774, some 4,000 protesters assembled on Cambridge Common. Although things started peacefully, the crowd soon turned rowdy. Benjamin Carp relates, 'When customs officer Benjamin Hallowell rode through Cambridge on his way from Salem, someone called out to him, 'Damn you! How do you like us now, you Tory Son of a Bitch!'

As Bryan Elson relates, it wasn't just the rebel Americans that Ben senior had to deal with. Admiral Graves had overall charge of all things naval in Boston. There was an issue regarding the supply of hay from Gallup's Island, near Nantucket, with Ben Hallowell senior owning the haying rights of the island. Hallowell refused the Admiral his order for the hay and the Admiral countered by refusing haying amongst the islands. 'In August 1775, the two encountered each other on the street. Hallowell called Graves a scoundrel, fisticuffs erupted, Graves drew his sword, and Hallowell took it from him and broke it over his knee.' There were numerous witnesses with the skirmish being reported both in Boston and London.

Benjamin Hallowell senior had displayed great physical courage, extreme obstinacy and disregard for authority when a principal was at stake. His younger son's career would illustrate that he had inherited these traits, perhaps in excess.

On 5 March, 1776 the American Revolution was now fully underway and General Washington had managed to gain and arm with cannon the heights around Boston, which spelt its doom as a Royalist stronghold. The Hallowell family, along with many of their friends and neighbours, fled the colony on the merchant ship *Hellespoint* which took them to Nova Scotia, arriving at Halifax on April 2nd. On 15 July, the family departed Halifax on board the *Aston Hall* and arrived in England later in the month.

There is little doubt that the loss of position in the colonial government and all of their American property, hit Benjamin Hallowell senior hard, and would have left an indelible impression on his son. It appears that young Ben was paying for his American background through being bullied at his schools, but he could take care of himself. In maturity Hallowell was described as both big and powerful and from the look of his portrait, his broken nose certainly speaks of a man who would fight for what he wants. The problem, however, was that although Ben could stand up for himself, he would do this at the cost of his education. When the Hallowell family were reunited in October 1776, the first thing Hallowell senior had to deal with was his recently expelled from school, son.

At fifteen years of age, Ben was too old for the normal route to being an officer in the Royal Navy. His father had to find a post for him as a midshipman, but without the requisite sea time. For some fathers, particularly those who had struck and humiliated an Admiral, this may have proved a particularly daunting task, but Hallowell senior was a man who was not without friends, and particularly friends within the Royal Navy. On 11 May 1777, Midshipman Benjamin Hallowell joined HMS *Sandwich* at Portsmouth. Captain Samuel Hood (afterwards 1st Viscount Hood), was in charge of Portsmouth, and it is thought that Hood and Hallowell senior were well acquainted as Hood commanded the Halifax station ten years previously when Hallowell was providing good service in the *King George*. At any rate, on 24 April 1778, young Ben was moved to HMS *Asia*, Captain Vandeput, and he began to gain sea time.

Hallowell's early career wasn't particularly promising. He was with Hood at the action off the Chesapeake shortly after joining the *Alcide* and after that moved to HMS *Alfred* and was involved in the engagements at St Christopher's and Dominica. It wasn't until April 1783 when his commission as lieutenant was confirmed. He was however fortunate to remain at sea following the American War and was made commander in November 1790.

He commanded the *Scorpion* sloop on the coast of Africa for a couple of years and in 1793 went to the Mediterranean in the *Camel* storeship which was followed by some short commissions. He took part in both the sieges of Bastia and Calvi as a volunteer, but without a ship. Nelson was most impressed with Hallowell and noted in July 1794 that he was full of zeal and played an important role in manning the guns. Lavery notes that for Hallowell, this was exactly the sort of support that was needed and in late 1795 he was given command of the *Lowestoft* frigate and a few months later moved to the *Courageux*, which he commanded during the action off Hyeres on 13 July 1795.

Hallowell continued in the *Courageux*, but then disaster struck on the night of 19 December 1796. Hallowell was on shore attending a court-martial and the *Courageux* was at anchor in Gibraltar Bay. David Hepper tells us what happened next. The weather was worsening with steadily rising wind and sea when *Courageux's* anchor cable parted. Another anchor was readied for letting go, but the ship had been carried across the bay and drew close to the Spanish guns. Lieutenant John Burrows was in command while Hallowell was absent, and decided to try and secure her original anchorage, with the wind and sea increasing strength all the time. The Master, John Morton, suggested that they take *Courageux* out to sea and try to gain an anchorage the next morning, but Burrows was persistent in staying within the Bay. In the end, *Courageux* put to sea, but a couple of hours later sighted the Moroccan coast and the effort to shorten sail proved too great for the hands on deck. Morton asked Burrows to call all hands on deck, but Burrows refused saying the watch below was exhausted and shouldn't be disturbed. Too late, and *Courageux* struck the rocks at the foot of Ape's Hill, swung broadside with the surf and was soon enough a wreck. Out of a ship's company of 600, only about 120 survived.

While being on board Admiral Jervis's flagship, HMS *Victory*, as a volunteer awaiting passage back to England, Hallowell was present at the Battle of Cape St Vincent, 14 February 1797.

On that fateful day Captain Calder was on *Victory's* quaterdeck and counting the number of enemy ships as the early fog cleared:

'There are twenty sail of the line, Sir John.'
'Very well, sir.'
'There are twenty-five sail of the line, Sir John.'
'Very well, sir.'
'There are twenty-seven sail of the line, Sir John.'
'Enough, sir, no more of that; the die is cast, and if there are fifty sail I will go through them.'
Meanwhile, the American Ben Hallowell became so excited that he thumped the Admiral on the back, 'That's right Sir John, and, by God, we'll give them a damn good licking!'

The other officers on the quarterdeck were struck dumb by Hallowell's action, but Sir John said nothing and probably held back a grin over the enthusiasm of this American.

Following the battle, Jervis then sent *Hallowell* back home with a duplicate set of the St Vincent dispatches and a strong recommendation from 'Old Jarvie' which resulted in Hallowell's immediate appointment to the *Lively* frigate with orders to return to the Mediterranean. From the *Lively* he moved to HMS *Swiftsure* which formed part of the inshore squadron commanded by Troubridge. It was thus that in May 1798, *Swiftsure* joined Rear-Admiral Nelson and the search for the French fleet that had escaped Toulon commenced.

Nelson's fleet approached from the west and passing Alexandria, Nelson ordered *Alexander* and *Swiftsure* to take a look in the harbour while the rest of the fleet continued to the east. *Alexander*'s signal at 12:40 that she had sighted the French fleet was not correct, as Ball was looking at shipping and not men-of-war. Ball's signal three minutes later tried to correct the mistake, although it must have been confusing on the receiving end! Within *Logs of the Great Sea Fights* by Jackson are given the meaning of some of the signals used at the Nile. That Jackson wasn't able to decipher them all was simply because he didn't have a contemporary signal book for the Nile. In this author's collection is such a book which has allowed me to decipher each of the signals recorded by Hallowell, which researchers may find useful.

In The National Archives is the *Journal of Captain Hallowell for the Battle of the Nile*. The following starts with the afternoon of 1 August 1798. 'Moderate breezes and pleasant weather. Unbent the small bower cable and got the end of it out at the larboard gun-room port, [per the order from Nelson to rig a cable for anchoring at the stern], and bent it again with an 8 1/2 inch cable from forward for a spring. At 12:40, the *Alexander* made the tabular signal No. 23 with a French flag at the mizen topmast head. [Fleet, having discovered it. French flag denotes the ships are French] At 12:43, the *Alexander* made the numeral signal No. 6. [That the signal made to the Admiral is not distinct or understood] At 1.23, spoke with the *Alexander*, who directed us to take possession of or drive on shore an enemy's galley or brig lying at anchor near the entrance of the old port of Alexandria. At 1.51, the *Vanguard* made the general signal No. 9. [To leave off chase or call in Ships otherwise separate from the Fleet.]; answered and tacked, ship then in 20 fathoms water, the Tower of Aguta bearing S by W, distance off shore about 2 leagues.

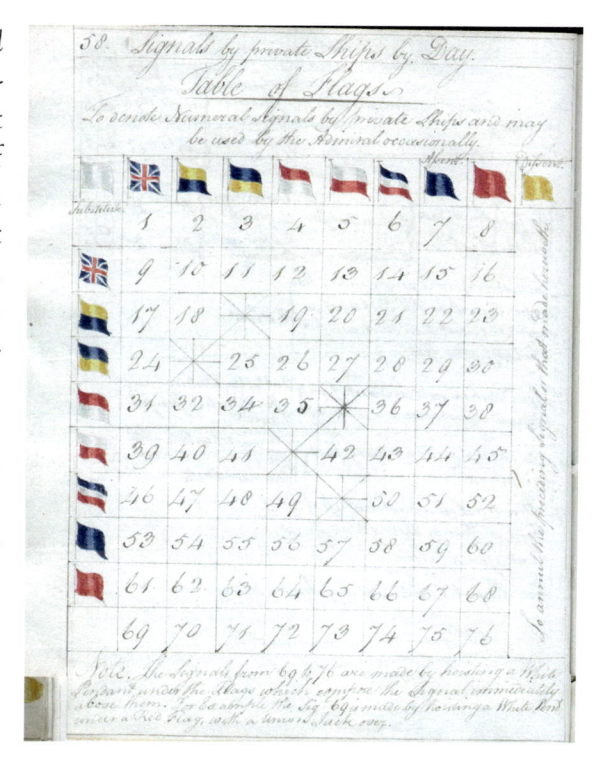

'Saw a number of French ships lying in the old port of Alexandria and French colours hoisted on the castles. At 3.15, the *Vanguard* made the general signal No. 53. [To Prepare for Battle]. At 3.38, discovered the French fleet, consisting of 13 sail of the line and 4 frigates, lying at anchor in the Bay of Aboukir.

'Got ready for action. Standing then to the NE; from 16 to 11 fathoms water. Answered the general signal No. 54 [To prepare for Battle; when it may be necessary to anchor with a Bower or Sheet Cable in abaft and Springs etc.], then in 11 fathoms of water, the island of Aboukir bearing SE, distance about 4 miles. At 5.12, observed the headmost ship of our fleet to bear up for the enemy's van ship. At 5.18 the *Vanguard* made the general signal No. 34 [For the ship leading the Line of Battle and others in turn to alter course by one point to Starboard in Succession etc.] to the leading ships. At 6.7, answered the general signal No. 66. [To make Sail after lying by the leading Ship first.] At 6.15, saw the enemy's van ship begin to fire at our leading ship, the *Goliath*. At 6.17, the *Goliath* began to fire at the enemy's van ship. At 6.18, the *Vanguard* made the general signal No. 5 with a red pennant over it. [To engage the Enemy. If closer, a Red Pennant will be shewn over the Flag.]

'At 6.32, the *Zealous* began to fire at one of the enemy's van ships. At 6.30, the *Culloden* made the tabular signal No. 43. [Striking and Sticking on a shoal] At 6.40 seven of our ships in hot action. At 7.11, bore up, then in 12 fathoms water. Saw the *Culloden* aground about ? miles from Aboukir Island. At 7.30 up foresail. At 7.39, lowered down the topsails, handed the topgallant sails and mainsail, and lowered the boats down from the quarter.

[Brian Lavery relates that as *Swiftsure* closed upon the enemy fleet in the dark, Hallowell 'saw a ship coming out under her foresail and foretopsail alone, showing no lights. Assuming she was French the crew got ready to fire, but Hallowell forbade it...' A good decision as the ship was *Bellerophon* coming out of the line as a near wreck after having been savaged by *L'Orient*.]

'At 8.3, let go our small bower anchor in 7 fathoms water with a spring. At 8.5, commenced firing at the enemy. A two-decked ship called the *Franklin* on our starboard quarter and a three-decked ship called *l'Orient* on the starboard bow. At 9.3, *l'Orient* caught fire and at 9.37, she blew up. Hove in the cable and spring occasionally.

Also from Brian Lavery we have, 'The *Swiftsure*, engaging both *L'Orient* and *Franklin*, was upwind of the French flagship and felt less danger, and even though the heat was beginning to melt the tar between her planks....,' Quoting Theophilus Lee, 'Hallowell saw, with the eye of judgement, that her present station was best calculated to secure her from danger. The explosion would naturally throw all up in the air and the *Swiftsure* being, as may be supposed, near the centre thereof, consequently the greater part of the fragments would naturally be projected beyond her.' Lavery continues, 'Hallowell ordered sentries to be posted on the cables to prevent anyone trying to cut them. As in the *Orion*, the gunports and magazine were closed and the men went under cover, taking wet swabs and buckets of water to put out any fires.'

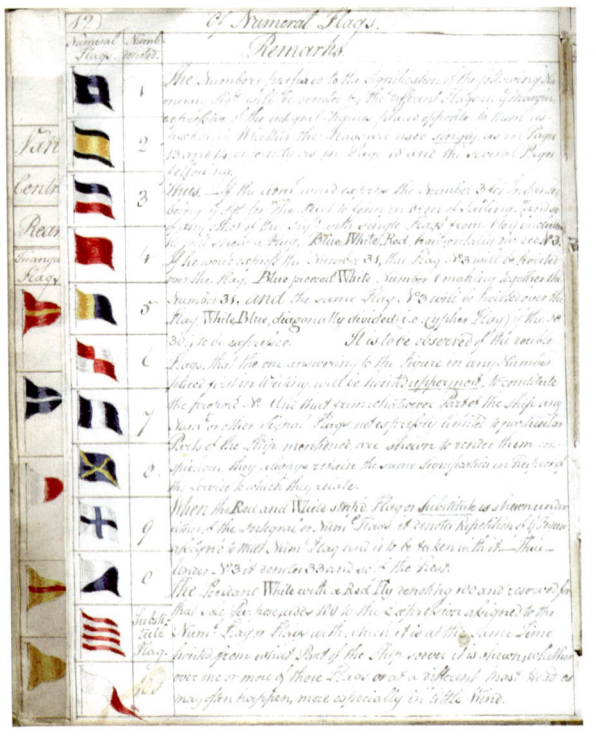

Hallowell's journal continues: 'Picked up 9 men, 1 lieutenant and commissary which escaped out of *l'Orient*. Ceased firing. Saw the *Alexander*'s bowsprit and her main topgallant sail to be on fire. At 5 minutes after, saw her driving to the SSE. At 10.20, sent Lieutenant Cowan to take possession of the enemy's ship that lay on our quarter, who hailed us that she had struck, with her main and mizen masts gone. At 10.35, he returned finding she was taken possession of by an officer from the *Defence*. At 10.40, saw the *Alexander* and *Majestic* engaging two of the enemy's ships to the S by E of us about 1 mile.

'2 August, A. M. - At 2.30, the *Alexander* and *Majestic* ceased firing. At 4.55 the *Theseus* dropped down to their assistance and renewed the action. At 5.17, the *Vanguard* made the signal No 55 to the *Leander*. [*Leander* to assist Ships in Battle.] At 5.27, *Vanguard* repeated d[itt]o. Saw 6 sail of the enemy's ships had struck their colours, most of them dismasted. Saw the *Bellerophon* lying about 4 miles to the eastward of us, with all her masts gone. At 6.20, saw an enemy's frigate strike to the *Theseus* after firing her broadside and then set her on fire. At 6.25, the *Goliath* went down to support the *Theseus*. At 6.54, the *Vanguard* made the *Zealous* signal No. 7 and compass south. [To chase ships in view on the bearing.] Seeing an enemy's frigate under way which made her escape with 2 line-of-battle ships and another frigate. Saw another frigate on shore dismasted. 2 line-of-battle ships aground SSE, and one dismasted S 1/2 E, with French colours flying. At 8, the two ships SSE struck their colour and at ? the other blew up. Made at the rate of 8 inches of water an hour. Carpenters employed stopping the shot holes. Found one of the cutters cut away and the other stove in such a manner as rendered her quite irreparable; cut her adrift; the ores masts, sails, and everything washed out and lost. Received several shot in the hull, masts, yards, &c. and a great part of the rigging cut to pieces.

'P.M. - Moderate breezes and pleasant weather. People employed knotting and splicing the rigging. At 6, the *Majestic* fired minute guns on interring her captain, who was killed in the action.'

Due to the judicious placement of *Swiftsure* by Hallowell, her ship's company suffered only 29 casualties, 7 killed and 22 wounded.

As a relic of this victory, Ben Hallowell had a coffin made from the mainmast of *l'Orient* which he presented to Nelson. In his letter to Nelson, Hallowell notes, 'that when you are tired of this life you may be buried in one of your own trophies', which is exactly what happened with Nelson being put to rest in St Paul's Cathedral within his *l'Orient* coffin.

R. J. Hamerton.]   [*From an Engraving.*
SIR BENJAMIN HALLOWELL-CAREW
(CAPTAIN HALLOWELL), 1760–1834.

Following the Nile, *Swiftsure* was employed along the coast of Egypt as detailed by Cooper Willyams. Later she formed part of Troubridge's squadron on the coast of Italy. She was then employed in various duties within the Mediterranean, at Gibraltar, Lisbon and Minorca. When on convoy duty to Malta in June 1801, Hallowell learned of a large French squadron which was on its way to land troops at Tripoli. Hallowell immediately left the convoy to investigate, but unfortunately was himself surrounded by the French and captured. In August he was released on parole, and at his court martial, was acquitted of any fault.

In 1802, he commanded the *Argos* on the coast of Africa and in 1803 was in the West Indies working for Commodore Samuel Hood during the reduction of St Lucia and Tobago. Later he gained command of the *Tigre* and in May and June 1805 accompanied Lord Nelson in the chase of the combined French and Spanish squadron to West Indies, but missed Trafalgar having been detached on other duties. He remained in the *Tigre* until 1811 when he gained his flag. He moved to HMS *Malta* of 80 guns and provided good service to Wellington on the east coast of Spain. Hallowell continued on board *Malta* until the close of the war.

He remained employed in various senior posts. In 1828, upon the death of a cousin Mrs Anne Paston Gee, he succeeded to the estates of the Carews of Beddington Park, Surrey with the proviso that he adopted the surname Carew, hence he was then named Benjamin Hallowell-Carew. He died at Beddington Park on 2 September 1834 and is buried there.

Provenance: Item 2486 at the Chelsea Naval Exhibition, 1891 details: 'A gilt medal commemorating the Victory at the Nile etc....presented by Alexander Davison to William Mead [Needs] who served on board the *Swiftsure*, has come down to the present holder as an heirloom. Lent by Mr. C. Burrough, late Chief Gunner's Mate'

Provenance: Medal fair, 1986.

References: The National Archives, Kew: ADM 36/13732, 13781-13782 & 13737 (*Swiftsure*).
ADM 101/121/3 (Surgeon Dalziel's journal).
The Sailing Navy List by David Lyon, Conway, London, 1993.
Dictionary of National Biography, Oxford University Press, 1975.
British Warship Losses in the Age of Sail (1650-1859) by David J Hepper, Boudriot, Rotherfield, East Sussex, 1994.
Logs of the Great Sea Fights 1794-1805 by Sturges Jackson, Navy Records Society, London, 1899-1900.
Manuscript *Royal Navy Signal Book*, watermarked 1796 and complete with the Numeric and Tabular signal codes. Sim Comfort Collection.
Three Articles pertaining to Royal Navy signal codes and Captain Popham's 'Marine Vocabulary' 1793 - 1815, by Sim Comfort, 23 page off print. 2009.
Nelson and His Times by Beresford, Harmsworth, London, circa 1897. (Hallowell portrait).
Defiance of the Patriots, The Boston Tea Party, by Benjamin Carp, Yale, New Haven & London, 2010.
Nelson's Yankee Captain by Bryan Elson, Fromac, Halifax, Nova Scotia, 2008.
Memoirs of the Life and Services of Sir J. Theophilus Lee, privately printed, London, 1836.
A Voyage up the Mediterranean in His Majesty's Ship Swiftsure, etc. by Reverend Cooper Willyams, White, London, 1802.
A Social History of the Navy 1793 - 1815 by Michael Lewis, George Allen and Unwin, London, 1960.

DN 32 Andrew Webb, Able Seaman, HMS Leander, Captain Thomas Boulden Thompson

Description: Jeweller gilt bronze medal engraved *Andrew Webb / Leander* in the reverse field. Weight: 39.1 grams. Very fine, but the medal has suffered from corrosion (salt water?) of some sort.

Background: HMS *Leander*, Captain Thomas Boulden Thompson, was the last ship to join the fight at the Nile. *Leander* was a 50-gun ship, Fourth Rate of the Portland class of 1767, built at Chatham and launched in 1780. She was 146 feet in length overall and 1,044 ton burthen. She mounted 22 x 24 pounders on the Gun Deck, 22 x 12 pounders on the Upper Deck, 4 x 6 pounders on the Quarterdeck and 2 x 6 pounders in the Forecastle. Her normal ship's company would be 350.

So, *Leander* was larger than a frigate, but much smaller and more lightly armed than a Third Rate of 74 guns. Her task, as part of Nelson's squadron, was often to act as a frigate, particularly by chasing down any strange craft in hope for intelligence of the French fleet. As Thompson approached the battle in total darkness, he came upon the stricken *Culloden* which was being assisted by Hardy in the *Mutine*. Thompson sent an officer on board *Culloden* to see if they wished further assistance, the normal offer from a Fourth Rate to a Third Rate in trouble, but Troubridge directed the officer to lose no time in joining the rest of the fleet in action.

Lavery quotes from Captain Berry on board the *Vanguard*, 'Captain Thompson of the *Leander* of 50 guns, with a degree of skill and intrepidity highly honourable to his professional character, advanced towards the enemy line on the outside and most judiciously dropped his anchor athwart [the] hawse of *Le Franklin*, raking her with great success, the shot from *Leander's* broadside which passed that ship all striking *L'Orient*, the flagship of the French commander in chief.' Lavery continues, 'At first the men of the *Orion* were confused, thinking that she [*Leander*], might be an enemy fireship. They hoisted a signal of four horizontal lights, which was returned, confirming the *Leander's* identity. She opened fire on the bows of the *Franklin* but in doing so she masked the more powerful guns of the *Orion*, which was forced to cease firing.'

Unfortunately, the log of *Leander* was lost when she was captured by *le Genéréux* a couple of weeks after the Nile, so we don't know how she fared during the rest of the night. What we do know is that with the dawn, Nelson signalled Thompson to move *Leander* in order to join Miller in the *Theseus*, along with the *Goliath* and *Zealous*, all in an attempt to cut off those French ships which had yet to strike, which included the *Genéréux* and *Guillaume Tell*. During the rest of the morning of the 2nd, all of the remaining French ships were now captured excepting the *Genéréux*, *Guillaume Tell* and two frigates, who made their escape.

Andrew Webb was from Dublin, aged 32 years and an Able Seaman at the time of the battle. He had joined *Leander* on 25 August 1795 at Sheerness and served on her continuously until her capture by the *Genéréux* on 18 August, 1798. The Lloyd's Patriotic Fund list of wounded at the Battle of the Nile, shows that Andrew Webb, AB, was amongst them. We lose sight of him following his capture by the French, but he appears to have returned to the Navy as is evidenced by his receipt of the Davison Nile medal.

Thomas Boulden Thompson (1766?-1828) was an officer who gave everything to the service, only withdrawing from action when his body had been so whittled away by enemy shot, that he could no longer stand on the quarterdeck. He was born at Barham in Kent on 28 February, probably in 1766. His parents were of slender means and unable to afford a proper education for Thomas, however his father, Mr Boulden, had the good fortune to marry Miss Thompson, whose brother was a captain in the Royal Navy, and who took a shine to his newly acquired nephew. It is to Captain Edward Thompson that young Thomas owes his education in the three Rs, and to navigation. In recognition of this support, Thomas took as his surname Thompson in the late 1770s.

Patronage continued with Thomas sailing with his uncle to Gibraltar in 1782 on board HMS *Hyaena* where he was present at the relief of Gibraltar and Rodney's victory over the Spanish off St Vincent, which was followed by Thomas's appointment as lieutenant. In 1783, Captain Thompson was appointed to the *Grampus* to cruise on the West African station where he passed away in late 1785 or early 1786. Command of the *Grampus* passed to another officer, but Lieutenant Thompson was given command of his old ship, HMS *Nautilus*. As Commander, Thompson fulfilled the original orders given to his uncle and cruised for a year on the West Africa station. He then returned to England and came ashore, where he remained until 1790 when he obtained Post rank, but remained unemployed until the autumn of 1796 when he took command of HMS *Leander*.

The *Naval Chronicle* tells us, 'In 1796, the *Leander* was ordered to Portsmouth to be refitted, and remained there till the summer of 1797, when she was directed to proceed to Gibraltar. It was shortly after Captain Thompson's arrival at that Port, that Admiral Earl St Vincent, from a variety of intelligence which he had received, was induced to believe that the town of Santa Cruz, in the island of Tenerife, was an assailable object. ...The command of the squadron which was appointed to this service was accordingly given to Rear-Admiral Nelson, with permission for

Captain Thomas Boulden Thompson

him to choose his officers. Captain Thompson was one of those on whom the Rear-Admiral's selection fell; and, with Captains Troubridge, Hood, Fremantle, Bowen, Miller and Walter, he volunteered his service to land the troops.

'On the evening of 25th July, the squadron anchored a few miles to the northward of Santa Cruz; and by eleven o'clock at night, all the men were in the boats, and rowed toward the shore in six divisions. In their progress some unfortunate accidents happened; and the night being extremely dark, the boats were unable to keep together. The Rear-Admiral, however, and the Captains Thompson and Freemantle, with four or five boats succeeded in landing at the Mole, which they stormed and carried, although defended by four or five hundred men, and half a dozen 24 pounders, which they spiked. But such a heavy fire of musketry and grape shot was kept up from the Citadel, and the houses at the Mole-head, that it was impossible for them to advance; and almost to a man, the whole party was either killed or wounded. Among the latter, was the brave Nelson, who lost his arm, and the Captains Thompson and Fremantle, who were slightly hurt.

'Notwithstanding the failure of this attempt, the merit of the officers employed shone conspicuous, and met with the full approbation of their gallant superior - Rear-Admiral Nelson, in his letter to Earl St Vincent on the occasion, etc.'

To this author, the experience of Santa Cruz fully bound those captains to Nelson, with Troubridge, Fremantle, Hood, Miller and Thompson remaining always available for the next adventure.

Santa Cruz was followed by the victory of the Nile. Although there is a criticism of Thompson's placement of *Leander* by a man on board *Orion*, I can think of no better situation for a lightly gunned ship than to be between the bow and stern of two enemy 74's, and there is little doubt that both enemy ships suffered heavy damage from *Leander*. Again, though excellent placement, *Leander* suffered only fourteen casualties during the action.

With *Leander* in fairly good condition, her frigate role again came forward and she was selected to take Captain Berry with the dispatches of the action to Earl St Vincent at Gibraltar. After transferring 80 men from his ship's company to assist in refitting other ships, Thompson departed the fleet on the 6th of August.

William James tells us what happened next: 'On the 18th, at daybreak, being within five or six miles of the west end of Goza di Candia, the *Leander* discovered in the south-west quarter, standing directly for her, a large sail, evidently a ship of the line; and which, although the *Leander* was becalmed, with bringing up a fine breeze from the southward. [The ship proved to be *le Генéreux* of 80 guns, Captain Lejoille, recently escaped from the Nile.] At 8 a.m. the *Généreux*, still retaining exclusive possession of the breeze approached within random-shot of the *Leander*, then steering under every stitch of canvas she could spread, with the wind on the larboard beam. At 9 a.m. the *Généreux* ranged up, within half gunshot, on the *Leander's* larboard and weather quarter. Finding that an action was inevitable, the *Leander* shortened sail and hauled up until her broadside could be brought to bear. The *Généreux* now fired a shot ahead of the *Leander*, and she later immediately replied to it by a broadside.

'A vigorous cannonade thus commenced on both sides; and the two ships continued nearing each other, keeping up a constant and heavy fire, until 10:30 a.m., when the *Généreux* evinced a disposition to run her opponent on board. Such was the shattered state of the latter's rigging, sails and yards, and so light the breeze, that the *Leander* could make no movement to evade the shock. The French 74, accordingly, struck the British 50 on the larboard bow, and dropping alongside, with a crash that bent double several of the *Leander's* loweredeck ports, continued there for some time.

'A spirited and well directed fire, however, from the *Leander's* remnant of marines, stationed on the poop, and commanded by the sergeant, and from the small-arm men on the quarterdeck, prevented the crew of the *Généréux*, numerous as they were, from taking advantage of the juxtaposition of the ships; and the Frenchmen every time they attempted to board were driven back with loss. Meanwhile such of the great guns of both ships, as would bear, continued in full activity.

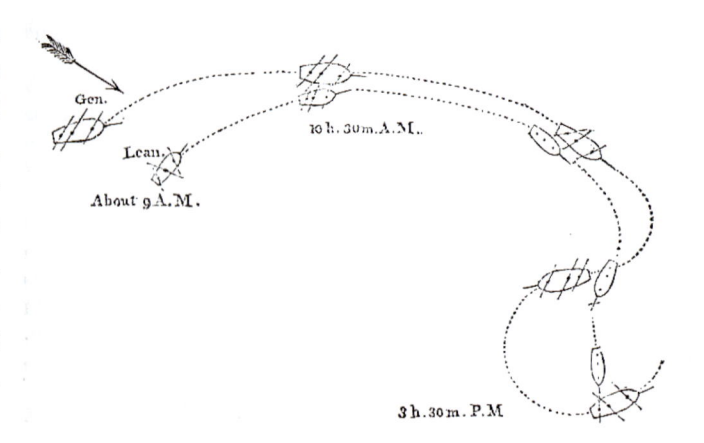

'After an interval of calm, a light air sprang up, still from the southward; and the *Généréux*, being from her lofty sails the first to feel its effects, forged ahead, and disentangled herself from the *Leander*, now lying with her mizenmast over the starboard quarter, her fore topmast over the larboard bow, and both her lower yards on the booms. The *Généréux*, soon afterwards, coming up in the wind on the starboard tack, the *Leander*, who by the aid of her spiritsail had succeeded in wearing, was enabled to luff under the stern of her antagonist. The opportunity was not lost, and the *Leander* deliberately discharged into the *Généréux* every gun upon her starboard broadside, which the wreck of her spars did not cover.

Action between H.M.S. "Leander" and "Le Généreux"

'The breeze again died away, and the sea became as smooth as glass; but no intermission took place in the mutual cannonade: it continued with unabated fury, until 3:30 p.m. By this time the *Généréux* having, by the aid of a light breeze, paid round off upon her heel, stood athwart the hawse of the *Leander*, and stationed herself on the latter's larboard bow. Here, unfortunately, the greater part of the guns, the foremost ones in particular, lay disabled with the wreck of the fallen spars. This gave a check to the *Leander's* firing, and the *Généréux* took the opportunity of hailing, to know if the British ship surrendered.

'The *Leander* was now totally ungovernable, having her lower yards on the booms, and no stick standing, save the bowsprit and the shattered remains of the fore and mizen masts: the ship's hull was also cut to pieces, and her decks were strewed on every side with killed and wounded. The *Généréux*, on the other hand, having lost only her mizen topmast, was gradually passing along the *Leander's* larboard beam, as if intending to take up a position across her stern. In the defenceless state of the British ship, what other reply to the question of surrender could be given, than the affirmative? It was given, by holding out a pike with the French jack on the end of it, and the *Généréux* took possession of her..

'In the six hours' close and bloody conflict, the *Leander* lost three midshipmen, 24 seamen, eight marines killed, her commander [Thompson] badly, in three places, Captain Berry, slightly, by a part of a man's skull which was driven through his arm, [and six other officers plus] 41 seamen and nine marines wounded. Her total loss therefore was 35 killed and 57 wounded, or a third of her gallant crew.'

The French were particularly hard on the officers and men of the *Leander* with all of their effects being plundered, contrary to normal practice. Thompson wasn't able to secure the services of *Leander's* surgeon until 1 September, when at last a musket ball was removed from his arm. It is a minor miracle that he survived the fight. The men were ultimately taken to Corfu and thence to Trieste. During captivity the French tried to lure the British seamen to join their cause which was met with a deaf ear, excepting George Bannister, a 34 year old Able Seaman from London, who responded, 'No, you damned French rascal, give us back our little ship, and we'll fight you again till we sink!'

James notes, 'Where is there a single-ship action which has conferred greater honour upon the conqueror than in this instance lights upon the conquered? Such a defence is unparalleled, even in the British navy, where to be brave is scarcely a merit.' The Admiralty too felt that Captain Thompson's conduct was 'deserving of every praise his country and court can give.' Thompson was awarded a pension of £200 per annum and a knighthood.

In the spring of 1799, Thompson was appointed to the *Bellona*, 74, and attached to the fleet off Brest until March 1801, when he was appointed to Admiral Hyde Parker's fleet destined for Copenhagen, with Nelson commanding a division of Hyde Parker's ships. This was probably Nelson's most difficult battle due to the shallow harbour at Copenhagen where the Danes had carefully arranged their floating batteries and shore guns.

Dudley Pope tells us of the *Bellona* on 2 April 1801. 'The *Bellona* was the next in the British line [to enter Copenhagen harbour]. The *Edgar*, *Ardent* and *Isis* were already in action by the time *Bellona* was under way, such was the short distance involved. Thompson had to follow *Isis*, which was so far ahead and frequently hidden by the drifting smoke that Thompson could not see the exact course she had steered.

'By the time the *Bellona* came within range of the *Provesteenen's* guns, the *Isis* had just anchored by the stern abreast of the *Wagrien*, and Thompson began passing between here and the Middle Ground, as laid down in his orders. Unknown to anyone in Nelson's ships there was a spur jutting out of the natural curve of the Middle Ground almost abreast of the *Provesteenen*; it protruded roughly one hundred yards into the channel and was about seven hundred yards long, with an even smaller spur sticking out a few score yards farther north. A ship coming up from the British anchorage but too close to the Middle Ground would run a mile - to abreast the *Provesteenen* and *Wagrien* - before reaching the main spur and until the last moment would be finding at least seven fathoms with the leadline, which was more than enough.

'And the *Bellona* did just that, she ran past the *Provesteenen* along the edge of the shoal and then touched on the spur. Sir Thomas had been standing up on the fourth quarter deck gun on the larboard side to see the Danish line better. His intended opponents were the tenth, eleventh and twelfth Danish ships, which meant he had to pass to turn the *Isis*, *Edgar*, *Ardent* and *Glatton*, anchoring ahead of Captain Bligh's ship.

'Suddenly Thompson realized [that he had lost headway]. The *Bellona* was aground. There was no shock or thump; she had slid imperceptibly onto soft sand. The *Wagrien* was almost bows on, about eight hundred yards away, in a perfect position for the *Bellona*'s guns to rake her, and from the angle the British ship was lying the *Provesteenen* was almost abeam. At once the *Bellona*'s guns fired.'

Nelson, however, was surprised to see the *Bellona* stop and signalled Thompson to 'Engage the enemy more closely'.

'Before Thompson could do anything - apart from ordering the signal to be acknowledged - he toppled from the gun on which he was standing: a shot had cut off his left leg. As he was carried below to the surgeon waiting amid his pile of instruments in the cockpit, Thompson ordered his First Lieutenant, Delafons, to take command.'

Shortly after, HMS *Russell* came up behind the *Bellona* and became stuck on the same spur of sand with her jib-boom almost over the *Bellona*'s taffrail, and Nelson's *Elephant* not far behind. Here, Nelson was faced with a dilemma, his pilots advised that the water continued to shoal on the inshore side of the Middle Ground and firmly advised that he should go around the outside. Nelson looked at the position of the enemy, and ignored this advice by taking *Elephant* by the inshore route, and in doing so probably averted a complete disaster at Copenhagen. *Bellona* continued to fight during the long day, but she suffered with eleven killed and 72 wounded, mainly caused below decks by 'bursting guns.'

Thompson recovered from the loss of his leg, his pension was increased to £500 and then a year later to £700 per annum. He was given command of the *Mary* yacht and in 1806 made Comptroller on the Navy, an office that he held until 1816, when he was appointed Treasurer of Greenwich Hospital and Director of the Chest. Advancements continued, but he was particularly attached to a farm he had bought near Bushy Park, Hertfordshire. It was here that he died on 3 March 1828.

Provenance: Medal fair, 1975.

References: The National Archives, Kew: ADM 36/12543-12546 & 13037 (*Leander*).
List of the Royal Navy by David Steel, Steel, London, 1802.
The Naval Chronicle, vol 14, Gold, London, 1805.
The Naval History of Great Britain...1793 to 1820 by William James, six vols., Richard Bentley, London, 1837 etc.
The Great Gamble, Nelson at Copenhagen by Dudley Pope, Weidenfeld & Nicolson, London, 1972.
The Sailing Navy List by David Lyon, Conway, London, 1993.

DN33 Presentation from Admiral Lord Nelson to Colonel William Stewart, HMS Elephant at Copenhagen, 2 April 1801

Description: Soho gilt bronze medal with the fields and legends chased. Attached at 12 o'clock is a loop suspension which is identical to the suspension found on the effigy of Admiral Lord Nelson at Westminster Abbey, believed to have been supplied by Lady Hamilton. Attached for wearing is a dark blue silk ribbon 1 cm wide and approximately 35 cms long. There is a small die break running through C. H. K. with a larger break below at the rim. The weight of the medal and ribbon is 40 grams. Extremely fine.

Background: The purchase of this marvellous Davison Nile in 1979 was one of the most exciting events in the long series of purchases of these medals. The Peninsular orders and medals to Sir William Stewart, being offered at Christie's by the 12th Earl of Galloway, were certainly going to fetch a great deal of money and were well beyond my wallet. They made £26,000. What really interested me was lot 171 which was a gilt bronze Davison Nile and also from the family. I had made up my mind to bid up to £100 for the medal, but it went for £140 to Stanley Gibbons, the stamp dealer. Fortunately, this auction was held in the days when the winning bidder's name was called out, so after the sale and checking my references again and hoping that Stanley Gibbons hadn't bought on behalf of a client, I contacted them and happily bought the medal for £175. Obviously, the medal posed a bit of a mystery because Stewart certainly wasn't at the Battle of the Nile, so why would an example of the Davison Nile be amongst his medals?

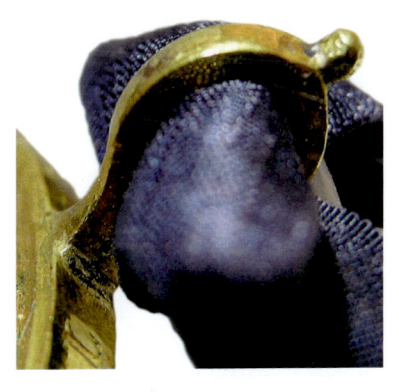

313

To me it had to have been a gift from Nelson to Stewart. At that time, the only reference I had that connected Davison Nile medals as having been made as gifts by Nelson at Copenhagen was the letter written after the battle from Nelson to Captain Hans Sneedorff of the Naval Academy in Copenhagen along with the image of the Davison Nile presented by Nelson, both published in Dudley Pope's *The Great Gamble*. The other medal described by Nelson in his letter was an example of the Ferdinand IV / *Foudroyant* medal also by Boulton and Küchler.

The purchase was a bet on my part as the whole idea of Nelson presenting Davison Nile medals to those he esteemed was pretty much wild speculation in medal collecting circles at that time. When I actually had Stewart's medal in my possession and then made the comparison with the Davison Nile medal worn by the effigy of Nelson in Westminster Abbey, which was thought to have been supplied by Lady Hamilton, and seen that the quite unusual loop suspension was identical with the Stewart medal; that was all that I needed to complete the connection of the medal with both Stewart and Nelson.

The purchase of the Lambert Davison Nile (DN 33) from Peter Dale in 1984 fully fixed the context of Nelson and Davison Nile medals at Copenhagen and Tancred's reference to a similar presentation to his uncle in 1803 further established this type of gesture by Nelson.

Returning to the Westminster Abbey effigy, we have the following from Mayo: 'There is reason to believe that Lord Nelson wore this [Nile] medal as one of his decorations, and a specimen is hung round the neck of the funeral effigy in Westminster Abbey.' Mayo also quotes a letter from Nelson's great-nephew, the then current Earl Nelson, writing from Trafalgar House, Salisbury, May 4, 1890: 'The Nile medal was given by Mr. A. Davison out of the profits made by him by the sale of the prizes taken at the battle of the Nile. I believe my great-uncle always wore it, and I have his medal in a red Russian leather case with a gold ring through the top of it by which it was hung round his neck.'

Nelson's orders and decorations had passed with his other effects to the first Earl Nelson's daughter, Lady Charlotte, upon his death in 1835. Lady Charlotte had married the Honourable Samuel Hood in 1810, who subsequently became Lord Bridport. So, the Nile medal in the possession of the then Earl Nelson in 1890, must have been a separate medal that didn't pass to the Bridports. Whether this medal is gold or gilt bronze we don't know. However, as the gold medal is quite heavy, for regular wearing a gilt bronze medal would be better as the Westminster Abbey effigy demonstrates. There is a real possibility that Colonel Stewart's Davison Nile medal, complete with a ribbon for wearing, had actually been worn by Nelson at Copenhagen, and with the exuberant generosity of Nelson, he may well have simply lifted the medal that he was wearing and gave it to Stewart, knowing he had another in his cabin. Nelson still had Davison Nile medals with him at Trafalgar which is evidenced by the inventory of his effects taken a by Captain Hardy.

Mayo also notes that on 13 July, 1895 Christie's auctioned the property of Lord Bridport which included Nelson's orders and decorations. Before the sale, the Nation stepped in and purchased for £2,500 his awards from the King (naval gold medals for St Vincent, the Nile, and Trafalgar), and his orders. There were two gold Davison Niles offered in the auction which the Nation didn't purchase. Each made 145 guineas, one to Spink and the other to Glendinning's, however, as Rina Prentice notes, one cannot be sure if these were gold or bronze gilt medals. The current whereabouts of these two medals is unknown. That they weren't purchased by the Nation has probably saved them because Nelson's gold medals awarded by the King were all stolen from the Painted Hall in Greenwich on 9 December, 1900 and have almost certainly been melted down for their bullion value.

For an account of General Stewart's life, I don't think one could improve upon that given in the Christie's catalogue by Raymond Sancroft-Baker:: 'Lieutenant General Sir William Stewart was born on January 10, 1774, the second son of the Seventh Earl of Galloway. He received a commission as ensign in the 42nd foot on March 8, 1786, became lieutenant in the 67th foot on October 14, 1787, and captain of an independent company on January 24, 1791. He was wounded in the unsuccessful attempt on Point-a-Pitre on July 2, 1794, when Guadeloupe had been recovered by the French. He returned to England in November and obtained a majority in the 31st foot.

'He was made lieutenant-colonel in the army and assistant adjutant-general to Lord Moira's corps on January 14, 1795, and in June he served on the staff of the expedition to Quiberon. On 1 September he was given command of the 67th foot, and went with it to San Domingo. Returning to Europe he obtained leave to serve with the Austrian and Russian armies in the campaign of 1799 and was present at the battle of Zurich.

'It was probably what he saw of Croats and Tyrolese in this campaign that led him to propose in concert with Colonel Coote Manningham that there should be a corps of riflemen in the British army. The proposal was adopted and an experimental 'corps of riflemen' was formed in January 1800. In August of that year he went with three companies of his rifles to Ferrol in Pulteney's expedition and was badly wounded in the first skirmish. He commanded the troops who served as marines in the fleet sent to the Baltic in 1801. He was on board Nelson's flagship at Copenhagen. Later, Nelson writing to St Vincent described him as 'the rising hope of the army' and there ensued a lasting friendship between them. By Nelson's wish Stewart's son was named Horatio. He was made a colonel on April 2.

Sir William Stewart

'In 1804 he was appointed brigadier of volunteers in the eastern counties, and in 1805 he published *Outlines of a Plan for the general Reform of the British Land Forces*. In December 1806 he took command of a brigade in Sicily, and three months afterwards went on to Egypt with Fraser's expedition. On April 3 he was sent to Rosetta with 2,500 men to avenge Wauchope's repulse. In his first reconnaissance he received a bullet wound in the arm. He laid siege to the town but did not risk an attack. On the 21st the Turks received reinforcements and cut to pieces a detachment of 700 men which he had placed at El Hamed, and had to fight his way back to Alexandria losing 300 more men on the road.

'The expedition returned to Sicily in September and Stewart was commandant of Syracuse until February 1809. He had been promoted major-general on April 25, 1808 and on August 31, 1809 he was made colonel of the 3rd battalion of the corps he had formed, the 95th rifles.

'In 1810 he was sent to the Peninsula to command the British and Portuguese troops which were to form part of the garrison at Cadiz. He was present at Busaco, but could not obtain the medal as he was not 'personally and particularly engaged.' In December, Hill was invalided and Stewart commanded his corps for a while but his self-distrust led Wellington to send Beresford to take Hill's place.

'In 1811, after Massena's retreat, the 2nd division - still forming part of Beresford's corps - shared in the first siege of Badajoz, and bore the brunt of the battle of Albuera. The 1st brigade of it (Colborne's) was nearly destroyed there by a sudden attack of French lancers on its rear as it was advancing to charge the French infantry. According to Napier, this happened because 'Stewart, whose boiling courage generally overlaid his judgement, heedlessly led up in column of companies', without waiting to deploy, as Colborne wished to do. But the charge was made by three deployed battalions (out of four), and, according to Sir Benjamin d'Urban, Beresford's Quarter Master-general, Stewart's fault lay rather in rejecting Colborne's proposal to keep a wing of one regiment in column. There can be no doubt that his impetuosity had something to do with the result; but the urgency of the case and the mist which hid the French cavalry go far to excuse him. Beresford had nothing but praise for him in his dispatch, and he was thanked by Parliament. In July he went home on account of ill-health, and was employed in the eastern district.

'In August 1812 he was again appointed to the army in the Peninsula, with the local rank of lieutenant-general. He joined on December 6 and was given command of the 1st Division. On June 4 he became lieutenant-general. At Vittoria he was on the right under Hill who spoke highly on his conduct. He was included in the thanks of Parliament and was made K.B. on September 11.

'Stewart took part in Hill's action at Buenza on the 30th and the next day he led the attack on the French rearguard at the Don Maria pass. In this attack he was badly wounded, having been already slightly wounded on the 25th. He was present at Nivelle, Nive and Orthes, and had a prominent part in the combat of Aire and also a minor part at Toulouse.

'He was popular with the men of his division, among whom he was known as 'auld grog Willie' on account of the extra allowances of rum which he authorised, and which Wellington made him pay for. For his services in the Peninsula he received the gold cross and two clasps, the Portuguese order of the Tower and Sword, and the Spanish order of San Fernando. On January 2, 1815 (on the enlargement of the order of the Bath) he received the G.C.B.

'Stewart had been M.P. for Saltash in 1795 and for Wigtonshire from 1796 onward, and on June 24, 1814 the speaker thanked him in his place, on behalf of the house, for his share in the victories of Vittoria and Orthes, and in the intermediate operations. He saw no further service. His health was broken by seventeen campaigns, in which he had received six wounds and four contusions, and in 1816 he resigned his seat in Parliament. In July 1818 he was transferred to the colonelcy of the 1st battalion of what had then become the Rifle Brigade. He settled at Cumloden on the borders of Wigton and Kirkcudbrightshire, near the family seat. He died there on January 7, 1827.'

In 1871 was published the *Copenhagen Journal* of Colonel Stewart which was drawn upon when Clark and M'Arthur produced their biography of Nelson. From Stewart's pen we have his observations regarding the recall signal made by Hyde Parker: 'About 10 o'clock [a.m.] the signal 39 (for leaving off action) was reported flying on board the *London*. After a long delay a few of our ships repeated it, but not observing our gallant Admiral, Lord Nelson, take any notice of it, soon hauled it down again. The only signal which he kept, on the contrary, flying, was the first one - for close action; and, with regard, to the other, was so much hurt at its being made that he merely hoisted the answering pennant, and never repeated or made the signal at all. He, on the contrary, at the very time observed that he was determined to give it to them till they should be sick of it, and that if three hours would not do, he would be responsible that four hours of such fire as we were then keeping up would do for them.'

Stewart worked with Nelson to create the treaty document to be agreed by the Danes and it was Stewart who delivered Nelson's dispatch for the battle to the King. His rank of Colonel was immediately confirmed for this service.

Provenance: Christie's, King Street, St. James auction of Orders, Decorations and Campaign Medals, 18 April 1979, Lot 171, part of the family medals of the 7th Earl of Galloway which included Lot 176, the Peninsular War gold medals to Lieutenant-General Sir William Stewart, G.C.B. who was with Lord Nelson at the battle of Copenhagen, 2 April 1801. Lot 171 sold to Stanley Gibbons, purchased from Stanley Gibbons, 19 April 1979.

References: Christie's catalogue for Orders, Decorations and Campaign Medals dated 18 April 1979, cataloguer Raymond Sancroft-Baker.
The Great Gamble, Nelson at Copenhagen by Dudley Pope, Weidenfeld & Nicolson, London, 1972.
Historical Record of MEDALS and Honorary Distinctions etc. by George Tancred, Spink, London, 1891. page 62.
Cumloden Papers containing the *Copenhagen Journal* of Colonel William Stewart, ed ?, published privately (50 copies only), Edinburgh, 1871.
Medals and Decorations of the British Army and Navy by J. H. Mayo, 2 vols. Constable, London, 1897.
The Authentic Nelson by Rina Prentice, National Maritime Museum, London, 2005.

Lord Nelson's flag ship, HMS *Elephant* at Copenhagen, 2 April 1801. Oil painting by Robert Dodd. Shown are the Blue Flag flying at the foremast to denote Nelson's rank as Vice-Admiral. At the main mast are flying Number 16 (yellow red yellow horizontal striped flag with a white and blue diagonally split flag) 'Engage the enemy more closely' which was Nelson's favorite signal. On the foremast and below Nelon's blue flag which denotes his rank as Vice-Admiral, is a flag with a red border and white centre, which is the Dissent Flag which is flown when a signal from a superior officer was not received clearly or to indicate a refusal to action the command. This in response to Hyde Parker's Number 39 'Disengage the Enemy'.
                                  Sim Comfort Collection.

DN 34   Presentation from Admiral Lord Nelson to Captain Robert Stuart Lambert, HMS Saturn at Copenhagen, 2 April 1801

Description: Bronze medal wrapped in contemporary sheet of paper which has inscribed, *Given by Lord Nelson to Capt. Lambert of the Saturn...[not decipherable] Baltic, 1801*. There is a small die break running through C. H. K. with a larger break below at the rim. Weight: 39.2 grams. Extremely fine.

Background: From John Marshall regarding Robert Stuart Lambert, we have:

'This officer is the eldest son of Robert Lambert, Esq., many years a Captain, R.N. He entered the naval service at an early age, and in 1791 was promoted to the rank of Lieutenant by the late Hon. Sir William Cornwallis, in the East Indies. He served as such on board the *Barfleur*, of 98 guns, bearing the flag of Rear-Admiral Bowyer, and commanded by the late Lord Collingwood, in the memorable battle of June 1, 1794, [The *Barfleur* lost 9 killed and 25 wounded with Rear-Admiral Bowyer losing a leg in the action.], after which he was made a Commander, into the *Swift* sloop of war. From that vessel he removed into the *Suffolk*, of 74 guns, as Flag-Captain to the late Admiral Rainier, with whom he served at the reduction of Ceylon, Amboyna, Banda, & etc., in the years 1795 and 1796. His Post commission bears the date April 11th in the latter year.

'Captain Lambert continued to command the *Suffolk*, till June 1798, when ill health compelled him to return to England. His next appointment was to the *Saturn* 74, in which ship he accompanied the expedition sent to the Baltic under Sir Hyde Parker, in 1801. [*Saturn* remained part of Hyde Parker's reserve during the battle. No doubt Nelson and Lambert met at some point, as is evidenced by Nelson's gift of the Davison Nile medal.] On his return from that station, he joined the *Alcmene* frigate, and was employed during the remainder of the war in affording protection to the Halifax, Newfoundland and Lisbon trade.

'Early in 1812, Captain Lambert was appointed to the *Duncan* of 74 guns, from which ship he removed into the *Royal Sovereign*, a first-rate, on the Mediterranean station, where he remained until the termination of hostilities. His advancement to the rank of Rear-Admiral took place August 12, 1819.

'Our officer soon after hoisted his flag in the *Vigo* of 74 guns, as Commander-in-Chief of the squadron employed at St Helena for the secure detention of General Bonaparte. He returned from that station January 1, 1822, and struck his flag on the 3rd of the same month.

'Rear-Admiral Lambert has three brothers now in his Majesty's service; viz, John, a Major-General and K.C.B.; Samuel, a Lieutenant-Colonel in the Grenadier Guards; and George Robert, a Commander R. N. Another, Henry, commanded the *Java* frigate, and was slain in an action with the American ship *Constitution*, at a moment when he had every prospect of obtaining a complete victory over his powerful opponent.'

Provenance: Peter Dale, 23 May 1984.

Peter had purchased from the Lambert family the Lloyd's Patriotic Fund £100 sword awarded to Captain Henry Lambert when commanding HMS *San Fiorenzo* at the capture of the French frigate *La Psyche*, 14 February 1805. Along with the sword were a number of other relics relating to members of the Lambert family who had served in the Royal Navy. Amongst them was this Davison Nile medal presented to Captain Robert Stuart Lambert by Lord Nelson at Copenhagen, 2 April 1801.

References: *Royal Naval Biography* by John Marshall, vol 2, Longman, London 1823.

BATTLE OF TRAFALGAR.

Painted by T. Whitcombe / Engraved by T. Sutherland

Euryalus — Victory — R. Sovereign — Temeraire

BT01   James Aldridge, Able Seaman, HMS Victory, Captain Thomas Hardy, Vice-Admiral, Lord Nelson

Description: Tin, fleet issue, cased and glazed in copper gilt frame. The reverse field engraved *J. Aldridge*. Weight: Medal only 40.5 grams, with case 71.6 grams. Extremely fine with no corrosion.

Background: Although no ship is given on the reverse inscription of this medal, the *Ayshford Trafalgar Roll* contains only one James Aldridge at Trafalgar and he was an Able Seaman on board *Victory*. James Aldridge was prest into the Royal Navy and joined *Victory* on 21 May 1803, aged 21 years. There is little doubt that he was a seasoned sailor as he was rated Able Seaman upon joining, most likely he had served in the merchant marine. His birthplace was Heath, Hampshire and he sent his mother 14 shillings a month to support her. I can only imagine that after he had his Boulton Trafalgar medal engraved, cased and glazed, he sent it to her as well for safe keeping as it has managed to avoid any corrosion one would find from a medal kept at sea. His prize money for Trafalgar came to just over £6 and ten shillings.

Interesting to note that upon being prest, he was first entered on board the cutter *Pigmy* as William Aldridge. Almost certainly a ploy upon his part to create a disguise in the event he managed to Run. However, later in May when he was signed on board *Victory*, he gave his correct name, James Aldridge. He served as an AB for his time on board *Victory*. When she entered Chatham dockyard for much needed repairs at the end of 1805, he was transferred to the *Ocean*, an even more powerful ship than *Victory* at 110 guns. He was again rated AB, but on 25 January 1809, he became Captain of the Main Top, the most senior and prestigious posting of all the topmen on board *Ocean*. As Captain of the Main Top, Aldridge was now a petty officer and responsible for the 60 to 70 men needed to manage the sails of the main mast.

From *Ocean*, he then moved to the *Milford*, Captain Henry Bayntun, and was rated Quarter Gunner, and then later in 1810 he was again rated Captain of the Main Top. He continued his service until August 1814 when he was discharged with the running down of the fleet following the end of the French war. He would have been 32 years old and apparently still in good health. Very possibly he went to sea again in the merchant marine as he was not only an experienced sailor and petty officer, but one of those very impressive seamen who men would instinctively follow at moments of crisis. A real sailorman's man.

The *Victory* as Nelson's flagship led the fleet at Trafalgar. Picture it. The combined fleets of France and Spain spread out in a roughly crescent shape over a distance of a mile. Two attacking columns of British ships, one led by Nelson and the other by Collingwood in the *Royal Sovereign*. The wind was light so the approach toward the enemy was slow which gave the French and Spanish plenty of time to fire broadsides at the attacking British who couldn't return fire. Awful moments while men died and ships took on damage until at last, *Victory* and *Royal Sovereign* broke the enemy line and their supporting ships also closed with the enemy and broke their line again and again.

From this point, the battle became a series of separate fights with perhaps the most severe being between *Victory* as she grappled the larboard side of the French 74-gun *Redoubtable*. The *Temeraire* then came to attack the starboard side of *Redoubtable* which meant that she had two of the most powerful British ships firing into her from each side, but the brave Captain Lucas, who commanded this stubborn French ship, would not stop fighting. At about 1:30 in the afternoon, a sharpshooter from *Redoubtable's* mizzen top fired upon and hit Nelson in the left shoulder with the bullet passing down into his body damaging his lung and breaking his spine. Nelson died a few hours later with the knowledge that the enemy had been crushed.

A battle of this type is unimaginable to us today. The constant crashing of cannon fire, the slaughter of those around you and it just kept going on hour after hour. James Aldridge was there not just as a witness, but as a man who would fight the enemy with cannon and be prepared to alter sails if need be, however for *Victory* after she grappled with *Redoubtable*, the manoeuvring for the day had ceased as battle raged with her single opponent until *Redoubtable* finally struck.

The victory at Trafalgar was greeted with joy and celebration, but also with a deep sorrow by mourning the loss of Lord Nelson, who had saved Britain at sea time and time again.

From Alexander Kent's *Passage to Mutiny*, we have the scene on board the frigate HMS *Tempest* just before she is about to be fired upon by pirate guns hidden ashore as the ship enters a treacherous cove. At the main mast fighting top are three marines and the Captain of the Top, a seaman named Wayth. A marine named Blissett had been sighting his musket toward something strange on the shore:

'The captain of the maintop, legs braced, his back against the massive blocks of the topmast shrouds, asked, 'Wot you dreamin' about, Blissett?' 'The captain of the top, a giant petty officer called Wayth, was very aware of his responsibility, the maze of cordage and spars, the great areas of canvas which he might be ordered to repair or reset at any moment of the day. And he disliked marines intensely without knowing why. .....The rest of his anger was blasted away by a crash of a heavy gun and the immediate shriek of iron as it smashed between *Tempest's* masts. Blissett fell to his knees, ears ringing, the breath pounded from his lungs by the closeness of a massive ball. Dazedly he stared at the length of severed rigging, and then, as he retched helplessly over the barricade, at the pulped remains of the maintop's captain. The ball had cut him completely in half, leaving his stomach against the mast like a pancake.'

Very grippy is Alexander Kent as he weaves a tale of battle at sea!

The incredible intensity of the fight between *Victory*, *Redoubtable* and *Temeraire* so inspired this author that with the combined effort of Malcolm Appleby, probably the finest engraver in Britain, and myself, The *Appleby Trafalgar Medal* was created and published in 2005. The medal won critical acclaim at the Goldsmiths' Company Competition of 2005 by winning the gold award for engraving and silver award for modelling. Examples are still available from Sim Comfort Associates.

Provenance: Sotheby's, Lot 9, 27 June 1985.
References: The National Archives, Kew: ADM 35/1996, 2515, 2974, 2938. ADM 36/16210. 15745. ADM 37/5115.
The Ayshford Complete Trafalgar Roll on cd, privately published, 2004.
England Expects by Dudley Pope, Weidenfeld & Nicolson, London, 1959.
Passage to Mutiny by Alexander Kent, Hutchinson, London, 1976

The Appleby Trafalgar Medal

The medal is based on the profile of Nelson from the A.W. Devis portrait. The obverse depicts *Victory* at Noon, just as she raised the *England Expects* signal. The reverse illustrates the situation at 1:45 pm, Nelson has fallen with *Victory* and *Temeraire* locked in mortal combat with *Redoutable* and her brave Captain Lucas.

Cast in sterling silver by Niagara Casting in Warwich, England, the edition is limited to 500 medals only, priced at £395.00 plus VAT and available from Sim Comfort Associates.

BT02 Midshipman Francis Edward Collingwood, HMS Victory

Description: Tin, fleet issue, silvered and engraved in the reverse field, *F. E. Collingwood / H.M.S. Victory*. Cased in silver and glazed. Medal variety with a clogged right leg of the first R in Trafalgar. Weight: Cased medal 58.8 grams. Exceptional extremely fine with no corrosion.

Background: From Mackenzie's *The Trafalgar Roll*, we have the following: 'Commander F. E. Collingwood was the only son of Francis Collingwood of Greenwich and grandson of Edward Collingwood, Master R. N., [who had sailed with Anson as a Midshipman on his trip around the world.] Born at Milford Pembrokeshire, 1785. Entered service 1799. Borne as A.B., but served as Midshipman of the *Victory* at Trafalgar and with Midshipman J. Pollard, is reputed to have shot the Frenchman who killed Lord Nelson. Lieut. 1806, Lieut. of *Pallas* at the destruction of five French men-of-war in Aix Roads, 1809. Was in the Walcheren Expedition 1809. Lieut. of *Iris* on the north coast of Spain [where he was regularly employed in the boats], and at the capture of three American letters of marque in 1813. Twice wounded in command of the *Kite*, revenue cutter, on the coast of Ireland 1820-23. Commander 1828, Died at Tralee, Ireland 1835, aged 50.'

Further, from Marshall's *Naval Biography* it is noted that following the surrender of *Redoubtable*, Collingwood was sent on board her with a few men to extinguish a fire and help to secure the ship. In December 1820, he obtained the command of the *Kite* revenue cutter employed on the coast of Ireland. During this time he had two ribs and his breast bone fractured, was wounded by a pike through the leg, and received two severe contusions on the head. He was also washed overboard in a heavy gale of wind, and must have perished, all his boasts having been previously lost, had not a following sea thrown him on the square-sail brace, to which he clung until assisted in-board. Francis Edward Collingwood was very plucky and lucky naval officer!

Provenance: 1987 auction of the medal collection of the Royal Norfolk Regiment Museum, Norwich.
References: *The Trafalgar Roll*, by Col. R. H. Mackenzie, George Allen, London, 1913.
Royal Naval Biography by Lieutenant John Marshall, R.N., Longman, London, 1822-1830, (12 vols.)

BT03 Thomas Randall, Able Seaman, HMS Victory

Description: Tin, fleet issue, silvered and engraved in the reverse field *Thos Randel / Victory*. Cased in copper gilt and glazed. Weight: Medal only 40.5 grams, medal and case 62.6 grams. Extremely fine, but with clouding of the design due to the silver wash.

Background: Thomas Randall or Randle or Randel was from Exeter, Devon and prest into the Royal Navy on 7 May 1803 aged 39 years. He was transferred to *Victory* on 11 May and was immediately rated AB, and then on the 20th promoted to Quarter Master. To say he was a prime hand is probably an understatement. To demonstrate your skills as an AB and then to be able to act as helmsman to such a massive ship of war, is something us armchair sailors can only dream of. For some infraction he was demoted back to AB on 10 November and then back to Quarter Master on 24 November 1804, but back to AB on 1 Feb 1805.

Like James Aldridge, who came on board *Victory* at the same time as Randel, they both were transferred to *Ocean* in January 1806. Thomas was again rated as an AB and stayed with her until 17 July 1809 when he transferred to the *Rhin*, which was a French built 44-gun frigate captured by the *Mars* off Rochfort on 28 July 1806. He was again promoted to Quarter Master's Mate on 1 December 1809, but then discharged the service on 7 November 1810. He was then 48 years old, which was a great age to be serving before the mast in those days. He did, however, live quite some time as is evidenced by a memorial to him in Topsham churchyard.

> THOMAS RANDLE
> WHO WAS FOR MANY YEARS
> IN THE ROYAL NAVY
> HAVING SERVED IN SEVERAL SHIPS
> AND AS QUARTER MASTER
> ON BOARD THE VICTORY
> AT THE BATTLE OF TRAFALGAR
> JAN 2ND 1851
> AGED 78

Also like James Aldridge, Thomas sent some of his pay to his mother, who lived in Topsham, what is now a suburb of Exeter. Thomas did receive the Naval General Service medal with Trafalgar clasp, which is rumoured to still be with the family.

Provenance: Private purchase, 1975.
References: The National Archives, Kew: ADM 35/1996, 2515, 2974, 3061. ADM 36/16413. ADM 27/14.

BT04 HMS *Temeraire*, recipient's initials J L or J P, Captain Eliab Harvey

Description: Tin fleet issue cased and glazed in a copper gilt case. The reverse field inscribed with a monogram *J L* or *J P* and below *Temeraire*. Weight: Cased medal 65.2 grams. Very good with extensive corrosion.

Background: *The Fighting Temeraire* was locked to the starboard side of *Redoubtable* as the French ship fought both the *Victory* and *Temeraire*. Within the Ayshford *Trafalgar Roll* there are 13 men with the initials J P and 10 with J L, so there is no room to speculate as to who this medal actually belonged to, however, whoever it was, they were certainly there!

From Mackenzie we have a good account of *Temeraire* at Trafalgar: 'She was the second ship in the weather line, closely following the *Victory* and her share of the action was particularly brilliant. When the *Victory* was engaged with the *Redoubtable*, the *Temeraire* came up to the starboard of the French 74 and also engaged her. This was after Nelson had fallen and the first broadside of the *Temeraire* checked an attempt at boarding the *Victory* which the French were about to make. The fight of the little two-decker against the pair of three-deckers was heroic. The top-men of the *Redoubtable* flung down hand-grenades and fire-balls till they set fire to the deck, larboard forechains, starboard foreshrouds and foresail: one fire-ball rolled into the magazine among the powder barrels, and only the presence of mind of a Master-at-arms saved the *Temeraire* from the fate of the *Orient* at the battle of the Nile.

'In the meantime a new antagonist, the French 80-gun *Fougueux* had come up on the starboard quarter of the *Temeraire* which had been suffering also from the fire of the French *Neptune*. She looked nothing but a cripple and the *Fougueux* came up determined to board her. When less than fifty yards separated the vessels, the starboard broadside of the *Temeraire* crashed into the French ship, sweeping her rigging and upper works bare, leaving her whole side a mass of splinters. She drove into the *Temeraire*, was lashed fast and twenty-eight men under Lieut. T. F. Kennedy sprang on to her deck - where the gallant French captain lay mortally wounded - and fought their way to the stump of the mainmast. In ten minutes they had British colours hoisted and the *Fougueux* was a prize to the *Temeraire*, which had also the *Victory's* prize, the *Redoutable*, lashed to her. Her losses amounted to 121 killed and wounded.'

Provenance: Private purchase, 1981.
References: *The Ayshford Complete Trafalgar Roll* on cd, privately published, 2004.
The Trafalgar Roll, by Col. R. H. Mackenzie, George Allen, London, 1913.

BT05 Philip Browne, Able Seaman, HMS Neptune, Captain Thomas Fremantle

Description: Tin fleet issue cased and glazed in a silver watch style case. The glass lunettes have long since been broken and lost.

The obverse fields are engraved HMS NEPTUNE and the reverse PHILIP BROWNE. Weight: Cased medal 46.7 grams. Very Fine with patchy light corrosion, but still original colour in places.

Background: From Mackenzie we have: 'The *Neptune* [98 guns] was the third ship in the weather column. She got into action about 1:45 p.m., when she hauled up for the nearest of the enemy's ships and passing immediately under the stern of the French *Bucentaure*, delivered her broadside into it with terrible effect. She then continued under the stern and along the starboard side of the Spanish *Santisima Trinidad* and luffed up to leeward of the huge four-decker, which had already suffered badly and which she fought until the Spaniard became wholly unmanageable. The *Neptune* was afterwards somewhat severely handled after they bore up. She lost 44 killed and wounded in the battle. Her masts and standing and running rigging were all more or less damaged and she had nine shots between wind and water.'

Philip Brown was from London and had found himself in Liverpool when the press gang from HMS *Princess* got him. He was 20 years old when transferred to the *Neptune* on 20 October 1803. There is no doubt he had experience of the sea as he was rated Ordinary Seaman when prest, however when he transferred to *Neptune*, he was not considered that skilled and was enrolled as a Landsman. The option all prest men had was to fight the system and live a miserable life in the King's service, or adapt and learn and hopefully advance. This is what Philip Browne did, although it took some time. He remained Landsdman while on board *Neptune*, but on 7 December 1806, he was transferred to the *Dreadnought* where in February 1808 he was promoted to Ordinary Seaman and then in February 1810 to Able Seaman.

He then served on board the *Latona*, the *Namur* and lastly the *Gloucester* where he was discharged as Unserviceable on 9 December 1813, aged 30. A hard time, one doesn't know if he was injured or wounded, and whether or not he was able to gain employment again with the merchant marine or ashore.

Provenance: Private purchase, 1990.
References: The National Archives, Kew: ADM 35/1187, 1188, 2345, 2191, 2715 - 2718, 3477. ADM 36/16433, 15573.
The Ayshford Complete Trafalgar Roll on cd, privately published, 2004.
The Trafalgar Roll, by Col. R. H. Mackenzie, George Allen, London, 1913.

BT06 Captain Henry Bayntun, HMS Leviathan

Description: Silver presentation medal with sliding silver suspension. The medal came in an envelope inscribed, *The silver medal for the Battle of Trafalgar presented to my Grandfather Henry William Bayntun Captain HMS Leviathan 74. Richard William Bayntun, Hereford 1906, Jany 29*. The inscription is now faded to a point of being largely unreadable. Weight: 62.0 grams with suspension. Very fine with light scratches. The lump at 11 o'clock on the reverse die is largely worn away, but still discernible under magnification.

Background: From Colin White's *The Trafalgar Captains* we have:

'Although Henry Bayntun was one of Sir John Jervis's pupils, his professional relationship with Nelson did not begin until 1804 when Bayntun, in the *Leviathan*, joined the Mediterranean squadron off Toulon. The *Leviathan* was also under Nelson's orders for the chase of the combined squadron of France and Spain to the West Indies and again at the Battle of Trafalgar.

'Bayntun's father was a diplomat stationed as Counsul-General at Algiers, and it was there that Henry was born in 1766. He entered the Royal Navy at an early age and gained his lieutenancy in 1783. In 1794, Bayntun was with Sir John Jervis in the West Indies and was involved in the capture of Martinique and gained command of the *Avenger* (16) following the death of her captain. With her boats, Bayntun took part in the boarding and capture of the French frigate *Bienvenue* (32) and other shipping in Port Royal Bay on 17 March 1794. This action was followed by the capture of Guadeloupe in the next month which resulted in his being promoted commander and then captain over the next few months.

Sir Henry Bayntun and his wife Sophia Mayhew by George Engleheart, 1810. Sim Comfort collection

'Bayntun then commanded the *Reunion* (36), which was unfortunately wrecked in December 1796. There followed appointments to the *Quebec*, frigate, *Thunderer* (74) and *Cumberland* (74). During this time, Bayntun stayed primarily in the West Indies. With the recommencement of the war in 1803, and in command of the *Cumberland*, Captain Bayntun captured on 30 June the French frigate *Creole* (40) with troops on board and a number of other vessels.

'After ten years spent mainly in the West Indies, Bayntun returned to Britain, took command in 1804 of the *Leviathan* (74) and joined Nelson in the Mediterranean. In the summer of 1805, he returned briefly to the West Indies during the chase of the Combined Squadron.

'At Trafalgar, the *Leviathan* was the fourth ship in Nelson's line, following in the wakes of the *Temeraire* and *Neptune*. Both the *Leviathan* and Fremantle's *Neptune* then passed under the stern of the *Bucentaure*, the *Neptune* moved into position to engage the *Santissima Trinidad*, while Bayntun conned the *Leviathan* toward the French *Neptune* (80), which had been giving Harvey's *Temeraire* much trouble, while Harvey tried to support *Victory* by engaging the *Redoutable*. The *Neptune* decided not to engage the *Leviathan* and fell off to leeward, so Bayntun turned his attentions toward the *Santissima Trinidad*.

'At 2:30pm, Bayntun saw Dumanoir's squadron of five ships bearing down on the *Victory*, so he disengaged from the *Santissima Trinidad* and, in company with a number of British ships recently arrived, set course for the French squadron. At about the same time, from the deck of the *Victory*, Hardy saw Dumanoir's squadron approaching and signalled the nearby British ships to come to the wind on the starboard tack and block the enemy. The *Leviathan* led this group and found herself on course to attack the Spanish *San Augustin* (74). She then turned out of the line and took position alongside the *San Augustin*, exchanging broadsides at very close quarters. Bayntun then grappled the Spanish ship, called for boarders and they carried her without much resistance. Unfortunately, the *San Augustin* was one of the prizes burnt during the great storm that followed the battle.

'Following Trafalgar, Bayntun took part in Nelson's funeral, carrying the 'guidon' in the splendid procession. He received the naval small gold medal and a sword from the Lloyd's Patriotic Fund. In 1807, he took part in the expedition to Buenos Ayres and in 1811, commanded the royal yacht *Royal Sovereign*. He advanced through the Navy List, reaching the rank of admiral in 1837 and, was made KCB in 1815, advanced to GCB in 1839. He died at Bath on 16 December 1840.'

Provenance: Private Purchase, 1983.
References: *The Trafalgar Captains*, edited by Dr Colin White, Chatham, 2005.

BT07 William Fullerton, Able Seaman, HMS Leviathan, Captain H. Bayntun

Description: Tin, fleet issue, inscribed in the reverse field, *William Fullertone / Leviathan*. The medal is fitted in a silver glazed case with loop suspension. The glass lunettes have long ago been broken and lost. Weight: 48.9 grams with silver mount. Fine with even corrosion overall.

Background: William Fullerton was a seaman from Cambeltown on the Kintyre peninsula in the west of Scotland. A hard and rugged land surrounded by difficult seas. He had been in the merchant marine when captured by the French in the early 1790s. Exchanged from a French prison, he joined the Royal

Navy as a volunteer and received a bounty of £2/10/-, however this author thinks that after the French had interrupted his life and put him in prison, he would have probably joined the RN just to get even!

On 31 July 1797, Fullerton was entered on the books of the *Leviathan* aged 28 years. He was initially rated as an Ordinary Seaman and then after Trafalgar, advanced to Able Seaman. He remained with *Leviathan* until the end of 1805 when she was taken into dock for a much needed refit following Trafalgar. Fullerton was transferred to *Formidable*, but then transferred to Plymouth hospital on the 1st of February 1806, suffering from breathing difficulties. Five years later he again was sent to hospital, this time to Haslar at Portsmouth and following examination, was discharged the service on 14 February 1811 as being unserviceable.

Here's a prime seaman who served for over thirteen years and appears to have been pretty well worn out when discharged. This was so often the case, but at least he was still alive after such a long time at sea.

Provenance: Private purchase, 1980.
References: The National Archives, Kew: ADM 35/959, 2246, 2789-2790. ADM 36/12429, 14750-14757, 15832-15837, 16572-16573. ADM 37/506-510, 2088-2089. ADM 102/294.

BT08 James Dennison, Able Seaman, HMS Leviathan, Captain H. Bayntun

Description: Tin, fleet issue, inscribed in the reverse field, *James Dennison* in script. The medal appears to have been fitted in a silver glazed case, which is now gone probably to melt down the silver for value. The engraving of both this medal and William Fullerton's medal are in the same hand which looks to be by a jeweller. Two Able Seamen having their medals preserved in the same way leads me to think they probably were friends on board *Leviathan*. Weight: 41.2 grams. Fine with even corrosion overall.

Background: From the report on James Dennison written by Gillian Hughes who researched this man: 'It would appear that James Dennison was an experienced seaman, probably from the merchant service, who volunteered to join *Leviathan* at Berbice in September 1800. [Berbice is located in Guyana and was a Dutch colony until captured by the British in 1797, returned to the Dutch in 1801 with the Peace of Amiens]. He was 22 years old and from Galloway and rated Able Seaman. [Galloway is in the south west of Scotland and I can imagine that both Fullerton and Dennison spoke Gaelic and shared their Scottish times together.] The ship was at that time Rear Admiral Duckworth's flagship in the West Indies until 1803 when she left Duckworth's command and returned to Spithead. She then sailed to the Mediterranean and after Trafalgar returned to England. Dennison transferred to *Formidable* [as did Fullerton], Captain Fayerman at the end of 1805. He was promoted Quarter Gunner in July 1806, then Quarter Master in January 1807, but then demoted to Quarter Master's Mate in July 1808. The ship was stationed in the Mediterranean returning to England at the end of 1810. Dennison was discharged seemingly to the *Namur* in May 1811.

'However, this was a rather complex part of Dennison's service, mostly due to missing muster lists for the end of his service in *Formidable*. It transpired that he was actually discharged to *Queen Charlotte*, from then to Plymouth Hospital, suffering from rheumatism. Four weeks later and as a supernumerary via first on board the *Prince Frederick* [hospital ship] and then the *Salvador del Mundo*, he eventually joined the 38-gun frigate *Diana*, Captain Ferris in October 1811. Six months later he was discharged, seemingly not well, though appears again as a supernumerary on the *Salvador del Mundo* before entering [the French built 42-gun frigate] *Niemen*, Captain Pym in May 1812.

'He was first rated Master at Arms and a few days later as Quarter Master. The ship first went to the Cape of Good Hope and after her return sailed for Bermuda, Halifax, Jamaica and took a large number of American vessels. It would seem that Dennison was sent in one of the prizes during June 1814. *Niemen* returned to England and was paid off on 6 May, 1815, which presumably was the end of his service in the Royal Navy.'

Again we have a prime seaman who joined the RN at age 22 and served fifteen years, leaving the service in fairly good health. Very strong men they were.

Provenance: Private purchase, 1997.
References: The National Archives, Kew: ADM 35/958-959, 2246, 2789-2790, 2946, 2743, 3643. ADM 36/ 14753-14757, 15832-15837, 16572-16573. ADM 37/506-510, 2088-2089, 3550, 3628-3629, 4359, 5375.

BT09 Richard Simmins [Symonds], Able Seaman, HMS Conqueror, Captain Israel Pellew

Description: Tin, fleet issue, inscribed in the reverse field, *Richard Simmins, Conqueror* in script. Holed for suspension. Weight: 43 grams. Very fine with even corrosion, but also some original colour.

Background: *Conqueror* was a 74-gun third rate line of battleship. From Mackenzie we have: 'At Trafalgar she was the fifth ship in the weather column, following immediately after the *Victory*, *Temeraire*, *Neptune* and *Leviathan* and completing in part the work which they had well begun. She engaged the French flagship *Bucentaure* and the Spanish four decker *Santissima Trinidad*. She shot away the former's main and mizen-masts by the board, her fore-mast in a few minutes sharing the same fate; when, after a loss of over four hundred killed and wounded, a white handkerchief was waved from her in token of submission and Captain Atcherley, Royal Marines, and a party from the *Conqueror* was sent on board the *Bucentaure*. There they received the swords of the French Commander-in-Chief, Villeneuve, and the senior military officer, General Contamin.

'The *Conqueror*, with the *Neptune*, then turned her attention to the *Santissima Trinidad*, whose main, mizen and fore-masts were soon shot away, and she also struck to the two Britishers, which were immediately borne down upon by five of the enemy's ships until other British ships came to their assistance.

'While the remainder of the combined fleet were making their escape to Cadiz, the *Conqueror* hauled across the course of one of them which had only her foresail set. Her brave captain stood upon the poop holding the lower corner of a small French jack while he pinned the upper corner with his sword to the stump of the mizen-mast. She fired two or three guns, probably to provoke a return and so perhaps spare the discredit of a tame surrender. The *Conqueror's* broadside was ready, but Captain Pellew, unwilling to injure the brave French officer, fired a single shot across her bow. The captain lowered the flag, took off his hat, and bowed his surrender.

'The *Conqueror's* losses in the battle amounted to twelve killed and wounded including four officers. [She suffered much amongst her masts and rigging]. One of the enemy's shot also cut away the head of the figure at the ship's bow, and the crew through the first lieutenant, asked permission to have it replaced by one of Lord Nelson. The request was granted and when the *Conqueror* arrived at Plymouth after towing the *Africa* to Gibraltar, a figure of the hero, remarkable for the correct likeness and superior workmanship, and which the crew ornamented at their own expense, was placed at her bow.'

This account shows how very skilled Israel Pellew was as a captain. One might remember that it was his focused gunnery that shot away the helm and mizen-mast of the *Cleopatre* when she fought the *Nymph*, then under the command of Pellew's brother Edward in 1793. Viewing results of individual ships at Trafalgar, it is common practice to look at the ships with the highest casualties as the most engaged. Not so! Pellew accounted for three enemy ships including the French commander-in-chief, and preserved the lives of his men through skilful placement of his ship and devastating gunnery.

Richard Simmins or Symonds as he is found in the ship's pay books, has a sad story. He was a young man from Eastdown in Devon who volunteered for the Royal Navy aged 21 in July, 1804. He was rated Landsman on board *Conqueror* and served his station well for the next eight years before being transferred to the *Barham* in February, 1812. *Barham* was a newly built 74-gun ship cruising in the West Indies. Symonds had excelled at his new profession with the Royal Navy. Although he was always rated as a Landsman when on board *Conqueror*, he was immediately rated as Able Seaman on board *Barham*. Then disaster struck when on the 25 of March, 1814 in Port Royal Harbour, Jamaica, Richard Symonds fell overboard and drowned. At least that is what the log reveals. More likely the many sharks in the harbour who enjoyed the offal thrown overboard from the ships, quickly reacted to the large splash and from there, all one would see is a swirl of grey fins and the water turn blood red. Not even time to get a boat into the water. I think Richard Symonds should have kept out of the tops and stayed a Landsman, much safer. His pay was allotted to his father back in Devon, small compensation for the loss of a loved son.

Provenance: Private purchase, 1980.
References: The National Archives, Kew: ADM 35/ 2149 -2150, 2657, 3314-3315. ADM 37/ 3307, 3901-3902.
The Trafalgar Roll, by Col. R. H. Mackenzie, George Allen, London, 1913.

BT10 John Blane, Able Seaman, HMS Conqueror, Captain Israel Pellew

Description: Tin, fleet issue, inscribed in the reverse field, *Jn Blane, Conqueror* in script. Weight: 40.9 grams. Very fine with even corrosion, but also some original colour.

Background: Both John Blane and Richard Symonds entered the Royal Navy on the same day, 23 July 1804 and came on board *Conqueror* on the same day. Symonds was a volunteer and Blane was Prest. Blane was 22 years old and came from the small seaport of Workington in Cumbria, just south of the Scottish Borders on the west coast of England.

He had experience at sea and was immediately rated Ordinary Seaman and then advanced to Able Seaman on 1 August 1806. On 22 February 1808, at sea in either the Bay of Biscay or off the coast of Portugal, John Blane slipped and fell into the sea. One can imagine the weather in February and with the sea running with a stiff wind, there was no chance for the ship to stop and rescue him, so DD for Discharged Dead was entered into the ship's pay book by his name. 'Drowned at Sea', is all of the additional information provided. Life for a topman was risky to say the least.

Provenance: Private purchase, 1988.
References: The National Archives, Kew: ADM 35/ 2149 -2150.

BT11 Thomas Leigh, Midshipman, HMS Conqueror, Captain Israel Pellew

Description: Tin, fleet issue, originally cased in gold and glazed, but the lunettes have disappeared long ago. Inscribed in the reverse field, *Thomas Leigh, Midshipman, HMS Conqueror* in script. Weight: 45 grams without the ribbon. Fine with some corrosion.

Background: From Mackenzie we have: 'Commander Thomas Leigh [was from Dartmouth] and entered the service as a volunteer in 1803. Rated as Ordinary Seaman [which was common practice when there were more Midshipmen on board than the allowed number], but served as Midshipman in the *Conqueror* in the pursuit of the combined fleets to the West Indies and back and at Trafalgar, 1805. Master's Mate in the *Pilot* in the action with gunboats, and the capture and destruction of a number of transports at Amanthea, 1810, when he was mentioned in dispatches. Lieutenant in 1814. Served in the Coastguard 1827-1835. During this period, Leigh was personally involved in several rescues at sea and received the Gold Medal and the Gold Boat from the Royal National Institution for the Preservation of Life from Shipwreck, which later became the Royal National Lifeboat Institution. An example of his bravery is found in his letter to the Secretary of the Royal Humane Society dated 26 December 1830. On Christmas Day, Leigh hastened waist deep in snow to get assistance to a brig whose hull was under water on a dangerous shoal located on the Norfolk coast near Winterton. After several attempts get a boat to the wreck, Leigh finally succeeded only to find 'the Master suspended from the main shrouds by his heels, a corpse..' Leigh managed to get the nearly frozen remainder of the crew into his boat and after a perilous return to shore with waves constantly breaking over them, managed to get everybody to a warm dry place. Leigh was promoted to Commander in 1835 and died in 1846.

Provenance: Spink auction, 16 July 1996, part lot 401, which was mainly a life saving group of medals. The Boulton Trafalgar medal was then bought privately from the group.

References: *The Ayshford Complete Trafalgar Roll* on cd, privately published, 2004.
The Trafalgar Roll, by Col. R. H. Mackenzie, George Allen, London, 1913.

BT12   Abraham Collier, Private Royal Marine, HMS Conqueror, Captain Israel Pellew

Description: Tin, fleet issue, inscribed in the reverse field, H. M. S. CONQUEROR *Abraham Collier*, in capital letters and script. Weight: 59.2 grams. The obverse is extremely fine while the reverse is fine with even corrosion overall. The medal had been cased in copper gilt and glazed, however the reverse lunette has been broken and lost long ago.

Background: Abraham Collier joined the Royal Marines on 24 February 1801, Plymouth Division. As a Private, 2nd Class Marine he joined *Conqueror* on 26 March 1803 and stayed with the ship until 26 February 1812, when she was paid off at Chatham. He remained in the Marines until 22 July 1814, and was discharged due to 'debility'.

The above doesn't tell us a great deal, however just looking at this length of continuous service and with the knowledge that *Conqueror* was a very active 74-gun ship, it is a very commendable record of service.

Provenance: Private purchase, 1993.

References: The National Archives, Kew: ADM 35/440, 2149-2150, 2657. ADM 158/214.

BT13 Thomas Curphy, Quarter Gunner, HMS Britannia, Captain Charles Bullen, flagship Rear-Admiral William, Earl of Northesk

Description: Tin, fleet issue, inscribed in the reverse field, *Tho Curphy Britannia* in script. This medal is the variety with the clogged foot on the first R in Trafalgar. Weight: 60.1 grams. The obverse is very worn, poor condition while the reverse is extremely fine. The medal had been cased and glazed in copper gilt. The obverse lunette has been lost which resulted in the extreme wear to that side of the medal.

Background: *Britannia*, another 100-gun three decker, followed *Conqueror* through the gap made by *Victory*. She fired broadsides at *Bucentaure* and *Santissama Trinidad*. Lieutenant Halloran wrote that the *Britannia* 'shattered the rich display of sculpture, figures, ornaments and inscriptions with which she was adorned. I never saw so beautiful a ship.'

There was little doubt of friction between Admiral Northesk and his flag Captain Charles Bullen. Bullen wished to bring *Britannia* more into the battle and Northesk wished to remain as support in case of need. In the end, Northesk had his way, but not before *Britannia's* powerful broadsides made herself felt during the battle. *Britannia* lost 50 men killed and wounded.

Thomas Curphy or Carphy, as he is recorded in the pay books, had an extraordinarily long career in the Royal Navy. He was born on the Isle of Man and it is noted that his name in Manx is spelled Curphy, however he had to suffer admiralty bureaucracy during his whole career with his name spelled Carphy. There is a mention in the *Manx Worthies* by A.W. Moor published in 1931, page 141, that Thomas Curphey was born in 1778, died in 1854 and had served in the Royal Navy, retiring a Boatswain and who had been present at Trafalgar in *Britannia*. He died aged 76 and had applied for and received the Naval General Service medal with Trafalgar clasp in 1848, and I can bet that his name is misspelled on that medal too! Only this engraved Boulton Trafalgar medal has his name in its correct form.

338

Above and right:
Earl Northesk's hanger that he wore at Trafalgar.

Left and below:
Silhouette of Captain Charles Bullen and his Lloyd's Patriotic Fund Trafalgar sword.

Sim Comfort collection.

There's no doubt that Curphy was a very skilled seaman who was also literate. He volunteered 21 September 1803 at Deal, Kent, aged 24 years old and very possibly served in the East Indiaman *Lord Nelson*. It was common practice to secure seamen from EIC ships as they returned from their 18 months voyage to the Orient and back. Hard on the seaman who really just wanted to visit with their families after such a long voyage, but the needs of the service prevailed.

On the 1st of October, he appeared on board *Britannia* and was immediately rated as Able Seaman, then on 1 February 1804 advanced to Quarter Gunner. One can see that on several occasions Thomas Curphy was lent to other ships, which is a strong indication that he was well versed in sorting out rigging and sails which was evidenced at his next ship *Royal George* where he was Yeoman of the Sheets, e.g. the man responsible for all of the ropes stored on board the ship.

On 24 June 1811 he passed his examination as Bo'sun at Plymouth. A tough examination with a Captain, Master and two Bo'suns as part of the reviewing board. As it should be because the Bo'sun was one of the key afterguard posts for any ship. The man who made sure all the masts, sails, anchors and rigging were as they should be so the line officers could make the best use of this powerful weapon of war.

Having served on several large line of battle ships, Curphy shipped on board the sloop *Elk* which made a trip to the East Indies in 1814 to 1816, following which the *Elk* went into ordinary, i.e. stripped of her upper masts and at anchor awaiting further service. However being the Bo'sun, Curphy remained on board to look after the ship until December, 1820. He then shipped as Bo'sun on the sloop *Lee* and remained in her until the end of 1821.

In March 1822, he transferred to the sloop *Cyrene* and cruised off the western coast of Africa fighting the slave trade. Very hard duty with sickness taking a toll on board as well as members of the ship's company being used to man captured slaver prizes. *Cyrene* returned to Portsmouth in 1824 and then cruised the eastern Mediterranean fighting pirates. Never boring in the Royal Navy!

He was discharged from the *Cyrene* at the end of 1825 at Woolwich, but then looked after ships being built and in ordinary at Portsmouth until 9 July 1831 when he was pensioned off due to Age and Infirmity after 29 years service. He was 53 years old and had spent near his whole mature life at sea.

Provenance: Private purchase, 1991. I'll never forget finding this medal on a dealer's table at a Britannia medal fair. The medal with the very worn obverse side looked very neglected, but I picked it up, turned it over and 'Oh my Goodness', the reverse side was just sensational! £50 was all it cost, however, the research by Gillian Hughes cost another £270 and worth every penny.

References: The National Archives, Kew: ADM 35/2140, 2404, 3057, 3083, 2587, 3258, 3728, 3451. ADM 36/15496, 16774, 15970, 15992-15997. ADM 37/556-562, 2204-2205, 2773, 2488-2489, 3512, 3127, 3854, 5546-5548, 6238, 6641-6643, 7404. ADM 27/14. ADM 6/122. PGM 16/1.ADM 35/ 440, 2149-2150, 2657. ADM 158/214.
England Expects by Dudley Pope, Weidenfeld & Nicolson, London, 1959.

BT14 James Boon, Captain of the Mast, HMS Africa, Captain Henry Digby

Description: Tin, fleet issue, inscribed in the reverse field, *James Boon, Africa* in script. Weight: 40.8 grams. Both the obverse and reverse are very fine with even corrosion overall.

Background: The *Africa* was a 64-gun ship built on the Thames in 1781. From Mackenzie: 'She was with Nelson watching Cadiz in 1805, and under Captain Henry Digby bore a conspicuous part in the battle of Trafalgar. She appears to have lost sight of the fleet in the course of the night before the battle and when the firing began was broad on the *Victory's* port beam and nearly also broad on the port beam of the leading ship of the enemy van. Nelson signalled to her to make all possible sail; but Digby seems to have misunderstood the order - which was intended to keep him out of danger - as meaning that he was to lose no time in closing with the enemy. He therefore, made the best of his way along the Franco-Spanish van exchanging broadsides with it and at length bore down ahead of the Spanish 140, *Santissima Trinidad*. Judging from her appearance that she had surrendered, Digby sent his first lieutenant to take possession of her. This officer reached her quarter-deck where he learned that the Spaniard had not surrendered and as he was not in a position to coerce her, he withdrew. No one, strange to say, made an effort to stop him.

'The *Africa* then at about 3:20 p.m., very gallantly brought to action the French 74 *Intrepid* and for about forty minutes fought her steadily, until the arrival of the British *Orion* upon the Frenchman's starboard quarter relieved her before she was silenced. The *Africa* had received terrible injury to mast and rigging and several shots between wind and water. Her losses in killed and wounded amounted to 62, including several officers.'

James Boon was another skilled seaman. He volunteered to join the Royal Navy just before Trafalgar on 3 September 1805 and was immediately rated Ordinary Seaman. He was 38 years old, and would have looked old indeed for the start of an adventure such as this. He appears to have been very well received and perhaps because of his mature age on 1 December 1806 was promoted to Captain of the Mast, a petty officer and the most senior topman on board the ship. He continued in this post until *Africa* was paid off at Portsmouth on 20 March 1813.

Provenance: Private purchase, 1993.
References: The National Archives, Kew: ADM 35/2102, 2563, 3257, 3480. ADM 37/99-103, 2000-2002, 2709-2710, 3300-3302, 3702, 3781. ADM 27/10.
The Trafalgar Roll, by Col. R. H. Mackenzie, George Allen, London, 1913.

BT15 James St Quintin, Volunteer 1st Class, HMS Agamemnon, Captain Sir Edward Berry

Description: Tin, fleet issue, cased in silver and glazed. Inscribed around the rim in script: *James St. Quintin H M S Agamemnon, Sir Edward Berry Capt.* Weight: 51.1 grams. Very fine with the obverse suffering from corrosion while the reverse is better with much original colour.

Background: From Mackenzie we learn that on the 13th of October, *Agamemnon* joined Lord Nelson, after having taken an active part in stopping the combined enemy fleet on 22nd July as they tried to enter the Channel during Sir Robert Calder's action. This battle decided for Napoleon that the invasion of Britain was not to be. During the pursuit of the enemy before Trafalgar, Berry nearly fell into their hands. On the morning of the 20th with a heavy French brig as prize in tow, she was unconsciously running into the midst of the enemy's ships, but eventually got clear. In the weather column, *Agamemnon* was a good deal engaged with Dumanoir's division. Her losses amounted to ten killed and wounded.

Commander James St. Quintin was born in Norwich in 1791 and entered the service as a Volunteer 1st Class in 1805. He served as Orderly Officer to his captain, Sir Edward Berry in the battle of Trafalgar, promoted Midshipman and was also in the battle of San Domingo, 1806 and in the expedition to Copenhagen in 1807. He was in the *Agamemnon* when she was wrecked at the mouth of the River Plate in 1809. St. Quintin commanded the barge of the *Barfleur* in an attack on the batteries at Cassio, 1813. He made Lieutenant in 1814, became a retired Commander in 1856 and died in 1865. He received the NGS with clasps for Trafalgar and San Domingo.

Both this Boulton Trafalgar medal and the next belonged to young gentlemen immediately under the command of Sir Edward Berry on board *Agamemnon*. As each medal is cased in silver and glazed in near identical form, and as each are engraved around the rim with nearly the same inscription which includes Berry's name, one wonders if it was Captain Berry who arranged for these two medals to be fitted in this manner? Could be, Berry was a generous man. Here again we have an example of medals belonging to junior officers, instead of their intended recipients in the lower deck.

Provenance: Private purchase, 1981.
References: *The Trafalgar Roll*, by Col. R. H. Mackenzie, George Allen, London, 1913.

BT16 Charles A. Johnston, Midshipman, HMS Agamemnon, Captain Sir Edward Berry

Description: Tin, fleet issue with the blocked leg in the first R in TRAFALGAR. The medal is cased in silver and glazed. Inscribed around the rim in block letters: C. A. JOHNSTON, Md, M. S. AGAMEMNON, Sr E. BERRY, BARt. Weight: 49.7 grams. Very Fine overall with light corrosion to the obverse and with the reverse having some bad patches of corrosion.

Background: Captain C. A. Johnston was the son of Lieutenant Charles Johnston, R.N. who died in 1804. He was born in Portsmouth and entered the service as a Volunteer 2nd Class in 1803. Johnston was promoted to Midshipman in 1805 and served as such in the *Agamemnon* at Trafalgar. He also was present at San Domingo in 1806, the capture of the *Lutine* in 1807 and the expedition to Copenhagen in the same year. He was on board *Agamemnon* when she was wrecked in 1809. Promoted to Lieutenant and part of the Coast Blockade 1825-31, then the Coastguard 1831-44. Promoted to Commander in 1844, retired Captain in 1860 and died the next year. He received the NGS with clasps for Trafalgar and San Domingo.

Provenance: Private purchase, 1981.
References: *The Trafalgar Roll*, by Col. R. H. Mackenzie, George Allen, London, 1913.

Silver tankard presented to Captain Berry by his officers following Trafalgar.   Private collection.

BT17 Richard Gurward, HMS Minotaur, Captain John Moore Mansfield

Description: Tin, fleet issue, cased in silver and glazed. Inscribed in the reverse field *Richard Gurward, Minotaur* in script. Weight: 53.1 grams. Nearly extremely fine with the obverse being free of corrosion while the reverse has a large lump of corrosion which partially obscures the engraved naming of the medal.

Background: *Minotaur* was a 74-gun ship and during the battle of Trafalgar, she worked with the *Spartiate* in the weather division. She forced the Spanish *Neptuno* to surrender and suffered three killed and 22 wounded.

Of Richard Gurward, there is absolutely no information at all. He wasn't listed anywhere in the *Minotaur's* pay books, which makes this medal both frustrating and highly interesting! This author is almost certain that he is on the muster for *Minotaur*, the medal is absolutely right, however, not under the name of Richard Gurward. He used an alias when he signed on and then after the battle received his Boulton's Trafalgar medal, had it cased and glazed and inscribed with his real name and then sent it home to Mother! William Williams notes that in the 1740's, he was pressed 'and shifted from one ship to another, till I found means to escape , going under different names, as best suited my purpose.' Men did want a way out if they felt the need to Run, and using an alias was the safest way.

Provenance: Private purchase, 1990.
References: *The Trafalgar Roll*, by Col. R. H. Mackenzie, George Allen, London, 1913.
The Journal of Llewellin Penrose, a Seaman, by William Williams, 4 vols. John Murray, London, 1815.

BT18 Lieutenant James Clephan, HMS Spartiate, Captain Sir Francis Laforey

Description: Silver, a restrike from the fleet issue dies circa 1880-1910?, engraved in script on the reverse: *James Clephan, Lieut., HMS Spartiate*. That the medal is a restrike is noted by the loss of detail in the centre of the large cloud of cannon smoke on the reverse and that the dies are the fleet issue dies by the lack of the lump on the reverse rim at 11 o'clock. The medal is cased in silver and glazed.

The Naval General Service medal bears the clasps 21 July 1801 Boat Action and Trafalgar. The rim is officially impressed block capitals: J. CLEPHAN, MASTER'S MATE.

The Boulton Trafalgar is Extremely Fine and the NGS is Very fine.

Background: The *Spartiate* was a 74-gun ship and with the *Minotaur* brought up the rear of the Weather Column. A critical point was reached in the battle when the French Admiral Dumanoir brought his five ships toward Villeneuve's flagship *Bucentaur*. Only the *Spartiate* and *Minotaur* stood in his way, but it was enough and they blocked the French Admiral's attempt to rejoin the conflict. The last of Doumanoir's five ships was the Spanish *Neptuno*, 84 guns, which surrendered to *Spartiate* after an hour's battle which left the Spaniard with 30 dead and 57 wounded where *Spartiate* had three killed and twenty wounded.

Dudley Pope commented: 'Dumanoir's descent with his five ships on the two lone British ships was a curious parallel with Nelson's approach in [doubling] the enemy line. Whereas Nelson succeeded, Dumanoir lost the *Neptuno* and had to report that 'the two vessels that I had intended to cut off managed to pass ahead of me at pistol shot and damaged me greatly.'

James Clephan was Second Lieutenant on board *Spartiate* at Trafalgar and rose to First Lieutenant shortly after the battle. His career is the stuff that keeps a naval novelist busy! He was born in Leven, Fifeshire, a small fishing village on the northern shore of the Firth of Forth. Clephan volunteered to join the Royal Navy on 23 July 1794, although this was after he had fallen into the hands of the Press Gang. He made the right choice to volunteer and not carry the stigma of being prest on board ship. He was 25 years old at the time and a seasoned man of the sea having served in the merchant service. He was immediately rated Able Seaman and then just a week later, rated as Quarter Gunner. Where did he gain his experience with cannon? We don't know, but he certainly had gunnery skills very likely gained in East India Company ships or perhaps as a privateer. A year later, he was rated Quarter Master's Mate which demonstrates his ability to steer and follow a compass bearing while keeping his ship as close to the wind as she could bear.

On the 6th of October, he appeared on board the newly built 18 pounder 36-gun frigate, HMS *Doris*, Captain Charles Jones, the 5th Lord Ranelagh. He entered the ship as Quarter Master, then on 9 May 1796 moved to Gunner's Mate, but then on 1 October 1796 to Master's Mate, a very senior petty officer station. All of this advancement and continued increase in responsibility demonstrates just how skilled he was at sea and his leadership qualities.

Doris was a very successful ship with captures of privateers as the war continued. I really can't think what would have been more exciting and fun than to be part of a ship's company of a frigate who had a smart and aggressive captain. Only a couple of hundred men on board the *Doris*, it was like a family and due to the close confines of the ship, everybody knew each other and worked together to keep the ship in fine trim, but also to use her to capture enemy ships and gain prize money which was shared by all on board.

Monday, 20 July 1801, was a mild day at the port of Brest. The moon was in quarter phase and there was a light breeze from the north east. Two British frigates, *Doris*, and *Beaulieu*, were anchored near the harbour keeping a watch on the Franco-Spanish fleet located deep within the harbour. Also near the mouth of the harbour and under the protective guns located on the cliffs above Camerate Bay, was the 20-gun French corvette, *La Chevrette* which looked a tempting prize to the hungry British sailors.

That night, boats from the *Doris* and *Beaulieu* pulled toward *La Chevrette*, but through poor leadership and confusion amongst the boats, they did not arrive together in order to mount an attack. However, the French were now alerted to the British plan and more men were brought on board *Chevrette* and its defences strengthened by moving the ship to an even more secure location within Camerate Bay.

The next night, the 21st, and having been joined by the frigate *Uranie*, boats again set forth, this time under the command of Lieutenant Keith Maxwell whose presence immediately cheered all those who had volunteered for this enterprise.

At about 1:00 a.m., the boats came in sight of the *Chevrette* who, hailing them, opened a heavy fire of musketry and grape upon their assailants. This was accompanied by musketry fired from the shore. The

Beaulieu's boats headed for the starboard bow and quarter while the boats from the *Uranie* and *Doris* boarded on the larboard bow.

The resistance from the French was fierce. James Clephan from the *Doris* tried to mount the larboard bow, but was wounded and thrown off the ship. No doubt this brought Clephan's blood up, and he managed to fight his way back on board the *Chevrette* and was the first man to gain the enemy's deck. Some accounts say he suffered nine wounds during the fight, but he kept on and supported now by the men boarding from both sides of the ship's bows. They fought their way toward the stern, having already cut *Chevrette's* anchor cable.

Maxwell had planned the attack well with different teams having different objectives. One group to get aloft and loose the sails, another to get to the helm and steer her free to open water. The British had lost the use of all their firearms, probably because of damp from the night before, so this fight was down to cold steel. And the French were very much up for it with their decks crowded with over 350 sailors defending their ship. We are now faced with one of the most ferocious examples of boarding actions, the defenders are just as much in the fight as the attackers and there is no place for anybody to retreat to. You either won or you died.

Detail from P. J. de Loutherbourg's painting of the cutting out of *La Chevrette*. The attacking British petty officer with the dark blue jacket standing by the bowsprit is thought to be James Clephan. Image courtesy of the Bristol City Museum and Art Gallery..

The British won at the cost to the French of 92 officers and men, including her captain, killed and 62 wounded, nearly 50% of those defending the ship. The British paid dearly for their success with 11 officers and men killed and 57 wounded. The number of casualties reflects upon the ferocity of the British attack.

For the gallantry shown by James Clephan on that fateful night, Admiral Cornwallis gave him an immediate promotion to Lieutenant, commenting 'You well deserve your promotion, few officers have earned it so hardly.'

Clephan joined a very special group of seaman, where only a dozen or so were promoted from the lower deck to the quarter deck during the long wars with France and Spain.

William James sums up those events of the 21st / 22nd of July by writing: 'It is such daring feats as these that ennoble the character of the British navy and long will be remembered, long held up as an example for imitation, the cutting out of *La Chevrette*.'

Later in the West Indies during 1811, Clephan was made Commander and given command of the sloop *Charybdis*. He captured several American vessels which included the privateer *Blockade*. He retired in 1840 aged 71 as a post captain and received the NGS with clasps for cutting out *La Chevrette*, 21 July 1801 Boat Action and Trafalgar. His NGS and silver Boulton Trafalgar medals were sold by the family at Sotheby's in 1980 for £2,300.

Above: Silhouette by an unknown artist of James Clephan, c. 1811. Right: The *Spartiate* Trafalgar flag. Courtesy, Charles Miller

What was a real surprise was when the family offered at a Charles Miller auction, the Union Jack that had flown at Trafalgar on board *Spartiate*. James Clephan had kept it as a memento of the action.

At the time of the auction in 2009, it was felt this was the only Union Jack to have survived Trafalgar and was estimated at £15,000. I attended the auction and will never forget the look on Charles Miller's face as the bidding reached £100,000, and then £200,000 and when it made £300,000, I thought he would collapse under the pressure! He didn't and in the end, the flag cost the new owner £384,000, a world record for a flag.

Provenance: Sotheby's auction in 1980 where the pair of medals made £2,300 to Peter Dale and then to myself.
References: The National Archives, Kew: ADM 35/734, 514-516, 1163. ADM 36 /13264-13266, 13015-13018, 14692-14694, 14727-14728, 15998-16002. ADM 37/139-142, 904-906.
The Trafalgar Roll, by Col. R. H. Mackenzie, George Allen, London, 1913.
The Naval Biographical Dictionary by W. R. O'Byrne, John Murray, London, 1849.
Royal Naval Biography by John Marshall, Longman, London, 1833.
The Naval History of Great Britain by William James, Richard Bentley, London, 1837.

BT19 Murdock McClode, Gunner's Mate, HMS Spartiate, Captain Sir Francis Laforey

Description: Tin, fleet issue, cased in silver and glazed. Inscribed in the reverse field M. *McClode* in script. Engraved around the rim in block capitals is: FROM M: BOULTON TO THE HEROES OF TRAFALGAR. Weight: 65.1 grams. An absolutely stunning Boulton Trafalgar medal where the protection provided by the glazed casing has preserved this medal perfectly for over 200 years.

Background: Murdock McCloed or MacLeod of Clan MacLeod of the Isle of Lewis in the Western Isles, Outer Hebrides was 28 years old when he volunteered for the Royal Navy on 7 May 1803. There is no doubt that he was an experienced seaman as he was rated Able Seaman upon joining the *Spartiate* and then on 1 June to Sailmaker's Crew. On 8 April 1804 to Quarter Master's Mate and then on 1 October to Gunner's Mate. All senior petty officer ratings.

On 23 November 1809 he transferred to the captured 36-gun French frigate *Desiree*, Captain Arthur Farquhar. He was immediately rated Gunner's Mate indicating that he had found the billet that best suited him and again as a senior petty officer. He remained on board until 1 March 1815, when he was discharged from the service at Portsmouth, probably along with most of the ship's company as the war at sea had come to an end.

His time on board *Desiree* was spent chasing enemy privateers and other shipping in the North Sea and later in the Baltic. In late 1813 there is a curious entry in the log: 'River Elbe. Detained 3 French prisoners from Shamrock and two spies.' Hate to have been one of the two spies!

Provenance: Private purchase, 1995.
References: The National Archives, Kew: ADM 35/1739-1740, 2437, 3092, 2740, 3418-3419. ADM 36 /15998-16002. ADM 37/139-142, 904-906, 2536-2537, 3553-3554, 4261, 5268. ADM 27/13.

BT20 Charles Doran, Ordinary Seaman, HMS Royal Sovereign, Captain Edward Rotherham, Vice-Admiral Cuthbert Collingwood

Description: Tin, fleet issue, holed for securing a suspension ring. On the obverse engraved in crude block capitals ROYAL SOVEREIGN and on the reverse C DORAN. Weight: 40.6 grams. Very Good, but much worn with just a bit of corrosion here and there.

Background: *Royal Sovereign*, a 100-gun three-decker, was Collingwood's flagship and led the Leeward Column into the attack at Trafalgar. From Dudley Pope: 'As the *Royal Sovereign* forged through the gap in the enemy line, she fired a whole broadside into the unprotected stern of the *Santa Ana*. The effect was even more dreadful than in the *Bucentaure* and *Santissima Trinidad*. As successive guns bore and fired their triple-shotted quota, much of the solid planking and rich carvings on the transom was smashed in as if by huge invisible fists, and the shot and splinters spun on down the decks, cutting down men and overturning fourteen guns. Rotherham ordered the helm to be put over and as the men worked swiftly in the choking smoke to reload the larboard guns, the *Royal Sovereign* swung round to larboard to come alongside the Spanish ship. But as she turned, Baudouin fired the *Fougueux*'s full broadside into her starboard quarter, and the 80-gun *Indomptable*, from only five hundred yards away on the British flagship's starboard beam, fired another.

'In the meantime the *Santa Ana*'s captain had guessed that the *Royal Sovereign* would swing round and come alongside to leeward, and had brought all the larboard-side guns' crews over to reinforce those on the starboard side. When the British ship came alongside, their yardarms touching as the two great vessels rolled in the swell, the Spanish gunners fired. *Royal Sovereign* heeled considerably under the impact of the 112-gun *Santa Ana*'s broadside. At the same time two more Spanish ships, the *San Justo* and *San Leandro*, which were well ahead, swung round and started firing into the *Royal Sovereign* and the French *Neptune*, which was in between them, followed suit. Collingwood's flagship was thus being engaged by three Spanish and three French ships.'

Thus the *Santa Ana* and *Royal Sovereign* continued until finally the Spaniard struck. In the meantime other British ships had arrived, particularly the *Belleisle* which gained the attention of *Royal Sovereign*'s antagonists and commenced her own battle for survival.

Royal Sovereign lost 144 killed and wounded during the battle.

Charles Duran hasn't been fully researched, however we can say that he grew up in Wicklow in Ireland. It is noted that Nelson couldn't have won or even fought the battle of Trafalgar without the Irish who made up nearly a third of the total men in his fleet. Duran Volunteered on 24 July 1803 and was rated as Ordinary Seaman, which shows that he had spent time at sea and was probably caught by a press gang and decided to take the King's shilling. He received a total of £6/10/0 in prize money for being at Trafalgar, which must have been a fine windfall for him.

Provenance: Royal Norfolk Regimental Museum auction in Norwich, 1987.
References: *The Ayshford Complete Trafalgar Roll* on cd, privately published, 2004.
England Expects by Dudley Pope, Weidenfeld & Nicolson, London, 1959.

BT21 Robert Collinson, Quarter Gunner, HMS Belleisle, Captain William Hargood

Description: Tin, fleet issue, cased and glazed in copper gilt. On the obverse is engraved *Defence 74 Guns* and on the reverse *Robt Collinson* in script. The ship Collinson was on board was actually the *Belleisle*. Weight: 64.6 grams. Extremely Fine for both obverse and reverse, although the reverse has some corrosion here and there.

Background: The 74-gun *Belleisle* suffered a fair amount in her approach to the enemy line. Dudley Pope takes up the story of her upon joining the *Royal Sovereign*. 'By this time the French and Spanish broadsides were beginning to tell against *Belleisle*. Lieutenant Nicolas later wrote, 'Although until that moment we had not fired a shot, our sails and rigging bore evident proofs of the manner in which we had been treated: our mizen-topmast was shot away and the ensign had been thrice rehoisted; numbers lay dead upon the decks,

Fougeux.   *Belleisle.*   *Indomptable.*   *Santa Ana.*   *Royal Sovereign.*

Painted by W.J. Huggins,
Marine Painter to His late Majesty.

Engraved by E. Duncan.

BELLEISLE. 15 minutes past Noon. Octr 21st 1805.

Dumanoir.   *Naiad.*   *Belleisle.*   *Sta Ana.*   *R. Sovereign.*   *Victory.*   *Achille.*

Painted by W.J. Huggins,
Marine Painter to His late Majesty.

Engraved by E. Duncan.

BELLEISLE. 4h. 15m. P.M. Octr 21st 1805.

and eleven wounded were already in the surgeon's care. The firing was now tremendous, and at intervals the dispersion of the smoke gave us a sight of the colour of our adversaries.'

'There was no need to send men aloft to cut the halyards and bring the studding-sails in with a rush at the last moment, for the enemy's swirling chain shot had torn them down, and before the *Belleisle* could bring her first broadsides to bear, more than fifty of her men had been killed or wounded. Soon she had the *Santa Ana* in the sights of her guns, and the whole larboard broadside crashed out; almost immediately the starboard broadside was fired into the *Fougueux*, and the smoke drifted on ahead of the *Belleisle*, almost hiding the *Indomptable* ahead and the *San Justo* beyond the *Santa Ana*.

'The Master brought the *Belleisle* round to starboard to go round the stern of the *Indomptable* and come up on her lee side, but suddenly out of the great banks of smoke, the *Fougueux* loomed up very close on the starboard quarter and in a few moments her larboard bow crashed against the *Belleisle's* starboard gangway.

'While the after guns of the *Belleisle's* starboard side fired into the *Fougueux* at the range of a few feet, the crews of those farther forward hastily got their handspikes under the carriages to heave them round to get them to bear. As the two ships drifted together almost covered in smoke, the condition on the gun decks were appalling. One man wrote, 'All that he knew was that he heard the crash of the shot smashing through the rending timbers, and then followed at once the hoarse bellowings of the captains of the guns, as men were missed at their posts, calling out to the survivors: 'Close up there! Close up!'

'The *Indomptable*, saved by the *Fougueux*, turned to starboard and fired a broadside into *Belleisle*. Then, as if she considered her part in the battle fulfilled, she drifted away to leeward into the smoke. Locked together, the *Fougueux* and *Belleisle* slowly fell away to leeward, hammering away at each other.'

From Mackenzie: 'At about 1 p.m. the *Fougueux* intervened and with her port bow ran on board the *Belleisle*, nearly midship on the starboard side. The two ships briskly engaged one another for about twenty minutes when the Frenchman dropped astern. The *Belleisle*, though by this time a wreck, was still further attacked until she was completely dismasted and shattered.

'But, she remained unconquered. She suspended a Union Jack at the end of a pike and held it up to view, while an ensign was made fast to the stump of the mainmast. She was however, succoured in time and though unable to take further active part in the fighting, she subsequently sent her last remaining boat to take possession of the Spanish *Argonauta* which had hauled down her colours and lay not far off. The losses of the *Belleisle* amounted to 127 killed and wounded. Her hull was knocked almost to pieces, both sides of it being about equally damaged, while her three masts, bowsprit, and figurehead were shot away, together with her boats and anchors.'

Dudley Pope provides detail of the surrender of the *Argonauta* which suffered 100 killed and 203 wounded out of a crew of 780. Lieutenant Owen of the *Belleisle* took possession of the enemy ship and wrote: 'On getting up the *Argonauta's* side, I found no living person on her deck; but on making my way, over numerous dead and a confusion of wreck, across the quarter-deck, I was met by the second captain at the cabin door, who gave me his sword.'

My records show that I bought this Boulton Trafalgar medal in 1980, but didn't have it researched by Gillian Hughes until 1990. I remember that there was a quick search amongst the pay books of HMS *Defence* and that there was no Robert Collinson listed. The medal and its engraving certainly looked contemporary, so I just marked it down to one of the vagaries of the Boulton Trafalgar medal, i.e. there were quite a number of men who used a *nom de guerre* when signing on with the Royal Navy, all to protect themselves if they decided to Run. When they received their un-named Boulton Trafalgar, they would have them engraved with their real name, and then send the medal home to Mother.

Gillian's research turned up a Robert Collinson who was on board HMS *Belleisle* at Trafalgar. The research was most complete as she had traced the man from 1793 to 1815 which was quite an effort.

Anyway, 25 years had now passed with no further advance on understanding Collinson's medal, and then in 2005 *The Nelson Dispatch*, the journal of The Nelson Society, published an article written by Eric Kirby, who is the great-great-great-grandson of Robert Collinson and who has researched his career in the Royal Navy at the National Archives at Kew. Quite a nice article and naturally I brought out Collinson's medal and the associated research papers to send a note to the author.

And there it was again, HMS *Defence* on the obverse of the medal!

With the aid of *The Ayshford Complete Trafalgar Roll*, I was able to confirm that Robert Collinson was the only man of that name at Trafalgar, and indeed the only Collinson at Trafalgar and that he served on HMS *Belleisle*. What went wrong with the naming of his Boulton Trafalgar medal?

From the research I could see that he transferred to HMS *London* upon the *Belleisle's* return to Plymouth, and also confirmation that he never served on HMS *Defence*.

If many of the men from the *Belleisle* transferred to a different ship upon arrival in England, what happened to the crew of the *Defence*?

As it happens I have a Boulton's Trafalgar to John Greenwood of HMS *Defence*, (BT 32), which was also fully researched by Gillian Hughes, and like the men of the *Belleisle*, they too changed ship, with Greenwood going to HMS *Kent*.

Well then, when was the Boulton Trafalgar distributed to the fleet? Tricky question because it had a lot to do with where the men were in 1807 when the medal was finally available for distribution. The *London* was stationed at Plymouth, so not a major problem getting the medal to the Trafalgar heroes who were on board her.

Next question, where was the *Kent* and her crew that came from the *Defence*, in 1807? Wonderful answer, the *Kent* was also stationed at Plymouth!

So, we have the medal probably showing up at the same time for men on both ships; we also know that because pay day in the Royal Navy was pretty much the same day everywhere, the men probably had money and their medals and those interested would have taken them to a local jeweller for engraving and perhaps to have them cased and glazed as well.

I then fetched John Greenwood's Boulton Trafalgar, and it was really a Eureka Moment!

Nearly all of the thirty plus Boulton Trafalgar medals in my collection are only engraved in the reverse field, above the battle scene. Sometimes the name of the man and his ship are given, and sometimes only the man's name, but it really is the reverse field that the jeweller used to do his engraving.

With Robert Collinson's medal, his name is engraved in the reverse field and his ship, albeit the wrong ship, is engraved in the obverse field.

For John Greenwood, his name is engraved in the obverse field and his ship, *Defence,* in the reverse field.

I then inspected both medals with my magnifying glass and looked carefully over the engraving for both medals.

They are by the same hand!!

Everything is explained. The same jeweller in Plymouth engraved both medals. He really did have men from *Defence* and *Belleisle* with money and medals and he was taking orders as fast as he could. It must have been even more confusing for him because these men were no longer on the ships that they were on at Trafalgar! That he spelled Collinson's surname correctly is a minor miracle.

All of this just underlines, that with engraved medals, it is best if the engraved detail agrees with the research, but in the case that it doesn't, this may not be cause to panic, at least not yet!

Robert Collinson (1772 - 1853) was from County Durham and joined the Royal Navy as an Able Seaman, aged 21, which shows he had already spent a number of years at sea in the merchant service. He showed real skill as during his service he was rated Coxswain, Quarter Gunner, and Quarter Master and continued in petty officer roles during his naval career which ended in 1815. He received the 1848 NGS with three clasps for Bridport's action of 17 June 1795 when on board HMS *Pallas* and Trafalgar when on board HMS *Belleisle* as a Quarter Master. His third clasp was *London* 13 March 1806 when that ship, following a five hour fight, captured the French 74 *Marengo*. After his naval service, Collinson continued his life at sea as a Master Mariner, and then later as a keelman and waterman. He resided in Bishopwearmouth, Sunderland, with his wife and eleven children.

For details regarding John Greenwood, please see BT 32.

Provenance: Private purchase, 1980.
References: *England Expects* by Dudley Pope, Weidenfeld & Nicolson, London, 1959.
The Ayshford Complete Trafalgar Roll on cd, privately published, 2004.
The Trafalgar Roll, by Col. R. H. Mackenzie, George Allen, London, 1913.
Robert Collinson 1772 - 1853 by Eric Kirby in The Nelson Dispatch, Vol. 8, pt. 10, pp. 630-33, April 2005.
Memoir of the Life and Services of Admiral Sir William Hargood etc. by Joseph Allen, Printed for private circulation only, Henry Richardson, Greenwich, 1841.
Admiralty pay books and logs for HMS Belleisle and Defence for 1805 and HMS London and Kent for 1807 and subsequent ships, kept at The National Archives at Kew.
The Naval General Service Medal Roll by C. Message, Message & Hayward, Ipswich, 1996.

BT22 Midshipman James Robinson, HMS Mars, Captain George Duff, succeeded by Lieutenant William Hannah

Description: Tin, fleet issue, cased and glazed in silver. On the reverse is engraved *Md Jas Robinson HMS Mars* in script. Weight: 60.2 grams. Near Extremely Fine with small patches of corrosion and tarnishing overall.

Background: From Dudley Pope: 'By now Captain Duff's 74-gun *Mars* was in action. The *Fougueux* going ahead to engage the *Royal Sovereign* and the *Belleisle*, had left a gap which the Spanish *Monarca* was slow to close. Captain Duff planned to pass through there, but Captain Cosmao Kerjulien in the 74-gun *Pluton*, quickly set all possible sail to pass the *Monarca* and head off the *Mars*. Captain Duff came down to fire a broadside into the *Monarca*, who turned away, but within a few minutes the *Pluton* had ranged ahead into the gap, nearly across the bows of the *Mars*, a position from which she would be able to pour in a raking broadside.

'To avoid this, Captain Duff luffed up the *Mars* to windward on to a course parallel with the *Pluton*, who kept up a heavy fire. By now the *Mars* was fast approaching the *Santa Ana*, who was still locked in a violent struggle with the *Royal Sovereign*, and Duff had to luff up and then heave to in order to avoid her. With the *Mars* stopped, the *Pluton* was in an ideal position on the starboard quarter of the British ship.

'A young Banffshire midshipman, James Robinson, wrote: Captain Duff walked about with a steady fortitude and said: 'My God, what shall we do? Here is a Spanish three-decker raking us ahead [*Santa Ana*] and a French one [*Pluton*] under our stern! In a few minutes our poop was totally cleared, the quarter-deck and foc's'le nearly the same, and only the Boatswain and myself and three men left alive.'

There is confusion regarding James Robinson, some authors attribute Hercules Robinson to the above quotation, but he was on board *Euryalus* during the whole of the action and the quotations aren't found in his book, *Sea Drift*. Elsewhere, Dudley Pope cites T. Robinson, where in fact it is J, for James. Clayton and Craig give the correct reference to James Robinson which is the letter to his father, dated 12 December 1805, MSS 1992/133 held at the National Museum of the Royal Navy Library in Portsmouth. The whole of this letter is transcribed below as it says a lot about the mental state of a 17 year old Midshipman who has just passed through a very traumatic event. You'll see that the letter varies from the above quotation and other quotations attributed to James Robinson which makes me think that there is more than one surviving letter. For completeness, I'll continue to use all of the quotes found attributed to James Robinson.

Returning to Dudley Pope: 'The British ship *Tonnant* was now entering the fray and bore down to rake the *Pluton*, who luffed to try to rake her first. But at this moment the *Fougueux*, in action with the *Belleisle*, shot away her antagonist's mizzenmast and drifted clear, getting into a perfect position to rake the stricken *Mars*.

'Captain Norman, commanding the Marines on board the *Mars* spotted her through the swirling smoke and ran to the quarter-deck to warn Captain Duff; but the *Mars* was hemmed in, and this combined with the fact that the wind had fallen away, prevented the ship from manoeuvring. Norman pointed out the *Fouguex*. 'Do you think our guns will bear on her?' asked Duff.

'I think not', replied Norman, 'but I cannot see for smoke.'

'Then we must point our guns on the ships on which they will bear', said Duff. 'I shall go and look, the men below may see better, as there is less smoke there.'

'He went to the end of the quarter-deck to look over the side, followed by his aide, Midshipman Arbuthnot. By leaning over he could just see the *Fouguex* on the starboard quarter through the smoke, and he told Arbuthnot to go below and order the guns to be pointed farther aft. The boy was just turning away toward the hatch when the *Fouguex* fired a full broadside into the British ship. One shot decapitated Duff and went on to kill two seamen who were standing just behind him. Duff's body fell on the gangway. Word was sent to Norwich below that his father had perished. When the men heard that their captain had been killed, wrote Midshipman Robinson, 'they held his body up and gave three cheers to show they were not discouraged by it, and then returned to their guns.'

'Lieut. William Hennah was now in command. The ship's maintopmast and the spanker-boom were shot away; the foremast was tottering, riddled with shot and about to crash over the side, and the other two masts were in little better condition, several guns had been smashed and the stern quarter and rudder were badly damaged. Already killed, in addition to Norwich's father, were Lachlan Duff's son Alexander, who died in his younger brother's arms, two midshipmen, seventeen seamen and eight Marines. Thomas Norman, the Captain of Marines, was dying, and five midshipmen [including James Robinson, slightly in the right arm], 44 seamen and sixteen Marines were wounded.

'Almost helpless, the stricken ship paid off, presenting her damaged stern to the *Pluton*. Cosmao, in the process of luffing round to port to rake the *Tonnant*, promptly flung the helm over the other way, paid off and raked the *Mars* with another broadside and then turned away, drifting to leeward after the *Fougueux* until she found the *Belleisle* lying helpless. Cosmao then hove-to the *Pluton* on the British ship's port quarter and opened fire.

'Mars was now near the recently surrendered *Bucentaure*, Villeneuve's flagship. Captain James Atcherley of the Marines and from the Pellew's *Conqueror* took the surrender of Villeneuve, but as *Mars* was now closer, he brought Villeneuve and his staff on board the *Mars* and Lieutenant Hennah took the surrender.'

From Midshipman James Robinson's letter we have, 'A circumstance happened which I cannot help telling you as it displays the soul of a British sailor. Villeneuve, the French commander in chief, came on board about the middle of the battle and seeing Captain Duff lying dead upon deck, began to smile to some of his attendants, which one of our sailors observing came running up to him and laid hold of him and said when my captain lived he was able to revenge an insult. Now he is dead it is my duty to revenge it for him at the same time throwing Villeneuve from him, covered the dead body with a flag that was laying near him.'

Now follows the complete letter of James Robinson to his father at 2 Hill Street, Edinburgh, Scotland, written on board the *Mars* at Gibraltar on 12 December 1805. I have inserted some punctuation, created some paragraphs and sorted out some spelling to aid reading what James has to say.

'My Dear Father,					H. M. S. *Mars* Dec 12th 1805

I wrote a hurried letter to my mother to keep her from that anxiety which becomes a mother occasioned by the late glorious although fatal victory. Great as former displays British valour may appear never did any of them equal this, the laurel which ever has crowned and adorned the Gallant Nelson's brow would have again done it in this, but God would have it otherwise therefore the Nation's thanks are due to Admiral Collingwood as the hero of that memorable day. In my letter to my mother I gave as official account as I could of the action and the results of it. I am proud to say it is a general remark the beautiful and steady manner Captain Duff brought the ship into the battle, he stood with his arms across [his chest and] looked with undaunted fortitude until his head and neck were entirely severed from his body.

The battle continued from twelve o'clock till three when there was a small intermission for the space of twenty minutes occasioned by the explosion of two French line of battle ships which was really dreadful as in them eight hundred men were driven into eternity being impossible to save them in [such] a critical moment.

Good fortune did not long attend us for never did ships experience such awful weather as we, without masts (they being shot away) we tossed about at the mercy of the winds and waves and what was worse, the sailors curse, the land close to us we burned and sunk our prizes as fast as possibly could, many of our own people perished who had been sent on board of them when the weather was moderate, the long renowned *Santissima Trinidad* sunk, I do not know the names of all the ships taken and destroyed however out of 34 [33] sail of the line, only 12 were left to carry home news of the action. They were eight sail superior to us at the commencement of the battle which lasted from 12 to sunset.

We lost an Admiral, two Captains, eleven lieutenants, the number of men is not yet certain. The French lost four Admirals, seven Captains and about five thousand men. We have been in Gibraltar since the action where we got jury masts. I saw my old friend Mosman [?] there.

I shall be in the greatest suspense until I hear from you. We have a Captain Oliver on board seemingly a good kind of man. I am told he is a native of Ireland. My dear father we must fight through all misfortunes, first the loss of Lord Maiveh [Nelson ?], now of Captain Duff. A man must not expect [the] road through life to be paved for him, but must make it as the maker does [?] in a field of corn.

The *Mars* is very much cut up. I daresay we will be in harbour six weeks. We have 110 men killed and wounded besides the Captain and four midshipmen and Captain of Marines. I wish to leave the *Mars* as soon as possible.

Captain Campbell has sent for me to sail with him in the *Nassau* 64 guns, now laying at Gravesend waiting for men. There is several line of Battle ships to be paid off as they require so much repair. The *Mars* will be one of the number.

My dear father, I should have written sooner but could not as I had my right arm a little bruised, indeed it almost appears to like a dream that I the Boatswain and four men were the only survivors out of sixteen in the *Mars*'s forecastle.

Write my dear father to Captain Campbell and thank him for his kindness, tell him to apply without delay for my discharge into the *Nassau* and I have no doubt that he will get it as Captain Oliver is unacquainted with me and has followers enough of his own. Now to accomplish this I will need a little money to pay my passage to London as I cannot receive a farthing of my pay for the *Mars* until I join the *Nassau*. I will also have in a month or two a considerable of prize money to receive [£37 in all]. I have made Mr. Hatful the purser my agent who is going to return to London and learn [?] the service for that purpose. When the prize money is payable you will receive mine from him which will be considerable.

Captain Duff told me a few days before the action that he had drawn upon you for twenty pounds, none of which he used on my account. You know the best way to recover this for I do not know who has taken upon hand to settle his affairs. You see now how I am situated. I want your advice how to act. I shall go entirely by your instructions.

Captain Duff acted so much of a father's part towards me that I hardly felt the want of your good advice, now he is no more. When you answer this let me know how Mrs. Duff is, poor woman. I pity her situation, but it is useless lamenting God's will must be done and many in the evening of the 21st besides her might weeping have said: 'When the sun rose this morning, I was a wife and this my child had a father, now I am a widow and this boy is an orphan! I often thank God I have such a father and time will show of God preserving my life when it will be your turn to say that you have such a son. I was a little astonished in a former letter I received from you in which you mentioned that I had chosen my profession and that I must continue in it.

It gave me much uneasiness. I confess I was almost tired of cruising in the Channel without seeing the world, but since we sailed from Portsmouth last, Captain Duff was such a favourite of the Admirals that we seldom remained off Cadiz. We went several times up the Mediterranean to Tuiton [Tetouan] in Africa for water. Captain Duff bought a most elegant dress for Mrs. Duff at Tangiers for which he gave twenty dollars, it was made of camel's hair. I should have liked very much to have got one for my mother, but it did not suit my purse. When I join Captain Campbell at Gravesend, I can go and see Betsy if it meets with your approbation. I believe she is not far from the Nore.

I wish very much to have an opportunity of embracing some of the family especially my mother. I long to kiss their lips which when at home, I never slept a night without doing and which at one time I thought I should never do again.

We threw the dead body of Captain Duff overboard on 24 Octr. A circumstance happened which I cannot help telling you as it displays the soul of a British sailor. Villeneuve, the French commander in chief, came on board about the middle of the battle and seeing Captain Duff lying dead upon deck, began to smile to some of his attendants, which one of our sailors observing came running up to him and laid hold of him and said when my captain lived he was able to revenge an insult. Now he is dead it is my duty to revenge it for him at the same time throwing Villeneuve from him, covered the dead body with a flag that was laying near him. Several others happened of the same nature, but we will defer relating them until I can do it verbally. Write without delay as I shall be in great suspense. Mr. Hatful location is, Mr. Hatful at Mr. James Hunts, Southampton Buildings, Covent Garden, London. He is a most gentlemanly man which you will find out by a letter correspondence and told me he will do everything that lay in his power to oblige me.

I can say no more until I get answers from you and remain your most affectionate son.

J. Robinson.'

From the research carried out about James Robinson, we have this: 'Robinson was discharged to *Nassau* on 4 January 1806', but he actually didn't join *Nassau*. Perhaps she had sailed before he could get to her, or perhaps he was delayed by spending time with Betsy who lived near Gravesend. Gillian Hughes did find that he spent some time on board the schooner *Whiting* and then ultimately joined HMS *Renown* in 1806 and stayed with her as a Midshipman until March 1809 when he briefly transferred to the *Elvin* and from there to the *Adamant* in May 1809. He continued in *Adamant* until he passed for Lieutenant on 6 February 1810, but from that point on, he is not found, except for a death notice in *The Scots Magazine*, vol. 74: 'On 16 September 1811 on passage home from Jamaica, Lieutenant James Robinson second son of George Robinson of Clermiston, writer to the Signet.' There aren't any more details, however the phrase 'on passage home' tends to indicate that he was a passenger as opposed to a serving officer on board the returning ship. If that was the case then he was probably returning home to recuperate from an illness contracted in Jamaica, which was a very common occurrence at that time.

Provenance: Private Purchase, 1995.
References: The National Archives, Kew: ADM 35/471-472, 2310. ADM 36/16241-42, 16261-16263. ADM 6/108/page 202. ADM 107/42 page 152.
The National Museum of the Royal Navy Library MSS 1992/133.
England Expects by Dudley Pope, Weidenfeld & Nicolson, London, 1959.
The Ayshford Complete Trafalgar Roll on cd, privately published, 2004.
The Trafalgar Roll, by Col. R. H. Mackenzie, George Allen, London, 1913.
Trafalgar, the men, the battle, the storm by Clayton & Craig, Hodder & Stoughton, London, 2004.
The Complete Navy List of the Napoleonic Wars by Patrick Malone' CD published Ageofnelson.org.Brussels, Belgium 2002.
Google Books, *The Scots Magazine*, vol. 74 for the death notice of 16 September 1811.

Watercolour sketch by Nicolas Pocock of HMS *Mars* at the end of the battle.
Courtesy The National Museum of the Royal Navy, Portsmouth.

A cypher found in Lieutenant Hennah's commonplace book in the Sim Comfort collection: 'By my worthy respected and esteemed friend Edward Hatfull [Purser to the *Mars*], this key was given to me on board the *Mars* January the eighteenth, one thousand eight hundred and five at anchor in Quiberon Bay when drinking a glass of grog and smoking a segar in commemoration of my wife's birthday in my cabbin.'

Miniature of Lieutenant George Lacey Decoeurdoux who served on board HMS *Lion* at the capture of the *Guillaume Tell* in 1800 and later as signal's lieutenant on board *Mars* at Trafalgar. He later served in the Transport Office, 1813-1817 and lived to receive the NGS with Trafalgar clasp.
Sim Comfort collection.

BT23 James Ryan, Landsman, HMS Mars, Captain George Duff, succeeded by Lieutenant William Hannah

Description: Tin, fleet issue. On the reverse is engraved *James Ryan HMS Mars* in script. Weight: 41.8 grams. Very fine with even light corrosion both sides.

Background: James Ryan was from Castle Coole in Northern Ireland and volunteered to serve the Royal Navy at 36 years of age. He appeared on board HMS *Mars* on 19 September 1803 and was rated Landsman. This could have been a real shock for James Ryan, what was he doing at sea at that age and still a Landsman? We don't know, very possibly just a strong back that was scooped up by the Press Gang and decided to take the King's shilling and make the best of what Fate had in store for him. He continued to serve right through Trafalgar where he was wounded and received £10 from the Lloyd's Patriotic Fund. What his wound was, we don't know, but £10 could relate to something such as the loss of fingers or toes or severe bruising from a flying splinter. Whatever it was, he stayed with the *Mars* and took part at the second battle of Copenhagen, 1807. With continued service his health deteriorated and at Deal Hospital on 12 February 1810 he was entered suffering from pneumonia and on 15 March, discharged as unserviceable. He was now 43 years old and one images his prospects weren't very good.

Provenance: Private purchase, 1979.
References: The National Archives, Kew: ADM 35/1054, 2310-2311, 2904-2905, 271. ADM 36/ 16260-16263. ADM 37/ 269-273, 2133-2135. ADM 102/183
The Ayshford Complete Trafalgar Roll on cd, privately published, 2004.

BT24 Francis Long, Private, Royal Marines, HMS Mars, Captain George Duff, succeeded by Lieutenant William Hannah

Description: Tin, fleet issue, cased and glazed in copper gilt. On the reverse is engraved *Francis Long RL Marines* in script. Weight: 65.7 grams cased. Obverse is a near perfect Extremely Fine while the reverse has suffered from light corrosion and discoloration, but still nearly Extremely Fine.

Background: We know a fair amount regarding Francis Long. He joined the Marines on 13 April 1793, clearly responding to the call to arms following the commencement of the war with Revolutionary France. He came from Croscombe, Somerset, just a few miles from Shepton Mallet where he enlisted. A labourer by trade, probably working on one of the estates in the area. He stood 5' 4" tall, his hair was brown, eyes blue and of a ruddy complexion. He was 17 years old and continued with the Marines until 23 November 1814 when he was discharged due to an ulcerous leg.

As a Private, he was attached originally with the 33rd Company until he joined the *Mars* on 29 March 1803 and changed to the 3rd Company, headquartered at Plymouth. His previous ships had been the *Russell* from 1797-1800, the *London* from 1800-1802. The next ten years were on board the *Mars* from 1803-1813. His final posting was to the *Royal Sovereign* in 1814. He took part in the first battle of Copenhagen in 1801, and the second battle in 1807. He appears to have survived Trafalgar unscathed, in fact he seems to have had a charmed life as he certainly saw a fair amount of action, but no wounds, just his bad leg which may have been caused by a minor wound. We know he was married because he paid 9 shillings and 4 pence every month to his wife and hopefully after his long service, the two of them enjoyed a good life together.

Provenance: Private purchase, 1990.

References: The National Archives, Kew: ADM 158/ 243. ADM 35/ 1468-1470, 943-944, 1054, 2310-2311, 2904-2905, 3610. ADM 36/ 12844-12847, 14065-14067, 16258-16263. ADM37/ 269-273, 2133-2136, 2794-2795, 3705-3706, 4117-4118. ADM 22/ 258.

BT25 Midshipman Henry Walker, HMS Bellerophon, Captain John Cooke, succeeded by Lieutenant William Pryce Cumby

Description: Tin, fleet issue, silvered, cased and glazed in copper gilt. There is no inscription on the medal. Weight: 84.4 grams cased. Extremely fine with the letters of the legend heightened by chasing. The medal has been given a silver wash which has, along with the casing, preserved it perfectly.

Background: From Mackenzie we have the brief details of the career of Henry Walker. He was born in Manchester and entered the service in 1803 as a Volunteer 1st Class. He served as a Midshipman in the *Bellerophon* at the blockades of Brest, Rochefort and Cadiz. He fought at the battle of Trafalgar and was present at the capture of the *Morengo* and *Belle Poule* in 1806. In the frigate *Nereide* he took part in the unsuccessful attack on Buenos Ayres in 1807. In the frigate *Cleopatra*, he contributed toward the capture of the French 40-gun frigate *La Topaz* and the reduction of Martinique, 1809. Promoted to Lieutenant in 1810 he joined the *Menelaus* and in her boats took part in the capture of three war vessels and convoy in the harbour of Corigeon in 1815. He was Lieutenant on board the *Leander* at the bombardment of Algiers in 1816 where he was wounded. He retired from the service in 1834 as Commander and died in Manchester in 1849. Mackenzie notes that Henry Walker received the Naval General Service medal with three clasps which would have been for Trafalgar, Martinique and Algiers, but the Message *NGS Roll* shows a medal with only the Trafalgar clasp, which is an error as the original roll shows all three clasps issued.

The bicentenary year of 2005 was certainly a year to be in London because all of the major and minor auction houses put on Trafalgar sales. Bonham's had a major sale on 5 July which was a great success and in fact drew such attention that Bonham's had another Trafalgar sale on 18 October. It was at this second sale that Henry Walker's Boulton Trafalgar medal was offered by the family. I was familiar with the letter that Henry had written to his mother after the battle and I knew I had to buy his medal. Fortunately, it wasn't that expensive, and a wonderful medal both in terms of condition and its history. I can't think of a better way to tell the story of *Bellerophon* than to transcribe Henry's letter in full, which comes from *Logs of the Great Sea Fights* by T. Sturges Jackson and published by the Navy Records Society in 1899-1900.

The *Bellerophon* was badly mauled at the Battle of the Nile, and Trafalgar was to prove no different.

Letter from Mr. Henry Walker, Midshipman, to his Mother, Mrs. R. Walker, Preston. (Now in the possession of his son, Mr. R.B.N. Walker [in 1898])

'*Bellerophon* at Sea, latitude 50 12 N, longitude 14 06 W.

22 November 1805

Dear Mother, I wrote you a few lines from on board the *Leviathan* in haste, to assure you of my safety after the late memorable action, and was in hopes before this time to have had the pleasure of giving you an account of my arrival in England, for which I am now on my passage, the *Bellerophon* being so much disabled in the action as to be in want of a thorough repair. The papers will have given you a much fuller account of the action than I can; but lest you should accuse me of idleness, I will give some particulars, which may, I hope, give you some amusement. Lord Nelson took the command of our fleet on the 29th of September, and though we had before that no doubt of success in the event of an action, yet the presence of such a man could not but inspire every individual in the fleet with additional confidence. Every one felt himself more than a match for any enemy that there was any probability of being opposed to; and as we knew the combined fleet had positive orders to put to sea, every eye was anxiously fixed toward the shore, and every signal that was seen flying on board our repeating frigates was expected to convey the welcome intelligence.

We were not long kept in this state of suspense, for about nine in the morning on the 19th October, a ship was observed firing guns and making signals for the enemy's fleet being getting under way. The Admiral immediately made signals for a general chase and to prepare for action. You may easily conceive with what alacrity this was obeyed. In a quarter of an hour 26 of the finest ships in the navy were under all sail, and formed a glorious sight; the wind was favourable and in a short time the *Bellerophon, Belleisle, Orion, Leviathan* and *Polyphemus* showed their superiority of sailing, and got far ahead of the fleet, which continued under a press of sail the whole ensuing night, steering for the Straits which was supposed to be the enemy's destination.

At daylight we were in sight of Gibraltar; a frigate made signals for a strange fleet N by E, when we were recalled and signals made for the order of sailing. We then stood back again to the northward; the weather was thick and squally so that we saw nothing of the enemy that day, though the *Agamemnon* and our frigates formed a chain betwixt them and us, and communicated by signals all their motions.

During the night we plainly discerned their signals and remained in the most anxious expectation till the next morning, when, at daylight, we saw them to leeward, and immediately beat to quarters and bore down on them in two columns with all sail set, Lord Nelson in the *Victory* leading one line, Admiral Collingwood, in the *Royal Sovereign*, the other, in which the *Bellerophon* was the fifth ship. The day was remarkably fine; our fleet consisted of 27 sail of the line, seven of which three-deckers, two 80-gun ships, fifteen seventy-fours, and there sixty-fours.

The combined fleet consisted of 33 sail of the line, four of which 3-deckers, six eighty-gun ships, twenty-two seventy-fours, and one sixty-four. Whilst we were bearing down on them they formed in a close order of battle, French and Spaniards alternately, and waited for us with great intrepidity. A few minutes before the firing commenced, Lord Nelson conveyed by telegraph the following sentence to the fleet: 'England expects that every man will do his duty.' This was received on board our ship with three cheers and a general shout of, 'No fear of that!'

At 10 minutes past twelve the *Royal Sovereign* opened fire on the enemy's centre; at 12:20, she broke their line and engaged the Spanish 3-decker to leeward; she was followed by the *Mars*, *Belleisle* and *Tonnant*, which engaged their respective opponents without breaking the line; at 12.25, we opened our fire; at 12:30, broke the line astern a Spanish 2-decker, fighting both sides in passing through; at 12:35, whilst hauling up, fell on board *l'Aigle*, a French 80-gun ship, our fore yard locking with her main yard. The action soon after became general, *l'Aigle* was the best manned ship in the combined fleet, and was full of picked grenadiers, who annoyed us most dreadfully with musketry.

The *Bellerophon* was equally manned, and had she been fairly alongside her opponent, would soon have carried her, and even in the disadvantageous situation in which we were placed, we very soon drove them from the lower deck; and though we could only bring our foremost guns to bear upon her, whilst we received her whole broadside and the fire of four other ships, we had nearly silenced her fire when she dropped astern of us. But you will be able to judge of our situation from an extract from our log:-

12:25. Fell on board the French two-deck ship *l'Aigle* whilst hauling to the wind, our fore yard locking with her main yard; kept up a brisk fire on her on our starboard bow, and a Spanish two-decker *Monarca*, on the larboard bow, at the same time receiving and returning fire from a Spanish two-decker on the larboard quarter, and receiving the fire of a Spanish two-decker athwart our stern and a French two-decker abaft the starboard beam. At 1, the main and mizzen topmasts fell over the side; at 1.5, the Master and at 1.11, the Captain fell; still foul of *l'Aigle*, and keeping up a brisk fire from the main and lower deck guns; quarter deck, poop and forecastle being nearly cleared away by the enemy's musketry chiefly from the troops on board *l'Aigle*. 1.20. The jib boom was shot away; at 1.40, *l'Aigle* dropped to leeward under a raking fire from us as she fell off; our ship at this time unmanageable from braces, bowlines, &c. shot away; 1.45. *l'Aigle* was engaged by *Defiance*; 2.5. She struck.

After we had thus got clear of our principal opponent, who did not return a single gun whilst we raked her, and two others of them had been engaged by the *Dreadnought* and *Colossus*, we were now only opposed to two Spanish seventy-fours, one of which, the *Monarca*, shortly afterwards struck, and was at 3 o'clock taken possession of by our second lieutenant, myself and 8 men.

The remaining one, the *Bahama*, struck to us in about half an hour afterwards, and was taken possession of by our fourth lieutenant. There was very little firing after this except from five French ships making off to windward, which fired on both the *Bellerophon* and *Monarca*. One of them was taken by the *Minotaur*, and at 7 minutes after 5 the firing ceased, when 21 of the enemy's ships remained in our possession and one on fire, which soon blew up; another sunk in action.

Among the prizes were three admirals' ships, the Commander-in-Chief, Admiral Villeneuve, was taken, as was the *Santissima Trinidad*, a Spanish 4-decker of 138 guns, the largest ship in the world. Such a victory

Situation of the *Bellerophon* at the moment of the death of her gallant commander, Captain John Cooke.

could not be obtained without great loss. Our ship as was to be expected from her situation, suffered very considerably, having 28 killed outright, 127 badly, and about 40 slightly wounded; 23 are since dead of their wounds. Our prize, the *Monarca*, had suffered still more, having upwards of 250 killed and wounded, and the ship very much injured in every respect.

Till now everything had been favourable to the British, and from the fineness of the day we had every prospect of bringing 20 of our prizes to England; but in the ensuing night a storm came on, such as I had never witnessed, and for the four following days we had a much severer struggle against the elements than the enemy. You will imagine what have been our sufferings, in a crippled ship, with 500 prisoners on board and only 55 Englishmen, most of whom were in a constant state of intoxication. We rolled away all our masts except the fore mast; were afterwards forced to cut away 2 anchors, heave overboard several guns, shot, &c. to lighten her; and were, after all, in such imminent danger of sinking that, seeing no ship near to assist us, we at length determined to run the ship on shore on the Spanish coast, which we should have done had not the *Leviathan* fortunately fallen in with and saved us, and all but about 150 Spaniards. The ship then went ashore and was afterwards destroyed. We were more fortunate than several of our countrymen, who were lost in the prizes; others were taken prisoners by the French and Spaniards, who rose upon and carried them into Cadiz. So dreadful was the storm that only four of the prizes, one of which is the *Bahama*, are left in our possession; they are now at Gibraltar. Three are got back into Cadiz, five on shore near that place, and the remainder either foundered in the gale or were destroyed by us to prevent their again falling into the enemy's possession.

All the British ships were fortunate enough to weather out the gale. Thirteen of the most disabled put into Gibraltar, the *Bellerophon* was one. I did not join till the 3rd inst., the day before she sailed in company with the *Victory* and *Belleisle* for England. I had the mortification to find my chest had been broken open in my absence, several of my clothes stolen, and nearly all my linen either lost or torn by the wounded for bandages, my hammock and bedding had likewise been shot away in the action, which is the more unfortunate as I can so ill afford to replace them. I suppose I have made about 20£ prize money in the late action, which would have brought me upwards of 100£ had we not met with the dreadful storm which destroyed our prizes; but when I shall receive this or get back to England is now equally uncertain, for we have lately had such violent easterly gales as have driven us far to the westward of England and Ireland; and till we get a fair wind it is impossible with crippled ships like ours to make any way towards home.

Henry Walker'

Provenance: Bonham's, 18 October 2005, lot 80, sold by family descendants of Midshipman Henry Walker.
References: *The Trafalgar Roll*, by Col. R. H. Mackenzie, George Allen, London, 1913.
Naval General Service Medal 1793-1840 by Colin Message, privately published, 1996.
Logs of the Great Sea Fights by T. Sturges Jackson, The Navy Records Society, London, 1899-1900.

BT26 Matthew Henley and his wife Betsy, Quarter Master, HMS Bellerophon, Captain John Cooke, succeeded by Lieutenant William Pryce Cumby

Description: Tin, fleet issue. On the reverse is engraved *Matt Henley* in script and BELLEROPHON in block capitals. On the obverse is engraved *Betsy Henley* in script. The engraving for both the obverse and reverse are in the same hand. Weight: 42 grams. Fine with both sides suffering from corrosion.

Background: From Admiral Smyth we have: 'The Quarter Master is a petty officer, appointed to assist the Master and Mates in their several duties, as stowing the hold, coiling the cables, attending the binnacle and steerage, keeping time by the watch glasses, assisting in hoisting signals and keeping his eye on general quarter deck movements.'

When I look at the research carried out by Gillian Hughes, which covers the period 1795 to 1826, one just wonders at the fortitude of a man such as this. Even more remarkable is his time on board *Bellerophon*, which he entered on 15 August 1801 and stayed with the ship until 28 October 1807. One then considers his stations while on board.

He was 20 years old, from London and Volunteered at Portsmouth on 25 May 1795 with his first ship being the 98-gun, second rate line of battle ship, *London*. He joined as an Ordinary Seaman, but was advanced to Able Seaman in December. Clearly a very experienced sailor at age 20. He joined the *Bellerophon* on 15 August 1801 as an Able Seaman and then on 1 March 1803, advanced to Quarter Gunner, then on 1 October of that year promoted to Midshipman, but only to 11 December when he was rated Coxswain. There is no doubt that he was well respected by his captains Viscount Garlies and John Loring.

Things changed in January 1805 when he was rated back to Able Seaman. It looks like Captain Loring came ashore at that time and that Matthew Henley was a favourite of his, but when he lost the support of Loring, he lost his position as Coxswain. This was only for a short while because on 2 March 1805, he was promoted to Quarter Master and it appears that Captain John Cooke, who took command on 1 April, was happy with this appointment of an important petty officer. Henley remained in that posting until discharged from *Bellerophon* 1807 to the 74-gun *Bedford*, where again he was rated as Quarter Master. His big step came in 1812 when he was examined for Boatswain, and was duly accepted and appointed to the 20-gun brig sloop *Rifleman*, where he remained until 31 October 1815. Although *Rifleman* only had 18 guns, 16 of them were 32 pound carronades, in a close fight, her broadside would have been devastating.

Now then, some speculation based on just a few facts, but with my romantic imagination, I really can't resist joining up the dots and hopefully coming to the right conclusion. Matthew Henley's Boulton Trafalgar medal is also inscribed to Betsy Henley. From the *Ayshford Trafalgar Roll* we have a note that Matthew Henley had submitted a Will in favour of Mart[ha] Thompson on 28 February 1806. Martha Thompson lived in London at the back of King Street and may have been a common law wife, or a married sister.

On the 25th of April, 1807 Matthew Henley arranged for an allotment of his pay, £1/1/0 per month to his wife Elizabeth [Betsy] to be paid in Plymouth and on 5 May 1807, he changed his Will to benefit Elizabeth.

To me, I can see Betsy as having been one of the women on board *Bellerophon* at Trafalgar and that this Boulton Trafalgar medal is their shared medal. Betsy was a Sea Wife, but it looks like she knew what she wanted and that she and Matthew were married. This probably took place when *Bellerophon* was again in Torbay in 1807 and both Matthew and Betsy had access to a church. It is also about this time that the Boulton Trafalgar medals arrived in Plymouth. Matthew was certainly a good catch for Betsy as his later advancement to Boatswain proved and I hope they had a long life together.

Matthew Henley saw a fair amount of action. When on board the *London*, he took part in Lord Bridport's action off the Isle of Groix on 23 June 1795, just a month after he came on board. He was also present at Copenhagen in 1801, but as Hyde Parker's flagship *London*, wasn't committed to the battle. With the *Bellerophon*, he was at Trafalgar along with several minor actions in the West Indies.

HMS *Bedford* had been used as a prison ship at Plymouth, but then was refitted for foreign service in 1807 when the petty officers and crew of the *Bellorophon* transferred to her under the command of Captain

James Walker. *Bedford* then joined Rear-Admiral Sir Sidney Smith who was assisting the Portuguese royal family in its flight from Lisbon to Rio de Janeiro where she continued to cruise until September 1810 and then returned to Portsmouth.

Matthew Henley then passed his examination as Boatswain and joined the *Rifleman* under the command of Joseph Pearce and cruised on the North American station during the War of 1812. Chasing and capturing privateers were her daily fare and *Rifleman* was successful.

On 8 June 1816, Henley moved to the 10-gun brig sloop *Briseis*, Commander George Dommett. These small ships were termed 'coffin brigs' because of their light construction and vulnerability in very bad weather. Almost as one would expect, she was lost off the north coast of Cuba, the Commander wasn't sure of their position and wanted to go closer in shore to check, much against the recommendation of the Master. Once inshore, the ship drifted and struck. There followed the inevitable as the sea was running high and *Briseis* in the end was rolled over. All the crew were saved. The court martial found Commander Dommett lacking in judgement and docked him two years seniority. The Master was found not to have pressed the danger forcefully enough and was dropped to the bottom of the Master's List and left on shore for three years to consider his position.

Upon his return to England in 1817, Henley was posted at Plymouth to look after several ships in Ordinary or building in his capacity as Boatswain. This must have been a good time for Betsy as very probably Matthew would be able to stay ashore during this period.

He joined the *Dartmouth*, a 36-gun 18 pounder frigate on 1 August 1824, again as Boatswain. *Dartmouth* cruised the Caribbean returning to Portsmouth in November 1826 when Matthew Henley was discharged as an invalid. There appears to have been a fair amount of sickness on board *Dartmouth*, malaria? Matthew was then 51 years old.

Hopefully he was able to regain his health being back in England and one also hopes that he and Betsy enjoyed a long life together.

Provenance: Private purchase, 1985.
References: The National Archives, Kew: ADM 35/ 227, 2129-2131, 939-943, 2628, 3306, 3796. ADM 36/ 15588-15590, 16497-16500, 11767-11769, 12572-12575, 14063-14066, 4088. ADM37/ 515-516, 2014-2017, 2722, 3311, 4788-4789, 5825, 5641, 6932-6935. ADM 27/ 12. ADM/ 11-12. ADM13 / 104. ADM 42/ 119, 183, 187.
The Sailor's Word-Book by Admiral W.H. Smyth, Blackie & Son, London, 1867.
The Ayshford Complete Trafalgar Roll on cd, privately published, 2004.

BT27 William Smart, Private Royal Marine, HMS Achille, Captain Richard King

Description: Tin, fleet issue. On the reverse is engraved *Wm Smart HMS Achille* in script. The medal has been given a silver wash and is cased in copper gilt and glazed. Weight: 69.2 grams cased. Extremely fine due to the silver wash and casing which have preserved the medal perfectly.

Background: From Dudley Pope we have an excellent account of the seventy-four gun *Achille* at Trafalgar. In addition to being the backbone of the Captain's authority on board ship, the Marines very often were deployed to support gun crews, particularly if casualties amongst the gunners were heavy. The Marines were regularly in the boats on cutting out expeditions and actions on shore.

'The seventh ship in Collingwood's division to get into action was Captain Richard King's *Achille*, not to be confused with the French ship of the same name. King, the son of an admiral, brought his ship down to pass through the enemy's line astern of the *Montañes* and ahead of the *San Ildefonso*. He chose the former for his victim, steered boldly under her stern and fired a broadside into her quarter as he passed.

'The British ship's broadside was perfectly controlled: the *Montañes*'s senior surviving officer, Lieut. Alejo de Rubalcava, wrote that the *Achille* 'poured a terrible fire into our larboard quarter, which caused great havoc amongst the crew, to the hull and to the rigging.'

'Captain Salzedo, commanding the Spanish seventy-four, at first set the topgallants and main-topmast-staysail to get more way on the ship so that he could luff up and bring his larboard broadside to bear on the British *Achille* before she reached him, but King was too quick and the *Achille*, after passing under the Spaniard's stern, came up alongside. Wreathed in thick smoke, the two ships lay close to each other, firing broadsides as boxers might exchange punches. Within half an hour Captain Salzedo was killed and his second-in-command carried wounded to the cockpit. Lieut. Perez, the only officer left alive on the quarter-deck, sent for the next senior officer, Rubalcava. And when he came to the quarter-deck he found nothing to inspire him. 'I observed in passing the main-deck that the crews of all the guns aft were out of action, many being stretched out dead and dying on the deck: the same thing was apparent in the chief guns on the quarter-deck, but it did not detain me from going up on the poop, where I instructed the midshipman entrusted with the charge of the Colours that he should stand by them and on no account should he haul them down.'

'While Rubalcava sent orders down to the gun-decks that all available men were to be collected to handle the guns left undamaged, Captain King realised the *Montañes* was beaten and up to the north-east through the smoke he could see the *Belleisle* being savagely attacked. While the *Montañes* sheered off out of the fight he turned away to starboard and a few minutes later, at 1:30 p.m., found another Spanish ship, the *Argonauta* (not to be confused with the French *Argonaute*) in the smoke on the starboard side. He promptly luffed up and hove-to on the *Argonauta's* larboard bow. For the best part of an hour the British gunners fired broadside after broadside into the Spanish ship.

'At the end of that time the *Argonauta*, according to her wounded commanding officer, Captain Pareja, 'had all the guns on the quarter-deck and poop dismounted, a great number of guns in the batteries out of action, as much as on account of the pieces [being damaged] as from the want of crews ... the whole of the rigging was destroyed, so that there were no shrouds left to the masts - save one to the mainmast - and they were threatening to fall every minute, being shot through.

'In this situation,' he adds, 'it was very evident that the ship could make but slight and feeble resistance ... With these inexpressible feelings I was taken below to have my wounds dressed, expecting every minute to find myself brought to the grievous point of having to surrender.' But for the moment the *Argonauta* had won a brief reprieve: the French *Achille* (which, as will be related later, had been in action with the *Revenge*) arrived on the British *Achille's* larboard side and opened fire.

'A short while afterwards the French *Berwick* sailed up on the British *Achille's* starboard side, between her and the stricken *Argonauta*. For a few minutes the British ship was sandwiched between two of the enemy while the *Argonauta* drifted away to leeward, masts tottering, more like a floating coffin than a ship of war.

'The French *Achille* then went ahead, leaving the British *Achille* and the *Berwick* to fight it out. Although King and his men had already silenced two ships - the *Montañes* and the *Argonauta* - they still had plenty of fight left in them, and within half an hour they forced the *Berwick* to strike. When one of the British *Achille's* officers went on board to take possession he 'counted upon her decks and in her cockpit and tiers fifty-one dead bodies, including that of her gallant captain, M. Camas'; and the wounded in the *Berwick*, according to the report of her few surviving officers, amounted to nearly 200: her loss in officers was very severe, 'the quarter-deck having thrice been cleared.'

The loss to the British *Achille* was 13 killed and 59 wounded which shows just how skilful Captain King was in placing his ship to inflict maximum damage on his enemies and minimum damage to his own ship.

This is one of the few medals that hasn't been fully researched, however from *The Ayshford Trafalgar Roll* we learn that William Smart joined the Royal Marines on 28 December 1804, aged 25 years old. He was from Wellington, Salop (Shropshire in England). He joined as a Volunteer and stood 5' 6" tall, fair complexion, hair brown and eyes grey and his trade is listed as labourer. He was attached to the Plymouth Division of Royal Marines and was discharged on 30 May 1814 due to a rupture, which was not an uncommon complaint due to all manner of physical exertions on board ship and when operating ashore.

As *Achille* remained in active service following Trafalgar, it is safe to think that Private William Smart stayed with her, as was the practice, until he was discharged in 1814.

For *Achille's* career following Trafalgar, we have this from Mackenzie:

'*Achille* joined Commodore Sir Samuel Hood's squadron, her boats assisted in the cutting out of the French corvette *Cesar*, 16, at the entrance of the river Gironde on the night of the 15th July 1806; and witnessed the capture off Rochefort, on the 24th September following, of the French 40-gun frigates *Armide*, *Minerve*, and *Gloire*. She was also in the expedition to Walcheren and the blockade of Flushing in the same year, and in the blockade of Cadiz 1810-1811. When commanded by Captain Askew P. Hollis, her boats, in conjunction with those of the *Cerberus*, captured twelve sail of Trabbacolles off Venice on the 17th July 1812; while in the same month, in conjunction with the *Milford*, she captured four other vessels.'

Provenance: Private purchase, 1979.

References: *England Expects* by Dudley Pope, Weidenfeld & Nicolson, London, 1959.
The Ayshford Complete Trafalgar Roll on cd, privately published, 2004.
The Trafalgar Roll, by Col. R. H. Mackenzie, George Allen, London, 1913.

The French *L'Achille* ablaze following broadsides from HMS *Prince*.
Image from Jenkins's *Naval Achievements* available from Sim Comfort Associates.

BT28 Henry Hore, Landsman, HMS Revenge, Captain Robert Moorsom

Description: Tin, fleet issue. On the reverse is engraved *Hen Hore HMS Revenge* in script. The medal is cased in silver and glazed and housed in a red leather case. Weight: 75 grams cased. Extremely fine, but with corrosion discolouring the medal across the obverse and here and there on the reverse.

Background: Henry Hore was a Dorset man from Hampreston, who joined the newly built 74-gun *Revenge* on 16 April 1805, aged 21 as a Landsman. Within the ships of Nelson's navy it was raw muscle power that hauled up anchors and made taut the lines of the great sails that gave power to a 74-gun ship of the line. Landsmen supplied that muscle power.

Dudley Pope recounts: 'At about 12:35 p.m. Captain Moorsom brought the *Revenge* into action. She was a new ship, built at Chatham and launched a few months earlier.

'While we were running down to them', wrote one of the sailors, 'we were favoured with several shots, and some of our men were wounded. Many of the men thought it hard the firing should be all on one side, and became impatient to return the compliment; but our Captain had given orders not to fire until we had got in close with them, so that all our shots would tell.'

'The *Revenge* came up to the line obliquely, running almost parallel to the *San Ildefonso* and the French *Achille* (before the latter went north to engage the British *Achille*). Captain Moorsom ordered the *Revenge's* gunners to open fire on both ships. His men were among the best trained in the Fleet, for Moorsom was one of the Navy's cleverest gunnery experts. One or more shot from the British ship's opening broadsides bit deep into the *Achille's* mizenmast five feet above the deck, and as the wood cracked and split, the officers on the poop scrambled to get clear. Slowly it toppled over the side, carrying with it the sharpshooters perched in the top.

'The French *Achille* had been sailing with her jib-boom very close to the stern of the *San Ildefonso*, but as the mizen went by the board she slowed down, and Moorsom seized the opportunity by taking the *Revenge* close across the *Achille's* bow to break through the line. He went so close to the French ship's jib-boom, sticking out from the bow like a massive tusk, caught the *Revenge's* mizentopsail and ripped it out. According to one of the *Revenge's* seamen, a number of the *Achille's* crew were perched on the bowsprit ready to jump on board, 'but they caught a Tartar; for their design was discovered, and our Marines with their small-arms and the carronade on the poop, loaded with canister shot, swept them off so fast that they were glad to sheer off'. The *Revenge* had by then fired two broadsides into her bows. Moorsom then luffed up, and put his ship on the *Achille's* starboard bow, where he could fire his larboard guns into her and aim his starboard broadside at the stern of the *San Ildefonso*.

'However, Admiral Gravina's flagship, the 112-gun *Principe de Asturias*, was just astern of the *Achille*, and she bore away to starboard so that she could rake the British ship. The *Revenge* then found herself in the midst of a triangle of fire from the *San Ildefonso*, *Achille* and *Principe de Asturias*, and she had to endure it for nearly twenty minutes before help arrived. This came in the form of the last four ships in Collingwood's division.

'Meanwhile Captain Moorsom and his *Revenge* had continued to battle with the French *Achille*. Finally the French ship wore and came round to starboard in an attempt to pass under the *Revenge's* stern; but Moorsom's gunners raked her and the mainmast - which had already lost its topmast - came tumbling down, leaving her with only a foremast standing.

'While the French *Achille* drifted away to leeward, Moorsom took the *Revenge* into action against the *Aigle* which had been involved with the *Bellerophon* and *Belleisle*, and raked her. Moorsom's ship had by now suffered badly: her bowsprit, all three lower masts and main-topmast were heavily damaged, nine shot had cut through the copper sheathing of the hull below the water-line and started leaks, and two midshipmen, eighteen seamen and eight Marines had been killed. Captain Moorsom, the Master and a lieutenant, the captain of Marines, 38 seamen and nine Marines had been wounded.'

Also on board *Revenge* was a seaman named William Robinson who wrote under the name of Jack Nastyface. His account of the *Revenge* at Trafalgar will give you some idea as to what it was like to be surrounded by four enemy ships, all determined to spew as much death and destruction upon you that they could.

'In this condition, we lay by the side of the enemy, firing away, and now and then we received a good raking from them, passing under our stern. This was a busy time with us, for we had not only to endeavour to repair our damage, but to keep to our duty. Often during the battle we could not see for the smoke, whether we were firing at a foe or a friend, and as to hearing, the noise of the guns had so completely made us deaf, that we were obliged to look only to the motions that were made. In this manner we continued the battle till nearly five o'clock, when it ceased.'

Henry Hore stayed with *Revenge* and was present in 1809 at the Battle of Basque Roads when Lord Cochrane tried to destroy a French squadron at anchor. *Revenge* was unlucky in running aground, which made her an easy target for the French shore batteries, and again she suffered.

Later, in 1809, *Revenge* took part in the secret expedition to Walcheren, which was a deadly place both from the resistance of the enemy and from a contagion called Walcheren Fever. At this time, Henry Hore is noted in the *Revenge's* muster list as 'lent to the *Sisiphone*' which is a ship we have no record of and may have been a hired troop transport. Henry continued to serve on board *Revenge* and learned the skills of a sailor with promotion to Ordinary Seaman and then to Able Seaman. On 11 Sept, 1814 when he was transferred to HMS *Namur*. Shortly after he was transferred to the *Glasgow* which was a newly launched 50-gun 4th rate. Henry would have been a topman on board *Glasgow*, but he died on board her on 17 January, 1815, probably due to an accident, perhaps a fall. Managing sails in the North Sea during January storms was always high risk for the topmen and fatal accidents were not uncommon. It is noted in the paylist that Henry sent his mother money every month. I think this Boulton Trafalgar was also sent to her for safe keeping.

Provenance: Private purchase, 1992.
References: The National Archives, Kew: ADM 35/ 2361, 2399-2400, 3032-3034, 3791. ADM 36/ 15978-15979, 16545-16547, 2828-2829. ADM37/ 154-158, 1184-1186, 2194-2195, 3436, 4104-4106, 5304. ADM 27/ 16.
England Expects by Dudley Pope, Weidenfeld & Nicolson, London, 1959.
Nautical Economy by William Robinson, privately published William Robinson, London, 1836. Reprinted as *Jack Nastyface, Memoirs of an English Seaman*, Naval Institute Press, Annapolis, 1973.

BT29 Thomas Mansell, Yeoman of the Sheets, HMS Revenge, Captain Robert Moorsom

Description: Tin, fleet issue. On the reverse is engraved *Ths Mansell HMS Revenge* in script. There is a silver loop attached for suspension. Weight: 41.4 grams. Very fine with some corrosion here and there on both sides of the medal.

Background: Thomas Mansell was a very experienced seaman who joined the *Drake*, which was the captured French privateer *Tigre*, 16-gun brig sloop. *Tigre* was captured in the Caribbean and it was there at Martinique Dockyard while *Drake* was being refitted that Thomas Mansell joined her as a Quarter Master on 7 October 1801. He was from South Shields and 25 year old. *Drake* formed part of Samuel Hood's squadron and took part in the capture of Surinam in April 1804. One can image life on board this beautiful ex-privateer with a ship's company of only 87 men and a Captain like William Ferris and an Admiral like Sam Hood. It must have been a very rewarding time for all on board her.

At Surinam, the Dutch 32-gun frigate *Amsterdam* was captured and Captain Ferris took command of her. Thomas Mansell followed his captain to his new command on 12 May 1804 and was again rated Quarter Master. In the *Amsterdam*, Commodore Samuel Hood returned to Portsmouth where the ship was paid off on 2 July 1805.

The change of command was fortunate for both Captain Ferris and Thomas Mansell because just a few months after leaving her, *Drake*, while escorting a convoy in company with the *Pandour* frigate off Nevis, struck a shoal which effectively tore her bottom out. Fortunately *Pandour* was close by and sent her boats to rescue the stricken officers and men from the *Drake* and all were saved.

No time for a break for Mansell as the next day after leaving the *Amsterdam*, he was transferred to the *Revenge*. He was initially rated as Able Seaman then Yeoman of the Sheets until 1 March 1806 when he was reinstated as Quarter Master. But it was not a happy end because on 10 September 1808 he was discharged to Haslar Hospital at Gosport along with 15 other men from the *Revenge*. All of the other men were returned to service, but Thomas Mansell died on the 14 of September. Hepatitis, acute liver failure, appears to have caused his death.

There is an anecdote from Landsman William Robinson, who served on board *Revenge* at Trafalgar, that is just so good, I'll give you all of it here. As a note, Robinson came from Farnham in Surrey and volunteered in May 1803 to join the newly built *Revenge*. He doesn't appear to have been literate upon joining, signed his name with His Mark, however he did serve until 1811 when he Ran and managed to escape detection. He later became a purser's steward, so he must have picked up his letters and numbers along the way. In 1836, he wrote *Nautical Economy, Memoirs of an English Seaman* under the pseudonym Jack Nastyface, but published the work in his own name, William Robinson. His recalling those hard days at sea has become a classic lower deck narrative.

      'The Advantage of learning to dance.

'As we were closely engaged throughout the battle [of Trafalgar], and the shots were playing their pranks pretty freely, grape as well as canister, with single and double headed thunderers all joining in the frolic; what was termed a slaughtering one, came in at one of the lower deck ports, which killed and wounded nearly all at the gun, and amongst them, a very merry little fellow, who was the very life of the ship's company, for he was ever the mirth of his mess, and on whatever duty he might be ordered, his spirits made light the labour. He was the ship's cobbler, and withal a very good dancer; so that when any of his messmates would serve us out a tune, he was sure to trip it on light fantastic toe, and find a step to it. He happened to be stationed at the gun when this messenger of death and destruction entered, and the poor fellow was so completely stunned by the head of another man being knocked against his, that no one doubted but that he was dead. As it is customary to throw overboard those, who, in an engagement are killed outright, the poor cobbler, amongst the rest, was taken to the port-hole to be committed to the deep, without any other ceremony than shoving him through the port; but, just as they were about to let him slip from their hand into the water, the blood began to circulate, and he commenced kicking. Upon this sign of returning life, his shipmates soon hauled the poor snob in again, and through wonderful to relate, he recovered so speedily, that he actually fought the battle out; and, when he was afterwards joked about it, he would say, 'it is well that I learned to dance; for if I had not shown you some of my steps, when you were about to throw me overboard, I should not be here now, but safe enough in Davy Jones's Locker!'

Provenance: Ex J. Coolridge Collection.
Bequethed 1913 to Wadsworth Antheneum.
1966 to the American Numismatic Society.
Morton & Eden, lot 8, 24 May 2006.

References: The National Archives, Kew: ADM 35/ 138, 2361, 2399-2400, 3032-3034, 3791. ADM 36/ 15525-15526, 15715, 15978-15979, 16545-16547, 2828-2829. ADM37/ 154-158, 1184-1186, 2194-2195, 3436, 4104-4106, 5304. ADM 27/ 16.

Nautical Economy by William Robinson, privately published William Robinson, London, 1836. Reprinted as *Jack Nastyface, Memoirs of an English Seaman*, Naval Institute Press, Annapolis, 1973.

The Past
Brutus to Cassius in *Julius Caesar* by W. Shakespeare.

BT30 Samuel Wise, Master's Mate, HMS Polyphemus, Captain Robert Redmill

Description: Tin, fleet issue with the blocked leg in the first R in TRAFALGAR. On the reverse is engraved *Saml Wise, HMS Polyphemus* in script. The medal is cased in silver and glazed. Engraved around the rim of the case in block letters is: FROM M : BOULTON TO THE HEROES OF TRAFALGAR. Weight: 59.9 grams. Extremely fine with some slight discoloration to the obverse while the reverse has remained in brilliant condition.

Background: *Polyphemus* as a 64-gun ship, was too light to stand face to face with the French or Spanish 74 gun ships at Trafalgar and tried to make herself useful by supporting the *Revenge* and other ships during the battle. She took the *Argonauta* in tow shortly after her surrender to *Belleisle* and then on the 23rd, following the great storm, took *Victory* in tow. So hard work for all on board her.

Samuel Wise was 28 years old, from Cumberland and entered the service as Able Seaman. He joined as a volunteer the captured French 20-gun corvette *La Percante*, renamed HMS *Jamaica*, on 12 November 1797 at Port Royal, Jamaica. She was actually part of a small force governed by the Council of Jamaica and given the task of fighting off privateers and trying to recapture ships belonging to the island that had been taken. The log of the *Jamaica* is full of captures and her captain Samuel Brooking was so revered by the Jamaican Council that he was award a hundred guinea sword upon his returning to England in 1799. Unfortunately his health had suffered much in the West Indies and he was never employed again.

During his time on board *Jamaica*, Samuel Wise was variously billeted as Able Seaman, then Midshipman and lastly as Master's Mate. There is little doubt that he was a very talented sailor. His return to England saw him transferred to the 64-gun *Stately*, Captain George Scott, and much work was carried out in the Mediterranean with the blockading of Genoa and Malta and being part of the expedition to Egypt in 1801. Although Samuel Wise was entered on board *Stately* as Master's Mate, this didn't last long and he was reduced to Able Seaman, which may have been not because of a lack of skill, but not able to control a strong will.

Stately was paid off at Chatham on 2 August 1804 and Samuel Wise moved directly to the *Polyphemus*. He was now 36 years old and married to Ann Wise. He made a will in her favour on the seventh of November 1806 around the time when he had been advanced from Master's Mate to Midshipman. It is probably to her that he sent his Boulton Trafalgar medal for safe keeping. But all was not well because late in 1806, he was disrated to Able Seaman and then, just as quickly again, rated Master's Mate. This may well have happened due to no fault in Samuel Wise, i.e. it may have been that his captain accepted on board a more influential young man as Midshipman which meant Wise had to step down to make room for the new appointment. Whatever the cause, we just don't know. What we do know is that when *Polyphemus* was in Portsmouth on 21 March 1808, in the ship's log beside the name Samuel Wise is the letter R. Samuel Wise decided enough was enough and Ran. I hope he was never caught because he would have most likely hung for his desertion.

Provenance: Private purchase, 1979.
References: The National Archives, Kew: ADM 35/ 884, 1634, 2369, 2985. ADM 36/ 12685-12686, 14856-14859, 15694-15694, 16505-16508. ADM37/ 1086-1088. ADM 48/103.
Royal Naval Biography by John Marshall, Longman, London, 1833.

BT31 Henry Wells, Purser, HMS Thunderer, Lieutenant John Stockham

Description: Tin, fleet issue. On the reverse is engraved *Henry Wells Purser HMS Thunderer* in script. There is a silver loop attached for suspension. Weight: 43.2 grams with suspension and ribbon. Fine, with discoloration to both sides, but no corrosion.

Background: Nelson was faced with one of those awful battles of wills amongst his captains. Robert Calder felt that his name had been besmirched due to his lack of full success in halting the combined squadrons of France and Spain on 22 July 1805 off Cape Finisterre as the enemy tried to gain control of the English Channel. He required a court martial to clear his name and three of Nelson's captains were involved with Captain William Lechmere of the *Thunderer* being one of them. Lechmere responded to the call and left

Lieutenant John Stockham to command his ship, which was a very lucky break for Stockham.

Mackenzie notes that *Thunderer*, 74 guns, at Trafalgar provided 'some assistance to the *Revenge* and subsequently was engaged with the Spanish 112-gun *Principe de Asturias* and the French 84-gun *Neptune*. Her losses amounted to sixteen killed and wounded, including three officers.'

Of Henry Wells, Mackenzie writes that he served as Clerk in the *Russell* in Lord Howe's victory of the 1st of June 1794 when he was wounded. Further, he was with Lord Bridport at his battle with the French fleet in 1795. Wells was promoted Paymaster and Purser in 1797 and served as Purser on board the *Thunderer* at both Sir Robert Calder's action and Trafalgar in 1805. He was present at the siege of Gaeta in 1806 and the forcing of the Dardanelles in 1807. He retired in 1843, aged 70 with 50 years of service to the Royal Navy. He received the NGS medal with three clasps, 1st of June 1794, 23 June 1795 and Trafalgar. He died in 1849.

From the research carried out by Gillian Hughes, it appears that Henry Wells had a patron in Sir Peter Parker and the original plan would have been for the young man to become a Midshipman and then progress through the officer corps. However, with his second ship, he became the Captain's Clerk and this role seemed to suit Henry who was clearly articulate and also good with numbers, which led to his ultimately being certified as a Purser. Being a Purser also offered the opportunity to make some money on the side and considering his very long service, one imagines that the job suited him very well.

Two of the ships that Henry served in before Trafalgar were hospital ships, the *Medusa* and the *Le Caton*. *Medusa* met with an unfortunate fate, being wrecked at Gibraltar. David Hepper provides the story: '26 November 1798, *Medusa*, Commander Alexander Beecher was at anchor off Gibraltar, when ordered to weigh and proceed. The wind was variable, the direction shifting and with occasional squalls. She weighed and loosed the foresail and fore-topsail, having previously set the driver and staysails. As she tried to put her head to seaward, the wind again shifted and took her down towards the shore. The sails were furled and she anchored, only to receive a testy message from Admiral Lord St Vincent indicating that he was very displeased with the display so far and inpatient with the delay. Signalling for assistance from the dockyard, the Master Assistant came aboard to direct the manoeuvre. Topsails and staysails were loosed and the cable hove in, the intention being to swing the head to seaward. The baffling winds again defeated them, the yards having to be braced constantly to take advantage of the wind, and she again failed to make headway, drifting down towards the shore. All sail was thrown aback and the anchors let go, but they did not bring her up before she struck the ground off Rosia Bay, where she bilged and filled with water.'

Commander Beecher and Henry Wells returned to England in the *Sourain*, with Beecher facing court martial. Henry continued his career and became Purser to *Le Caton* at Plymouth until he joined the *Thunderer* and took part at Trafalgar.

Provenance: Christie's Lot 12, 20 November 1984.
References: ADM 35/ 1474-1475, 1465-1467, 857, 1074-1075, 375-376, 2502, 3099, 3846-3847, 4046-4048, 4450-4452. ADM 36/ 15455-15457, 11412-11415, 12825, 13400, 15154, 14090-14091. ADM 37/ 526, 192-198, 2249-2251, 4160-4161, 5161-5162, 6026-6028, 6312, 7612-7617, ADM 12/81.
The Trafalgar Roll by Col. R.H. Mackenzie, George Allen, London, 1913.
Naval General Service Medal 1793-1840, Colin Message, privately published, 1996.
British Warship Losses in the Age of Sail (1650-1859), David Hepper, Jean Boudriot Publications, East Sussex, 1994.

BT32 John Greenwood, Able Seaman, HMS Defence, Captain George Johnstone Hope

Description: Tin, fleet issue. On the obverse is engraved *John Greenwood* and the reverse *Defence* in script. Weight: 40.6 grams. The obverse is Extremely Fine and without corrosion while the reverse is Very Fine with some corrosion.

Background: From Mackenzie we learn that the *Defence*, 74-guns, was one of the most illustrious ships under Nelson's command at Trafalgar. She was launched in 1763 and served with Rodney, taking part in many of his actions, most notably in the defeat of Langara's Spanish fleet in January 1780, which effected the Relief of Gibraltar. Rodney then sailed west to the West Indies, while *Defence* sailed east and joined Sir Edward Hughes, thus taking part in the last battle against the French Admiral Suffren off Pondicherry on 20 June 1783.

She played an important role at Lord Howe's victory of the 1st of June, was with Nelson at the Nile and again at Copenhagen in 1801 and continued in the Baltic for a while. She was again at Copenhagen in 1807, but unfortunately wrecked along with the *St George* on the east coast of Jutland on Christmas Eve, 1811. Of her crew of 530, only a handful survived that terrible night.

At Trafalgar, *Defence* was at the end of Collingwood's column and only got into action two and a half hours after its start. She did some useful mopping up and managed to secure the capture of *San Ildefonse* of 74 guns which had already been heavily engaged by other ships. The Spanish 74 weathered the storm after Trafalgar and was one of the few surviving prizes.

This is a particularly interesting Boulton Trafalgar medal as it was engraved by the same jeweller at Plymouth that engraved the Robert Collinson medal, BT21. I think the medal to Greenwood was also originally cased and glazed which is evidenced by the fine condition of the obverse and that the casing was probably in silver which meant that with the corrosion to the reverse, the casing was removed and melted down for its cash value. It is perhaps fortunate that Greenwood transferred to the *Kent* following Trafalgar, or he and his medal may have suffered the fate of the *Defence* on Christmas Eve, 1811.

John Greenwood was from Eltham in Kent and at 22 years of age volunteered to join *Defence* on 15 June 1803. He was immediately rated Able Seaman, so was a prime hand. Following Trafalgar, *Defence* returned to Plymouth and Greenwood transferred to HMS *Kent* on Christmas Day, 1805. He continued in the *Kent* until January 1813 when he was transferred to HMS *Woolwich* which conveyed Sir James Yeo and his special team of men that formed the Naval Establishment of the Lakes of Canada. On the 30th of April, 1814, he moved to the newly built *Princess Charlotte*. HMS *Princess Charlotte*, later HMS *Burlington*, was a 42-gun fifth rate frigate built at the Kingston Royal Naval Dockyard in Kingston, Ontario. She had originally been named as *Vittoria*, but was renamed before being launched. She was built to a design by George Record, and was constructed under a private contract by Master Shipwright John Goudie. She served on Lake Ontario, having been commissioned on 5 May 1814 under Captain William Mulcaster.

The ship took part in British attacks on Fort Oswego and Sackett's Harbour on Lake Ontario in 1814. In November that year she came under the command of Captain Edward Collier, and was renamed HMS *Burlington* on 9 December 1815 after *Princess Charlotte* had returned to England. Captain Nicholas Lockyer took command in June 1816. *Burlington* was offered for sale in January 1833, but there were no buyers and she was later towed away and scuttled.

From the gazetted letter by Commodore Yeo, he notes that Captain Mulcaster of the *Princess Charlotte* commanded the 200 seamen armed with pikes that played an important role in the capture of Fort Oswego and its subsequent securing of naval stores and destruction of the fort. Mulcaster was severely wounded during the action. One would think that John Greenwood was right up front with the rest of the *Princess Charlotte's* lads as they attacked the fort at Oswego and later at Sackett's Harbour.

On his return to England on board the *Princess Charlotte*, Greenwood was rated Sailmaker. He was finally discharged on 27 June 1815 and one hopes that such an experienced seaman found further employment in the merchant service.

Provenance: Private purchase 1992.
References: The National Archives, Kew: ADM 35/ 507-508, 2291, 2881, 3536. ADM 37/ 4455, 5000, 5245.
A Signal Victory, The Lake Erie Campaign by Skaggs and Altoff, Naval Institute Press, Annapolis, 1997.
The Trafalgar Roll, by Col. R. H. Mackenzie, George Allen, London, 1913.
Royal Naval Biography by John Marshall, Longman, London, 1833.

Commadore Sir James Yeo, miniature painted by an unknown Canadian artist. SCC

BT33 William Harkins, 2nd Class Boy, HMS Naiad, Captain Thomas Dundas

Description: Tin, fleet issue cased in copper gilt and glazed with the reverse lunette missing. On the reverse is engraved *W Arkins Naiad* in script. Weight: 54.4 grams. The obverse is extremely fine and with spots of corrosion, while the reverse is very fine with some corrosion and a very dark patina.

Background: The Boulton Trafalgar medal wasn't intended to be distributed amongst the men on board frigates, only line of battle ships were to receive the medal. The *Naiad* was a 36-gun frigate with her home port being Plymouth and was in Plymouth when the Boulton Trafalgar medal was distributed by Admiral Young, the Port Admiral. Nicholas Goodison cites a letter from John Woodward to Matthew Robinson Boulton dated 9 February 1808, that at Plymouth, Admiral Young 'distributed medals indiscriminately as long as supplies lasted.'

Perhaps it is the Luck of the Irish that William Harkins (or Farkins) from Londonderry received a medal. He was 16 years old when he volunteered on 1 September 1804 and was rated a Boy, Second Class. We know that he wasn't destined for the Quarterdeck because in August, 1806 he was rated Landsman and later in on the 1st of January 1810, he became the ship's barber.

On the 8th of April 1812, he transferred to the 44-gun frigate *Junon* where he served on the North American station during the War of 1812, spending a lot of time in the Chesapeake Bay area as *Junon's* men were involved various activities against American gun boats and privateers.

On the 3rd of November, William Harking was discharged as a barber to HMS *St Lawrence*, on Lake Ontario, but no further information was found regarding him.

From Wikipedia: HMS *St Lawrence* was a 112-gun first-rate wooden warship of the Royal Navy that served on Lake Ontario during the War of 1812. She was the only Royal Navy ship of the line ever to be launched and operated entirely in fresh water.

The *St Lawrence* had her keel laid on 12 April 1814, and was launched on 10 September 1814. British naval commodore Sir James Lucas Yeo commissioned her as his flagship, with Captain Frederick Hickey as Flag Captain, in the Kingston Royal Naval Dockyard in Kingston, Upper Canada.

At the time, Lake Ontario was effectively landlocked for any but the smallest vessels, due to shallow water and rapids on the St Lawrence River downstream and Niagara Falls upstream. As a result, warships operating on Lake Ontario had to be built on site, either in Kingston or in the American naval dockyards at Sackett's Harbour, or converted from merchant ships already operating in the lake.

Control of the lake, which was the most important supply route for the British for military operations to the west, had passed back and forth between the Americans and the British over the course of the war. The construction of a first rate ship of the line, in a campaign that had been dominated by sloops and frigates, gave the British uncontested control of the lake during the final months of the war. HMS *St Lawrence* never saw action, because her presence on the lake deterred the U.S. fleet from setting sail.

After the war in 1815, the ship was decommissioned. In January 1832, the hull was sold to Robert Drummond for £25. Between May and August, the hull was towed out of Navy Bay. It later formed the end of a pier attached to Morton's Brewery in Kingston and was used as a storage facility by the brewery, for cordwood among other materials. Later, it was sunk in 30 feet (9.1 m) of water close to shore, and is now a popular diving attraction.

Provenance: Private purchase 1989.
References: The National Archives, Kew: ADM 35/ 2340, 2350- 3532. ADM 36/ 16157, 15734, 16798- 16800. ADM 37/ 3599, 4322, 5330, 2617-2618, 3627, 1420-1421, 1419.

Matthew Boulton's Trafalgar Medal by Nicholas Goodison, Birmingham City Council, 2007.

Bird's-eye view of Nelson's attacking fleet at Trafalgar. From Jenkins's *Naval Achievements*.

Survival during the Age of Fighting Sail

Having read a fair number of the modern naval novels written by Forester, O'Brian, Stockwin and Kent, one gains a very clear view of just how awful a fierce encounter between two opposing ships of the line would be. Also we have Jack Nastyface of the *Revenge* at Trafalgar telling us about the 'slaughtering' shot from the enemy that tears through your gun port killing and maiming all of the men at that gun and then those on the other side of the deck. The absolute carnage of such a battle really seems beyond our imagination. That these men stayed at their guns and continued to fight, I find most remarkable. Then one understands that they fought for each other and their ship, which was both their home and their livelihood. They were a team in the best sense of the word and whatever it took, they stuck together to come out on top.

In this catalogue of medals received by men who were there and survived both the Battle of the Nile and Trafalgar, I began to notice something that didn't have to do with the butcher's bill of battle, but the ordinary casualties that occurred during normal sailing of a 3rd rate 74-gun ship. I know this is a very small sample to draw any conclusions from, but there is a message amongst the stories of these men's lives and that is being a seaman or marine during the Age of Fighting Sail was a risky business and the men paid with their lives and health just to keep those ships in action at sea.

One problem with the Davison Nile medal is that with the Peace of Amiens and the decommissioning of so many ships, we lose track of the men who fought at the Nile. However, the Boulton Trafalgar medal gives us a more complete view as the men may be traced to the end of the wars in 1815.

There are some comments that may be made regarding the Nile though. Thirty-four medals are listed and amongst them is one man, James Dean of the *Defence*, who was killed in action. Somebody took the time to get a bronze medal to his family, which underlines that a caring nature survived such a brutal existence. Captain Ralph Miller of the *Theseus* died in 1799 due to an accidental explosion on board ship at Acre. Four men where captured by the French after the Nile and one thinks they were all exchanged in good health because all four of them received the Nile medal. Twenty-two of the medals went to officers and men who were discharged or paid off in good health. One man, Robert Lewis of the *Minotaur*, Ran, he'd had enough and so took his chances ashore. Six men were discharged in poor health and no longer of value to the Royal Navy.

The Trafalgar medal provides more information. Thirty-three medals in all. Amongst the recipients are three men whose fates we don't know. Seventeen officers and men were discharged at the end of the war in good health. One man, Samuel Wise of the *Polyphemus* Ran in 1808, he'd had enough. Four men were Discharged Dead through accident on board their ships. All four were Able Seamen and it appears that all four fell out of the tops and drowned. One officer, Lieutenant James Robinson, died at sea, most likely from a fever picked up in the West Indies. Seven men were discharged as Unserviceable, i.e. no longer fit for fulfilling their roles on board ship.

The Boulton Trafalgar recipients offer a most striking picture. It was clearly dangerous being an Able Seaman and working in the tops in all weathers. The wider picture shows that nearly half of the men who received the medal and fought at Trafalgar didn't last until the end of the war ten years later and I'm not surprised! Just how hard was it to continue year after year on board ship in all weathers, being involved in small fights with the enemy and living in very difficult conditions with not the best food and not the best of medical care.

One also wonders about mental health amongst these men. Just having been through a battle like Trafalgar would have left scars on the mind that could haunt any man through the rest of his life. Perhaps some of the men discharged as Unserviceable were suffering from demons and the officers simply knew that they would infect the mental state of the ship if they continued on board. One just doesn't know.

Lastly, we have three women to mention. Mary Williams on board *Goliath*, Ann Crumwich on board *Alexander*, both at the Nile, and Betsey Henley on board the *Bellerophon* at Trafalgar. They were never recognised, not on the ship's books, but they were there and no doubt helped to nurse the wounded and generally assisted in the domestics of shipboard life as best they could. One does, however, remember the Shield Maidens of the Viking Age. I could well imagine a female shipmate with cutlass in hand or serving a gun if the battle required her strength. These women on board ship certainly weren't delicate flowers!

All I can say is that by cataloguing this collection, it has certainly brought me much closer to these sailors and what they went through. So I salute them, all part of Nelson's *Band of Brothers ...and Sisters*!

#	Ship	Name	Fate
1	Victory	James Aldridge, AB	D. good health
2	Victory	F. E. Collingwood, Mid	D. good health
3	Victory	Thomas Randall, AB	D. good health
4	Temeraire	J L or J P	?
5	Neptune	Philip Browne	D poor health 1813
6	Leviathan	Capt. H. Bayntun	D. good health
7	Leviathan	W. Fullertone	D. poor health 1811
8	Leviathan	James Dennison	D. good health
9	Conqueror	R. Simmins	DD. Accident 1814
10	Conqueror	John Blane	DD. Accident 1808
11	Conqueror	Thomas Leigh	D. good health
12	Conqueror	Abraham Collier	D. poor health
13	Britannia	Thomas Carphy	D. good health
14	Africa	James Boon	D. poor health 1813
15	Agamemnon	J. St Quntin	D. good health
16	Agamemnon	C. A. Johnston	D. good health
17	Minataur	Richard Gurward	?
18	Spartiate	Lt. J. Clephan	D. good health
19	Spartiate	M. McClode	D. good health
20	Royal Sovereign	C. Doran	?
21	Belleisle	Robert Collinson	D. good health
22	Mars	Lt. J. Robinson	DD. accident diease?
23	Mars	James Ryan	D. poor health 1810
24	Mars	Francis Long	D. poor health 1814
25	Bellerophon	Mid H. Walker	D. good health
26	Bellerophon	M. Henley	D. good health
27	Achille	William Smart	D. poor health 1814
28	Revenge	Henry Hore	DD. Accident 1815
29	Revenge	Thomas Mansell	DD disease 1808
30	Polyphemus	Samuel Wise	Run! 1808
31	Thunderer	Henry Wells	D good health
32	Defence	John Greenwood	D good health
33	Naiad	W. Harkins	D good health

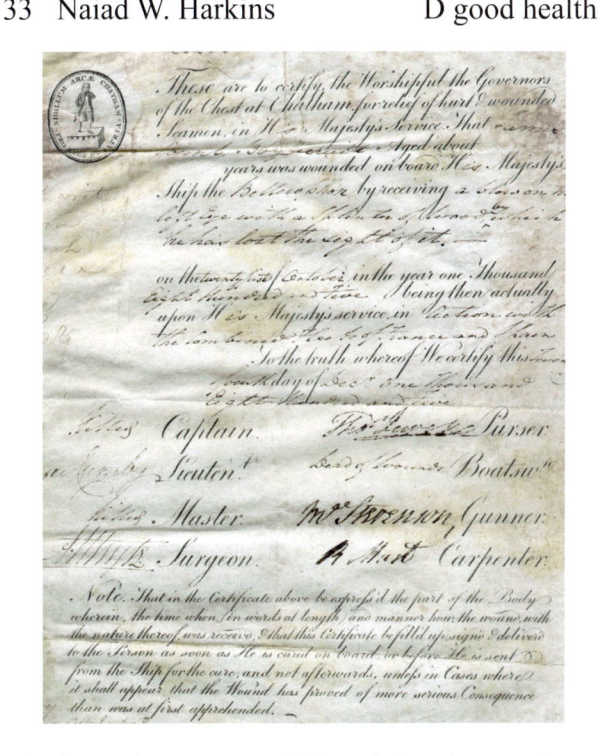

Chatham Chest Hurt and Wound Certificate to James Count, Boy on board *Bellerophone* who received 'a blow on the left eye with a splinter of wood by which he has lost the sight of the eye.' SCC

Image Credits: All images used are subject to copyright and require permissions from the image holders. The page location in noted in **bold** print.

Birmingham Museum Trust.
Frontispiece

Bonham's auction house, London, England.
244,

Britannia Royal Naval College.
281

Bristol City Museum and Art Gallery.
347

Charles Miller Auctions Ltd.
135, 348

Dean and Chapter of Westminster, Westminster Abbey, London, England.
Nelson Effigy 282

Glendining's.
10, 36

Hasler Royal Naval Hospital, Portsmouth
172

Iceland Tourism
24

Morton & Eden
149

Randy Maffit
149

Sim Comfort Collection, England.
XIV, 9, 11, 33, 35, 37 - 40, 48, 51-52, 54-55, 57, 60-61, 63-64, 66-67, 69, 73, 75, 77, 88-89, 94-95, 97-98, 101-102, 108-113, 115, 117, 122-123, 126-127, 129-132, 135, 141, 143, 145, 147, 149, 150, 152-157, 159-164, 166, 171, 174, 176-177, 179-181, 183-186, 189, 191-194, 197-198, 200, 202-204, 206-208, 210-212, 214, 219-221, 227, 229-230, 234-235, 237, 239, 240, 246, 249-251, 255, 257-261, 263-264, 270, 273, 275, 285-286, 292, 297, 303-308, 310, 313, 315, 317-320, 321, 323-333, 335-339, 341-345, 349-352, 356, 361-364, 367-368, 370-371, 373-374, 376, 378-380, 382-385, 387.

Randy Maffit
149

Royal Numismatic Society
119

Skyler Liechty Collection
26

Sotheby's auction house, London, England.
78, 83-84, 89-91, 278-279

Stack's Bowers Galleries.
9

State Library, New South Wales.
216

Tahiti Tourisme
12

The National Maritime Museum, Greenwich, England.
BHC 2957 20, BHC 2396 22, MEC 1445 49, PAD 4121 68, 87, D4424 89, PAG9745 121, BHC2527 **289**

The National Museum of the Royal Navy, Portsmouth.
361

The National Portrait Gallery, London, England.
MW05868 25, MW00394 62,

The Trustees of the British Museum, London.
34-35

A UK Private Collection.
266, 269

Wellington Museum, Wellington, New Zealand.
14, 47

Wikipedia
13, 52, 291

Woolly & Wallis.
140

Index

British Regiments

11th Regiment of Foot 226
31st of Foot 315
42nd of Foot 315
49th of Foot 148
67th of Foot 315
88th of Foot, The Connaught Rangers 237 - 239
90th of Foot 186 - 187
90th Perthshire Volunteers 187
95th of Foot, The Rifle Brigade 148, 315

A

Abbott, Lemuel Francis 62, 78, 281
Aberdeen University 172
Able Seaman 153, 207, 236, 241 - 242, 247, 251, 258, 260, 263, 276, 307, 321, 325, 328, 331 - 335, 340, 346, 349, 355, 369, 382
Aboukir Bay 63 - 66, 87, 107 - 108, 113 - 116, 167, 218, 254, 259, 273, 290
Acre 108
Adam, James 3
Adams, John xi
Adams, William 146
Addington, Henry 86
Admiralty 10, 13, 15, 17, 31, 33, 42 - 43, 57, 65, 125, 136 - 137, 142
Admiralty Chart office 18
Aldridge, James 131, 322, 326
Aldridge, John 321
Alexander Ball monument at Valletta, Malta. 291
Alexandria 99, 108, 113, 114, 199
Allemand, Captain 205
Allendrake, Joseph 189
American Numismatic Society 378
American Revolutionary War 49 - 50
Ancient Gregorians 85, 88
Anderson, William 44
Andras, Catherine 134 - 135
Angerstein, John Julius 249
Anson, Admiral George 191, 324
Antarctic Circle 24, 45
Anti-Jacobin Review and Magazine 87
Appleby, Malcolm 76, 323
Appleby Trafalgar Medal 323
Arbuthnot, Mid. Alexander 357

Aris's Birmingham Gazette 120
Armourer and Mate 259, 262
Arnold, John 45
Assay Office Collection, Birmingham 140
Atcherley RM, Captain James 334, 358
Atkins, Captain David 276
Attwood, Philip xi, 76
Aubrey, Captain Jack 70
Aunger, Oliver 258
Austen, Captain F.W. and Jane 211
Australia 21, 23, 216
Aylmer, Captain Frederick 195
Ayshford, Pam and Derek xi

B

Baldwin's 37
Ball, Captain Alexander 102, 283, 286 - 292, 303
Baltic service 97
Band of Brothers 90, 167
Banks, Sir Joseph 3, 11 - 12 - 34, 42 - 47, 55, 64, 213
Banks, Sarah Sophia 12, 34, 38, 41, 55
Bannister, George 311
Barber, Ship's 384
Barham, Lord 138, 142
Barrett, Captain John 208
Barrington, Vice-Admiral 164
Basque Roads, Battle of 244, 276, 375
Batavia 23
Bates, John 178
Bates, Sarah 178
Battenberg, Prince Louis xv
Battison, Ebenezer and Thomas 207 - 208
Baudouin, Captain 350
Bayly, William 45
Bayntun, Captain Henry 141, 322, 329 - 332
Bayntun, Richard William 329
Bayntun, Sophia Mayhew 330
Beaglehole, J. C. 17, 19 - 23, 43, 46
Beanes, Dr William 228
Beaufort, Admiral 288
Beckford, William 85
Bedford, Lieut. John 227
Beecher, Commander Alex 381
Beechey, Sir William and Lady 134, 138
Bellerophon engraver 250, 259 - 261
Bell, Surgeon 209
Berkeley, Sir George and Anne Louisa Emily 284
Bermuda Penny 8, 9
Berridge, John 268

Berry, Captain Sir Edward 100, 195, 197 - 206, 209, 211, 280, 284, 288 - 289, 307 - 311, 342 - 343
Berry, Marcy xi
Betts, Jonathan xi, 144
Birmingham 3 - 5, 18, 28, 120
Birmingham Assay Office Collection xvi, 140
Birmingham City Archives 72, 142
Birmingham City Council xvi, 133
Birmingham Museum and Art Gallery xvi, 51, 145
Blackwood, Captain Henry 202
Blake, William 124
Blane, John 335
Bligh, Captain Richard 287
Bligh, Captain William 16 - 17, 38, 47, 218 - 219, 312
Board of Longitude 19
Board of Ordnance 262
Boatswain and Mate 236, 340, 369
Bonaparte, Napoleon 63 -65, 69 - 70, 99, 110, 113, 132, 167 - 168, 250, 253, 273, 290, 319, 342
Bonham's 227, 244, 297, 364, 368
Boon, James 341
Boston, Comptroller of Customs 299
Boston Tea Party 300
Boswell, James 3
Botany Bay 23, 213, 215
Boulogne 112
Boulton, Anne 4, 5
Boulton & Fothergill 28, 29, 30 - 33, 44, 51
Boulton, Matthew xi, 2 - 8, 10, 12, 17 - 19, 24 - 34, 39, 41 - 77, 87 - 88, 112, 117 - 124, 131 - 138, 142 - 145, 157, 282, 314
Boulton, Matthew Robinson 4 - 5, 134 - 138, 143, 384
Boulton, Matthew senior 3
Boulton, Nancy 5
Boulton, P.W. 139
Boulton's Trafalgar Medal 2, 42, 74, 120, **131 - 134**, 138, 140 - 144, 386
Boulton & Watt 44
Bounty paid 234, 236
Bowden, Thomas 155, 156
Bowen, Captain George 266
Bowen, Captain Richard 181, 309
Bowen, Lieut. 164
Bowers & Marena 37
Bowers, Q. David 7
Bowyer, Admiral 318
Boys, 1st, 2nd and 3rd class 241 - 242, 261, 276, 384, 387
Bradley, Lieut. William 214, 216

Brenton, Captain J. 256
Bridport, Admiral Lord 44, 191, 208, 283, 287, 314, 381
Bridport Collection 120
Britannia Royal Naval College 281
British Art Medal Society 76
British Museum 11, 12, 18, 34, 37, 41, 55, 76, 112, 223
Broadbent, Michael xi
Brodie, Lieut. Thomas 103, 104, 107
Broke, Captain Philip 148
Brooking, Captain Samuel 379
Browne, Philip 328, 329
Brown, James 139
Brown, Laurence xi, xv, 56
Brown, Master Robert 214
Bruff, Peter Shuyler 190
Bryon, Captain John 16
Buchan, Alexander 19
Buckler's Hard 256, 276
Bullen, Captain Charles 338
Burke, Edmund 50
Burnett, Sir William 171 - 174
Burney, James and Fanny 44 - 45, 47
Burnham Thorpe 79
Burrows, Lieut. John 302
Burton, Anthony 53
Butler, Roy collection 263
Bynon, Joanna 277

C

Cabareta Point, Battle of 193
Calder, Admiral Sir Robert 112, 132, 195, 302, 342, 380 - 381
Caldwell, Admiral Benjamin 265
Camas, Captain M. 372
Campbell, John 280
Campbell, Nicola xi
Camp Cove 215
Cape Finisterre, Battle of 132
Cape St Vincent, Battle of 126 - 127, 167, 192, 195, 198, 247, 284, 302
Cape St Vincent Large Gold Medal 62
Cappell [Capel], Captain T. B. 139
Captain of the Forecastle 276
Captain of the Main Top 229 - 233, 321 - 322, 341
Captain's Clerk 381
Captains of guns 234
Captain's Servant 241 - 242, 276
Caracciolo, Admiral 118

Carp, Benjamin 299, 300
Cartwheel Twopence 8
Casabianca, Cadet 116
Cases, 48 mm 119
Chain Cent 8, 9
Chaplain 174
Charles XII, King 201
Chatham Chest 387
Chatterton, Joseph 250 - 251, 256 - 259
Chelengk 83
Chelsea Naval Exhibition 306
Christian, Fletcher 47
Christie and Ansell, auctions 5
Christie, Mary 207
Christie's 36, 133, 203, 211, 278 - 283, 313 - 315, 381
Christ's Hospital 45
Clarence, Duke of 268, 279
Clayton, Peter xi
Clayton, Tim 356
Clephan, Lieut. James 345 - 348
Clerke, Charles 16, 24, 44, 47
Cleveley, John 64, 124
Cleveley, Robert 64, 66, 68, 138
Cnut, King 168
Cobbler, Ship's 377
Cochrane, Admiral Sir Alexander 210, 228
Cochran, Thomas Lord 232-233, 244, 375
Cocker, W.G. 259, 261
Cocker, William 262
Coin and Medal News 133
Colen, Joseph 128, 156, 158
Collier, Captain Edward 383
Collier, Private Abraham 337
Collingwood, Admiral Cuthbert 79, 81, 128, 133, 138, 142, 172, 224, 228, 272, 318, 322, 350, 358, 365, 371, 382
Collingwood, Francis 324
Collingwood, Master Edward 324
Collingwood, Mid. F.E. 324, 325
Collins, Judge David 215
Collins, Lieut. John 290
Collinson, Robert 351, 354 - 355, 382
Colonial Williamsburg 230
Colville, Admiral 299
Comitia Americana 57
Committee of Safety 109
Comte de Lapérouse 157
Conrad, Joseph 218
Conseil, Captain 165

Constable, Archibald xv
Contamin, General 334
Cook, Ship's 220, 223
Cook, Captain James 3, 10, 13 - 14, 16 - 24, 31, 38 - 39, 42, 44 - 47, 124, 213, 215, 217
Cooke, Captain John 228, 364, 367 - 369
Cook, William Hemmings 157
Cooper, Robert Palliser 44
Copenhagen, 1807 Battle of 243
Copenhagen, 1801 Battle of 65, 167 - 168, 217, 226, 245, 284 - 285, 311, 313 - 319
Copenhagen, Naval Academy 314
Corbet, Captain Robert 293 -296
Corbett, Benjamin 237, 239 - 240
Cordingly, David 251 - 254
Cork Historical and Archaeological Society 146
Cornwallis, Admiral William 128, 164, 225, 253, 318, 347
Cornwallis, General Charles 50
Cornwallis's Retreat 253
Cotes, Captain Thomas 204
Cotton, Admiral Sir Charles 226, 265
Count, James 387
Covent Garden Theatre 2
Cowan, Lieut. Thomas 304
Coxswain 247, 355, 369
Cracraft, Captain 295, 296
Craigie, Andrew 194
Craig, Phil 357
Cranston, Captain James 253
Creswell, Captain RM 290
Crimmin, P.K. 125
Crocombe, Lieut. Richard 218
Crossman, Lieut. Richard 276
Crumwich, Ann 66, 292, 387
Cumby, Lieut. W.P. 364, 368
Cumming, Captain James 163
Curphy, Thomas 338, 340
Cuthbert, Lieut. Robert 225, 263 - 268, 275, 279, 281

D

Dale, Peter 314, 319, 348
Dalrymple, Alexander 17, 18
Dalziel, Surgeon James 297
Danelaw 168
Daniel, Lieut. R.S. 254
Daniel, Robert Savage 101
Darby, Captain Henry 101, 107, 250 - 262, 283
Dardanelles 211

Darling, Margaret 249
David, J. L. 109 - 110
Davison, Alexander xi, 3, 63 - 94, 197, 269, 278 - 283
Davison, Alexander Horatio Nelson 92
Davison, Harriett 92 - 93
Davison, Katy 79
Davison Nile Medal 2, **63,** 66, 68, 71, 77, 86 - 89, 119, 124, 143, 171, 198, 386
Davison, William 90, 91
Davy Jones's Locker 378
Day, Robert 146, 148
Dean, James 386
Dean, John 248, 249
Debenham's 283
Decoeurdoux, Lieut. G.L. 361
De Graaff, Govenor 50
Delafons, Lieut. 312
Dennison, James 332
Denon, Vivant 108 - 109, 112 - 114
Deptford Dockyard 167
Derby porcelain factory 82, 86
Devis, Arthur William 91, 95, 323
Dickinson, H. W. xvi
Dies, Creating 76
Digby, Captain Henry 341
Dillon, Lieut. William 243
Dix, Nimrod xi, 70, 170, 241, 245
Dix Noonan and Webb 246 - 247, 277
Dixon, Christopher xi, 160, 228
Dodd, Robert 66, 67, 101, 317
Dogger Bank, Battle of 191
Dommett, Captain George 370
Doran, Charles 350
Doty, Dr Richard xvi, 6 - 8, 145
Douglas-Morris, Captain Kenneth 173, 176, 228, 277
Downer, Martyn xi, 64 - 65, 68, 79, 204, 279, 283
Drawwater, Benjamin 44
Droz, Jean-Pierre 7, 8, 57, 77
Drummond, Robert 385
Duckworth, Admiral Sir J. T. 118, 133, 191, 210, 333
Duff, Alexander, Lachlan, & Norwich 357
Duff, Captain George 227, 228, 356 - 362
Duke of Bronte 117
Dumanoir, Admiral 203, 331, 342, 345 - 346
Duncan, Admiral Adam 64
Duncan, Captain C. 257
Dundas, Captain G.H. 257
Dundas, Captain Thomas 384
Dundas, Henry 65, 86, 87

Dupeyrat, Jean Baptiste 77
Dupré, Augustin 57
Duran, Charles 351
Durham, Captain Philip 172 - 173
Dusky Bay 45
Dutch West Indies Company 49

E

Earl St Vincent's Medal of Approbation 2, **123**
Earth to the Sun, distance 15
East India Company 8, 80, 140, 294, 340, 346
Eddy, Ray xi
Edgar, Thomas 47
Edgeworth, Richard Lowell 4
Edwin Wolf Collection 203
Egyptian Club 90, 280
Egyptian Revival 110
Eimer, Christopher xi, xvi, 76
Elliott, John 44
Elson, Bryon 299 - 301
Endeavour Bay 23
England expects that every man will do his duty. 366
England, Lieut. Thomas 105 - 106
Engleheart, George 330
Etienne, Captain 268
Eustace, William 185, 186
Exmouth, Viscount 293

F

Fabian, Captain 163
Faddy, Lieut. William RM 206
Fannin, Peter 45
Farquaharson, James 18
Farquhar, Captain Arthur 349
Faulknor, Captain Robert 163 - 165
Fayerman, Captain 333
Fearney, William 247
Fearon, Daniel xi, 76
Ferdinand IV, King 68, 109, 117 - 119, 275, 280, 283
Ferdinand IV Medal **117,** 120, 314
Ferris, Captain William 256, 333, 377
First Fleet to Australia 213 - 214
First of June 1794, Battle of 8, 55 - 59, 87, 242 - 243, 252, 265, 271, 276, 318
First of June Medal **55,** 68, 77
Flaxman, John 64, 124, 196
Fletcher, Ian 238, 239
Flinn, Private William & Elizabeth 66, 292, 295, 296

Foley, Captain Thomas 70, 163 - 182, 283, 285
Foote, Captain Edward 118
Forester, C.S. 386
Format Coins xi, 51, 76, 126, 133
Forster, George 44, 45
Forster, John Reinhold 44
Fort Royal, Martinique 164
Fort Saint Elmo 118
Fothergill, John 5, 10, 26 - 30, 32, 43 - 44
Franklin, Benjamin 3, 5
Franklin, Sir John 159
Frazier, Lieut. John 218
Freemasonry 85
Fremantle, Captain Thomas 309, 328
French and Indian War 15
French Revolutionary Wars 57
French, William and Mary 178
Fullerton, William 331 - 333
Furneaux, Captain Tobias 45

G

Gage, General 300
Galaup, Jean-Francois de 157
Galloway, Earl of 313, 315
Galwey, Lieut. Edward 200
Gambier, Captain James 242 - 244
Gardner, D.G.M 152
Garlies, Viscount 369
Gee, Anne Paston 306
Gell, Admiral John 167
George III, King 5, 10 - 11, 21, 23, 26, 34, 38, 40, 55,
    65, 88, 128, 133, 138, 198, 252, 275, 279, 283
George IV, King 172
Germany, Emperor of 283
Gibraltar 50 - 51, 99, 108, 164
Gilbert, Joseph 44
Glass, John 263, 267
Glendining's 10, 36 - 38, 41, 70, 314
Glover, John 179, 181, 182, 183
Goldsmiths' Company, London 72, 323
Goldstein, Erik 230
Goodison, Nicholas xvi, 133, 142, 384
Gore, John 16, 47
Gosling, Harriett 80
Goudie, John 383
Gould, Captain Davidge 186, 188, 283
Gould, Rupert T. 144
Graham, Sir James 284
Graham, Sir Thomas 187

Grasse, Admiral Count de 50, 51, 53, 128, 253, 266
Graves, Admiral 50, 301
Graves & Nicholson 250
Gravina, Admiral 375
Great Barrier Reef 23
Greaves, Edward 250
Green, Charles 19, 23
Green, Geoffrey 230
Green, Valentine 51
Greenwich Hospital & Painted Hall 277, 312, 314
Greenwich Mean Time 15
Greenwood, John 354 - 355, 382, 383
Grenier, General 209
Grenville, Lord 89
Grimsby 38
Grimwade, Mark xi, 72
Guardi, Giacomo 121
Guichen, Admiral de 213, 266
Gunner & Mate 234, 349
Gurward, Richard 344
Gutterry, Don Juan Antoine 181

H

Hadaway, Lieut. John 254
Hailes Roll 146
Halifax, Earl of 18
Hall, Basil 262
Halloran, Lieut. 338
Hallowell, Benjamin senior 300, 301
Hallowell, Captain Benjamin 102, 283, 297 - 306
Hallowell, Robert 299
Hamilton, Lady Emma 3, 70, 79 - 94, 109, 118 - 119,
    134, 138, 141, 200, 222, 282 - 283, 313 - 314
Hamilton, Sir William 65, 85, 109, 119 - 120, 124, 222
    - 223, 273, 280, 283
Hammond, James xi, xvi, 133, 142, 235, 236
Hancock, John 300
Hannah, Lieut. William 356, 362
Harding, George Perfect 95
Hardy, Captain Thomas Masterman 65, 70, 100, 118,
    146, 206, 259, 268, 275 - 284, 307, 314, 321, 331
Hardy, Joseph 284
Hardy, Mary Charlotte 278
Hardy, Thomas A. xi, xvi, 119, 120
Hargood, Captain William 351
Harkins, William 384
Harrison, John 15, 19, 21, 45, 144
Harvey, Captain Eliab 326
Harvey, Captain John 55 - 59

Harvey, William 44
Haslar Hospital 218, 377
Hastings, Marquis of 86
Hatfull, Purser Edward 359, 361
Hawaii 47
Hawkins, Lieut. Richard 104, 105, 107
Hayward, John xi, 2, 148, 237
Heaton Mint 140
Henley, Betsy 368, 369, 387
Henley, Matthew 368, 369, 370
Hennah, Lieut. William 227, 357 - 358, 361
Hepper, David 217, 266, 302, 381
Heritage Auctions 26
Heywood, Mary 251
Hickey, Captain Federick 385
Hicks, Zachary 16, 21, 23
Hill, Colonel Richard 187
Hill, David 214 - 215
Hodges, John 51
Hodges, William 22, 44
Holles, Captain A.P. 257
Hollingrick, Joseph 189 - 192
Hollis, Captain Askew P. 373
Home, Captain Roddam 79
Hood, Admiral Lord 44, 191, 195, 226, 301
Hood, Alexander 44
Hood, Captain Samuel 44, 103 - 104, 128, 179 - 185, 256, 267 - 268, 283, 305, 309, 373, 377
Hope, Captain G.J. 382
Hope, Captain W.J. 252 - 253
Hopping, Ann 177
Hore, Henry 374 - 376
Hore, Peter xi
Hoste, Lieut. William 104
Hotham, Admiral 244
Howe, Admiral Lord 8, 55 - 59, 64, 77, 124, 191, 209, 243, 251 - 252, 258, 265, 271, 276, 381 - 382
Huahine 21
Hudson Bay Company 128, 156 - 159
Hughes, Admiral Sir Edward 271, 382
Hughes, Gillian xi, 185, 189, 221, 236, 332, 340, 354, 360, 369, 381
Hunter, Captain John 213, 215, 216, 217, 218
Hunter, Robert 80
Hunt, Graham xi
Hunts, Mr. James 360

I

Iceland 24, 26

Impress Service 208
Indian Peace Medal 41
Irish sailors 238
Irving, Hasting 148
Isham, Charles Thomas 157
Israel, Nigel xi

J

Jack-of-the-dust 286
Jackson, T. Sturges 99, 196, 303, 365
Jamaica, Council of 379
James, William 164 - 165, 179, 204 - 205, 287, 309, 311, 348
Jefferson, Thomas 57
Jervis, Captain William 226
Jervis, Admiral Sir John (see Earl St Vincent) xv, 127, 164, 179, 192, 195, 209, 288, 302, 330
Jewish Pedlars & Jewellers 143, 230
Jingling Johnny 239
John Adams Collection 52
Johnson, Dr Samuel 124
Johnson, [Johnston] Joseph. 148
Johnston, Charles A. 343
Jolliffe, Lieut. George 254
Jones, Captain Charles 346
Jones, Isaac 153
Jones, John Paul 57
Joyeuse, Admiral Villaret de 56 - 57

K

Keats, Captain R.G. 192 - 193, 256 - 257
Keep Museum, Dorchester 279
Keith, Admiral Lord 210, 218, 259
Keltie, James 194
Keltie, Master James 194, 212 - 219
Kemp, Arthur 45
Kempenfelt, Admiral Richard 213, 265
Kemp, Peter 178
Kendall, Larcum 45
Kennedy, Lieut. T.F. 327
Kent, Alexander 322 - 323, 386
Kerjulien, Captain Cosmao 356
Key, Francis Scott 228
King, Captain Richard 371 - 372
King, James 47
King's Bench 93
Kingston, Ontario 383, 385
Kinsman, Nathaniel 231

Kirby, Eric 354
Kirby, Master Edward 254
Knighton, George 229, 233 - 234
Knighton, Lieut. Charles 233
Knight, Roger 118
Knowles, Captain Sir Charles 167
Koster, Simon de 134 - 135
Küchler, Conrad Heinrich 8, 55 - 57, 59, 63 - 65, 68, 77, 87, 119, 124, 131 - 134, 283, 314
Kydd, Thomas 236

L

Laforey, Captain Sir Francis 345, 349
Lakes of Canada 383
Lambert, Captain Henry 319
Lambert, Captain R.S. 314, 318 - 319
Lambert, Col. Samuel 319
Lambert, Commander G.R. 319
Lambert, General John 319
Landsman 176, 235- 237, 248, 286, 297, 362, 374, 377
Lángara, Admiral 51, 382
La Riviere, Lucien 37
Laughton, J.K. 263, 293 - 295
Launder, Lieut. P.W. 254
Laurie and Whittle 68
Lavery, Brian xi, 65, 167 - 168, 182, 195, 199 - 200, 209, 244, 267 - 268, 272, 287 - 289, 302 - 307
Lawrence-Archer, Major 187
Lawrence, Lieut. G. B. 184
Lawson, Master W. 290
Lechmere, Captain William 380
Lee, Lieut. Theophilus 304
Légion d'honneur 113
Leigh, Mid. Thomas 336
Lejoille, Captain 309
Lewis, Michael 174 - 177, 185 - 190, 212, 223, 241 - 242, 298
Lewis, Robert (William) 229, 235 - 236, 261, 386
Liechty, Skyler xi, 26
Lind, James 24
Linois, Admiral 256
Lloyd, Christopher 271, 272
Lloyd's Coffee-House 249
Lloyd's of London 249
Lloyd's Patriotic Fund 227, 249, 308, 319, 331, 339, 362
Locker, Captain William 81, 288
Lockyer, Captain Nicholas 383
Loggie, Charles 44

Longitude 15, 21
Long, Private Francis 362, 363
Long, W.H. 192, 202, 256
Loring, Captain John 253, 369
Louis, Captain Thomas 207 - 212, 218 - 229, 233 - 235, 237, 283
Louisiana Territory 70
Louis XVI, King 57, 109, 251
Louis XV, King 109
Loutherbourg, P.J. de 347
Louvre 110
Lucas, Captain Jean 322
Lunar Society 5
Lyons, John 146

M

Macbride, Captain John 208
MacGregor of MacGregor 278
Mackaness, George 38, 218
Mackenzie, Col. R.H. 171, 324, 327 - 328, 334, 336, 341 - 342, 353, 364, 381 - 382
Mafit, Randy xi, 148
Magon, Captain 227
Maitland, Captain Frederick 250
Mangin, Reverend Edward 174 - 175
Manley, Isaac George 16, 44
Manningham, Col. Coote 315
Mansell, Thomas 376, 377
Mansfield, Captain J.M. 344
Marines, Royal 125, 126, 204
Marshall, John 188, 192, 224 - 225, 295, 318, 324
Marten, Humphrey 157
Martin, Captain T.B. 223 - 225
Martin, Sir Henry 218
Masefield, John 223, 231, 234
Maskelyne, Nevil 19, 45
Masonic 68, 85 - 88, 204, 280
Massaredo, Admiral 180
Master-at-Arms 185, 223, 333, 327
Masterman, Thomas & Nanny 284
Master of a ship 212, 247, 355, 370
Master's Mate 236, 264, 336, 346, 379
Matcham, George 82
Matthew Boulton Trust 140
Matthews, William 30, 32, 42
Maurice, Lieut. J. W. 183
Maxwell, James 44
Maxwell, Lieut. Keith 346, 347
Mayo, J. H. xv

McClode, Murdock 349
McCouaig, Simon 239
Medals, 48 mm cases 73
Medals, engraving 74
Medals, gilding 71, 263
Medical Department 172
Medlen, Virginia xi, 178, 189
Merton Place 79, 83, 93, 97
Midshipman 241, 251, 265, 324, 336, 342 - 343, 356, 364, 369, 379
Milford Haven, Marquess xv, 56
Military General Service Medal 237
Miller, Captain Ralph Willett 65 - 67, 99, 108, 181, 194 - 198, 209, 259, 280 - 283, 308 - 309, 386
Miller, Charles xi, 135, 348
Millet, Timothy xi
Milne, Lieut. David 165 - 166
Minotaur engraver 231 - 236, 259
Mitchell Library xvi, 32, 46
Moira, Lord 81, 86, 88, 93, 315
Molyneux, Robert 16, 23
Monkhouse, Jonathan 16, 23
Monkhouse, William Brougham 16, 23
Monnier, Lieut. 219
Montagu, Honourable Mr. 138
Montagu, John 23
Montesque, Baron 4
Moody's Toyshop 120
Moonlight Battle, Rodney 1780 51
Moor, A.W. 338
Moore, Arthur Leslie & Leslie Wakefield 159
Moore, Elizabeth 178
Moore, Sir John 187
Moore, William 178
Moorsom, Captain Robert 374, 376
Moreno, Admiral de 256
Morpeth 80
Morrice, John 300
Morris, Richard 223
Morton & Eden 378
Morton, Master John 302
Morton, Master Micah 213, 214
Morton's Brewery 385
Motuara 21
Mulcaster, Captain William 383
Murray, Colonel 154
Murray, John xv
Murray of Polmaise, Colonel 246
Museum Napoleon 110

Museum of Mankind 39
Mutiny of 1797 124, 265
Mutiny of the Bounty 47

N

Nagle, Jacob 216 - 217
Naples 68, 109, 118 - 119
Nastyface, Jack 375, 377, 386
National Archives, Kew xi, 175, 185, 213, 219, 221, 263, 303, 354
National Army Museum 221, 239
National Maritime Museum, Greenwich xi, 20, 22, 49, 68, 144, 169, 197
National Portrait Gallery, London 25, 62
Nautical Standard 139
Naval Chronicle 2, 133
Naval General Service Medal 70, 146, 221, 228, 277, 282, 345, 364, 381
Naval Gold Medals 65, 133, 198, 243, 268, 275 - 276, 279, 285, 331
Nave, William 298
Navy Board 81, 137, 199
Navy Office 81 - 82, 125, 138
Navy Records Society 99, 175
Naxton, Michael xi
Neads, William 297, 306
Nelson, Admiral Lord 2 - 3, 23, 51, 59, 62 - 70, 79 - 126, 131 - 138, 141, 143, 167 - 169, 176, 179, 181, 192, 195, 197 - 204, 209 - 211, 226, 228, 244 - 253, 259, 265, 268 - 296, 302 - 324, 330 - 331, 334, 341 - 342, 346, 358, 365 - 366, 380
Nelson, Alice 159
Nelson, Earl William 120, 138, 314
Nelson, Edmund 80, 83, 93
Nelson Effigy 282 - 283, 313 - 314
Nelson, Ernest 159
Nelson, Fanny 80 - 85, 89, 92 - 93, 120, 280
Nelson, Horatia 93
Nelson, Lady Charlotte 314
Nelson, Maurice 81 - 82
Nelson's Coffin 305
Nelson Society xvi, 119 - 120
Nepean, Evan 47, 268, 280
Newgate prison 80
New Guinea 23
New Orleans, Battle of 228
New South Wales 82, 213 - 214, 219
New Zealand 21 - 24

Nicol, Andrew 66, 176 - 177
Nicolas, Lieut. 351
Nicolas, Paul Harris 139
Nicolas, Sir Nicholas Harris 81, 280, 285
Nicol, John 177 - 178
Nielly, Admiral 287
Nile, Battle of 2, 63 - 74, , 82, 86, 99, 113, 118, 386
Nisbet, Captain Josiah 120, 280
Noble Auctions 46
Nom de guerre 261, 344
Norfolk Island 217
Norman RM, Captain Thomas 357
Northesk, Earl of 338
North, Lord 299
Northumberland, Duke of 86
Northwest Company 157 -158
North West Passage 47
Norwich, City of 134
Nugent, Captain 164
Numismatic Chronicle 56, 64, 77, 119, 133 - 134

O

O'Brian, Patrick 386
O'Bryen, Captain Lucius 264
Oldfield, Captain Thomas 106
Oliver, Captain Robert 358
Ontario, Lake 384
Oranje Bay 49
Orde, Admiral John 79
Order of Merit 146
Order of St Ferdinand 210, 275
Orders and Medals Research Society 148
Ordinary Seaman 155, 179, 189, 220, 236, 262, 270, 276, 298, 350
Ori, Chief 21
Orkney Yole 158
Orme, Daniel 156
Oswego, Fort 383
Otaheite 16, 17, 19, 21, 22, 46, 47
Otaheite Medal (Resolution & Adventure Medal) 8, 10, 13, 26 - 28, 30, 32, 34, 37, 39, 41, 43, 45, 49, 51, 53, 68, 76
Owen, Lieut. 353

P

Palermo 65, 118
Palliser, Hugh 45
Pareja, Captain 372

Paris Mint 57, 112
Parker, Admiral Sir Hyde 167 - 169, 226, 245, 265, 311, 316 - 318
Parker, Admiral Peter 86, 88, 280, 381
Parker, Admiral William 271 - 272
Parker, Captain Edward 92
Parkinson, Sydney 19, 23
Parr, Captain Thomas 217
Parsons, George 200 - 201, 224
Pasley, Captain Thomas 250 - 253
Patten, James 44
Paulet, Captain Lord Harry 245
Payne, A.A. collection 261
Payne, Anthony xi
Pearce, Captain Joseph 370
Peard, Captain S. 256
Pellew, Captain Israel 333, - 358
Pellew, Captain Sir Edward (Lord Exmouth) 226 - 275, 293, 334
Pengelly, Colin 250, 255
Percy family at Alnwick Castle 80
Percy, Hugh 80
Perree, Rear-Admiral 200 - 201
Perry, William 16
Peyton, Captain John 241, 244, 246, 248, 283
Philadelphia Mint 7 - 9
Phillip, Commodore Arthur 213 - 217
Pickernell, Captain 139
Pickersgill, Richard 16, 44
Picton, General Thomas 239
Pinches, John 132 - 141
Pingo, Thomas 26
Pitcairn Island 47
Pitt, William 86, 189
Plant, Samuel 204 - 206
Plenderleath Copenhagen medal. 149
Plymouth 142
Plymouth Hospital 153
Pocock, Nicolas 58, 60, 61, 66, 202, 361
Poedua 20 - 21
Pollard, J. G. xvi, 56, 64, 77, 119, 133 - 134
Pollard, Mid. John 324
Pope, Dudley 172, 311, 314, 346, 350 - 351, 353, 356 - 357, 371, 374
Port Jackson 215
Port Mahon, Minorca 168
Post Captain 212
Prentice, Rina 282, 314
Press Gang 189, 346, 362

397

Price, Richard xi, 73
Prince of Wales 86
Prisoners of War 172, 260 - 267, 271, 277, 298, 332
Public Record Office 18
Purser 380 - 381
Puzzle Picture, Captain Samuel Hood's 184
Pym, Captain 333
Pyramids, Battle of 113

Q

Quarter Gunner 234, 247, 265, 322, 333, 338, 346, 351, 355, 369
Quarter Master 194, 247, 325, 333, 355, 368, 377
Quarter Master's Mate 246, 247, 346, 349
Quebec 15, 18, 79, 80, 86
Quiberon Bay, Battle of 15
Quota System & Man 189 - 190, 298

R

Rainier, Admiral Peter 318
Randall, Thomas 241, 325, 326
Ranelagh, Lord 346
Record, George 383
Redmill, Captain Robert 379
Renaudin, Admiral 244
Resolution and Adventure Medal (See Otaheite Medal)
Reward for Gallantry Medal 146, 148
Reward for Gallantry Medal at Copenhagen 146
Reward of Merit Medal 146
Reynolds, John 23
Reynonds, Josuha 25
Richards Marindin & Co 120
Richards, Theophilus 120
Richards, Thomas B. 119, 120
Rich, Captain Thomas 276
Rickman, John 47
Rifle Brigade (See 95th Foot) 315 - 316
Riley, Mary Ann 177
Riou, Captain Edward 47, 164, 217
Risk, James 170
Roberts, Henry 44
Robinson, Anne 3
Robinson, Captain Isaiah 50
Robinson, George 360
Robinson, Hercules 356
Robinson, Lieut. James 356 - 360, 386
Robinson, Mary 3
Robinson, William 375, 377

Rodger, N.A.M. 231, 234
Rodney, Admiral Lord 49 - 53, 195, 253, 266, 308, 382
Roebuck, John 18
Rose, Master John 273 - 275
Rosetta 113
Ross, Hercules 81
Rotherham, Captain Edward 350
Rotton, Master's Mate 214
Rowe, Robert 286, 291
Rowley, Commodore 294
Royal Academy 26, 124
Royal Collection 12
Royal Geographical Society 8
Royal Humane Society 336
Royal Marines 226, 337, 362 - 363, 371
Royal Mint 6, 76
Royal National Lifeboat Institution 336
Royal Naval College 164
Royal Naval Hospital 90 - 91, 285
Royal Navy Library, Portsmouth 357
Royal Norfolk Regimental Museum 325, 351
Royal Numismatic Society 145
Royal Observatory, Greenwich 19, 144
Royal Society 6, 13, 15 - 18
Rubalcava, Lieut. Alejo de 371 - 372
Ruffo, Cardinal 118
Russell, Captain T.M. 276
Russia, Emperor of 138, 283
Ryan, James 362

S

Sackett's Harbour 383, 385
Sailmaker 383
Saint Eustatia Medal **49** -51, 53
Saints, Battle of the 51, 53, 128, 191, 253, 266, 287
Salter, John 91
Salzedo, Captain 371
Sancroft-Baker, Raymond 315
San Domingo, Battle of 203, 210, 342 - 343
Sandwich, Earl of 23 - 24, 45
Santa Cruz, Tenerife 180 - 181
Saumarez, Captain James 272, 275
Saumarez, Captain Philip 191
Saumarez, Captain Sir James 107, 189 - 193, 254 - 257, 272, 275, 288
Saumarez's Action 193
Schomberg, Captain Isaac 276, 296
Scott, Captain George 379
Seaby xv, 174

398

Sea Fencibles 226
Sea Wife 176, 369
Selim III, Sultan of Turkey 90-91, 283
Selkirk, Lord Douglas 158
Seringapatam Medal 140
Seven Years War 15
Shanks, James 45
Ships
  American
    Andrew Doria 50
    Blockade 348
    Bonhomme Richard 57
    Constitution 319
    Liberty 300
  British
    Achille 136, 371-374
    Adamant 360
    Adventure 10-11, 22, 24, 31, 39, 42, 44-46
    Africa 136, 334, 341
    Africaine 294-295
    Agamemnon 136, 143, 198, 202-203, 211, 342-343, 365
    Agincourt 47
    Aigle 226
    Ajax 136, 178
    Albemarle 79-81
    Alcide 301
    Alcmene 318
    Alexander 66, 99, 103-104, 108, 168, 192, 215, 268, 273 275, 286-292, 303, 387
    Alfred 301
    Amazon 47, 169, 217
    Amphitrite 293
    Anson 295
    Ardent 311
    Argos 305
    Ariel 163
    Artois 208
    Asia 164, 301
    Assurance 163, 217
    Aston Hall 301
    Athenian 171
    Audacious 100, 105, 107, 168, 181-182, 186 200, 256-257
    Avenger 330
    Barfleur 318, 342
    Barham 334
    Beaulieu 217, 346
    Bedford 369, 370

    Belleisle 136-137, 142, 226, 287, 350-357, 365-366, 368, 372, 375, 379
    Bellerophon 68-69, 74, 100-101, 107, 136, 182, 226, 228, 250-255, 258-262, 267, 274, 304, 364-369, 375, 387
    Bellona 16, 168-169, 170, 173, 311-312
    Bienfaisant 208
    Bittern 292-296
    Blanche 165-167, 171
    Blenheim 272, 275, 281
    Bloom 237
    Boadicea 294
    Boreas 252
    Bounty 47
    Bourbonnaise 294
    Briseis 370
    Bristol 191
    Britannia 137, 164, 167, 338, 340
    Brunswick 55-61, 68, 253
    Burford 198
    Burlington 383
    Caesar 192-193, 256-257
    Calpe 257
    Cambridge 223, 298
    Camel 302
    Canada 217, 287
    Canceaux 85
    Canopus 210, 247
    Captain 136, 195, 198, 272
    Castor 271
    Caton 381
    Censor 219
    Centaur 183, 184
    Cerberus 373
    Ceres 185
    Charybdis 348
    Circe 228
    Cleopatra 288, 364
    Colossus 136-137, 142, 222, 366
    Conqueror 136, 143, 202, 210, 333-338, 358
    Courageux 179, 182-183, 185-186, 302
    Crescent 191
    Culloden 99-102, 169, 181, 209, 245, 270-276, 279, 290, 304, 307
    Cumberland 208, 222, 231-234, 330
    Cyrene 340
    Dartmouth 370
    Defence 101, 103, 107, 136, 241-249, 254, 274, 304, 354-355, 382-383, 386

Defiance 136, 169, 171 - 173, 177, 366
Desiree 169
Diadem 226
Diamond Rock 183
Diana 333
Dictator 218
Director 47
Discovery 16, 46 - 47
Dolphin 16, 19, 271
Doris 346 - 347
Drake 377
Dreadnought 136, 329, 366
Duncan 319
Edgar 176, 178, 311
Elephant 65, 167, 169, 176, 178, 284 - 285, 312 - 313, 317
Elk 340
Elvin 360
Emerald 181
Endeavour 16 - 17, 19, 21, 23
Entreprenant 137
Eurus 258, 259
Euryalus 137, 356
Excellent 272
Fisgard 223 - 225
Fishburn 214
Formidable 332 - 333
Foudroyant 68, 117 - 118, 175, 200 - 202, 280
Fox 181
Franklin 244
Friendship 214 - 215
Fulminette 293
Ganges 136
Gladiator 262
Glasgow 376
Glatton 47, 312
Glory 238
Gloucester 174, 329
Goliath 66, 70, 99 - 105, 163, 167 - 168, 171, 174 - 182, 190, 199, 245, 267, 274, 303 - 308, 387
Grampus 308
Growler 276
Guardian 217
Hannibal 256
Harrier 275
Haughty 236
Hecate 223
Helena 284
Hellespoint 301

Hite 244
Hyaena 213 - 214, 308
Impregnable 265
Invincible 265
Iphigenia 294
Iris 324
Irresistible 299
Isis 164, 311
Jamaica 379
Java 275, 319
Jeddah 218
Juno 267
Junon 384
Jupiter 266
Kent 354, 382 - 383
King George 299, 301
Kite 324
Latona 252, 329
Lavinia 137
Leander 99, 102 - 106, 168 - 169, 181, 188, 191, 200, 206, 273 - 274, 304, 307 - 311, 364
Lee 340
Leopard 210
Leviathan 136, 141, 143, 207, 233, 252, 329, 330 - 334, 365 - 367
Lion 202, 361
Lively 266 - 267, 283, 302
London 316, 354 - 355, 363, 369
Lord Nelson 340
Louisa 257
Lowestoffe 190 - 192
Lowestoft 302
Mackworth 208
Madras 296
Magicienne 294
Majestic 99, 101, 103 - 104, 107, 168, 225, 263, 265 -268, 273 - 275, 279, 281 - 282, 304 - 305
Malabar 217 - 218
Malta 305
Mariner 187 - 188
Mars 44, 136, 143, 226 - 228, 253, 326, 356 - 362, 366
Martha of Whitby 218
Mary 312
Medusa 381
Meleager 226, 284
Menelaus 294, 364
Mignonne 195
Milford 322, 373

Minerva 265-266
Minerve 284
Minotaur 69, 74, 100 - 107, 136, 153, 194, 207 - 212, 218, 220, 222, 229 - 231 - 238, 244, 261, 344 - 345, 366, 386
Montagu 266, 268 - 269
Mulgrave 228
Mutine 65, 99 - 100, 206, 268, 274 - 275, 278 - 284, 307
Naiad 137, 142, 384
Namur 219, 329, 333, 376
Nassau 359 - 360
Nautilus 308
Nemesis 288
Neptune 136, 202, 328 - 329, 330, 334
Nereide 293 - 294, 364
New Zealand 207
Niemen 333
Northumberland 200 - 201, 210, 211
Nottingham 178
Nymph 334
Ocean 136, 321 -322, 326
Orion 100, 103, 107, 136, 181, 189 - 192, 196, 199, 209, 244 - 245, 269, 272, 274, 288, 304, 307, 341, 365
Otter 294
Pallas 232 - 324, 355
Pandour 377
Pegasus 58
Penelope 202
Perseus 258
Phoebe 137
Pickle 137
Pigmy 321
Pilot 336
Polyphemus 136, 365, 379 - 380, 386
Pompee 256
Prince 85, 136, 373
Prince Frederick 333
Prince George 238
Princess 328
Princess Charlotte 383
Princess Royal 276
Quebec 208, 330
Queen 175, 213
Queen Charlotte 56 - 58, 68, 252, 280, 333
Ramilies 178
Regulus 218
Renown 265, 360

Resolution 10 - 11, 14, 22, 24, 31, 37, 42 - 47, 68
Reunion 330
Revenge 136 - 137, 172, 372, 374 - 377, 379, 381, 386
Rhin 326
Rifleman 369 - 370
Rose 164 - 165
Royal George 340
Royal Sovereign 134, 136 - 137, 142, 226, 253, 319, 322, 331, 350 - 356, 363 - 366
Royal William 176 - 178, 247, 262
Russell 169, 191, 312, 363, 381
Salisbury 213
Salvador del Mundo 333
Sampson 153, 219
Sandwich 236, 266, 287, 301
San Fiorenzo 224, 226, 319
Saturn 318
Scarborough 215
Scipio 251
Scorpion 302
Seahorse 118, 181, 270 - 271
Serapis 57
Shannon 148, 149
Sirius 137, 213 - 217, 294
Sisiphone 376
Solebay 264
Sourain 381
Spartiate 136, 143, 200, 218, 344, 345 - 346, 348 - 349
Spencer 251, 256, 262
Spitfire 191
Stately 379 - 380
Staunch 294
St George 284, 382
St Lawrence 384 - 385
Success 200 - 201
Suffolk 318
Sultan 271
Superb 192, 210 - 211, 256 - 257, 271
Supply 213, 215, 217
Swift 318
Swiftsure 99, 102 - 108, 136, 142 - 143, 175, 273 - 275, 290, 297 - 298, 302 - 306
Temeraire 136, 322 - 323, 326 - 327, 330, 334
Tempest 322 - 323
Terpsichore 181, 238
Terrible 195
Texel 194

401

Thames 204 - 205, 256, 257, 271
Theseus 99 - 100, 104 - 108, 168, 181 - 182, 194 - 196, 199 - 200, 209, 281, 304 - 305, 308, 386
Thorn 267
Thunder 180
Thunderer 136, 143, 265, 330, 380 - 381
Tigre 120, 196, 305
Tonnant 136, 149, 220 - 222, 225 - 228, 357, 366
Trimmer 226
Unite 195
Uranie 346, 347
Vanguard 85, 99 - 101, 103, 118, 121, 181, 197 - 209, 267, 273, 275, 280, 284, 288 - 289, 303 - 305, 307
Venerable 183, 193, 256 - 257
Vengeance 185
Vengeur 60
Veteran 164
Victory 65, 70, 90, 94, 127 - 128, 131, 136, 143, 146, 167, 193, 195, 203, 210, 213, 228, 241, 265, 271 - 272, 284, 321 - 334, 338, 341, 365, 368, 379
Vigo 319
Ville de Paris 123 - 124, 128 - 129, 152 - 156
Vittoria 383
Warrior 218, 226
Whiting 360
Woolwich 383
Zealand 194, 236, 238
Zealous 99, 100, 103 - 105, 168, 179 - 185, 190, 199, 244, 254, 304 - 305, 308
Zebra 163 - 165

Danish
  Provesteenen 311, 312
  Wagrien 311, 312

Dutch
  Amsterdam 377
  Java 275
  Texel 194
  Waaksamheyd 217

French
  Achille 372 - 375
  Aigle 172, 375
  Alerte 225
  Alexandre 211, 287
  Aquilon 101, 103, 107, 209, 218, 244
  Argonaute 372
  Armide 373
  Artemise 168
  Astree 294
  Beaulieu 347
  Belle Poule 364
  Berwick 372
  Bienvenue 164, 330
  Bucentaur 345
  Bucentaure 328, 330, 334, 338, 350, 358
  Carmagnole 205
  Caroline 293 - 294
  César 53, 373
  Chevrette 346 - 348
  Cleopatre 334
  Comte d'Artois 208
  Concorde 265
  Conquerant 100 - 102, 107, 167, 188
  Courageux 16, 207
  Creole 330
  Desiree 349
  Diane 105, 114, 182
  Diomede 211
  Dragon 225
  Formidable 257, 287
  Fougueux 226 - 227, 327, 350, 353, 356 - 357
  Franklin 102 - 103, 107, 245, 247, 254, 304, 307
  Généréux 104 - 105, 107, 114, 168, 182, 200 - 201, 308 - 311
  Gironde 225
  Gloire 373
  Guerrier 100, 102, 107, 181 - 182, 196
  Guillaume Tell 104 - 105, 107, 114, 182, 188, 201 - 202, 308, 361
  Hercule 44, 114
  Imperiale 211
  Indomptable 350, 353
  Intrepid 341
  Iphigenie 294
  Justice 105, 114, 182
  L'Achille 60
  l'Aigle, 366
  La Peuple Souverain 103
  l'Artemise 104
  Le Patriote 58
  Le Vengeur 58
  l'Heureux 101, 104, 107, 267, 268, 290
  L'Hirondelle 296
  l'Immortalite 224
  l'Orient 100 - 108, 114, 168, 191, 245, 250, 254 - 255, 267 - 268, 290, 304 - 305, 307
  Lutine 343

Marengo 355
Mercure 101, 104, 107, 268, 290
Minerve 373
Morengo 364
Neptune 327, 330, 350, 381
Ocean 276
Percante 379
Peuple Souverain 100 - 101, 107, 244 - 245, 254
Pique 165 - 167
Pluton 226 - 227, 356 - 357
Psyche 319
Redoubtable 322 - 324, 327, 330
Resistance 224
Reunion 191
Revolutionaire 252
Sanspareil 271
Serieuse 100, 103, 107
Spartiate 100, 103, 107, 199, 209
Tigre 287, 377
Timoleon 105, 106, 107
Tonnant 104 - 108, 267 - 268, 290
Topaz 364
Tortue 205
Uranie 204 - 205
Vengeur du Peuple 55 - 61
Venus 225
Ville de Paris 253
Portuguese
  Carlotta 257
Russian
  Sevolod 183
Spanish
  Algesiras 227
  Argonauta 353, 372, 379
  Bahama 366 - 367
  Hermangildo 192 - 193, 257
  Monarca 227, 356, 366 - 367
  Montañes 371 - 372
  Neptuno 344 - 346
  Principe de Asturias 172, 375, 381
  Real Carlos 192 - 193, 257
  Salvador del Mundo 272
  San Antonio 193, 257
  San Augustin 331
  San Ildefonso 371, 374 - 375, 382
  San Josef 198, 272
  San Juan Nepomuceno 227
  San Justo 350, 353
  San Leandro 350

  San Nicolas 126, 198, 272
  Santa Ana 226, 350, 353, 356
  Santissima Trinidad 192, 203, 272, 328, 330 - 334, 338, 341, 350, 358, 366
  Vivo 225
Ship's Corporal 185
Ship's Cove 46
Ship's forge 262
Ship's Steward 223
Simmins, Richard 333 - 334
Simpson, Mary 81
Sint Eustatius 49
Slade, Sir Thomas 167
Slessor, Tim xi
Small Arms 262
Small, Dr William 5
Smart, Private William 371 - 373
Smith, Isaac 16, 23, 44
Smith, L. Richard xvi, 46
Smith, Robert 146
Smith, Shirlee Anne 157 - 158
Smith, Sir Sidney 108, 120, 195 - 196, 224, 370
Smyth, Admiral W.H. 186, 212, 247, 262, 274, 286, 368
Sneedorff, Captain Hans 314
Society for the Encouragement of Arts, Manufactures, and Commerce 157 - 158
Society Islands 21
Society of Civil Engineers 6
Soho, Birmingham 5 - 6, 29, 44, 112, 120, 133
Soho gilding 262
Soho Mint xi, 6, 8 - 9, 51, 76, 120, 126, 134, 136, 138 - 139, 143
Soho Mint Archives 134, 136
Solander, Daniel Carl 17 - 19, 23 - 24, 26, 28, 42, 44, 64
Sotheby's 38, 78, 84, 89 - 91, 146, 148, 278, 282, 348
South Island, New Zealand 39, 45
Southouse, Chaplain Edward 174 - 175
Spence, James 157
Spencer, Countess 90, 124, 126
Spencer, Earl 124, 256
Spink xv - xvi, 11, 36, 37, 41, 154, 159, 174, 246, 314, 336
Spithead Mutiny 1797 208
Spratt, Jack 172 - 173
Stack's Bowers Galleries 9, 170
Stack, William 148
Stamp Act, 1765 299

Stanhope, Lord 18
Stanhope, Lieut. Michael 266, 267
Stanley Gibbons 313
St Anthony's Head 170
Steel, David 249
Stein, Glenn xi, 178, 249
Steward's Mate 286
Stewart, Archibald [John] 260 - 261
Stewart, Col. William 63, 176, 283, 313 - 317
Stewart, Horatio 315
Stewart, John 259
Stewart, William 65
St James's Square 92, 93, 94
St Jean d'Acre 196
Stockham, Lieut. John 380 - 381
Stockholm Tar 230
Stockwin, Julian 236, 386
Stonelake, Elizabeth 222
Stonelake, James 222
Stonelake, Martha 228
Stonelake, William 220 - 225, 228
Stormont, Lord 50
Stothard, Thomas 66, 124, 177
Stott, Captain John 265, 266
St Paul's Cathedral 56, 86, 124, 133, 196, 305
St Quintin, James 342
Strachan, Admiral Richard 133
St Vincent, Battle of 1797 81, 125, 171
St Vincent, Earl (see John Jervis) 3, 64, 86, 88, 107, 118, 123 - 128, 138, 153 - 159, 167, 180 - 181, 196 - 200, 226, 245, 253 - 255, 265, 271 - 273, 280 - 283, 308 - 309, 315
St Vincent's Medal of Approbation **123**, 153
Styles's Hotel 120
Suckling, Maurice 80
Surgeon 171
Sydney Cove 216 - 217
Sydney, Lord 216
Sykes, John 180

T

Tahiti 13, 20 - 23
Talbot, Mary Anne 58
Tancred, George xv, 154, 246, 314
Tann, Jennifer 53
Tar, Jack 74
Tarrant, William 146
Tasmania 21, 45

Taylor, Ann 178
Taylor, Jeremy 94
Taylor, John 58
Taylor, Stephen 295
Taylor, William 178
Taylor, W.J. 120, 132, 139, 141
Terra Australis Incognita 15
The Nelson Society 354
Theophilus Richards & Co 120
The Royal Society 47
The Thanksgiving Medal 88
Thickness, Philip 4
Thomas, Donald 232
Thomason, Edward 112
Thompson, Captain Edward 308
Thompson, Captain T.B. 168 - 170, 181, 200 - 201, 206, 307 - 312
Thompson, Commodore 164
Thompson, George 242
Thompson, John 17
Thompson, Martha 369
Thompson, Mid. George 240, 241, 245
Tierze, Franz 146
Timmins, Major 137
Timor 47
Tippett, Charles 270, 276 - 277
Tomison, William 157 -158
Tomlinson, Barbara xi
Topmen 231
Torres Straits 23
Townley, Captain 139
Townshend, Jane 177
Trafalgar, Battle of xv, 2, 59, 65, 112, 131 - 133, 146, 171 - 172, 202, 228, 314, 322, 386
Trafalgar Square 86
Transit of Venus 15 - 16, 19, 21
Troubridge, Captain Thomas 102, 181, 209, 244, 253, 265, 268, 270 - 276, 279, 281, 283, 305 - 309
Trout, William 186 - 188
T & T Richards Toy-shop 120
Tuffin, J. Furnel 134, 138
Tupaia 21, 23
Turner, Thomas 229, 234 - 235
Tyler, Captain Sir Charles 220, 226 - 228, 284
Tyrason, Don Miguel 180

U

Union Flag 124

United States of America. 50
Ushant, Second battle of 213

V

Vaere, John de 64
Valetta, Malta 188
Vancouver, George 44, 47
Vandeput, Captain 301
Van Diemen's Land 215
Vaughan, Samuel & Sarah 300
Venus to the Earth, distance 15
Vesuvius 117
Vice, David xi, xvi, 51, 64, 76, 126, 133, 140, 142
Viking long ship 158
Villeneuve, Admiral 210, 334, 345, 358, 366
Voigt, Henry 8
Volunteer 1st Class 241 - 242, 342, 364

W

Wainwright, Captain John 228
Wales, Prince of 90
Wales, William 45
Walker, Captain James 370
Walker, Mid. Henry 364 - 365, 368
Wallace, Colonel J. A. 239
Waller, Lieut. 257
Wallis, Captain Samuel 16, 21
Wallis & Wallis 263
Walpole, Horace 252
Walpoles at Houghton Hall 80
Walter, Captain 309
Walton, Lieut. 267
Warner, Oliver 242, 243, 268, 271, 276
Warren, Commodore J.B. 224
Warwick, Peter xi
Washington, General George 50, 301
Watkins, Lieut. Frederick 165
Watt, James 3, 4, 5, 6, 8, 26 - 27, 51
Watts, James 246, 247
Webb, Andrew 307, 308
Webber, John 14, 20, 21, 47
Wedgwood, Josiah 3, 4, 6, 64, 124
Weeks, Lieut. John 276
Weir, Captain James, RM 187
Wellington, Duke of 239, 305, 315
Wellington Museum 14, 47
Wells, Captain Thomas 244
Wells, Purser Henry 380, 381

Westcott, Captain George 101, 263 - 267, 279 - 283
Westminster Abbey 59, 70, 198, 282 - 285, 313 - 314
Westwood, Arthur xvi
Westwood, John senior 26, 30, 43
Wheeler, Sir John xi
Whitby 38
White, Colin 202, 329
White, Lieut. 139
White, Surgeon John 214
Wilkinson, Francis 16
Wilks, John and Margaret 163
Wilks, Lieut. Thomas 163 -170
Williams, Captain David 187
Williams, Mary 66, 176, 177, 387
Williamson, John 47
Williams, William 244, 344
Willis, Sam xi, 58
Willock, Elizabeth 269
Willoughby, Captain Nesbit 294
Willyams, Reverend Cooper 175. 305
Wilson, Robert 223
Winchester, Marquis of 245
Wise, Ann 380
Wise, Samuel 379 - 380, 386
Wood, James 154 - 155
Woodward, John 137, 142, 384
Woolley & Wallis 38, 140
Woolstone, Gloucester 175
Wörlitzpark 85

X

XRF gun 144

Y

Yeo, Commodore Sir James 383, 385
Yeoman of the Powder Room 242
Yeoman of the Sheets 241 - 242, 250 - 251, 340, 376
York Boat 158, 159
York Cape 23
York, Duke of 226
York Factory, Hudson Bay 156
Young, Admiral 142, 384

Z

Zoffany, Johann 24
Zootman, Admiral 191

Sim Comfort Associates

127 Arthur Road, Wimbledon Park
London, SW19 7DR, England
Tel: 44 (0) 20 8944 8747
Email: sim@simcomfort.co.uk
Website: www.simcomfort.co.uk

2017 Stock List

- David Steel's *Elements and Practice of Naval Architecture*: One volume quarto and One Elephant Folio with 38 plates. Hand bound in blue buckram. 500 limited edition. £650.00 plus shipping.

- David Steel's *Elements and Practice of Rigging and Seamanship*: Two volumes quarto with 99 plates and two movable vovelles. Hand bound in blue buckram. 500 limited edition. £400.00 plus shipping.

- Jenkins's *Naval Achievements of Great Britain 1793 – 1816*: One Large Quarto volume with 57 aquatints. Hand bound in blue buckram for £275.00 or half blue goat for £500.00 plus shipping. 150 in half leather and 500 in buckram limited edition.

- Sim Comfort's *Naval Swords and Dirks*. A study of fighting edged weapons used by the British, French and Americans, with the period being the Age of Fighting Sail. Two volumes quarto. Boxed set sewn bound with dust wrappers. 750 limited edition. £150.00 plus shipping.

- Sim Comfort's *Lord Nelson's Swords*. Vol III to *Naval Swords and Dirks* details Lord Nelson's fighing sword and City of London, Egyptian Club and Lloyd's Patriotic Fund swords. One volume quarto sewn bound with dust wrapper. 500 limited edition. £75.00 plus shipping.

- Sim Comfort's *Forget Me Not*. A study of naval and maritime engraved coins and plate. One volume octavo, hand bound with dust wrapper. 500 limited edition. £75.00 plus shipping.

- Sim Comfort's *Matthew Boulton's Naval Medals*. A survey of seven medals which include the Otaheite, Earl St Vincent's, the Davison Nile and Boulton's Trafalgar medals. One volume quarto sewn bound with dust wrapper. 500 limited edition. £125.00 plus shipping.

- *The Appleby Trafalgar Medal* in sterling silver. 500 limited edition. £395.00 plus VAT and shipping.

- *The South Polar Race Medal* in sterling silver. 100 limited edition. £395.00 plus VAT and shipping.

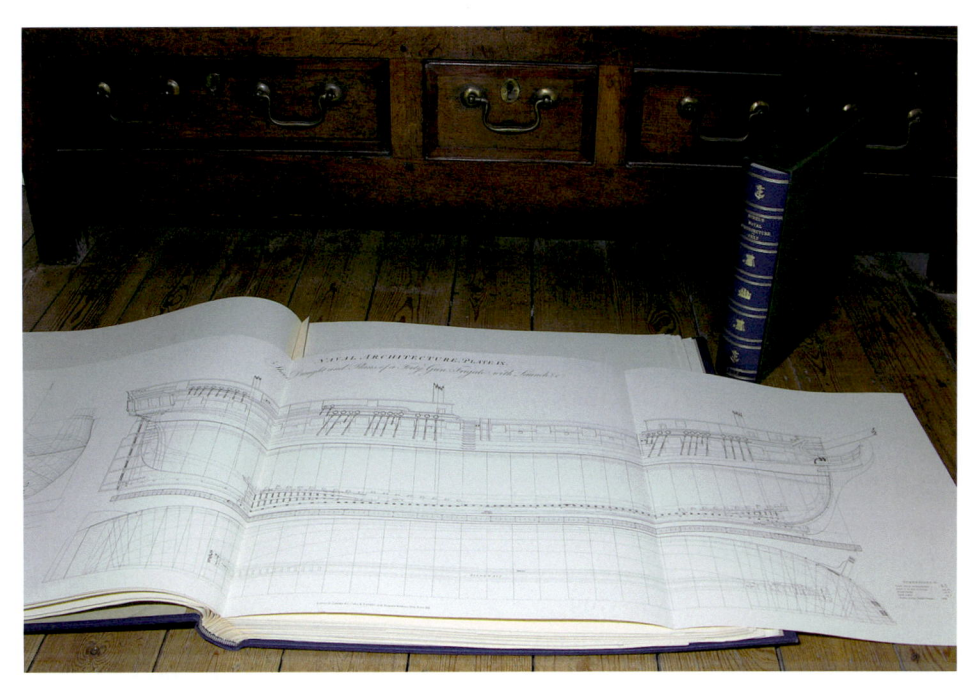

David Steel's *Naval Architecture* elephant folio with 38 ships' draughts and text volume. £650 the set.

David Steel's *Rigging and Seamanship*, two volumes with 99 plates. £400 the set.

The Naval Achievements of Great Britain, From the Year 1793 to 1817.
by
James Jenkins

Originally published in 1817, Sim Comfort Associates now offers a fine colour facsimile of the complete work which includes 57 aquatints, mainly by Thomas Whitcomb.

List of Plates
Portrait of Lord Nelson.
Portrait of Earl St. Vincent.
1) View of Gibraltar.
2) Capture of *La Cleopatre*, 18 Jun 1793.
3) Capture of *La Reunion*, 21 Oct 1793.
4) Destruction of the French Fleet at Toulon, 18 Dec 1793.
5) Capture of *La Pomone*, *L'Engageante* & *La Babet*, 23 Apr 1794.
6) Capture of the *Castor*, 29 May 1794.
7) Lord Howe in the *Queen Charlotte*, Breaking the Enemy's Line, 29 May 1794.
8) Lord Howe's Victory, 1 Jun 1794.
9) Capture of *La Pique*, 5 Jan 1795.
10) Lord Hotham's Action, 14 Mar 1795.
11) Capture of *La Gloire*, 10 Apr 1795.
12) Capture of *La Prevoyante* and *La Raison*, 17 May 1795.
13) Lord Bridport's Action off L'Orient, 23 Jun 1795.
14) Capture of *La Minerve*, 24 Jun 1795.
15) Capture of the *Mahonesa*, 13 Oct 1796.
16) Capture of *La Proserpine*, 13 Jun 1796.
17) Capture of *La Tribune*, 8 Jun 1796.
18) Capture of *Le Desius*, 25 Nov 1796.
19) Battle of Cape St. Vincent, 14 Feb 1797.
20) Capture of *L'Hercule*, 20 Apr 1797. [1798]
21) Action off Camperdown, 11 Oct 1797.
22) Capture of *La Nereide*, 21 Dec 1797.
23) Capture of *La Confiante*, 31 May 1798.
24) Capture of the *Dorothea*, 15 Jul 1798.
25) Capture of the *Liguria*, 7 Aug 1798.
26 & 27) Battle of the Nile, 1 Aug 1798.
28) Capture of *La Loire*, 18 Oct 1798.
29) Capture of *L'Immortalite'*, 20 Oct 1798.
30) Capture of the *Furie* & *Waakzamheid*, 23 Oct 1798.
31) Capture of *La Forte*, 28 Feb 1799.
32) Capture of *La Vestale*, 20 Aug 1799.
33) Cutting out the *Hermione* from the Harbour of Porto Cavallo, 25 Oct 1799.
34) Capture of *La Desiree*, 7 Jul 1800.
35) Capture of *La Vengeance*, 21 Aug 1800.
36 & 37) Destruction of the Danish Fleet before Copenhagen, 2 Apr 1801.
38) Battle off Cabareta Point, 12 Jul 1801.
39) Capture of *La Chiffonne*, 19 Aug 1801.
40) Capture & Distruction of Four Spanish Frigates, 5 Oct 1804.
41) Sir Robt. Calder's Action, 22 Jul 1805.
42, 43 & 44) Battle of Trafalgar, 21 Oct 1805.
45) Sir Richard Strachan's Action, 4 Nov 1805.
46) Sir J. T. Duckworth's Action off St. Domingo, 6 Feb 1806.
47) Capture of the *Maria Riggersbergen*, 18 Oct 1806.
48) Capture of the *Badere Zaffer*, 6 Jul 1808.
49) Destruction of the French Fleet at Basque Roads, 12 Apr 1809.
50) Capture of *Le Sparviere*, 3 May 1810.
51) Capture of the Island of Banda, 9 Aug 1810.
52) Capture of the USS *Chesapeake*, 1 Jun 1813.
53) Capture of the USS *Argus*, 14 Aug 1813.
54) Capture of *La Clorinde*, 26 Feb 1814.
55) Bombardment of Algiers, 27 Aug 1816.

Overall Size: Large Quarto, 34 x 27cm (13 1/2 x 10 1/2 inches). 288 pages printed on Mohawk Superfine softwhite eggshell (matt finish, acid free), 148 gsm paper. Stochastic Process is employed for colour reproduction of the plates.

A Limited Edition of 600 copies: Numbers 1 to 150 bound in half blue goat: £500 plus p & p.

Numbers 151 to 600 bound in full blue buckram: £275 plus p & p.

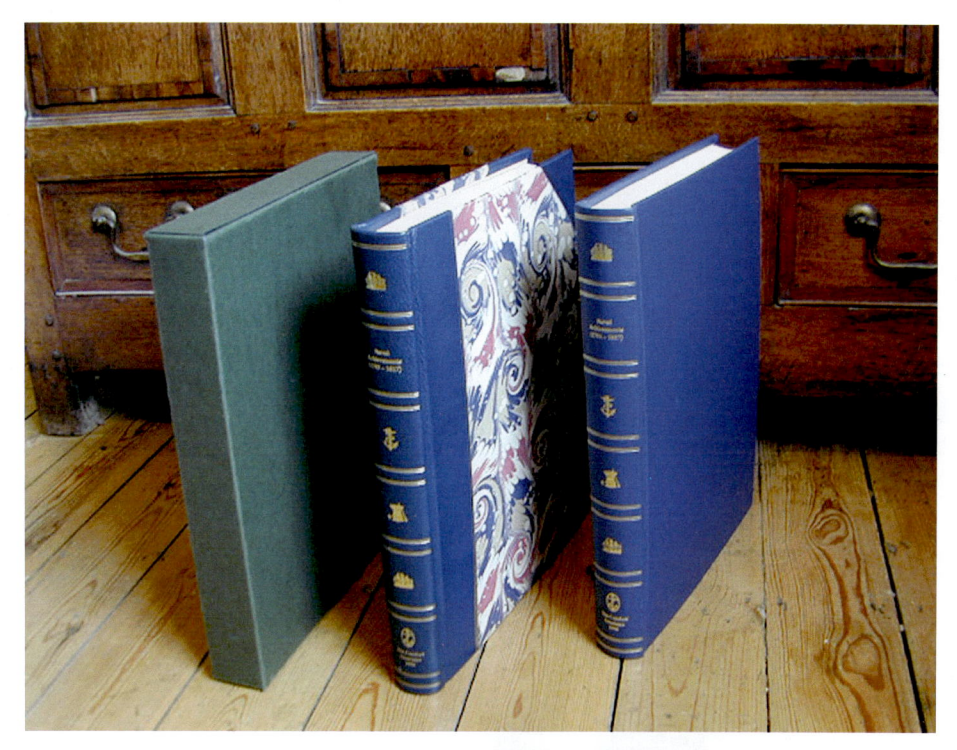

Corech d'en Baus,
66190 Collioure,
France
Telephone 04-68-82-14-01

30·IX·98

Dear Mr Comfort,

Many thanks for Naval Achievements and for your letter.

I think the reprint of Jenkins is a quite remarkably successful piece of book-production and I send you my hearty congratulations on the quality of your paper, colour reproduction, letterpress and binding. And to descend to details, let me say that the parcel survived its journey well, the contents perfectly unharmed.

Yours truly

Patrick O'Brian

PS I enclose a cheque for the packing and postage.

Naval Swords & Dirks reflects the weapons that a naval officer and his men would have used to gain their fame. Included are 174 British, 21 French and 33 American hangers, cutlasses officers' swords and dirks all illustrated with over 1,000 colour images which include all makers' marks. The text provides a lively commentary written by a collector for fellow collectors and museum curators. A glossary and comprehensive index is also provided. The whole very finely printed in two bound volumes and special supplement contained as a boxed set and limited to 750 numbered sets. £150 plus p&p.

Lord Nelson's Swords contains a review of all the swords associated with Admiral Lord Nelson, whether they be genuine or dubious! More importantly, the goal of identifying the sword that Nelson actually used to gain is fame is achieved by studying Nelson portraiture. As the whereabouts of the sword are unknown, everything you need to identify it is detailed, so happy hunting.

In addition are the swords associated with Admirals Collingwood and Northesk and Captain Hardy, plus a full survey of Egyptian Club swords and Lloyd's Patriotic Fund swords. Finely printed and limited to 500 copies, £75 plus p&p.

Lord Nelson's Swords

Sim Comfort

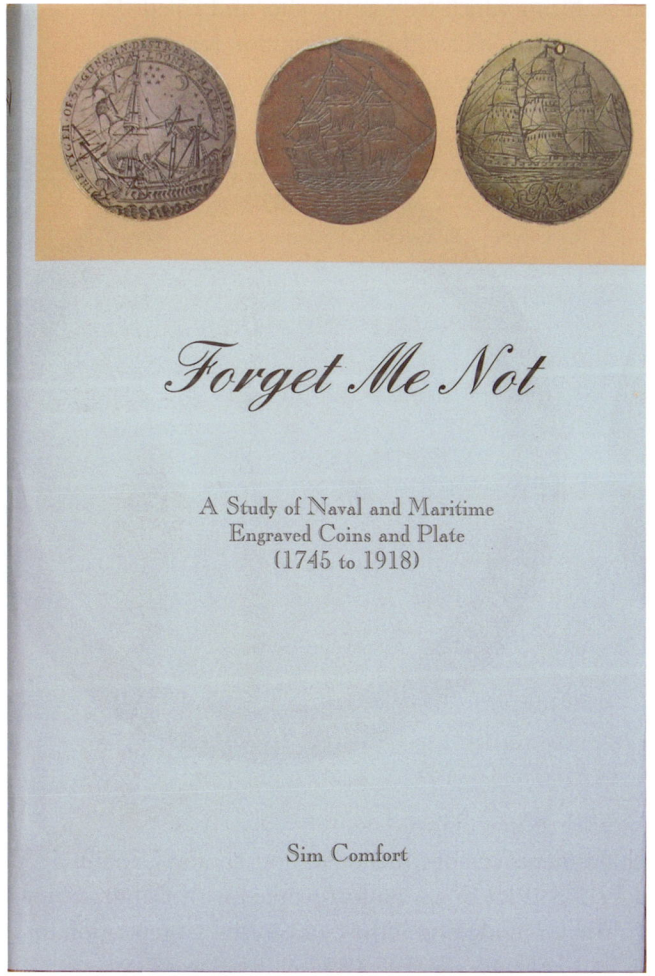

Forget Me Not explores the art of the sailor which closely reflected his world. He used devices such as fish, the sun, anchors and mermaids to scrimshaw whale teeth and decorate tobacco boxes and sea chests. But the most potent of all his images was that of the ships he sailed in, and possibly the most personal of all the things the mariner created was his gift to the loved one that he left behind. The engraved coin is small in size, but ideally suited as a medium to detail his ship and declare his affection.

Contained in this octavo volume is the first full study of maritime engraved coins and all the various types of ships found in this rare art form. The time span is from the mid 18th to the beginning of the 20th century. Included are 140 pieces that depict the great men-of-war during the age of fighting sail, Indiamen, privateers, convict ships, slavers and numerous merchantmen. Where research is available the story of the men and ships is provided. Finely printed and limited to 500 copies, £75 plus p&p.

The Appleby Trafalgar Medal

To commemorate the 200th anniversary of the Battle of Trafalgar, Sim Comfort and Malcolm Appleby worked together to create something really special. The shape of the medal echos the Devis portrait of Nelson, the obverse shows *Victory* as she is about to break the enemy line and flying the *England Expects* signal. The reverse details the awful fight between the *Victory*, *Redoubtable* and *Temeraire* during which Nelson was shot and killed. The medal won the gold prize for engraving and silver prize for modelling at the Goldsmiths' Competition for 2005.

Available in hallmarked sterling silver with the edition limited to 500 medals: £395 plus vat and shipping.

The South Polar Race Medal

To commemorate the centenary of the remarkable achievements of both Roald Amundsen and Captain Scott and their teams in their quest to reach the South Pole in 1911 / 1912, Sim Comfort worked with Danuta Solowiej to crate an outstanding silver medal which won the silver prize for modelling at the Goldsmiths' Competition for 2012.

Available in hallmarked sterling silver with the edition limited to 100 medals: £395 plus vat and shipping.

Notes